Drafting

* How will the group approach the drafting stage? By dividing the wor[k] ~~among different writers? By writing~~ together as a group? By assigning the work to one person?
* Has the group agreed on format elements such as spacing, typography, table and graph design, headings, and documentation?
* Has the group set deadlines for the work to be completed?
* Should the group appoint a coordinator for the project?
• Do you have a comfortable place to work?
• Where in your organizational plan can you begin confidently?

Revision

• Have you stated clearly and specifically the purpose of the report?
• Have you put into the report everything required? Do you have sufficient supporting evidence? Have you stated the implications of your information clearly?
• Are all your facts and numbers accurate?
• Have you answered the questions your readers are likely to have?
• Does the report contain anything that you would do well to cut out?
• Does your organization suit the needs of your content and your audience?
• Are your paragraphs clear, well organized, and of reasonable length? Are there suitable transitions from one point to the next?
• Is your prose style clear and readable?
• Is your tone appropriate to your audience?
• Have you satisfied the needs of an international audience?
• Are all your statements ethical? For example, have you avoided making ambiguous statements or statements that deliberately lead the reader to faulty inferences?
• Are your graphs and tables clear and accurate? Are they well placed? Do they present your information honestly?
• Is your document readable, accessible, and visually effective?
• Are there people you should share your draft with—for example, members of the target audience—before going on to a final draft?

Editing

• Have you checked thoroughly for misspellings and other mechanical errors?
• Have you included all the formal elements that your report needs?
• Are design elements such as headings, margins, spacing, typefaces, and documentation consistent through-out the draft?
• Are your headings and titles clear, properly worded, and parallel? Do your headings in the text match those in the table of contents?
• Is your documentation system the one required? Have you documented wherever appropriate? Do the numbers in the text match those in the notes?
• Have you keyed the tables and figures into your text, and have you sufficiently discussed them?
• Are all parts and pages of the manuscript in the correct order?
• Will the format of the typed or printed report be functional, clear, and attractive?
• Does your manuscript satisfy stylebook specifications governing it?
• Have you included required notices, distribution lists, and identifying code numbers?
• Do you have written permission to reproduce extended quotations or other matter under copyright? (Permission is necessary only when your work is to be published or copyrighted.)
• While you were composing the manuscript, did you have any doubts or misgivings that you should now check out?
• Have you edited your manuscript for matters both large and small?
• What remains to be done (such as proofreading the final copy)?

TENTH EDITION

Reporting Technical Information

Kenneth W. Houp
Late, The Pennsylvania State University

Thomas E. Pearsall
Emeritus, University of Minnesota

Elizabeth Tebeaux
Texas A&M University

Sam Dragga
Texas Tech University

New York   Oxford
OXFORD UNIVERSITY PRESS
2002

Oxford University Press

Oxford New York
Athens Auckland Bangkok Bogotá Buenos Aires Calcutta
Cape Town Chennai Dar es Salaam Delhi Florence Hong Kong Istanbul
Karachi Kuala Lumpur Madrid Melbourne Mexico City Mumbai
Nairobi Paris São Paulo Shanghai Singapore Taipei Tokyo Toronto Warsaw

and associated companies in

Berlin Ibadan

Published by Oxford University Press, Inc.
198 Madison Avenue, New York, New York 10016
http://www.oup-usa.org

Oxford is a registered trademark of Oxford University Press

Library of Congress Cataloging-in-Publication Data

Pearsall, Thomas E.
    Reporting technical information / Thomas E. Pearsall, Elizabeth Tebeaux, Sam
Dragga.—10th ed.
    p. cm.
    Rev. ed. of: Reporting technical information / Kenneth W. Houp, c1998.
    Includes index.
    ISBN 0-19-514612-3 (pbk.: alk. paper)
    1. Technical writing. I. Tebeaux, Elizabeth. II. Dragga, Sam. III. Houp, Kenneth W.,
1913- Reporting technical information. IV. Title.

T11 .P3925 2001
808'.066—dc21   00-053079

Printing number: 9 8 7 6 5 4 3 2 1
Printed in the United States of America
on acid-free paper.

Brief Contents

Preface **xvii**

1 An Overview of Technical Writing **1**

Part I. Foundations **11**

2 Composing **13**

3 Writing Collaboratively **35**

4 Writing for Your Readers **55**

5 Achieving a Readable Style **81**

6 Writing Ethically **107**

7 Writing for International Readers **125**

Part II. Techniques **155**

8 Gathering, Evaluating, and Documenting Information **157**

9 Presenting Information **175**

10 Analyzing Information **211**

11 Document Design **231**

12 Using Illustrations **279**

Part III. Applications **327**

13 Correspondence **329**

14 The Strategies and Communications of the Job Hunt **355**

15 Proposals and Progress Reports **393**

16 Recommendation Reports **441**

17 Empirical Research Reports **483**

18 Instructions **503**

19 Oral Reports **541**

Appendix A. Handbook **573**

Appendix B. Formal Elements of Technical Documents **607**

Chapter Notes **683**

Index **689**

Contents

Preface xvii

1 An Overview of Technical Writing 1

Some Matters of Definition 2

The Substance of Technical Writing 2

The Nature of Technical Writing 4

The Attributes of Good Technical Writers 6

The Qualities of Good Technical Writing 7

A Day in the Life of Two Technical Writers 7

Marie Enderson: Computer Specialist and Occasional
Technical Writer 7

Ted Freedman: Technical Writer and Company Editor 8

Exercises 10

▶ PART I. FOUNDATIONS 11

2 Composing 13

Situational Analysis 15

Topic and Purpose 15

Audience and Persona 16

Discovery 20

Brainstorming 20

Using Arrangement Patterns for Discovery 21

Other Successful Discovery Techniques 22

Arrangement 22

Drafting and Revising 23

The Rough Draft 23

Revision 26

Editing 28

Checking Mechanics 28

Checking Documentation 28

Checking Graphics 29

Checking Document Design **29**

Editing with Word Processing Programs **29**

Exercises **33**

3 **Writing Collaboratively 35**

Planning **37**

Drafting **40**

Dividing the Work **40**

Drafting in Collaboration **40**

One Person Doing the Drafting **40**

Revising and Editing **41**

Revising **41**

Editing **42**

Collaboration in the Workplace **43**

Collaboration on the Internet **44**

E-Mail **44**

FTP Sites **45**

Synchronous Discussions **45**

Group Conferences **47**

Conference Behavior **47**

Group Roles **49**

Exercises **51**

4 **Writing for Your Readers 55**

Goals of Communication **56**

The Planning Process **56**

Determining Your Readers **57**

Asking Questions to Analyze Your Readers **60**

Determining Your Purpose **71**

Understanding Your Role as a Writer **72**

Planning the Content **73**

Anticipating the Context in Which Your Writing
Will Be Received **75**

Thinking about Your Readers: A Summary of
Considerations **75**

Exercises **79**

5 Achieving a Readable Style 81

The Paragraph 82

    The Central Statement 83

    Paragraph Length 83

    Transitions 84

Lists and Tables 85

Clear Sentence Structure 86

    Sentence Length 86

    Sentence Order 87

    Sentence Complexity and Density 88

    Active Verbs 91

    Active and Passive Voice 92

    First-Person Point of View 93

    A Caution about Following Rules 94

Specific Words 94

Pomposity 96

    Empty Words 96

    Elegant Variation 97

    Pompous Vocabulary 97

Good Style in Action 98

Choosing a Style for International Readers 100

Exercises 102

6 Writing Ethically 107

Understanding Ethical Behavior 108

    What Makes an Act Unethical? 108

    Why Should We Act Ethically? 109

Recognizing Unethical Communication 111

    Plagiarism 111

    Deliberately Using Imprecise or Ambiguous Language 112

    Making False Implications 112

    Manipulating the Data 112

    Using Misleading Visuals 113

Behaving Ethically 116

Dealing with Unethical Behavior in Others 118

Exercises 120

7 Writing for International Readers **125**

Establishing a Perspective on International
Communication **126**

Understanding Readers from Various Cultures **127**

Individualism versus Collectivism: Valuing Either
Individuals or Groups **129**

Separation of Business and Private Relationships **130**

Power Distance between Social Ranks **131**

Universal or Relative View of Truth **133**

Whether the Entire Message Is Contained in the
Text **134**

Whether Uncertainty Is to Be Avoided or Accepted **135**

The Power and Value of Time **135**

Masculine versus Feminine **136**

Considering Culture in the Planning Process **136**

Example International Documents for Examination **139**

Writing Business Communications to Readers in
Other Cultures **143**

Culture and Graphics **147**

A Final Word **148**

Guides to Doing Business in Cultures around the
World **149**

Exercises **151**

▶ PART II. TECHNIQUES   **155**

8 Gathering, Evaluating and Documenting Information **157**

Asking the Right Questions **158**

Looking for Answers **158**

Interviews **159**

Newsgroups **160**

World Wide Web **161**

Library **163**

Evaluating Answers **168**

Citing Sources **171**

Exercises **172**

9   Presenting Information 175

Chronology 176

Topical Organization 178

Exemplification 178

Analogy 179

Classification and Division 180

Definition 185

  Sentence Definitions 185

  Extended Definitions 186

  Placement of Definitions 187

Description 188

  Visual Language 190

  Mechanism Description 192

  Process Description 194

Exercises 208

10 Analyzing Information 211

Classical Argument 213

  Major Proposition 214

  Minor Propositions and Evidence 214

  Organization 215

Pro and Con 217

Induction and Deduction 218

  Induction 218

  Deduction 220

  Logical Fallacies 221

Comparison 222

  Alternatives 222

  Criteria 223

Toulmin Logic 223

  Applying Toulmin Logic 224

  Arranging Your Argument for Readers 226

Exercises 228

11 Document Design 231

Understanding the Basics of Document Design 232

  Know What Decisions You Can Make 232

Choose a Design That Fits Your Situation **237**

Plan Your Design from the Beginning **237**

Reveal Your Design to Your Readers **239**

Keep Your Design Consistent **239**

Designing Effective Pages and Screens **241**

Leave Ample Margins **242**

Use Blank Space to Group Information **242**

Set the Spacing for Easy Reading **246**

Use a Medium Line Length **246**

Use a Ragged Right Margin **247**

Choosing Readable Type **248**

Choose a Legible Type Size **249**

Choose a Typeface (Font) That Is Appropriate
for the Situation **250**

Use Special Typefaces Sparingly **251**

Use Highlighting Effectively **252**

Use a Mixture of Cases, Not All Capitals **255**

Use Color Carefully **255**

Helping Readers Locate Information **256**

Write Descriptive Headings **257**

Design Headings to Organize the Page **260**

Use Page Numbers and Headers or Footers in
Print Documents **264**

Appreciating the Importance of Document Design **266**

Exercises **267**

12 Using Illustrations **279**

Choosing Illustrations **280**

Consider Your Purpose **280**

Consider Your Audience **281**

Consider Your Audience Again **282**

Consider Your Purpose Again **282**

Creating Illustrations **297**

Designing Tables **298**

Designing Bar and Column Graphs **300**

Designing Circle Graphs **305**

Designing Line Graphs **308**

Designing Illustrations Ethically **311**

Exercises **321**

▶ PART III. APPLICATIONS   327

13 Correspondence **329**

Determining Your Purpose **330**

Analyzing the Audience **333**

Composing Letters, Memos, and E-Mail **337**

Finding the Appropriate Style **340**

　Direct versus Indirect Style **340**

　Conversational Style **342**

Special Considerations for E-Mail **345**

Special Considerations for International Correspondence **346**

Keeping Copies of Correspondence **347**

Exercises **350**

14 The Strategies and Communications of the Job Hunt **355**

Preparation **356**

　Self-Assessment **356**

　Information Gathering **359**

　Networking **362**

The Correspondence of the Job Hunt **364**

　Letter of Application **364**

　The Résumé **368**

　Follow-Up Letters **380**

Interviewing **382**

　The Interview **383**

　Negotiation **385**

　Before and After the Interview **386**

Exercises **390**

15 Proposals and Progress Reports **393**

The Relationship between Proposals and Progress
　Reports **394**

Proposals **395**

The Context of Proposal Development **398**

Effective Argument in Proposal Development **399**

Standard Sections of Proposals **401**

Progress Reports **406**

Physical Appearance of Proposals and Progress Reports **425**

Style and Tone of Proposals and Progress Reports **425**

Other Forms of Proposals and Progress Reports **425**

Exercises **435**

16 Recommendation Reports **441**

An Informal Report: The Church Repair Project **442**

The Situation **442**

Important Features of Report **443**

A Formal Report: The Oil Spill Problem **443**

The Situation **448**

Important Features of Report **448**

A Feasibility Report: Department Store Location **464**

Logic of the Feasibility Study **464**

Preparation of the Feasibility Report **466**

The Situation **469**

Important Features of Report **469**

A Final Word **479**

Exercises **480**

17 Empirical Research Reports **483**

Audience Adaptation **492**

Introduction and Literature Review **492**

Statement of Objectives **493**

Choice of Materials or Methodology **493**

Rationale for Investigation **494**

Verb Tense in Literature Reviews **494**

Materials and Methods **495**

Design of the Investigation **495**

Materials **495**

Procedures **496**

Methods for Observation, Analysis, and Interpretation **496**

Voice in Materials and Methods Section **497**

Results **497**

Discussion **497**

A Final Word **498**

Exercises **500**

18 Instructions **503**

Situational Analysis for Instructions **505**

What Is the Purpose of My Instructions? **505**

What Is My Reader's Point of View? **505**

How and Where Will My Reader Use These Instructions? **505**

What Content Does My Reader Really Need and Want? **506**

How Should I Arrange My Content? **506**

Possible Components of Instructions **506**

Introduction **507**

Theory or Principles of Operation **508**

List of Equipment and Materials Needed **512**

Description of the Mechanism **513**

Warnings **516**

How-To Instructions **521**

Tips and Troubleshooting Procedures **525**

Glossary **528**

Accessible Format **528**

Reader Checks **531**

Exercises **536**

19 Oral Reports **541**

Preparation **542**

Delivery Techniques **543**

The Extemporaneous Speech **543**

The Manuscript Speech **544**

Arranging Content **545**

Introduction **545**

Body **546**

Conclusion **548**

Presentation **548**

    Physical Aspects of Speaking **548**

    Audience Interaction **551**

Visual Aids **554**

    Purpose of Visual Aids **554**

    Criteria for Good Visual Aids **555**

    Visual Content **557**

    Visual Presentation Tools **562**

Exercises **571**

Appendix A. Handbook 573

Appendix B. Formal Elements of Document Design 607

Report Format **607**

Letter and Memorandum Format **637**

Documentation **649**

Designing a World Wide Web Site **675**

Outlining **681**

Chapter Notes 683

Index 689

Preface

Reporting Technical Information has a new publisher, Oxford University Press. In 1999 our former publisher, Allyn & Bacon, was bought by an English firm, Pearson Education. As part of its conditions for approving the sale, the U.S. Department of Justice required Allyn & Bacon to divest itself of some of its most successful books. *Reporting Technical Information* was one of the books divested and was ultimately bought by Oxford. We are happy in our new home and look forward to a long relationship.

Also, we now welcome Professor Sam Dragga, formerly a contributor to *Reporting Technical Information,* as a full coauthor. Professor Dragga, an accomplished teacher and researcher of technical writing and a former president of the Association of Teachers of Technical Writing, has made major contributions to this tenth edition.

▶ CHANGES TO THE TENTH EDITION

In keeping with our touchstone that all writing is subject to infinite improvement, we have freshened many examples and made many small changes in style and substance in this edition. We have also made some major changes. This tenth edition has four new chapters and four thoroughly rewritten chapters.

New Chapters

Chapter 6, Writing Ethically To aid the teaching of ethics in the classroom, we have expanded the material on ethics from the ninth edition and made it into a separate chapter. The new chapter includes illustrative material from the codes of various professional groups, such as the Institute of Electrical and Electronics Engineers. The chapter tells readers where they can go online for more information on ethics and provides realistic exercises dealing with ethical dilemmas. When appropriate, other chapters deal with ethics as well; see for example, Chapter 12, Using Illustrations.

Chapter 7, Writing for International Readers Reflecting the increasing globalization of business and technology, this chapter provides a concise but comprehensive introduction to the differences among world cultures and the effects of the differences on communication. The chapter covers such issues as the importance of personal relationships, individualism versus collectivism, differing views of truth, and the power and value of time. Included as part of the chapter is an extensive bibliography that encourages further study. When appropriate, information and exercises dealing with international differences are also included in other chapters.

Chapter 8, Gathering, Evaluating, and Documenting Information This new chapter helps students in formulating their research questions and then guides them to sources of information, such as interviewing, the electronic library catalog, indexes, and the Internet. The chapter pays particular attention to evaluating information, especially that information found on the Internet.

Chapter 17, Empirical Research Reports In response to many reviewer suggestions, we have broken empirical research reports out into a separate chapter. We have also provided a complete empirical research report as an example.

Rewritten Chapters

Four existing chapters have been extensively rewritten.

Chapter 4, Writing for Your Readers We now use six on-the-job situations to help students deal with such questions as these: Who will read your message? How technical should you be in explaining your situation? What is your purpose in writing? What is your business relationship to the reader?

Chapter 12, Using Illustrations This chapter offers the latest information on constructing and using visual aids. It provides numerous examples of both good and inadequate visuals, with appropriate commentary. The chapter concludes with an extensive section on how to avoid constructing graphs that violate principle of ethics.

Chapter 13, Correspondence This chapter offers advice on when to use e-mail rather than conventional letters and memos and describes how to conduct correspondence in all three formats.

Chapter 14, The Strategies and Communications of the Job Hunt We recognize that most people now gather needed information about jobs and potential employers from the Internet rather than from print sources, and we advise students accordingly.

Appendixes We have also reorganized and rewritten portions of our appendixes. Appendix A, Handbook, now deals exclusively with the conventions of usage and punctuation. Appendix B, Formal Elements of Technical Documents, is divided into five sections: Report Format, Letter and Memorandum Format, Documentation, Designing a World Wide Web Site, and Outlining. The two appendixes should provide ready reference for students who need help in these matters.

Finally, before each chapter you will find what we have called a scenario. Each scenario depicts a situation in which the student will use the information illustrated in the chapter in an on-the-job context. We hope that these realistic vignettes will help students understand how the skills and techniques they are learning transcend the academic environment. For the total plan of the tenth edition, please see the table of contents.

▶ ACKNOWLEDGMENTS

The chapter notes provide detailed acknowledgments of the many sources we have used in this edition. In addition, we thank the many colleagues who took time to review our work and make many useful suggestions, in particular, the following: Carol A. Serf, The Georgia Institute of Technology; Marilyn Sandidge, Westfield State College; Dave Clark, Iowa State University; Cecelia Hawkins, Texas A & M University; and Randal Woodland, University of Michigan-Dearborn. We also thank Professor James Connally, University of Minnesota, for his contributions to Chapter 19, Oral Reports. We thank our new editor at Oxford University Press, Tony English, for his thoughtful assistance. Finally, we express our love and gratitude to our spouses, Anne, William Jene, and Linda, for their loving and loyal support.

▶ AN INVITATION

We invite students and teachers to send comments and suggestions directly to Tom Pearsall at his e-mail address: tpearsall@aol.com

Thomas E. Pearsall
Elizabeth Tebeaux
Sam Dragga

Reporting Technical Information

SCENARIO

You are an engineer for General Power Equipment, Inc. Your work is mainly in research and development. GPE is a medium-sized company that makes machinery powered by small engines and motors, such as lawn mowers, power generators, and pumps. GPE has recently acquired North Star Snow Throwers, an acquisition that seems likely to fit well with the company's other products.

Helen Bergen, the vice president for research and development, has been given the task of integrating North Star into GPE. She asks you to come to a meeting in her office. When you enter her office, you find Jack Kumagai, of GPE's legal staff already there.

Helen greets you, but she has a worried look on her face. She has some printouts in front of her. "Jack and I have just been going over this information that I got off the Web," she says. "Do you know that snow throwers are an open invitation to litigation? Listen to this:

"'Last year there were over a thousand amputations caused by snow throwers and over 5,000 emergency room visits resulting from their use. These things kill people. People get caught in them or run them in the garage and die from carbon monoxide.'"

"Are North Star snow throwers more dangerous than any other?" you ask.

"Not really," answers Jack. "but the warnings on their machines and the instructions in their manuals are inadequate in my opinion."

"That's where you come in," Helen says to you. "We want to avoid litigation, sure, but what we really want is for people to use any of our products safely. Work with Jack. Write warnings that really do the job. Write a manual that makes safe operations of these things as foolproof as possible." She smiles and adds, "When you're finished with the manual, put your engineer's hat back on and work on making these machines safer."

Warnings and manuals are just two of the many things you may have to do in technical communication. This first chapter introduces you to that world in a general way. The chapters that follow show you how to do manuals and warnings and much more.

An Overview of Technical Writing

▶ Some Matters of Definition

▶ The Substance of Technical Writing

▶ The Nature of Technical Writing

▶ The Attributes of Good Technical Writers

▶ The Qualities of Good Technical Writing

▶ A Day in the Life of Two Technical Writers
Marie Enderson: Computer Specialist and
    Occasional Technical Writer
Ted Freedman: Technical Writer and Company Editor

This first chapter is purely introductory. It is intended to give you the broadest possible view of technical writing. Beginning with Chapter 2, we go into details, but in order to be meaningful, these details must be seen against the background given here.

► SOME MATTERS OF DEFINITION

As you work your way through this book, you will see that technical writing is essentially a problem-solving process that involves the following elements at one or more stages of the process:

- A technical subject matter that is peculiar to or characteristic of a particular art, science, trade, technology, or profession.
- A recognition and accurate definition of the communication problem involved.
- The beginning of the solution through the establishment of the role of the communicator and the purpose and audience (or audiences) of the communication.
- Discovery of the accurate, precise information needed for the solution of the problem through thinking, study, investigation, observation, analysis, experimentation, and measurement.
- The arrangement and presentation of the information thus gained so that it achieves the writer's purpose and is clear, useful, and persuasive.

The final product of this problem-solving process is a piece of technical writing that may range in size and complexity from a simple memorandum to a stack of books. To expand our overview of technical writing, we discuss it under these five headings:

The Substance of Technical Writing
The Nature of Technical Writing
The Attributes of Good Technical Writers
The Qualities of Good Technical Writing
A Day in the Life of Two Technical Writers

► THE SUBSTANCE OF TECHNICAL WRITING

Organizations produce technical writing for internal and external use. Internally, documents such as feasibility reports, technical notes, e-mail, and memorandums go from superiors to subordinates, from subordinates to superiors, and between colleagues at the same level. If documents move in more than one direction, they may have to be drafted in more than one version. Company policy, tact, and the need to know are important considerations for intra-company paperwork.

Many examples come to mind. The director of information services studies and reports on the feasibility of providing middle management with personal computers. The research department reports the results of tests on new products. The personnel department instructs new employees about company policies and procedures. In fact, the outsider cannot imagine the amount and variety of paperwork a company generates simply to keep its internal affairs in order. Survey research indicates that college-educated employees spend about 20% of their time on the job writing.[1] In fact, most college-educated workers rank the ability to write well as very important or critically important to their job performance.[2]

Externally, letters and reports of many kinds go to other companies, the government, and the users of the company's products. Let us cite a few of the many possibilities: a computer company prepares instructional manuals to accompany its computers; a university department prepares a proposal to a state government offering to provide research services; an architectural firm prepares progress reports to inform clients of the status of contracted building programs; an insurance company writes letters accepting or denying claims by its policyholders.

The manufacture of information has become a major industry in its own right. Much of that information is research related. Many government agencies, scientific laboratories, and commercial companies make research their principal business. They may undertake this research to satisfy their internal needs or the needs of related organizations. The people who conduct the research may include social scientists, computer scientists, chemists, physicists, mathematicians, psychologists—the whole array of professional specialists. They record and transmit much of this research via reports. The clients for such research may be government agencies or other institutions that are not equipped to do their own research. Reports may, in fact, be the only products of some companies and laboratories.

Much technical writing goes on at universities and colleges. Professors have a personal or professional curiosity that entices them into research. If they believe that their findings are important, they publicize the information in various ways—books, journal articles, papers for professional societies, the Internet. Students assigned research problems present what they have done and learned in laboratory reports, monographs, and theses.

Many reports are prepared for public use. For example, a state department of natural resources is entrusted not only with conserving woodlands, wetlands, and wildlife but also with making the public aware of these resources. State and federally supported agricultural extension services have as a major responsibility the preparation and dissemination of agricultural information for interested users. Profit-earning companies have to create and improve their public image and also attract customers and employees. Airlines, railroads, distributors of goods and services, all have to keep in the public view. Pamphlets, posted notices, World Wide Web sites, and radio and television announcements are commonly used to meet these needs.

Myriad applications such as these—company memos and reports, government publications, research reports, public relations releases—create a great flood of information. Some of it is of only passing interest; some of it makes history. Some of it is prepared by full-time professional writers, but most of it is prepared by professionals in a technical field who are writing about their own work.

▶ THE NATURE OF TECHNICAL WRITING

Technical writing, whether done by professional writers or professionals in a technical field, is a specialty within the field of writing as a whole. It requires a working knowledge of the technical subject matter and terminology. People working with technical documents need to learn about document design, standards for abbreviations, the rules that govern the writing of numbers, the uses of tables and graphs, and the needs and expectations of people who use technical documents.

And yet a broad and sound foundation in other writing is a tremendous asset for those who write technical documents, for it gives them versatility both on and off the job. They can write a good letter, prepare a brochure, compose a report. In this comprehensive sense, they are simply *writers*. The same writing skills that are important in a college classroom are important on the job. Surveys show that workers rank writing skills in this order of importance:[3]

1. Clarity
2. Conciseness
3. Organization
4. Grammar

Writers understand, too, that not all writing is done in the same tone and style. As writers, they have not one style but a battery of them:

. . . the very nice plant my mother had on her table in the front hall.	Everyday, homey diction; much depends on the reader's imagination
. . . in a shaft of yellow sunlight, a white-flowering begonia in a red clay pot.	Pictorial, vivid, sensory; shows, rather than tells
. . . a 12-inch begonia propagated from a 3-inch cutting; age, 42 days.	Specific, technical, factually informative

As someone who writes technical documents, whether part-time or full-time, you may have to use all of these styles, for your job will be to convey your message to your intended readers. By playing the right tune with these styles in different combinations, and by adding other writing skills in generous measure, you can produce leaflets, proposals, brochures, sales literature, reports to stockholders, and a great variety of letters.

In writing intended for your professional colleagues, you will be nearer to the third begonia example than to the first two. Your diction will be objective and accurate. By relying on this style, you can produce operating manuals, feasibility reports, research reports, progress reports, and similar materials. When your audience and purpose are appropriate for this style, your writing is likely to have these characteristics:

- Your purpose is usually spelled out in the first one or two paragraphs. All included information bears upon the accomplishment of the stated purpose. For example, a technical paper on smoke detectors may set forth only one major objective: to determine the relative effectiveness of photoelectric and ionization chamber types in detecting smoldering fires, flaming fires, and high temperatures. Other major topics would be reserved for other papers.
- The vocabulary tends to be specialized. Some of the terms may not appear in general dictionaries. If the audience shares the writer's specialization, such terms may not be defined within the text, on the assumption that professional colleagues will be familiar with them. At other times, the terms may be listed and defined in accompanying glossaries.
- Sentences are highly specific and fact filled.
- When appropriate to the material, numbers and dimensions are plentiful.
- Signs, symbols, and formulas may pepper the text.
- Graphs and tables may substitute for prose or reinforce and expand on the surrounding prose. Figures and illustrations of all sorts are widely used, sometimes to supplement prose, sometimes to replace it.
- Documentation and credits appear in notes and bibliographies.

As this list makes clear, audience analysis is tremendously important to successful technical writing. What is appropriate for your professional colleagues may be inappropriate for the general public. In matters of definition, for example, terms are not normally defined if the audience is expected to know them. But the indispensable corollary to that proposition is that terms *have to be defined* when your audience, for whatever reason, cannot be expected to know them. Sentences can be fact filled when the audience is highly professional and highly motivated. However, when your readers do not share your motivation, profession, and enthusiasm, you should slow your pace and make your prose less dense. In technical writing, you have to know your audience as well as your objectives and adapt your style and material to both.

▶ THE ATTRIBUTES OF GOOD TECHNICAL WRITERS

To write clear and effective reports, you build on the natural talents you have in communicating ideas to others. How can you build successfully? What skills, characteristics, and attitudes are of most value to the technical writer? From experience, we can summarize some of the major attributes that will stand you in good stead:

- Be reasonably methodical and painstaking. Plan your work for the day and for the rest of the week. Look up from time to time to take stock of what you and others are doing, so that you do not squander your time and energy on minor tasks that should be put off or dispensed with altogether. File your correspondence. Keep at your desk the supplies you need to do your work. Keep a clear head about ways and means for accomplishing your purpose.
- Be objective. Try not to get emotionally attached to anything you have written; be ready to chuck any or all of it into the wastebasket. While reading your own prose or that of your colleagues, do not ask whether you or they are to be pleased but whether the intended audience will be pleased, informed, satisfied, and persuaded.
- In your research, keep in mind that most of what you do will eventually have to be presented in writing. Do your work so that it will be honestly and effectively reportable. Keep a notebook, a computer journal, or a deck of note cards. Record what you do and learn.
- Never forget that *clarity* is your most important attribute. Until the sense of a piece of writing is made indisputably clear, until the intended reader can understand it, nothing else can profitably be done with it.
- As someone who writes, understand that writing is something that can be learned, even as chemistry, physics, and mathematics can be. The rules of writing are not as exact as those of science, but they can never be thrown overboard if you are to bring your substance home to your reader.

One writer, who knew well the nature and substance of technical writing, summed up the way to be successful with three imperatives that underlie much of this book:

1. Know your reader.
2. Know your objective.
3. Be simple, direct, and concise.[4]

▶ THE QUALITIES OF GOOD TECHNICAL WRITING

Because the qualities of good technical writing vary, depending on audience and objective, we cannot offer you a list that applies equally to everything you write. However, some qualities are apparent in good technical writing. Good technical writing

- Arrives by the date it is due.
- Is well designed. It makes a good impression when it is picked up, handled, and flipped through or read online.
- Has the necessary preliminary or front matter to characterize the report and disclose its purpose and scope.
- Has a body that provides essential information and that is written clearly, without jargon or padding.
- When appropriate, uses tables and graphs to present and clarify its content.
- Has, when needed, a summary or set of conclusions to reveal the results obtained.
- Has been so designed that it can be read selectively—for instance, by some users, only the summary; by other users, only the introduction and conclusions; by still other users, the entire report.
- Has a rational and readily discernible plan, such as may be revealed by the table of contents and a series of headings throughout the report.
- Reads coherently and cumulatively from beginning to end.
- Answers readers' questions as these questions arise in their minds.
- Conveys an overall impression of authority, thoroughness, soundness, and honest work.

Beyond all these basic characteristics, good technical writing is free from typographical errors, grammatical slips, and misspelled words. Little flaws distract attention from the writer's main points.

▶ A DAY IN THE LIFE OF TWO TECHNICAL WRITERS

To summarize, let us describe two representative writers, whom we shall identify as Marie Enderson and Ted Freedman.

Marie Enderson: Computer Specialist and Occasional Technical Writer

Marie has a bachelor's degree in engineering technology. She works in the information services division of a small electronics company that employs some 400 people. Marie has been with the company for a little over a year.

Since her childhood, she has been recognized as a whiz at mathematics. In college, she was drawn to the use and design of computing systems. Her major responsibility is to provide technical support for computer systems users in the company.

Marie's first project with the company was to design an automated system for the shipping department. She interviewed the supervisors and workers in the department to establish the department's needs. She then matched the needs to available off-the-shelf equipment and programs and designed a system to automate much of the department's work. After finishing her design, she had to prepare a written report and oral briefing describing it for the shipping department and her boss. She had a ghastly time the next two weeks. She found, as do many novice writers, that she knew what she wanted to say but not where or how to say it. The ten-page report did somehow get written and, after a thorough overhaul by Ted Freedman (whom we'll meet next), was presented. Her oral report was a summary of the written report, and it was well received. Her system design was accepted and will be implemented in several months.

Marie's first experience with on-the-job technical writing taught her four important things: (1) An engineer is not simply a person whose only product is a new design or a gadget that works; (2) things that go on in your head and hands are lost unless they are recorded; (3) writing about what you have thought and done is a recurring necessity; and (4) technical writing, strange and difficult as it may seem at first, is something that can be learned by anyone of reasonable intelligence and perseverance.

Marie's present project is to write a set of instructions for the accounting department to help them use an automated system that was installed over a year ago. Marie's predecessor had installed the equipment and furnished the accountants a set of the manuals produced by the computer and program manufacturers. The manuals are well written, but because they are written by different manufacturers for a general audience, they do not integrate the components of the system in a way meaningful to the accountants. Marie has studied the system and interviewed the users to determine their needs. She has drafted a twenty-page booklet that supplements the manufacturer's manuals and shows the accountants how to use the new equipment and programs in their work. She has sent the draft to Ted Freedman for his comments.

Ted Freedman: Technical Writer and Company Editor

Ted Freedman was hired three years ago by the company as a technical writer–editor. He holds a bachelor's degree in technical communication. His office is a sparsely furnished cubicle down the hall from the publications and mailing departments. His office furnishings include a brand-new personal computer and printer, a four-foot shelf of dictionaries and reference manuals, and an extra-large wastepaper basket.

At 8:45 this morning Ted is scheduled for a project review session in the company auditorium. He arrives at the auditorium with five minutes to spare. For the next hour he studies flip charts, slide projections on the huge screen, chalk-and-blackboard plans for company reorganization (minor), and staffing proposals for three new projects totaling $778,400. From the platform, Chief Scientist Muldoon requests that Ted develop research timetables and preview reporting needs.

At 10:20 he meets with a commercial printer to examine the artwork and layout for a plush report the company is preparing for a state commission. The work looks good but needs a little typographical variety, he suggests.

At 12:55, back from lunch in the company cafeteria, Ted glances over the memos that collected on his desk during the morning—nothing urgent. Then he opens the manila envelope lying in his mail rack. In it is a computer disk that contains Marie's instructional booklet and a printout of the booklet.

At 1:30 he calls Marie and arranges for a meeting at 3:00 so that they can run through the draft together. In the meantime he looks over the printout. He notices some computer jargon. He is pretty sure the accountants would not have a clear idea of the distinction between Standard Generalized Markup Language (SGML) and American Standard Code for Information Interchange (ASCII). He circles both phrases. Reading on, he finds a spot where the text should be supported by a graphic. He makes a note of it in the margin. He realizes that the booklet would be more accessible to the reader with more headings in it. He puts Marie's disk into his word processor and, scrolling through her text on the screen, inserts headings that fit her arrangement and material. Thus, the afternoon wears on.

At 3:00, Marie arrives and the two confer, make changes, and plan later alterations in the draft. As before, they work amicably together. They intersperse their writing and editing with an occasional trip to the water cooler, a chat with a department head, and a visit to the World Wide Web to consult a specialized reference work.

Ted is good at his work and is considered to have a great future with the company.

Marie and Ted are roughly representative of many thousands of technical writer–editors. Most of them, like Marie, are not professional technical writers. They write as the need arises, to report or instruct. To gain a more rounded understanding of their duties and behavior, we would have to pay them many additional visits; however, certain things are evident even from this brief visit. Like most writers on the job, they work in collaboration with others. Also, much of the time they are not writing at all, in the popular sense. Some of the time they are simply listening hard to what people are saying to one another—trying to clarify, simplify, and translate into other terms. A generous portion of their time is spent on tasks that have little direct connection with writing but eventually provide grist for the writing mill. The techniques, tools, and processes that writers such as Ted and Marie need to accomplish their work are the subject matter of this book.

▶ EXERCISES

1. As your instructor directs, bring to class one or more documents that you believe to be technical. In groups of four or five discuss the documents. In what respects is the writing technical? Subject matter? Purpose? Tone? Specialized vocabulary? How has the writer used numbers, formulas, tables, and graphs? Are there headings and transitional features that guide readers through the document? Is it easy to scan the document and select certain parts of it for more intensive reading? In a class discussion, present your group's conclusions to the class.

2. Rewrite a brief paragraph of technical prose (perhaps a document submitted in Exercise 1) to substantially lower its technical level. Explain what you have done and why.

3. Examine several periodicals in your discipline. In what ways and to what extent does your examination of such periodicals confirm or change your first impressions of technical writing?

4. As your instructor directs, bring to class examples of technical and scientific writing for a lay audience, as opposed to a technical audience. You can find such examples in *Discover* or the science section of a news magazine like *Time* or *Newsweek*. Also, instructions for mechanisms such as compact disc players and VCRs are written for a lay audience. In groups of four or five, compare these examples to examples chosen from the periodicals you examined for Exercise 3. Present the conclusions your group reaches from this examination in a class discussion.

5. In two columns, list your assets and limitations as a technical writer.

Foundations

PART I emphasizes the composing process, introducing the book's central focus. Chapter 2 discusses how to analyze a writing situation and how to discover, arrange, revise, and edit technical information. Chapter 3 suggests strategies for working on collaborative writing projects. Chapter 4 shows how to adapt reports for various audiences. Chapter 5 emphasizes elements of style at the paragraph, sentence, and language level. Chapters 6 and 7 are new for this edition. Chapter 6 explains what it means to be ethical and how to be ethical in your writing. Chapter 7 deals with the reality of globalization and offers advice on how to write for non-American readers.

SCENARIO

With your new engineering degree, you went to work for Southwest Coal Power (SCP), a company that builds coal-burning power plants. In the six months you've been with SCP, you've learned how new technologies are making the burning of coal cleaner and safer for the environment. SCP has contracted to build a new power plant in Roll, Arizona. Before SCP can build the plant, however, it must file an Environmental Impact Statement that details any environmental problems the plant may cause and ways that such problems would be mitigated. You have been assigned to the team writing the statement. The proposed plant will use a boiler called a "fluidized-bed boiler," and the head of the team has assigned you the task of explaining the boiler.

In your first attempt, you wrote a highly technical textbook description of the fluidized-bed boiler, and the head of the team didn't like it at all. "Think of your readers," he said. "They're not engineers. They're bureaucrats and politicians and concerned citizens. They won't understand most of this, and when people don't understand something, they get suspicious and hostile. Give me something a nonengineer would understand."

So now you are putting on paper some thoughts about your readers. They won't understand engineering terminology. They need some sort of analogy, maybe. You've seen the fluidized-bed boiler compared to a giant pressure cooker. That might work. And you have some good drawings that show the boiler in action, pretty easy to visualize, really.

What's the reader's point of view? They probably think coal is a dirty fuel and that the new power plant will endanger the environment. You can show them how this new kind of boiler "fluidizes" more than 90 percent of the sulfur and nitrogen pollutants out of coal. You begin to realize that thinking about your readers can be a good way to discover the content you need and even to organize it.

This chapter explains how audience analysis fits into the composing process and identifies the other steps of the process.

chapter 2

Composing

▶ Situational Analysis
  Topic and Purpose
  Audience and Persona

▶ Discovery
  Brainstorming
  Using Arrangement Patterns for Discovery
  Other Successful Discovery Techniques

▶ Arrangement

▶ Drafting and Revising
  The Rough Draft
  Revision

▶ Editing
  Checking Mechanics
  Checking Documentation
  Checking Graphics
  Checking Document Design
  Editing with Word Processing Programs

The composing process is similar to all high-level reasoning processes in that we don't understand it completely. As one authority points out, "There are more neurons in the human brain than stars in the Milky Way—educated estimates put the number of neurons at about 10^{12} or one trillion. Each of those cells can 'talk' to as many as 1,000 other cells, making 10^{15} connections."[1] Given that level of complexity and those kinds of numbers, no one can map out completely how any complex, high-level, problem-solving process works. And the composing process is precisely that: a complex, high-level, problem-solving process.

Since classical times we have understood some things about the composing process. Aristotle, for example, recognized the wisdom of taking one's audience into account. In recent years, empirical research has revealed additional useful facts about the process. What we tell you in this chapter is based on those classical concepts that have stood the test of time and modern research. We don't pretend to have all the answers, or even that all our answers are right for you. But we can say that the process we describe draws on the actual practices of experienced writers, and it works for them.

For most skilled and experienced writers, the composing process breaks up into roughly five parts. The first part involves **situational analysis,** that time when you're trying to bring a thought from nowhere to somewhere. It's a time when you think about such things as your audience, your topic, and your purpose. In the second stage, you "discover" the material you need to satisfy your purpose and your audience. That **discovery** process may go on completely within the trillion cells of your brain or, as is often the case in technical writing, in libraries, laboratories, and workplaces as well.

When the discovery stage is almost complete, you pass into a stage in which you **arrange** your material. That is, before writing a draft, you may rough out a plan for it or even a fairly complete outline.

With your arrangement in hand, you are ready for the fourth part of the composing process, the **drafting and revising** of your document. For many competent writers, drafting and revising are separate steps; for others, they are almost concurrent.

In the final stage of the writing process, you **edit** your work to satisfy the requirements of standard English and proper format.

Time spent on these five parts is usually not equal. Situational analysis, discovery, and arrangement for a complicated piece of work may take 80 percent or more of the time you spend on the project. For an easy piece of routine writing, these first three stages may take a few minutes, and drafting and revising may take up the bulk of the time. Some situations call for careful, scrupulous editing; others do not.

The process is often not linear. If the drafting bogs down, you may have to return to the situational analysis stage to resolve the problem. Drafting and revising may alternate as you write for a while, then stop to read and revise. But, in rough outline, what we have described for you is the competent writer's composing process. Throughout this book, we frequently deal with the process. We remind you again and again of the needs of your audience and provide ways to discover material to satisfy different purposes and topics. In the rest of this chapter we provide some strategies you can use to develop a competent writing process of your own. Because any part of the process can be done in cooperation with others, we provide information on how to write collaboratively (Chapter 3).

▶ SITUATIONAL ANALYSIS

In this section we discuss situational analysis, dealing first with topic and purpose, and then with audience and persona.

Topic and Purpose

The topics and purposes of technical writing are found in the situations of technical writing. The topics are many. You may have a mechanism or process to explain—that is your topic. You may have to define a term or explain a procedure. You may have to report the results and conclusions of a scientific experiment or a comparison shopping study. New research has to be proposed. Work delays have to be explained. All these and many more are the topics of technical writing.

Although the topics of technical writing are varied, the purposes are more limited. Generally, your purpose is either to inform or to argue. Most topics can be handled in one of these two ways, depending on the situation. Often, you are simply informing. For example, the situation may call for you to describe a mechanism so that someone can understand it. As you will see in Chapter 9, Presenting Information, mechanism description will often call for you to divide the mechanism into its component parts and then describe these parts, perhaps as to size, shape, material, and purpose. As another example, you may have to define a term from your discipline. In your definition, you may tell what category the thing being defined belongs to and what distinguishes it from other members of the same category. You may give an example of the thing described.

On the other hand, when dealing with your mechanism or definition, you may be really mounting an argument. You may not be merely describing a mechanism; you may be attempting to demonstrate its superiority to other mechanisms of the same type. To do so, you'll need to argue, perhaps by showing how your mechanism is more economical and easier to maintain than other mechanisms. In the same way, you may not be simply defining a term; you may be arguing that your definition is more comprehensive or more correct than previous definitions of the same term.

Be sure to have your topic and purpose in hand before you proceed on in your writing project. It's good practice to write them down, something like this:

> I will define alcoholism in a way that reflects recent research. Further, I will demonstrate that my definition, which includes the genetic causes of alcoholism as well as the environmental ones, is more complete and accurate than definitions that deal with environmental causes alone.

Will the topic and purpose change as you proceed with your project? That depends on the situation. Frequently, the situation will call for you to stick closely to a narrow topic and purpose: *We have to explain to our clients our progress (or lack of progress) in installing the air conditioning system in their new plant.* Or, in another typical situation, *We have to provide instructions for the bank tellers who will use the computer consoles we have installed at their stations.* Although the way you handle such topics and purposes is subject to change as you explore them, the topics and purposes themselves really are not subject to change. On the other hand, the situation may call for you to explore a topic, perhaps the potential effect of the rising age of the American population on the restaurant business. Although you have defined your topic well enough to begin your exploration, the precise topic and the purpose may have to wait until you discover more information about your subject.

Audience and Persona

Writers make important decisions about content and style based on consideration of the audience and the persona the writer wants to project. **Persona** refers to the role the writer has, or assumes, when writing. It relates to, among other things, the position of the writer and his or her relationship to the audience and the situation. For example, a bank lending officer might assume one persona when writing to a loan applicant and a different persona when writing to a supervisor to justify a loan that has been made.

Professional people consider both audience and persona seriously when composing, as this quote from a hydrology consultant at an engineering firm indicates:

> We write about a wide range of subject matters. Some things are familiar to a lay audience. Most people can understand a study about floods. They can understand a study that defines a 100-year flood plain. They can imagine, say, water covering a street familiar to them. But other subjects are very difficult to communicate. We work with three-dimensional models of water currents, for example, that are

based upon very recondite hydrologic movements. We also have a wide audience range. Some of our reports are read by citizen groups. Sometimes we write for a client who has a technical problem of some sort and is only interested in what to do about it. And sometimes we write for audiences with high technical expertise like the Army Corps of Engineers. Audiences like the Army Corps expect a report to be written in a scientific journal style, and they even want the data so they can re-analyze it. A lot of times the audience is mixed. A regulatory agency may know little about the subject of one of our reports, but they may have a technically trained person on the staff who does. In any case, we must understand what it is that the client wants, and we must be aware of what he knows about the subject. We must convince clients that we know what we are doing. We depend upon return business and word-of-mouth reputation, and we must make a good impression the first time. Much of the technical reputation of this company rides on how we present ourselves in our technical reports.[2]

Here are some questions you need to ask about your audience and persona when you are preparing to write.

What Is the Level of Knowledge and Experience of Your Readers? In technical writing, the knowledge and experience your readers possess are key factors. Do your readers understand your professional and technical language? If they do, your task is easier than if they do not. When they do not, you have to be particularly alert to your word choice, choosing simpler terms when possible, defining terms when simpler choices are not possible. Awareness of your readers goes beyond word choice. There are whole concepts that a lay audience may not have. Geologists, for example, thoroughly understand the concept of plate tectonics and can assume that geologists in their audience understand it equally well. When addressing a lay audience, however, the geologist writer would be wise to assume little understanding of the concept. If the geologist wishes to use the concept, he or she will have to take time to explain it in a way that the audience can grasp.

What Is the Reader's Point of View? Point of view relates to the reader's purpose and concerns. Suppose that you are writing about a procedure. People may read about procedures for many reasons. In one case, the reader may wish to perform the procedure. In another, the reader may have to make a decision about whether to adopt the procedure. In yet another, readers may simply want generalized information about the procedure, perhaps because they find it interesting.

Each case calls for a different selection of content and a different style. Readers wishing to perform the procedure need a complete set of step-by-step instructions. The decision maker needs to know by what criteria the procedure has been evaluated and why, under these criteria, it is a better choice than other procedures. Those who read for interest want the general concept of the procedure explained in language they can understand.

What Is Your Relationship to the Reader? Are the readers your bosses, clients, subordinates, peers, or students? If you are a public employee, are you writing to a taxpayer who contributes to your salary? Writers in the workplace, when interviewed about how they write, reveal that they pay a good deal of attention to the effect of such relationships on tone, as these quotations demonstrate:[3]

- Writing to my boss, I try to pinpoint things a little more.
- When you have something as personal as a phone call or a conversation back and forth . . . I feel free to use "I" rather than "we."
- We always want them to realize they can call on us if they have any questions.
- This [referring to a statement] is a bit more on a personal level. . . . The other [statement] is much too formal.
- Just to say "Send his address" would, I think, be a little too authoritarian.

The roles writers find themselves in also affect their choice of content. Imagine the difference in approach between a Chevrolet sales representative trying to sell a fleet of Chevrolets to a company, and a young executive of the same company reporting to his or her superiors that the results of a feasibility study demonstrate Chevrolets to be the best purchase. In the first instance, the sales representative is likely to be more enthusiastic about Chevrolets than other makes. The decision makers would expect and understand such enthusiasm and would allow for it. In the second instance, the decision makers will expect a more balanced approach from the young executive.

What Is Your Reader's Attitude about What You Are Going to Say? Audiences can be suspicious and hostile. They may be apathetic. Of course, they may be friendly and interested. Their attitude should affect how you approach them. If you have an unfriendly audience, you must take particular care to explain your position carefully in language that is understandable but not patronizing. You may need more examples than you would with a friendly audience. A friendly audience may be persuaded with less information. With a friendly audience, you may present your conclusions first and then support them. With an unfriendly audience, it's a sound idea to present your support first and then your conclusions.

Readers may have attitudes about the language you use. For example, public health officials have had a difficult time expressing how to avoid exposure to AIDS. Such advice, to be effective, must refer very explicitly to sexual practices. Newspapers have had to change their usual practice to allow such language to be printed, and some readers have found the language offensive. In most cases, the interest in AIDS prevention has won out over reader sensibilities, but the problem illustrates well the social context of audience analysis.

What Persona Do You Wish to Project? If you have read many scientific journals, you have probably noticed that they have a certain tone about them, a tone to which words such as *objective*, *formal*, and *restrained* readily apply. Scientists, to find acceptance in such journals, must adopt such a tone. A breezy, light journalistic style, though it might be just as clear, would not be acceptable. In the same way, bankers must present themselves in a careful, formal way. We're not likely to give our money for safekeeping into the hands of someone who comes on like a television used-car dealer. Young executives writing to their bosses are likely to be a bit deferential. The bosses, in turn, want to sound firm but reasonable and not authoritarian. What has come to be called "corporate culture" plays a role in the persona a writer may adopt. In writing, you must project the values and attitudes of the organization you work for. To do so, you may look over past correspondence and reports to see what practices have been used, what sort of tone writers in the organization have adopted.

Taking on a persona when you write is something like taking on a persona when you dress. The student who exchanges his blue jeans and running shoes for a business suit and wing tips when he reports for a job interview is slipping out of one persona into another. The teacher who exchanges a comfortable sweater and skirt for a businesslike dress when she leaves the classroom to consult in industry is exchanging one persona for another. It's a common enough experience in life, and you should not be surprised to find such experiences in writing situations. Both dressing and writing have their own rhetorics. However, don't misinterpret anything we have said as a rationale for being obscure or jargony. You should be clear no matter what persona you adopt.

What Is the Influence of International Cultures? You can no longer be certain that you will be writing or speaking to a North American audience only. Because many organizations operate internationally, technical professionals often need to communicate with people from other countries. When they do so, they must take the culture of the country they are dealing with into account.

Anthropologists have defined culture in a number of ways:

- Culture is a shared system of meanings, derived from the environment in which people live and work.
- Culture is a mind-set, the response by people to their physical and human environment. It is the survival mechanism they develop and pass on consciously and unconsciously to succeeding generations.
- Culture is a transmitted system of values, ideas, and behaviors. It is a set of common understandings.

Thinking that people are the same everywhere would be a major error in analyzing your audience. Countries, and cultures within those countries, do differ. Cultures differ because of climate, topography, population density, natural resources available, religion, family structure, educational systems, and political systems. To understand a person, you must understand the culture through which that person interprets the world. Only when you know what approach and persona readers from other cultures expect from you will you be able to communicate with them. As you plan any document, always consider the culture of your readers. In Chapter 7, Writing for International Readers, we discuss specific cultural differences and ways to deal with them. We remind you of cultural differences in discussing style, graphics, correspondence, and oral reports.

▶ DISCOVERY

At some point in your writing process you must "discover" the material you will use in your writing. Discovery is teasing out of your mind the information you will use and modify to meet the needs of your topic, purpose, audience, and persona. Discovery is making connections. It's putting together two pieces of information to create a third piece that didn't exist before the connection. A mind that is well stocked with information will probably be successful at discovery. Those trillion neurons need something to work with; the more you read, observe, and experience, the better writer you are likely to be.

Of course, all the material you need may not be in your mind when you begin. Discovery includes using libraries, the Internet, and laboratories to fill in the gaps in your knowledge. You may also use interviews, on-site inspections, letters of inquiry, and the like to gather information. The techniques we discuss here will enable you to explore your own mind. (See also, Chapter 8, Gathering, Evaluating, and Documenting Information.)

Brainstorming

In brainstorming you uncritically jot down every idea about a subject that pops into your head, without thought of organization. The key to successful brainstorming is that you do not attempt to evaluate or arrange your material at the first stage. These processes come later. Evaluation or arrangement at the first critical stage may cause you to discard an idea that could prove valuable in the context of all the ideas that the brainstorming session produces. Also, avoiding evaluation at this point prevents the self-censorship that often blocks a writer.

Because brainstorming is a fairly painless process, it's frequently a good device to break down the normal resistance most of us have to hard thinking. It can result in your writing down a good deal more information than you ever thought you possessed. It can quickly reveal holes in your knowledge, which can be filled with information you gather later.

Using Arrangement Patterns for Discovery

Although you do not arrange your material in the discovery stage, you can use familiar arrangement patterns as aids in discovering your material. For example, suppose your purpose is to describe a procedure for a reader who wishes to perform the procedure. If you were familiar with writing instructions, as you will be after reading Chapter 18, Instructions, you would know that a set of instructions often lists and sometimes describes the tools that must be used to perform the procedure. Furthermore, instructions describe the steps of the procedure, normally in chronological order. Knowing what is normally required for a set of instructions, you can brainstorm your material in a more guided way.

You can begin by writing down the tools that will be needed for the procedure. Think about what you know about your audience. Are they experienced with the tools needed? If so, simply list the tools. If they are not experienced, jot down some information they'll need to use the tools properly.

When you are done with the tools, write down the steps of the procedure. Keep your readers in mind. Are there some steps so unfamiliar to your readers that you need to provide additional information to help them perform the steps? If so, list what that information might be.

As in brainstorming, in very little time you can get information out where you can see it. Also, as in brainstorming, if there are gaps in your knowledge, you can discover them early enough to fill them.

Another task frequently encountered in technical writing is arguing to support an opinion. In discovering an argument, you can begin by stating that opinion clearly, perhaps something like "Women should get equal pay for equal work." Next, you can turn your attention to the subarguments that might support such an opinion. For example, first, you would have to establish that in many instances women are not getting equal pay for equal work, and, therefore, a problem really does exist. Then you might think of a philosophical argument: Ethically, women have a right to equal pay for equal work. You might think of an economic argument: Women's needs to support themselves and their families equal those of men. And so forth. As you think about subarguments, you will begin to think about the information you will need to support them. Some of it you may have; some you may need to research. The very form and needs of your argument serve as powerful tools to help you discover your material.

Other Successful Discovery Techniques

Most experienced writers develop their own discovery techniques. In the workplace, writers often use past documents of a similar nature to jog their minds. Many professional writers keep journals that they can mine for ideas and data. Scientists keep laboratory notebooks that can be invaluable when it's time to write up the research. In the workplace, people talk to each other to discover and refine ideas.

Asking questions, particularly from the reader's point of view, is a powerful discovery technique. Suppose you were describing the use of computers for word processing. What questions might the reader have? *Do I have to be an expert typist to use a word processor? What are the advantages of word processing? The disadvantages? How do I judge the effectiveness of a word processor? What do word processors cost? Will word processing make writing and revising easier?* As you ask and answer such questions, you are discovering your material.

When you have established your topic and purpose, analyzed your audience, and discovered your material, it's time to think about arrangement.

▶ ARRANGEMENT

When you begin your arrangement, you should have a good deal of material to work with. You should have notes on your audience, purpose, and persona. Your discovered material may take various forms. It may be a series of notes produced by brainstorming or other discovery techniques. You may have cards filled with notes taken during library research or notebooks filled with jottings made during laboratory research. You may have previous reports and correspondence on the topic you are writing about. You may have ideas for graphs and tables to use in presenting your material. In fact, you may have so much material that you do not know where to begin.

You can save yourself much initial chaos and frustration if you remember that certain kinds of reports (and sections of reports) have fairly standard arrangements (see Chapter 9, Presenting Information, and Chapter 10, Analyzing Information). The same arrangement patterns that helped you discover your material can now serve you as models of arrangement. For instance, you might divide your subject into a series of topics, as we have done with the chapters of this book. If you're describing a procedure and know that your readers wish to perform that procedure, you may use a standard instruction arrangement: introduction, tool list and description, and steps of the procedure in chronological order. If you are arranging an argument, you have your major opinion, often called the major thesis, and your subarguments, often called minor theses. You'll probably want to consider the strength of your minor theses when you arrange your argument. Generally, you want to start and finish your argument with strong minor theses. You'll place weaker minor theses in the middle of your argument.

Documents such as progress reports, proposals, and empirical research reports have fairly definite arrangements that we describe for you in Part III, Applications. Not all the arrangements described will fit your needs exactly. You must be creative and imaginative when using them. But they do exist. Use them when they are appropriate.

How thorough you are at this stage depends on such things as the complexity of the material you are working with and your own working habits. Simple material does not require complicated outlines. Perhaps nowhere else in the writing process does personality play such a prominent role as it does at the arrangement stage. Some people prepare fairly complete arrangement patterns; others do not.

Most experienced writers are usually thorough but informal in writing down their arrangement patterns. However, if you need a formal outline and need instruction in preparing one, see Outlining in Appendix B.

In technical writing, graphs and tables are important techniques for presenting material. It's not too early to think about them while you are arranging your material. For help in planning and selecting graphs and tables, see Chapter 12, Using Illustrations.

▶ DRAFTING AND REVISING

When you have finished arranging your material, you are ready to draft and revise your report. Keep in mind that writing is not an easy mechanical job. But we do give you suggestions that should make a tough job easier.

The Rough Draft

Writing a rough draft is a very personal thing. Few writers do it exactly alike. As you have seen, most write from a plan of some sort; a few do not. Some write at a fever pitch; others write slowly. Some writers leave revision for an entirely separate step. Some revise for style and even edit for mechanics as they go along, working slowly, trying to get it right the first time. All we can do is describe in general the practices of most professional writers. Take our suggestions and apply them to your own practices. Use the ones that make the job easier for you and revise or discard the rest.

Probably our most important suggestion is to begin writing as soon after the prewriting stage as possible. Writing is hard work. Most people, even professionals, procrastinate. Almost anything can serve as an excuse to put the job off: one more book to read, a movie that has to be seen, anything. The following column by Art Buchwald describes the problem of getting started in a manner that most writers would agree is only mildly exaggerated.

MARTHA'S VINEYARD—There are many great places where you can't write a book, but as far as I'm concerned none compares to Martha's Vineyard.

This is how I managed not to write a book and I pass it on to fledgling authors as well as old-timers who have vowed to produce a great work of art this summer.

The first thing you need is lots of paper, a solid typewriter, preferably electric, and a quiet spot in the house overlooking the water.

You get up at 6 in the morning and go for a dip in the sea. Then you come back and make yourself a hearty breakfast.

By 7 A.M. You are ready to begin Page 1, Chapter 1. You insert a piece of paper in the typewriter and start to type "It was the best of times . . ." Then you look out the window and you see a sea gull diving for a fish. This is not an ordinary sea gull. It seems to have a broken wing and you get up from the desk to observe it on the off chance that somewhere in the book you may want to insert a scene of a sea gull with a broken wing trying to dive for a fish. (It would make a great shot when the book is sold to the movies and the lovers are in bed.)

It is now 8 A.M. and the sounds of people getting up distract you. There is no sense trying to work with everyone crashing around the house. So you write a letter to your editor telling him how well the book is going and that you're even more optimistic about this one than the last one which the publisher never advertised.

It is now 9 A.M. and you go into the kitchen and scream at your wife, "How am I going to get any work done around here if the kids are making all that racket? It doesn't mean anything in this family that I have to make a living."

Your wife kicks all the kids out of the house and you go back to your desk . . . You look out the window again and you see a sailboat in trouble. You take your binoculars and study the situation carefully. If it gets worse you may have to call the Coast Guard. But after a half-hour of struggling they seem to have things under control.

Then you remember you were supposed to receive a check from the *Saturday Review* so you walk to the post office, pause at the drugstore for newspapers, and stop at the hardware store for rubber cement to repair your daughter's raft.

You're back at your desk at 1 P.M. when you remember you haven't had lunch. So you fix yourself a tuna fish sandwich and read the newspapers.

It is now 2:30 P.M. and you are about to hit the keys when Bill Styron calls. He announces they have just received a load of lobsters at Menemsha and he's driving over to get some before they're all gone. Well, you say to yourself, you can always write a book on the Vineyard, but how often can you get fresh lobster?

So you agree to go with Styron for just an hour.

Two hours later with the thought of fresh lobster as inspiration, you sit down at the typewriter. The doorbell rings and Norma Brustein is standing there in her tennis togs looking for a fourth for doubles.

You don't want to hurt Norma's feelings so you get your racket and for the next hour play a fierce game of tennis, which is the only opportunity you have had all day of taking your mind off your book.

It is now 6 P.M. and the kids are back in the house, so there is no sense trying to get work done any more for that day.

So you put the cover on the typewriter with a secure feeling that no matter how ambitious you are about working there will always be somebody on the Vineyard ready and eager to save you. [Reprinted by permission of Art Buchwald.]

But you must begin, and the sooner the better. Find a quiet place to work, one with few distractions. Choose a time of day when you feel like working, and go to work.

Where should you begin? Usually, it's a good strategy to begin not with the beginning but with the section that you think will be the easiest to write. If you do so, the whole task will seem less overwhelming. As you write one section, ideas for handling others will pop into your mind. When you finish an easy section, go on to a tougher one. In effect, you are writing a series of short, easily handled reports rather than one long one. Think of a 1,500-word report as three short, connected, 500-word reports. You will be amazed at how much easier this attitude makes the job. We should point out that some writers do prefer to begin with their introductions and even to write their summaries, conclusions, and recommendations (if any) first. They feel this sets their purpose, plan, and final goals firmly in their minds. If you like to work that way, fine. Do remember, though, to check such elements after you have written the discussion to see whether they still fit.

How fast should you write? Again, this is a personal thing, but most professional writers write rapidly. We advise you not to worry overmuch about phraseology or spelling in a rough draft. Proceed as swiftly as you can to get your ideas on paper. Later, you can smooth out your phrasing and check your spelling, either with your dictionary or your word processor's spelling checker. However, if you do get stalled, reading over what you have written and tinkering with it a bit is a good way to get the flow going again. In fact, two researchers of the writing process found that their subjects spent up to a third of their time pausing. Generally, the pauses occurred at the ends of paragraphs or when the writer was searching for examples to illustrate an abstraction.[4]

Do not write for more than two hours at a stretch. This time span is one reason you want to begin writing a long, important report at least a week before it is due. A report written in one long five- or six-hour stretch reflects the writer's exhaustion. Break at a point where you are sure of the next paragraph or two. When you come back to the writing, read over the previous few paragraphs to help you collect your thoughts and then begin at once.

Make your rough draft very full. You will find it easier to delete material later than to add it. Nonprofessional writers often write thin discussions because they think in terms of the writing time span rather than the reading time span. They have been writing on a subject for perhaps an hour and have grown a little bored with it. They feel that if they add details for another half-hour they will bore the reader. Remember this: At 250 words a minute, average readers can read an hour's writing output in several minutes. Spending less time with the material than the writer must, readers will not get bored. Rather than wanting less detail, they may want more. Don't infer from this advice that you should pad your report. Brevity is a virtue in professional reports. But the report should include enough detail to demonstrate to the reader that you know what you're talking about. The path between conciseness on one hand and completeness on the other is often something of a tightrope.

As you write your rough draft, indicate where your references will go. Be alert for paragraphs full of numbers and statistics, and consider presenting such information in tables and graphs. Be alert for places where you will need headings and other transitional devices to guide your readers through the report. (See Chapter 11, Document Design.)

Whether your planning has been detailed or casual, keep in mind that writing is a creative process. Discovery does not stop when you begin to write. The reverse is usually true. For most people, writing stimulates discovery. Writing clarifies your thoughts, refines your ideas, and leads you to new connections. Therefore, be flexible. Be willing to revise your plan to accommodate new insights as they occur.

Revision

Some writers revise while they are writing. For them, revision as a separate step is little more than minor editing, checking for misspellings and awkward phrases. For other writers—particularly those who write in a headlong flight—revising is truly rewriting, and sometimes even rearranging, the rough draft. Naturally, there are many gradations between these two extremes. Whether you revise while you write or in a separate step, you should be concerned about arrangement, content, logic, style, graphics, and document design. In some situations you may want to show your work to others and seek their advice.

Arrangement and Content In checking your arrangement and content, try to put yourself in your reader's place. Does your discussion take too much for granted? Are questions left unanswered that the reader will want answered? Are links of thought missing? Have you provided smooth transitions from section to section, paragraph to paragraph? Do some paragraphs need to be split, others combined? Is some vital thought buried deep in the discussion when it should be put into a prominent position at the beginning or end? Have you avoided irrelevant material or unwanted repetitions?

In checking content, be sure that you have been specific enough. Have you quantified when necessary? Have you stated that "In 2000, 52 percent of the workers took at least twelve days of sick leave" rather than "In a previous year, a majority of the workers took a large amount of sick leave"? Have you given enough examples, facts, and numbers to support your generalizations? Conversely, have you generalized enough to unify your ideas and to put them into the sharpest possible focus? Have you adapted your material to your audience?

Is your information accurate? Don't rely on even a good memory for facts and figures that you are not totally sure of. Follow up any gut feeling you have that anything you have written seems inaccurate, even if it means a trip back to the library or laboratory. Check and double-check your math and equations. You can destroy an argument (or a piece of machinery) with a misplaced decimal point.

Logic Be rigorous in your logic. Can you really claim that A caused B? Have you sufficiently taken into account other contributing factors? Examine your discussion for every conceivable weakness of arrangement and content, and be ready to pull it apart. All writers find it difficult to be harshly critical of their own work, but a critical eye is essential.

Style After you have revised your draft for arrangement and content, read it over for style. (We treat this as a separate step, which it is. But, of course, if you find a clumsy sentence while revising for arrangement and content, rewrite it immediately.) Use Chapter 5, Achieving a Readable Style, to help you. Rewrite unneeded passive voice sentences. Cut out words that add nothing to your thought. Cross out the pretentious words and substitute simpler ones. If you find a cliché, try to express the same idea in different words. Simplify; cut out the artificiality and the jargon. Be sure the diction and sentence structures are suitable to the occasion and the audience. Remember that you are trying to write understandably, not impressively. The final product should carry your ideas to the reader's brain by the shortest, simplest path.

Graphics Much technical information is presented in tables and graphs. When dealing with content that has visual components, you should probably present at least some of that content graphically. When you have numerous statistics, particularly statistics that you are comparing to each other, you probably should display them in tables or graphs. (For help in such matters, see Chapter 12, Using Illustrations.)

Document Design Good document design—the use of tables of contents, headings, the right typeface, proper spacing, and so forth—is integral to good technical writing. We offer detailed guidance in this area in Chapter 11, Document Design, and in Report Format in Appendix B.

Sharing Your Work In actual workplace situations, writers often share their drafts with colleagues and ask for their opinions. Often, someone who is not as close to the material as the writer can spot flaws far more quickly than the writer can. As you'll see when we discuss revising and editing with word processing programs, you may also share your work with your personal computer.

When you are writing instructions, it's an excellent idea to share an early draft with people who are similar in aptitude and knowledge to the people for whom the instructions are intended. See whether they can follow the instructions. Ask them to tell you where they had trouble carrying out your instructions or where poor vocabulary choice or insufficient content threw them off track.

▶ EDITING

Editing is a separate step that follows drafting and revising. It's the next-to-final step before you release your report to its intended audience. When you're drafting and revising a manuscript, you may have to backtrack to the discovery or the arranging stage of the process. But when you are editing, it's either because you are satisfied with your draft or because you have run out of time. In the editing stage, you make sure your report is as mechanically perfect as possible, that it meets the requirements of standard English and whatever format requirements your situation calls for. If you are working for a large organization or the government, you may have to concern yourself with things such as stylebook specifications, distribution lists, and code numbers.

Checking Mechanics

Begin by checking your mechanics. Are you a poor speller? Check every word that looks the least bit doubtful. Some particularly poor spellers read their draft backwards to be sure that they catch all misspelled words. Develop a healthy sense of doubt and use a good dictionary or the spelling checker of your word processing program. Do you have trouble with subject–verb agreement? Be particularly alert for such errors. In Appendix A we have provided you with a handbook that covers some of the more common mechanical problems. A word processor can help by allowing you to check for some of the errors a computer program is able to detect.

Checking Documentation

When you are satisfied with your mechanics, check your documentation. Be sure that all notes and numbers match. Be sure that you have used the same style throughout for your notes. For help in documentation, see Documentation in Appendix B.

Checking Graphics

Check your graphics for accuracy, and be sure you have mentioned them at the appropriate place in the report. Are your graphics well placed? If they are numbered, be sure that their numbers and the numbers you use in referring to them match.

Checking Document Design

In your drafting and revision, you should have made sure that your design makes your document readable and accessible for your readers. When editing, check for more mundane but nevertheless important things. For instance, is your table of contents complete? Is it accurate? Does it match the headings you have used? Do your headers or footers accurately portray your material?

When you are satisfied that you have done all that needs to be done, print your final draft, then proofread it one more time before you turn it over to your audience. The author of a report is responsible for all errors.

Editing with Word Processing Programs

To help the writer with editing, spelling checkers and grammar and style checkers are available in word processing programs.

Spelling Checkers You may have a spelling checker in your word processing program or one that you have bought separately. Spelling checkers work by looking up every word of your text in the dictionary that is a part of the program. Most spelling checkers have no sense of grammar or usage. They will stop on a word spelled correctly if that word does not happen to be in the program's dictionary, as is true of many technical terms. More important, they will not stop at a word that is in the program's dictionary when that word is used incorrectly in context. A spelling checker won't catch errors like these:

> The *student's* all came to class today.
> They wanted to *here* your speech.
> They wanted to hear *you* speech.

(For a list of words that sound alike but have different spellings and meanings, such as *weather* and *whether*, see the entry for Spelling Error in the Handbook.) Use a spelling checker first, but then make sure to proofread as well.

Grammar and Style Checkers You can get programs that check your work for grammar, punctuation, and style. Some will flag sentences in the passive voice, long sentences, wordy phrases, double words (such as *and and*), unpaired quotation marks, and other problems. Some also flag subject–verb agreement problems, incorrect possessives, and other grammatical faults. Some give your text a "readability rating" according to one or more formulas.

Grammar and style checkers can be helpful. They can make you more aware of your writing style. If you tend to write in the passive voice, they'll press you to change to active voice. If you tend to use wordy phrases or unnecessarily long words, they'll give you shorter, crisper alternatives.

Use grammar and style checkers with great caution, however. Some current text-analysis programs are too rule-bound to be flexible, and some of the rules may be of doubtful validity. Consider the advice grammar and style checkers give you in light of the purpose and audience for your document. Not every passive voice sentence should be rewritten as an active sentence. Not every sentence of more than twenty-two words is too long. Grammar and style checkers work only at the sentence and word level, but the most serious problems with many documents are in their content and overall organization. If you change words and sentences here and there without considering larger issues of content and arrangement, you may actually be making your document less useful and understandable.

▶ PLANNING AND REVISION CHECKLISTS

The following questions are a summary of the key points in this chapter, and they provide a checklist you can use when you are composing.

Situational Analysis

- What is your topic?
- Why are you writing about this topic? What is your purpose (or purposes)?
- What are your readers' educational levels? What are their knowledge and experience in the subject matter area?
- What will your readers do with the information? What is their purpose?
- Do your readers have any expectations as to style and tone (serious, light, formal)?
- What is your relationship to your readers? How will this relationship affect your approach to them?
- What are your readers' attitudes about what you are going to say?
- Do you have an international audience whose culture may differ from that of the United States?

Discovery

- What discovery approach can you use? Brainstorming? Using arrangement patterns? Other?
- Are there documents similar to the one you are planning that would help you?
- Do you have notes or journal entries available?
- What questions are your readers likely to want answered?
- Do you have all the information you need? If not, where can you find it? People? Library? Laboratory research? World Wide Web?
- What tables, graphs, diagrams, or other graphic aids will you likely need?

Arrangement

- Are there standard arrangement patterns that would help you—for example, instructions, argument, proposals?
- Will you need to modify any such standard pattern to suit your needs?
- Do you need a formal outline?
- When completed, does your organizational plan fit your topic, material, purpose, and audience?
- What headings and subheadings will you use to reveal your organization and content to your readers?
- Is everything in your plan relevant to your topic, purpose, and audience?
- If you have a formal outline, does it follow outlining conventions? Are entries grammatically parallel? Is each section divided into at least two parts? Have you used correct capitalization? Are entries substantive?

Drafting

- Do you have a comfortable place to work?
- Where in your organizational plan can you begin confidently?
- Where will your graphical elements be placed?

Revision

- Have you stated clearly and specifically the purpose of the report?
- Have you put into the report everything required? Do you have sufficient supporting evidence? Have you stated the implications of your information clearly?
- Are all your facts and numbers accurate?
- Have you answered the questions your readers are likely to have?

- Does the report contain anything that you would do well to cut out?
- Does your organization suit the needs of your content and your audience?
- Are your paragraphs clear, well organized, and of reasonable length? Are there suitable transitions from one point to the next?
- Is your prose style clear and readable?
- Is your tone appropriate to your audience?
- Have you satisfied the needs of an international audience?
- Are your graphs and tables clear and accurate? Are they well placed?
- Is your document readable, accessible, and visually effective?
- Are there people you should share your draft with—for example, members of the target audience—before going on to a final draft?

Editing

- Have you checked thoroughly for misspellings and other mechanical errors?
- Have you included all the formal elements that your report needs?
- Are design elements such as headings, margins, spacing, typefaces, and documentation consistent throughout the draft?
- Are your headings and titles clear, properly worded, and parallel? Do your headings in the text match those in the table of contents?
- Is your documentation system the one required? Have you documented wherever appropriate? Do the numbers in the text match those in the notes?
- Have you keyed the tables and figures into your text, and have you sufficiently discussed them?
- Are all parts and pages of the manuscript in the correct order?
- Will the format of the typed or printed report be functional, clear, and attractive?
- Does your manuscript satisfy stylebook specifications governing it?
- Have you included required notices, distribution lists, and identifying code numbers?
- Do you have written permission to reproduce extended quotations or other matter under copyright? (Permission is necessary only when your work is to be published or copyrighted.)
- While you were composing the manuscript, did you have any doubts or misgivings that you should now check out?
- Have you edited your manuscript for matters both large and small?
- What remains to be done (such as proofreading the final copy)?

► EXERCISES

1. Describe accurately and completely your current writing process. Be prepared to discuss your description in class.

2. Interview someone who has to write frequently (such as one of your professors). Ask about the person's writing process. Base your questions on the process described in this chapter; that is, ask about situational analysis and arranging, drafting, revising, and editing techniques. Take good notes during the interview, and write a report describing the interviewee's writing process.

3. Choose some technical or semitechnical topic you can write about with little research—perhaps a topic related to a hobby or some school subject you enjoy. Decide on a purpose and audience for writing about that topic. For example, you could instruct high school seniors in some laboratory technique. You could explain some technical concept or term to someone who doesn't understand it—to one of your parents, perhaps. Analyze your audience and persona, following the suggestions in this chapter. With your purpose, audience, and persona in mind, brainstorm your topic. After you complete the brainstorming, examine and evaluate what you have. Reexamine your topic and purpose to see whether information you have thought of during the brainstorming has changed them. Keeping your specific topic, purpose, audience, and persona in mind, arrange your brainstorming notes into a rough outline. Do not worry overmuch about outline format, such as roman numerals, parallel headings, and so forth.

4. Turn the informal outline you constructed for Exercise 3 into a formal outline (see Outlining in Appendix B).

5. Write a rough draft of the report you planned in Exercises 3 and 4. Allow several classmates to read it and comment on it. Revise and edit the rough draft into a final, well-written and well-typed draft. Submit all your outlines and drafts to your instructor.

6. On page 19, we describe culture as a "transmitted system of values, ideas, and behavior. It is a set of common understandings." In groups of six or seven, discuss and describe the values, ideas, behavior, and common understandings that govern your culture. Are there disparities of opinion within the group about these matters? Prepare two lists: one composed of the group's agreements and another composed of the disparities of opinion within the group. Be prepared to present and talk about both lists in a full class discussion.

SCENARIO

It had been a day that started badly but ended rather well. You and five of your colleagues at the Rock Hill Power Company were drafting the company's five-year strategic plan. You were plugging the need for a statement concerning ethical behavior on the part of the company, and Charlie Burke kept objecting to your idea. Things were getting kind of hot.

"Look, Charlie," you said, "Companies need to be ethical to stay in business. Remember what happened to. . ."

Charlie cut you off with, "Look, I don't need you to lecture me on the need for ethical behavior, so I wish you would quit pontificating about it."

You were about to really tell him off when Carla broke in. "I thought only popes had the right to pontificate," she said. "Why don't we look at the need for the company to help its customers move toward more environmentally sound heating systems. We need to set realistic goals for that."

The group was pretty well agreed about the goals to be set in that area. You discussed them amiably and, in about thirty minutes, achieved a good draft statement on that topic.

Then Carla said, "About ethics. You know, the National Science Foundation supports an ethics help line on the Net run by the National Institute for Engineering Ethics."

"So?" said Charlie.

"Well," said Carla, "You've made clear your objections to a statement in the strategic plan about ethics. You think it could be perceived as an admission that we haven't been ethical in the past, right?"

"You got it," Charlie said.

"Maybe so," Carla said, "but ethics in engineering has become a really hot topic. People are concerned about it. A statement in our strategic plan about ethics could be perceived as a sign that we are up-to-date and ethically aware, as, indeed, we really are."

"I think Carla's right," Jerry said.

"I suppose we could talk about it," Charlie said.

And the group did talk about it, and in about twenty minutes had worked out an ethics statement that satisfied everyone, even Charlie and you.

Planning documents collaboratively and having group discussions are common experiences in the workplace. As we have just seen, they often lead to tense, even personal arguments. How Carla defused the tension in this situation and moved the group on to a good resolution is explained in this chapter.

chapter 3

Writing Collaboratively

▶ Planning

▶ Drafting
   Dividing the Work
   Drafting in Collaboration
   One Person Doing the Drafting

▶ Revising and Editing
   Revising
   Editing

▶ Collaboration in the Workplace

▶ Collaboration on the Internet
   E-Mail
   FTP Sites
   Synchronous Discussions

▶ Group Conferences
   Conference Behavior
   Group Roles

As we point out in Chapter 2, you can write collaboratively as well as individually. Organizations conduct a good deal of their business through group conferences. In a group conference, people gather, usually in a comfortable setting, to share information, ideas, and opinions. Organizations use group conferences for planning, disseminating information, and, most of all, for problem solving. As a problem-solving activity, writing lends itself particularly well to conferencing techniques. In fact, collaborative writing is common in the workplace.[1]

In this chapter, we discuss some of the ways that people can collaborate on a piece of writing. We conclude with a brief discussion of group conferencing skills, skills that are useful not only for collaborative writing but for any conference situation you are likely to find yourself in.

People cooperate in many ways in the workplace. One of the ways they cooperate is to share their writing with one another. Someone writing a report may pass it to a coworker and ask for a general comment or perhaps specifically for feedback on the report's style, tone, accuracy, or even grammar.

However, the collaborative writing we discuss in this chapter is more complex than a simple sharing. Rather, it is the working together of a group over an extended period of time to produce a document. In producing the document, the group shares the responsibility for the document, the decision making, and the work. Figure 3-1 shows the major steps of the collaborative process. Collaborative writing can be two people working together, or five or six. Writing groups with more than seven members are likely to be unwieldy. In any case, all the elements of composing—situational analysis, discovery, arrangement, drafting and revising, and editing—generally benefit by having more than one person working on them. Student groups doing collaborative writing in the classroom found that it developed their interpersonal communication skills, aided in the generation of ideas and topics, and lowered the stress of writing.[2]

There is a downside in that groups sometimes digress and stray from the point of the discussion. Some students in collaborative groups found that they generated more ideas than they could use and that conflicts sometimes slowed the process.[3] Therefore, it helps to have some set procedures that guide discussion down the right pathways and yet do not stifle it. To that end, we have provided a planning and revision checklist at the end of this chapter and many others. The checklist provided on the front endpapers of this book combines the checklist from Chapter 2, Composing, with key elements from the checklist that follows this chapter. Following these checklists will help you stay on track. The checklists raise questions about topic, purpose, and audience that will guide either the individual or the group to the answers needed.

Planning	Drafting	Revising	Editing
• Keep all discussions objective.	• Choose a drafting plan:	• Revise for content, organization, style and tone.	• Edit for format and standard usage.
• Record discussion.	—Divide the work.	• Be concerned with accuracy and ethics.	• Check and double-check for inconsistencies in such things as margins, typeface, documentation, and headings.
• Analyze situation and audience.	—Draft in collaboration.	• Make criterion-based comments.	
• Establish purpose.	—Choose a lead writer.	• Make reader-based comments.	
• Discover content.	• Consult with group when needed.	• Be objective in discussion, not personal.	
• Organize content.	• Stick to deadlines.	• Remember that people get attached to their writing.	
• Agree on style and tone.		• Accept criticism gracefully.	
• Agree on format.		• Don't avoid debate, but keep discussions as friendly and positive as possible.	
• Choose coordinator.		• Know when to quit revising.	
• Seek opinion on plan from outside group.		• Seek opinion from outside of group.	

FIGURE 3-1 • The Collaboration Process

▶ PLANNING

The advantage of working in a group is that you are likely to hit on key elements that working alone you might overlook. The collaborative process greatly enhances situational analysis and discovery. Shared information about audience is often more accurate and complete than individual knowledge. By hammering out a purpose statement that satisfies all its members, a group heightens the probability that the purpose statement will be on target.

The flow of ideas in a group situational analysis and in a discovery brainstorming session will come so rapidly that you risk losing some of them. One or two people in the group should serve as recorders to capture the thoughts before they are lost. It helps if the recording is done so that all can see—on a blackboard, a pad on an easel, or a computer screen. During the brainstorming, remember to accept all ideas, no matter how outlandish they may appear. Evaluation and selection will follow.

The group can take one of the more organized approaches to discovery. For instance, if instructions are clearly called for, the group can use the arrangement pattern of instructions to guide discovery. If discovery includes gathering information, working in a group can speed up the process. The group can divide the work to be done, assigning portions of the work according to the expertise of each group member.

When the brainstorming and other discovery techniques are finished, the group must evaluate the results. This is a time when trouble can occur. When everyone is brainstorming, it's fun to listen to the flow. There is a synergy working that helps to produce more ideas than any one individual is likely to develop working alone. When the time comes to evaluate and select ideas, however, some ideas will be rejected, and tension in the group may result. Feelings may be ruffled. Keep the discussion as open but as objective as you can. Where possible, divorce the ideas from the people who offered them.

Evaluate the ideas on their merits—on how well they fit the purpose and the intended audience. Whatever you do, don't attack people for their ideas. Again, someone should keep track of the discussion in a way that the group can follow.

In collaborative writing, a good way of evaluating the ideas and information you are working with is to arrange them into an organizational plan. The act of arranging will highlight those ideas that work, without shining too bright a spotlight on those that don't. A formal outline is not always necessary, but a group usually needs a tighter, more detailed organizational plan than does an individual (see Outlining in Appendix B).

Do not be in a hurry at this stage (or any other stage) to reach agreement. Collaborative groups should not be afraid of argument and disagreement. Objective discussion about such elements as purpose, content, style, and tone are absolutely necessary if all members of the group are to visualize the report in the same way. A failure to get a true consensus on how the report is to meet its purpose and how it should be written can lead to serious difficulties later in the process.

While in the planning stage, a group should take four other steps that can save a lot of hassle and bother later on:

1. Using Chapter 11, Document Design, to help you, make up a style sheet for everyone to follow. Agree on and record such matters as these:

   - Font type and size and spacing for text
   - Line length and margins
   - Highlighting (boldface, italics, and so forth)
   - Placement and style of page numbers
   - Format for headers and footers

- Placement, caption style, and identification (numbers or letters) for figures and tables
- Format for at least three levels of headings, to include font size and type, grammatical structure, capitalization, placement, and spacing (see pages 256–264)
- Format for lists and informal tables [bullets (•), numbers, spacing, indentation, and so forth]
- Documentation for both text and graphics (see Documentation in Appendix B or use the documentation format in some guide, such as *The Chicago Manual of Style*)

When the style sheet is finished, print out copies for everyone in the group. If you take the time to provide examples of such things as headings, your style sheet will be even more useful.

2. Set deadlines for completed work and stick to them. The deadlines should allow ample time for the revising stage and for the delays that seem inevitable in writing projects.

3. Choose a coordinator from among the group. In choosing a coordinator, group members should avoid both passive and dominating personality types. The group should give the coordinator the authority to enforce deadlines, call meetings, and otherwise shepherd the group through the collaborative process. Unless the coordinator abuses his or her authority, the group should give the coordinator full cooperation.

4. Schedule frequent review sessions. In them, group members should offer support and encouragement and check to see if group goals are being met. Such sessions are also useful in identifying any who may be shirking their work and those whose load may be unfair. In either case group members must move to correct the situation, usually by talking out the problem. Workloads can be adjusted and shirkers can be asked to meet their assigned responsibilities.

When the planning is finished, you may want to take one more step. Collaborative writing, like individual writing, can profit from networking with individuals or groups outside your immediate working group. You may want to seek comments about your content and organizational plan from people with particular knowledge of the subject area. If you're writing in a large organization, it might pay to seek advice from people senior to you who may see political implications your group has overlooked. In writing instructions, you would be wise to discuss your plan with several members of the group to be instructed. Be ready to go back to the drawing board if your networking reveals serious flaws in your plan.

▶ DRAFTING

In the actual drafting of a document, a group can choose one of several possible approaches.

Dividing the Work

For lengthy documents, perhaps the most common drafting procedure is to divide the drafting among the group. Each member of the group takes responsibility for a segment of the organizational plan and writes a draft based on the group plan. It's always possible, even likely, that each writer will alter the plan to some degree. If the alterations are slight enough that they do not cause major problems for group members working on other segments of the plan, such alterations are appropriate. However, if such changes will cause problems for others, the people affected should be consulted.

Allow generous deadlines when you divide the work. Even when a group has agreed on the design features, there will be many stylistic differences in the first drafts. A group that divides the work must be prepared to spend a good deal of time revising and polishing to get a final product in which all the segments fit together smoothly.

Drafting in Collaboration

In a second method of drafting, a group may want to draft the document in collaboration, rather than dividing up the work. Word processing, in particular, makes such close collaboration possible. Two or three people sitting before a keyboard and a screen will find that they can write together. Generally, one person will control the keyboard, but all collaborators can read the screen and provide immediate feedback as changes are made to the document. Although such close collaboration is possible, it is a method seldom used in the workplace, probably because it is time consuming and, therefore, costly. Its use is most often reserved for short, important documents in which the writers must weigh every word and nuance.

One Person Doing the Drafting

The third method of drafting is to have one person draft the entire document. This produces a uniformity of style, but in a classroom the obvious disadvantage is that not everyone will get needed writing experience. An alternative approach is to divide the work but then appoint a lead writer to put the segments together, blending the parts into a stylistic whole. The group may even give the lead writer the authority to make editorial decisions when the group cannot reach agreement on its own. In large organizations you will find all of these methods, or combinations of them, in use.

▶ REVISING AND EDITING

Collaboration works particularly well in revising and editing. People working in a group frequently will see problems in a draft, and solutions to those problems, that a person working alone will not see.

Revising

In revising, concern yourself primarily with content, organization, style, and tone. Be concerned with how well a draft fits purpose and organization. When the group can work together in the same location, everyone should have a copy of the draft, either on paper or on a computer screen. Comments about the draft should be both criterion based and reader based.[4]

Criterion-Based Comments Criterion-based comments measure the draft against some standard. For example, the sentences may violate stylistic standards by being too long or by containing pretentious language. (See Chapter 5, Achieving a Readable Style.) Perhaps in classifying information, the writer has not followed good classification procedures (see Chapter 9, Presenting Information). The group should hold the draft to strict standards of ethics and accuracy. Whatever the problem may be, approach it in a positive manner. Say something like, "The content in this sentence is good. It says what needs to be said, but maybe it would work better if we divided it into two sentences. A sixty-word sentence may be more than our audience can handle."

Reader-Based Comments Reader-based comments are simply your reaction as a reader to what is before you. Compliment the draft whenever you can: "This is good. You really helped me understand this point." Or you can express something that troubles you: "This paragraph has good factual content, but perhaps it could explain the implications of the facts more clearly. At this point, I'm asking, What does it all mean? Can we provide an answer to the 'so-what' question here?"

Word Processing Word processing offers an attractive technique for revising, particularly when geography or conflicting schedules keep group members apart. Each member can do a draft and then via electronic file transfer, send a copy to one or more coauthors. The coauthor can make suggested revisions and send the file back to the original author. It helps if the revisions are distinguished in some way, perhaps through the use of asterisks or brackets. Many word processors include a feature for this very purpose.

The original author can react to the changes in a way he or she thinks appropriate. If the collaborators can get together, they can download the revised file and work on the draft side by side. As we point out on pages 44–47, the Internet (or a local area net) can also be used for collaboration.

Comments from Outside the Group As with the organizational plan, you should consider seeking comments on your drafts from people outside the group. People senior to you in your organization can help you to ensure that the tone and content of your work reflect the values and attitudes of the organization.

Problems in the Group Although it is effective, collaborative revision can cause problems in the group. We all get attached to what we write. Criticism of our work can sting as much as adverse comments about our personality or habits. Therefore, all members of the group should be particularly careful in the revising stage. Support other members of the group with compliments whenever possible. Try to begin any discussion by saying something good about a draft. As in discussing the plan, keep comments objective and not personal. Be positive rather than negative. Show how a suggested change will make the segment you are discussing stronger—for instance, by making it fit audience and purpose better.

If you are the writer whose work is being discussed, be open to criticism. Do not take criticism personally. Be ready to support your position, but also be ready to listen to opposing arguments. Really *listen*. Remember that the group is working toward a common goal—a successful document. You don't have to be a pushover for the opinions of others, but be open enough to recognize when the comments you hear are accurate and valid. If you are convinced that the revision is necessary, make the changes gracefully and move on to the next point. If you react angrily and defensively to criticism, you poison the well. Other group members will feel unable to work with you and may find it necessary to isolate you and work around you. Harmony in a group is important to its success. Debate is appropriate and necessary, but all discussions should be kept as friendly and positive as possible.

Know when to quit revising. As we have said in every preface to every new edition of this book, "All writing is subject to infinite improvement." However, none of us has infinity in which to do our work. When the group agrees that the document satisfies the situation and purpose for which it is being written, it's time to move on to editing.

Editing

Make editing a separate process from revision. In editing, your major concerns are format and standard usage. Editing by a group is more easily accomplished than is revision. Whether a sentence is too long may be debatable. If a subject and verb are not in agreement, that's a fact. Use the Handbook of this text to help you to find and correct errors. Final editing should also include making the format consistent throughout the document. This is a particularly important step when the work of drafting has been divided among the group. Even if the group agrees beforehand about format, inconsistencies will crop up. Be alert for them. All the equal headings should look alike. Margins and spacing should be consistent. Footnotes should all be in the same style, and so forth.

The final product should be seamless. That is, no one should be able to tell where Mary's work leaves off and John's begins. To help you reach such a goal, we provide you with some principles of collaborating.

▶ COLLABORATION IN THE WORKPLACE

The collaboration process we have described in this chapter, or one very much like it, is the one you will probably use in a classroom setting. It is also the one you are likely to use in the workplace when a group voluntarily comes together to produce a piece of work. As such, it is a fairly democratic process. However, in the workplace, collaboration may be assigned by management rather than being a voluntary decision made by members of a group. In such a case the process may be significantly different from what we have described.

In an assigned collaboration, people may be placed in the group because they can provide technical knowledge and assistance the group may need to carry out its assignment. For example, within a state department of transportation, a group might be assigned to produce an environmental impact statement in preparation for building a new highway. The group might include a wildlife biologist, a civil engineer, a social scientist, and an archaeologist. Furthermore, a professional writer may be assigned to the group to help with the composing process from planning to editing.

Rather than the group's choosing a leader or a coordinator, management may assign someone to be the leader. Good leadership encourages democratic process and collaboration and enables people to do what they do best. However, there are times in the workplace when an assigned leader may act in an arbitrary way—for example, about work assignments and deadlines.

Finally, in the workplace, there is often a prescribed process for reviewing the collaborative results. This process may involve senior executives and people with special knowledge, such as attorneys and accountants. The reviewers may demand changes in the document. The group may have some right of appeal, but, in general, the wishes of the review panel are likely to prevail.

▶ COLLABORATION ON THE INTERNET

One important tool for collaboration in the workplace is the Internet, specifically e-mail, FTP (file transfer protocol), and synchronous discussions. Using the Internet, group members can work together on a project from remote locations. For example, consider the group working to produce the environmental impact statement for the department of transportation. The biologist might be on part-time loan to the project from the department of parks and wildlife. The civil engineer might be located at the highway construction site. The social scientist and archaeologist could be affiliated with two different universities in two different cities. The professional writer might be located at the department of transportation. Without the Internet to bring these five people together, collaboration on the environmental impact statement would be inefficient, impractical, or impossible.

E-Mail

The group just described might initiate collaborative work on their project by creating a distribution list for e-mail. Each member of the group could then mail a message to a common e-mail address, and all the members of the group would receive a copy of the message. That is, instead of mailing several e-mail messages, a group member would only have to mail one—a considerable reduction in time and effort. In addition, all members of the group would know that they were all getting the same message, leading to feelings of equality and trust among the group members.

A group leader could use such a distribution list to mail messages about scheduling, deadlines, funding, or other information that might affect the operations of the group. Group members could also use the list to exchange research findings, ask questions, or discuss issues that arise during the project.

Individual e-mail could also assist in other phases of the group's collaboration. For example, in drafting the environmental impact statement, the professional writer might have specific questions for the civil engineer. In reviewing the writer's draft, the civil engineer might identify several necessary corrections and e-mail the writer only with that information.

For both individual e-mail and its distribution list, the group would want to use e-mail software that allows users to attach files to their e-mail messages. Such software compresses a file, translates it to binary code, and transmits it over the Internet, complete with all original formatting, graphics, and special characters. When the e-mail message is received, the attached file is displayed on the recipient's computer screen, ready to be accessed by appropriate software. If all group members have compatible systems, it's easy to circulate drafts for review, editing, and revision.

For example, the professional writer could e-mail a message to the group's distribution list and attach a draft of the environmental impact statement for members to review. The e-mail message might identify specific passages that the writer would like the reviewers to pay attention to. Or, the writer might list a series of questions about the document for each reviewer to address. The members of the group would receive a copy of the e-mail message and the attached file. Each would review the draft, make corrections, and individually e-mail the writer, attaching the revised document to his or her e-mail message.

FTP Sites

FTP (file transfer protocol) sites allow you to upload files from your computer to a remote computer or to download files from a remote computer to your computer. FTP is thus a potential tool for collaboration because it creates a common electronic work site. That is, instead of continually e-mailing information to the group and attaching a copy of a document to your e-mail message, you can easily upload a copy of a file to the group's designated FTP site and allow each member of the group to download a copy at his or her convenience.

The five people working on the environmental impact study, for example, might house at their FTP site a schedule listing the tasks assigned to each member of the group. As each member completed a designated task, he or she would download a copy of the schedule, note the completion of the task, upload the revised schedule, and discard the previous schedule. Using FTP, the group could also make drafts of documents available for review. Each member of the group could download a copy of the document, make the necessary corrections, and upload the revised version—and all without e-mailing a single message.

Synchronous Discussions

Synchronous discussions can be useful to a group at several points in the collaborative process. Unlike e-mail, synchronous communication is almost simultaneous, with the participants gathered together in real time in a virtual meeting room. Such discussions are often called MUDs (multiple user dimension, dialogue, domain, or dungeon) or MOOs (multiple user domain object-oriented). A number of sites are available on the Internet for synchronous discussions.

Consider again the group asked to write the environmental impact statement. As soon as this group is assigned to the project, members could meet each other in a synchronous discussion for planning. Group members could introduce themselves, discuss purpose and audience, brainstorm regarding topics to cover, consider guidelines for organization and style, divide the project, and establish a schedule.

Once the project has started, group members might meet periodically in a synchronous discussion to monitor their progress, discuss problems and solutions, and offer each other support. Together they might also compose brief sections of the document that require careful wording or especially sensitive treatment.

They might also use synchronous discussions to conduct a joint review of a draft of the document. That is, instead of each member of the group responding individually to a draft, the entire group would meet at the same time to make corrections and suggestions for revision. Such joint reviews are often helpful, especially if individual reviews yield contradictory suggestions. In a joint review, members have the opportunity to negotiate their differences of opinion and reinforce each other's comments. To arrange a joint review, the group leader could e-mail a message to the group's distribution list, specifying the subject of the synchronous discussion and attaching a copy of the draft for members to examine before the review.

Synchronous discussions are also valuable at the end of a project. A final meeting allows the group to examine its operations, congratulate itself on its successes, identify its mistakes, and evaluate the collaborative experience.

Like all conferences, synchronous discussions require appropriate collaborative behaviors to be successful. Many of the suggestions in the next section, Group Conferences, can be applied in electronic meetings as well as in face-to-face situations. Here are some suggestions that apply more specifically to synchronous discussions:

- **Don't monopolize the conversation.** Gauge the frequency with which other participants are contributing messages and do likewise. Other participants may not type as well as you do or have as much experience with synchronous discussions. In addition, other participants may be experiencing a long transmission lag time. Give your colleagues time to compose and convey their ideas.
- **Pay attention to other contributors, especially those just entering the conversation.** Acknowledge and reply to their messages. Nobody likes to be ignored. New participants often need to be encouraged and will appreciate your consideration and support.
- **Keep your participation interactive by switching often from writing to reading and vice versa.** Keep in mind that the other participants can't see you and so must gauge your involvement in the conversation by the frequency of your messages. If you stop to write long messages or to read for a long period of time, the other participants will wonder why you have disappeared from the conversation. If you write long messages, you

will also force the other participants to disappear from the conversation while they read what you've written. Sooner or later they will start skimming or ignoring your long messages.

▶ GROUP CONFERENCES

Collaborative writing is valuable as a means of writing and learning to write. In a school setting, collaborative writing is doubly valuable because it also gives you experience in face-to-face group conferencing. You will find group conferencing skills necessary in the workplace. Most organizations use the group conference for training, problem solving, and other tasks. In this section we briefly describe good conference behavior and summarize the useful roles conferees can play. You'll find these principles useful in any conference and certainly in collaborative writing.

Conference Behavior

A good group conference is a pleasure to observe. A bad conference distresses conferees and observers alike. In a bad group conference, the climate is defensive. Conferees feel insecure, constantly fearing a personal attack and preparing to defend themselves. The leader of a bad conference can't talk without pontificating; advice is given as though from on high. The group punishes members who deviate from the majority will. As a result, ideas offered are tired and trite. Creative ideas are rejected. People compete for status and control, and they consider the rejection of their ideas a personal insult. They attack those who reject their contributions. Everyone goes on the defensive, and energy that should be focused on the group's task flows needlessly in endless debate. As a rule, the leader ends up dictating the solutions—perhaps what he or she wanted all along.

In a good group conference, the climate is permissive and supportive. Members truly listen to one another. People assert their own ideas, but they do not censure the opinions of others. The general attitude is, "We have a task to do; let's get on with it." Members reward each other with compliments for good ideas and do not reject ideas because they are new and strange. When members do reject an idea, they do it gently with no hint of a personal attack on its originator. People feel free to operate in such a climate. They come forward with more and better ideas. They drop the defensive postures that waste so much energy and instead put the energy into the group's task.

How do members of a group arrive at such a supportive climate? To simplify things, we present a list of **dos** and **don'ts.** Our principles cannot guarantee a good conference, but if they are followed they can help contribute to a successful outcome.

Dos

- Do be considerate of others. Stimulate people to act rather than pressuring them.
- Do be loyal to the conference leader without saying yes to everything. Do assert yourself when you have a contribution to make or when you disagree.
- Do support the other members of the group with compliments and friendliness.
- Do be aware that other people have feelings. Remember that conferees with hurt feelings will drag their feet or actively disrupt a conference.
- Do have empathy for the other conferees. See their point of view. Do not assume you know what they are saying or are going to say. Really listen and hear what they are saying.
- Do conclude contributions you make to a group by inviting criticism of them. Detach yourself from your ideas, and see them objectively as you hope others will. Be ready to criticize your own ideas.
- Do understand that communication often breaks down. Do not be shocked when you are misunderstood or when you misunderstand others.
- Do feel free to disagree with the ideas of other group members, but never attack people personally for their ideas.
- Do remember that most ideas that are not obvious seem strange at first, yet they may be the best ideas.

Don'ts

- Don't try to monopolize or dominate a conference. The confident person feels secure and is willing to listen to the ideas of others. Confident people are not afraid to adopt the ideas of others in preference to their own, giving full credit when they do so.
- Don't continually play the expert. You will annoy other conferees with constant advice and criticism based on your expertise.
- Don't pressure people to accept your views.
- Don't make people pay for past mistakes with continuing punishment. Instead, change the situation to prevent future mistakes.
- Don't let personal arguments foul a meeting. Stop arguments before they reach the personal stage by rephrasing them in an objective way.

Perhaps the rule "Do unto others as you would have them do unto you" best summarizes all these dos and don'ts. When you speak, you want to be listened to. Listen to others.

Group Roles

You can play many roles in a group conference. Sometimes you bring new ideas before the group and urge their acceptance. Perhaps at other times you serve as information giver and at still others as harmonizer, resolving differences and smoothing ruffled egos. We describe these useful roles that you as a conference leader or member can play. We purposely do not distinguish between leader and member roles. An observer of a well-run conference would have difficulty knowing who the leader is. We divide the roles into two groups: task roles, which move the group toward the accomplishment of its task; and group maintenance roles, which maintain the group in a harmonious working condition.

Task Roles When you play a task role, you help the group accomplish its set task. Some people play one or two of these roles almost exclusively, but most people slide easily in and out of most of them.

- **Initiators** are the idea givers, the starters. They move the group toward its task, perhaps by proposing or defining the task or by suggesting a solution to a problem or a way of arriving at the solution.
- **Information seekers** see where needed facts are sparse or missing. They solicit the group for facts relevant to the task at hand.
- **Information givers** provide data and evidence relevant to the task. They may do so on their own or in response to the information seekers.
- **Opinion seekers** canvass group members for their beliefs and opinions concerning a problem. They might encourage the group to state the value judgments that form the basis for the criteria of a problem solution.
- **Opinion givers** volunteer their beliefs, judgments, and opinions to the group or respond readily to the opinion seekers. They help set the criteria, including ethical criteria, for a problem solution.
- **Clarifiers** act when they see the group is confused about a conferee's contribution. They attempt to clear away the confusion by restating the contribution or by supplying additional relevant information, opinion, or interpretation.
- **Elaborators** further develop the contributions of others. They give examples, analogies, and additional information. They might carry a proposed solution to a problem into the future and speculate about how it would work.
- **Summarizers** draw together the ideas, opinions, and facts of the group into a coherent whole. They may state the criteria that a group has set or the agreed-upon solution to the problem. Often, after a summary, they may call for the group to move on to the next phase of work.

Group Maintenance Roles When you play a group maintenance role, you help to build and maintain the supportive group climate. Some people are so task oriented that they ignore the feelings of others as they push forward to complete the task. Without the proper climate in a group, the members will often fail to complete their tasks.

- **Encouragers** respond warmly to the contributions of others. They express appreciation for ideas and reward conferees by complimenting them. They go out of their way to encourage and reward the reticent members of the group when they do contribute.
- **Feeling expressers** sound out the group for its feelings. They sense when some members of the group are unhappy and get their feelings out in the open. They may do so by expressing the unhappiness as their own and thus encourage the others to come into the discussion.
- **Harmonizers** step between warring members of the group. They smooth ruffled egos and attempt to lift conflicts from the personality level and objectify them. With a neutral digression, they may lead the group away from conflict long enough for tempers to cool, allowing people to see the conflict objectively.
- **Compromisers** voluntarily withdraw their ideas or solutions in order to maintain group harmony. They freely admit error. With such actions, they build a climate in which conferees do not think their status is riding on their every contribution.
- **Gatekeepers** are alert for blocked-out members of the group. They subtly swing the discussion away from the forceful members to the quiet ones and give them a chance to contribute.

► PLANNING AND REVISION CHECKLISTS

The following questions are a summary of the key points in this chapter, and they provide a checklist for composing collaboratively. To be most effective, the questions in this checklist should be combined with the checklist questions following Chapter 2, Composing. To help you use the two checklists together, we have combined Chapter 2 questions with the key questions from this list and printed them in the front endpapers of this book.

Planning

- Is the group using appropriate checklists to guide discussion?
- Has the group appointed a recorder to capture the group's ideas during the planning process?

- At the end of the planning process, does the group have an organizational plan sufficiently complete to serve as a basis for evaluation?
- How will the group approach the drafting stage? By dividing the work among different writers? By writing together as a group? By assigning the work to one person?
- Has the group agreed on format elements such as spacing, typography, table and graph design, headings, and documentation?
- Has the group set deadlines for the work to be completed?
- If the group will be using electronic communication, has the group agreed on a site and conventions for exchanging information?
- Should the group appoint a coordinator for the project?
- Are there people you should share your draft with? Supervisors? Peers? Members of the target audience?

Revision

- Are format elements such as headings, margins, spacings, typefaces, and documentation consistent throughout the group's documents?
- Does the group have criteria with which to measure the effectiveness of the draft?
- Is the document accurate and ethical?
- Do people phrase their criticisms in an objective, positive way, avoiding personal and negative comments?
- Are the writers open to criticism of their work?
- Is the climate in the group supportive and permissive? Do members of the group play group maintenance roles as well as task roles, encouraging one another to express opinions?

▶ EXERCISES

1. By following the techniques outlined in this chapter, groups could do most of the writing exercises in this book as collaborative exercises. For a warm-up exercise in working collaboratively, work the following problem:

   - Divide into groups of three to five people. Consider each group to be a small consulting firm. An executive in a client company has requested a definition of a technical term used in a document the firm has prepared for that company.

- The group plans, drafts, revises, and edits an extended definition for the client (see Chapter 9, pages 185–188). Use a memo format (see Letter and Memorandum Format in Appendix B).

2. Following the completion of the memo, the group critiques its own performance. Before beginning the critique, the group must appoint a recorder to summarize the critique.

   - How well did the members operate as a group?
   - What methods did the group use to work together to analyze purpose and audience and to discover its material?
   - What technique did the group use to draft its memo?
   - Was the group successful in maintaining harmony while carrying out its task?
   - What trouble spots emerged?
   - What conclusions has the group reached that will help participants in future collaborative efforts?

3. The recorders report to the class the summaries of the groups. Using the summaries as a starting point, the class discusses collaborative writing.

4. Divide into groups of six to seven people. Each group is a consulting firm that deals in Web site design and content. The group has been asked to evaluate a Web site (assigned by the instructor) and write a report to the webmaster that recommends ways to improve the site (see Chapter 16, Recommendation Reports).[5] Some of the questions the group may wish to consider in the evaluation are the following:

   - Does the site seem to have clearly defined objectives?
   - Is the audience for which the site is intended apparent, and will the site suit that audience?
   - Is the site easy to navigate?
   - Is the text readable?
   - Are graphics, videos, and audio portions used appropriately?
   - Are useful links provided?

   See Designing a World Wide Web Site in Appendix B; also, the following two Web sites will be helpful to you in your evaluation:

   - *Yale Style Manual* http://info.med.yale.edu/caim/manual/index.html
   - *Pointers on How to Create Business Web Sites That Work* http://www.viacorp.com/pointers.html

5. Work Exercise 1 without having face-to-face contact within the group. Rather, use electronic means, such as e-mail, FTP sites, Instant Messaging, and synchronous discussion.

6. After working Exercise 5, the group meets to discuss the advantages and disadvantages of collaborating electronically. What can be done to mitigate the disadvantages? Appoint a recorder to summarize the discussion. The recorder reports the summary to the class. Using the summaries as a starting point, the class discusses collaborating electronically.

SCENARIO

Kevin Arrington is a system analyst in charge of the help desk at a large insurance company. Kevin's group is responsible for responding to hardware and software problems at the company. When questions arise from various offices, Kevin sends a technical person to investigate and then reports to the person who asked for help with the problem.

Kevin receives a call from the customer service department, which has been trying to use a new customer complaint tracking program. Kevin investigates and finds that the customer service staff had not installed the program as Kevin's team had instructed. Now the program has shut down. Kevin types this response to Foster Davey, who had made the call for help:

TO: f-davey@ign-mail

If your employees had read the procedures before installing the program, AS WE SPECIFICALLY TOLD THEM TO DO, particularly the installation warnings, they would have seen that the program takes 40 full minutes to install. Not allowing the full 40 minutes, which includes a short break before the final 3 minutes, caused the entire program to shut down. This is a simple program to install, IF all instructions are followed. Tell your people to read the manual with specific attention to p. 1, which warns that the program is not fully loaded after 37 minutes. After a 40-second interval, the program will automatically begin the final installation segment. A "program installed" note will appear at the end.

Kevin winces, and starts over:

Foster, we have found the problem with your new CS tracking program. Please note, on page 1 of the installation manual, that the program takes a full 40 minutes to install. The program may appear to be ready to go after 37 minutes. However, a 40-second interval, during which the screen is blank, except for the blinking cursor, precedes the final 3 minutes of program installation. After this final stage, a "program installed" note will appear. If the program is not allowed to load correctly, it will shut down. Praba Raghaven explained the importance of following the load time requirement to your group, but he will help your group reload the program before tomorrow morning. Everything else appears normal, so the program should operate correctly. Let us know if other problems arise.

Kevin feels better about the second version and sends the message.

chapter 4

Writing for Your Readers

▶ Goals of Communication

▶ The Planning Process
Determining Your Readers
Asking Questions to Analyze Your Readers
Determining Your Purpose
Understanding Your Role as a Writer
Planning the Content
Anticipating the Context in Which Your Writing
    Will Be Received

▶ Thinking about Your Readers: A Summary of
    Considerations

As we discussed in Chapter 2, developing effective documents requires a process involving at least five stages: planning the document, discovering content, arranging ideas, drafting and revising, and editing. While each of these stages can be a separate activity, when you write you will more than likely be moving back and forth from one activity to the other, as you develop your document. Following this process will help ensure that content is appropriate as well as correctly and effectively presented.

Planning is the most important of the five stages, but it is much more than just collecting information and then arranging it in some kind of order. Planning requires that you (1) understand as precisely as possible who will be reading and using what you write, (2) determine your purpose in sharing the content with your readers, and (3) know the context in which your writing will be received and used and how that context has led to the need for your document.

Too often, writers become absorbed in the ideas and information they either want or need to write and forget that the person or group who will read the document may have a very different view of the content. As a writer, you must never forget that your reader(s) cannot climb into your mind and know exactly what you are thinking. Written documents, designed after careful analysis of some of characteristics of those who will read them, become your way of helping readers understand what's in your mind.

▶ GOALS OF COMMUNICATION

Before studying the planning process, remember that in developing any communication, you have three main goals that show the relationship among reader, purpose, and context:

1. You want your reader(s) to understand your meaning exactly in the way you intend.

2. You want your writing to achieve its goal with the designated reader(s).

3. You want to keep the good will of those with whom you communicate.

▶ THE PLANNING PROCESS

To achieve the three goals just listed, you must pursue the following five tasks, both before you begin to write and while you are actually composing your document:

1. Determine as fully as possible *who* will read what you write.

2. Know what goals you want your writing to achieve.

3. Understand your role in the organization as a writer and how this should be reflected in what you write.

4. Determine the content by considering your readers' frame of reference and your purpose in writing.

5. Understand the business context in which you are communicating.

We introduced these concepts in Chapter 2, but in this chapter we want to discuss each one in more depth.

Determining Your Readers

Academic versus Nonacademic Readers In understanding your readers' point of view, it's helpful to examine how the writing you have been doing in school differs from the writing that you will do as an employee in an organization. Writing in school is very different from writing in the workplace. Understanding the differences is critical to your becoming an effective employee writer.

Writing in School The writing you have done as a student has been directed toward teachers and professors. Your goal has been to convince them that you understand and have mastered concepts and facts presented in a course. In school, your teachers are a captive audience: They are paid to read what you write (no matter how good or bad, how clear or muddled it is), to assess the accuracy of the content, and to determine your grade. Your teachers are knowledgeable about the subject you are writing about. They expect a specific response, and part of their job is to determine what you are trying to say.

Academic writing follows a predictable sequence. In a class setting, your written assignments are submitted, graded, and then returned to you. These assignments have relevance for a specific course of study for a specific time, usually several months. Even when you do team projects, you usually work with the students whose backgrounds are similar to yours.

In a work context, however, the writing situation is very different.

Writing at Work—Different Readers, Different Purposes In a work context, the reader for whom you write is no longer a single reader, a professor who is an expert in the subject area. On the job, employees write to many readers who have varied educational and technical backgrounds. The person for whom you work, for example, may have an educational background very different from yours, or your supervisor's responsibilities may have channeled his or her technical knowledge into other areas. For example, you may report directly to a person with an educational background in physical chemistry or electrical engineering and present job responsibilities in personnel management, data-base administration, quality control, or financial analysis. You may have been hired because you bring a specific kind of expertise to the organization, an expertise that your immediate supervisor does not have. One of your tasks may be to share your knowledge with your supervisor and other employees who are not well informed about the work you have been hired to do. Some times you will write to people who are interested in the financial aspects of an issue. At other times, you will write to people who are interested only in the technical, the personnel, or perhaps the liability aspects of the same issue.

You will often need to communicate with employees from other departments within your organization. They will read what you write based on their own jobs, backgrounds, educational profiles, and technical expertise. You may also find yourself writing to customers outside the organization. Unlike students with whom you took classes in college, many of those with whom you work and communicate will be older than you and will have different educational and technical backgrounds. Your ability to communicate with these customers and coworkers will depend on your ability to perceive the unique background each brings to the job and the way individual backgrounds differ from yours.

In short, you may have a single reader or a variety of readers. Your reader(s) can and likely will change with every document you have to write. You can count on one important fact: These readers, all of whom have their own job tasks and come from a variety of age, cultural, educational, and disciplinary backgrounds, will not approach what you write as your professors did. They will feel no commitment to read what you write unless your message is useful to them as they do their own jobs.

Information Overload and Indifferent Readers Because we live in an information age where the quantity of information grows rapidly, where people have more to read than they can ever hope to read, few documents are read completely. Most are skimmed. Because writing at work is not material for leisure reading, your readers—all involved in doing their own jobs—will read as little as possible, and they will focus only on the parts of your document that will be helpful to them. As they pick up your report, for example, they will immediately be asking: What is this? Why should I read it? How does it affect me? What am I going to have to do? They will want to find the main points quickly, and they will become impatient if they are unable to do this by glancing at the page. They will not usually read any document completely or bother to respond to it unless the message at the beginning indicates that they should do so. How they respond to the first few sentences of your writing will often determine how much more of it they will read.

The Challenge of the Indifferent Reader As you make the transition from student writer to employee writer, remember that unlike your teachers, your readers in your job context do not have to read what you write. If you want your writing to be read, you must make your message clear and easy to read. You must make your message as interesting and relevant to them as possible. Because your readers have to read selectively, conciseness and clarity are basic ingredients of effective writing. Mechanical correctness remains a desirable quality, but correct writing that cannot be read easily and quickly will not be considered effective. Few readers will be either patient or impressed with verbose, disorganized writing, even if each sentence is mechanically correct. Without conciseness and clarity—topics that are discussed in Chapter 5—few people will read what you write, much less respond to it.

Who Will Read What You Write?
Who Will Act on What You Write?

The Potential for Unknown Readers In a work context, you will never know for sure who will read what you write, thanks to copy machines that allow documents to be duplicated and shared and the ease with which e-mail messages can be forward. But in most organizations, you will be expected to send copies of what you write to a specific group of individuals, called a distribution list. However, you should still anticipate that what you write will be disseminated to others unknown to you. Thus, you will have a primary reader (the person to whom the report is addressed), secondary readers (those who receive copies—the distribution list, often labeled DIST or cc, for copy), and unknown readers (those who receive copies from any of your expected readers). The memorandum heading (Figure 4-1) shows how complex the

TO: Computing Support Staff [primary readers]
DATE: November 21, 2001
SUBJECT: Customer Complaints, Jan–Oct 2001
FROM: Darren Herscowitz
DIST: Melanie Stuart, Operations
            Mack Schropshire, Sales   [secondary readers—distribution list]
            Aston Conolee,
            Gif Small,
            File 2301.5   [potential unknown readers who may
                                             have access to the report from this file]

FIGURE 4-1 • Internal Report Heading

problem of determining readers can be. And, copies of anything you write will be filed, either in paper or electronic form.

Among those receiving copies, you need to attempt to determine who will act on what you write. In many cases, your primary reader will transmit your document to someone else for action. Perhaps this individual is one of your secondary readers. Or, the person who will be responsible for acting on what you write may be unknown to you. Thus, assessing your readers—WHO will act on what you write—is critical because your assessment of this reader's perspective will tell you how you will compose the message to be conveyed.

Asking Questions to Analyze Your Readers

When you consider your reader (or readers), you will want to determine as much as you can about them.

- **How much do they know about what you are writing?**
- **Is your reader an expert in the area about which you are writing?**

Readers who are technical experts in an area about which you are writing have different needs from readers who are not experts.

- **Does your reader know anything at all about your topic?**
- **What is your reader's educational level?**
- **What is the reader's cultural background?**

If your reader is from a culture other than your own, you will want to review material covered in Chapter 7, Writing for International Readers. Culture affects communication style. For example, in the United States, readers value direct, concise letters. In most other countries, this approach is considered rude. In the United States, business documents focus on business only. In many other countries, individuals do not separate business and personal relationships. Therefore, business communication prepared for such readers may contain "personal," non-business-related elements. In short, you often cannot write to a person in another culture as you would write to a person in your own. If you fail to adopt your content and your style to the perspectives of readers in the culture in which you wish to do business, you can easily ruin any possibility of a successful business relationship.

- **Will your reader(s) be interested in what you write? If not, how could you present your message to make it appealing?**
- **What kind of relationship do you have with this reader? What is the reader's attitude toward you, the subject matter you need to communicate, the job you have, and your area within the organization? Do you have credibility with this reader?**

In short, when you ask yourself these questions, you are trying to determine your reader(s)' perception, which is determined by a host of factors: education, family, geographical and cultural background, job responsibilities, rank in the organization, age, life experiences—just to name a few demographics that define how people see the world. How much your reader knows about your topic is critical because it determines what you say and the technical level of your presentation. The following situation illustrates this point.

Situation 1

Josh Means is the computer information system manager for a civil engineering company. Josh has been asked to write a report to explain whether the company should purchase personal computers or workstations, which are more powerful and more costly than PCs, to run the popular design application AutoCad. Josh decides to write a summary memo, which will be attached to the longer report, addressed to the vice president of operations, Greg Monaco. The summary memo will also be given to members of the board of directors, since the decision to purchase either PCs or workstations will require a substantial expenditure of funds.

In planning the memo, which will be read by Greg and by the board of directors, Josh decides on a short memo that highlights his reasons for recommending workstations rather than PCs. Josh also plans to use the memo as an agenda for discussing the two options when he gives his oral recommendation to the board. Thus, he builds his explanation about five points, which will be the outline for his presentation. Because he is writing to a nontechnical audience, he is careful to explain all technical terms (see Figure 4-2). Josh also knows that the board will be interested only in the main reasons for his recommendations, rather than technical detail.

Josh also decides to write a memo to Regina Huang, who is head of the Purchasing Department. Regina has extensive knowledge of computer hardware and is a supporter of PCs because of their lower cost.

Before you read each of Josh's memos, ask yourself: How will Regina's perspective differ from Greg's perspective? How will Regina's outlook differ from the perspective of the board of directors.

In writing to Regina Huang, Josh knows that he is communicating with someone who is familiar with the hardware side of personal computers but is less informed about the merits of workstations in comparison to PCs. Because of her technical expertise, Josh can use a more sophisticated explanation than would have been appropriate for the Board of Directors (see Figure 4-3).

DATE: September 7, 2001

TO: Greg Monaco

FROM: Josh Means

SUBJECT: **Analysis of Hardware for AutoCad Platform**

After analyzing the benefits and deficiencies of both personal computers and workstations for running AutoCad, I recommend that we purchase workstations instead of personal computers. Workstations were designed to run complex applications, like AutoCad, efficiently in today's networked environments. PCs, in contrast, were designed to run less complex problems for use in a home, or small business, environment. Manufacturers are attempting to upgrade the technology of PCs while still retaining the level of simplicity needed for home use. These opposite design goals create an abundance of problems when PCs are configured to be used in an industrial environment like ours.

In considering the value of workstations, I focused on five hardware considerations that target critical differences between UNIX workstations and PCs that use DOS. The sixth consideration, cost, favors DOS, but the difference does not override the value of UNIX workstations.

1. Networking Capabilities

Workstations perform better in a networked environment than personal computers do. Workstations were developed to utilize networks efficiently and effectively. PCs, on the other hand, were engineered as stand-alone machines. Extra software and hardware must be added if they are to be networked. Simply stated, workstations were specifically tailored to run in networks, while PCs are not.

UNIX, the major operating system employed by workstations, has inherent networking capabilities. DOS, or Disk Operating System, provides the PC with no networking capabilities. UNIX makes excellent use of networked systems, allowing network file sharing and load distribution. DOS does not have these capabilities.

2. Multitasking/Multiprocessing

Several people can use a workstation simultaneously (multitasking). Each person can be running several programs simultaneously (multiprocessing). A PC can be used by only one person and can run only one program.

UNIX is a multitasking/multiprocessing operating system. DOS with Windows does permit some applications to be run concurrently, but only to a very limited extent, requiring cooperation between the application and the operating system.

FIGURE 4-2 • Situation 1: Response to a Nonexpert Reader

3. Peripherals

Hundreds of different peripherals (printers, scanners, speakers) can be attached to workstations. Only a small subset of these can be used with a personal computer. AutoCad may use a large number of peripherals, many of which will not connect to a PC.

4. Architecture

The CPU, or central processing unit, of a workstation is faster than the CPU of a PC. This difference means that AutoCad will run faster on a workstation than a PC.

Most workstations CPUs utilize reduced instruction set computing (RISC), while the CPUs for PCs use complex instruction sets (CISC). RISC chips perform arithmetic operations much quicker than CISC chips. AutoCad, a mathematically intense program, will execute faster on RISC processors than it will on CISC processors.

5. Operating System

The operating system is the program that manages the computer. Workstations utilize state-of-the-art operating systems designed to increase the performance of complex programs such as AutoCad. The operating system currently powering about 90% of the PCs is DOS, which is virtually the same operating system personal computers used a decade ago. It was not designed to manage the computers now available, and was definitely not designed to support programs like AutoCad.

6. Cost

Despite the increased cost of workstations, the power they offer, in comparison to PCs, will provide a more efficient platform for running AutoCad. Given the problems of networking PCs, the power of workstations will be more cost effective for AutoCad.

Attachment: Analysis of Workstations vs Personal Computers for Running AutoCad

FIGURE 4-2 • (Continued)

The educational and knowledge level of your reader provides one critical difference with which you are already familiar as a student. What you knew about your major field has and will change dramatically as your move through the sequence of required courses in your major. The more a reader knows about a field of study, the more technical the language appropriate to that field can be used in reports about that filed of study. The less the reader knows about a field, the less complex the discussion about the topic will need to be. Being able to adapt your presentation to the technical level of your reader will be critical to the success of your message:

DATE: September 7, 2001

TO: Regina Huang

FROM: Josh Means

SUBJECT: **Information on Workstations vs PCs**

As you are aware, I am recommending that we purchase workstations instead of PCs for running AutoCad. Several considerations are involved, but principally the decision is one of power.

The Limits of DOS

When DOS was introduced, there was no anticipation that it would be called upon to run packages as sophisticated as AutoCad. To get around the memory limitation of 640K, programming tricks of all kinds, such as DOS extenders were introduced. These work, but they have to step around the operating system to get work done.

For example, when the program is run, the extender is called first. It appears to DOS to be the program running in real mode. Once running, the extenders switches the PC into protected mode. It then loads the application and begins its execution. As the application runs, the extender traps all calls to DOS. To the degree possible, the extender simulates the results of the call to DOS, doing as much of the housekeeping as possible. However, if the call necessitates interaction with DOS, the extender momentarily switches the PC into real mode, lets DOS perform the DOS call, then switches the PC back to protected mode. It is the extender's job to make sure that the DOS call and the switch between modes does not disturb the running application. In short, a very klutzy operation.

The Value of Workstations

Today even ordinary workstations, such as the SparcStation 10 from Sun Microsystems, the largest workstation vendor, include 32 MB of RAM, expandable to 512 MB. This capacity, coupled with high-performance graphics and math operations, make such workstations optimal for large CAD projects. Far more capable (and yes, expensive) versions are available from Silicon Graphics. Most workstations are used in networked environments, and many vendors are currently exploring the technology of distributed computing whereby some of a workstation's processing can be offloaded to idle workstations on the network, boosting performance even further.

FIGURE 4-3 • Situation 1: Response to a Technical Reader

The Value of UNIX

The real performance boost conferred by workstations stems not so much for the factors I've just discussed but from the architecture of the CPU. Intel CPUs used complex instruction sets (CISC). Typically, they combine simple instructions and complex instructions. A classic example of the latter is the SLAT instruction, which looks up a byte in a user-supplied table and translates its value. This rarely used instruction requires eleven clock cycles to execute. In addition, instructions are of varying lengths, meaning that the retrieval time of the instructions occurs more slowly. CISC chips generally perform floating-point operations poorly.

While workstations cost more, the freedom from having to work with the problems of DOS extenders is, to my mind, worth the difference

FIGURE 4-3 • (Continued)

Situation 2 (Figure 4-4)

A zoology graduate student was asked to teach a short course on bird-watching for the university's continuing education program. The four paragraphs in Figure 4–4 were part of a longer explanation that he wrote for people in the class, all of whom were adults who were experienced bird-watchers.

The student was also asked to discuss migratory birds with a members of middle school science class who were also going to attend a continuing education session. He translated his material on "Flocking" to fit their knowledge level and what they may have observed about birds. (see Figure 4-5).

In short, a reader's expertise about a topic will tell you how technical you can be, what level of language you can use.

• **How well do you know your reader?**

Many times you may know your reader(s) personally. However, if you know an individual's level in the organization, the responsibilities associated with that level, and the kind of technical expertise your reader has, this information will help you decide what you need to say and how to present your information. Knowing a person's responsibilities in the organization can be particularly useful in helping you anticipate your reader's attitude—how interested he or she will be in your subject. Because people tend to read only what is useful to them, try to relate your message to your reader's job. That knowledge can tell you whether the reader will be interested, mildly curious, indifferent, negative, or uninterested. Knowing the readers' attitude toward your message the topic addressed in will help you determine how to present your information.

The Function of Flocking in Long-Distance Soaring Migrants

Studies by ornithologists have shown that soaring birds migrate in flocks. Since most migratory broad-winged hawks are observed in flocks and form groups even in the early morning, flocking must have some specific advantages for these raptors.

Some researchers believe that flocking assists hawks in navigating and in orienting themselves in the proper direction. Other biologists conclude that flocking enables hawks to locate thermals, the rising currents of warm air that allow the birds to soar and thus gain altitude. A hawk that has reached the top of a thermal, can then glide down to the base of the next thermal, soar up, and glide down again, thermal-hopping until it reaches its destination.

Some researchers also suggest that thermal travel conserves energy and time for migrating raptors hawks' ability to find these thermals for soaring (wings spread for circular motion) and gliding (wings spread for forward motion). This method of flight is essential to conserve energy. In contrast, flapping flight uses over five times as much energy. Thermals also increase hawks' flight speed, since they use air currents both while soaring within the thermal and while gliding to the next one, rather than relying on their own powered flight.

These researchers also believe that flocking behavior enhances hawks' chances for encountering these life-saving thermals. A group of hawks moving together, as in (a) will more likely find thermals, which are produced randomly by the heating of the earth's surface, than will a bird traveling alone across the vast expanse of sky, as in (b). Interestingly, a computer simulation program has been designed to find optimum dimensions for encountering thermals produced by a geometric shape similar to that of hawk flocks.

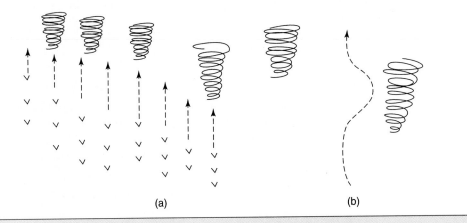

(a)   (b)

FIGURE 4-4 • Situation 2: Response for an Knowledgeable Audience

What Is Flocking?

Why do hawks fly together in a group? Haven't you noticed that you often see hawks flying together rather than just one hawk flying all by itself?

Soaring birds, such as hawks and vultures, migrate in flocks, groups of birds that fly close together. Scientists have studied why hawks like flying together in flocks. These scientists have concluded that hawks travel as a group to help each other fly in the right direction. Another possible reason is that a group of hawks traveling together can more easily find thermals than can one hawk flying all by itself.

What are thermals and why are they important to soaring birds? Thermals are bubbles of warm air that rise from the ground into the sky. Hawks get inside these thermals and circle high in the air. When they reach the top of the thermal, they glide down to the bottom of the next one, then up again and down until they arrive home. Their flight looks like this:

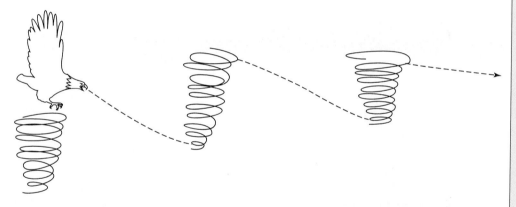

So hawks, by using thermals, which are natural warm air currents, can circle and glide rather than flap their wings. As a result, they save energy as well as time. That's why you see hawks flying together. Working together, they can find these thermals, rather than looking for them alone.

FIGURE 4-5 • Situation 2: Response for a Nonexpert Audience

- **Who else is likely to read what you write?**

   Many times the person to whom you are addressing your report will not be the one to act on it. For that reason, you need to know who else will read your document.

   Most reports and letters have distribution lists: the names of those who receive copies (see Figure 4-1). A person on the distribution list may be the person who will ultimately act on what you write. Thus, the needs and perceptions of those who receive copies should be considered.

- **Why is each person on the distribution list receiving a copy?**
- **How much does each person on this list know about your topic?**

Sometimes your primary reader may know the situation your are discussing, and the purpose of the report may be to inform others within the organization by going through proper channels.

- **What situation led to the need for this document?**

Many times you can better understand your reader's perspective if you understand the situation that requires you to write this document. The need for written communications develops from interactions of people involved in a work environment. To be able to select content, level of language (technical or general), and the amount of explanation needed in a business context, a writer must be careful to determine the needs of each reader. Closely examining a situation requiring a written response may even help you determine what you need to tell your readers and how to present your message.

Situation 3

Andrew Williams, a tax specialist for an accounting firm, needs to write a client, Michele Miller, who owns a ranch, to explain how she can deduct from her income tax the costs of new ranch equipment. Michele, who studied animal science in college, is not a tax expert. She has asked Andrew a specific question, and Andrew needs to answer her question in language she can understand (see Figure 4-6).

Assume, however, that Andrew's supervisor, Paul Wagner, who has received a paper copy of one letter to Michele, asks Andrew to provide a summary of recent rules for deducting business expenses from an individual's annual income tax obligation. Paul is a tax specialist, and he is interested in the IRS rules governing

---

January 16, 2001

Ms. Michele Miller
St. Rt. 2, Box 483
Victoria, TX 75384

Dear Ms. Miller:

I have reviewed the financial information you have given me about your ranching operations during 1999–2000 and have determined that you are eligible to use a portion of the amount you have spent on ranch equipment to reduce your current taxable income. According to the information you have given me, you will be able to reduce your taxable income by $10,000, based on the $19,500 you spent on ranch equipment in the past year.

FIGURE 4-6 • Situation 3: Response to a Nonexpert Reader

Qualifications for the Deduction

The IRS allows businesses to choose to deduct the costs of certain assets instead of recording those assets on the balance sheet and deducting only a small portion of their cost as depreciation each year. However, several qualifications must be met before the current deduction is allowed.

1. The purchased assets must be tangible assets that depreciate (such as barns or tractors, rather than land).

2. You must start using the asset in your business the same year that you choose to take the current deduction.

3. You must let the IRS know that you choose to take the current deduction by making an election—noting the amount your spent—on your tax return. You need to use Form 4562 to record your purchase and the deduction.

Limitations on the Deduction

The IRS also places limits on the amount of the deduction you can take each year for all equipment you purchased:

1. The maximum deduction allowed is $10,000, even if, as in your case, you spent more than you earned. If you had spent less than $10,000, the deduction would be limited to the amount you had spent.

2. The remaining deduction allowed cannot exceed the taxable income that your business earns for the year.

How to Take the Deduction

To be able to take the $10,000 deduction, complete Part I of Form 4562 and file that form when you file your 1040 tax return for the current year. Instructions for making the election are on the back of the form. A copy of Form 4562 can be obtained at your IRS office in Victoria.

If your business circumstances change, of if you have questions, please call me at 800 453-1859.

Sincerely,

Andy Williams

Andrew Williams, C.P.A.

Pc: Paul Wagner

FIGURE 4-6 • (*Continued*)

business expenses as deductions. In one letter shown in Figure 4–7, Andrew uses the full range of specialized tax jargon to summarize the relevant rules.

You will find that your readers differ according to their knowledge of the topic about which you are writing, what they need to know, and the ways in which they will use what you write. In Situation 3, Michele, a rancher, wants a clear answer to her question: Can she deduct the cost of new equipment

---

DATE: January 16, 2001

TO: Paul Wagner

FROM: Andrew Williams

SUBJECT: Section 179 Election to Expense Certain Depreciable Business Assets

Under Section 170 of the IRC, U.S. taxpayers are allowed to expense, at their election, the cost of certain tangible property, called Section 170 property, rather than capitalizing that property to an asset account. The deduction is allowed in the year that the property is placed in service.

Section 179 Property

The property that qualifies for expensing is called Section 179 property and is any property subject to depreciation that is

1. tangible personal property, other than air conditioning and heating units;
2. other tangible property, not including a building or structural component of a building;
3. elevators and escalators;
4. research facilities and facilities for the bulk storage of fundible commodities;
5. single-purpose agricultural or horticultural structure;
6. qualified rehabilitation expenditures;
7. qualified timber property; or
8. storage facilities used in connection with the distribution of petroleum or its primary products.

This list of properties and further explanation about them can be found in Section 48(a) of the IRC.

Limitations on Amount Expenses

Several limitations exist on the amount allowed to be expenses during one taxable year. These limitations are listed in Section 179(b) of the IRC:

1. The maximum amount that can be expensed in one year is $10,000 ($5,000 for married persons filing separately).

FIGURE 4-7 • Situation 3: Response to an Expert Reader

2. This $10,000 maximum is reduced dollar for dollar by the cost of Section 179 property placed in service during the taxable year that exceeds $200,000. Therefore, the deduction is completely phased out when the cost of Section 179 property in service during one year equals $210,000.

3. The remaining deduction (after limitations 1 and 2 have been applied) is further limited to the taxable income of the trade or business. In this instance, taxable income is computed without taking into account the Section 179 amounts in question. Any amounts disallowed under this limitation can be carried forward indefinitely.

Making the Election to Expense

The election to expense the cost of Section 179 property is made on Par I of Form 4562 and should be filed with the taxpayer's original tax return for the year the property is placed in service. This election must be made for each taxable year in which a section 179 expensing is claimed.

NOTE: Once this election has been made, it can be revoked only with the consent of the Secretary of the Treasury.

More detailed information on 179 expensing, including examples, can be found in Treasury Regulations, Sec. 1.179-1 through Sec. 1.179-5. If I can be of help, please contact me at extension 2905.

FIGURE 4-7 • (*Continued*)

she has purchased for her ranch and, if so, how should the deduction be calculated and reported? In contrast, Paul Wagner wants to know the Internal Revenue Service rules for deducting purchases. How Andrew Miller presents the information to these readers is determined by what each one knows and needs to know about the topic.

Determining Your Purpose

- **Why are you writing?**
- **What do you want to achieve with your document?**

Determining why you are writing—what you want to achieve—is as important as determining your readers. *Purpose is always related to readers.* And, you may have more than one purpose. For example, you may be writing to inform readers, to provide information, to recommend a course of action. In addition, what you say may serve as documentation, proof of your efforts—to show that you have provided the information requested. Written messages that document employees' activities serve a major function in today's business organizations. Without documentation, you may find it difficult to prove that you performed specific tasks.

Situation 4

Karen Thorpe, a project director, supervises nine engineers, who submit monthly project reports on the engineering work they are doing. Karen uses these monthly reports to compile reports to her supervisor and to keep track of how each project is progressing. For the past three months, Sharon Hall, one of the engineers, has submitted her project reports two weeks late. This past month, Sharon did not submit her report until a week before the next one was due. Talking with Sharon has not produced results. Thus, Karen writes Sharon a memo that has two purposes: (1) to notify Sharon officially that she needs to submit all project reports on time from now on and (2) to provide documentation for Sharon's personnel file that she has been informed that her tardy reports are affecting the project group and asked to comply with team deadlines (see Figure 4-8). In addition, the memo can emphasize that Sharon's contribution is important, while firmly but objectively warning her that a consistent pattern of lateness is unacceptable.

Understanding Your Role as a Writer

• What is your position in the organization?

As an employee in an organization, you will be hired to perform the duties that define a particular job. As the individual responsible for performing specific tasks, you will be communicating with employees above you, below

---

DATE: February 6, 2001

TO: Sharon Hall

FROM: Karen Thorpe

SUBJECT: Timely Submission of Monthly Project Reports

As I discussed in our meeting of January 20, submission of status reports on each engineering project is a standard requirement for all team members in our group. These reports provide critical information for tracking progress and problems on each project. When one team member's reports are missing, the status of the group's effort is affected. Your input is important.

Since October 1999, your reports have been one to two weeks late. Last month, your January report was submitted three weeks late, one week before the February report was due. Late submission of any person's status report affects our ability to inform the division office of our progress.

Please see that your monthly reports are submitted by the first work day of each month.

FIGURE 4-8 • Response to Situation 4

you, and on your own level in the organization. In writing to individuals in any group, you will communicate, not as you would with a friend or family member, but as the person responsible for the work associated with that position in the organization. That is, when you write, you create a personality that should fit the position you hold.

If your are to have credibility as a writer in an organization, the image that you project should be appropriate to your position. What you say and how you say it should reflect your level of responsibility in the organization—the power relationship that exists between you and the reader. The image you project will change, depending on your readers. You will project the image of a subordinate when you write to those higher than you in the organization, but you will transmit the image of the supervisor to those who work directly under you. When you communicate with others on your own job level, you will convey the image of a colleague. Good writers have the ability to fit their message to each reader. Situation 5 provides examples that illustrate this technique.

Situation 5

Bill Ramirez, director of training, finds himself in a dilemma. He must write his supervisor (Marshall Collins), an associate (Kevin Wong), and his assistant director (Joyce Smith) about the same issue: unqualified people have been enrolled in a training course, and not enough seats are available for qualified employees who need the class. Kevin is frustrated that employees in his office are not being scheduled for the class. Joyce is responsible for scheduling the class. Marshall Collins needs to know about how Bill is handling this dilemma Note how Bill's e-mails to Joyce (Figure 4-9) Kevin (Figure 4-10), and Marshall (Figure 4-11) differ.

From reading the three e-mails, explain how Bill shifts his message, depending on the position and needs of each reader in the organization. How does the perspective of each reader determine what Bill sends in each e-mail?

Planning the Content

- **What ideas should be used to achieve the goals of the message?**
- **What ideas should be omitted?**
- **How should your ideas be arranged?**

Once you have analyzed your reader(s) and your purpose, you can begin to decide what you want and need to say, then how you will phrase your ideas. Knowing what your reader(s) need(s) to know will help you decide how to arrange your message.

- **What tone do you want to convey?**

Knowing how your message sounds will always be critical. Review the e-mails in Figures 4-9, 4-10, and 4-11. Note differences in the sound of each message. You should always try to convey a tone that is respectful and

TO: <Joyce Smith> jsmith@ibc.com

SUBJ: Unqualified Enrollees in DM Classes

Please remove everyone with less than six months experience from the June Database Management classes. I know you need help in determining the hiring dates of all the people who apply, but we have a three-month waiting list of people, not to mention district supervisors who are unhappy with our inability to meet their training needs. Please stop by before you leave at 5:00 so that we can figure out how to make the screening process easier. Please call Marc Jacz in personnel. He developed a selection procedure for our C++ courses last year and has agreed to work with us.

FIGURE 4-9

TO: <Kevin Wong> wong@ibc.com

SUBJ: Meeting Training Requirements in DM Classes

Thanks for your message. I appreciate your telling me about your problem.

We will see to it that your people who signed up for the June DM classes are taken care off. Joyce's group is understaffed, and they don't have enough people to check experience records of applicants. However, we are working on the problem. Your employees will receive priority. Kevin, I apologize for the situation, and I will appreciate your patience as we get this problem resolved. Please call me if you want to talk. We will schedule your people as quickly as possible.

FIGURE 4-10

TO: <Marshall Collins> mcollins@ibc.com

SUBJ: Update on Training Enrollments

You may hear that we have been having difficulties meeting the demand for our Database Management classes. That's true. We can enroll only those who have completed the basic six months with IBC. Determining who is qualified has been a problem because of the demand for these classes. We have to have priorities on who is admitted. My associate and I are working with personnel to develop an efficient plan for screening enrollees, but we need more people who are qualified to train new hires in database management. In the past six months we have been unprepared for the demand. I'll keep you informed.

FIGURE 4-11

commensurate with your position in the organization. How a message is conveyed may often be as important as the content.

Anticipating the Context in Which Your Writing Will Be Received

• How will your writing be used?

Knowing what will happen to your writing when it is received also helps you know who might read it and what you need to say. For example, once it has reached its primary destination, a document may be quickly skimmed and filed; it may be skimmed and then routed to the person who will be responsible for acting on it; it may be read, copied, and distributed to readers unknown to you; it may be read and used as an agenda item for discussing a particular point; it may be read carefully and later used as a reference. Being able to visualize the context in which it will be read and used can often guide you in deciding not only what to say but also how to organize the information and arrange it on the page. The following example explains how consideration of the context helped a writer know how to plan a letter:

> **Situation 6**
>
> Katheryn Stone is employed by the American Farm Bureau Federation. She tracks congressional legislation and reports to various community groups about legislation that effects them. Katheryn needs to report to the Dos Palos Ag Boosters the results of legislation passed by the 104th Congress that directly affects them.
>
> Katheryn writes the president of Dos Palos Ag Boosters. She knows that the letter will be copied and distributed widely in the community as well as in the organization. Thus, she designs a letter (see Figure 4–12) that clearly summarizes the main points of the legislation. She uses a listing arrangement to enhance readability of the news. Because this letter will be read by a wide audience, she avoids discussing the legal issues involved in transferring the property.
>
> Katheryn extracted her letter from the House of Representatives Bill shown in Figure 4–13.

▶ THINKING ABOUT YOUR READERS: A SUMMARY OF CONSIDERATIONS

As you think about those whom you want to read what you will write, keep in mind the following questions, which evolve from the preceding discussion. Throughout the writing process, you will need to consider each question. While the process may seem complicated, with practice, considering your reader(s) will become a natural part of your planning, your writing, and your revision processes:

January 4, 1997

Mr. Daniel Halpern
10046 Camelia Drive
Dos Palos, CA

Dear Mr. Halpern:

SUBJECT: News from Congress

Greetings from Washington! I am happy to inform you that Bill 4041 has been Approved. This bill allows the Secretary of Agriculture to sell a parcel of government-owned land to the Dos Palos Ag Boosters to use as a farm school.

Contents of the Bill

In summary, Bill 4041 contains the following provision:

- Congress agreed to give 22 acres of land located at 18296 Elgin Avenue, Dos Palos, California, to the Dos Palos Ag Boosters to use as a farm school.

- The farm school will educate students and beginning farmers in principles of farming.

- The Dos Palos Ag Boosters will pay the Secretary of Agriculture for the land.

- The Secretary of Agriculture will survey the land to determine the exact acreage transferred to the Ag Boosters and the price of this land will be determined by the market price of the land.

- The Secretary of Agriculture may transfer the land to the Dos Palos School District if the Dos Palos Ag Boosters ask the Secretary to do so.

- The sale of this land is final.

Please contact our office or your state representative regarding this bill. Transfer of land must follow specific procedures and will take approximately one year to complete all legal requirements.

Sincerely,

Katheryn Stone

Katheryn Stone

FIGURE 4-12 • Situation 6: Response to a Broad Nonexpert Audience

HR 4041 IH
104th CONGRESS
2d Session

To authorize the Secretary of Agriculture to convey a parcel of used agricultural land in Dos Palos, California, to the Dos Palos Ag Boosters for use as a farm school.

SECTION 1. LAND CONVEYANCE, UNUSED AGRICULTURAL LAND, DOS PALOS, CALIFORNIA.

1. CONVEYANCE AUTHORIZED—Notwithstanding any other provision of law, including section 335 (c) of the Consolidated Farm and Rural Development Act (7 U.S.C. 1985 (c)), the Secretary of Agriculture may convey to the Dos Palos Ag Boosters of Dos Palos, California, all right, title, and interest of the United States in and to a parcel of real property (including improvements thereon) held by the Secretary that consists of approximately 22 acres and is located at 18296 Elgin Avenue, Dos Palos, California, to be used as a farm school for the education and training of students and beginning farmers regarding farming. Any such conveyance shall be final with no future liability accruing to the Secretary of Agriculture.

2. CONSIDERATION—As consideration for the conveyance under subsection(a), the transferee shall pay to the Secretary an amount equal to the fair market value of the parcel conveyed under subsection (a).

3. ALTERNATIVE TRANSFEREE—At the request of the Dos Palos Ag Boosters, the Secretary may make the conveyance authorized by subsection (a) to the Dos Palos School District.

4. DETERMINATION OF FAIR MARKET VALUE AND PROPERTY DESCRIPTION—The secretary shall determine the fair market value of the parcel to be conveyed under subsection (a). The exact acreage and legal description of the parcels shall be determined by a survey satisfactory to the Secretary. The cost of any such survey shall be borne by the transferee.

5. ADDITIONAL TERMS AND CONDITIONS—The Secretary may require such additional terms and conditions in connection with the conveyance under this section as the Secretary considers appropriate to protect the interests of the United States.

FIGURE 4-13 • Situation 6: Legal Notification

1. **Who will read your message?** Always try to assess your readers: Who will act on what you write? Who else may read your document? For example, your reader may forward an e-mail message to one or many other people; you can never be sure. Who will act on what you write? Considering this point may help you anticipate other possible readers.

2. **How much does your reader know about your topic?** Does your reader have a strong background in and knowledge about your topic?

Or, does your reader know little about it? If your reader is not an expert on your topic, you will need to define terms, explain concepts, and provide background information.

3. **Is your reader interested in your topic?** Writing to a reader who is interested in what you are presenting is much easier than writing to an uninterested or indifferent reader. Nevertheless, look for ways to make your writing interesting to your reader. Be concise: Provide your reader only what is necessary. Use graphics if possible to help your reader "see" what you are saying. Chapter 5 deals with ways to create clear sentences.

4. **How technical should you be in explaining your position?** The answer to this question depends on the education and level of knowledge of your reader(s). Sometimes, the technical level of a presentation depends on a reader's position in the organization.

5. **What does your reader need to know? What is your purpose in writing?** Based on your reader profile, you will need to determine how much information you must give your reader, based on what you are trying to accomplish with your message and your reader's level of understanding and interest in the topic.

6. **How will your reader approach your document?** Most readers will likely skim or scan a document and then read parts of it critically or analytically, depending on their own needs or interest level. **NOTE:** Do not get into the habit of including extra information in a document "just in case" your reader needs it. Give readers what they needs. Supply additional material in attachments. Remember: We live in an information age where people are given more to read than they can possibly handle. Designing documents that target the needs and backgrounds of readers helps ensure the effectiveness of written communications.

7. **What is your business relationship to your reader?** Knowing your role in the organization and the level in the organization of your readers will also help you decide what to say and how to say it. Writing to your supervisor will be different from writing to customers or to your peers in the organization. A person's job responsibilities will shape how the individual approaches any document. Be aware of your relationship to your reader as you select the tone of your message. Try reading aloud what you have written. Does the message sound appropriate for your reader(s). Your writing needs to be clear and concise, but it also needs to convey an attitude that is appropriate for the reader, the occasion, and the context.

In short, once you have thought about your readers and your purpose in writing—these two aspects of communication are inextricable—you can make decisions about content, style, visual aids, and even the length of the document you will write.

▶ EXERCISES

1. Select an article in a specialized trade journal or publication in your field of study. Write a summary of the article to an audience unfamiliar with the information. Describe your intended audience as precisely as possible.

2. Use a database to locate three articles on the same topic. These articles should be selected from three different publications. Examine each article, and if possible the entire issue in which the article appeared. To what audience is each article directed? How do the articles differ? To what type of audience is each publication directed? How does each writer target a specific article to the audience of the publication?

3. You have just received a letter from the dean of your college explaining that a college-wide study is under way to evaluate the required courses in each department. As part of this evaluation, the dean asks you to explain what you found to be the worst required course(s) you have taken. He also asks you to evaluate the best course(s) you have taken. In analyzing each course, he wants you to state specifically why you consider these courses to be best and worst. A committee composed of faculty from each department, from outside the department, and from the dean's office will be examining each curriculum. To help in assessing the curriculum in each major, the dean wants input from students with majors in each department.

4. Draft a letter to a faculty member from whom you have received a lower grade than you believe you should have received. Compare your letter with those of other students. Ask them to assess the effectiveness of your letter.

Collaborative Assignments

1. The president of your university has asked student groups to outline what they believe to be the major problems students confront on campus and to describe each problem briefly. Solutions can also be suggested. Work as a team. Assume your team is a fraternity, service organization, or student activity group.

2. Assume that the president of the university has taken a stand on an issue which your group finds objectionable. Write the president, stating your position and your reasons for that position.

    As you and your team members plan your response in each situation, discuss each of the seven questions presented in the last section of this chapter as your consider your reader and how you want him or her to respond to your message.

SCENARIO

As a new project engineer for the state highway department, you were asked—well, told, really—to be part of a team that was writing a new policy and procedure memorandum (PPM). The purpose of the PPM was to increase citizen participation in highway planning. The team spent an afternoon discussing the PPM and its purpose. The team leader, Chief Engineer Rosenberg, asked you to have a written purpose statement ready for the next meeting. "It will give us a good start for our next discussion," he said.

That night, you gave up watching your favorite TV shows to write the statement and have ready it for the next day. You wanted to be sure the statement covered everything and would be taken seriously by its readers. Of course, you also wanted it to impress Chief Engineer Rosenberg. By midnight you were satisfied with your statement:

> The purpose of this PPM (Policy and Procedure Memorandum) is to ensure, to the maximum extent practicable, that highway locations and designs reflect and are consistent with federal, state, and local goals and objectives. The rules, policies, and procedures established by this PPM are intended to afford full opportunity for effective public participation in the consideration of highway location and design proposals before submission to the federal Department of Transportation for approval. They provide a medium for free and open discussion and are designed to encourage early and amicable resolution of controversial issues that may arise.

At the next day's meeting the chief was impressed all right, but in the wrong way. He read your statement aloud, and said, "A bit on the pompous side, don't you think?" He then proceeded to rewrite the statement. You had to admit that his version was easier to read and understand.

This chapter discusses the principles the chief used to achieve clarity and avoid pomposity.

chapter 5

Achieving a Readable Style

▶ The Paragraph
The Central Statement
Paragraph Length
Transitions

▶ Lists and Tables

▶ Clear Sentence Structure
Sentence Length
Sentence Order
Sentence Complexity and Density
Active Verbs
Active and Passive Voice
First-Person Point of View
A Caution about Following Rules

▶ Specific Words

▶ Pomposity
Empty Words
Elegant Variation
Pompous Vocabulary

▶ Good Style in Action

▶ Choosing a Style for International Readers

A readable text is one that an intended reader can comprehend without difficulty. Many things can make a text difficult to read. For example, the content may include unexplained concepts that the reader does not understand. Material that is new to the reader may not be explained in terms of material already familiar to the reader. The material may not be arranged or formatted in a way to make it accessible to the reader. We cover such aspects of readability else where, notably in Chapter 2, Composing, Chapter 4, Writing for Your Readers, and Chapter 11, Document Design. In this chapter, we deal with style elements at the paragraph, sentence, and word level that can make your text clearer and more readable.

Examples of unclear writing style are all too easy to find, even in places where we would hope to find clear, forceful prose. Read the following sentence:

> While determination of specific space needs and access cannot be accomplished until after a programmatic configuration is developed, it is apparent that physical space is excessive and that all appropriate means should be pursued to assure that the entire physical plant is utilized as fully as feasible.

This murky sentence comes from a report issued by a state higher education coordinating board. Actually, it's better than many examples we could show you. Although difficult, the sentence is probably readable. Others are simply indecipherable. When you have finished this chapter, you should be able to analyze a passage like the one just cited and show why it is so unclear. You should also know how to keep your own writing clear, concise, and vigorous. We discuss paragraphs, lists, clear sentence structure, specific words, and pomposity. We have broken our subject into five parts for simplicity's sake, but all the parts are closely related. All have one aim: readability.

If there is a style checker in your word processor, it will incorporate many of the principles we discuss in this chapter. Nevertheless, use it with great care. Style checkers used without understanding the principles involved in good style can be highly misleading. (We discuss style checkers and problems associated with them more fully in Chapter 2, Composing.)

▶ THE PARAGRAPH

In Chapters 9 and 10, we discuss various ways to arrange information, such as exemplification, narration, and description. Any of these arrangement strategies may be used not only to develop reports but also to develop paragraphs within reports. This short paragraph uses exemplification:

> Until recently, virtually all medical products had terrestrial sources. For example, organisms found in all soil have yielded products such as penicillin, amoxicillin,

and other antibiotic compounds responsible for saving millions of Americans from suffering and death.[1]

The following longer paragraph depends on narration:

The body starts to form most of its bone mass before puberty, the beginning of sexual development, building 75 to 85 percent of the skeleton during adolescence. Women reach their peak bone mass by around 25 to 30, while men build bone mass until about age 30 to 35. The amount of peak bone mass you reach depends largely on your genes. Then, gradually, with age, the breakdown outpaces the buildup, and in late middle age bone density lessens when needed calcium is withdrawn from bone for such tasks as blood clotting and muscle contractions, including beating by the heart.[2]

Thus, paragraphs vary in arrangement and length, depending on their purpose and content, but a mark of a well-written paragraph is clear organization around a central statement.

The Central Statement

In technical writing, the central statement of a paragraph more often than not appears at the beginning of the paragraph. This placement provides the clarity of of statement that good technical writing must have. In a paragraph aimed at persuasion, however, the central statement may appear at the close, where it provides a suitable climax for the argument. Wherever you place the central statement, you can achieve unity by relating all the other details of the paragraph to the statement, as in this paragraph of fact and speculation:

The central statement concerning Yellowstone National Park is underlined. The rest of the paragraph presents facts and speculation in support of the central statement.

The Earth's crust beneath Yellowstone National Park is still restless. Precise surveys have detected an area in the center of the caldera that rose by as much as 86 centimeters between 1923 and 1984 and then subsided slightly between 1985 and 1989. Scientists do not know the cause of these ups and downs but hypothesize that they are related to the addition or withdrawal of magma beneath the caldera, or to the changing pressure of the hot ground water system above Yellowstone's large magma reservoir. Also, Yellowstone National Park and the area immediately west of the park are historically among the most seismically active areas in the Rocky Mountains. Small-magnitude earthquakes are common beneath the entire caldera, but most are located along the Hebgen Lake fault zone that extends into the northwest part of the caldera. A magnitude 7 earthquake occurred along this zone in 1959.[3]

Paragraph Length

Examination of well-edited magazines such as *Scientific American* reveals that their paragraphs seldom average more than a hundred words in length.

Magazine editors know that paragraphs are for the reader. Paragraphing breaks the material into related subdivisions to enhance the reader's understanding. When paragraphs are too long, the central statements that provide the generalizations needed for reader understanding are either missing or hidden in the mass of supporting details.

In addition to considering the reader's need for clarifying generalizations, editors also consider the psychological effect of their pages. They know that large blocks of unbroken print have a forbidding appearance that intimidates the reader. If you follow the practice of experienced editors, you will break your paragraphs whenever your presentation definitely takes a new turn. As a general rule, paragraphs in reports and articles should average one hundred words or fewer. In letters and memorandums, because of their page layout, you should probably hold average paragraph length to fewer than sixty words.

Transitions

Generally, a paragraph presents a further development in a continuing sequence of thought. In such a paragraph, the opening central statement will be so closely related to the preceding paragraph that it will provide a sufficient transition. When a major transition between ideas is called for, consider using a short paragraph to guide the reader from one idea to the next.

The following four paragraphs provide an excellent example of paragraph development and transition:

Repetition of the key word *fossil* provides transition throughout the passage. The first sentence expresses the passage's central theme: Fossils provide clues to the past. In the second paragraph, the phrase "will tell even more" alerts readers that the paragraph will examine another role for fossils. The next sentence clarifies that role: to reveal the former boundaries between ancient lands and seas. The third paragraph's central statement looks both backward and forward, first summarizing the preceding paragraph and then announcing yet another role for fossils: to provide

The distribution of fossils (skeletons, shells, leaf impressions, footprints and dinosaur eggs) in rocks of a certain age tells something about the ancient distribution of lands and seas on the Earth's surface. The remains of coral and clamshells found in the very old limestones in parts of Pennsylvania and New York indicate that this region was once covered by a shallow sea. Similarly, the remains of ancestral horses and camels in rocks of South Dakota show that the area was then dry land or that land was nearby.

A closer look at these fossils will tell even more. Their distribution identifies the ancient areas of land and sea and also determines the approximate shoreline. The distribution of living forms shows that thick-shelled fossil animals once lived in shallow seas close to shore, where their shells were built to withstand the surging and pounding of waves. Thin-shelled, delicate fossil animals probably lived in deeper, calmer water offshore.

In addition to providing a measure of water depth, fossils can also be used to indicate the former temperature of water. In order to survive, certain types of present-day coral must live in warm and shallow tropical saltwaters, such as the seas around Florida and the Bahamas. When similar types of coral are found in the ancient limestones, they provide a good estimate of the marine environment that must have existed when they were alive.

information about the temperature of ancient seas. The final paragraph rounds off the passage by summarizing its main points.

All these factors—depth, temperature, currents, and salinity—that are revealed by fossils are important, for each detail tends to sharpen and clarify the picture of ancient geography.[4]

The four paragraphs illustrate that you will develop paragraphs coherently when you keep your mind on the central theme. If you do so, the words needed to provide proper transition will come naturally. More often than not, your transitions will be repetitions of key words and phrases, supported by such simple expressions as *also, another, of these four, because of this development, so, but*, and *however*. When you wander away from your central theme, no amount of artificial transition will wrench your writing back into coherence.

▶ LISTS AND TABLES

One of the simplest things you can do to ease the reader's chore is to break down complex statements into lists. Visualize the printed page. When it appears as an unbroken mass of print, it intimidates readers and makes it harder for them to pick out key ideas. Get important ideas out into the open where they stand out. Lists help to clarify introductions and summaries. You may list by (1) starting each separate point on a new line, leaving plenty of white space around it, or (2) using numbers within a line, as we have done here. Examine the following summary from a student paper, first as it might have been written and then as it actually was:

The exploding wire is a simple-to-perform yet very complex scientific phenomenon. The course of any explosion depends not only on the material and shape of the wire but also on the electrical parameters of the circuit. In an explosion the current builds up and the wire explodes, current flows during the dwell period, and "postdwell conduction" begins with the reignition caused by impact ionization. These phases may be run together by varying the circuit parameters.

Now, the same summary as a list:

The exploding wire is a simple-to-perform yet very complex scientific phenomenon. The course of any explosion depends not only on the materials and shape but also on the electrical parameters of the circuit.
    An explosion consists primarily of three phases:

1. The current builds up and the wire explodes.
2. Current flows during the dwell period.
3. "Postdwell conduction" begins with the reignition caused by impact ionization.

These phases may be run together by varying the circuit parameters.

The first version is clear, but the second version is clearer, and readers can now file the process in their minds as "three phases." They will remember it longer.

Some writers avoid using lists even when they should use them, so we hesitate to suggest any restrictions on the practice. Obviously, there are some subjective limits. Lists break up ideas into easy-to-read, easy-to-understand bits, but too many can make your page look like a laundry list. Also, some journal editors object to lists in which each item starts on a separate line. Such lists take space, and space costs money. Use lists when they clarify your presentation, but use them prudently.

Tables perform a function similar to lists. You can use them to present a good deal of information—particularly statistical information—in a way that is easy for the reader to follow and understand. We discuss tables and their functions in Chapter 12, Using Illustrations.

▶ CLEAR SENTENCE STRUCTURE

The basic English sentence structure follows two patterns, *subject-verb-object* (SVO) and *subject-verb-complement* (SVC):

Americans(S) love(V) ice cream(O).
She(S) planned(V) carefully(C).

Around such simple sentences as "Americans love ice cream" the writer can hang a complex structure of words, phrases, and clauses that modify and extend the basic idea. In this case, the writer actually wrote "Americans love ice cream, but ice cream is made from whole milk and cream and therefore contains a considerable amount of saturated fat and dietary cholesterol."

In this section on clear sentence structure, we discuss how to extend your sentences without losing clarity. We discuss sentence length, sentence order, sentence complexity and density, active verbs, active and passive voice, and first-person point of view.

Sentence Length

Many authorities have seen sentence length as an indicator of how difficult a sentence is. More recent research has found that although sentence length and word length may be indicators, they are not the primary causes of difficulty in reading sentences. Rather, the true causes may be the use of difficult sentence structures and words unfamiliar to the reader. This position is summed up well in this statement:

A sentence with 60, 100, or 150 words needs to be shortened; but a sentence with 20 words is not necessarily more understandable than a sentence with 25 words.

The incredibly long sentences that are sometimes found in technical, bureau-cratic, and legal writing are also sentences that have abstract nouns as subjects, buried actions, unclear focus, and intrusive phrases. These are the problems that must be fixed, whether the sentence has 200 words or 10.

Similarly, short words are not always easier words. The important point is not that the words be short, but that your readers know the words you are using.[5]

In general we agree with such advice. Sentence density and complexity cause readers more grief than does sentence length alone. Nevertheless, it's probably worth keeping in mind that most professional writers average only slightly more than twenty words per sentence. Their sentences may range from short to fairly long, but, for the most part, they avoid sentences like this one from a bank in Houston, Texas:

> You must strike out the language above certifying that you are not subject to backup withholding due to notified payee underreporting if you have been noti-fied that you are subject to backup withholding due to notified payee under-reporting, and you have not received a notice from the Internal Revenue Service advising you that backup holding has terminated.

Sentence Order

What is the best way to order a sentence? Is a great deal of variety in sentence structure the mark of a good writer? One writing teacher, Francis Chris-tensen, looked for the answers to those two questions. He examined large sam-ples from twenty successful writers, including John O'Hara, John Steinbeck, William Faulkner, Ernest Hemingway, Rachel Carson, and Gilbert Highet. In his samples, he included ten fiction writers and ten nonfiction writers.[6]

What Christensen discovered seems to disprove any theory that good writing requires extensive sentence variety. The writers whose work was ex-amined depended mostly on basic sentence patterns. They wrote 75.5 per-cent of their sentences in plain **subject–verb–object (SVO)** or **subject–verb–complement (SVC)** order, as in these two samples:

Doppler radar increases capability greatly over conventional radar. (SVO)
Doppler radar can be tuned more rapidly than conventional radar. (SVC)

Another 23 percent of the time, the professionals began sentences with short **adverbial openers:**

Like any radar system, Doppler does have problems associated with it.

These adverbial openers are most often simple prepositional phrases or single words such as *however, therefore, nevertheless*, and other conjunctive adverbs. Generally, they provide the reader with a transition between thoughts.

Following the opening, the writer usually continues with a basic SVO or SVC sentence.

These basic sentence types—*SVO(C)* or *adverbial + SVO(C)*—were used 98.5 percent of the time by the professional writers in Christensen's sample. What did the writers do with the remaining 1.5 percent of their sentences? For 1.2 percent, they opened the sentence with **verbal clauses** based on participles and infinitives such as "*Breaking* ground for the new church" or "*To see* the new pattern more clearly." The verbal opener was again followed most often with an SVO or SVC sentence, as in this example:

> Looking at it this way, we see the radar set as basically a sophisticated stopwatch that sends out a high-energy electromagnetic pulse and measures the time it takes for part of that energy to be reflected back to the antenna.

Like the adverbial opener, the verbal opener serves most of the time as a transition.

The remaining 0.3 percent of the sentences (about one sentence in three hundred) were **inverted constructions,** in which the subject is delayed until after the verb, as in this sentence:

> No less important to the radar operator are the problems caused by certain inherent characteristics of radar sets.

What can we conclude from Christensen's study? Simply this: Professional writers are interested in getting their content across, not in tricky word order. They convey their thoughts in clear sentences not clouded by extra words. You should do the same.

Sentence Complexity and Density

Research indicates that sentences that are too complex in structure or too dense with content are difficult for many readers to understand.[7] Basing our observations on this research, we wish to discuss four particular problem areas: openers in front of the subject, too many words between the subject and the verb, noun strings, and multiple negatives.

Openers in Front of the Subject As Christensen's research indicates, professional writers place an adverbial or verbal opener before their subjects about 25 percent of the time. When these openers are held to a reasonable length, they create no problems for readers. The problems occur when the writer stretches such openers beyond a reasonable length. What is *reasonable* is somewhat open to question and depends to an extent on the reading ability of the reader. However, most would agree that the twenty-seven words and five commas before the subject in the following sentence make the sentence difficult to read:

Opening phrase
too dense

Because of their ready adaptability, ease of machining, and aesthetic qualities that make them suitable for use in landscape structures such as decks, fences, steps, and retaining walls, preservative-treated timbers are becoming increasingly popular for use in landscape construction.

The ideas contained in this sentence become more accessible when spread over two sentences:

Puts central idea
before supporting
evidence

Preservative-treated timbers are becoming increasingly popular for use in landscape construction. Their ready adaptability, ease of machining, and aesthetic qualities make them highly suited for use in structures such as decks, fences, steps, and retaining walls.

The second version has the additional advantage of putting the central idea in the sequence before the supporting information.

The conditional sentence is a particularly difficult type of sentence in which the subject is too long delayed. You can recognize the conditional by its *if* beginning:

Subject too
long delayed

If heat [20–35°C (or 68–95°F)-optimum], moisture (20%+ moisture content in wood), oxygen, and food (cellulose and wood sugars) are present, spores will germinate and grow.

To clarify such a sentence, move the subject to the front and the conditions to the rear. Consider the use of a list when you have more than two conditions:

List helps to clarify

Spores will germinate and grow when the following elements are present:

- Heat [20–35°C (or 68–95°F) optimum]
- Moisture content (20%+ moisture content in wood)
- Oxygen
- Food (cellulose and wood sugars)

Words between Subject and Verb In the following sentence, too many words between the subject and the verb cause difficulty:

Subject and
verb too widely
separated

Creosote, a brownish-black oil composed of hundreds of organic compounds, usually made by distilling coal tar, but sometimes made from wood or petroleum, has been used extensively in treating poles, piles, cross-ties, and timbers.

The sentence is much easier to read when it is broken into three sentences and first things are put first:

Revised

Creosote has been used extensively in treating poles, piles, cross-ties, and timbers. It is a brownish-black oil composed of hundreds of organic compounds. Creosote is usually made by distilling coal tar, but it can also be made from wood or petroleum.

You might break down the original sentence into only two sentences if you felt your audience could handle denser sentences:

Revised

Creosote, a brownish-black oil composed of hundreds of organic compounds, has been used extensively in treating poles, piles, cross-ties, and timbers. It is usually made by distilling coal tar, but it can also be made from wood or petroleum.

Noun Strings Noun strings are another way in which writers sometimes complicate and compress their sentences beyond tolerable limits. A noun string is a sequence of nouns that modifies another noun; for example, in the phrase *oxidization filtration process*, the nouns *oxidization* and *filtration* modify *process*. Sometimes the string may also include an adjective, as in *special oxidization filtration process*.

Nothing is grammatically wrong with the use of nouns as modifiers. Such use is an old and perfectly respectable custom in English. Expressions such as *firefighter* and *creamery butter*, in which the modifiers are nouns, go virtually unnoticed. The problem occurs when writers string many nouns together in one sequence or use many noun strings in a passage, as shown in this paragraph (Italics added):

Six noun strings
in one paragraph

We must understand who the initiators of *water-oriented greenway* efforts are before we can understand the basis for *community environment decision making* processes. *State government planning* agencies and commissions and *designated water quality planning and management* agencies have initiated such efforts. They have implemented *water resource planning and management* studies and have aided *volunteer group greenway initiators* by providing technical and coordinative assistance.[8]

In many such strings, the reader has great difficulty in sorting out the relationships among the words. In *volunteer group greenway initiators*, does *volunteer* modify *group* or *initiators?* The reader has no way of knowing.

The solution to untangling difficult noun strings is to include relationship clues such as prepositions, relative pronouns, commas, apostrophes, and hyphens. For instance, a hyphen in *volunteer-group* indicates that *volunteer* modifies *group.* The strung-out passage just quoted was much improved by the inclusion of such clues:

Relationship clues
help to clarify
noun strings

We must understand who the initiators of efforts to promote water-oriented greenways are before we can understand the process by which a community makes decisions about environmental issues. Planning agencies and commissions of the state government and agencies that have been designated to plan and manage water quality have initiated such efforts. They have implemented studies on planning and managing water resources and have aided volunteer groups that initiate efforts to promote greenways by providing them with technical advice and assistance in coordinating their activities.[9]

The use of noun strings in technical English will no doubt continue. They do have their uses, and technical people are very fond of them, but avoid using them excessively. When you do use them, check to be sure you are clear.

Multiple Negatives Writers introduce excessive complexity into their sentences by using multiple negatives. By *multiple negative*, we do not mean the grammatical error of the *double negative*, as in "He does *not* have *none* of them." We are talking about perfectly correct constructions that include two or more negative expressions, such as these:

Negative statements
- We will not go unless the sun is shining.
- We will not pay except when the damages exceed $50.
- The lever will not function until the power is turned on.

The positive versions of all of these statements are clearer than the negative versions:

Positive statements
- We will go only if the sun is shining.
- We will pay only when the damages exceed $50.
- The lever functions only when the power is turned on.

Research shows that readers have difficulty sorting out passages that contain multiple negatives. If you doubt the research, try your hand at interpreting this government regulation (italics added):

Excessive use of negatives
§928.310 Papaya Regulation 10. Order. (a) *No* handler shall ship any container of papayas (*except* immature papayas handled pursuant to §928.152 of this part): (1) During the period January 1 through April 15, 1980, to any destination within the production area *unless* said papayas grade at least Hawaii No. 1, *except* that allowable tolerances for defects may total 10 percent. Provided, that *not* more than 5 percent shall be for serious damage, *not* more than 1 percent for immature fruit, *not* more than 1 percent for decay: Provided further, that such papayas shall individually weigh *not* less than 11 ounces each.[10]

Active Verbs

The verb determines the structure of an English sentence. Many sentences in technical writing falter because the finite verb does not comment on the subject, state a relationship about the subject, or relate an action that the subject performs. Look at the following sentence:

Action in a noun
Protection of the external corners is accomplished by a metal strip.

English verbs can easily be changed into nouns, but sometimes, as we have just seen, the change can lead to a faulty sentence. The writer has put the true action into the subject and subordinated the metal strip into the object of a preposition. The sentence should read:

Action in a verb

A metal strip protects the external corners.

The poor writer can ingeniously bury the action of a sentence almost anywhere, With the common verbs *make, give, get, have*, and *use*, the writer can bury the action as an object:

Action in an object

We have the belief that oxidized nitrogen is a significant nutrient in the upper trophogenic zone.

Properly revised, the sentence puts the action in the verb:

Action in a verb

We believe that oxidized nitrogen is a significant nutrient in the upper trophogenic zone.

Some writers can even bury the action in an adjective:

Action in an adjective

The new understanding of phytoplankton bloom dynamics in the Ross Sea produced an excited reaction in the biologists.

Revised:

Action in a verb

The new understanding of phytoplankton bloom dynamics in the Ross Sea excited the biologists.

When writing, and particularly when rewriting, you should always ask yourself, Where's the action? If the action does not lie in the verb, rewrite the sentence to put it there, as in this sample:

Action in nouns

Music therapy is the scientific application of music to accomplish the restoration, maintenance, and improvement of mental health.

This sentence provides an excellent example of how verbs are frequently turned into nouns by the use of the suffixes *-ion, -ance* (or *-ence*), and *-ment*. If you have sentences full of such suffixes, you may not be writing as actively as you could be. Rewritten to put active ideas into verb forms, the sentence reads this way:

Action in verbs

Music therapy applies music scientifically to restore, maintain, and improve mental health.

The rewritten sentence defines *music therapy* in one-third less language than the first sentence, without any loss of meaning or content.

Active and Passive Voice

We discuss active and passive voice sentences in Chapter 9, but let us quickly explain the concept here. In an active voice sentence, the subject performs the action and the object receives the action, as in "The heart pumps the blood." In a passive voice sentence, the subject *receives* the action, as in "The blood is pumped." If you want to include the doer of the action, you must add this information in a prepositional phrase, as in "The blood is pumped *by the heart.*" We urge you to use the active voice more than the passive. As the *CBE Style Manual*, published by the Council of Biology Editors, points out, "The active is the natural voice in which people usually speak or write, and its use is less likely to lead to wordiness and ambiguity."[11]

However, you should not ignore the passive altogether. The passive voice is often useful. You can use the passive voice to emphasize the object receiving the action. The passive voice in "Influenza may be caused by any of several viruses" emphasizes *influenza.* The active voice in "Any of several viruses may cause influenza" emphasizes the *viruses.*

Often the agent of action is of no particular importance. When such is the case, the passive voice is appropriate because it allows you to drop the agent altogether:

Appropriate passive   Edward Jenner's work on vaccination was published in 1796.

Be aware, however, that inappropriate use of the passive voice can cause you to omit the agent when knowledge of the agent may be vital. Such is often the case in giving instructions:

Poor passive   All doors to the biology building will be locked at 9 P.M.

This sentence may not produce locked doors until it is rewritten in the active voice:

Active voice   The custodian will lock all doors to the biology building at 9 P.M.

Also, the passive voice can lead to dangling participles, as in this sentence:

Passive with dangling modifier   While conducting these experiments, the chickens were seen to panic every time a hawk flew over.

Chickens conducting experiments? Not really. The active voice straightens out the matter:

Active voice   While conducting these experiments, we saw that the chickens panicked every time a hawk flew over.

(See also Dangling Modifier in the Handbook.)

Although the passive voice has its uses, too much of it produces lifeless and wordy writing. Therefore, use it only when it is clearly appropriate.

First-Person Point of View

Once, reports and scientific articles were typically written in the third person—"This investigator has discovered"—rather than first person—"I discovered." The *CBE Style Manual* labels this practice the "passive of modesty" and urges writers to avoid it.[12] Many other style manuals for scientific journals now recommend the first person and advise against the use of the third person on the grounds that it is wordy and confusing. We agree with this advice.

The judicious use of *I* or *we* in a technical report is entirely appropriate. Incidentally, such usage will seldom lead to a report full of *I's* and *we's*. After all, there are many agents in a technical report other than the writer. In describing an agricultural experiment, for example, researchers will report how *the sun shone, photosynthesis occurred, rain fell, plants drew nutrients from the soil*, and *combines harvested*. Only occasionally will researchers need to report their own actions. But when they must, they should be able to avoid such roundabout expressions as "It was observed by this experimenter." Use "*I* observed" instead. Use "We observed" when there are two or more experimenters.

A Caution about Following Rules

We must caution you before we leave this section on clear sentence structure. We are not urging upon you an oversimplified primer style, one often satirized by such sentences as "Jane hit the ball" and "See Dick catch the ball." Mature styles have a degree of complexity to them. Good writers, as Christensen's research shows, do put information before the subject. Nothing is wrong with putting information between the subject and verb of a sentence. You will find many such sentences in this book. However, you should be aware that research shows that sentences that are too long, too complex, or too dense cause many readers difficulty. Despite increasingly good research into its nature, writing is a craft and not a science. Be guided by the research available, but do not be simplistic in applying it.

▶ SPECIFIC WORDS

Semanticists have developed the concept of the abstraction ladder, which is composed of rungs that ascend from very specific words such as *table* to abstractions such as *furniture, wealth*, and *factor*. The human ability to move up and down this ladder enabled us to develop language, on which all human progress depends. Because we can think in abstract terms, we can call a moving company and tell it to move our furniture. Without abstraction, we would have to bring the movers into our house and point to each object we wanted moved. Like many helpful writing techniques, however, abstraction is a device you should use carefully.

Stay at an appropriate level on the abstraction ladder. Do not say "inclement weather" when you mean "rain." Do not say "overwhelming support" when you mean "62% percent of the workers supported the plan." Do not settle for "suitable transportation" when you mean "a bus that seats thirty-two people."

Writing that uses too many abstractions is lazy writing. It relieves writers of the need to observe, to research, and to think. They can speak casually of "factors," and neither they nor their readers really know what they are talking about. Here is an example of such lazy writing. The writer was setting standards for choosing a desalination plant to be used at Air Force bases.

Too abstract
- The quantity of water must be sufficient to supply a military establishment.
- The quality of the water must be high.

The writer here thinks he has said something. He has said little. He has listed slovenly abstractions when, with a little thought and research, he could have listed specific details. He should have said:

Use of specific detail
- To supply an average base with a population of 5,000, the plant should purify 750,000 gallons of water a day (AFM 88-10 sets the standard of 150 gallons a day per person).
- The desalinated water should not exceed the national health standard for potable water of 500 parts per million of dissolved solids.

Abstractions are needed for generalizing, but they cannot replace specific words and necessary details. Words mean different things to different people. The higher you go on the abstraction ladder, the truer this is. The abstract words *sufficient* and *high* could be interpreted in as many different ways as the writer had readers. No one can misinterpret the specific details given in the rewritten sentences.

Abstractions can also burden sentences in another way. Some writers are so used to thinking abstractly that they begin a sentence with an abstraction and *then* follow it with the specific word, usually in a prepositional phrase. They write,

Poor   The problem of producing fresh water became troublesome at overseas bases.

Instead of

Revised   Producing fresh water became a problem at overseas bases.

Or

Poor   The circumstance of the manager's disapproval caused the project to be dropped.

Instead of

Revised   The manager's disapproval caused the project to be dropped.

We do not mean to say you should never use high abstractions. A good writer moves freely up and down the abstraction ladder. But when you use words from high on the ladder, use them properly—for generalizing and as a shorthand way of referring to specific details you have already given.

▶ POMPOSITY

State your meaning as simply and clearly as you can. Do not let the mistaken notion that writing should be more elegant than speech make you sound pompous. Writing *is* different from speech. Writing is more concise, more compressed, and often better organized than speech. But elegance is not a prerequisite for good writing.

A sign at a gas station reads, "No gas will be dispensed while smoking." Would the employees in that service station speak that way? Of course not. They would say, "Please put out that cigarette" or "No smoking, please." But the sign had to be elegant, and the writer sounds pompous—and illiterate as well.

If you apply what we have already told you about clear sentence structure, you will go a long way toward tearing down the fence of artificiality between you and the reader. We want to touch on just three more points: empty words, elegant variation, and pompous vocabulary.

Empty Words

The easiest way to turn simple, clear prose into elegant nonsense is to throw in empty words, such as these phrases that begin with the impersonal *it:* "It is evident," "It is clear that," or, most miserable of all, "It is interesting to note that." When something is evident, clear, or interesting, readers will discover this for themselves. If something is not evident, clear, or interesting, rewrite it to make it so. When you must use such qualifying phrases, at least shorten them to "evidently," "clearly," and "note that." Avoid constructions like "It was noted by Jones." Simply say, "Jones noted."

Many empty words are jargon phrases writers throw in by sheer habit. You see them often in business correspondence. A partial list follows:

to the extent that	is already stated
with reference to	in view of
in connection with	inasmuch as
relative to	with your permission
with regard to	hence
with respect to	as a matter of fact

We could go on, but so could you. When such weeds crop up in your writing, pull them out.

Another way to produce empty words is to use an abstract word in tandem with a specific word. This produces such combinations as

20 in number *for* 20
wires of thin size *for* thin wires
red in color *for* red

When you have expressed something specifically, do not throw in the abstract term for the same word.

Elegant Variation

Elegant variation will also make your writing sound pompous.[13] Elegant variation occurs when a writer substitutes one word for another because of an imagined need to avoid repetition. This substitution can lead to two problems: The substituted word may be a pompous one and the variation may mislead the reader into thinking that some shift in meaning is intended. Both problems are evident in the following example:

Elegant variation

Insect damage to evergreens varies with the condition of the plant, the pest species, and the hexapod population level.

Confusion reigns. The writer has avoided repetition, but the reader may think that the words *insect, pest,* and *hexapod* refer to three different things. Also, *hexapod*, though a perfectly good word, sounds a bit pompous in this context. The writer should have written,

Revised

Insect damage to evergreens varies with the condition of the plant, the insect species, and the insect population level.

Remember also that intelligent repetition provides good transition. Repeating key words reminds the reader that you are still dealing with your central theme (see pages 84–85).

Pompous Vocabulary

Generally speaking, the vocabulary you think in will serve in your writing. Jaw-breaking thesaurus words and words high on the abstraction ladder will not convince readers that you are intellectually superior. Such words will merely convince readers that your writing is hard to read. We are not telling you here that you must forgo your hard-won educated vocabulary. If you are writing for readers who understand words such as *extant* or *prototype*, then use them. But use them only if they are appropriate to your discussion. Don't use them to impress people.

Nor are we talking about the specialized words of your professional field. At times these are necessary. Just remember to define them if you think your reader will not know them. What we are talking about is the desire some writers seem to have to use pompous vocabulary to impress their readers.

The following list is a sampling of heavy words and phrases along with their simpler substitutes.

accordingly: so	*due to the fact that:* because
acquire: get	*facilitate:* ease, simplify
activate: begin	*for the purpose of:* for
along the lines of: like	*in accordance with:* by, under
appreciative of: appreciates	*in connection with:* about
assist: help	*initiate:* begin
compensation: pay	*in order to:* to
consequently: so	*nevertheless:* but, however
in the event that: if	*prior to:* before
in the interests of: for	*subsequent to:* later, after
in this case: here	*supportive of:* supports
make application to: apply	*utilize:* use

You would be wise to avoid the word-wasting phrases on this list and other phrases like them. You really don't need to avoid the single words shown, such as *acquire* and *assist*. All are perfectly good words. But to avoid sounding pompous, don't string large clumps of such words together. Be generous in your writing with the simpler substitutes we have listed. If you don't, you are more likely to depress your readers than to impress them. Don't be like the pompous writers who seek to bury you under the many-syllable words they use to express one-syllable ideas.

We urge you to read as much good writing—both fiction and nonfiction—as time permits. Stop occasionally and study the author's choice of words. You will find most authors to be lovers of the short word. Numerous passages in Shakespeare are composed almost entirely of one-syllable words. The same holds true for the King James Bible. Good writers do not want to impress you with their vocabularies. They want to get their ideas from their heads to yours by the shortest, simplest route.

▶ GOOD STYLE IN ACTION

A final example will summarize much that we have said. Insurance policies were verbal bogs for so long that most buyers of insurance gave up on finding one clearly written. However, the St. Paul Fire and Marine Insurance Company decided that it was both possible and desirable to simplify the wording of its policies. The company revised one of its policies, eliminating empty words and using only words familiar to the average reader. In the revision, the company's writers avoided excessive sentence complexity and used predominantly the active voice and active verbs. They broke long paragraphs into shorter ones. The insurance company became *we* and the insured *you*. Definitions were included where needed rather than segregated in a glossary. The resulting policy is wonderfully clear. Compare a paragraph of the old with the new.[14]

Old:

Cancellation

Passive voice

Average sentence length: 29 words

Empty words

This policy may be canceled by the Named Insured by surrender thereof to the Company or any of its authorized agents, or by mailing to the Company written notice stating when thereafter such cancellation shall be effective. This policy may be canceled by the Company by mailing to the Named Insured at the address shown in this Policy written notice stating when, not less than thirty (30) days thereafter, such cancellation shall be effective. The mailing of notice as aforesaid shall be sufficient notice and the effective date of cancellation stated in the notice shall become the end of the policy period. Delivery of such written notice either by the Named Insured or by the Company shall be equivalent to mailing. If the Named Insured cancels, earned premium shall be computed in accordance with the customary short rate table and procedure. If the Company cancels, earned premium shall be computed pro rata. Premium adjustment may be made at the time cancellation is effected or as soon as practicable thereafter. The check of the Company or its representative, mailed or delivered, shall be sufficient tender of any refund due the Named Insured. If this contract insures more than one Named Insured, cancellation may be effected by the first of such Named Insureds for the account of all the Named Insureds; notice of cancellation by the Company to such first Named Insured shall be deemed notice to all Insureds and payment of any unearned premium to such first Named Insured shall be for the account of all interests therein.

Unfamiliar words

All one paragraph

A 66-word sentence

New:

Can This Policy Be Canceled?

Active voice

Average sentence length: 15 words

Clear, specific language

Short paragraphs

Yes it can. Both by you and by us. If you want to cancel the policy, hand or send your cancellation notice to us or our authorized agent. Or mail us a written notice with the date when you want the policy canceled. We'll send you a check for the unearned premium, figured by the short rate table—that is, pro rata minus a service charge.

If we decide to cancel the policy, we'll mail or deliver to you a cancellation notice effective after at least 30 days. As soon as we can, we'll send you a check for the unearned premium, figured pro rata.

Examples that substitute specific, familiar words for the high abstractions of the original policy are used freely. For instance:

> You miss a stop sign and crash into a motorcycle. Its 28-year-old married driver is paralyzed from the waist down and will spend the rest of his life in a wheelchair.
>
> A jury says you have to pay him $1,300,000. Your standard insurance liability limit is $300,000 for each person. We'll pay the balance of $1 million.

Or:

> We'll defend any suit for damages against you or anyone else insured even if it's groundless or fraudulent. And we'll investigate, negotiate and settle on your behalf any claim or suit if that seems to us proper and wise.
>
> You own a two-family house and rent the second floor apartment to the Miller family. The Millers don't pay the rent and you finally have to evict them. Out of sheer spite, they sue you for wrongful eviction. You're clearly in the right, but the defense of the suit costs $750. Under this policy we defend you and win the case in court. The whole business doesn't cost you a penny.

Incidentally, there is no fine print in the policy. It is set entirely in 10-point type, a type larger than that used in most newspapers and magazines. Headings and even different-colored print are used freely to draw attention to transitions and important information. Most states now require insurance policies sold within their borders to meet "plain language" requirements. We can hope, therefore, that the impossible-to-read insurance policy is a thing of the past.

You can clean up your own writing by following the principles discussed in this chapter and demonstrated in the revised insurance policy. Also, if you exercise care, your own manner of speaking can be a good guide in writing. You should not necessarily write as you talk. In speech, you may be too casual, even slangy. But the sound of your own voice can still be a good guide. When you write something, read it over; even read it aloud. If you have written something you know you would not speak because of its artificiality, rewrite it in a comfortable style. Rewrite so that you can hear the sound of your own voice in it.

▶ CHOOSING A STYLE FOR INTERNATIONAL READERS

In the United States, good technical and business style calls for clarity and succinctness. It's a style that is suitable in English-speaking Canada. The Canadian edition of this text, revised specifically for Canadian readers by two Canadian teachers, has no significant changes in this chapter.[15] It's a style that, with some modification, will not offend members of most Western European cultures. However, cultures in which romance languages—such as

French, Spanish, and Italian—predominate do prefer a more formal style where conciseness is not an issue.

Asian readers and, to a lesser degree, Mexican and Latin American readers, may find the directness of the North American style blunt and aggressive, even rude. Their style compared to the North American style is more formal, and ideas, particularly dissenting ideas, are presented much more indirectly. In short, the success of any style depends on how readers react to it. We offer our major advice about some of the adjustments you can make in Chapter 7. Writing for International Readers.

▶ PLANNING AND REVISION CHECKLISTS

You will find the planning and revision checklists following Chapter 2, Composing, and inside the front cover valuable in planning and revising any presentation of technical information. The following questions apply specifically to style. They summarize the key points in this chapter and provide a checklist for revising.

Planning

You can revise for good style, but you can't plan for it. Good style comes when you are aware of the need to avoid the things that cause bad style: ponderous paragraphs, overly dense sentences, excessive use of passive voice, pomposity, and the like. Good style comes when you write to express your thoughts clearly, not to impress your readers. Good style comes when you have revised enough writing that the principles involved are ingrained in your thought process.

Revision

- Do you have a style checker in your word processing software? If so, use it, but exercise the cautions we advocate in Chapter 2, Composing.
- Are the central thoughts in your paragraphs clearly stated? Do the details in your paragraphs relate to the central thought?
- Have you broken up your paragraphs sufficiently to avoid long, intimidating blocks of print?
- Have you guided your reader through your paragraphs with the repetition of key words and with transition statements?
- Have you used lists or tables when they would help the reader?
- Are your sentences of reasonable length? Have you avoided sentences of sixty to one hundred words? Does your average sentence length match that of professional writers—about twenty words?

- Professional writers begin about 75 percent of their sentences with the subject of the sentence. How does your percentage of subject openers compare to that figure? If your average differs markedly, do you have a good reason for the difference?
- When you use sentence openers before the subject, do they provide good transitions for your readers?
- Have you limited sentence openers before the subject to a reasonable length?
- Have you avoided large blocks of words between your subject and your verb?
- Have you used noun strings to modify other nouns? If so, are you sure your readers will be able to sort out the relationships involved?
- Have you avoided the use of multiple negatives?
- Are your action ideas expressed in active verbs? Have you avoided burying them in nouns and adjectives?
- Have you used active voice and passive voice appropriately? Are there passive voice sentences you should revise to active voice?
- Have you used abstract words when more specific words would be clearer for your readers? Do your abstractions leave unintended interpretations open to the reader? When needed, have you backed up your abstractions with specific detail?
- Have you avoided empty jargon phrases?
- Have you chosen your words to express your thoughts clearly for your intended reader? Have you avoided pompous words and phrases?
- Is your style suitable for international readers?

▶ EXERCISES

1. You should now be able to rewrite the example sentence on page 82 in clear, forceful prose. Here it is again; try it:

   While determination of specific space needs and access cannot be accomplished until after a programmatic configuration is developed, it is apparent that physical space is excessive and that all appropriate means should be pursued to ensure that the entire physical plant is utilized as fully as feasible.

2. Here is the pompous paragraph from page 80. Rewrite it in good prose:

   The purpose of this PPM [Policy and Procedure Memorandum] is to ensure, to the maximum extent practicable, that highway locations and designs reflect and are consistent with federal, state and local goals and objectives. The rules, policies, and procedures established by this PPM are intended to afford full opportunity for effective public participation in the consideration of highway location and design proposals before submission to the federal Department of Transportation for approval. They provide a medium for free and open discussion and are designed to encourage early and amicable resolution of controversial issues that may arise.

3. Following are some expressions that the Council of Biology Editors believes should be rewritten.[16] Using the principles you have learned in this chapter, rewrite them:

- an innumerable number of tiny veins
- as far as our own observations are concerned, they show
- ascertain the location of
- at the present moment
- at this point in time
- bright green in color
- by means of
- (we) conducted inoculation experiments on
- due to the fact that
- during the time that
- fewer in number
- for the purpose of examining
- for the reason that
- from the standpoint of
- goes under the name of
- if conditions are such that
- in all cases
- in order to
- in the course of
- in the event that
- in the near future
- in the vicinity of
- in view of the fact that
- it is often the case that
- it is possible that the cause is
- it is this that
- it would thus appear that
- large numbers of
- lenticular in character
- masses are of large size
- necessitates the inclusion of
- of such hardness that

- on the basis of
- oval in shape, oval shaped
- plants exhibited good growth
- prior to (in time)
- serves the function of being
- subsequent to
- the fish in question
- the tests have not as yet
- the treatment having been performed
- there can be little doubt that
- throughout the entire area
- throughout the whole of this experiment
- two equal halves
- If we interpret the deposition of chemical signals as initiation of courtship, then initiation of courtship by females is probably the usual case in mammals.
- A direct correlation between serum vitamin B_{12} concentration and mean nerve conduction velocity was seen.
- It is possible that the pattern of herb distribution now found in the Chilean site is a reflection of past disturbances.
- Following termination of exposure to pigeons and resolution of the pulmonary infiltrates, there was a substantial increase in lung volume, some improvement in diffusing capacity, and partial resolution of the hypoxemia.

4. Turn the following sentence into a paragraph of several sentences. See whether listing might help. Make the central idea of the passage its first sentence.

> If, on the date of opening of bid or evaluation of proposals, the average market price of domestic wool of usable grades is not more than 10 percent above the average of the prices of representative types and grades of domestic wools in the wool category which includes the wool required by the specifications [see (f) below], which prices reflect the current incentive price as established by the Secretary of Agriculture, and if reasonable bids or proposals have been received for the advertised quantity offering 100 percent domestic wools, the contract will be awarded for domestically produced articles using 100 percent domestic wools and the procedure set forth in (e) and (f) below will be disregarded.

5. Lest you think all bad writing is American, here are two British samples, quoted in a magazine devoted to ridding Great Britain of gobbledygook.[17] Try your hand with them.

- The garden should be rendered commensurate with the visual amenities of the neighborhood.
- Should there be any intensification of the activities executed to accomplish your present hobby the matter would have to be reappraised.

6. The following description of how liposome technology may lead to better medical treatment is intended for an educated lay audience, an audience probably much like you. Analyze the description using the principles of this chapter: paragraph development, lists and tables, clear sentence structure, the use of specific words, and the avoidance of pomposity. You should consider such elements of style as transitions; paragraph length; sentence length, order, density, and complexity; and active and passive voice. Using your analysis, decide whether this description succeeds. Write a memo to your teacher stating and justifying your decision (see Letter and Memorandum Format in Appendix B).

> Can microscopic artificial membranes help doctors treat cancer, angina, and viral infections more effectively, and lead to better vaccines, bronchodilators, eye drops, and sunscreens? The researchers who are developing liposome technology hope so. A liposome is a tiny sphere of fatty molecules surrounding a watery interior. Because they are made of the same material as cell surface membranes, liposomes stick to cells and are not toxic. These characteristics make them attractive candidates for drug delivery vehicles.
>
> In 1980, two groups of researchers used liposomes filled with a common antibiotic to cure mice having a severe, but localized, infection. The infected cells were of a kind that is specialized to take up foreign bodies, and so they readily engulfed the liposomes. However, getting other kinds of cells to take up drug-filled liposomes has proven to be more difficult. A number of groups of researchers are experimenting with antibody-tagged liposomes filled with an anticancer drug. The liposomes are guided to the diseased tissue by the antibodies, which seek out cancerous cells but spare healthy ones. This selectivity allows smaller amounts of a drug to be used with greater effect, an important advantage considering the serious toxicity of many anticancer drugs.
>
> Other research teams are developing liposome-drug compounds that would be injected into muscle to release growth hormone or anticancer agents over a period of weeks. Scientists also hope to use liposomes to improve the safety and effectiveness of vaccines, including an influenza vaccine. As the cost of both natural lipids (extracted from egg yolk and soybeans) and artificial lipids declines, the future may bring many other liposome-containing medical products as well as nonmedical items, such as cosmetics.[18]

SCENARIO

After a year on the job with Pace Electronics, you are pleased to be assigned to work with Dr. Sean Barry on a proposal for a large research project. Dr. Barry is new to Pace, but he has a huge reputation in the field. You've worked well together on the rationale for the project, and you are both pleased with the section describing why the proposed research needs to be done.

When it is time to write the section of the proposal that describes the research methodology to be used, Dr. Barry hands you a thick manual and says, "We'll be using the same methodology that's described in there on pages 12 through 18; just copy it as is." Thumbing through the manual, you notice that it has been copyrighted by the company Dr. Barry worked for before he came to Pace.

You draw the copyright information to Dr. Barry's attention.

"Don't sweat it," he says. "Actually, I wrote that section myself."

"Yes," you say, "but it's the company that holds the copyright."

Dr. Barry is annoyed. "Look," he says, "it's all boilerplate. Just copy it and get the job done."

You do as you are told. But you worry about whether the short-cut was ethical. Maybe Dr. Barry is right and it's ethical to copy boilerplate, even when another company holds the copyright. After all, he wrote the material.

You realize you don't know enough to decide the ethics of the situation. You decide to talk your problem over with a few of your colleagues, some of whom have been at Pace for several years.

As you'll see when you read this chapter, this was a wise decision. You will also find in this chapter ways of recognizing and dealing with unethical behavior.

chapter 6

Writing Ethically

▶ Understanding Ethical Behavior
What Makes an Act Unethical?
Why Should We Act Ethically?

▶ Recognizing Unethical Communication
Plagiarism
Deliberately Using Imprecise or Ambiguous Language
Making False Implications
Manipulating the Data
Using Misleading Visuals

▶ Behaving Ethically

▶ Dealing with Unethical Behavior in Others

Because technical writing often has consequences for large numbers of people, ethical considerations frequently play a role in the writing process.[1] For example, it is sometimes a temptation in a feasibility report to soft-pedal results that do not support the recommendation the writer wishes to make. It may seem advantageous in a proposal to exaggerate an organization's ability to do a certain kind of research. A scientist may be too willing to ignore results that do not fit his theory and report those that do. Each of these acts would be unethical.

▶ UNDERSTANDING ETHICAL BEHAVIOR

What makes an act unethical? Why should we be ethical? Let us briefly answer those two questions and then offer a few suggestions about how to behave ethically.

What Makes an Act Unethical?

Most of us carry around ethical rules in our head. Most of us, no doubt, would agree that it is unethical to lie, cheat, and steal. Further extended, we would likely agree that it is wrong to make promises we don't intend to keep or to plagiarize a paper. Where do such ethical rules come from? In part, they are rules learned at home or through religious training or simply in the rough-and-tumble of growing up. The loss of friends who catch one in a lie can be a lasting ethical lesson. Philosophers have long attempted to develop theories to support ethical behavior. Most embrace either logic, consequences, or some combination of the two.

Logically, as the eighteenth-century German philosopher Immanuel Kant proposed, we should not act in a way that we cannot will to be universal behavior. For example, you might make a promise that you have no intention of keeping, but you cannot will that to be universal behavior. For, if you did, all promises would be worthless, and it would be pointless to make a promise, false or otherwise.

Another group of philosophers, the utilitarians, make consequences their test for ethical behavior. An act should do the greatest good for the greatest number of people or, conversely, create the least amount of evil for the fewest people. For example, causing an industrial plant to clean up its smokestack emissions may be an economic evil for the company and its stockholders, but be the greatest good for the large general population that must breathe those emissions. Medical scientists who fudge their data to produce impressive conclusions may become famous, but unsuspecting people may be injured as a result of the deception.

No matter how philosophers explain ethical behavior, one thing seems clear: Acting ethically often involves putting selfish interests aside for the sake of others. George F. R. Ellis, a modern-day student of ethics, stated this as a universal principle of ethical behavior:

> The foundational line of true ethical behavior, its main guiding principle valid across all times and cultures, is the degree of freedom from self-centeredness of thought and behavior, and willingness freely to give up one's own self-interest on behalf of others.[2]

Why Should We Act Ethically?

We, after all, don't have to act ethically. We don't have to will that our acts become universal behavior, as Kant would have us do. Nor, despite the utilitarians, must we constantly seek the greatest good for the greatest number. We don't have to set self-interest aside for the sake of others. Ethical behavior is inner-directed; we can ignore the dictates of our conscience when we choose to do so. If acting ethically is a voluntary act, why bother?

It's possible to list some pragmatic, nonaltruistic reasons for acting ethically. For one thing, some unethical acts are also illegal. You can end up in prison for stealing or otherwise bilking people of money. For another reason, organizations that intend to prosper over the long term need to have a reputation for ethical behavior. Unethical acts can help a organization or an individual temporarily, but in the long run, they usually do more harm than good.

Professionals, such as engineers and scientists, must act with integrity to survive in their work environments. For that reason most professional groups have a professional code that calls for ethical behavior. Most such codes draw upon the utilitarian philosophy of ethics.

The code for the Society for Technical Communication (STC) reproduced in Figure 6-1 is an example of such a code. Notice that beyond legality, the code calls for promoting "the public good." Further, under *Fairness*, the code makes clear that technical communicators may serve the interests of their clients only so long "as they are consistent with the public good."

The first principle of the Code of Ethics of the Institute of Electrical and Electronics Engineers (IEEE) also puts public welfare above all else. It agrees that members of IEEE will "accept responsibility in making engineering decisions consistent with the safety, health, and welfare of the public" and will "disclose promptly factors that might endanger the public or the environment." Such codes will help guide professionals through many ethical dilemmas, but like all such codes really don't answer the question we began with: Why should we act ethically?

STC Ethical Principles for Technical Communicators

As technical communicators, we observe the following ethical principles in our professional activities.

Legality

We observe the laws and regulations governing our profession. We meet the terms of contracts we undertake. We ensure that all terms are consistent with laws and regulations locally and globally, as applicable, and with STC ethical principles.

Honesty

We seek to promote the public good in our activities. To the best of our ability, we provide truthful and accurate communications. We also dedicate ourselves to conciseness, clarity, coherence, and creativity, striving to meet the needs of those who use our products and services. We alert our clients and employers when we believe that material is ambiguous. Before using another person's work, we obtain permission. We attribute authorship of material and ideas only to those who make an original and substantive contribution. We do not perform work outside our job scope during hours compensated by clients or employers, except with their permission; nor do we use their facilities, equipment, or supplies without their approval. When we advertise our services, we do so truthfully.

Confidentiality

We respect the confidentiality of our clients, employers, and professional organizations. We disclose business-sensitive information only with their consent or when legally required to do so. We obtain releases from clients and employers before including any business-sensitive materials in our portfolios or commercial demonstrations or before using such materials for another client or employer.

Quality

We endeavor to produce excellence in our communication products. We negotiate realistic agreements with clients and employers on schedules, budgets, and deliverables during project planning. Then we strive to fulfill our obligations in a timely, responsible manner.

Fairness

We respect cultural variety and other aspects of diversity in our clients, employers, development teams, and audiences. We serve the business interests of our clients and employers as long as they are consistent with the public good. Whenever possible, we avoid conflicts of interest in fulfilling our professional responsibilities and activities. If we discern a conflict of interest, we disclose it to those concerned and obtain their approval before proceeding.

Professionalism

We evaluate communication products and services constructively and tactfully, and seek definitive assessments of our own professional performance. We advance technical communication through our integrity and excellence in performing each task we undertake. Additionally, we assist other persons in our profession through mentoring, networking, and instruction. We also pursue professional self-improvement, especially through courses and conferences.

Adopted by the STC Board of Directors
September 1998.

FIGURE 6-1 • The Ethics Code of the Society for Technical Communication

Perhaps the real justification for acting ethically is less obvious than these individual and professional reasons. Acting ethically is a price we pay for living in a free, civilized society. A nonethical society would either be barbaric or totalitarian. That is, a world without ethics would be a world in which anything goes: murder, theft, rape, pillage, lying, and cheating in all their forms. It would be a society unfit to live in. Conversely, when ethics are lacking, the state, in order to maintain a civilization, would have to have laws restricting all kinds of unethical behavior.

In part, because we have unethical people, we live in such a society right now. We do have laws, for example, condemning theft, murder, and insider trading. We would not need environmental laws if every company voluntarily acted in the best interests of the general population. But a state that attempted to control everything covered by ethical behavior would be a totalitarian state, in its own way almost as bad as a barbaric one.

You can easily name nations in which the rule of law has broken down and corruption and unethical behavior are commonplace, with unfortunate consequences for the citizens of those nations. So, perhaps the best motivation for acting ethically is that it allows us to live in a civilized society without the heavy hand of government constantly on us.

▶ RECOGNIZING UNETHICAL COMMUNICATION

Perhaps the first step to communicating ethically is to recognize the ways in which people can be unethical when they communicate. Chief among the ways are plagiarism, deliberately using imprecise or ambiguous language, making false implications, manipulating data, and using misleading visuals.

Plagiarism

Ethical writers acknowledge the sources of the words, ideas, and findings they use. In some forms of writing, journalism for example, the acknowledgment may be in the text in a statement like, "As Dr. Ken Olson discovered, it's possible to vaccinate mosquitoes to prevent their developing and passing dengue on to human beings."

In more formal and scholarly writing, some system of documentation—notes and citations—is used to show the source of the information and to give full credit to Dr. Olson (see Documentation in Appendix B). To present the words and work of others as your own is plagiarism. It's a form of lying and highly unethical. Take every precaution to avoid even the appearance of plagiarism. For example, make sure that even your acknowledged paraphrases and summaries do not track the original so closely that they border on stealing another person's words.

Deliberately Using Imprecise or Ambiguous Language

In Chapter 5, Achieving a Readable Style, we discuss ways in which you can write clearly and help your readers to understand you. We urge you to write with precision and to avoid ambiguous language. Most often, an unclear style results from a faulty style, but, unfortunately, not always. It can result from a deliberate attempt to mislead or manipulate the reader by hiding unfavorable information.

Imagine the writer of a feasibility report who wishes to convey the impression that a certain change in company policy is desirable. He takes a survey of all the workers in the company and finds that 50.1 percent of the 20 percent who returned his survey favor the change. In his report he writes "A majority of those who returned the survey favored the change." By using *majority*, he makes a stronger case for change than if he reported the actual precise figure of 50.1 percent. In addition, by not revealing that this "majority" represents only 10 percent of the company's workers, he further strengthens what is actually rather weak support for his case. He has not lied, but through imprecision he has certainly misled his audience.

Making False Implications

Writers can imply that things are better than they are by manipulating their language. For example, a writer answering an inquiry about her company's voltage generator could reply, "Our voltage generator is designed to operate from the heat of Saudi Arabian deserts to the frozen tundra of Greenland." It may be true that the generator was *designed* that way, but if it *operates* well only between Atlanta and Toronto, the writer has made a false implication without telling an outright lie.

For another example, imagine a mutual fund that led its market in returns for ten years. In the eleventh year, the original fund manager retires and a new manager takes over. In that year and the next, the fund drops to the bottom tenth of its market in returns. The writer of an advertising brochure for the fund writes the following: "Our fund has led the market for ten of the last twelve years." Again the writer avoids an outright lie, but clearly has made an unethical statement.

Manipulating the Data

In the book, *Honor in Science*. Sigma Xi, the Scientific Research Society, lists three ways scientists can present their results unethically:

- *Trimming*: the smoothing of irregularities to make the data look extremely accurate and precise.
- *Cooking*: retaining only results that fit the theory and discarding others.
- *Forging*: inventing some or all of the research data that are reported, and even reporting "data" from experiments that were never performed.

Only the last of these three manipulations is clearly a lie, but all misrepresent the data, and all are unethical.

Using Misleading Visuals

Like words, visuals can misrepresent data and mislead unwary readers. The fundamental principle in constructing an ethical visual is to represent the data accurately and proportionally.[3]

Pictographs are particularly prone to misrepresentation. For example, Figure 6–2 is a line graph that shows the per capita health care expenditures in the United States from 1976 to 1996. The graph shows an increase from $671 in 1976 to $3,521 in 1996, an increase of 525 percent.

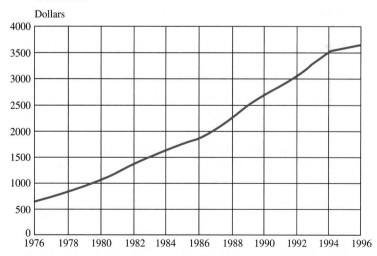

Personal Health Care Expenditures per Capita: 1976 to 1996

FIGURE 6-2 • Line Graph
Source: U.S. Department of Commerce, *Statistical Abstract of the United States: 1998*, 118th ed. (Washington, DC: GPO, 1998), 119.

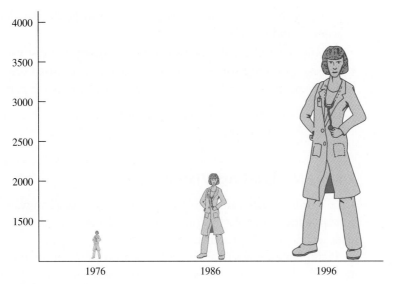

FIGURE 6-3 • Misleading Pictograph

Suppose now, as in Figure 6-3, we represent three of those years (1976, 1986, 1996) as human figures. Because the figures grow in two dimensions, while the data grow in only one dimension, the pictograph greatly exaggerates the increase in expenditures. Even when the actual figures are shown on the graph, as they are in Figure 6-3, naive or careless reader may be misled. Experienced graph readers may not be misled, but they will distrust the motives of the graph maker.

Actually, there is significant distortion even in the graph in Figure 6-2. When reporting dollar amounts in graphs and tables, you must be aware of the inflation of the dollar over time. To show true change in cost, you must use a device called the *constant dollar*. The government publishes tables that show the true value of the dollar compared to a base year. The table in Figure 6-4 shows 1982 as the base year and gives percentage figures for other years that factor in inflation.

Applying constant-dollar percentages in Figure 6-2, we can produce the graph in Figure 6-5, which shows a much smaller growth in expenditures than does the graph in Figure 6-2. The growth in constant dollars is actually from $1,179 in 1976 to $2,323 in 1996—a 202 percent increase rather than the 525 percent increase shown in Figure 6-2.

Unfortunately, many ways exist to distort graphic material beyond the ones illustrated here. Too narrow graphs can exaggerate the steepness of a

No. 771. Purchasing Power of the Dollar: 1950 to 1997

[**Indexes: PPI, 1982 = $1.00; CPI, 1982–84 = $1.00**. Producer prices prior to 1961, and consumer prices prior to 1964, exclude Alaska and Hawaii. Producer prices based on finished goods index. Obtained by dividing the average price index for the 1982 = 100, PPI; 1982 = 100. CPI base periods (100.0) by the price index for a given period and expressing the result in dollars and cents. Annual figures are based on average of monthly data]

YEAR	ANNUAL AVERAGE AS MEASURED BY—		YEAR	ANNUAL AVERAGE AS MEASURED BY—		YEAR	ANNUAL AVERAGE AS MEASURED BY—	
	Producer prices	Consumer prices		Producer prices	Consumer prices		Producer prices	Consumer prices
1950....	$3.546	$4.151	1966....	2.841	3.080	1982....	1.000	1.035
1951....	3.247	3.846	1967....	2.809	2.993	1983....	0.984	1.003
1952....	3.268	3.765	1968....	2.732	2.873	1984....	0.964	0.961
1953....	3.300	3.735	1969....	2.632	2.726	1985....	0.955	0.928
1954....	3.289	3.717	1970....	2.545	2.574	1986....	0.969	0.913
1955....	3.279	3.732	1971....	2.469	2.466	1987....	0.949	0.880
1956....	3.195	3.678	1972....	2.392	2.391	1988....	0.926	0.846
1957....	3.077	3.549	1973....	2.193	2.251	1989....	0.880	0.807
1958....	3.012	3.457	1974....	1.901	2.029	1990....	0.839	0.766
1959....	3.021	3.427	1975....	1.718	1.859	1991....	0.822	0.734
1960....	2.994	3.373	1976....	1.645	1.757	1992....	0.812	0.713
1961....	2.994	3.340	1977....	1.546	1.649	1993....	0.802	0.692
1962....	2.985	3.304	1978....	1.433	1.532	1994....	0.797	0.675
1963....	2.994	3.265	1979....	1.289	1.380	1995....	0.782	0.656
1964....	2.985	3.220	1980....	1.136	1.215	1996....	0.762	0.638
1965....	2.933	3.166	1981....	1.041	1.098	1997....	0.759	0.623

FIGURE 6-4 • Tabular Data
Source: U.S. Department of Commerce, *Statistical Abstract of the United States: 1998* 118th ed. (Washington, DC: GPO, 1998), 487.

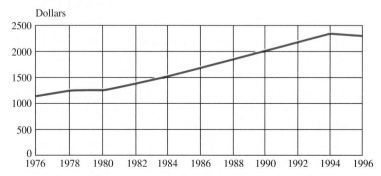

Per Capita Health Care Expenditures in Constant Dollars: 1976 to 1996

FIGURE 6-5 • Line Graph Created by Using Constant Dollars

curve, too wide the shallowness of the curve. Comparing data for six months on one bar to data for a year on another bar can mislead. Neglecting to show clearly that a graph does not begin at zero can seriously affect the reading of the graph.

Ethical graphs of the kind we show in Chapter 12, Using Illustrations, avoid the distortions and ambiguity we have demonstrated here. They do not lie or misrepresent the data.

▶ BEHAVING ETHICALLY

We are probably most tempted to behave unethically when either our own interests or the interests of our organization are at stake. For example, you may be writing a proposal for your research laboratory to do a significant and costly piece of research for a large government agency. It's sensible practice to cast your laboratory in its best light—a proposal is a sales document, after all. But the temptation to go too far is ever present. You may be tempted to exaggerate the expertise of your scientists who will carry out the job. Through imprecise language, you may hide the deficiencies of your laboratory or overstate its attributes.

On the other hand, you may write unethically simply by not recognizing the consequences of what you have written. A way to bring the consequences of your writing to the foreground is to construct a fault tree diagram at the point in your planning or writing where you recognize that there are various options open to you. As you construct your fault tree, you would draw each of your possible options as a branch, and list the consequences for each branch. If any of the listed consequences leads to another consequence, draw another branch showing that consequence, and so on, until you have exhausted all reasonable options. Let us illustrate.

Imagine yourself to be a newly graduated civil engineer. You are hired by a land developer to develop plans for streets and sewage disposal for a large parcel of land on which your client plans to build 45 houses. In walking the parcel, you discover that about half of it is a waste dump filled with trees and other vegetation covered over with several feet of soil. When you draw this to the developer's attention, he tells you that he has used the parcel of land as a dump for debris from other development project. Upon further questioning, he reveals that he has never sought a county permit for these activities, which means that the dump is an unauthorized land use. You realize that a dump filled with vegetation could become a source of substantial amounts of highly explosive methane gas. You recognize three possible options you can recommend to the developer:

1. Proceed with the development as planned.
2. Delay building until the contents of the dump have been removed.
3. Cancel the development plans.

To help yourself sort out the consequences of the actions, you develop the fault tree shown in Figure 6-6.

Your fault tree makes it clear that you cannot ethically recommend option 1. Option 2 is ethically acceptable, despite some costly negative consequences. You realize you'll need some further work to determine the cost of removing the dump. Option 3 is ethical but probably not cost-effective. If the developer chooses either option 2 or 3, you have fulfilled your ethical duty. Should the developer decide to go ahead with the development, you have another ethical choice. Should you remain quiet, but keep a copy of your report to protect yourself, or should you "blow the whistle" on the developer?

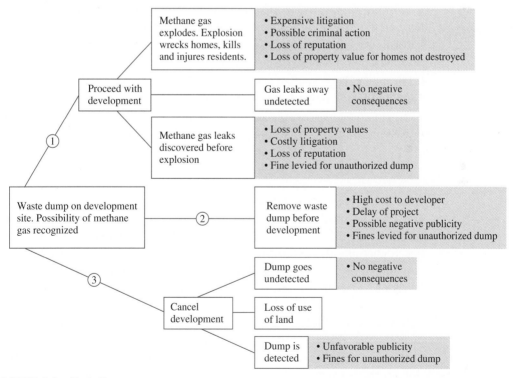

FIGURE 6-6 • Fault Tree

Here, the professional codes are helpful. Almost all place responsibility to public welfare above that of responsibility to the client. Given the possible cost in human misery if the developer goes ahead, there seems to be little choice; you'll have to blow the whistle.

▶ DEALING WITH UNETHICAL BEHAVIOR IN OTHERS

In most workplaces, most the time, people act ethically. But the temptation not to do so is often present, and sometimes the line is crossed. Sometimes you will perceive that others are acting unethically, or you may be asked or ordered to act unethically. For example, a supervisor may order you to shade the truth when writing a proposal or a feasibility report. Such a request or order is, in itself, unethical. Some of the cases reported on the Online Ethics Center for Engineering and Science are instructive in arriving at a definition of unethical conduct:[4]

- Writing instructions that risk an environmental health hazard.
- Allowing unsafe work practices to continue.
- Working for a private firm and a government agency at the same time when the firm and the agency may have conflicting interests.
- Writing a feasibility study with the opportunity to make a decision in the writer's own financial or professional interest.
- Hiring a college graduate and then withdrawing the offer after the graduate has already refused other offers.
- Accepting expensive gifts and favors from a supplier.
- Paying bribes to foreign officials to obtain contracts.
- Not giving proper authorship credit to a graduate student for a research paper.

In not every case mentioned here has the ethical line necessarily been crossed. For example, sometimes there are honest disagreements as to whether something really is an environmental hazard or an unsafe work practice. Sometimes the obligation to maintain a client's confidentiality makes it very difficult to draw the ethical line where it needs to be. Because whether behavior is unethical is often ambiguous, it pays to check on your own perceptions.

Talk to your colleagues about what you perceive to be unethical behavior, including unethical requests or orders. Talk to your supervisor. Talk to the person you think is behaving unethically. There may be satisfactory explanation for the behavior, or perhaps the person will agree to modify it. The table in Figure 6–7 lists the responses of 48 experienced technical communicators

Subjects	Comments
33	Talk to colleagues
27	Decide myself
20	Talk to boss
4	Talk to mentor
4	Talk to family
3	Talk to friend
3	Talk to whoever requested dubious action

FIGURE 6-7 • Sources of Advice Making Moral Choices
Source: Sam Dragga, "A Question of Ethics: Lessons from Technical Communicators on the Job," *Technical Communication Quarterly*, spring 1997, 169.

when they were asked what they would do if asked to enter gray areas of ethical behavior.

If after careful investigation you remain convinced that unethical behavior will continue and is harmful, then you should act. Some organizations have standing committees that will consider reports of unethical behavior and evaluate such situations. In other firms you may have to deal with higher management. Report the facts and the implications of those facts only. Do not make accusations that could land you in legal trouble; leave any formal complaint for those who deal with the matter.

What if the person who is in your opinion behaving unethically is your supervisor or your client? In the case of the waste dump with the methane gas problem, you could have detailed for the client in writing and orally the possible consequences of proceeding. If this presentation had failed, then given the very real risk to life and property, you would have had no alternative to reporting the matter to the proper authorities. This would have meant reporting the presence of the dump and documenting the possibility of a methane gas explosion there by citing situations at comparable dumps. Having done this, you would have met your ethical responsibility.

In this chapter, we have made you aware of some of the ethical situations you may encounter on the job and suggested ways to deal with them. To become more skillful at recognizing and dealing with unethical behavior, find and read the ethical code that covers your discipline. You can probably find it online at the Illinois Institute of Technology Center for the Study of Ethics in the Professions <http://csep.iit.edu>. This center also provides links to other sites that deal with ethics.

The Online Ethics Center for Engineering and Science <http://onlineethics.org> offers many aids, such as essays on ethics, case histories, and descriptions of exemplary ethical behavior by scientists and engineers. However, no amount of reading about ethics will make you or anyone else ethical. That result requires a good will, good judgment, moral sense, and, frequently, courage. In the end, it's character that counts.

▶ EXERCISES

1. Radon is an odorless, radioactive gas produced by the breakdown of uranium in the soil. Exposure to radon at sufficient levels can cause lung cancer. The U.S. Surgeon General considers radon to be second only to smoking as a cause of lung cancer in the United States. Imagine that you live in an area where radon in houses is a potential health threat. Concerned residents frequently hire radon removal contractors to test for radon levels in their houses and, when necessary, to install radon removal systems.

   You obtain summer employment with one such contractor. His name is John May and his firm is called May Radon Removal. Typically, the contractor tests the house for radon and then presents a proposal to the householder detailing any work determined to be necessary and naming a price. To obtain more information about radon and its reduction, you read a government booklet entitled *Consumer's Guide to Radon Reduction*.[5] From this reliable source, you learn that the most expensive radon reduction systems are needed for houses that are built either on concrete slabs or with basements. Systems for such houses can run as high as $2,500. Houses built over crawl spaces can almost always obtain adequate reduction by increasing the ventilation of the crawl space, a measure that seldom costs more than $500. You realize that you have been helping Mr. May install expensive systems suitable for basement and slab-constructed houses in houses built over crawl spaces.

   You look at a proposal being presented to a householder who owns a house with crawl space construction. In the proposal, you find that Mr. May has recommended suction depressurization, a system normally used under basements or slabs. It requires an expensive installation of pipes and fans in the soil under the house to trap and suck away radon. Your employer offers no alternatives to this system. In the proposal, Mr. May justifies the suction depressurization system with this statement: "Suction depressurization is the most common and usually the most reliable radon reduction method." From your research on radon, you know this is a true statement.

What should you do? Write a memorandum to your instructor describing your conclusions and any actions you plan to take (see Chapter 13, Correspondence, and Letter and Memorandum Format in Appendix B).

2. Form collaborative groups of five or six people and let each group discuss the following problem, using the bulleted questions as an aid:

> Thelma Miller has been working on her new job as systems analyst in Oglethorpe Consulting for some three months now. It is her first job out of college and she is enjoying it. She has made friends with Jim Brown, whose workstation is next to hers. At lunch time, Jim frequently eats at his workstation while playing electronic games at his computer. One day Thelma mentions to Jim that she wonders how he can afford such a variety of expensive games. Jim smiles, and says, "No problem."
>
> Later that day, Thelma gets an e-mail message from Jim directing her to a bulletin board (BB) that he maintains. Logging on to the BB, she finds that it a repository of copyrighted business and game software, as well as free shareware, that any user of the BB can download without cost. There are warnings on the BB that any users should maintain complete confidentiality about the board's existence.
>
> Upon asking her coworker where all the software comes from, Thelma learns that Jim set the BB up a year ago and has gradually established a network of people who share any software they obtain. She asks Jim if he thinks the distribution of copyrighted software is unethical.
>
> Jim smiles and says, "No problem." He adds, "Some of the people right here at Oglethorpe Consulting download business stuff from the BB that they need on the job. It saves the time it takes to fill out the requisitions to get the firm to buy it. Hey, the firm monitors all our e-mail; they must know what's going on."
>
> When Thelma frowns, Jim says, "Hey, don't use it if you don't want to, but keep quiet about it, OK?"

> - Is Jim being unethical? Why? Why not?
> - Is anyone being harmed? Who?
> - Are the people who download software from the BB being unethical? Why? Why not?
> - What is the company's stake in what is going on?
> - What should Thelma do?

Each small group will compose a memo to the instructor that summarizes the group's discussion and gives its conclusions (see Chapter 13, Correspondence, and Letter and Memorandum Format in Appendix B).

3. You are the head of Bangor Testing, a medium-sized consulting firm. Dana Anderson is your director of research. One of his projects, contracted for by the Maine Department of Transportation (MDOT) has just finished. The report has been printed and is ready for transmittal to the MDOT. At that moment, Dana learns that one of the technicians assigned to the project has not followed the proper procedure in one of five tests that were part of the contracted research; therefore, the results of that particular test are worthless. Dana and his test crew are sure that the results of the other tests conducted support the report's conclusions, and that the report is valid without the invalidated test. You agree with that conclusion.

   To redo the test and print a corrected report would both prevent the MDOT's from moving forward promptly with an important project and hurt the reputation of Bangor Testing. Dana comes to you with the problem. What will you advise him to do, and why? Write him an e-mail message advising him on a proper course of action and giving the rationale for your advice.[6]

4. The instructor will assign a case that may involve unethical conduct to five students and ask them to role-play the members of a board of review looking at the case. The board must discuss the case and decide whether the conduct involved is unethical.

   For advice on role-playing, see "Role Playing in an Engineering Ethics Class" on the Online Ethics Center for Engineering and Science <http://onlineethics.org/edu/loui2.html>.

5. Whether professional organizations should have codes of ethics is a matter of controversy. Some believe the codes provide useful standards by which to judge professional conduct. Others believe that professional ethics is no different from the ethics of any moral person and, therefore, such codes are pointless or, worse, misleading and harmful.

   In groups of four or five, discuss this matter. For guidance in the discussion, the group should go to the Center for Study of Ethics in the Professions: Codes of Ethics Online Project <http://csep.iit.edu/codes/index.html>. See particularly the introduction to the project.

   Following the discussion, each small group should prepare a position paper that reflects the consensus of the group about the value of professional codes of conduct. These position papers can become the basis for a class discussion on the subject.

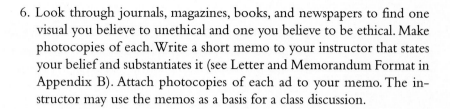

6. Look through journals, magazines, books, and newspapers to find one visual you believe to unethical and one you believe to be ethical. Make photocopies of each. Write a short memo to your instructor that states your belief and substantiates it (see Letter and Memorandum Format in Appendix B). Attach photocopies of each ad to your memo. The instructor may use the memos as a basis for a class discussion.

SCENARIO

Paul Miller looks at his watch. He needs to leave for the airport to catch a plane. Paul has been in Honduras for three days, trying to close a deal for the purchase of a small local textile plant. He made the trip after initial fax contact and some third-party mediation to establish contact with Miguel Mujarez, who wants to sell the plant. Paul was told by his friend Raul Peña that a solid relationship with the Mujarez family is essential because so many employees in the company have worked for the plant for decades. The plant, which has been in the Mujarez family since the early 1950s, is very much a family operation.

Paul had scheduled four days for the trip. He spent half a day with the plant manager, two days and two evenings with Miguel Mujarez, one day with a cousin, Juan Mujarez, and one day with the plant employees. Paul is anxious to get a positive response from Miguel, sign the contract, and return to Atlanta.

At dinner, on his last night in Honduras, Paul asked Miguel point-blank when they could complete the deal. Miguel acted as if he hadn't heard the question and continued to discuss one of his sons' feats in soccer. Then he asked Paul about universities in Atlanta, since he hoped to interest his oldest son in attending a school there. He spoke at length about the fine workers at the plant and asked numerous questions about Paul's family and other matters that Paul felt were not relevant. The discussion seemed to be going in circles.

On the final day of Paul's visit, Miguel was supposed to meet him at the office at 10:00. It's now after 12:30, and Miguel is not there. Paul has asked the secretary when Miguel will arrive. She'd said "Soon" several times but finally acknowledged that Miguel probably won't arrive until the late afternoon because his parents have arrived in town. Paul tries to control his frustration: if the secretary knew at 9:30 that Miguel would not be coming to the office, why hadn't she told him? Why wait until only a short time remains before he must leave for the airport?

Juan Mujarez arrives at that moment, expresses great happiness at seeing Paul, and says he hopes all the parties can discuss the sale in a few weeks. Paul is amazed and tells Juan that he came to Honduras to complete the deal. Juan expresses regret and begins discussing an appropriate time for Paul's next visit.

On the way to the airport, Paul recalls the experience of a friends who had not completed a business transaction with a Japanese firm that had just moved to Ohio until the company had been in Ohio for nearly a year. Paul decides that he cannot spend any more time on this matter. Miguel obviously does not want to sell the company soon, and Paul cannot determine a price that will persuade Miguel to sell. He has wasted nearly a week in trying to close the sale. He admits, wearily, that he just doesn't know how to do business with Central Americans.

chapter 7

Writing for International Readers

▶ Establishing a Perspective on International
   Communication

▶ Understanding Readers from Various Cultures
   Individualism versus Collectivism: Valuing Either
      Individuals or Groups
   Separation of Business and Private Relationships
   Power Distance between Social Ranks
   Universal or Relative View of Truth
   Whether the Entire Message Is Contained in the Text
   Whether Uncertainty Is to Be Avoided or Accepted
   The Power and Value of Time
   Masculine versus Feminine

▶ Considering Culture in the Planning Process

▶ Example International Documents for Examination

▶ Writing Business Communications to Readers in
   Other Cultures

▶ Culture and Graphics

▶ A Final Word

▶ Guides to Doing Business in Cultures around the World

When you as an employee in a business organization think about your audience while planning a report, letter, proposal, or e-mail, you may realize that some or all of your readers do not have English as their first language. Because of the power of technology to link cities and countries around the world, we now live in a global village. Business and technical organizations are becoming increasingly international. Many have offices in countries around the globe, as diminishing trade barriers enable U.S. organizations to do business throughout the world. Because of the globalization of business, effective written communications are as important in dealing with people in other countries as they are in dealing with U.S. residents. However, communication is culture specific: You cannot write to people in other countries the way you write to people in the United States. How you communicate is determined by the culture of the readers with whom you wish to communicate. In this book, we primarily emphasize strategies for developing business and technical documents for U.S. readers. However, we also want to introduce you to a procedure for planning documents that will be effective with readers in other cultures. In today's global market, you must be able to communicate with people everywhere.

A number of books have been written about protocols for doing business in other countries. These books explain business etiquette that must be followed when individuals wish to do business in another country. At the end of this chapter, we will list several of the growing number of books that you will find useful as well as interesting as you attempt to understand how culture determines the proper ways to meet and do business with individuals in other countries: greeting individuals according to the traditions of other countries, the appropriateness of shaking hands, the design and presentation of your business card, proper format for business letters and reports, proper deportment during dinner parties, gift giving, and the significance of holidays and colors are only a few matters that you need to learn about before you make contact with individuals in another country.

The study of international communication is a separate area of study, but here we provide guidelines for written business communications that will enable you to make the transition between the U.S. culture and other cultures. Some of the example documents we provide here (and in Chapter 13, Correspondence), will help you see how culture influences the preparation of documents for readers of different traditions.

▶ ESTABLISHING A PERSPECTIVE ON INTERNATIONAL COMMUNICATION

Designing effective written business communications for readers in other countries requires that you approach the development of international communication documents from four perspectives:

The Fatal Communication Error: Assuming that the United States is the greatest country in the world. Thus, you can do and say whatever you want: business people in other cultures will automatically follow your lead because the U.S. way is obviously the best way.

No perspective could be more detrimental to your success with people from other cultures. Outside the United States, you must learn to operate by another set of rules.

1. Cultures vary, but no one culture is inherently superior to any other.
2. Communicating successfully with people from other cultures requires that you play by their "ground rules." When your audience is an individual or an organization in another country, you need to carefully analyze this audience to understand its perspective.
3. The U.S. culture differs dramatically from most cultures in the world.
4. Everyone thinks his or her culture is "the best." You may not like many of the characteristics of the cultures of people with whom you need to communicate, but you must respect the differences between cultures and the perspectives of readers from outside your own tradition.

▶ UNDERSTANDING READERS FROM VARIOUS CULTURES

Anthropologists tell us that cultures differ in a number of specific ways. As a result, readers in different cultures have different expectations. Cultural anthropologists such as Geert Hofstede,[1] Fons Trompenaars,[2] Edward Hall,[3] and Lisa Hoecklin[4] have isolated a number of cultural characteristics—differences in values—that enable us to understand differences among cultures based on our understanding of how values differ among cultures. We will discuss nine major values that shape differences among cultures. These points of difference are drawn from the research of these cultural anthropologists. For our purposes, these values are important because they can affect written communication. We will show you example documents that illustrate how values affect communications. To be an effective global communicator, you must first understand the U.S. culture and know how characteristics of our culture shape written documents prepared for distribution in the United States. Understanding specific cultural differences that affect communication will give you a good beginning for understanding how to communicate with business people the world over.

In Table 7-1, you will see how a number of major countries rate on four of the value dimensions measured by Geert Hofstede, who is perhaps the leading expert on intercultural differences. The higher the score, the more a particular value is stressed in the culture.

▲ TABLE 7-1	Cultural Dimension Scores of Representative Countries			
Country	Individualism	Power Distance	Uncertainty Avoiding	Masculinity
United States	91	40	46	62
Australia	90	36	51	61
Great Britain	89	35	35	66
Canada	80	39	48	52
Italy	76	50	75	70
Belgium	75	65	94	54
Denmark	74	18	23	16
Sweden	71	31	29	5
France	71	68	86	43
Ireland	70	28	35	68
Norway	69	31	50	8
Switzerland	68	34	58	70
Germany	67	35	65	66
South Africa	65	49	49	63
Finland	63	33	59	26
Austria	55	11	70	79
Israel	54	13	81	47
Spain	51	57	86	42
India	48	77	40	56
Japan	46	54	92	95
Argentina	46	49	86	56
Iran	41	58	59	43
Jamaica	39	45	13	68
Brazil	38	69	76	49
Arab countries	38	80	68	53
Turkey	37	66	85	45
Greece	35	60	112	57
Philippines	32	94	44	64
Mexico	30	81	82	69
East Africa	27	64	52	41
Portugal	27	63	104	31
Malaysia	26	104	36	50
Hong Kong	25	68	29	57
Chile	23	63	86	28
West Africa	20	77	54	46
Singapore	20	74	8	48
Salvador	19	66	94	40
South Korea	18	60	85	39
Taiwan	17	58	69	45
Peru	16	64	87	42
Pakistan	14	55	70	50
Indonesia	14	78	48	46
Venezuela	12	81	76	73
Panama	11	95	86	44
Guatemala	6	95	101	37

Source: Geert Hofstede, *Cultures and Organizations: Software of the Mind* (New York: McGraw-Hill, 1991).

Individualism Versus Collectivism: Valuing Either Individuals Or Groups

In the United States, individualism is a predominant cultural characteristic. As Lisa Hoecklin states:

> Individualism is a concern for yourself as an individual as opposed to concern for the priorities and rules of the group to which you belong. The majority of the people in the world live in societies where the interests of the group take precedence over the interests of the individual. In these societies, the group to which you belong is the major source of your identity and the unit to which you owe lifelong loyalty. For only a minority of the world's population do individual interests prevail over group interests.[5]

Individualism is the driving force behind all other U.S. cultural characteristics. As Table 7-1 shows, the United States tends to be the most individualist country in the world. Reverence for individualism expresses itself in a number of major ways, which can be generalized as follows: In the United States, children learn to think in terms of "I." Individual achievements are often valued over team achievement, and even in team efforts, specific team members are usually singled out for outstanding contributions. Common sayings like "every man for himself," "the winner takes all," "be independent," "look out for yourself" illustrate the pronounced individualism in the United States. Emphasis is placed on the individual's responsibility for his or her own destiny. Another common theme you have probably heard: If you fail, then you failed because you didn't work or try hard enough. Only within the past two decades have students and employees learned to work as teams. U.S. business people tend to separate their business lives from their personal lives. In the U.S. business culture, how one feels about an individual should not interfere with sound business decisions involving that person. Americans tend to be direct and to the point. They are hard driving, pragmatic, and competitive in work and often in recreation. It is often said that Americans live to work. Because of the Puritan influence that has long dominated U.S. culture, a strong work ethic is highly valued. Thus, work—success through work—often takes precedence over family and friendships. Because of the importance of success, the individual's self-worth is often bound up with his or her career achievements.

In group-valuing (collectivist) cultures, individuals are a part of tight social networks in which members identify closely with their families and business organization. They are motivated by the group's needs and achievements. The individual's success is valued as it reflects the success of the group. In collectivist societies, the success of the team is more important than the success of the individual. Decisions are made by groups. Employees in collectivist societies act according to the interest of the group, which may not always mesh with the individual's desires. Self-effacement along with deference to the interest of the group is the standard. Earnings may be shared with relatives. Promotions are based on seniority within the groups. Often relatives of employees are hired, as relationships among those in the group are seen as more important than benefiting from the talents of someone from outside the group.

People's business lives and their personal lives are merged. People are polite, formal, and indirect, and concerns about the welfare of the group are emphasized over the success and needs of any one person. Collectivist cultures allow individuals to be expressive within the group, even though formality and deference are valued within the group and to individuals outside the group. Many collectivist societies value family welfare over business issues. That western cultures are more individualist than Latin American, Pacific Rim, and Third World countries is illustrated by the patterns discernible in the ratings of Table 7-1.

Implications for Communication Written communications are valued in the United States because they are often used to document individual actions. Because the U.S. culture is heterogeneous, written documents are very important to ensure precise understanding and compliance. In contrast, group-valuing organizations tend to prize oral communication over written communication. When you are writing to individuals within a group-valuing culture, you will want to focus on how the issues you are discussing reflect on the organization and the actions of the group. You will want to de-emphasize yourself: Avoid excessive use of "I" in discussing business and focus on establishing rapport with the organization, rather than specific individuals. Emphasize your relationships with the group before launching into discussion of the business you wish to transact.

Documents prepared in collectivist cultures may not be as explicit or as detailed as they are in individualist cultures, like the United States. Because collectivist cultures value "group think," individuals in groups share values and ideas: They do not have to illustrate every idea and document every fact by explicit verbal and numerical communication. In collectivist societies, action is decided and agreed on by the group, and therefore the fact-finding process occurs in a relative rule-free environments. However, the more heterogeneous the group, the more explicit documents will need to be.

Separation of Business and Private Relationships

How a culture treats and values relationships is critical in understanding that culture and in determining how best to communicate with people in that culture. The treatment of relationships is directly connected with a society's emphasis on groups or individuals, as collectivist (group-valuing) cultures are generally more relationship oriented than individualist cultures. For example, in the United States personal relationships are usually kept separate from business relationships. Business decisions are based on business information only. Keeping one's private life separate from one's business life is expected, and attempts to establish or preserve this boundary are respected. When doing business, individuals are expected to present an opaque, objective deportment.

In cultures that value individualism, people have more open public space, but private space is more closely guarded. The U.S. approach to business is direct, open, rapid, and extroverted. Many people outside the country, perceive the U.S. tendency always to be to the point as harsh and abrasive. Americans, who separate work and private lives, tend to view business relationships differently from personal relationships. In business dealings, the focus is on business objectives. Relationships are viewed only as a necessary, brief prelude to initiating and completing a business transaction.

In collectivist cultures, like those in Mexico and in the Pacific Rim nations, people do not separate public and private lives. One is influenced by the other without any shame or excuse. To representatives of cultures that separate business from personal affairs, however, collectivist-oriented business persons appear indirect, non committal, and evasive. In a collectivist culture, promotions are often made on the basis of friendship rather than competence. What is right depends on the relationships involved. Many organizations are composed of family members. Business is conducted in accordance with family needs. A culture that does not distinguish business from private relationships bases its notion of efficiency not on time to completion but on how well one understands others. In such a culture, you can expect to spend extensive time building relationships with individuals in the company with which you want to do business.

Implications for Communication Unlike U.S. communications which focus on business, communications in relationship-oriented cultures de-emphasize business and emphasize the relationships among the individuals involved in a given business transaction. Cultures that do not separate business and private relationships will expect communications that are formal, reserved but positive, and indirect in dealing with business issues. Emphasizing the relationship between you and your business organization and your reader will be paramount. An extremely efficient business presentation may be perceived as inappropriately direct, and your ideas may be rejected accordingly.

Power Distance between Social Ranks

Inequalities exist in any society, and some people have more power, respect, status, and wealth than others. Hofstede defines power distance as the degree of closeness, or interdependence, that exists among members of organizational hierarchies. Do superiors consult subordinates about decisions? Do employees feel comfortable in disagreeing or questioning superiors' decisions? Is interdependence on authority evident in supervisor–subordinate relationships, and if so, to what extent? In short, power distance is measured in terms of the prevalence of ranks or levels of authority. Column 2 of Table 7-1 shows how various cultures were rated on power distance.

In high-power-distance cultures, employees manage their work according to their superior's specifications, and authoritarian attitudes are readily accepted. Inequalities among people are both expected and desired. Hierarchies in organizations are pronounced; the powerful have privileges that the less powerful do not have, and subordinates expect to take orders. In high-power-distance cultures, bosses are expected to make unilateral decisions. Employees do what they are told without asking questions. Superiors are authoritarian figures. Disagreeing with "the boss" is unacceptable. High-power-distance cultures are characterized by steep organizational pyramids and close supervision of employees. In high-power-distance cultures, age is a positive factor and a major qualification for leadership roles. In high-power-distance cultures, formality and politeness in communications are considered extremely important. One is never openly aggressive.

In low-power-distance cultures, the individual is freer to follow his or her own preferences and criticize management. Inequalities among people are minimized, subordinates are consulted, and decentralization in responsibility is popular. Employees have upward mobility, and teamwork is valued because interdependence exists between the less and the more powerful.

U.S. business organizations vary in terms of the power structures. The number of levels in an organization—and the power at each level—vary significantly with the size and type of organization. This range of power explains why you were told in Chapter 4 to determine the relationships between you and your reader, to choose your content and tone in terms of that relationship. The power distance within the organization tells you how open, direct, or formal you can be in stating your ideas. The United States, however, is generally a mid-level power-distance country. Because of the emphasis on the responsibility of the individual and the individual's responsibility for his or her destiny, Americans like to be involved in decision making. Central decision making is accepted, but those in the organization below the leaders expect to be heard. Great differences in rank are expected, but those who have rank ideally have earned it through extreme individual effort, success in achieving business goals, and hard work. While hierarchies in organizations are dominant, U.S. organizations are moving toward "flatter" organizations and participatory management.

In many of today's U.S. organizations, strong individuals must become "team players" who can lead the group. Youth is often more revered than age. Low-power-distance business cultures and business organizations have flatter organizations, more team decision making, fewer autonomous "bosses," and more decisions coming from group (committee) recommendations. The variations in power distance in the U.S. culture explains why the country has a score of 40 in Table 7-1. Understanding the extent of teamwork in a particular U.S. company, as well as an international company, can be critical to your success in dealing and working with that company.

Implications for Communication In high-power-distance cultures, using correct forms of address can be extremely important: knowing specifically who should receive a report or letter, the title or rank of that person, the names of all individuals who should appear on the distribution list. Establishing the correct tone in addressing the intended reader(s) is thus important in establishing the correct "distance" between writer and reader. Therefore, tone in documents prepared for readers in high-power-distance cultures may need to be more formal if the writer is preparing a document for someone who holds a relatively superior position. In contrast, in preparing documents for readers in low-power-distance cultures, strict recognition of business hierarchies and the use of formal address gain less favor. The style of the message can be more casual.

Universal or Relative View of Truth

Cultures also differ in how they perceive truth. A universal view of truth means that what is true can be discovered, defined, and applied in all situations. In other cultures, truth is relative. It changes depending on the needs of the situation or the group affected by the decision. In many collectivist cultures, relationships and the needs of people in the organization (many who may be relatives or family members) are more important than the objective truth of a situation. The United States exemplifies what Trompenaars calls a universalist culture: "Truth" exists; clear differences exist in "right" and "wrong," and people should be guided by universal rules of behavior that are considered to apply to everyone. "Rules" should be laid down in strictly worded agreements and contracts. Once defined, the "rules" govern business and behavior. This concept of truth evolves from the Puritan roots of the United States: Truth exists; it should transcend and guide the actions of individuals, and at times it may take precedence over the immediate needs of people.

"Particularist" cultures, in contrast to "universalist" cultures, believe that truth is relative. What is "true" and what should be done depend on a particular situation. Human relationships are more important than rules, and written contracts are not held to be binding, if situations arise that make certain provisions undesirable. If a problem involving people arises, then a written contract is less important than the human issues that affect the contract. In particularist cultures, people are more important than contracts.

Implications for Communication In a universalist culture, writers are advised to be as specific and concrete as possible. Clarity and precision in format, language, and meaning are valuable. In a culture in which truth is relative, comments may be less direct and more dependent on the situation. The message may appear vague. Oral communications may be more significant than written communications. Rules that apply in one business situation may cease to apply when a different situation arises. In collectivist cultures, be sure to discuss the impact of the situation on the group.

Whether the Entire Message Is Contained in the Text

In the United States, documents are expected to "contain" the complete meaning. The "truth" of the situation must be contained in the text because texts document facts and human actions. These are the hallmart of a text-oriented culture. Written agreements and statements are very important. "Talk is cheap." What you say you will do means little if you do not put your promises in writing. Documents contain all details needed. Conditions not included in the written document are not recognized as applicable, and obligations not spelled out in the text are not legally binding.

In other cultures, the "meaning" of a business situation or a document is much more than the document. Meaning comes from the people and the human issues involved in a given decision. The meaning of a document—such as a contract—depends on the situation. The document may be ignored, even if it is a contract. In such cultures, schedules are flexible; being late to dinner, meetings, or other engagements is expected and acceptable. Establishing relationships is seen as more important than doing business. Business lives and work lives are intertwined. Thus, business days and documents are less structured, less efficient, less direct than U.S. documents.

Implications for Communication The text of U.S. documents is expected to contain all facts necessary to arrive at a solid business decision. Contracts are considered binding. In non textual cultures, the language is suggestive, oblique, and theoretical; documents themselves are often wordy, tending to focus on organizational situations rather than pristine factual details. What a document ultimately "means" may be a function of the circumstances under which it was prepared. Business obligations may not be clearly or completely stated.

Whether Uncertainty Is to Be Avoided or Accepted

Another important cultural difference focuses on how a culture tolerates uncertainty. (How cultures vary on this value is presented in column 3 of Table 7-1.) Members of cultures that avoid uncertainty appear to be anxiety-prone people who perceive the uncertainties inherent in life as threats that must be fought. In these cultures, employees fear failure, take fewer risks, resist change, and place a premium on job security, career patterning, and company benefits. The manager is expected to issue clear instructions, and subordinates' initiatives are tightly controlled. Employees in cultures that dislike uncertainty accept formal procedures, wide power distances within hierarchies, and highly structured organizations. Societies that dislike uncertainty exhibit high stress and anxiety levels, need structured environments, believe that time is money, and believe in the value of hard work.

In contrast, people raised in cultures that accept uncertainty are more likely to take each day as it comes. Conflict and competitiveness can be used constructively, and dissent will be tolerated. Needs for written rules and regulations are relatively few, and rules that turn out to be unrealistic or unenforceable can be easily changed. Time is seen as a framework for orientation; rules are flexible; precision and punctuality are not paramount. Emotions are not shown, and rules that are highly restrictive are avoided. The United States scores about midway on the continuum of avoiding/accepting uncertainty.

Implications for Communication In *cultures* that accept uncertainty, written documents may be less problematic than they are in cultures that seek to avoid uncertainty, where documents are valued for documentation and governance purposes. In *companies* that dislike uncertainty, precisely written documents, forms, tables, graphs, procedures, policies, and style sheets are valued because they create uniformity and clarity. While tolerance for uncertainty varies in the United States, fear of litigation is driving more companies toward insistence on precision in documents.

The Power and Value of Time

Another cultural value that affects communication is the value a culture places on time. The United States is one of the most time-conscious cultures in the world. People in this country value not only productivity, but also efficiency in process and product. Effective use of time—time management: doing more and more work in less and less time—is a cherished U.S. ideal. While many collectivist cultures value relationships before work, here we tend to value work before relationships. Many cultures consider relationships with friends and family, the need to enjoy each day, and the time spent in building and maintaining relationships as more important than efficient execution of work. Cultures that value time usually value productivity. Cultures that value relationships place people before business. In these cultures, efficient use of time is less valuable than the slower paced focus on relationship building and weaving business with relationships.

Implications for Communication When you address members of cultures that value relationships rather than productivity, emphasize relationships with the persons with whom you are doing business. Make business secondary to the relationship. In contrast, in preparing documents for U.S. readers, emphasize the business goal: Be precise, direct, and complete. Make goals, expectations, and commitments known.

Masculine versus Feminine

Many cultures give males superior positions. Men, rather than women, serve in positions of authority. Occupations tend to be segregated by gender, and inequality of the sexes is generally accepted. Expectations to pursue and succeed in careers apply more to men than to women, who are primarily homemakers. Masculine cultures exemplify high job stress, achievement, aggressiveness, competitiveness, and financial success. Feminine cultures, in contrast, feature less occupational segregation by gender. Women occupy well-paid jobs, and the work environment shows less stress, more awareness of individuals' personal needs, and more concern for the importance of family and social issues. Feminine cultures value nurturing relationships, consensus, compromise, and negotiation. Column 4 of Table 7-1 shows how cultures rate on this dimension. Clearly, the United States tends to be a masculine culture.

Implications for Communication American women need to avoid assuming a domnieering stance when working with men from cultures outside of the United States where males assume positions of authority. When American women write to men in these masculine cultures, the tone should be formal and polite. Avoiding immediate, direct discussion of business issues is imperative. Establishing rapport with the individual within the organization is critical. In general, communications for feminine cultures should focus on relationships, while communications for non-U.S. masculine cultures should be assertive and decisive, with an emphasis on the business transaction.

▶ CONSIDERING CULTURE IN THE PLANNING PROCESS

The most important factors influencing how you plan and then draft your document are your audience and your purpose. Thus it is essential to understand to whom you are writing and why you are writing. As you consider these factors in planning communications that include international readers, you will want to answer the following questions. Because many of these questions pertain to U.S. documents, you can see how effective use of international communications requires that you broaden your perspective as you plan a document:

- To whom is this message directed?
- What do you know about the reader(s)? Age? Interests? Education? Job responsibilities? Title?
- What is their attitude toward you, and how do they perceive the topic?
- What are their particular characteristics, as gleaned from messages they have written or encounters you have had with them?
- If the document is being directed to a reader in a non-U.S. culture, what are its characteristics?

> Is it oriented toward the individual or toward the group?
>
> Do people separate their business and private relationships?
>
> Does this culture value success of individuals or success of groups?
>
> Do people see truth as universal or as relative to particular circumstances?
>
> Is the entire message–and what it means—usually contained in the text?
>
> Do the people value time and efficiency?

- How well are the members of your target audience able to read English?
- What is the situation that has led to your need to write this document?
- What purpose do you hope to achieve? What do you want to happen as a result of this document?
- Based on the broad value characteristics of the culture, what choices do you need to make about

> Structure (deductive or inductive)
>
> Organization of ideas
>
> Degree of specificity about business purpose
>
> Type of information disclosed about you and your organization
>
> Quantity of detail presented about you and your organization
>
> Style
>> Sentence length
>> Word choice
>> Address protocols
>> Tone
>> Formatting techniques
>> Graphics

In short, considering culture is simply another dimension of considering your audience and the context in which your message will be read. As the guidelines in Table 7-2, suggest, your answer to these questions will affect how you write to any audience.

▲ TABLE 7-2	Guide for Designing International Written Business Communications
Non-Western business characteristics	**Western business characteristics**
Prefers face-to-face communication *Use a style in written documents that is conversational reflecting oral, narrative discourse; nonlinear discourse*	Insists on written communication as documentation *Structure documents by standard business protocol; use paragraphs; linear discourse*
Values intuitive, aesthetic written communication *Deemphasize structured response and use of headings/page design*	Values analytical, logical, denotative written communication *Emphasize structured, logical messages; use headings/page design*
Values indirect communication *Deemphasize "main point" or place it at the end of the message* *State message obliquely*	Values direct communication *Highlight main point; begin with most important ideas first* *State point clearly and objectively*
Values slower pace of communication *Conciseness not valued* *Include comments about nonbusiness issues* *Use opulent style*	Values rapid, efficient pace of communication *Conciseness valued* *Minimize nonbusiness remarks* *Use clear, brief, simple style*
Values formal communications *Emphasize use of formal titles, forum, and audiences for messages*	Values informal communications *Deemphasize titles, consistent decorum, and occasion for communication*
Focuses more on the situation *Focus on the issues as these are bound up with the welfare of the organization*	Focuses more on the ideas involved in the situation *Focus more on issues as business decisions only*
People work near one another or share space and responsibilities *Understand that messages may be shared with many in the group*	Individuals are assigned separate spaces/specific duties *Direct messages toward specific individuals having specific tasks*
Content reflects interdependencies crucial to intra-/inter-organizational communication Decision making via consensus *Focus message on all groups that are affected by the message*	Interdependence, which is mistrusted in communications, is deemphasized Decision making via designated leaders *Focus on hierarchies in the organization and those receiving copies; focus on those responsible for acting on the message*
Content and presentation are conciliatory Harmony should be maintained and confrontation avoided. *Control tone to allow everyone to save face in unpleasant situations; avoid blame on individuals or groups*	Content and presentation are argumentative or at least very direct Honesty in communication is desirable. *State the issues squarely but tactfully* *Use design to highlight facts and desired outcomes*
Organizational relationships are highest priority. Relationships more important than rules. *Emphasize company background and rationale for business actions*	Organizational tasks/goals are highest priority; rules and goals before relationships. *Emphasize recommendations, procedures, policies in written form*

▲ TABLE 7-2	Guide for Designing International Written Business Communications *(cont'd)*
Non-Western business characteristics	**Western business characteristics**
Long-term organizational agendas *Discuss business in terms of larger human and company concerns*	Short-term organizational agendas *Emphasize action required and time tables for achieving goals*
Clear distinctions between surface communication and business objective *Messages should be oblique; building relationships carefully and futuristically with business in the background* *Elegance more important than brevity*	Less distinction between business objective and surface communication *Messages should aim to capture and summarize the desired goal of the communique; ambiguity in goals not desirable* *Conciseness more important than elegance*
Agreements easily modified and ignored	Agreements legally binding
Perceived truth may be modified by changing realities; it is not confined to written discourse Documentation in relationships	Perceived truth is defined by written agreements; facts have one interpretation Documentation in written documents
Truth is a product of several perspectives: written, spoken, felt; messages often evade issues; are closed and introverted. *Messages may be formal, but they are revocable*	Truth is one textualized statement having one meaning contained in the text *Messages are to the point; often abrasive* *Messages are binding; they contain truth, which can be defined and agreed upon by all parties.*
Approach is theoretical and indirect; specific implementation is omitted *Goal required may be hard to explain; linear prose, more undifferentiated text*	Approach is practical; action-oriented; problem-solving approach is used *Goal should be visually clear; bulleted lists, numbered steps*
Time/deadlines are relative and flexible *Do not emphasize time in the message*	Deadlines/commitments are firm *Always include specific time requirements*
High-context communication; work and life intertwined; emphasis on the group responsibility shared by groups *Use message to link aspects of the culture; personal/ public/corporate lives shared* *Tone of document: subjective and oblique.*	Low-context communications; work and life separate, emphasis on individuals, responsibility directed toward specific individual(s) *Keep message strictly business; personal life is separate from business life* *Tone of document: objective, direct, and precise*

Note: Written communication strategies are set in italics

▶ EXAMPLE INTERNATIONAL DOCUMENTS FOR EXAMINATION

To see how cultural characteristics can effect document design, consider the following example documents, which were written by individuals in the United States, Mexico, and Pakistan.

Figure 7-1 is a typical U.S. business letter. Note that it is direct, concise, and focused on the business issues at hand. The main point of the letter appears in the opening paragraph. The closing paragraph indicates the action required and the time constraints. The middle paragraphs are denotative, and the content is developed in a logical sequence with no digressions. The style

Water Authority
District 4

CITY OF GLENDALE
4000 First Street, Room 202
Glendale, TX 77863

March 30, 2001

Mr. Harold Jonas
9515 Richmond Way
Houston, TX 77381

Dear Mr. Jonas:

The City of Glendale Water Authority regrets the continuing problems with insufficient water supply to River Forest Business Park. Irregular pumping has occurred because of faulty release mechanisms, which have not been functioning when water storage sinks below a specified point. We have ordered a new release regulation system, which suppliers have assured us will arrive by April 20. As soon as the systems arrives, installation will begin. The system should be operating within five-to-seven working days.

Water regulation is a complex process because of the need to conserve water while guaranteeing that residents of every area served by every pump station are served without interruption of service. For the past three months, to avoid overfill of storage tanks, we have assigned technicians the responsibility of visually monitoring the refill boundary indicators. Once they see that storage capacity is approaching the refill zone, they manually activate the pumping stations. This method has worked well during the recent rainy months, when water requirements are low. Manual operation has allowed us to examine every aspect of the pump system to determine exactly where the problem occurs when the equipment fails to activate in time to avoid water shortages to your neighborhood. During the recent drought, however, manual release has not been efficient, as technicians are often not able to react quickly enough.

Although our analysis of the water system has been lengthy, we have been able to locate the problem and order new equipment. By locating and replacing only the faulty problem, we will save Glendale over $1 million dollars. Unfortunately, the testing process has been lengthy and at times inconvenient for residents of subdivisions dependent on Station 3. However, the problem should be eliminated no later than May 1. We will appreciate your patience as we attempt to implement a long-term solution while conserving both tax money and water.

Sincerely,

M H Marks

M. H. Marks
Director

FIGURE 7-1 • U.S. Business Letter

is informal but efficient. The point is straightforwardly presented: that is, the "medium is the message." Because of a cultural preoccupation with efficient use of time, commitment to achievement, and aggressive business practices, most U.S. business letters are direct and concise. Business is separate from personal issues, even if the writer knows the reader in a nonbusiness context.

U.S. business letters usually follow this development scheme Illustrated in Figure 7-2.

Figure 7-3: is a Pakistani business letter. Note that the style is formal and courteous. The point is politely stated. As Table 7-1 indicates, Pakistan is a collectivist country with a high score in uncertainty avoidance. Thus, a letter that seeks to collect a debt uses an extremely tactful approach. The main news occurs in the second paragraph. The writer attempts to build a solid case—asking the reader to examine the invoice amounts—before venturing the request. Note the courteous closing. Note the differences in letter format between this letter and Figure 7-1, which uses U.S. block style. The Pakistani business letter follows the development scheme of Figure 7-4.

Figure 7-5, a translation of a letter by a Mexican business consultant in Mexico City, introduces his services to a U.S. company that has recently opened an office in Mexico City. The consultant has been working through a friend at the U.S. consulate. In Mexico, as in many Latin American countries, you must establish relationships and credibility with friends of those with whom you wish to do business before directly contacting the individuals in the target company. Thus, the reader will know about the writer, and the writer quickly alludes to the mutual friend.

Because Mexico is a collectivist culture in which relationships are considered more valuable than time, there is a more relaxed approach to doing business. This characteristic of Mexico's culture expresses itself in the inexpe-

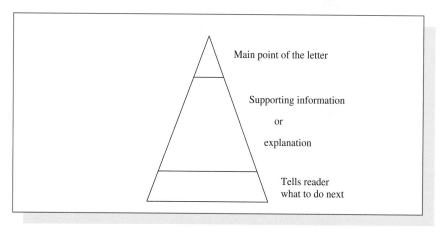

FIGURE 7-2 • Scheme of U.S. Business Letter

TELEGRAMS: RUNYON

CABLES   : Tomichi

PHONE: 8632137

Telex: 41212 RUNYON

Fax: 00 82 24 683-9215

Runyon Finnly & Co. Pakistan (PVT.) LTD
Merchants, Engineers & Contractors
IMPORT REGISTRATION NO. K0156
EXPORT REGISTRATION NO. W003971

OUR REF h/1299/TR-54

YOUR REF_____

G.P.O. BOX NO451

KARACHI 74200 (PAKISTAN)

Date Jan. 23, 2001

The Chief Executive

Contractors, Ltd.

Jamson Square Building,

Karachi

for the kind attention of

_____

Dear Sir,

RE: PENDING BILLS

We draw your kind attention to the long pending Bills which we know you will understand our need to discuss with you. Our business relationship has occurred for many years and for that we are grateful:

1) Bill No. DRM/65/2158 dt. 8. 8. 94		Rs..50,000.00
2) " " JM/JC/443 " 30. 11.95		Rs., 45,000.00
3) " " GM/PE/215/7 " 12.10.95		Rs. 2,950.00
		97,950.00

During our visit last month, your Mr. Vibras very kindly promised to settle the above Bills by the first week of Jan. The Bills are pending for more than a year and in addition we are in urgent need of funds. We, therefore, request you to please send us your Cheque in settlement of our above Bills soon after receipt of this letter.

Your co-operation is solicited,

faithfully yours,

for RUNYON FINNLY & CO, PAKISTAN (PVT) LTD.

Asad Paravichi

DIRECTOR

FIGURE 7-3 • Pakistani Business Letter

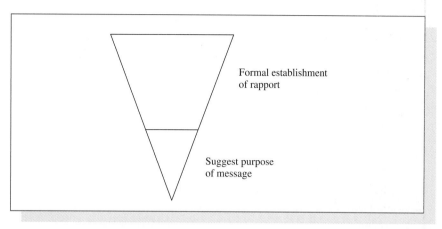

FIGURE 7-4 • Scheme of Pakistani Business Letter

diency of the sentences themselves. Directness, conciseness, and efficiency are not major issues because the process of doing business, of building relationships is what is important. The liquid quality of the language is, in an important sense, preserved by the masculine focus of the culture, which exudes a formal bravado. Note that no time frame is suggested; no plan of action stipulated. The style is ornate, effusive, aesthetic—certainly not concise or direct. The style is more complex; the sentences, less efficiently structured. The ideas presented seem more theoretical and less pragmatic. Many non Western business cultures that are collectivist will allude to the purpose about midway through the letter. However, the business issue is obliquely stated. Figure 7-6 shows the development scheme of this letter, which also differs from the U.S. letter (Figure 7-1) in format.

▶ WRITING BUSINESS COMMUNICATIONS TO READERS IN OTHER CULTURES

If you find that you will be communicating with people from other cultures, particularly in a business context, be sure that you do research on business etiquette for each country. These procedures include understanding the use of business cards, dressing appropriately, making proper introductions and greetings, knowing how business decisions are made and knowing what topics to discuss and to avoid in all conversations, business or social. An increasing number of books and videos, as well as information on the World Wide Web, are available to help you understand the perspectives of readers in other cultures.

Initially, however, what is important is that you understand that what is acceptable in written communications in the United States will likely be unacceptable in many other countries. Knowing this fact is an important first step

13 Agosta de 2001

Lic. Felix Ortiz Fraga
General Director
Pintural Chihuahua, S.K.A. de C.V.
44 Salgado, Monterrey, Nuevo Leon

Estimado Lic. Ortiz:

Because of the relationship that exists between us, our mutural desire to enable the effective pursuit of business in Mexico City, it is my pleasure to greet you and present for your consideration the special services in Consulting and Executive Training that is offered by Grupo Empresarial SIA, which has as its object to support your organization in the achievement of the objectives of competitiveness and leadership that are demanded by the economic and social environment in which we actually live. I am greatly indebted to Lic. Julio Montevezos, whose family has long been associated with my family here in Mexico City. It is indeed an honor to greet you upon your arrival in Mexico City.

Among those services offered by Empresarial SIA, you will encounter the following:

☐ Consulting for diagnosis and analysis of processes subsequent to the implantation of operative models oriented to produce knowledge of Mexican business practices integral to your organization.

☐ Training at an executive level in the development of general abilities, such as updating courses for administrative and technical personnel.

As a complement to what was previously mentioned, we offer specialized support for the analysis, definition and implementation of computer systems, along with the infrastructure necessary for your organization.

We would feel very honored to have the opportunity to discuss personally with you the solutions we would be able to propose to you, and by which we would be in contact with you or the person that you indicate to us, in order to agree upon a an interview in this respect.

Atentamente

Ing. Raul Orosco Jeminez

FIGURE 7-5 • Mexican Business Letter

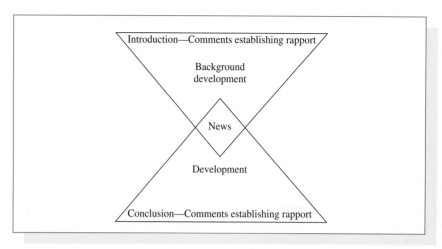

FIGURE 7-6 • Scheme of Mexican Business Letter

in learning how to communicate about technical and business issues with people in other countries.

Even though you may be able to use English to a reader in another culture—English is becoming the international technical language—you should attempt to assess aspects of that country's culture and values that may affect communication. For example, for collectivist countries, try to emphasize the group rather than individuals. Attempt to establish rapport with your readers rather than emphasizing the business objective. For countries that exemplify and expect differences in ranks (high power distance), be aware of the possible need for titles, respect for those in powerful positions within the organization, and the status of women in the country. Use Appendix B (Letter and Memorandum Format) to learn how to set up business letters.

You can see how these broad cultural characteristics are embedded in written communications by examining a letter written by a woman real estate agent in the United States to a Japanese reader who has just moved to Texas.

Situation 1 (Figure 7-7)

Katherine Ashcroft, a commercial leasing agent, contacts Keisuke Ashizawa, a Japanese engineer whose team is currently working on a research project in Texas. Mr. Ashizawa, who has discovered that he will need to remain in the United States longer than he had expected, has expressed to his American colleague Kevin Graham, an interest in leasing a condominium. He has also discussed with Kevin a desire to find a local book. With these requests in mind, Kevin has offered to introduce Mr. Ashizawa to Ms. Ashcroft. The businesswoman would like to work with Mr. Ashizawa (and hopefully other members of his team's research group). After receiving a call from Kevin, she writes the letter shown in Figure 7-7.

March 27, 2001

Mr. Keisuke Ashizawa
1402 Louisiana
Suite 651
Houston, TX 77002

Dear Mr. Ashizawa:

Mr. Kevin Graham, a close friend of our family, has informed me of your arrival in Houston to pursue work for Remco during the next 24 months. We are delighted that you have arrived in Houston during the early spring. Houston is famous for its azalea gardens and flowering fruit trees. Texas is also known for its state flower, the Bluebonnet, which blooms in profusion along the Texas highways. While Houston lacks cherry blossoms, we hope that you will find our azalea gardens an acceptable substitute.

To assist in making your stay in Houston pleasant as well as productive, arrangements have been made for representatives from several Houston banks to contact you. They will be sending you information about their services prior to arranging an appointment. You can then contact those banks that interest you. Or, if these are not acceptable, we would be happy to locate others. My husband, who is senior vice-president of Texas Commerce Bank, is eager to be of service in helping you select whatever financial services you require. We are honored to be able to help you.

Mr. Graham has invited me to meet you during the Offshore Technology Conference, which my husband will also attend. As Kevin has told you, as a residential leasing agent, I am interested in assuring that any visitors to our city receive appropriate accommodations in accordance with their needs. I will look forward to meeting you and hearing more about your work and answering any questions you may have about our culture. We will be pleased to work with Kevin to enable you to see other parts of Texas during the coming months, if you wish.

Sincerely,

Katherine Ashcroft

Katherine Ashcroft

FIGURE 7-7 • Request to a Japanese Engineer

Figure 7-7 is concise and polite rather than aggressive. The main issue is not discussed until the final paragraph, and this is not the ultimate goal of the writer, who wishes to become Mr. Ashizawa's real estate agent. In addition, the request in the letter is indirectly stated. The style is formal, even though the writer attempts to establish rapport with the reader before even mentioning the request. Because the writer is a woman and the reader, a man, the writer is careful to sound appropriately deferential, since the Japanese culture scores high on the masculine/feminine scale. No time-table is mentioned on any of the issues. Japan is a collectivist culture in which relationships must be established before business can be conducted. It also scores high on avoiding uncertainty. Building trust and de-emphasizing the business goal are critical.

▶ CULTURE AND GRAPHICS

Decisions about graphics as well as text need to be determined by the culture of your intended readers.[6] For example, what are the reading processes of your audience? Do they read left to right or from right to left? This information will help you know how to arrange graphics so that they will be viewed by the reader in the proper sequence.

1. If you are unsure about reading habits, consider using arrows with graphics to show the direction that your graphics flow, (see Figure 7-8). Or, use numbers on graphics to show the order in which something should be read.

2. Concepts of good and bad can also differ among cultures. In U.S. tables, what is considered acceptable and preferable is usually placed on the right, while in Asian cultures the left-hand side is one place of honor.

3. Avoid acronymns, abbreviations, jargon, slang, and colloquialisms. Use plain typefaces. Do not attempt to use humor, as what is humorous varies among cultures.

(a)

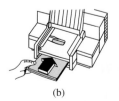

(b)

FIGURE 7-8 • Examples of Graphics Using Arrows

(a)   (b)   (c)   (d)   (e)

FIGURE 7-9 • Examples of Internationally Recognized Graphics: (a) airport; (b) fragile; (c) keep dry; (d) bar; and (e) hotel

4. Be sure to use graphics that are internationally recognized, (see Figure 7-9).

5. Avoid graphics that may be interpreted differently in other cultures—animals, religious symbols, national emblems, hand gestures, and colors. For examples, dogs are considered pets in much of the West. To many Asians, they are food. Cattle have an honored position in India, but in the United States their meat is eaten.

6. Remember that colors can be particularly problematic, so black and white graphics are usually the safest choice, (see Table 7–3).

7. Because of differences in gender roles among cultures and differences in how body language is interpreted, make graphics of people as gender-neutral as possible. Also avoid depicting hand gestures in graphics, as positions of fingers, hands, and arms have different meanings in different cultures.

8. If possible, try to determine how fluent your readers will be in English. For example, if your readers lack such fluency, use simple, concrete words and short sentences. Avoid abbreviations.

9. Watch how you use document design. Many cultures do not use bold-face headings or pay much attention to document design principles. Many Mexican documents, for example, will use few headings, and these are underlined. Many cultures do not use extensive tables and graphs. Format strategies for correspondence—salutations, dates, subject lines, closings, and titles—also differ among cultures. American word processing programs have helped unify document design through use of common templates among international corporations, but differences still exist and should be respected.

▶ A FINAL WORD

A number of reference books are available that provide writers extensive guidance on where to place dates, inside addresses, and reference lines in in-

▲ TABLE 7-3	**Color Associations in Different Cultures**				
Culture	Red	Yellow	Green	Blue	Purple
Bolivia		Yellow flowers—contempt			Funerals
Europe, and North America	Danger	Caution Cowardice	Safe Sour	Masculine Truth, authority	
Japan	Anger funerals	Grace Nobility Childish gaiety	Future Youth Energy	Villainy	
China	Joy Festivity	Honor Royalty		Funerals	
Arab countries		Happiness Prosperity	Fertility Strength	Virtue Faith Truth	

ternational documents. These books can also be helpful in explaining what titles to give individuals. These details are important, but none are as important as how you develop the content of the letter. As you saw in Chapter 5, the word order of English, its emphasis on concreteness and brevity can be construed as rude, insulting, and improperly aggressive by readers in other cultures. Particularly in Romance language cultures, sentences are more fluid, more complex, and the meaning more oblique. Understanding how to capture in English the tone expected by your international reader is the challenge. Remember that culture determines rhetoric. Germans prefer details and background information. The French like a formal and authoritative approach. U.S. readers like everything short and direct. The Japanese like instructions that are accurate but polite. Middle Eastern readers value grandiloquent, florid prose and impassioned style. In China, theory is stated, and readers are expected to determine details. However, the important point is to remember that just as we are steeped in our culture people from other countries are steeped in theirs. To communicate effectively with them, we must understand the concept and role of culture and some of the ways that our traditions diverge from other throughout the world. Ultimately, we must respect those differences.

▶ GUIDES TO DOING BUSINESS IN CULTURES AROUND THE WORLD

An increasing number of books and videotapes are available on differences between the U.S. culture and other cultures around the world. Understanding some of these differences, as they apply to doing business in other countries, will help you understand how to communicate, orally and in writing, with individuals in other countries. Videotapes that discuss the meaning of gestures and body language can be particularly helpful in illustrating such differences. The following books have been selected because they provide concise, useful information about different cultures and will help you understand how culture affects communication styles and methods.

Axtell, Roger E. *Do's and Taboos of Hosting International Visitors*. New York: Wiley, 1990.

———. *Do's and Taboos of Using English around the World*. New York: Wiley, 1995.

———. *Gestures: The Do's and Taboos of Body Language around the World*. New York: Wiley, 1998.

Axtell, Roger E., Tami Briggs, Margaret Corcoran, and Mary Beth Lamb, eds. *Do's and Taboos around the World for Women in Business*. New York: Wiley, 1997.

Bosrock, Mary Murray. *Put Your Best Foot Forward, Europe: A Fearless Guide to International Communication and Behavior*. St. Paul, MN: International Education Systems, 1995.

———. *Put Your Best Foot Forward, Mexico/Canada: A Fearless Guide to Communication and Behavior/NAFTA*. St. Paul, MN: International Education Systems, 1995.

———. *Put Your Best Foot Forward, Russia: A Fearless Guide to International Communication and Behavior*. St. Paul, MN: International Education Systems, 1995.

Cole, Gregory. *Passport Indonesia: Your Pocket Guide to Indonesian Business, Customs, and Etiquette*. San Rafael, CA: World Trade Press, 1997.

Doing Business Internationally: The Resource for Business and Social Etiquette. Princeton, NJ: Princeton Training Press, 1997.

Gannon, Martin J. *Understanding Global Cultures: Metaphorical Journeys through 23 Countries*. 2d ed. Thousand Oaks, CA: Sage, 2001.

Gao, Ge, and Shella Ting-Toomey. *Communicating Effectively with the Chinese*. Thousand Oaks, CA: Sage, 1998.

Goldman, Alan. *Doing Business with the Japanese: A Guide to Successful Communication, Management, and Diplomacy*. Albany: SUNY Press, 1994.

Hofstede, Geert H. *Cultures and Organizations; Software of the Mind*. 2d ed. New York: McGraw-Hill, 1997.

Hall, Edward T., and Mildred Reed Hall, *Understanding Cultural Differences: Germans, French, and Americans* Yarmouth, ME: Intercultural Press, 1990.

Hamlet, Janice D., ed. *Afrocentric Visions: Studies in Culture and Communication*. Thousand Oaks, CA: Sage, 1998.

Hoecklin, Lisa. *Managing Cultural Differences: Strategies for Competitive Advantage*. Wokingham, UK: Addison-Wesley, 1995.

Irvin, Harry. *Communicating with Asia: Understanding People and Customs*. St. Leonards, NSW, Australia: Allen & Unwin, 1996.

Joshi, Monaj. *Passport India: Your Pocket Guide to Indian Business, Customs, and Etiquette*. San Rafael, CA: World Trade Press, 1997.

Kim, Eun Young. *A Cross-Cultural Reference of Business Practices in a New Korea*. Westport, CT: Quorum Books, 1996.

Leppert, Paul. *Doing Business with Mexico*. Fremont, CA: Jain, 1996.

Li, Jenny. *Passport China: Your Pocket Guide to Chinese Business, Customs, and Etiquette*. San Rafael, CA: World Trade Press, 1996.

March, Robert M. *Working for a Japanese Company: Insight into the Multicultural Workplace*. Tokyo: Kodansha International, 1992.

McKinniss, Candace B., and Arthur Natella, Jr. *Business in Mexico: Managerial Behavior, Protocol, and Etiquette*. New York: Haworth, 1994.

Moran, Robert T., and Jeffrey Abbott, *NAFTA: Managing the Cultural Differences*. Houston, TX: Gulf, 1994.

Morrison, Terri, Wayne A. Conaway, and George A. Borden. *Kiss, Bow, or Shake Hands: How to Do Business in 60 Countries*. Holbrook, MA: B. Adams, 1994.

O'Hara-Devereaux, Mary, and Robert Johansen *Globalwork: Bridging Distance, Culture, and Time*. San Francisco: Jossey-Bass, 1994.

Pinelli, Thomas E. *A Comparison of the Technical Communication Practices of Japanese and U.S. Aerospace Engineers and Scientists*. Washington, DC: American Institute of Aeronautics and Astronautics, NASA. Springfield, VA: National Technical Information Service, 1996. NAS 1.15.111924.

Trompenaars, Fons, and Charles Hampden-Turner. *Riding the Waves of Culture: Understanding Diversity in Global Business*. 2d ed. New York: McGraw-Hill, 1998.

► EXERCISES

1. The U.S. government publishes a series of books on individual countries and marketing strategies for each country. Over 200 reports are available on 200 different countries. Over 100 are recent. Some examples include:

   Holen, Leslie, and Elena Mikalis. *Marketing in France*. Washington, DC: U.S. Department of Commerce, International Trade Administration, 1989.

   Lyons, Maryanne B., and Maria H. Rauhala. *Marketing in Iceland*. Washington, DC: U.S. Department of Commerce, International Trade Administration, 1991.

   Marketing in India. Washington, DC: U.S. Department of Commerce, International Trade Administration, 1990.

   McLaughlin, Robert. *Marketing in the United Kingdom*. Washington, DC: U.S. Department of Commerce, International Trade Administration, 1990.

   McQueen, Cheryl. *Marketing in Pakistan*. Washington, DC: U.S. Department of Commerce, International Trade Administration, 1992.

   Write a report, choosing two or three countries from the books in this series available in your library. Explain the differences in marketing strategy among the countries you choose to investigate.

2. Another series published by various branches of the U.S. government, and available from the Government Printing Office in Washington, DC, focuses on important aspects of individual countries. For example:

   Hudson, Rex, ed. A. *Chile: A Country Study*. 3d ed. Washington, DC:

   Worden, Robert L., Andrea Matles Savada, and Ronald E. Dolan, eds., 1994. *China: A Country Study*. Washington, DC: Headquarters, Department of the Army, 1988.

   Heitzman, James, and Robert L. Worden. *India: A Country Study*. 5th ed. Washington, DC: Federal Research Division, 1996.

   Metz, Helen Chapin, ed. *Iraq: A Country Study*. 4th ed. Federal Research Division, Library of Congress 4th ed., 1990. Washington, DC: Headquarters, Department of the Army, 1990.

Shinn, Rinn S., ed. *Italy, a Country Study.* 2d ed. Foreign Area Studies, the American University. Washington, DC: Headquarters, Department of the Army, 1987.

Watkins, Chandra D. *Marketing in Kenya.* Washington, DC: U.S. Department of Commerce, International Trade, 1992.

Chose two or three different books in this series. Books are available on over 100 different countries. Write a report comparing and contrasting these countries in major categories of your choice.

Collaborative Projects

1. Prepare a written report on the challenges associated with doing business in a specific country. Focus your report on issues such as the following: management styles, corporate culture, negotiation style, social values, economics, and political systems. Allow each team member to choose and focus on one issue. After each person has completed research, come together as group. Decide how you will prepare each segment in the written report. Prepare each segment, then make copies of the segment for each team member. Following discussion of each team member's findings, write, as a team, a summary of the findings.

   The following works provide useful, more advanced information on culture and its effects on business, economics, and politics than the general guides to doing business in various countries:

   Caroll, Raymond. *Cultural Misunderstandings: The French–American Experience.* Chicago: University of Chicago, 1988.

   Child, John. *Management in China during the Age of Reform.* Cambridge: Cambridge University Press, 1994.

   Clegg, Stewart, and S. Gordon Redding. *Capitalism in Contrasting Cultures.* New York: de Gruyter, 1990.

   Curry, Jeffrey. *A Short Course in International Negotiating: Planning and Conducting International Commercial Negotiations.* San Raphael, CA; World Trade Press, 1999.

   Durlabhji, Subhash, and Norton E. Marks, eds. *Japanese Business: Cultural Perspectives.* Albany: SUNY Press, 1992.

   Kline, John M. *Foreign Investment Strategies in Restructuring Economies: Learning from Corporate Experience in Chile.* Westport, CT: Quorum Books, 1992.

   Jain, Subhash C. *Market Evolution in Developing Countries: The Unfolding of the Indian Market.* New York: International Business Press, 1993.

   Kato, Hiroki, and Joan S. Kato. *Understanding and Working with the Japanese Business World.* Englewood Cliffs, NJ: Prentice-Hall, 1992.

   Maccoby, Michael, ed. *Sweden at the Edge: Lessons for American and Swedish Managers.* Philadelphia: University of Pennsylvania Press, 1991.

Saik, Yasutaka. *The Eight Core Values of the Japanese Businessman: Toward an Understanding of Japanese Management.* Binghamton, NY: International Business Press, 1999.

Simons, George F., Carmen Vázquez, and Philip R. Harris. *Transcultural Leadership: Empowering the Diverse Workforce.* TX, Houston: Gulf Publishing, 1993.

Soufi, Wahib Abdulfattah, and Richard T. Mayer. *Saudi Arabian Industrial Investment: An Analysis of Government–Business Relationships.* New York: Quorum Books, 1991.

Wilson, Peter W., and Douglas F. Graham. *Saudi Arabia: The Coming Storm.* Armonk, NY: M. E. Sharpe, 1994.

Whitley, Richard. *Business Systems in East Asia: Firms, Markets, and Societies.* London: Newbury Park; Thousand Oaks, CA: Sage, 1992.

Divergent Capitalisms: The Social Structuring and Change of Business Systems. New York: Oxford University Press, 1999.

PART II

Techniques

PART II is the bridge between the foundation skills of Part I and the applications of Part III. Chapter 8 tells you how to lay the groundwork for successful reports by gathering the information you need. Chapters 9 and 10 together show you how to organize your information in a meaningful way, whether it be to define, describe or argue. Chapters 11 and 12 deal with the visual elements that are so important in technical communication. Chapter 11 demonstrates how to produce documents that both look good and function well. Chapter 12 explores the world of graphics and tables.

SCENARIO

You are the supervisor for the general contractor on a major construction project. This is your first assignment as supervisor on a building of this size, and you are eager to make a good impression on your bosses.

You have hired a number of subcontractors for various portions of the project. The subcontractors, in turn, have hired workers to complete specific jobs. Today you learned that some of the workers are not legal U.S. residents. If you keep them on the payroll, you will be breaking the law. You don't know what the precise penalties are for hiring undocumented workers, but if their illegal immigrant status were discovered you would probably lose your job. Yet if you cause the workers to lose their jobs, you will be depriving them of money that they and their families desperately need. Moreover, a delay in construction may cause you to miss the promised completion date, obliging your company to pay damages to the property owner. A delay wouldn't look good on your record.

You would like to speak to your bosses, but you decide that it would be foolish to go in to such a meeting without a better understanding of the law as well as your professional ethical responsibilities. You need information—a lot of it and soon.

chapter 8

Gathering, Evaluating, and Documenting Information

▶ Asking the Right Questions

▶ Looking for Answers
Interviews
Newsgroups
World Wide Web
Library

▶ Evaluating Answers

▶ Citing Sources

On the job you will often find yourself in situations requiring good research skills. You will need to know what questions to ask, where to look for answers, and how to evaluate the responses you receive from various sources. The ability to gather credible information efficiently will make you a more productive and valuable member of your organization.

Keep in mind that research is a continuous process of asking questions and receiving answers that prompt more questions. Whenever possible, try to cycle through this process again and again until you are sure that you have all the pertinent and reliable information necessary to make confident decisions or to take appropriate actions.

▶ ASKING THE RIGHT QUESTIONS

Efficient research starts with the right questions. You have to determine as specifically as possible what you already know and what you don't yet know about your subject. Consider these five questions:

- **What personal experience do I have regarding this subject?**
- **What have I read about this subject?**
- **What have I heard from friends or colleagues about this subject?**
- **What specific questions would I ask a specialist about this subject?**
- **What keywords would I use to investigate this subject in a library's catalog or on the World Wide Web?**

These five questions will give you a good start on your research by helping you to inventory your existing knowledge of the subject and to identify the gaps that you need to fill. As you proceed with your research and learn more about your subject, you will be able to refine and revise your research questions, and the answers to some of your questions will lead you to new questions and new answers.

For example, as you examine the issue of hiring undocumented workers, several good questions might come to mind: What are my legal responsibilities as a citizen? As the supervisor on this construction project? As a representative of my company? What is my company's responsibility here? What is its potential liability? Has a situation like this ever occurred at my company? If so, how was it resolved? Does my company's code of conduct address this issue? If so, what does it advise? What are my professional responsibilities as a civil engineer? Does my professional association's code of conduct address this issue? If so, what does it advise?

▶ LOOKING FOR ANSWERS

Once you know what you're looking for, you must decide where to start looking. Ordinarily, you will start with the most readily available sources and keep investigating until you have answered all your questions, exhausted your sources of information, or run out of time (and often you will run out of time).

A wide variety of information sources are typically available to you.

Interviews

Interviewing subject specialists is a highly efficient way of researching. You ask specific questions and receive answers tailored to your specific questions. Whether the interview is conducted in person, over the telephone, by letter, or through e-mail, good preparation is essential to getting full and pertinent answers to your questions.

First, do enough background reading on your subject to allow you to ask sophisticated questions. Subject specialists will typically appreciate your research efforts and cooperate with the interview. On the other hand, if you could have answered your questions by reading a good encyclopedia, subject specialists are likely to think you are wasting their time.

Second, find out as much as possible about your subject specialists. What qualifies them to advise you in this area? Is it their education? Their job experience? Both? What have they said or written about this subject? What is their particular approach to the subject? What is their potential bias? What is their reputation within the profession?

Third, compose your list of questions, carefully targeting the areas of expertise of your subject specialists. For example, don't ask a practicing engineer about the origins of engineering ethics; instead, ask the president of the professional association of engineers or a scholar who has specifically studied this topic. Ask a practicing engineer about his or her experiences with ethical dilemmas. Don't ask a police officer your questions about immigration regulations; ask the director of the local immigration office or a lawyer who specializes in such cases. Ask the police officer about his or her experiences in working with the federal Immigration and Naturalization Service in matters involving undocumented workers.

Fourth, politely request the interview. Keep in mind that subject specialists won't be entirely forthcoming unless they understand your purpose. Identify the topic of the interview, explain how and when you would like to conduct the interview, tell why you chose this individual or group of individuals to interview, and let the party or parties know what you will do with the information you receive. Request permission to quote your subject specialists; with a personal or telephone interview, ask permission to record the session to assure the accuracy of your quotations.

In developing your list of questions, consider the following guidelines:

Create questions that require explanations or evaluations instead of a simple yes or no answer. Instead of "Does your professional association prohibit the use of undocument workers?" ask "What does your professional association advise about the hiring of workers who are not legal U.S. residents?"

Ask follow-up questions to encourage elaboration. Solicit details and examples. If you ask "What are the hiring risks for local contractors?" ask a follow-up such as "How likely is it that a local contractor will be caught?" or "When was the last time a local contractor was caught?"

Ask follow-up questions for clarification whenever you don't understand a given answer. If possible, restate the answer in your own words and ask your subject specialist if your understanding is correct. For example, "So you believe the hiring of undocumented workers by local contractors is a fairly common practice? Is that right?" Here the yes/no question is necessary to prompt your source to confirm or discount your interpretation.

Early on, include questions that acknowledge your subject specialist's expertise. By demonstrating that you have prepared for the interview by acquiring a basic understanding of the subject, such questions will encourage the specialist to give candid and comprehensive answers. For example, you could ask "In your 1999 article, "Ethics in Civil Engineering," you said . . . Why do you adopt this position?" Or you might ask "You've been an INS agent for five years. In that time, how has the . . .?"

Keep your interview focused, always steering the comments of the subject specialist to your topic. Intercept the specialist if he or she drifts from the topic: for example, "That's a good observation about the legal requirements. But let me ask you more about professional ethics. How did . . .?"

Following the interview, write a thank-you letter or e-mail message to each of your subject specialists.

Newsgroups

Newsgroups are electronic communities of people from all over the world who exchange information about a common interest or affiliation by posting questions and answers to online bulletin boards. You will find one or more newsgroups to answer almost every question you might ask. For example, if you have a question regarding the immigration regulations of the United States, you could try the misc.immigration.usa newsgroup or the alt.visa.us newsgroup. To find a newsgroup appropriate to your research, visit a directory site on the World Wide Web such as www.cyberfiber.com.

Newsgroups are either moderated or unmoderated. In a moderated newsgroup, all messages posted to the bulletin board are initially reviewed by the newsgroup's moderator. Acting as the group's editor, the moderator will accept timely, relevant messages for publication on the bulletin board, while declining to publish submissions that repeat earlier posts or are irrelevant to the group or otherwise of little merit. In unmoderated newsgroups, all messages are posted directly to the bulletin board without filtering or editing by a moderator.

If you are doing research within a newsgroup, keep in mind the following guidelines:

- **Upon joining a newsgroup, observe the discussion before you start to ask questions.** Remember that you're joining a conversation that is already in progress. It is polite to listen for a while before speaking yourself. By briefly "lurking" in this way, you will develop a clearer understanding of the purpose of the newsgroup, the nature and style of messages on the bulletin board, and the appropriate way to ask and answer questions.

- **If the newsgroup offers archives of previous messages or FAQs (frequently asked questions), review this material.** It will familiarize you with the major topics of conversation and keep you from raising a subject or asking a question that has already been discussed thoroughly.

- **Compose a clear and specific subject line to your message.** You want to be certain that participants who really know something about your topic will notice your message; you also don't want to waste the time of participants whose expertise lies elsewhere.

- **Keep your message to the point.** Don't ask newsgroup participants to scroll through paragraphs of unnecessary information to locate the questions you are asking or the answers you are offering. If you are asking a question, be as specific as possible. If you are answering a question, copy only the pertinent passages of the original question and try to give a brief but thorough answer.

- **Don't engage in "flaming" within the newsgroup.** Deliberately provocative and insulting comments disrupt the collaborative community that the newsgroup is designed to establish. If you consider a message genuinely offensive, comment off list to either the contributor of the message or the moderator of the newsgroup.

World Wide Web

On the World Wide Web, billions of pages of information await your visit. For example, if you were investigating information on the professional ethics of civil engineers, you could visit the sites of the following professional associations:

ACI American Concrete Institute: www.aci-int.org
AISC American Institute of Steel Construction: www.aiscweb.com
ASCE American Society of Civil Engineers: www.asce.org
ASTM American Society for Testing and Materials: www.astm.org

AWWA American Water Works Association: www.awwa.org
BOCCA Building Officials and Code Administrators: www.bocai.org
CERF Civil Engineering Research Foundation: www.cerf.org
IISI International Iron and Steel Institute: www.worldsteel.org
ITE Institute of Transportation Engineers: www.ite.org

With millions of sites and billions of pages, the World Wide Web is the biggest library of information resources available. The entire government of the United States, for example, is accessible through the World Wide Web (see www.fedworld.gov). But how do you know what's out there? And how do you find what you're looking for? To help you navigate the World Wide Web, a variety of search engines are available, such as Alta Vista, Excite, InfoSeek, Lycos, and Yahoo. A search engine is a research service that scours the Internet looking for sites with keywords pertinent to your subject, listing the sites it discovers usually according to relevance to your subject.

A simple search looks only for the presence of keywords (e.g., *ethics*). A focused search looks for the presence or absence of specific combinations of keywords, using plus signs and minus signs as prefixes. For example, a search for *civil engineering ethics* asks for all files containing at least one of the three words: *civil, engineering,* or *ethics*. A search for *+civil +engineering +ethics* narrows the focus to only those files containing all three words: *civil, engineering,* and *ethics*. A search for *−civil +engineering +ethics* asks for all files containing both *engineering* and *ethics* but not the word *civil*.

Each service is a little different from the others—more or less comprehensive, more or less specialized. You might wish to try several search engines to see which directs you most quickly to the most appropriate sources for your subject or field. Also keep in mind that search engine firms are often paid to give priority to specific sites in their listings: that is, while one search engine might have been paid to list a site among its first five, a different search engine might list the same site tenth or twentieth in relevance to your subject.

Also available are metasearch engines such as MetaCrawler (www.metacrawler.com) and Search.com (www.search.com). A metasearch service will submit your key words to several search engines simultaneously, thus offering you a kind of one-stop shopping in your research process.

Keep in mind, however, that a visit to the World Wide Web can be a little confusing and intimidating. There is so much information available, and it is so easy to jump from site to site and link to link, that you may lose track of the pages you have already visited. Here are several tips to keep you from losing your way:

- Check the GO menu item. The GO menu item of your browsing software shows the footprints of your search: it lists all the pages you have visited since you left your home page. Clicking on a page from the GO list will immediately take you back to that page.

- Use the BACK and FORWARD buttons. When you leave your home page, your browsing software activates a BACK button that will take you back to pages you have already visited. When you back up, the FORWARD button is activated: it allows you to reverse direction and proceed to the last new page you visited. The BACK and FORWARD buttons allow you to retrace your steps. If you found useful information early in your search, but didn't note the specific page, use the BACK and FORWARD buttons to help you look for it.

- Use the BOOKMARK or FAVORITES function. When you find a page that you think will be particularly useful to you, especially a page that you might wish to visit often, use the BOOKMARK or FAVORITES function to note the location of that page. This menu item lists all the pages that have been so noted. Clicking on a page from the BOOKMARK or FAVORITES list will take you immediately to that location on the World Wide Web.

- Open multiple windows. Using multiple windows allows you to keep a page of information readily available while you continue browsing for additional information.

Library

If possible, visit your local library and discuss your subject with a research librarian. Librarians are familiar with the library's resources—both paper and electronic—and are trained to assist visitors in finding answers to research questions. Librarians won't find the answer for you, but they will help to point you in the right direction.

On the job, however, you typically won't have time to make a physical visit to an outside library. A virtual visit will often have to do. In addition to the physical copies of books, journals, indexes, newspapers, and specialized encyclopedias, more and more libraries are subscribing to electronic sources of information, permitting you to do your library research simply by accessing the library's World Wide Web site. By acquiring and organizing the electronic versions of research materials, your local library thus opens the door to a world of information that might otherwise be unavailable to you.

Encyclopedias A good way to start your library search is by looking at the specialized dictionaries and encyclopedias that summarize key information on a subject. Such materials give you the basic understanding you will need before reading advanced books and articles or before interviewing subject specialists for pertinent details and up-to-date information.

In addition to paper versions of encyclopedias and dictionaries (typically housed in the library's reference room), a variety of electronic sources are available, such as *Encyclopedia Americana Online, Grolier Multimedia Encyclopedia Online*, or *Encyclopedia Britannica*.

Such electronic sources allow you to search quickly and efficiently by subject. For example, checking the word *immigration* in the *Grolier Multimedia Encyclopedia Online* leads you immediately to a brief history of immigration law in the United States, including discussion of the Immigration Reform and Control Act of 1986, which imposed penalties on employers who knowingly and willfully hired undocumented workers. It is this law that is pertinent to the situation on the construction project. The information in the encyclopedia thus allows you to focus your investigation. And your familiarity with this law gives you credibility during your interviews with subject specialists.

Electronic Library Catalog The electronic library catalog is a listing of all the books, periodicals, and miscellaneous materials such as maps, films, and audio and video recordings that a library houses. Traditionally, the library catalog was a series of file drawers of index cards listed in alphabetical order by author, title, and subject. Today, almost all libraries have computerized their catalogs, permitting quick electronic search by author, title, subject, and keyword (see Figure 8-1). For example, you might do a subject search using the words *engineering ethics*. Your search would identify several promising books and list all the information that you would need to locate the books in the library (see Figure 8-2).

The location of each item in a library has a specific numeric identifier known as a call number. Call numbers operate on one of two systems: the Dewey decimal system, dividing materials into 10 categories (see Figure 8-3), or the Library of Congress system, dividing materials into 21 categories (see Figure 8-4). Maps of your library show where the different categories of books are located.

```
Enter a search word or phrase:
Select a search option:     Keyword     Author      Title       Subject
Limit your search by:       Languages:              Material types:
Enter a keyword or keyword phrase:
Select a search option:     Keyword     Author      Title       Subject
(Selecting the keyword option permits the use of qualifiers.)
Limit your search:          Select one or more databases:
Languages:                  Material types:
```

FIGURE 8-1 • Searching the Electronic Library Catalog

```
* Brief Record Hitlist * Full Record Hitlist * Refine Search *
Holdings Display * MARC Display * Download Full Citation for Record *
------------------------------------------------------------------------
Previous Record        Next Record
------------------------------------------------------------------------
Record # 4

Title:                 Thinking like an engineer: studies in the ethics of a
                       profession / Michael Davis.
Author:                Davis, Michael, 1943-
Call number:           TA157 .D32 1998
Publisher:             New York: Oxford University Press [1998]
Subject heading(s):    Engineering ethics.

Description:           xii, 240 p.; 25 cm.

Notes:                 At head of title: Association for Practice and
                       Professional Ethics. Includes bibliographical
                       references (p. 227-235) and index.
ISBN:                  *0195120515 (alk. paper)
DBCN:                  ALS-6049
Holdings:
                                 Holdings
         Location            Call number            Material    Status
      Main Library—Stacks    TA157 .D32 1998 c.1    Book        Available
```

FIGURE 8-2 • Listing for a Book in an Electronic Library Catalog

```
000    General knowledge (encyclopedias and other reference works)
100    Philosophy
200    Religion
300    Social sciences
400    Language (linguistics)
500    Pure sciences (mathematics, chemistry, physics)
600    Applied sciences (engineering)
700    Arts (music, painting, athletics)
800    Literature
900    History and geography
```

FIGURE 8-3 • Dewey Decimal Classification System

Knowing how materials are classified in your local library allows you to go to a specific section of the library to browse the shelves. Often through simple browsing you will discover materials that you might never have otherwise located—a useful book, for example, that because of its unusual title failed to show up during your search of the electronic catalog.

A	General works
B	Philosophy and religion
C	Auxiliary science of history
D	History of Europe, Asia, and Africa
E	History of United States
F	History of United States local, Canada, Latin America, and South America
G	Geography and anthropology
H	Social sciences
J	Political science
K	Law
L	Education
M	Music
N	Fine arts
P	Language and literature
Q	Science and mathematics
R	Medicine
S	Agriculture
T	Technology
U	Military science
V	Naval science
Z	Library science

FIGURE 8-4 • Library of Congress Classification System

Indexes While the electronic library catalog identifies the titles of the magazines and journals in your library, it can't tell you the titles of the specific articles published. To locate that information, you go to electronic indexes such as the Online Computer Library Center's FirstSearch, which includes both WorldCat (a database of all books in over 8,000 libraries) and ArticleFirst (a database of over 12,500 journals in a wide variety of fields). FirstSearch also gives you access to specialized databases such as the following:

- **Applied Science and Technology Abstracts**: abstracts of applied science and technology research
- **Business Dateline**: index of articles on regional business activities in over 500 magazines and newspapers
- **New York Times**: abstracts of all articles in the *New York Times*
- **Newspaper Abstracts**: abstracts of articles in 30 national and regional newspapers
- **Index to Legal Periodicals & Books**: index of articles in over 600 legal journals
- **GPO Monthly Catalog**: index of all publications of the Government Printing Office

- **Periodical Abstracts**: abstracts of articles in over 2,000 journals in a variety of fields
- **Social Science Abstracts**: abstracts of articles in over 400 journals in anthropology economics, geography, political science, law, and sociology,
- **Wilson Business Abstracts**: abstracts of articles in over 300 business magazines

For example, your research on the subject of *illegal immigration* would uncover a citation of a promising publication from the U.S. Department of Justice (see Figure 8-5).

```
GOVDOC NO:    J 1.103:
AUTHOR:       United States. Dept. of Justice.
TITLE:        Administrative decisions under employer sanctions, unfair
              immigration-related employment practices, and civil penalty
              document fraud laws
PLACE:        [Washington, DC]:
PUBLISHER:    The Dept. For sale by the U.S. G.P.O., Supt. of Docs.
YEAR:         1993, 9999
PUB TYPE:     Serial
LANGUAGE:     English
FORMAT:       v.; 24 cm.
FREQUENCY:    Irregular
NUMBERING:    Vol. 3 (Jan. 1992 to Dec. 1993)
NOTES:        Title varies slightly. Decisions and orders of the Chief Ad-
              ministrative Hearing Officer, of the U.S. Dept. of Justice
              Executive Office for Immigration Review
SUBJECT:      Alien labor, legal status, laws, etc. United States Cases.
              Emigration and immigration law United States Cases.
              Illegal aliens, employment. United States Cases.
              Alien labor certification. United States Cases.
              Alien labor certification, corrupt practices. United States
              Cases.
ALT TITLE:    OCAHO
              United States. Dept. of Justice. Administrative decisions
              under employer sanctions & unfair immigration-related
              employment practices laws
              United States. Dept. of Justice. 8 USC 1324 . . . proceeding
OTHER:        United States. Dept. of Justice. Executive Office for
              Immigration Review. Office of the Chief Administrative Hear-
              ing Officer.
ITEM NO:      0717-C-20
STOCK NO      U.S. Govt. Print. Off., Supt. of Docs., Mail Stop: SSOP,
              Washington, DC 20402-9328
OCLC NO:      37879193
```

FIGURE 8-5 • Citation of a Government Publication in FirstSearch

▶ EVALUATING ANSWERS

With all the information that is available to researchers today, the difficulty isn't so much finding answers to your questions as it is determining which answers to trust.

With interviews, for example, you have quick access to the newest information on a subject, such as the findings from yesterday's experiment, but you sacrifice the review process that serves as a check and balance on the research of subject specialists. You receive the information directly from a subject specialist without a good gauge on the accuracy of the person's findings or the potential bias of his or her conclusions and recommendations. Unless you have a separate method for verifying the findings or judging the reputation of a subject specialist, you could be receiving erroneous or misleading information.

With newsgroups and the World Wide Web, similarly, you have the blessing of the widest possible participation in the creation and distribution of information: everybody's ideas and opinions are readily available for your consideration. The curse of such wide participation, however, is that misinformation is easily distributed by unreliable or unscrupulous sources.

With books and journal articles, on the other hand, the information you receive is often considered credible because it has been through a review process. Before publication of the material scholars in the field as well as editors and publishers examine the typescript—usually several times—to identify any incorrect or inconsistent material, which the authors of the original manuscript are then asked to eliminate or correct. While such information has high credibility, the review and publication process may well last as long as a couple of years. The information you receive, as a consequence, is never the newest information available.

Ideally, you will have several sources of information that will help you to achieve a credible balance of the most authoritative information available and the most up-to-date information available. If you receive identical information from both books and interviews, for example, you likely have good answers to your questions.

In addition, a variety of aids are available to assist you in judging the credibility of your sources. For example, erroneous information distributed in a newsgroup is often challenged by other newsgroup participants. So don't accept the earliest answer to your question in a newsgroup: wait to see if others support or dispute the posting.

In judging a book, check the book reviews written by specialists in the field to determine their opinion of the book's credibility. For articles, check the Letters to the Editor feature in later issues of the magazine or journal to see if readers have questioned any findings or conclusions. With published research, a good gauge of a source's credibility is the frequency with which it is cited by other scholars in the field.

To assist you in evaluating World Wide Web sites, rating services are available. For example, britannica.com is a service of Encyclopedia Britannica that classifies, describes, indexes, and evaluates World Wide Web sites. The editors of *Encyclopedia Britannica* rate sites on a scale of one to five stars according to the following criteria:

- Accuracy, usefulness, depth, and breadth of information
- Credentials and authority of the author or publisher
- Quality of design, graphics, and multimedia
- Ease of navigation
- Timeliness of revision
- Quality of graphics or multimedia

Sites considered by the editors to be without merit are excluded from the Britannica listings.

A search of britannica.com on the keywords *illegal* + *immigration* yields eight citations. The highest rated is the following:

```
1996 Statistical Yearbook of the Immigration and
Naturalization Service
U.S. Department of Justice
Rating: ***
Overview of immigration to the U.S. with statistical
tables.
Covers such topics as programs on immigration,
refugees,
asylum, temporary admissions, and naturalization.
Also presents statistics on illegal immigration and
apprehension.
This site is an excellent source of data.
```

Similarly, a site such as about.com offers guided access to the World Wide Web. A trained legion of subject specialists directs you to pertinent sites offering credible information and monitors additional resources such as discussion groups and bulletin boards. Or consider a site such as askme.com, which allows you to ask questions of specialists in a variety of fields. The credentials of all specialists are listed, and each is rated on the usefulness of his or her answers to previous questions. You also have a choice of either reviewing answers to previous questions or asking a new question.

Ultimately, however, the decision to trust a source is yours. If you are using and distributing information, it is your reputation as a professional—your judgment as a researcher—that is at risk. To assess the credibility of your sources and the reliability of their answers to your questions, consider the following:

Interviews

- What are the individual's credentials? Does he or she have appropriate and pertinent education and job experience?
- What is the individual's reputation in the field? Is he or she considered to be a national, regional, or local authority on the subject?
- Do you know a trustworthy specialist in the field who would recommend this individual as a source of information?
- Did you notice bias in the individual's comments? Was he or she cautious and careful in offering explanations and opinions or impulsive and imprecise?
- Did the individual support his or her opinions with sufficient and plausible evidence?
- Did the expert tell you anything that is contradicted by your other sources?
- Did the expert tell you anything that is verified by your other sources?

Newsgroups

- Who participates in this newsgroup? Is it restricted to specialists in the field or accessible to the public? Do the participants have appropriate and pertinent education and job experience?
- What is the newsgroup's reputation? Is it widely considered a good source of credible information?
- Do you know a trustworthy specialist in the field who would recommend this newsgroup as a source of information?
- Did you notice bias in the answers to your question? Are the participants cautious and careful in offering explanations and opinions or impulsive and imprecise?
- Did participants support their opinions with sufficient and plausible evidence?
- Did participants tell you anything that is contradicted by your other sources?
- Did participants tell you anything that is verified by your other sources?

World Wide Web sites

- Who operates this World Wide Web site? Does the site display the credentials of that organization or individual? Does that organization or individual have appropriate and pertinent credentials?
- What is the site's reputation? Is it widely considered a good source of credible information?
- Do you know a trustworthy specialist in the field who would recommend this site as a source of information?

- Do you notice bias in the information? Is the site designed to advertise? Or does it offer fair and impartial coverage of its topic?
- Does the site support opinions with plausible evidence? Does it try to educate or entertain?
- How timely is the information? Does the site display the date it was last modified?
- Is any of the information at this site contradicted by your other sources?
- Is any of the information at this site verified by your other sources?

Books and articles

- Who wrote this book or article? Does the author (or authors) have appropriate and pertinent education and job experience?
- What is the reputation of the journal or book publisher? Is this journal widely considered to be a good source of credible information? Does this publisher ordinarily publish highly regarded books?
- Do you know a trustworthy specialist in the field who would recommend this book or article as a source of information?
- How often is this book or article cited in other publications on this subject?
- Do you notice bias in the book or article? Is the author cautious and careful in offering explanations and opinions or impulsive and imprecise?
- Does the author support opinions with sufficient and plausible evidence?
- How timely is the information?
- Is any of the information in this book or article contradicted by your other sources?
- Is any of the information in this book or article verified by your other sources?

▶ CITING SOURCES

If you use information from interviews, newsgroups, World Wide Web sites, books, or articles for a document you are writing or a presentation you are delivering, you have a moral and a rhetorical obligation to acknowledge your sources. Your moral obligation is to give appropriate credit to the individuals who deserve it—the people who composed the words, created the illustrations, or developed the ideas you are borrowing. Citing sources also serves the rhetorical function of bolstering the credibility of your investigation because it allows you to attribute your findings to pertinent subject specialists.

Depending on the rhetorical situation, you may choose a formal or informal method for acknowledging your sources. In a formal system of citation, your references will require specific and consistent formatting (see

Documentation in Appendix B for examples). A formal system of citation is particularly important if your document or presentation might be used by others to conduct subsequent research. The consistent formatting of citations will assist researchers in locating the sources you used.

If your document or presentation will be used by others chiefly to make decisions or take actions (i.e., by individuals managing information instead of creating information), a formal system of citation may be unnecessary). If informal citation is appropriate, you might acknowledge your sources by simple tagging:

- According to Lew Pauley's *Immigrants and Immigration*, . . .
- In a recent interview, Timothy Cooper of the Immigration and Naturalization Service told me that . . .
- Information from the Department of Labor (www.dol.gov) indicates that . . .

Keep in mind that the citation of sources offers you the opportunity to demonstrate that your research has been fair and thorough. If your list of sources, for example, omits a major book on your topic or the World Wide Web site of the organization you are investigating, your readers would have cause to doubt the validity of your findings. Similarly, if all your information comes from a single source or a single kind of source (e.g., all interviews), your readers would likely consider your research to be biased or incomplete. Your list of sources is often a good indicator of the quality of your investigation and the merits of your conclusions and recommendations.

▶ EXERCISES

1. Choose a topic of importance to your major or minor. Familiarize yourself with the topic by reading the information available in one of the online encyclopedias such as www.encyclopedia.com. After you have completed this introductory reading, devise a series of questions about the topic that you would like to ask a subject specialist.

2. Interview a professional in your major or minor regarding your topic. List the criteria according to which you chose this individual and assessed the credibility of his or her answers to your questions.

3. Find a newsgroup that might offer answers to questions about your topic? How did you locate this newsgroup? Who are its participants? How active is it? How helpful are the participants? How credible is the information that is exchanged?

4. To locate information on the World Wide Web, use a series of keywords regarding your subject on four different search engines. Note the similarities and differences in the listings of the four search engines? Which sites appear on all four lists? Which sites appear on only one list? Are the same sites listed higher or lower on different lists? Why?

5. Using the rating service britannica.com, submit the same series of keywords regarding your subject. Which World Wide Web sites are listed by this rating service? Which sites identified by the rating service as credible sources were also listed by the search engines? Do you agree or disagree with britannica.com's evaluation of the sites?

6. By interviewing professionals in your major or minor or by researching in the library, identify a noted authority on your specific subject. What speeches or publications are the basis for this individual's reputation as a highly authoritative scholar? Locate copies of his or her publications. How readily available are such publications? How often is this individual cited by other scholars in the field? Give examples of such citations from books, magazine and journal articles, or World Wide Web sites.

SCENARIO

It's a relaxed Saturday morning and you stop by a friend's apartment to say hi. You find her struggling to unplug a clogged sink drain by using a plunger.

"Look," you say, "you ought to buy yourself a plumber's snake. It would unclog that drain in a couple of minutes.

"Really? What's a plumber's snake?"

"Well, it's a tool for unplugging drains. Mostly, it's a flexible, springlike, steel cable about five feet long and with the diameter of a pencil. The cable has a football-shaped boring head on its working end. The head is about two inches long, and at its widest point it's twice the diameter of the cable. The whole business looks a bit like a snake—hence its name."

"That so? Anything to it besides the cable and head?"

"Uh-huh. There's a crank. It's a hollow steel tube in the shape of an opened-up Z. It's about ten inches long, so you can get both hands on it. You slip the crank over the cable. With it, you can rotate the cable after you've inserted it in the drain, so that the head operates something like a drill to bore through the clog."

"Sounds like a handy gadget. I'll have to get one."

In an impromptu way, you have applied the organizational strategy used to describe things to the description of a mechanism. And that's what this chapter is all about. It reviews organizational strategies, such as chronology and definition, and gives them a technical writing twist.

If you need such a review, you may find this chapter useful.

chapter 9

Presenting Information

- ▶ Chronology

- ▶ Topical Organization

- ▶ Exemplification

- ▶ Analogy

- ▶ Classification and Division

- ▶ Definition
  Sentence Definitions
  Extended Definitions
  Placement of Definitions

- ▶ Description
  Visual Language
  Mechanism Description
  Process Description

If you follow our advice in Chapters 2 and 4 about situational analysis and writing for your readers, you will likely come up with an organizational strategy that fits your purpose and your audience. Nevertheless, being aware of the full array of organizational strategies available to you can be useful at both the discovery and organizing stages of composing. Therefore, this chapter reviews the strategies that have stood the test of time for presenting information: chronology, topical organization, exemplification, analogy, classification and division, definition, and description. In the next chapter we deal with analyzing information.

Taken together, Chapters 9 and 10 lay the groundwork for organizing the numerous technical reports you may be called upon to write. You can use any of the strategies in these two chapters as an overall organizing principle for an entire report. But you will also use them as subordinate methods of development within a larger framework. For example, within a paper arranged topically you may have paragraphs or small sections based upon chronology, exemplification, classification, and so forth. Within a set of instructions you are likely to have both mechanism and process descriptions. The two uses are mutually supportive and not in conflict with each other.

▶ CHRONOLOGY

When you have reason to relate a series of events for your readers, arranging the events chronologically—that is, by time—is a natural way to proceed. In your chronological narrative, be sure your readers always know where they are in the sequence of events. In the example that follows, a description of the volcanic eruption of Mount St. Helens, we have printed in boldface the phrases the authors use to orient their readers.

MOUNT ST. HELENS, WASHINGTON. The catastrophic eruption on **May 18, 1980**, was preceded by 2 months of intense activity that included more than 10,000 earthquakes, hundreds of small *phreatic* (steam-blast) explosions, and the outward growth of the volcano's entire north flank by more than 80 meters. A magnitude 5.1 earthquake struck beneath the volcano at **08:32 on May 18**, setting in motion the devastating eruption.

Within seconds of the earthquake, the volcano's bulging north flank slid away in the largest landslide in recorded history, triggering a destructive, lethal lateral blast of hot gas, steam, and rock debris that swept across the landscape as fast as 1,100 kilometers per hour. Temperatures within the blast reached as high as 300 degrees Celsius. Snow and ice on the volcano melted, forming torrents of water and rock debris that swept down river valleys leading from the volcano. **Within minutes**, a massive plume of ash thrust 19 kilometers into the sky, where the prevailing wind carried about 520 million tons of ash across 57,000 square kilometers of the western United States.[1]

Chronology can be used to project forward as well as to describe the past. In the next example, the Bureau of the Census forecasts how the population of the United States will change during the first half of the twenty-first century:

> The United States population would increase by 50 percent, from 263 million in 1995 to 394 million in 2050, under the Census Bureau's middle-series population projections. The population would grow to 275 million in 2000, and 347 million in 2030. The average annual growth rate, however, would decrease from 1.05 percent for the 1990–1995 period to 0.63 percent for the 2040–2050 period.
>
> In 1995, there were 34 million people ages 65 and over representing 13 percent of the population. The middle-series projection for 2050 indicates that there will be 79 million people ages 65 and over, representing 20 percent of the population. . . . The population ages 85 and over is growing especially fast. It is projected to more than double from nearly 4 million (1.4 percent of the population) in 1995 to over 8 million (2.4 percent) in 2030, then to more than double again in size from 2030 to 2050 to 18 million (4.6 percent).[2]

In technical writing, graphics of all kinds are frequently useful in presenting and analyzing information, and you should always be alert for opportunities to use them. In the case of the population projection just quoted, the Census Bureau used the graph shown in Figure 9-1 to illustrate the predicted trends.

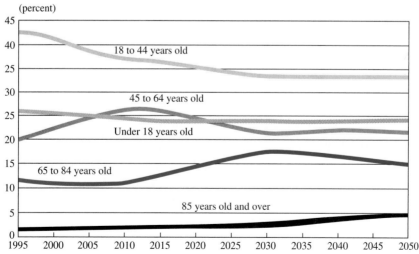

Distribution of the Population by age
(1995 to 2050: middle-series projections)

FIGURE 9-1 • Population Graph
Source: U.S. Department of Commerce, *How We're Changing* (Washington, DC: Bureau of the Census, 1997), 1.

Because the arrangement of your material follows the sequence of events you relate, arrangement is not a particular problem for you when you use chronological order. Choosing the level of detail you need may be a problem. Obviously, the narrator of the events at Mount St. Helens and the person who reported the population projection could have used more or less detail. As in most kinds of writing, purpose and audience are your best guides in these matters. If your purpose, for example, is to give a broad overview for a lay or executive audience, you will limit the amount of detail. If you have, on the other hand, an expert audience who will wish to analyze carefully the sequence you describe, you will need to provide considerable detail.

▶ TOPICAL ORGANIZATION

Technical writing projects often begin with a topic, say, Christmas tree farming. One way to deal with topics is to look for subtopics under the major topic. Under these subtopics you can gather yet smaller sub-subtopics and related facts. In the case of the Christmas tree topic, the subtopics might very well be production and marketing. Production could be broken down further into planting, maintaining, and harvesting. Marketing could be broken down into retail, wholesale, and cut-your-own. With some thought, you can break most topics down into the appropriate subtopics and sub-subtopics.

Be sure to choose topics and subtopics that suit your purpose and audience. Suppose your audience to be a group of executives who may have an interest in the use of robotics in their industries. Your audience analysis tells you that their major interest in robotics is application, not history or theory. You limit yourself, therefore, to application as a topic. You refine your purpose. You decide you want to give them some idea of the range of robotics. To do so, you reach into your knowledge of robotics and choose several illustrative applications:

- Installing windows in automobiles as the automobiles pass on an assembly line
- Arc welding in an airplane plant
- Mounting chips in a computer factory

By using these three applications as your subtopics, you can illustrate a wide range of current robotics practice. Within a few minutes, you have limited your topic to manageable size and made a good start on arrangement.

▶ EXEMPLIFICATION

Technical writing sometimes consists largely of a series of generalizations supported by examples. The writer makes statements, such as this one about earthquakes:

The actual movement of ground in an earthquake is seldom the direct cause of death or injury.

Having made a generalization, the writer must now support it:

Most casualties result from falling objects and debris because the shocks can shake, damage, or demolish buildings and other structures. Earthquakes may also trigger landslides and generate huge ocean waves (seismic sea waves), each of which can cause great property damage and considerable loss of life. Earthquake-related injuries are commonly caused by: (1) partial building collapse, such as toppling chimneys, falling brick from wall facings and roof parapets, collapsing walls, falling ceiling plaster, light fixtures, and pictures; (2) flying glass from broken windows (this danger may be greater from windows in high-rise structures); (3) overturned bookcases, fixtures, and other furniture and appliances; (4) fires from broken chimneys, broken gaslines, and similar causes (this danger may be aggravated by a lack of water caused by broken mains); (5) fallen powerlines; and (6) drastic human actions resulting from panic.[3]

There are two common ways to use examples. One way is to give one or more extended, well-developed examples. This method is illustrated in the paragraph about earthquake damage. The other way is to give a series of short examples that you do not develop in detail, as in the following paragraph:

I use the term culture to refer to the "system of knowledge" that is shared by a large group of people. The "borders" between countries usually, but not always, coincide with political boundaries between countries. To illustrate, we can speak of the culture of the United States, the Japanese culture, and the Mexican culture. In some countries, however, there is more than one culture. Consider Canada as an example. There is the Anglophone (i.e., English-speaking) culture derived from England and there is the Francophone culture derived from France.[4]

Like most everything else in writing, the use of examples calls for judgment on your part. Too few examples, and your writing will lack interest and credibility. Too many examples, and your key generalizations will be lost in excessive detail.

▶ ANALOGY

Analogies are comparisons—they compare the unfamiliar to the familiar in order to help readers better understand the unfamiliar. You should frequently use short, simple analogies, particularly when you are writing for lay people. For example, many lay people have difficulty comprehending the immense power released by nuclear reactions. A completely technical explanation of $E = mc^2$ probably would not help them very much. But suppose you tell them that if one pound of matter—a package of butter, for instance—could be converted directly to energy in a nuclear reaction, it would produce enough electrical power to supply the entire United States for 35 hours (that is, over 11 billion kilowatt hours). Such a statement reduces $E = mc^2$ to an understandable idea.

Scientists recognize the need for analogy when they are called upon to explain difficult concepts. A scientist working with microelectronic integrated circuits—that is, microchips—when asked to explain how small the circuits are, said, "Your grope for analogies. If you wanted to draw a map of the entire United States that showed every city block and town square, it would obviously be a *very* big map. But with the feature sizes we're working with to create microcircuits right now, I could draw that entire map on a sheet of paper not much larger than a postage stamp."[5]

A writer looking for a way to explain the immense age of the universe relative to humankind put it this way:

> Some 12 to 20 billion years ago, astronomers think a "primeval atom" exploded with a big bang sending the entire universe flying out at incredible speeds. Eventually matter cooled and condensed into galaxies and stars. Eons after life began to develop on Earth, humans appeared. If all events in the history of the universe until now were squeezed into 24 hours, Earth wouldn't form until late afternoon. Humans would have existed for only two seconds.[6]

Besides being practical, analogies can liven up your writing. Here is a writer having fun with some far-fetched analogies that, nevertheless, help the reader grasp the enormousness of the quantities he is discussing:

> If all the Coca-Cola ever produced were dumped over Niagara Falls in place of water, the falls would flow at a normal rate for 16 hours and 49 minutes . . . Two ships the size of the Queen Elizabeth could be floated in the ocean of Hawaiian Punch Americans consume annually.[7]

Analogies can be presented visually, and in technical writing they frequently are. Figure 9-2 is a graphic that uses the familiar—water pressure and flow—to explain the unfamiliar—*voltage* and *current*.

Throughout your writing, use analogy freely. It's one of your best bridges to the uninformed reader.

▶ CLASSIFICATION AND DIVISION

Classification and division, like chronological and topical arrangement, are useful devices for bringing order to any complex body of material. You may understand classification and division more readily if we explain them in terms of the *abstraction ladder*. We borrow this device from the semanticists—

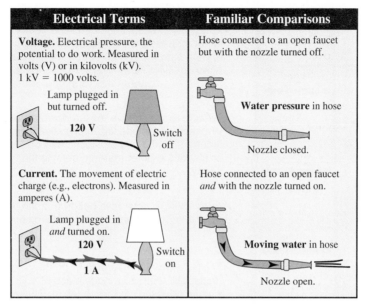

Electrical Terms	Familiar Comparisons
Voltage. Electrical pressure, the potential to do work. Measured in volts (V) or in kilovolts (kV). 1 kV = 1000 volts.	Hose connected to an open faucet but with the nozzle turned off.
Lamp plugged in but turned off. 120 V Switch off	**Water pressure** in hose Nozzle closed.
Current. The movement of electric charge (e.g., electrons). Measured in amperes (A).	Hose connected to an open faucet *and* with the nozzle turned on.
Lamp plugged in *and* turned on. 120 V Switch on 1 A	**Moving water** in hose Nozzle open.

Voltage produces an electric field and current produces a magnetic field.

FIGURE 9-2 • Visual Analogies
Source: U.S. Department of Energy, *Emf in the Workplace* (Washington, DC: DOE, 1996), 6.

people who make a scientific study of words. We construct the ladder in Figure 9-3 by beginning with a very abstract word on top and working down the ladder to end with a specific term.

While looking at Figure 9-3, keep one important distinction in mind: Even "John Smith's kitchen table" is not the table itself. As soon as we have used a word for an object, the abstraction process has begun. Beneath the word is the table *we see*; and beneath that is the table *itself*, consisting of paint, wood, and hardware that consist of molecules that consist of atoms and space.

In classification, you move *up* the abstraction ladder, seeking higher abstractions under which to group many separate items. In division, you move *down* the abstraction ladder, breaking down higher abstractions into the separate items contained within them. We will illustrate classification first.

Suppose for the moment that you are a dietitian. You are given a long list of foods found in a typical American home and asked to comment on the value of each. You are to give such information as calorie count, carbohydrate count, mineral content, fat content, vitamin content, and so forth. The list is as follows: onions, apples, steak, string beans, oranges, cheese, lamb chops, milk, corn flakes, lemons, bread, butter, hamburger, cupcakes, and carrots.

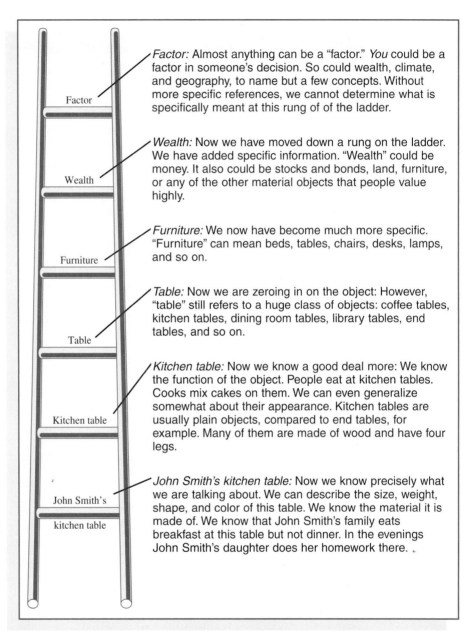

Factor: Almost anything can be a "factor." *You* could be a factor in someone's decision. So could wealth, climate, and geography, to name but a few concepts. Without more specific references, we cannot determine what is specifically meant at this rung of of the ladder.

Wealth: Now we have moved down a rung on the ladder. We have added specific information. "Wealth" could be money. It also could be stocks and bonds, land, furniture, or any of the other material objects that people value highly.

Furniture: We now have become much more specific. "Furniture" can mean beds, tables, chairs, desks, lamps, and so on.

Table: Now we are zeroing in on the object: However, "table" still refers to a huge class of objects: coffee tables, kitchen tables, dining room tables, library tables, end tables, and so on.

Kitchen table: Now we know a good deal more: We know the function of the object. People eat at kitchen tables. Cooks mix cakes on them. We can even generalize somewhat about their appearance. Kitchen tables are usually plain objects, compared to end tables, for example. Many of them are made of wood and have four legs.

John Smith's kitchen table: Now we know precisely what we are talking about. We can describe the size, weight, shape, and color of this table. We know the material it is made of. We know that John Smith's family eats breakfast at this table but not dinner. In the evenings John Smith's daughter does her homework there.

FIGURE 9-3 • Abstraction Ladder

   If you try to comment on each item in turn as it appears on the list, you will write a chaotic essay. You will repeat yourself far too often. Many of the things you say about milk will be the same things you say about cheese. To avoid this repetition and chaos you need to classify the list, to move up the abstraction ladder seeking groups like the following:

Food

Vegetables	*Cereal*	*Meat*
Onions	Corn flakes	Steak
String beans	Bread	Lamb chops
Carrots	Cupcakes	Hamburger
Fruit	*Dairy*	
Apples	Milk	
Oranges	Cheese	
Lemons	Butter	

By following this procedure, you can use the similarities and dissimilarities of the different foods to aid your organization, rather than having them disrupt it.

In division, you move down the abstraction ladder. Suppose your problem now is the reverse of the former one. You are a dietitian, and someone asks you to list examples of foods that a healthy diet should contain. In this case you start with the abstraction, *food*. You decide to divide this abstraction into smaller groups such as vegetables, fruit, meat, cereal, and dairy. You then subdivide these groups into typical examples such as cheese, milk, and butter for dairy. Obviously, the outline you could construct here might look precisely like the one already shown. But in classification, we arrived at the outline from the bottom up; in division, from the top down. Figure 9-4 shows the

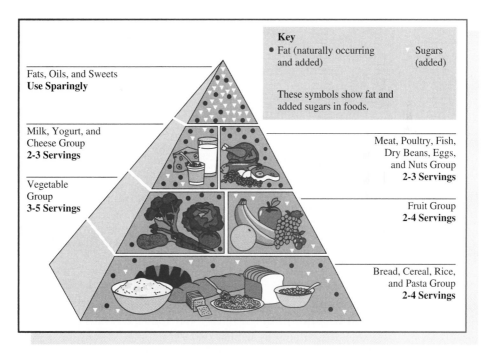

FIGURE 9-4 • The Food Guide Pyramid: An Example of Classification
Source: U.S. Department of Agriculture, *Making Healthy Food Choices* (Washington, DC: GPO, 1993), 2.

Food Guide Pyramid, an excellent example of classification and division in action.

Very definite rules apply in using classification and division.

1. **Keep all headings equal**. In the food classification example, you would not have the headings Meat, Dairy, Fruit, Cereal, and Green Vegetables, because Green Vegetables does not take in a whole class of food as the other headings do. Under the heading of Vegetables, however, you could have subheadings of Green Vegetables and Yellow Vegetables.

2. **Apply one rule of classification or division at a time**. In the example, the classification is done by food types. You would not in the same classification include headings *equal* to the food types for such subjects as Mineral Content and Vitamin Content. You could, however, include these as subheadings under the food types.

3. **Make each division or classification large enough to include a significant number of items**. In the example, you could have many equal major headings such as Green Vegetables, Yellow Vegetables, Beef Products, Lamb Products, Cheese Products, and so forth. In doing so, however, you would have over-classified or overdivided your subject. Some of the classifications would include only one item.

4. **Avoid overlapping classifications and divisions as much as possible**. In our example, if you had chosen a classification that included Fruits and Desserts, you would have created a problem for yourself. The listed fruits would have to go in both categories. You cannot always avoid overlap, but keep it to a minimum.

As you choose your classification and division strategies, keep your situational analysis in mind. In a brochure about controlling termites, the authors chose to classify them according to their habitat:

> Based on ecological considerations, three types of termites occur in the United States: (1) drywood, (2) dampwood, and (3) subterranean. Drywood termites build their nests in sound dry wood above ground. Dampwood species initially locate their nests in moist, decaying wood but can later extend tunnels into drier parts of wood. Subterranean termites are more dependent on an external moisture source, and they typically dwell in the soil and work through it to reach wood above ground.[8]

The authors chose to classify termites in this way because, as they put it, "this information provides a foundation for control methods based on the habits and behavior of the termites." Obviously, termites can be classified in many ways. Classifying by habitat seemed the best way to these authors in view of the brochure's purpose and the needs of the audience.

▶ DEFINITION

Everyone in a trade or a profession uses a specialized vocabulary that suits that occupation. Plumbers know the difference between a *globe valve* and a *gate valve*. Electrical engineers talk easily about *gamma rays* and *microelectronics*. Statisticians understand the mysteries of *chi-squared tests* and *one-way analyses of variance*. In fact, learning a new vocabulary is a major part of learning any trade or profession. Unfortunately, as you grow accustomed to using your specialized vocabulary, you may forget that others don't share your knowledge—your language may be incomprehensible to them. So, the first principle in understanding definition is to realize that you will have to do it frequently. You should define any term you think is not in your reader's normal vocabulary. The less expert your audience is, the more you will have to define. And sometimes, when you use a new specialized term or use an old term in a new way, you will even need to define for your fellow specialists.

Definitions range in length from a single word to long essays or even books. Sometimes, but not usually, a synonym inserted into your sentence will do, as in this example:

> The oil sump—*that is, the oil reservoir*—is located in the lower portion of the engine crankcase.

Synonym definition serves only when a common interchangeable word exists for some bit of technical vocabulary you wish to use.

Sentence Definitions

Most often you will want to use at least a one-sentence definition containing the elements of a logical definition:

> term = genus or class + differentia

Although you may not have heard of the elements of a logical definition, you have been giving and hearing definitions cast in the logical pattern most of your life. In the *logical definition*, you state that something is a member of some genus or class and then specify the differences that distinguish this thing from other members of the class. For instance:

Term	=	*Genus or Class*	+	*Differentia*
An ohmeter	is	an indicating instrument		that directly measures the resistance of an electrical circuit.

A legume   is   a fruit   formed from a single
carpel, splitting along
the dorsal and the
ventral sutures, and
usually containing a
row of seeds borne
on the inner side of
the ventral suture.

The second of these two definitions, particularly, points out a pitfall you must avoid. This definition of a legume would satisfy only someone who was already fairly expert in botany. Real lay people would be no further ahead than before, because the terms *carpel* and *dorsal and ventral sutures* are not familiar to them. When writing for nonexperts, you may wish to settle for a definition less precise but more understandable:

A legume is a fruit, such as a pea pod, formed of an easily split pod that contains a row of seeds.

Here you have stayed with plain language and given an easily recognized example. Both of these definitions of a legume are good. The one you would choose depends on your audience.

Extended Definitions

To make sure you are understood, you will often want to extend a definition beyond a single sentence. The most common techniques for extending a definition are description, example, and analogy. However, any of the arrangement techniques, such as chronology, topical order, classification, and division may be used. The following definition, from *Chambers*, a respected technical dictionary, goes beyond the logical definition to give a description:

anemometer. An instrument for measuring the velocity of the wind. A common type consists of four hemispherical cups carried at the ends of four radial arms pivoted so as to be capable of rotation in a horizontal plane, the speed of rotation being indicated on a dial calibrated to read wind velocity directly.

Our lay definition of legume gave an example: "such as a pea pod." Often analogy is valuable, as demonstrated by this comparison, from the same source.

A voltmeter is an indicating instrument for measuring electrical potential. It may be compared to a pressure gauge used in a pipe to measure water pressure.

The following definition of a hurricane is a good example of an extended definition intended for an intelligent lay audience. In it, the writer makes extensive use of both process and mechanism descriptions. Notice, also, that the writer begins by defining other terms needed in understanding hurricanes:

Defines related terms

A hurricane is defined as a rotating wind system that whirls counterclockwise in the northern hemisphere, forms over tropical water, and has sustained wind speeds of at least 74 miles/hour (119 km/hr). This whirling mass of energy is formed when circumstances involving heat and pressure nourish and nudge the winds over a large area of ocean to wrap themselves around an atmospheric low. Tropical cyclone is the term for all wind circulations rotating around an atmospheric low over tropical waters. A tropical storm is defined as a cyclone with winds from 39 to 73 mph, and a tropical depression is a cyclone with winds less than 39 mph.

Describes process

It is presently thought that many tropical cyclones originate over Africa in the region just south of the Sahara. They start as an instability in a narrow east-to-west jet stream that forms in that area between June and September as a result of the great temperature contrast between the hot desert and the cooler, more humid region to the south. Studies show that the disturbances generated over Africa have long lifetimes, and many of them cross the Atlantic. In the 20th century an average of 10 tropical cyclones each year whirl out across the Atlantic; six of these become hurricanes. The hurricane season is set as being June 1 through November 30. An "early" hurricane occurs in the 3 months before the season, and a "late" hurricane takes place in the 3 months after the season.

Describes mechanism

Hurricanes are well-organized. The 10-mile-thick inner spinning ring of towering clouds and rapid upper motion is defined as the hurricane's eyewall; it is here that the condensation and rainfall are intense and winds are most violent. Harbored within the eyewall is the calm eye of the hurricane—usually 10–20 miles across—protected from the inflowing winds and often free of clouds. Here, surface pressure drops to a minimum, and winds subside to less than 15 mph. Out beyond the eyewall, the hurricane forms into characteristic spiral rain bands, which are alternate bands of rain-filled clouds. In the typical hurricane, the entire spiral storm system is at least 1,000 miles across, with hurricane-force winds of 100 miles in diameter and gale-force winds of 400 miles in diameter. A typical hurricane liberates about 100 billion kilowatts of heat from the condensation of moisture, but only about 3% of the thermal energy is transferred into mechanical energy in the form of wind. Sustained wind speeds up to 200 mph have been measured, but winds of about 130 mph are more typical. It is estimated that an average hurricane produces 200 billion tons of water a day as rain.[9]

As this writer has done, extend your definition as far as is needed to ensure the level of reader understanding desired.

Placement of Definitions

You have several options for placement of definitions within your reports: (1) within the text itself, (2) in footnotes or endnotes, (3) in a glossary at the beginning or end of the paper, and (4) in an appendix. Which method you use depends on the audience and the length of the definition.

Within the Text If the definition is short—a sentence or two—or if you feel most of your audience needs the definition, place it in the text with the word defined, as in this example:

> Besides direct electric and magnetic induction, another source of power-frequency exposure is contact currents. Contact currents are the currents that flow into the body when physical contact is made between the body and a conducting object carrying an induced voltage. Examples of contact current situations include contacts with vehicles parked under transmission lines and contacts with the metal parts of appliances, such as the handle of a refrigerator.[10]

When you are using key terms that must be understood before the reader can grasp your subject, define them in your introduction.

In Footnotes and Endnotes If your definition is longer than a sentence or two and your audience is a mixed one—part expert and part lay—you may want to put your definition in a footnote at the bottom of the page or in an endnote at the end of your report. A lengthy definition placed in the text could disturb the expert who does not need it.

In a Glossary If you have many short definitions to give and if you have reason to believe that most members of your audience will not read your report straight through, place your definitions in a glossary (see Figure 9-5 and pages 617–618, 620). Glossaries do have a disadvantage: Your readers may be disturbed by the need to flip around in your paper to find the definition they need. When you use a glossary, be sure to draw your readers' attention to it, both in the table of contents and early in the discussion.

In an Appendix If you need one or more lengthy extended definitions (say, more than two hundred words each) for some but not all members of your audience, place them in an appendix (see pages 634–635). At the point in your text where readers may need the definitions, be sure to tell readers where they are.

▶ DESCRIPTION

In technical writing you will chiefly have to describe two things: mechanisms and processes. The two are closely related. That is, many mechanisms are performing a process of some sort—think of the engine in an automobile. In describing the mechanism, you necessarily describe the process it performs. Conversely, many processes use one or more mechanisms in performing the process.

Terms are printed in boldface.

When necessary, definitions are extended in complete sentences.

Grammatically parallel sentence fragments are used for definitions (see Parallelism in Appendix A).

GLOSSARY

Alternator—a device that supplies alternating current.

Anemometer—a device for measuring wind speed.

Crossflow turbine—a drum-shaped water turbine with blades fixed radially along the outer edge. The device is installed perpendicularly to the direction of stream flow.

DC-to-AC Inverter—a device that converts electrical current from direct to alternating.

FERC—The Federal Energy Regulatory Commission, established by Congress to regulate nonfederal hydroelectric projects.

Flow—the quantity of water, usually measured in gallons or cubic feet, flowing past a point in a given time.

Generator—a device that converts mechanical energy into electrical energy—a large number of conductors mounted on an armature that rotates in a magnetic field.

Head—the vertical height in feet from the headwater (with a dam) or where the water enters the intake (no dam) to where the water leaves the turbine.

Induction generator—an alternating current generator whose construction is identical to that of an AC motor.

Intake structure—a structure that diverts the water into the penstock; a small dam.

Isolation transformer—a device used to isolate the utility grid system from an earth-grounded electric generating system.

Net energy billing—an electric metering system in which the meter turns backwards when electricity flows from the generating system to the utility lines and forward when the utility is supplying electricity to the residence.

Pelton wheel—a water turbine in which the pressure of the water supply is converted to velocity by a few stationary nozzles, and the water jets then impinge on buckets mounted on the rim of the wheel.

Penstock—the pipe that carries pressurized water from the intake structure to the turbine.

Photovoltaic array—several photovoltaic modules connected together, usually mounted in a frame.

Photovoltaic module—several solar cells connected together on a flat surface.

PURPA—Public Utility Regulatory Act, a federal regulation requiring utilities to buy back power generated by small producers.

Solar easements—a written agreement with a person's neighbors that protects his/her access to the sun through the prohibition of any structures that might block their access.

Synchronous Inverter—a device that links the output from a wind generator to the power line and the domestic circuit. The varying voltage and frequency generated by the windmill is instantly converted to exactly the same type of electricity distributed by a utility's power grid.

FIGURE 9-5 • Definitions in a Glossary
Source: U.S. Department of Energy, *Homemade Electricity: An Introductory to Small-Scale Wind, Hydro, and Photovoltaic Systems* (Washington, DC: GPO, n.d.), 57.

Often, whether a description is labeled a mechanism or process description is a matter of purpose and emphasis. For example, the graphic in Figure 9-6 has as its purpose the description of the flat-plate collector and places its emphasis on the collector. The graphic in Figure 9-7, while it shows the mechanism, emphasizes the process the mechanism performs. Whether you are writing a mechanism or a process description, as always in technical writing, your goal should be to satisfy your purpose and the needs of your audience.

After explaining the use of visual language in description, we deal with the two types of description.

Visual Language

As Figures 9-6 and 9-7 illustrate, graphics play an important role in many mechanism and process descriptions. But, visual language plays its part also. The following brief description shows how a combination of analogy and a

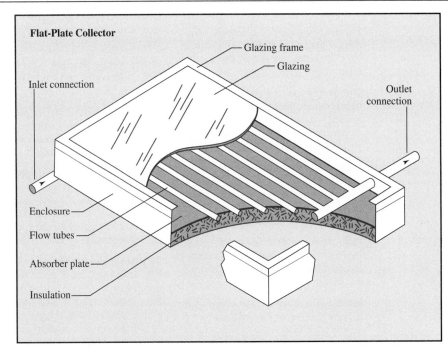

A flat-plate collector is an insulated, weatherproofed box containing a dark absorber plate. The plate heats up and transfers the heat to the fluid flowing through tubes in or near the absorber plate.

FIGURE 9-6 • Mechanism Description
Source: U.S. Department of Energy, *Solar Water Heating* (Washington, DC: DOE, 1996), 2.

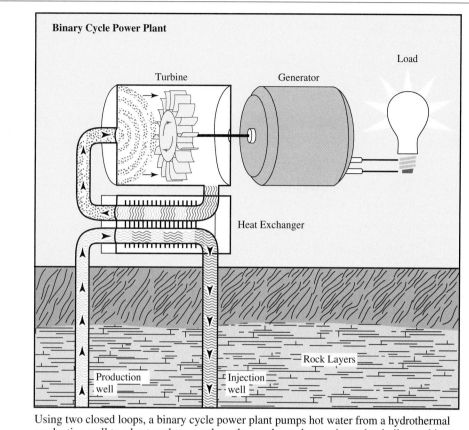

Binary Cycle Power Plant

Using two closed loops, a binary cycle power plant pumps hot water from a hydrothermal production well to a heat exchanger where the geothermal water is used to boil a working fluid. The resulting working-fluid vapor turns a turbine/generator that generates electricity. After passing through the heat exchanger, the geothermal water is returned to the reservoir via an injection well, and the working-fluid vapor is condensed and recirculated through the working-fluid loop.

FIGURE 9-7 • Process Description
Source: U.S. Department of Energy, *Geothermal Energy . . . Power from the Depths* (Washington, DC: DOE, 1997), 5.

few words indicating shape can help a reader accurately visualize a DNA molecule:

> DNA is a deceptively simple molecule, consisting of a series of subunits, called bases, linked together to form a double helix that can be visualized as an immensely long, corkscrew-shaped ladder. Each rung in the ladder is made up of two bases fitted together, and the ends of the rung are attached to chains of sugar-phosphates that are like the upright rails of a ladder.[11]

We visualize things in essentially five ways—by shape, size, color, texture, and position—and we have access to a wide range of terms to describe all five. In addition, comparison of the unfamiliar to the familiar through analogy is a powerful visualization tool.

Shape You can describe the shape of things with terms such as *cubical, cylindrical, circular, convex, concave, square, trapezoidal,* or *rectangular.* You can use simple analogies such as *C-shaped, L-shaped, Y-shaped, cigar-shaped, cork-screw,* or *spar-shaped.* You can describe things as *threadlike* or *pencil-like* or as *saw-toothed* or *football-shaped.*

Size You can give physical dimensions for size, but you can also compare objects to coins, paper clips, books, and football fields.

Color You can use familiar colors such as red and yellow and also, with some care, such descriptive terms as *pastel, luminous, dark, drab,* and *brilliant.*

Texture You have many words and comparisons at your disposal for texture, such as *pebbly, embossed, pitted, coarse, fleshy, honeycombed, glazed, sandpaper-like, mirrorlike,* and *waxen.*

Position You have *opposite, parallel, corresponding, identical, in front, behind, above, below, right, left, north, south,* and so forth to indicate position.

Analogy The use of analogy will aid your audience in visualizing the thing described. In the following example, a simple comparison to a balloon (which we have set in boldface) helps the reader visualize the swelling of a volcano before eruption:

> As magma enters the shallow summit reservoir, the volcano undergoes swelling or *inflation* (**a process similar to the stretching of a balloon being filled with air**). This swelling in turn causes changes in the shape of the volcano's surface. During inflation, the slope or *tilt* of the volcano increases, and reference points (benchmarks) on the volcano are uplifted relative to a stable point and move further apart from one another. For Hawaiian volcanoes, pre-eruption inflation generally is slow and gradual, lasting for weeks to years. However, once eruption begins, the shrinking or *deflation* typically occurs rapidly as pressure on the magma reservoir is relieved—**a process not unlike deflating a balloon.** During deflation, changes in tilt and in vertical horizontal distances between benchmarks are opposite to those during inflation.[12]

Mechanism Description

The physical description of some mechanism is perhaps the most common kind of technical description. It is a commonplace procedure with little mystery attached to it.

For example, the description of a plumber's snake on page 174 demonstrates most of the techniques of good technical description. It does all the following:

- Describes the overall appearance of the plumber's snake and names the material it is made of—steel.
- Divides the mechanism into its component parts—cable, boring head, and crank.
- Describes the appearance of the parts, gives their functions, and explains how they work together.
- Points out an important implication, a *so-what*, of one of the descriptive facts: "It's about ten inches long, *so you can get both hands on it.*"
- Gives only information important in this description. For example, because it is of no consequence in this description, you are not told the color of the mechanism.
- Uses figurative language—such as *springlike* and *football-shaped*—and comparisons to familiar objects—such as pencils, snakes, and drills—to clarify and shorten the description.

Planning Despite certain elements that most mechanism descriptions have in common, there is no formula for writing them. You must use your judgment, weighing such matters as purpose and audience. As you plan your mechanism description, you'll need to answer questions like these

- **What is the purpose of the description?**
- **Why will the intended reader read the description?**
- **What are the purpose and function of the mechanism?**
- **How can the mechanism be divided?**
- **What are the purpose and function of the parts?**
- **How do the parts work together?**
- **How can the parts be divided? Is it necessary to do so?**
- **What are the purpose and function of the subparts?**
- **Which of the following are important for understanding the mechanism and its parts and subparts:**
    - **Construction?**
    - **Materials?**
    - **Appearance?**
    - **Size?**
    - **Shape?**
    - **Color?**
    - **Texture?**
    - **Position?**
- **Are there any so-whats that you need to express explicitly for the reader?**

- **Would the use of graphics aid the reader?**
- **Would analogies clarify the description for the reader?**

The answers to those questions will largely determine how you arrange your description and the details you elect to provide your readers.

Examples of Mechanism Descriptions In Figure 9-8, the annotations draw your attention to the various features of a mechanism description, as exemplified in the descriptive overview of the Hubble Space Telescope. Figure 9-9 is one of several graphics that accompany the telescope's description. As Figure 9-9 demonstrates, such graphics are frequently labeled and are shown cutaway, to display the interior of the mechanism described.

Many of the principles of mechanism description have nonmechanical applications. For example, we don't usually think of skin as a mechanism, but the same rational principles we have been discussing are found in the passage in Figure 9-10 about skin. The subject is divided, objective physical details are described, function is discussed, so-whats are given, and a graphic is provided.

Process Description

Process description is probably the chief use of chronological order in technical writing. By process we mean a sequence of events that progresses from a beginning to an end and results in a change or a product. The process may be humanly controlled—such as the manufacture of an automobile—or it may be natural—the metamorphosis of a caterpillar to a butterfly, for example.

Process descriptions are written in one of two ways:

- **For the doer**—to provide instructions for performing the process.
- **For the interested observer**—to provide an understanding of the process.

A cake recipe provides a good example of instructions for performing a process. You are told when to add the milk to the flour, when to reserve the whites of the eggs for later use. You are instructed to grease the pan *before* you pour the batter in, and so forth. Writing good instructions is an important application of technical writing, and we have devoted all of Chapter 18 to it. In this chapter we focus on the second type of process description—providing an understanding of the process.

Verb Tense, Mood, and Voice In writing process description, it's important to make the correct choice between present and past tense and to decide which voice and mood to use.

The Hubble Space Telescope is just over 13 meters (43 feet) long and 4 meters (14 feet) in diameter, about the size of a bus or tanker truck. Upright, it is a five-story tower; carried inside the Space Shuttle for the trip to orbit, it fills the payload bay.

The Hubble Space Telescope is made up of three major elements: the Optical Telescope Assembly, the focal plane scientific instruments, and the Support Systems Module, which is divided into four sections, stacked together like canisters:

Aperture Door and Light Shield: protecting the scientific instruments from light of the sun, Earth, and moon and also from contamination

Forward Shell: enclosing the Optical Telescope Assembly mirrors

Equipment Section: girdling the telescope to supply power, communications, pointing and control, and other necessary resources

Aft Shroud: covering the five focal plane instruments and the three fine guidance sensors

Solar energy arrays and communications antennas are attached to the exterior shell. Doors allow astronauts to remove instruments and components from the equipment bays. Handrails and sockets for portable foot restraints attached to the external surface aid the astronauts in performing maintenance and repair tasks.

Space Telescope Vital Statistics

Length:	13.1 m (43.5 ft)
Diameter:	4.27 m (14.0 ft)
Weight:	11,000 kg (25,500 lb)
Focal Ratio:	f/24

Primary Mirror

Diameter:	2.4 m (94.5 in)
Weight:	826 kg (1,825 lb)
Reflecting Surface:	Ultra-low expansion glass covered by aluminum with magnesium-fluoride coating

Secondary Mirror

Diameter:	0.3 m (12 in)
Weight:	12.3 kg (27.4 lb)
Reflecting Surface:	Ultra-low expansion glass covered by aluminum with magnesium-fluoride coating

Systems

	Optical Telescope Assembly
	Support Systems Module
	Focal Plane Science Instruments
	Wide Field/Planetary Camera
	Faint Object Camera
	Faint Object Spectrograph
	Goddard High Resolution Spectrograph
	High Speed Photometer
	Fine Guidance Sensors (for astrometry)
Data Rate:	Up to 1 mbps

Margin notes:

Description by size and analogy

Division of telescope into its component parts

Functions of key subdivisions of Support Systems Module

Miscellaneous details

Lists for ease of reference

FIGURE 9-8 • Mechanism Description of the Hubble Space Telescope
Source: National Aeronautics and Space Administration, *Exploring the Universe with the Hubble Space Telescope* (Washington, DC: GPO, n.d.), 57.

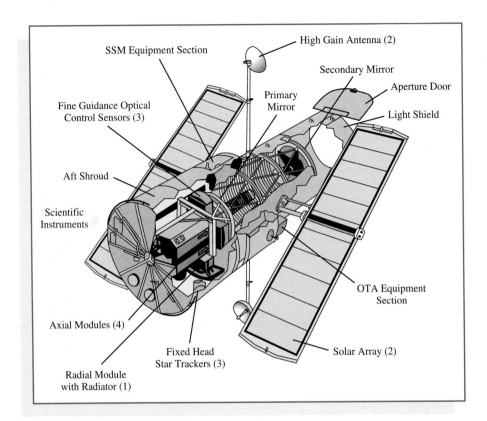

FIGURE 9-9 • Graphic for the Hubble Space Telescope
Source: National Aeronautics and Space Administration, *Exploring the Universe with the Hubble Space Telescope* (Washington, DC: GPO, n.d.), 58.

Processes that are ongoing are usually described in the present tense, as if each step were unfolding before the reader's eyes (we have set the verbs in boldface):

Blood from the body **enters** the upper chamber, atrium, on the right side of the heart and **flows** from there into the lower chamber, the ventricle. The ventricle **pumps** the blood under low pressure into the lungs where it **releases** carbon dioxide and **picks** up oxygen.

Completed processes that have already occurred in the past are usually described in the past tense. In empirical research reports, for example, the researcher describes the procedures that were followed in past tense (verbs in boldface):

During the excavation delay we **accomplished** two tasks. First, we **installed** a temporary intake structure and **tested** the system's efficiency. Second, we **designed**, **built**, and **installed** a new turbine and generator.

Skin

Function

Division into parts

The skin is the protective covering of the body. The epidermis, the outer layer of skin, contains no blood vessels or nerves. The layer of skin below the epidermis is the dermis. The dermis contains the blood vessels, nerves, and specialized structures such as sweat glands, which help to regulate body temperature, and hair follicles. The fat and soft tissue layer below the dermis is called subcutaneous fat tissue (Figure 1-3). The skin is one of the most important organs of the body. The loss of a large part of the skin will result in death unless it can be replaced.

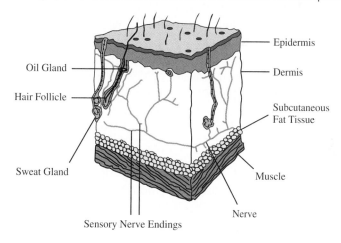

Figure 1–3. Skin.

Function

The protective functions of the skin are many. Skin is watertight and keeps internal fluids in while keeping germs out. A system of nerves in the skin carries information to the brain. These nerves transmit information about pain, external pressure, heat, cold, and the relative position of various parts of the body.

Skin provides information to the first aider concerning the victim's condition. For example, pale, sweaty skin may indicate shock.

FIGURE 9-10 • Skin Described as a Mechanism
Source: U.S. Department of Labor, *First Aid Book* (Washington, DC: GPO, 1993), 9.

In writing instructions, you will commonly use the active voice and the imperative mood:

Clean the threads on the new section of pipe. **Add** pipe thread compound to the outside threads.

In following your instructions, the reader, after all, is the doer. With its implied *you*, the imperative voice directly addresses the reader. But in a process description written for understanding, which will be read by a reader who is not the doer, the use of imperative mood would be inappropriate and even misleading.

In writing a process description for understanding, therefore, you will ordinarily use the indicative mood in both active and passive voice:

> Active voice: The size of the cover opening **controls** the rate of evaporation.
> Passive voice: The rate of evaporation **is controlled** by the size of the cover opening.

In active voice, the subject does the action. In passive voice, the subject receives the action. Use of the passive emphasizes the receiver of the action while de-emphasizing, or removing completely, the doer of the action. (Incidentally, as the preceding examples illustrate, neither doer nor receiver has to be a human being or even an animate object.) When the doer is unimportant or not known, you should choose passive voice. Conversely, when the doer is known and important, you should choose the active voice. Because the active is often the simpler, more direct statement of an idea, choose passive voice only when it's clearly indicated. We have more to say on this subject on pages 92–93.

Examples of Process Description As with all technical writing, you can write process descriptions for varied audiences. In the following excerpt, the writer describes how a star like our sun derives energy from fusion, until eventually it depletes its sources and destroys itself. The intended audience is educated lay persons. The writer uses present tense throughout and, predominantly, the active voice.

Overview of process

In their hot, high-pressure and high-density interiors, stars produce energy through the fusion of low-mass atomic nuclei to high-mass nuclei. In normal stars like the Sun, hydrogen nuclei are joined together to make helium, in a process that liberates large amounts of energy.

Description of process

A star like the Sun can persist in its normal state, deriving energy from the fusion of hydrogen to helium, for some 10 billion years. Upon the inevitable depletion of its internal, hydrogen-based energy source, a star proceeds through more advanced evolutionary stages in which it converts successively more massive nuclear species into yet higher mass nuclei, to satisfy its needs for energy and prevent collapse under the influence of its strong self-gravity. After converting hydrogen to helium, it proceeds to convert the helium to carbon and oxygen, then to silicon-like nuclei, and so on, until, in the more massive stars, the nuclear fusion products approach the mass of iron nuclei. Beyond this point, no further energy can be extracted by building nuclei of increasing mass. Atomic nuclei with masses near that of iron are the most stable of nuclei; conversion of these nuclei to other species, through either nuclear fusion or nuclear fission, requires not the extraction of energy but the injection of energy.

Having depleted all its nuclear energy sources, a star begins to cool and can no longer resist the pull of its own gravity. In the more massive stars, we believe that this process leads to a sudden catastrophic collapse. The gravitational collapse of the star's interior is thought to release a large amount of energy which, flowing from the star, blows the star's outer layers away into space, to disperse and mix with the interstellar matter. At the same time, the exploding material in the ensuing supernova explosion is compressed and heated to the point that fast nuclear reactions occur, resulting in a buildup of very massive atomic nuclei, which are dispersed with the star's outer layers into the preexisting interstellar matter.[13]

In writing process descriptions to provide understanding, you'll find that extensive detail is not always necessary or even desirable. As in mechanism description, the amount of detail you give relates to the technical level and technical interests of your readers. When *Time* magazine, for example, publishes an article about open-heart surgery, its readers do not expect complete details on how such an operation is performed. Rather, they expect their curiosity to be satisfied in a general way. The author of the description of a star's fusion process used a level of detail he felt would satisfy his lay audience.

The words and graphic in Figure 9-11 describe the process by which a dry steam power plant operates. The intended readers are business owners who might be considering installing a new power plant. The language is simple, and the level of detail is meant to satisfy the needs of a lay audience.

Figure 9-12 shows a process description written for an executive audience. It deals with shipworms, marine organisms that attack wood immersed in salt water. As with the description written for a lay audience, the writer has chosen her level of detail carefully. As you read it, notice that no attempt is made to give the full information about shipworms that an entomologist might desire. We don't learn, for example, how shipworms reproduce, nor do we even learn very clearly what they look like. For the intended readers of the letter, such information is not needed. They do need to know what is presented—the process by which shipworms lodge on the wood and how they bore into it. The readers do need to know that the damage done by shipworms is largely invisible from the exterior of the wood and, finally, that they must take action and what that action has to be.

Empirical research reports written for experts use process description to describe the *methods* used by the researcher. Writers of such reports must include enough detail about their methods to allow their fellow experts to duplicate the research. Because of that requirement, the level of detail in an expert report is normally much higher than that in a lay or executive report. The writer, having an expert audience, uses technical language freely. The following excerpt is the method section from a report of research that tested

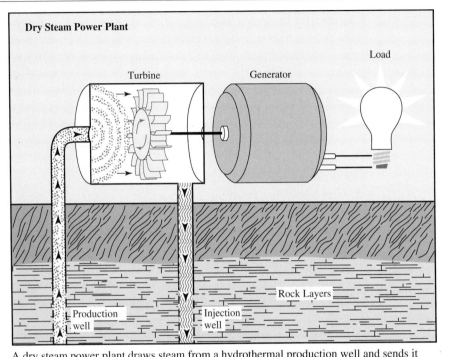

Dry Steam Power Plant

A dry steam power plant draws steam from a hydrothermal production well and sends it to a turbine/generator. The steam turns the turbine to generate electricity and is then condensed and returned to the geothermal reservoir via an injection well.

FIGURE 9-11 • Process Description
Source: U.S. Department of Energy, *Geothermal Energy . . . Power from the Depths* (Washington, DC: DOE, 1997), 4.

whether students taught to revise globally would revise better than those who were not. (To *revise globally* means to deal with such things as purpose, organization, and audience, as opposed to dealing with only surface things such as spelling and grammar.)

The study was conducted in two writing classes during the ninth week of a sixteen-week semester. Half of the students in each class were randomly assigned to the treatment group; the other half served as the control group. The mean SAT verbal score for the control group (532.2) was slightly higher than that for the treatment group (514.4); however, a *t*-test revealed that the difference between these means was not significant.

After giving brief instructions about the nature of the study, an experimenter (not the instructor for the course) asked the students in the control group to go with another experimenter to a nearby room to complete the experiment. The experimenters read the same brief instructions to both the treatment and control

Marine Consultants
42 Oceanside Avenue
East Hampton, NY 11515
(631) 286-3563

Fax (631) 286-2249

17 July 2001

Mr. Avery Brandisi
Chief Executive Officer
Maritime Transport Inc.
864 Third Avenue
New York, NY 10022

Dear Mr. Brandisi:

We have as you requested examined the condition of the pilings that support the Maritime Transport East River pier. The pilings show only minor shipworm damage. However, because of the high probability that your pilings will suffer further shipworm damage if not protected, we recommend that you take action as soon as possible.

Shipworms are mollusks that bore into submerged wood and do extensive damage to it. The shipworms, so called because when fully grown they resemble worms, begin life as small organisms looking for a place to lodge. When a shipworm comes to rest on wood, it changes into a wormlike animal with a pair of shells on its head. Using these shells, the shipworm bores its way into the wood. As the head bores in, the end of the wormlike body remains at the entrance hole. The shipworm lives on the wood borings and the organisms in the seawater it passes through itself.

Although shipworms may reach lengths up to four feet, the entrance hole remains the same size. Thus, the wood can be completely honeycombed with shipworms and except for small entrance holes look perfectly sound. This is what can happen to your pilings, if they are not properly treated.

Ironically, your firm and many other waterside businesses in New York harbor are victims of the progress made in cleansing the water in the harbor. When the harbor was polluted, it would not support most marine animals, including shipworms. In the now relatively clear water of the harbor, shipworms have returned and are causing major damage that will take millions of dollars to repair.

Either sheathing or chemical treatment would offer your pilings a good measure of protection. If you like, we can help you choose the best treatment and recommend reputable contractions to do the work.

Sincerely,

Mary Chen

Mary Chen
Consulting Entomologist

FIGURE 9-12 • Executive Process Description

groups. These task instructions [not included in this quoted excerpt] informed students that they would have 30 minutes to revise a short text about the operation of a water treatment plant so that it could be used as a handout for high school students who tour the plant. The instructions specifically cued students to revise so that the handout would be "clear, organized, easy to read, and free of errors." The instructions also directed students to mark deletions, additions, changes, and movements of text in standard ways such that a typist could easily retype their revised texts.

After reading the instructions and asking for questions, the experimenters reminded the students that they had 30 minutes to complete their revisions and instructed them to begin. The students were informed when they had 15 minutes and 5 minutes remaining. For each of the treatment and control groups, the procedure was completed within the 50-minute class period.

Procedures for the two groups were identical except that an experimenter presented eight additional minutes of instruction to the treatment group. The eight minutes taken for the special instruction of the experimental groups was approximately equal to the time it took to change rooms for the control groups.

The purpose of this instruction was to cue students to revise globally by illustrating how an expert writer and a novice writer revised a similar text. The experimenter illustrated differences between the revision activities of the expert and the novice writers using overhead transparencies. First, he explained the differences in basic approach and procedure—the expert writer read through the entire text to identify major problems and then focused on improving the whole text. In contrast, the novice writer began making changes immediately and proceeded to search through the text for local errors.

After this overview, the experimenter illustrated differences in the amount and types of changes that the two writers made using transparencies of the two writers' actual revisions of the sample text. The transparencies illustrated that the expert writer not only made more revisions but made different kinds of revisions. The effect was rather dramatic: while the novice writer limited himself to eliminating spelling, wordiness, and grammar errors, the expert writer also addressed global issues, adding an initial purpose statement, selecting and deleting information for the specified audience, reorganizing the text, and providing explicit cues to the new overall organization.[14]

Given the premises on which this book is based, we are pleased to report that the students taught to revise globally revised more successfully than those who were not. For more information about writing method sections in empirical research reports, see pages 494–495.

Planning As with writing mechanism descriptions, there are no easy formulas to follow in writing process descriptions. You must exercise a good deal of judgment in the matter. As in all writing, you must decide what your audience needs to know to satisfy its purpose and yours. However, the following questions should provide guidance to aid you in exercising your judgment:

- What is the purpose of the description?
- Why will the reader read the description?
- What is the reader's level of experience and knowledge regarding the process?
- What is the purpose of the process
- Who or what performs the process?
- What are the major steps of the process?
- Can the major steps be broken down into substeps?
- Are there graphics and analogies that would help the reader?

▶ PLANNING AND REVISION CHECKLISTS

You will find the planning and revision checklists that follow Chapter 2, Composing, and Chapter 4, Writing for Your Readers, valuable in planning and revising any presentation of technical information. The following checklists specifically apply to organizational strategies. As well as aiding in planning and revision, they summarize the key points in this chapter.

CHRONOLOGICAL ARRANGEMENT

Planning

- Do you have a reason to narrate a series of events? Historical overview? Background information? Drama and human interest for a lay audience? Forecast of future events?
- What are the key events in the series?
- In what order do the key events occur?
- Do you know or can you find out an accurate timing of the events?
- How much detail does your audience need or want?
- Will graphics help?

Revision

- Is your sequence of events in proper order?
- Are all your time references accurate?
- Have you provided sufficient guidance within your narrative so that your readers always know where they are in the sequence?

- Is your level of detail appropriate to your purpose and the purpose and needs of your audience?
- Did you use graphics?

TOPICAL ARRANGEMENT

Planning

- What is your major topic?
- What is your purpose?
- What is your audience's interest in your topic? How do their interest and purpose relate to your purpose?
- Given your purpose and your audience's purpose, how can you limit your topic? What subtopics are appropriate to your purpose and your audience's purpose? Can you divide your subtopics further?

Revision

- Do your topics and subtopics meet your purpose and your audience's purpose and interests?
- Did you limit your subject sufficiently so that you can provide specific facts and examples?
- Do you have headings? Do your headings accurately reflect how your reader will approach your subject matter? Are your headings phrased as questions? If not, would it help your readers if they were?

EXEMPLIFICATION

Planning

- Do your generalizations need the support of examples?
- Do you have or can you get examples that will lend interest and credibility to your document?

Revision

- Have you left any generalizations unsupported? If so, have you missed a chance to interest and convince your readers?
- Have you provided sufficient examples to give interest and credibility to your material?

ANALOGY

Planning

- What is your audience's level of understanding of your subject matter?
- Would the use of analogy provide your readers with a better understanding of your subject matter?
- Are there things familiar to your readers that you can compare to the unfamiliar concept—for example, water pressure to voltage?
- Will graphics help?

Revision

- Have you provided analogies wherever they will help reader understanding?
- Do your analogies really work? Are the things compared truly comparable?
- Did you use graphics?

CLASSIFICATION AND DIVISION

Planning

- Where is your subject on the abstraction ladder? Are you moving up the ladder, seeking higher abstractions under which you can group your subject matter (classification)? Are you moving down the ladder, breaking your abstractions down into more specific items (division)?
- What is your purpose in discussing your subject matter?
- What is your audience's purpose and relationship to your subject matter?
- What classification or division will best meet your purpose and your audience's needs?
- Will graphics help?

Revision

- Are all the parts of your classification equal?
- Have you applied one rule of classification and division at a time?
- Is each classification or division large enough to include a significant number of items?
- Have you avoided overlapping classifications and divisions?
- Does your classification or division meet your purpose and your audience's needs?
- Did you use graphics?

DEFINITION

Planning

- Do your readers share the vocabulary you are using in your report? Or do you need to make a list of the words you need to define?
- Do any of the words on your list have readily available synonyms known to your readers?
- Which words will require sentence definitions? Which words are so important to your purpose that they need extended definitions?
- How will you extend your definition? Description? Example? Analogy? Chronology? Topical order? Classification? Division? Graphics? Are there words within your definition that you need to define?
- Does everyone in your audience need your definitions? How long are your definitions? How many definitions do you have?
- Where can you best put your definitions? Within the text? In footnotes? In a glossary? In an appendix?
- Will graphics help?

Revision

- In your sentence definitions, have you put your term into its class accurately? Have you specified enough differences so that your readers can distinguish your term from other terms in the same class?
- Will your readers understand all the terms you have used in your definitions?
- Have you used analogy and graphics to help your readers? If not should you?
- Does the placement of your definitions suit the needs of your audience and the nature of the definitions?
- Did you use graphics?

MECHANISM DESCRIPTION

Planning

- What is the purpose of the description?
- Why will the intended reader read the description?
- What are the purpose and function of the mechanism?
- How can the mechanism be divided?
- What are the purpose and function of the parts?
- How do the parts work together?

- How can the parts be divided? Is it necessary to do so?
- What are the purpose and function of the subparts?
- Which of the following are important for understanding the mechanism and its parts and subparts: Construction? Materials? Appearance? Size? Shape? Color? Texture? Position?
- Are there any so-whats that you need to express explicitly for the reader?
- Will analogies clarify the description for the reader?
- Will graphics help?

Revision

- Does your description fulfill your purpose?
- Does the level of detail in your description suit the needs and interests of your readers?
- Have you made the function of the mechanism clear?
- Have you divided the mechanism sufficiently?
- Do your descriptive language and analogies clarify the description?
- Have you clarify stated your so-whats?
- Did you use graphics? If so, are they sufficiently annotated?

PROCESS DESCRIPTION

Planning

- What is the purpose of the description?
- Why will the reader read the description?
- What is the reader's level of experience and knowledge regarding the process?
- What is the purpose of the process?
- Who or what performs the process?
- What are the major steps of the process?
- Do the major steps break down into sub-steps?
- Are there graphics and analogies?

Revision

- Does your description fulfill your purpose?
- Does your description suit the needs and interests of your readers?
- Have you chosen the correct tense—either past or present?
- Have you chosen either active or passive voice appropriately?
- Are the major steps of the process clear?
- Have you provided enough graphics? Are your graphics sufficiently annotated?

▶ EXERCISES

1. Write a memo to an executive. The purpose of the memo is to inform the executive about the subject matter of the memo. Base the arrangement of the memo on one of the techniques described in this chapter. With your memo include a short explanation of why you chose the arrangement technique you did. Your explanation must show how your purpose and your reader's purpose and interests led to your choice. For instruction on the format of memos, see Letter and Memorandum Format, Appendix B.

2. Write a chronological narrative of several paragraphs that is intended to serve as a historical overview. Choose as a subject for your narrative some significant event in your professional field. Accompany your narrative with a description of your audience and an explanation of how their purpose and yours led you to the level of detail you use in your narrative.

3. Write an analogy several paragraphs long that will make some complicated concept in your discipline comprehensible to a fourth-grade student.

4. Write an extended definition of some term in your academic discipline. Use a graphic if it will aid the reader. In a paragraph separate from your definition, explain to your instructor your purpose and audience.

5. Write a description of some mechanism in your field. If you have no mechanisms in your field, choose three common household tools—such as a can opener, vegetable scraper, screwdriver, carpenter's level, or saw—and write a one-paragraph description of each. Include at least one graphic as a part of each description. In a paragraph separate from your description explain to your instructor your purpose and audience.

6. Write two versions of a process description intended to provide an understanding of a process. The first version is for a lay audience whose interest will be chiefly curiosity. The second version is for either an expert or an executive audience that has a professional need for the knowledge. The process might be humanly controlled—for instance, buying and selling stocks, writing computer programs, fighting forest fires, giving cobalt treatments, or creating legislation. It could be the

manufacture of some product—paint, plywood, aspirin, digital watches, maple syrup, fertilizer, extruded plastic. Or you might choose to write about a natural process—thunderstorm development, capillary action, digestion, tree growth, electron flow, hiccuping, the rising of bread dough. In a separate paragraph accompanying each version, explain to your instructor how your situational analysis guided your strategy.

SCENARIO

You and Ms. Cranshaw, your college career placement counselor, are discussing how to write an application letter.

"What's the point of the letter?" Ms. Cranshaw asks.

"To let them know, I'd like to work for them," you say.

"That's obvious, but what's the real point of your letter?"

"I guess that they should hire me."

"You're getting close." Ms. Cranshaw says. "But why should they hire you?"

"Well, because I would fit into the company well. I can do the kinds of things they do."

"Is that a fact or an opinion?" Ms. Cranshaw asks.

"I guess it's an opinion," you say.

"Right, and what do you need to support opinions?" Ms. Cranshaw asks.

"Facts, in this case, facts about what I have studied and what I have done and can do," you say.

"Now, we're on target," Ms. Cranshaw says. "A letter of application is like any argument. You have to have a clear idea of what your purpose is, gather the facts you need to support that purpose, present those facts in a logical format, and make sure your conclusion is obvious—inescapable, if you can manage that."

Arguments are everywhere in technical writing, from letters of application to proposals to the analysis sections of research reports. This chapter lays the groundwork for organizing those arguments logically and presenting them well.

chapter 10

Analyzing Information

▶ Classical Argument
Major Proposition
Minor Propositions and Evidence
Organization

▶ Pro and Con

▶ Induction and Deduction
Induction
Deduction
Logical Fallacies

▶ Comparison
Alternatives
Criteria

▶ Toulmin Logic
Applying Toulmin Logic
Arranging Your Arguments for Readers

Analytical reports are common in technical writing. We describe four types in Part III, Applications: proposals, progress reports, recommendation reports, and empirical research reports. Other types are evaluation reports, environmental impact statements, and economic justification reports. No matter what label is given to an analytical report, and no matter what its format, it has one thing in common with all other analytical reports: It goes beyond the facts to reach a conclusion or conclusions. You may, further, base recommendations, decisions, and actions on your conclusions.

A fact is by definition something known with certainty, something that can be objectively verified. Conclusions, by contrast, are opinions. We have more confidence in some opinions than others, but, again by definition, we can never know an opinion with the absolute certainty of a fact. Because they are opinions, conclusions based on insufficient or ill-organized facts are not convincing.

What you have learned in Chapter 9, Presenting Information, will help you organize the information you use in your analyses. In the following excerpt, the authors use exemplification (see pages 178–179) to support their opinion that Southeast wetlands play an integral role in the region's quality of life.

> Southeast wetlands play an integral role in the region's quality of life—maintaining water quality and quantity, supporting diverse and plentiful fish and wildlife habitat, and providing economic livelihood and recreation for millions of people.
>
> A few specific examples of the contribution of wetlands to the region are noted here.
>
> A single 2,300-acre Georgia floodplain wetland naturally provides pollution control benefits worth an estimated $1 million each year (Wharton 1970). The 552,000-acre Green Swamp complex northeast of Tampa, Florida, stores water for eventual aquifer recharge with an estimated value of $25 million annually (Brown 1984). The value of standing timber in southern wetland forests has been estimated at $8 billion (Tiner 1984).
>
> The wetlands of the Gulf Coast from Alabama to Louisiana provide winter habitat for more than 400,000 geese and three million ducks (Mississippi Flyway Council 1991). Louisiana is second only to Alaska in volume of commercial fishery landings with a harvest of over 1.2 billion pounds, with a value of $264 million in 1989 (National Marine Fisheries Service 1991). Louisiana's catch is made up primarily of wetland-dependent species such as brown shrimp, white shrimp, blue crab, seatrout and spot (Gosselink 1984).
>
> Freshwater fishes of the region also depend on wetlands. For example, 53 species of fish are known to use flooded bottomland hardwood wetlands during their life cycles (Wharton et al. 1981).

Wetlands provide the region with a variety of recreational opportunities as well. In 1985 alone, more than two million people fished Florida's fresh waters. Nearly one million people each year visit Everglades National Park, America's largest wetland park and a designated Wetland of International Importance (Ramsar Convention Bureau).[1]

This chapter is designed to aid you in reaching sound opinions and in presenting them convincingly. To meet these goals, we introduce five methods of analysis: classical argument, pro and con argument, induction and deduction, comparison, and Toulmin logic.

▶ CLASSICAL ARGUMENT

In argument, you deal with opinions that lie somewhere on a continuum between verifiable fact and pure subjectivity. Verifiable fact does not require argument. If someone says a room is thirty-five feet long and you disagree, you don't need an argument, you need a tape measure. Pure subjectivity cannot be argued. If someone hates the taste of spinach, you will not convince him or her otherwise with argument. The opinions dealt with in argument may be called propositions, premises, claims, conclusions, theses, or hypotheses, but under any name they remain opinions. Your purpose in argument is to convince your audience of the probability that the opinions you are advancing are correct.

Typically, an argument supports one major opinion, often called the major proposition. In turn, the major proposition is supported by a series of minor propositions. Minor propositions, like major propositions, are opinions, but generally they are nearer on the continuum to verifiable fact. Finally, the minor propositions are supported by verifiable facts and frequently also by statements from recognized authorities.

To understand how you might construct an argument, imagine for the moment that you are the waste management expert in an environmental consulting firm. Land developers constructing a new housing subdivision called Hawk Estates have turned to your firm for advice. Hawk Estates, like many such new subdivisions, is being built close to, but not in, a city called Colorful Springs. The problem at issue is whether Hawk Estates should build its own sewage disposal plant or tap into the sewage system of Colorful Springs. (The developers have already ruled out individual septic tanks because Hawk Estates is built on nonabsorbent clay soil.) Colorful Springs will allow the tap-in. You have investigated the situation and thought about it a good deal, and you have decided that the tap-in is the most desirable alternative. The land developers are not convinced. It's their money, so you must write a report to convince them.

Major Proposition

In developing your argument, it helps to use a chart like the one in Figure 10-1. The chart is a way of clearly separating and organizing your major proposition, minor propositions, and evidence. First, you must state your major proposition: Hawk Estates should tap into the sewage system of the city of Colorful Springs.

Minor Propositions and Evidence

Now you must support your major proposition. Clearly, your most relevant minor proposition is that Colorful Springs' sewage system can handle Hawk

Major Proposition	Minor Proposition	Evidence
Hawk Estates should tap into sewage system of Colorful Springs.	Colorful Springs can handle Hawk Estates sewage	• Estimate of waste from Hawk Estates • City engineer's statement that Colorful Springs can handle estimated waste
	Overall cost to Hawk Estates taxpayers only slightly higher if tapped into Colorful Springs	• Initial cost of plant vs. cost of tap-in • Yearly fee charged by Colorful Springs vs. operating cost of sewage lagoon • Cost per individual taxpayer
	Proposed plant, a sewage lagoon, will be a nuisance to homeowners	• Well-maintained lagoons okay • Lagoons hard to maintain, often small bad, experts say • Lagoon has to be located upwind of development

FIGURE 10-1 • Argument Arrangement Chart

Estates' waste. Questions of cost, convenience, and so forth would be irrelevant if Colorful Springs could not furnish adequate support, so you lead off with this proposition. To support it, you give the estimated amount of waste that will be produced by Hawk Estates, followed by a statement from the Colorful Springs city engineer that the city system can handle this amount of waste.

The minor proposition that the overall cost to Hawk Estates taxpayers will be only slightly more if they are tapped into the city rather than having their own plant is a difficult one. It's actually a rebuttal of your argument, but you must deal with it for several reasons. First and foremost, you must be ethical and honest with the developers. Second, it would be poor strategy not to be. Should they find that you have withheld information from them, it would cast doubt on your credibility. You decide to put this proposition second in your argument. In that way you can begin and end with your strongest propositions, a wise strategy. To support this proposition, you list the initial cost of the plant versus the cost of the tap-in. You also state the yearly fee charged by the city versus the yearly cost of running the plant. You might anticipate the opposing argument that the plant will save the homeowners money. You could break down the cost per individual homeowner, perhaps showing that the tap-in would cost an average homeowner only an additional ten dollars a year—a fairly nominal amount.

Your final minor proposition is that the proposed plant, a sewage lagoon will represent a nuisance to the homeowners of Hawk Estates. Because the cost for the tap-in is admittedly higher, your argument will probably swing on this minor proposition. You state freely that well-maintained sewage lagoons are not particularly smelly. But then you point out that authorities state that sewage lagoons are difficult to maintain, and if not maintained to the highest standards, they emit an unpleasant odor. To clinch your argument, you show that the only piece of land in Hawk Estates large enough to handle a sewage lagoon is upwind of the majority of houses, during prevailing winds. With the tap-in, of course, all wastes are carried away from Hawk Estates and represent no problem of odor or unsightliness whatsoever.

Organization

When you draft your argument, you can follow the organization shown on the chart, adding details as needed to make a persuasive case. Although your major proposition is actually the recommendation that your argument leads to, you present it first, so that your audience will know where you are heading. In executive reports such as this, major conclusions and recommendations are often presented first.

In summing up your argument, you draw attention once again to your key points. You acknowledge that in cost and the ability to handle the produced wastes, the proposed plant and the tap-in are essentially equal. But, you point out, the plant will probably become an undesirable nuisance to Hawk Estates. Therefore, you recommend that the builder choose the tap-in over the plant.

The following argument presents background information that supports a later conclusion that advanced automotive technology is needed to lower pollution and to conserve gasoline. The major premise of the argument is first supported by statistical examples and second by the chronology (see pages 176–178) of several trends (We have omitted fourteen footnotes documenting the argument and the superscripts that designate them in the source.)

> The automobile is also associated with many of the ills of a modern industrial society. Automotive emissions of hydrocarbons and nitrogen oxides are responsible for as much as 50 percent of ozone in urban areas; despite improvements in air quality forced by government regulations, 50 million Americans still live in counties with unsafe ozone levels. Automobiles are also responsible for 37 percent of U.S. oil consumption, in an era when U.S. dependence on imported oil is more than 50 percent and still increasing. A concern related to automotive gasoline consumption is the emission of greenhouse gases, principally carbon dioxide, which may be linked to global climate change.
>
> The automobile fleet, which accounts for 15 percent of the U.S. annual total, is one of this country's single largest emitters of carbon dioxide.
>
> Recent technological improvements to engines and vehicle designs have begun to address these problems, at least at the level of the individual vehicle. Driven by government regulation and the gasoline price increases of the 1970s, new car fuel economy has doubled between 1972 and today, and individual *vehicle* emissions have been reduced substantially. Several trends have undercut a portion of these gains, however, with the result that the negative impacts of automobiles are expected to continue.
>
> An important trend has been a 40 percent drop in the real price of gasoline since its peak in 1981. This decline has reduced the attractiveness of fuel-efficient automobiles for consumers and encouraged more driving; vehicle-miles traveled (VMT) have been increasing at 3 percent per year. Expanding personal income has meant that more new vehicles (especially less fuel-efficient light trucks and vans) are being added to the fleet; there were approximately 15.1 million new light-duty vehicles purchased in 1994. With more drivers and expected increases in individual travel demand, automotive oil consumption and carbon dioxide emissions are expected to increase by 18 percent from 1993 to 2010, when U.S.

oil imports are expected to reach 64 percent. Although highway vehicle emissions have been dropping and air quality improving, the rates of improvement have been slowed greatly by the increase in travel. Similar trends in automobile purchasing and use are occurring in other industrialized countries, even with motor fuel prices far higher than those in the United States, and the problems will be compounded as developing countries such as China continue to industrialize and expand their use of automobiles.

With these trends as background, it is clear that a major advance in automotive technology that could dramatically reduce gasoline consumption and emissions would have great national and international benefits.[2]

Throughout any argument, you appeal to reason. In most technical writing situations, an appeal to emotion will make your case immediately suspect. Never use sarcasm in an argument. You never know whose toes you are stepping on or how you will be understood. Support your case with simply stated, verifiable facts and statements from recognized authorities.

▶ PRO AND CON

The pro and con form of analysis looks at one side of a question and then looks at the other side before reaching a conclusion. The analysis excerpted here is typical.

Advantages

There are many advantages to earth-sheltered construction. An earth-sheltered home is less susceptible to the impact of extreme outdoor air temperatures, so you won't feel the effects of adverse weather as much as in a conventional house. Temperatures inside the house are more stable than in conventional homes, and with less temperature variability, interior rooms seem more comfortable.

Because earth covers part or all of their exterior, earth-sheltered houses require less outside maintenance, such as painting and cleaning gutters. Constructing a house that is dug into the earth or surrounded by earth builds in some natural soundproofing. Plans for most earth-sheltered houses "blend" the building into the landscape more harmoniously than a conventional home. Finally, earth-sheltered houses can cost less to insure because their design offers extra protection against high winds, hailstorms, and natural disasters such as tornados and hurricanes.

Disadvantages

As with any type of unusual construction, there are some disadvantages associated with earth-sheltered housing. Principal downsides are the initial cost of construction, which may be up to 20% higher, and the level of care required to avoid moisture problems, during both the construction and the life of the house. It can take more diligence to resell an earth-sheltered home, and buyers may have a few more hurdles to clear in the mortgage application process. . . .

A Home for the Future
If you are looking for a home with many energy efficient features that will provide a comfortable, tranquil, weather-resistant atmosphere, an earth-sheltered home could be right for you.[3]

► INDUCTION AND DEDUCTION

Much of your thought, whether you are casually chatting with friends or are on your most logical and formal behavior, consists of induction and deduction. In this section we cover both induction and deduction and discuss some of the fallacies you'll want to avoid in using them.

Induction

Induction is a movement from particular facts to general conclusions. It's a method of discovering and testing the inferences that you can draw from your information. The inductive process consists of (1) looking at the evidence, (2) making an educated guess to explain the evidence, and (3) investigating to see whether the guess fits the evidence. The educated guess is called a hypothesis. No matter how well constructed your hypothesis is, remember, it's still only a guess. Be ready to discard it in an instant if it doesn't fit your facts.

The whole process of gathering evidence, making hypotheses, and testing hypotheses against the evidence is, of course, the scientific method at work.

The following description of the beginnings of the theory of continental drift illustrates well how induction works in forming and supporting scientific thought:

The belief that continents have not always been fixed in their present positions was suspected long before the 20th century; this notion was first suggested as early as 1596 by the Dutch map maker Abraham Ortelius in his work *Thesaurus Geographicus*. Ortelius suggested that the Americas were "torn away from Europe and Africa. . . by earthquakes and floods" and went on to say:"The vestiges of the rupture reveal themselves, if someone brings forward a map of the world and considers carefully the coasts of the three [continents]." Ortelius' idea surfaced again in the 19th century. However, it was not until 1912 that the idea of moving continents was seriously considered as a full-blown scientific theory—called *Continental Drift*—introduced in two articles published by a 32-year-old German meteorologist named Alfred Lothar Wegener. He contended that, around 200 million years ago, the supercontinent Pangaea began to split apart. Alexander Du Toit, Professor of Geology at Johannesburg University and one of Wegener's staunchest supporters, proposed that Pangaea first broke into two large continental landmasses, *Laurasia* in the northern hemisphere and *Gondwanaland* in the southern hemisphere. Laurasia and Gondwanaland then continued to break apart into the various smaller continents that exist today.

Wegener's theory was based in part on what appeared to him to be the remarkable fit of the South American and African continents, first noted by Abraham Ortelius three centuries earlier. Wegener was also intrigued by the occurrences of unusual geologic structures and of plant and animal fossils found on the matching coastlines of South America and Africa, which are now widely separated by the Atlantic Ocean. He reasoned that it was physically impossible for most of these organisms to have swum or have been transported across the vast oceans. To him, the presence of identical fossil species along the coastal parts of Africa and South America was the most compelling evidence that the two continents were once joined.

In Wegener's mind, the drifting of continents after the break-up of Pangaea explained not only the matching fossil occurrences but also the evidence of dramatic climate changes on some continents. For example, the discovery of fossils of tropical plants (in the form of coal deposits) in Antarctica led to the conclusion that this frozen land previously must have been situated closer to the equator, in a more temperate climate where lush, swampy vegetation could grow. Other mismatches of geology and climate included distinctive fossil ferns (*Glossopteris*) discovered in now-polar regions, and the occurrence of glacial deposits in present-day arid Africa, such as the Vaal River valley of South Africa.

The *theory of continental drift* would become the spark that ignited a new way of viewing the Earth.[4]

Continental drift was the forerunner of the modern theory of plate tectonics—the theory that the surface of the earth is composed of plates upon which the continents ride.

Looking for similarities and differences as Wegener did is a major tool in testing hypotheses. Examining similarities and differences in the population has led medical authorities, including the Surgeon General of the United States, to declare that cigarette smoking is hazardous to your health. Researchers began this examination by looking at the population, and they saw a difference. There are those who smoke and those who don't. Within each of these two groups, medical authorities looked for similarities. Smokers had in common a high incidence of respiratory problems, including emphysema and lung cancer. Nonsmokers had in common a low incidence of such problems. The higher incidence of such problems in the smoking group when compared to the nonsmoking group was a significant difference.

Induction is the chief way we have of establishing casualty—that A caused B. In the following example, the author uses induction to support the proposition that pollution and overfishing are stressing the oceans of the world. The proposition is then supported by evidence of the pollution and overfishing.

The oceans, ravaged by pollution and overfishing, are in trouble. World fisheries are under unprecedented stress as competition for these finite resources increases. Pollution caused by the deliberate dumping of debris, chemical contaminants, agricultural and industrial runoffs, sewage, and vessel discharge has endangered marine life and habitats. Coral mining, blast fishing, the dumping of contaminated dredge material, and other human activities have destroyed or dramatically damaged ocean and coastal habitats and the wildlife they sustain. The Food and Agriculture Organization of the United Nations estimates that 70 percent of the world's commercially important fish stocks are fully or over-exploited. Chronic overfishing has depleted Atlantic cod and halibut stocks and resulted in the loss of thousands of American jobs. Stocks of some large ocean fish—tunas, sharks, swordfish, and marlin—have declined 60–90 percent in the last two decades. Every year, 27 million tons of fish, marine mammals, sharks, sea turtles, and seabirds, one third of the world's catch, are caught unintentionally and thrown back dead or dying into the ocean.

The United States, with one of the longest coastlines in the world and as a major maritime power and seafood consumer, has vested economic and environmental interests in protecting the oceans. In addition to providing a major food source, the oceans are maritime highways for efficient commerce and national security. They also serve as a source for oil, for medicine, and for recreation. The health and economic well-being of the world's coastal populations and communities are intimately linked to the quality of the marine environment.[5]

Remember that despite the terminology used—conclusion, proposition, thesis—generalizations based on particulars are opinions, nothing more and nothing less. Therefore, the better you support general statements with facts, the more likely they are to be strong and convincing.

Deduction

Deductive reasoning is another way to deal with evidence. Whereas in inductive reasoning you move from the particular to the general, in deductive reasoning you move from the general to the particular. You start with some general principle, apply it to a fact, and draw a conclusion concerning the fact. Although you will seldom use the form of a syllogism in writing, we can best illustrate deductive reasoning with it:

1. All professional golfers are good athletes.
2. Judy is a professional golfer.
3. Therefore, Judy is a good athlete.

In expressing deductive reasoning, we commonly present the syllogism in abbreviated form. You might say, for instance, "Because Judy was a professional golfer, I knew she was a good athlete."

Although induction is the more common organizing technique in argument, deduction is sometimes used, as in this example:

> Layered rocks form when particles settle from water or air. Steno's *Law of Original Horizontality* states that most sediments, when originally formed, were laid down horizontally. However, many layered rocks are no longer horizontal. Because of the *Law of Original Horizontality*, we know that sedimentary rocks that are not horizontal either were formed in special ways or, more often, were moved from their horizontal position by later events, such as tilting during episodes of mountain building.[6]

Presented formally, the syllogism in this paragraph would go something like this:

1. Steno's *Law of Original Horizontality* states that most sediments when originally formed were laid down horizontally.
2. However, some sedimentary rocks are not horizontal.
3. Therefore, these sedimentary rocks either were formed in special ways or were moved from their horizontal orientation by later events such as mountain building.

Logical Fallacies

Many traps exist in induction and deduction for the unwary writer. When you fall into one of these traps, you have committed what logicians call a fallacy. Avoid a rush to either conclusion or judgment. Take your time. Don't draw inferences from insufficient evidence. Don't assume that just because one event follows another, the first caused the second—a fallacy that logicians call *post hoc, ergo propter hoc* ("after this, therefore, because of this"). You need other evidence in addition to the time factor to establish a causal relationship.

For example, tobacco smoking was introduced into Europe in the sixteenth century. Since that time, the average European's life span has increased severalfold. It would be a fine example of the *post hoc* fallacy to infer that smoking has caused the increased life span, which in fact probably stems from improvements in housing, sanitation, nutrition, and medical care.

Another common error is applying a syllogism backwards. The following syllogism is valid:

1. All dogs are mammals.
2. Jock is a dog.
3. Therefore, Jock is a mammal.

But if you reverse statements (2) and (3) you have an invalid syllogism:

1. All dogs are mammals.
2. Jock is a mammal.
3. Therefore, Jock is a dog.

Jock, of course, could be a cat, a whale, a Scotsman, or any other member of the mammal family. You can often find flaws in your own reasoning or that of others if you break the thought process down into the three parts of a syllogism.

▶ COMPARISON

In business and technical situations, you frequently have to choose between two or more alternatives. When such is the case, the method of investigating the alternatives will usually involve comparing the alternatives one to another. (Contrast is implied in comparison.) To be meaningful, the comparisons should be made by using standards, or criteria. Perhaps you have bought a car recently. When you did, you had to choose among many alternatives. In reaching your decision, you undoubtedly compared cars using criteria such as price, comfort, performance, appearance, gas mileage, and so forth. Perhaps you even went so far as to rank the criteria in order of importance, for example, giving price the highest priority and appearance the lowest. The more consciously you applied your criteria, the more successful your final choice may have been.

After you bought your car, no one asked you to make a report to justify your decision. However, in business it's common practice for someone to be given the task of choosing among alternatives. The completion of the task involves a report that states the decisions or recommendations made and justifies them. When such is the case, a comparison arrangement is a good choice. You can arrange comparison arguments by alternatives or by criteria.

Alternatives

Assume you work for a health organization and that you are comparing two alternative contact lenses: daily wear and extended wear. Your criteria are cost, ease of use, and risk of infection. After the necessary explanations of the lenses and the criteria, you might organize your material this way:

- Daily wear
  Cost
  Ease of use
  Risk of infection
- Extended wear
  Cost
  Ease of use
  Risk of infection

In this arrangement, you take one alternative at a time and run it through the criteria. This arrangement has the advantage of giving the whole picture for each alternative as you discuss it. The emphasis is on the alternatives.

Criteria

In another possible arrangement, you discuss each alternative, criterion by criterion:

- Cost
  Daily wear
  Extended wear
- Ease of use
  Daily wear
  Extended wear
- Risk of infection
  Daily wear
  Extended wear

The arrangement by criteria has the advantage of allowing sharper comparison. It also is advantageous for readers who read selectively. Not every reader will have equal interest in all parts of a report. For example, an executive reading this report might be most interested in cost; a consumer, in ease of use; an ophthalmologist, in risk of infection.

▶ TOULMIN LOGIC

When you construct an argument by yourself, it's difficult at times to see the flaws in it. When you expose the same argument to your friends, even in casual conversation, they, being more objective about it, can often spot the flaws you have overlooked. Toulmin logic provides a way of checking your own arguments for those overlooked flaws. It can also help you arrange your argument.[7]

Applying Toulmin Logic

Because using Toulmin logic is a way of raising those questions readers may ask, its use will make your arguments more reader oriented. Toulmin logic comprises five components:

1. Claim: the major proposition or conclusion of the argument
2. Grounds: the evidence upon which the claim rests—facts, experimental research data, statements from authorities, and so forth
3. Warrant: justification for the grounds and what makes them relevant to the claim
4. Backing: further evidence for accepting the warrant
5. Rebuttal: counterarguments; exceptions to the claim, warrant, or backing; or reasons for not accepting them

Arguments are rather complex chains of reasoning in which you have to make the case not only for your claim but also for the grounds upon which the claim is based. Toulmin logic helps you construct the chain. For an example, let's consider the greenhouse effect hypothesis.

Claim

The accumulation of gases, particularly carbon dioxide (CO_2), emitted from the burning of fossil fuels will trap heat in the atmosphere, which will cause global warming, resulting in droughts, severe storms, floods, and food shortages.

Grounds

In past 100 years, CO_2 concentration in the atmosphere has risen from 270 parts per million (ppm) to 350 ppm. That this rise has been caused by the increased burning of fossil fuels seems indisputable. Various computer models predict global temperatures rising by as much as 4°C in the next 50 years.

Warrant

The United Nations sponsored Intergovernmental Panel on Climate Change has reached the conclusion that "the balance of evidence suggests that there is a discernible human influence on climate."[8]

Backing

The CEO of American Electrical Power has said that "It's clear to me that there is an increase in CO_2 that is probably not for the good, and we ought to do something about it."[9] In June 1992 the nations of the world at the Earth Summit conference in Rio de Janeiro signed a treaty that states a dangerous global warming has already started. In 1997 Europe, the United States, and Japan at an environmental conference in Kyoto, Japan, agreed to "reduce greenhouse emissions" beginning in 2008.[10]

Up to this point, the argument for the greenhouse hypothesis and its effects seems to be going well. But, if you dig further, you will find rebuttals.

Rebuttal

Satellite and balloon measurements show no significant warming over the last 18 years. Harvard climatologist Brian Farrell says, "There really isn't a persuasive case being made" for the detection of greenhouse warming.[11] Climate modeler Max Suarez of the NASA Goddard Space Flight Center says that it is "iffy" to say if greenhouse warming has begun, "especially if you're trying to explain the very small [temperature] change we've already seen. I certainly wouldn't trust the [computer] models at that level of detail yet."[12] NASA records indicate that despite some recent violent hurricanes, the frequency and intensity of hurricanes are decreasing overall.[13]

And so on. Digging for evidence on the greenhouse effect shows a sharp division with reputable scientists coming down on both sides of the question. The claim has to be qualified, perhaps something like this: "Some scientific studies show a correlation between the rise of CO_2 in the atmosphere and global warming, but the evidence and methodology of such studies have not convinced all scientists that the results claimed are valid." Applying Toulmin logic has resulted in a weaker claim, but it is a claim that can be supported with the existing evidence.

The following release from the U.S. Department of Energy shows the effect of the rebuttals. It deals with the rebuttal by acknowledging the possibility that influences other than human activity may be causing the earth's temperature to vary. But its conclusion, favoring the theory that greenhouse warming is occurring, is qualified by the phrase "appears to be."

> Perhaps no single environmental issue is as complex or holds such potentially profound implications for the world's inhabitants than the issue of global climate change.
>
> There is little question that human activity is changing the make-up of the atmosphere that surrounds our planet. As world economies have become more industrialized over the last century, we have begun emitting more greenhouse gases into the air than natural processes can remove. Deforestation and clearing land for agriculture have accelerated the buildup of greenhouse gases in the atmosphere, both by releasing significant quantities of these gases and by reducing the capacity of green plants to absorb carbon dioxide, one of the chief greenhouse gases.
>
> In 1995, a panel of more than 2,000 of the world's top climate scientists concluded that the Earth was indeed warming and that the "balance of evidence suggests a discernible human influence" on climate. Yet, there are still large gaps in the scientific data. The warming in the last century—about 1 degree Farenheit—is still small enough to fall within the range of normal climatic changes for a planet that has fluctuated in and out of ice ages for at least the last 200,000 years. A small part of that single degree of warming may have come from variations in the sun's intensity, which can raise or lower the Earth's temperatures in ways not yet fully understood.

Nonetheless, the bulk of recent evidence—from rising sea levels and retreating glaciers to freak storms and floods—appears to be falling within the boundaries of scientists' predictions of greenhouse warming.[14]

Arranging Your Argument for Readers

You can use Toulmin logic to arrange your argument as well as to discover it. Though you would not want to follow Toulmin logic in a mechanical way, thinking in terms of claim, grounds, warrant, backing, and rebuttal can help you to be sure you have covered everything that needs to be covered.

Obviously, claim and grounds must always be presented. In most business situations, as we have pointed out, the claim is likely to be presented first, particularly in executive reports. However, in a situation in which the readers might be hostile to the claim, it may be preferable to reverse the order. If the grounds are strong enough, readers may be swayed to your side before they even see the claim. On the other hand, if a hostile audience sees the claim first, they may not pay enough attention to the grounds to be convinced.

Rebuttals should always be considered, and, if serious, they should be included in your presentation. You have an ethical responsibility to be honest with your readers. Furthermore, if your readers think of rebuttals you haven't responded to, it will damage your credibility. If you can counter the rebuttals successfully, perhaps by attacking their warrant or backing, your claim can stand. If you cannot counter them, you will have to qualify your claim.

How deeply you go into warrants and backing depends on your readers. If your readers are not likely to realize what your warrant is (for example, that respected scientists agree with this hypothesis), then you had better include the warrant. If your readers are likely to disagree with your warrant or discount its validity, then you had better include the backing.

All in all, Toulmin logic can be a considerable help in discovering and arranging an argument. It is also extremely useful in analyzing the soundness of other people's arguments.

▶ PLANNING AND REVISION CHECKLISTS

You will find the planning and revision checklists that follow Chapter 2, Composing, and Chapter 4, Writing for Your Readers, valuable in planning and revising any presentation of technical information. The following checklists specifically apply to organizational strategies. As well as aiding in planning and revision, they summarize the key points in this chapter.

Planning

- What is your claim, that is, the major proposition or conclusion of your argument?
- What are your grounds? What is the evidence upon which your claim rests—facts, experimental research data, statements from authorities, and so forth?
- Do you need a warrant that justifies your grounds and makes them relevant?
- Do you need further backing for your grounds and warrant?
- Are there rebuttals—counterarguments; exceptions to the claim, warrant, or backing; or reasons for not accepting them? Can you rebut the rebuttals? If not, should you qualify your claim? Will you present your argument unethically if you do not state the rebuttals and deal with them honestly?
- Are you choosing among alternatives? If so, what are they?
- What are the criteria for evaluating the alternatives?
- Is your audience likely to be neutral, friendly, or hostile to your claim? If your audience is hostile, should you consider putting your claim last rather than first?

Revision

- Is your claim clearly stated?
- Do you have sufficient grounds to support your claim?
- If needed, have you provided a warrant and backing for your grounds?
- Does any of your evidence cast doubt on your claim? Have you considered all serious rebuttals?
- Have you dealt responsibly and ethically with any rebuttals?
- Have you remained fair and objective in your argument?
- Have you presented evidence for causality beyond the fact that one event follows another?
- If you have used deductive reasoning, can you state your argument in a syllogism? Does the syllogism demonstrate that you have reasoned in a valid way?
- Is your argument arranged so that it can be read selectively by readers with different interests?

▶ EXERCISES

1. Write a memo to an executive that recommends the purchase of some product or service the executive needs for the conduct of his or her business. Your memo should establish criteria and justify choosing the product or service you recommend over other alternatives. See Letter and Memorandum Format in Appendix B. for information on memo format.

2. Your new boss on your first job knows how important it is for the organization to stay aware of trends that may affect the organization. He or she asks you to explore such a trend. The possibilities are limitless, but you may be happier exploring some trend in your own field. For example, are you in computer science? Then you might be interested in the latest trends in artificial intelligence. Are you in forestry? Trends in the use and the kinds of wood products might interest you. Develop a claim about the trend, for example:

   • If trend A continues, surely B will result.
   • Trend A will have great significance for X industry.

   Support your claim with a well-developed argument that demonstrates your ability to use induction, deduction, and Toulmin logic. Write your argument as a memorandum to your boss. See Letter and Memorandum Format in Appendix B. for information on memo format.

3. You are a member of a consulting firm. Your firm has been called in to help a professional organization deal with a question of major importance to the members of the organization. For example, nurses have an interest in whether nurses should be allowed to prescribe medication and therapy. You will probably be most successful in this exercise if you deal with organizations and questions relevant to your major. Investigate the question and prepare a short report for the executive board of the organization. Your report should support some claim—for example, nurses should be allowed to prescribe medication and therapy. Use Toulmin logic in discovering and presenting your argument. That is, be aware of the need to provide grounds, warrants, backings, and qualifiers. Anticipate rebuttals and deal with them ethically and responsibly. Use Appendix B for help with format and documentation.

4. You are the scientific adviser for a newly elected congressman from your home district. He has a college degree in history and is a self-avowed scientific illiterate (which is why he has hired you).

He says to you, "I need to have a position on global warming. Is it or isn't it happening? If it is happening, how serious is it? Write a position paper on the subject for me. Take a strong stand and defend it, but do it ethically and in language I can understand."

Write the position paper the congressman has requested. Use both Internet and print sources. Document your paper. See Appendix B for help with format and documentation.

SCENARIO

K elly Flick in the company post office needs to notify the offices in the company about new mail pickup and delivery procedures. She prepares the following memo:

TO: All Departments

FROM: Kelly Flick

SUBJECT: Results of Survey Concerning Mail Procedures

Last fall we surveyed offices to determine the effectiveness of our mailing procedures. We have used your input to revise our procedures to improve the handling of all incoming and outgoing mail. The result should be more timely performance in both respects.

On February 4 we will initiate new pickup and delivery times for mail to ensure that we get all our outgoing mail to the post office by the closing time and that incoming mail is delivered to all offices the day it arrives at our post office.

Be sure that all your mail is delivered to the mail room before 3:00 p.m. every day. The mail room will close at 3:00 sharp to allow us time to sort, bag, and load all mail, which must arrive at the Maberry post office branch by 4:30. Bring large mailings to the mail room by 1:00 p.m. Mail clerks can pick up incoming mail at 8:30 each morning. We will retrieve incoming mail at Maberry during dropoff each afternoon, sort it before 6:00, and have priority items ready for pickup shortly before 6:00. Other mail will be ready for pick up by 8:00 the following morning. As usual, we will see that all Express Mail is delivered as soon as it arrives.

Amanda, Kelly's assistant, does not think there will be much compliance with the new procedures. However, Kelly decides to send the memo anyway. A week later, Amanda tells Kelly that she has received calls from three people complaining that they brought outgoing mail to the mail room at 4:00 and were told that they were late. None of the callers remembered having received a memo about new mail procedures. Kelly is stunned, for she knows that every office received multiple copies of the memo for distribution to employees in the various departments.

How can document design strategies be used to improve this memo? Assuming that everyone received this memo, why don't people remember reading it?

chapter 11

Document Design

▶ Understanding the Basics of Document Design
Know What Decisions You Can Make
Choose a Design That Fits Your Situation
Plan Your Design from the Beginning
Reveal Your Design to Your Readers
Keep Your Design Consistent

▶ Designing Effective Pages and Screens
Leave Ample Margins
Use Blank Space to Group Information
Set the Spacing for Easy Reading
Use a Medium Line Length
Use a Ragged Right Margin

▶ Choosing Readable Type
Choose a Legible Type Size
Choose a Typeface (Font) That Is Appropriate
for the Situation
Use Special Typefaces Sparingly
Use Highlighting Effectively
Use a Mixture of Cases, Not All Capitals
Use Color Carefully

▶ Helping Readers Locate Information
Write Descriptive Headings
Design Headings to Organize the Page
Use Page Numbers and Headers or Footers in Print
Documents

▶ Appreciating the Importance of Document Design

As you have seen in the previous chapters, effective writing requires a number of composing strategies, based on your audience's needs. But effective writing is more than *writing*, more than just words on the page or computer screen, more than correct sentences arranged in logical paragraphs. To be effective, your document must also work visually.

With the ever-increasing capabilities of software to change the appearance of text, to incorporate graphics with text, even to include animation and sound with text, you have many choices in how your document will look on paper or online. This chapter will help you make wise choices for designing both paper and online documents.[1]

► UNDERSTANDING THE BASICS OF DOCUMENT DESIGN

Readers judge your work from the presentation as well as from the content of the document and the style of your writing. In fact, a reader's first impression comes from the appearance of your work, not from what it says. A dense page of information that is difficult to read will often discourage a reader. In contrast, a page designed to help readers locate important information may add to the persuasiveness of your position or convince your readers to put a little more effort into finding what they need and understanding what they find.

Figure 11-1 is a vacation policy for a business organization. Figure 11-2 is a revision of that policy that incorporates principles of document design we will discuss in this chapter. Examine Figure 11-1 and then Figure 11-2. Which one would you rather read? Why is one more readable than the other? Now consider Figure 11-3, which is very unattractively formatted. Compare Figure 11-4, which invites reading and use because it's broken into manageable chunks. The headings, list, and table all help the reader to quickly see the structure of the writer's points and to grasp the important information.

These five principles will help you plan your document's visual design:

- Know what decisions you can make.
- Choose a design that fits your situation.
- Plan your design from the beginning.
- Reveal your design to your readers.
- Keep your design consistent.

Know What Decisions You Can Make

Many companies have a standard format for reports, letters, or proposals. Many journals have standard formats that all manuscripts must follow. Companies have also been developing standards and style sheets for online documents and World Wide Web sites. Before you develop your document,

Joint Practice 27: Vacation Days for Management

General

The purpose of this Joint Practice is to outline the vacation treatment applicable to management employees.

Eligibility

Vacations with pay shall be granted during the calendar year to each management employee who shall have completed six months' employment since the date employment began. Vacation pay will not be granted if the employee has been dismissed for misconduct. Vacation allowed will be determined according to the following criteria: (a) One week's vacation to any such management employee who has completed twelve months of service but who could not complete seven years of service within the vacation year. (b) Two weeks' vacation to any such management employee who has completed twelve months of service but who could not complete seven years of service within the vacation year. Two weeks will be allowed if the employee initially completes six months' service and twelve months' service within the same vacation. (c) Three weeks' vacation to any management employee who could complete seven or more but less than fifteen years' service within the vacation year and to District level who shall have completed six months' employment within the vacation year. (d) Four weeks' vacation to any management employee who completes fifteen or more but less than twenty-five years' service within the vacation year and to Division level who shall have completed six months' employment within the vacation year. (e) Five weeks' vacation to any management employee who completes twenty-five or more years of service within the vacation year and to Department head level and higher management who shall have completed a period of six months' employment within the vacation year.

The foregoing criterion is Net Credited Service as determined by the Employees' Benefit Committee. Where eligibility for a vacation week under (a) or (b) above first occurs on or after December 1 of a vacation year, the vacation week may be granted in the next following vacation year if it is completed before April 1 and before the beginning of vacation for the following year. When an authorized holiday falls in a week during which a management employee is absent on vacation, an additional day off (or equivalent time off with pay) may be taken in either the same calendar year or prior to April 1 of the following calendar year. When the additional day of vacation is Christmas Day, it may be granted immediately preceding the vacation or prior to April 1 of the following calendar year.

FIGURE 11-1 • Original Policy

Joint Practice 27: Vacation Time Allowed Management Employees

The following schedule describes the new vacation schedule approved by the company. This schedule is effective immediately and will remain in effect until a further update is issued.

Vacation Eligibility

1. Vacation with pay shall be granted during the calendar year to each management employee who has completed 6 months' service since the date of employment. Employees who have been dismissed for misconduct will not receive vacation with pay.

Net Credited Service	Eligible Weeks
6 months–12 months	1
12 months–7 years	2
7 years–15 years and to District level with 6 months service	3
15 years–25 years and to Division level with 6 months service	4
25 years or more and to Department head or higher management with 6 months service	5

Net Credited Service is determined by the Employee Benefits Committee.

2. If eligibility occurs on or after December 1 of a vacation year,

   • vacation may be granted in the next following year if it is taken before April 1.

3. If an authorized holiday falls in a vacation week,

   • an additional day may be taken in either calendar year or before April 1 of the following year.

4. If the additional day of vacation is Christmas Day,

   • it may be taken immediately preceding the vacation or before April 1 of the following year.

FIGURE 11-2 • Revised Policy

With the substantial growth in computing in the College of Engineering during the past decade, the issue of linking the departments through a computer network has become critical. The network must satisfy a number of criteria to meet the needs of all of the engineering departments. We first state these criteria and then discuss them individually in detail.

To adequately serve both faculty and student needs in the present environment, the network must be able to handle the number of computers currently in use. In addition, the system must be able to expand and link in additional computers as the number of computers increases over the next few years. The different types of computers that the departments presently possess must all be linkable to the network, and the types of computers that are scheduled for purchase must also be able to be connected to the network. The network should permit the transfer of files in both text and binary form in order to facilitate student access to files and collaborative exchange among faculty and research associates. The network must also have adequate bandwidth in order to handle the expected traffic. Finally, the network must permit both students and faculty to link to the existing national networks.

Each department currently has both computer laboratories for students and computers that are associated with faculty research projects. The various departments possess different numbers of computers. The Aeronautical Engineering Department at present has 27 computers, while Civil Engineering has 12. The Electrical Engineering Department has the most in the College with 46. Mechanical has 22, and Nuclear Engineering, the smallest department in the College, presently has 7. This means that the entire College presently has 114 computers which will need to be networked.

In order to meet their different needs, each department has focused on the purchasing of computers with differing strengths. The computers provide for faculty and advanced students to program in a variety of languages including Pascal, C, and Fortran.

The page with just text looks dense and uninviting.

Readers can't tell at a glance what the text is about.

FIGURE 11-3 • An Example of Poor Formatting

find out what format requirements are already in place. Don't change formats arbitrarily, just to be different. If you think the format you are being asked to use doesn't work well for your audience and your content, find out who makes decisions on format and present a case for the changes that you want.

You don't have to use sophisticated software to apply basic principles of document design. You can use a basic word processing program to produce a visually effective document like the one shown in Figure 11-4.

With the substantial growth in computing in the College of Engineering during the past decade, the issue of linking the departments through a computer network has become critical. The network must satisfy a number of criteria to meet the needs of all the engineering departments. We first list these criteria and then discuss them individually in detail.

What must the network do?

To serve both faculty and students, the network must be able to
- handle the number of computers currently in use
- link different types of computers
- expand as the number of computers increases
- link to the national networks
- transfer and store both text and binary files

The network must also have adequate bandwidth to handle the expected traffic.

Handling the number of computers currently in use

Each department has both computer laboratories for students and computers that are associated with faculty research projects. The following table shows the number of computers in each department at the end of the last fiscal year.

Aeronautical Engineering	27
Civil Engineering	12
Electrical Engineering	46
Mechanical Engineering	22
Nuclear Engineering	7
Total	114

Linking different types of computers

In order to meet its different needs, each department has focused purchasing on machines with different strengths.

A Proposal to Install a Computer Network
for the College of Engineering   page 3

Sidebar annotations (left margin):

Large headings make the topics and structure obvious.

A bulleted list makes the points more memorable.

Each item in the list becomes the heading for a subsection.

The subsection headings are also bold but smaller than the main section heading.

The shorter line length makes the text easier to read and makes the headings stand out.

The numbers are much clearer in a table.

The footer on every page reminds readers of the overall topic.

FIGURE 11-4 • The Page from Figure 11-3, Reformatted

Choose a Design That Fits Your Situation

Don't make your document any more complex than the situation requires. You don't need a table of contents or a glossary for reports that are under five pages. Add appendix material only if it is necessary and will be useful for your readers.

You'll impress readers most by providing just the information they need in a way that makes it easy for them to find and understand it. Many people read technical and business documents selectively. They scan the document, looking for sections that are relevant to their needs. They try to grasp the main points quickly because they are busy and have far too much to read.[2]

Similarly, users working with a computer program are not likely to read the entire user's manual. They go to the manual or to online help when they have a specific problem or need instructions for a specific task. They want to get to the right page or screen immediately. They want the instructions to stand out on the page or screen. Look at Figures 11-5 and 11-6. The numbered steps in Figure 11-6 are easier to read and follow than the prose paragraph in Figure 11-5.

Plan Your Design from the Beginning

Think about how you will arrange and present your information as you plan the document. Ask basic questions like these:

- How will people use the document? Will most people read it from beginning to end? Will they want to skim it and grab the main points without reading more? Will they want to jump to a specific topic? Even if they read the document through once, will they want to come back later and find a specific point quickly?

Drawing Product Help

To draw a box:

Decide where to put one corner of the box and move the mouse so that the cursor is in that position on the screen. Press and hold the left mouse button, sliding the mouse along the diagonal of the box which will appear on the screen as you move the mouse. When the box is the desired size, release the mouse button.

FIGURE 11-5 • Instructions in Paragraph Style
This format is difficult to follow, both online and on paper.

> ## Drawing Product Help
>
> **To draw a box:**
>
> 1. Decide where to put one corner of the box.
>
> 2. Move the mouse so that the cursor is in that position on the screen.
>
> 3. Press and hold the left mouse button, sliding the mouse along the diagonal of the box.
>
>   The box appears as you move the mouse.
>
> 4. When the box is the size you want, release the mouse button.

FIGURE 11-6 • Instructions in List Form
Instructions formatted like this are easier to follow.

- Will most people see this document on paper or on a computer screen?
- Will you be able to include graphics easily? Will you be able to use color?
- What type of print document are you creating? (Other chapters in this book give you specific ideas for preparing letters and memos, instructions, proposals, and different types of reports.)
- What type of online document are you creating? There are many types of online documents, including e-mail messages, online resumes, online help that comes with a product, world wide web pages, online forms, and computer presentations.[3] (For more about e-mail, see Chapter 13. For more about print and online resumes, see Chapter 14. For more about designing visuals to accompany oral presentations, see Chapter 19. For more about the World Wide Web, see Appendix B.)

As you answer these questions, think about these points: If people will skim and scan your document, the table of contents and page layout can help them find information quickly. (The rest of this chapter includes techniques for developing effective designs to help people find what they need.) If the document is going to be read on a computer screen, you may have both more constraints and more opportunities than if the document were printed on paper. We read more slowly from the computer screen than from paper,[4] so limiting the amount of information and leaving blank space between paragraphs or list items is crucial in an online document. Graphics and color may be easier and less expensive to include in an online document than in a paper document.

Reveal Your Design to Your Readers

Seeing the text is the first step in reading a document. Research on how people read and process information shows that readers have to understand how the material is organized before they can make sense of it.[5] Headings reveal the organization of your document so that readers can see what you are writing even before they try to grasp your message on the sentence level. A few well-placed and well-written headings that show the structure and logic of the discussion can help readers, even in a memo. Longer reports definitely need headings and a table of contents that lists the headings. In online documents—such as World Wide Web pages—a contents list leads to pages whose titles are like the headings in paper documents. You'll learn more about how to write and design effective headings later in this chapter. (see Figure 11-21.)

Keep Your Design Consistent

Consistency in design is essential to easy reading. When you have considered your audiences, the content you have to deliver, and the ways that people will read and use your document, you can develop a page layout (a design) that will work well for your situation. Once you have the page layout planned, don't change it for arbitrary reasons. In this book, you know when you are beginning a new chapter, when you are at a new section, and when you are at another part of the same section, because the headings at each level are consistent throughout the book. Look again at Figure 11-4. Is it obvious where the major section starts? Is it obvious that there are two parallel subsections?

To help yourself maintain consistency as you create a document, you can use templates in your word processing program. Most programs let you design each element of a document and then set the design as a repeatable style. The style includes the type size; the typeface, or font; placement of an element on the page; whether the text has a border (also called a line or a rule) over or under it; whether the text or headings are bold or italic; the amount of space that comes before and after a heading; the style of the text that follows each kind of heading; and so forth.

Another part of planning in order to keep your design consistent is thinking about the types of information that you have. Once you have a list of the types of information, you can plan a design that shows the same type of information in the same way throughout the document.

Figure 11-7 shows a letter using document design to reveal the content and the relationships among the sections. This example shows how any document, including routine letters and memoranda, will benefit from the use of document design.

Wilson, Wilson, and Fitch
2202 Winding Parkway, Suite 400
Glendale, Arizona 85320

September 14, 1998

Mr. Nick Marshall
Vice President
Multi-TechCompany
34454 Meadows Avenue
Glendale, AZ 85320

SUBJECT: Tax Treatment of Moving Expenses for Employees

Dear Mr. Marshall:

The moving expenses of your employees are regarded as itemized deductions subject to several requirements and limitations. Your employees should have no problem meeting the requirements for deductibility, but they should be informed of the limitations that apply to these expenses.

Conditions for Eligibility

1. **Distance Test.** The distance between the old residence and the new residence and the new place of employment must be at least 35 miles farther than the distance between the old residence and the new place of employment. Because your employees will be moving across the country, they will meet this test.

2. **Minimum Period of Employment after the Move.** There is a 39-week minimum period of employment following the move. This minimum should have no effect on your employees as long as they continue to work for your company.

Limitations of Expenses

Once the foregoing conditions have been met, the moving expenses qualify as itemized deductions. However, some of these expenses are limited by specific dollar amounts, depending on whether the expense is direct or indirect.

Direct Expenses

Expenses directly associated with moving to the new residence are not limited, except to say that they must be reasonable. Direct expenses include

- Traveling from the old residence to the new residence
- Moving all household goods to the new location.

FIGURE 11-7 • Letter That Uses Document Design Principles

Mr. Nick Marshall
September 14, 1998
Page 2

Indirect Expenses

House hunting and temporary living expenses are limited to a total of $1,500 as a deduction.

1. **House hunting expenses** are all expenses incurred while you are actually looking for a house or dwelling. You must be working for your new company and looking for a house to use these expenses as indirect expenses.

2. **Temporary living expenses** include food and lodging expenses you incur after you move to the area of the new place of employment but before you move into a permanent residence.

   Note: Temporary living expenses will be allowed during a maximum 30-day period only.

3. Residence expenses are costs you incur in selling the old residence and/or costs incurred in locating a new one. Examples of these expenses include

   - Closing costs
   - Real estate commissions
   - Expenses necessary in acquiring or settling a lease.

Total deductible expenses in the indirect category, including house hunting costs, temporary living expenses, and residence expenses are limited to $3,000. Any amount incurred in excess of this amount cannot be taken as an itemized deduction.

If you need any further clarification, please call me at 303 444-5609.

Sincerely,

Kelly Jones

Kelly Jones, C.P.A.
Wilson, Wilson, and Fitch

FIGURE 11-7 • *Continued*

▶ DESIGNING EFFECTIVE PAGES AND SCREENS

Visually effective pages and computer screens are inviting. They are designed on a grid, so readers know where to look for information. They have space inside the text, around the graphics, and in the margins, so they look open and information is easy to locate. The line length and margins help people read easily. You can use the following suggestions to help you develop visually effective pages and screens:[6]

- Leave ample margins.
- Use blank space to group information.
- Set the spacing for easy reading.
- Use a medium line length.
- Use a ragged right margin.

Leave Ample Margins

Look at Figure 11-8. Do you want to read it? Too little space makes the page look dense and uninviting. Now look at Figure 11-9. Wouldn't you rather read this version? Blank space (often called *white space* on paper) makes the page look inviting and makes information easier to find and read.

You can incorporate blank space into documents in several ways. One place for blank space is at the margins—the space around the edges of the paper, computer screen, or window on the computer screen. If your document will be read on paper, also think about how it will be bound. If you are putting your work in a binder, be sure to leave room for the binding. Don't punch holes through the text. Similarly, think about whether a reader will want to punch holes in a copy later or put the work in a binder. Figure 11-10 shows how these guidelines appear proportionately for margins on a standard 8½-by-11-inch page:

top margin	1 inch
bottom margin	1 inch
left margin	1 inch, if material is not being bound
	2 inches, if material is being bound
right margin	1 inch

If you are going to photocopy on both the front and back of the page, leave space for the binding in the left margin of odd-numbered pages and in the right margin of even-numbered pages. Some word processing programs let you set the margins so that they alternate for right-hand (odd-numbered) pages and left-hand (even-numbered) pages. If you cannot set alternating margins, set both the right and the left margin at about 1½ inches to allow for binding two-sided copies.

Use Blank Space to Group Information

Don't think of blank space as wasted or empty space. Space is a critical element in the layout, for both paper and screens. Look at how all the examples

TO: All Department Heads

SUBJECT: New Copy Procedures

Long lines and the uninterrupted flow of text obscure the new procedures.

A recent study of our copy center request procedures indicates that we are not fulfilling copy requests as efficiently as possible. A number of problems surfaced in the survey. First, many requests, particularly large orders, are submitted before the copy center opens. Others are submitted after the copy center closes. As a result, the copy center has an enormous backlog of copy orders to fill before it can begin copy orders submitted after 8:30 A.M., when the center officially opens. This backlog may throw the center two or three hours behind schedule. All copy requests throughout the day then require over two hours to complete. By 2:00 P.M., any copy requests submitted may not be filled that day. If large orders arrive unexpectedly even a routine copy request may take two days to complete.

To remedy the situation, we will change to the following copy request procedure beginning Monday, February 3. The copy center will close at 3:00 every afternoon. Two work-study employees will work at the center from 3:00 until 5:00 to complete all orders by 4:00. If you submit copy requests by 3:00, the center will have them ready by 4:00. In short, all requests will be filled the day they are submitted. However, do not leave copy requests after 3:00, as these will not be processed until the following day. However, we guarantee that if you leave your request for copies with us between 8:30 and 3:00, you will have them that day.

Requests for copies of large orders—over 100 copies of one item, single/multiple copies of any document over 25 pages, of front/back photocopying of one item up to 50 copies—will require that a notice be given the copy center one day in advance. That way, the center can prepare for your copy request and be sure to have it ready for you. Copies of the request form are attached. Please complete one of these and send it to Lynda Haynes at the copy center so that she can schedule all big jobs. If you submit a big copy request without having completed the form, your request will be completed after other requests are complete.

Allow plenty of time for routine jobs—at least two hours, and three if possible. Beginning February 3, give all copy requests to the receptionist at your office number. Be sure you attach complete instructions. Give your name, your phone number, and your office number. State the number of copies required and any special instructions. Specify staples or clips, color paper, and collation on multipage copies.

Pick-up procedures also change February 3. All copy jobs, after they are complete, will be placed in each department's mail box. No copies will be left outside the copy center after closing time. No copies will be left with the receptionist. Large orders that will not fit mail boxes will be delivered to your office.

If you have questions about this new procedure, please contact Lynda Haynes at 2257.

FIGURE 11-8 • Memo That Violates Format Guidelines

TO: All Department Heads   DATE: January 27, 2001

FROM: Lynda Haynes

SUBJECT: **New Procedures for Ordering Copies from the Copy Center**

EFFECTIVE DATE: MONDAY, FEBRUARY 5, 2001

To handle orders more quickly and efficiently, the Copy Center is changing its procedures. Please inform everyone in your department and ask them to follow these new procedures.

Large Orders and Routine Requests

First, you must decide if you have a large order or a routine request. A large order is

- more than 100 copies of any item
- more than 50 copies of any item to be copied two-sided (front/back)
- single or multiple copies of any document over 25 pages.

Procedures for a Large Order

1. Fill out one of the attached Requests for Copying a Large Order forms.

2. Send the completed form to Lynda Haynes at the Copy Center at least one day in advance of the day you need the copying done.

   That way, Lynda can schedule big jobs, and you will avoid delays in getting your copying completed.

Procedure for a Routine Request

1. Attach complete instructions to your request. Include
   - your name, phone number, and office number
   - the number of copies you need
   - for multiple-page copies: instructions on collating and staples or clips
   - any special instructions, such as paper color

2. Give all copy requests to the Copy Center receptionists.

3. Allow 2 to 3 hours for your order to be filled.

NOTE:

Routine requests left between 8:30 A.M. and 3:00 P.M. will be processed by 4:00 P.M. on the same day.

The Copy Center will close at 3:00 P.M. Orders left after that time will be processed the next day.

Copy Pick up Procedures

Copies will be delivered to your department's mailbox. If the order is too large for your mailbox, it will be delivered to your office.

If You Have Questions . . .   Contact Lynda Haynes at ext. 2257.

The information is in the order in which users need it.

The page with lots of white space is easier to read.

The headings in bold break the text into meaningful sections.

FIGURE 11-9 • A Revision of Figure 11-8

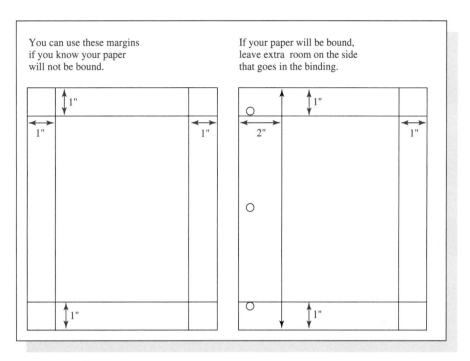

FIGURE 11-10 • Page Layouts Showing Margins
These margins are for 8¹/₂-by-11-inch paper. (Some people prefer a larger, 1¹/₂-inch margin at the bottom of the page.)

in this chapter use space, and note all the ways that the more visually effective examples use space well. The space in the margins is important, but it's not enough. Graphic designers call margins *passive space* because margins only define the block of the page or screen that readers should look at. Graphic designers know that *active space* inside the text is really what makes the difference in an effective layout.

For online documents, passive margin space is not as critical as it is on paper. However, active space inside the text is even more critical in online documents than it is on paper. Most online documents are not read continuously; rather, users consult them in an effort to quickly locate and act on information. Space helps users locate information quickly, helps them keep their place, and gives them smaller, more manageable "chunks" to deal with.

Here are several techniques to get space onto your pages and screens:

- Use headings frequently. Put them above the text or to the left of the text and put space before them.
- Use bulleted lists for three or more parallel points. Use numbered lists for steps in instructions. Lists are often indented inside the text, and each item may be separated from the others by a blank space.

- Use pictures, tables, and other graphics, both because they provide relief from paragraphs of text and because they make points visually obvious that would take many words to explain. (See Chapter 12, Using Illustrations.)
- Separate paragraphs with an extra blank line, or indent the first line of each paragraph. In online documents, make your paragraphs even shorter than you would in paper documents so that there is space even in a small window. Online, one instruction or one short sentence may make an appropriate paragraph. Look again at Figures 11-5 and 11-6. The space is an active design element that makes the instructions in Figure 11-6 much easier to follow than the instructions in Figure 11-5.

Set the Spacing for Easy Reading

It's common in paper documents such as letters and memos to use single spacing, unless the document is very short. When you use single spacing, put an extra line between paragraphs. Figures 11-2 and 11-9 show you this style.

Drafts are usually double-spaced to give writers and editors more room in which to write their corrections and notes. When you use double spacing in drafts, you have to have some way to show where new paragraphs begin. Indent the first line of each paragraph or add an extra line between paragraphs. Even final reports are often done in double spacing or space-and-a-half.

For documents that will be read on the computer screen, set the spacing so each line can be read easily but so there is more space between paragraphs than between lines within the paragraph. Double spacing is not usually used for continuous text on the screen because a typical screen holds only about one-third of what a paper page holds.

Use a Medium Line Length

Long lines of uninterrupted text are tiring to read. Moreover, readers are likely to lose their place in moving from the right margin of a long line back to the left margin of the next line. Very short lines are also difficult to read. They make the text appear choppy, and readers may have trouble keeping the sense of what they are reading. Figure 11-11 illustrates the problems with both very long and very short lines of text.

The number of characters that fit in a certain amount of space depends in part on the size and style of type that you are using. (See the section entitled Choosing Readable Type in this chapter for more on this subject.) If you have one column of text on paper or in a full-width computer screen, try to keep the lines of text to about fifty to seventy-five characters, or about ten to twelve words. That's what this book does.

In a format with two equal columns, keep each column to about thirty-five characters, or about five words. If your online document comes up in a

Long lines of type are difficult for many people to read. Readers may find it difficult to get back to the correct place at the left margin. The smaller the type, the harder it is for most people to read long lines of type.

Very short lines
takes up too
much space
and make
comprehension
difficult.

FIGURE 11-11 • Line Length
Very long lines and very short lines are hard to read.

window on the computer, you will, of necessity, use short lines. Set the default line length so that a typical short instruction fits well on one line.

Use a Ragged Right Margin

Since you first began writing by hand on ruled notebook paper and then once you began typing, you have been accustomed to having a firm left margin in your documents. The first line of a paragraph of text either starts at that left margin (called *block style*) or is indented two or five spaces (called *indented style*). This book uses indented style for paragraphs. Many letters and memos today use block style. Figure 11-1 is an example of the indented style for paragraphs. Figure 11-7 is in block style. In both styles, all the lines after the first one in a paragraph start at the same firm left margin.

Although text is almost always lined up on the left margin, it is not always also lined up evenly on the right margin. The text of this book is even on both the left and the right. Most of the examples in the figures in this chapter are even on the left but not on the right. The technique of making all the text align exactly on the right margin is called *justifying the text*. When the text is lined up on the left but is not justified on the right, we say it has a *ragged right margin*. Figure 11-12 shows the four ways that you can align text.

Be careful if you decide to justify type on the right margin. Some word processing programs create unsightly gaps in justified type that make the text very difficult to read. Research shows that regular spacing eases the reading process. If all the extra space needed to fill out a line of text is put between just two of the words, the words will not be evenly spaced across the line. Readers' eyes tend to focus on the large space between words rather than on the words themselves.[7]

Even if your computer can microjustify—divide extra space evenly across the line so that you can hardly tell there is any—think about the purpose and audience for your work. Justified type gives a document a formal tone.

This text is justified only on the left. It has a ragged right margin. This is the preferred style for most on-line documents and documents that are printed on desktop printers.

This text is justified on both the right and the left. This is typical of books and other materials printed on high-resolution printers. If the computer cannot put the space in evenly across the rows, the text will include "rivers" of white that make reading difficult.

This text is justified on the right, but not on the left. This is highly unusual, except sometimes in headings.

This text has each line centered. Centering is sometimes used for headings and title pages.

FIGURE 11-12 • The Four Ways to Line Up (Justify) Text

Unjustified (ragged right) type gives a document a more friendly, personal tone. Many journals have changed from justified type to ragged right because ragged right is more readable and because they want to look modern. Readers like unjustified text.[8] Poor readers have more difficulty reading justified text.[9] Online documents almost always have ragged right margins, both because reading from the screen is more difficult than reading from paper and because writers want to make their online documents look modern and friendly.

► CHOOSING READABLE TYPE

Today's technology gives you many choices for the shape of the letters, numbers, and other characters in your text. These different shapes are called *type, typefaces,* or *fonts.* Companies, or groups within companies, often have style guidelines that tell you what fonts to use for official reports, letters, manuals, and online documents. If you aren't in one of those companies, or if you are writing a document that is not covered by the style guidelines, you are likely to have to make decisions about what to use.

These six suggestions will help you choose type that is easy to read:

• Choose a legible type size.
• Choose a typeface (font) that is appropriate for the situation.

- Use special typefaces sparingly.
- Use highlighting effectively.
- Use a mixture of cases, not all capitals.
- Use color carefully.

Choose a Legible Type Size

Type is measured in *points*. A point is $1/72$ of an inch, so a letter in 36-point type is about $1/2$ inch high. On a computer, you have a wide choice of point sizes, from very small to very large, as you can see in Figure 11-13.

Research conducted before word processing was commonplace suggested that 8- to 10-point type was best, but that was for typeset documents like this book that are printed at very high resolution. Most documents today are printed on desktop printers at a resolution of only 300 or 600 dots per inch. At that resolution, 8-point, even 10-point type, is difficult to read.

For most word-processed documents, you will find that 11- or 12-point type works well for the regular text. You may want to use 9- or 10-point type for headers, footers, and footnotes. You can then use larger sizes for titles and headings, but don't make them so large that they destroy the balance of the page. (A later section, Design Headings to Organize the Page, has more on type size for headings. Figure 11-23 shows an example of good style and placement for headings.)

In some online situations, such as e-mail, you may not have a choice of what type size or font to use. In writing other online documents, make sure the type is large enough to be read by most users at the distance they sit from their monitors and with the monitors they use. Both on paper and online, experiment with different fonts in different sizes to see what is most readable, with the technology that you have—and, for online, with the technology that most of your readers have.

This is 8-point type.
This is 10-point type.
This is 12-point type.
This is 14-point type.
This is 18-point type.
This is 24-point type.
This is 36-point type.

FIGURE 11-13 • Type Comes in Different Sizes

Times New Roman	The quick brown fox jumped over the lazy dog.
Century Schoolbook	The quick brown fox jumped over the lazy dog.
Arial	The quick brown fox jumped over the lazy dog.
Courier New	The quick brown fox jumped over the lazy dog.

FIGURE 11-14 • Different Fonts
The same text in the same point size but in different fonts takes up different amounts of space on the page.

The shape and spacing of the letters also affect how much room the font takes up on a page or screen and how readable it is. Type in one font may look much tighter and smaller than type in the same point size in another font because of the way the letters are shaped and how they are spaced when typed next to each other. Figure 11-14 shows four fonts, all in 13-point type.

Choose a Typeface (Font) That Is Appropriate for the Situation

There are thousands of type fonts, and you may have a wide selection to choose from with your technology. Type fonts can be divided into two main groups: *serif type*, which has extenders on the letters, and *sans serif type*, which does not have extenders. Figure 11-15 shows the difference between serif and sans serif type. Many computer programs give you a choice of several different serif and sans serif fonts. Figure 11-16 shows you examples of some of those choices from one program.

Serifs draw the reader's eye across the page, so most books and other long paper documents are printed with serif type. Sans serif type works well in brochures and other short documents. Sans serif type also works well for visuals with oral presentations because viewers are at a distance from the words, and they're reading single lines at a time. (See Chapter 19, Oral Reports, for more on presentations.)

Experts are still discussing whether serif or sans serif type is better for online documents. Many writers prefer sans serif typefaces for their online doc-

FIGURE 11-15 • Styles of Type
Type comes in two major styles: serif and sans serif (without serifs).

Serif Typefaces	Sans Serif Typefaces
Times	Helvetica
Palatino	Futura Light
Garamond	Franklin Gothic
Schoolbook	Helvetica Narrow
Courier	OCRA

FIGURE 11-16 • Examples of Typefaces
Some traditional and new typefaces (fonts) available on the Macintosh computer.

uments because, with the poor resolution of many screens, serifs can make individual letters more difficult to read. Also, sans serif type, like ragged right margins, gives a document a more modern look.

In general, once you decide on a font for your document, use that font throughout the document. An exception to that rule is that even if you are using a serif font for the text, sans serif works well in tables, figure captions, and the legends with your graphs. You can also switch to a sans serif font for the headings and headers or footers.

Use Special Typefaces Sparingly

Some computers offer unusual typefaces, as you see in Figure 11-17. These typefaces are not generally appropriate for technical reports or for online documentation. They are not as readable as the typefaces in Figure 11-16.

THIS FONT LOOKS LIKE OLD-FASHIONED COMPUTER WRITING.

This might be appropriate for invitations.

Use outline fonts sparingly.

This looks like Ye Olde Font.

FIGURE 11-17 • Special Typefaces
Unusual typefaces should be used with caution and only in appropriate situations.
Source: Fonts from Arts & Letters. Computer Support Corporation, Dallas, TX 75244.

Use Highlighting Effectively

There are many ways to highlight material—to draw the reader's attention to parts of your document that you want to emphasize. We have already discussed two ways: changing the size of the type to indicate a heading and using space to set off specific elements such as headings, lists, and tables. You have several other choices for highlighting:

boldface

italics

<u>underlining</u>

changing the color

Placing information in a box

Cautions or warnings often are printed with rules set above and below the material

---

As you design your documents and decide on highlighting techniques, keep these three points in mind:

- Don't use too many techniques.
- Don't use any technique for more than a short sentence.
- Be consistent in the way you use each technique.

Don't Use Too Many Techniques Highlighting calls attention to specific elements in the text. If you use too many different kinds of highlighting or use one kind too often, you dilute the effect.

Don't Use Any Technique for More Than a Short Sentence Whole paragraphs underlined, set in boldface or italics, or printed a different color are difficult to read. Instead of enticing readers to pay attention to the material, long sections in highlighting turn readers away.

Figure 11-18 is a memo that uses too much underlining in an attempt to emphasize the major points. Despite the underlining, it does not invite reading. Figure 11-19 shows how white space, bold headings, and a judicious use of bold in the text make the memo more inviting and easier to read and, especially, make the major points more obvious.

Be Consistent in the Way You Use Each Technique Highlighting helps readers quickly grasp different elements in the text. Once you choose a technique for highlighting a particular kind of information, use that technique consistently for that kind of information. If you use italics for specially

TO: David Stewart   DATE: February 19, 2001

FROM: Kathy Hillman

SUBJECT: Short Course Request from Ocean Drilling

Because I will be away on a three-week teaching assignment, I would appreciate your handling the following request, which came in just as I was preparing to leave today.

Randy Allen, director of the offshore drilling research team, would like a short-course in writing offshore safety inspection reports. He would like the short-course taught from 2–4 P.M. <u>Monday–Friday afternoons, beginning week after next</u>. The class must be scheduled then, as the team leaves the following week for their next research cruise.

The drilling research team spends <u>two weeks each month on cruise</u>. After they return, they have one week to complete their reports before briefing begins for the next research expedition. Because of their rigid schedule, <u>they cannot attend our regularly scheduled writing classes</u>.

Allen says that the cultural and educational backgrounds of the team are varied. Five of the ten regular researchers are native Europeans who attended only European universities. Of the remaining five, two have degrees from U.S. institutions, and three attended Canadian universities. <u>As a result of their varied educational backgrounds, their reports lack uniform handling of English and organization</u>. All the researchers have expressed interest in having a short review of standard English usage so that their reports to management will be more uniform.

<u>Sarah Kelley</u> says she can develop a class for the drilling team. We have materials on reports, style, and standard usage in the files. She can work with Ocean Drilling to determine the best report structure and develop a plan. These <u>items can be easily collected and placed in binders</u>. We also have <u>summary sheets</u> on each topic that will be good reference aids when the researchers write their reports following their cruise.

<u>Sarah will contact you Monday morning. If her teaching the class meets with your approval, please give Randy Allen a call, at extension 721, before noon. He has a staff meeting scheduled at 1:30 and would like to announce the short course then. In fact, if the course cannot be scheduled this month, it cannot be taught for seven months because of off-season cruise schedules. Allen wants this course before the team begins a series of four reports during the off-season.</u>

Please arrange a time for Sarah to meet with Allen so they can go over several previous reports. Sarah wants to be sure that what she covers in the course is what they need.

If you need to talk to me about this request, I will be staying at the Hyatt in New Orleans.

FIGURE 11-18 • Memorandum That Overuses Underlining and Lacks Headings

| TO: | David Stewart | DATE: | February 19, 2001 |

FROM: Kathy Hillman

SUBJECT: Request from Offshore Drilling Team for a Special Short Course

**ACTION
REQUIRED: Decision from you by Monday, February 24 at noon**

Because I will be away on a three-week teaching assignment, I would appreciate your handling the following request, which came in just as I was preparing to leave today.

Offshore Drilling Wants a Special Short Course

Randy Allen, director of the offshore drilling research team, would like a short course in how to write offshore safety inspection reports. He would like the short course taught from 2 to 4 P.M. Monday to Friday afternoons, beginning the week after next. Allen wants this course before they begin a series of four reports during the off-season.

They Cannot Attend Our Regular Writing Classes

The class must be scheduled at the time Randy has requested because the team leaves the following week for their next research cruise. The team spends two weeks each month on cruise. After they return, they have one week to complete their reports before briefing begins for the next research expedition. Because of this rigid schedule, they cannot attend our regularly scheduled writing classes. In fact, **if the course cannot be scheduled this month, it cannot be taught for seven months** because of the off-season cruise schedules.

The Offshore Drilling Team Needs Help with Their Writing

Allen says that the cultural and educational backgrounds of the team are varied. Five of the ten regular researchers are native Europeans who attended only European universities. Of the remaining five, two have degrees from U.S. institutions, and three attended Canadian universities. As a result of their varied educational backgrounds, their reports lack uniform handling of English and report organization. Allen says that all the researchers have expressed interest in having a short review of standard English usage so that their reports to management will be more uniform.

Sarah Kelley Can Develop the Class

Sarah Kelley says she can develop a class for the offshore drilling team. We have materials on reports, style, and standard usage in the files. She can work with the ocean drilling group to determine the best report structure and develop a plan. These items can be easily collected and put in binders. We also have summary sheets on each topic that will be good reference aids when the researchers write their reports following their cruise.

Please Decide by Monday Noon and Call Randy Allen—Extension 721

Sarah will contact you Monday morning. If you approve of her teaching the class, please call Randy Allen at extension 721, before noon. **He has a staff meeting scheduled for 1:30 and would like to announce the short course then.**

Please arrange a time for Sarah Kelley to meet with Randy Allen so they can go over several previous reports. Sarah wants to be sure that what she covers in the course is what they need.

FIGURE 11-19 • Revision of Figure 11-18

CAPITAL LETTERS GIVE US NO CLUES TO DISTINGUISH ONE LETTER FROM ANOTHER. THEREFORE, THE LETTERS BLUR INTO EACH OTHER VERY QUICKLY, AND WE WANT TO STOP READING. LOWERCASE LETTERS GIVE US CLUES TO THE SHAPES OF THE WORDS, AND WE USE THOSE SHAPES AS WE READ.

Capital letters give us no clues to distinguish one letter from another. Therefore, the letters blur into each other very quickly, and we want to stop reading. Lowercase letters give us clues to the shapes of the words, and we use those shapes as we read.

FIGURE 11-20 • A Comparison of Text in All Capitals and Text in Mixed Case

defined words, do so throughout. If you decide to set off cautions and warnings with rules above and below the text, use that technique for all cautions and warnings and don't use it for anything else.

Use a Mixture of Cases, Not All Capitals

Don't use all capitals for text. A sentence in all capitals takes about 13 percent more time to read than a sentence typed in the regular uppercase and lowercase letters that we expect.[10] As Figure 11-20 shows, all capitals slow down reading because we use the shapes of letters to help us read, and the shapes disappear with all capitals.

A sentence in all capitals also takes up about 30 percent more space than the same sentence in lowercase letters. Mixed case is especially important online because space is always at a premium on screen and because text is harder to read on the screen. In addition, if you use all capitals in e-mail, readers think you're shouting at them.

Use Color Carefully

On paper, avoid printing the text in color. Black ink on white paper provides the best contrast, and high contrast between paper and ink is necessary for easy reading. Colored paper may be a better choice if it enhances the effectiveness of your document. For example, some companies use light gray, cream, or light blue paper for major reports and proposals. Some companies use paper of one color for the main body of the report and another color for the appendices. Some use colored sheets as dividers between sections of reports. If you use colored paper, choose a very light shade to keep the contrast between ink and paper high.

You may be able to print a document in more than one color. If so, use color judiciously. Color works well in headings and in visuals such as graphs, charts, and pictures, but it doesn't work well for text on paper. This book, for example, uses green-blue for headings and other elements on the page, but the regular text is black.

When planning to use color in a printed report or other document, think about what may happen to the document in the future. If it is likely to be photocopied, make sure that color is not the only indicator of any particular feature, because the color will be lost in photocopying. Also, remember that some people are colorblind; they cannot distinguish certain colors.

There is often an added cost to printing paper documents in color. Online, color is free, but don't go overboard using a rainbow of colors. Also, keeping a high contrast between the text and the background is important on screen as well as on paper. For example, a solid light blue makes a good background color for the screen, but blue is not a good color for text because our eyes don't focus well on blue letters.[11] Don't create artistic backgrounds that make the text difficult to see. You want readers to pay attention to your words and pictures, not to the background.

The golden rule for all aspects of document design, both on paper and on screen, is to make the page or screen look clear, uncluttered, and consistent. Keep it simple.

▶ HELPING READERS LOCATE INFORMATION

To help your readers find what they need and understand your document, you have to plan a useful structure for the document (organize it well), and you have to show that structure to the readers (design it well). In the previous sections of this chapter, we showed you how to use page layout and fonts to make your document clear and easy to use. In this section, we show you how to give readers clues to the document's overall structure.

As we pointed out earlier in the chapter, most people read technical and business documents selectively, both in print and online. With a print document, readers may glance over the table of contents to see what the document is about and then pick and choose the sections to read by looking for headings that match their needs and interests. They may skim through the pages, stopping when a heading or example or graphic strikes them as relevant or important. They may need to go back to the document later to check specific facts, and they'll want to find the relevant pages quickly.

Readers seldom work through an online document from beginning to end. They *use* an online document World Wide Web site rather than *read* it. They jump from the contents page (which corresponds to the table of contents of a paper document) or from the search function (which corresponds to an index) directly to a topic that interests them. To help readers (users) find what they need quickly, you have to arrange your document well and then give them clues to your arrangement.

Following are three ways to help your readers find information easily:

- Write descriptive headings.
- Design useful headings.
- Use page numbers and headers or footers in print documents.

Write Descriptive Headings

Headings are the short lines—the titles—that you put above each section and subsection of your document. Even short documents, such as memos, instructions, and letters, can benefit from headings. Compare Figures 11-19 and 11-18 to see how useful headings can be, even in a short memo.

In longer documents, headings are essential to break the text into manageable pieces. Furthermore, in longer documents, the first few levels of headings become the table of contents. Online documents, such as World Wide Web pages, use headings too. Those headings may become a contents page in an online document, or they may be the home page or top of the page of a World Wide Web site. Each heading becomes a link to the relevant section so that a user can click on the heading and jump directly to that section.

Headings are the road map to your document. For a print document, the headings come from your outline, although you usually don't use Roman numerals or letters in headings. If you are creating an online document, you should first develop an outline for it, too, and think carefully about the headings. These five suggestions will help you write useful headings:

- Use concrete language.
- Use questions, verb phrases, and sentences instead of nouns alone.
- Use standard keywords if readers expect them.
- Make the headings at a given level parallel.
- Make sure the headings match the table of contents.

Use Concrete Language Generic headings such as *Part I* or *Section 2* give no clues about the content of your work. Make your headings tell your story. Readers should be able to read only your headings, without any of your text, and understand the overall content as well as the structure (the arrangement) of your document.

Use Questions, Verb Phrases, and Sentences Instead of Nouns Alone The best way to write headings is to put yourself in your readers' place. Will readers come to your document with questions? Then questions will make good headings. Will they come wanting instructions for doing tasks? Then verb phrases that match the actions they need to take will make good headings. Will they come seeking knowledge about a situation? Then statements of fact about that situation will make good headings. Figure 11-21 shows how effective it can be to use questions, verb phrases, and statements as headings.

To see headings like these in actual documents, look back at figures that appeared earlier in this chapter. Figure 11-9 shows two levels of headings on the same page. The memo in Figure 11-19 has only one level of heading. Here the writer uses sentences as headings so that a busy reader can skim through the headings and grasp the important messages in the memo.

Use Standard Keywords If Readers Expect Them You may be working on a document for which readers expect to see a certain set of headings in a certain order, as in a standard proposal format. In that case, you

---

Questions are useful as headings in a brochure.
> What does the gypsy moth look like?
> How can we protect trees from gypsy moths?
> How often should we spray?

Verb phrases are useful in instruction manuals.
Verb phrases can be gerunds, like these:
> Adding a graphic
> Selecting the data
> Choosing type of graph to use
> Adding a title

Verb phrases can be imperatives, like these:
> Make your attendance policy clear.
> Explain your grading policy.
> Announce your office hours.
> Supply names of texts to be purchased.
> Go over assignments and their due dates.

Short sentences are useful in memos and reports.
> Our workload has doubled in the past year.
> We are also being asked to do new tasks.
> We have logged 560 hours of overtime this year.
> We need three more staff positions.

FIGURE 11-21 • Different Structures You Can Use for Effective Headings

Project Summary	Facilities and Equipment
Project Description	Personnel
Rationale and Significance	Budget
Plan of Work	

FIGURE 11-22 • Keywords as Headings in a Proposal

should organize your material in the order and with the headings that your readers expect. Figure 11-22 shows the headings you might use in a standard proposal format.

However, be wary of using single nouns or strings of nouns as headings in most documents. Headings that are only nouns may be ambiguous, overly technical, or too general. Research shows that people have a great deal of difficulty predicting what information comes under noun headings.[12]

Make the Headings at a Given Level Parallel Like list items, headings at any given level in a document should be parallel. Parallelism is a very powerful tool in writing. See for yourself the difference parallelism makes by comparing the two sets of headings in Figure 11-23.

Make Sure the Headings Match the Table of Contents To check how well your headings tell your story and to check how well you've maintained parallel structure in headings, use your word processing program to create an outline view, or a table of contents, for your draft document in print or online. Both in print and online, the headings become the table of contents. In a print document, readers can use the table of contents to turn to a particular section. They know they're in the right place if the heading for that section matches the wording in the table of contents. The same is even more true online, where readers almost always move by jumping directly from a heading in the contents to a screen of information. If the heading (the title) on the screen they come to doesn't match the heading that they clicked on in

Nonparallel Headings	**Parallel Headings**
Graph Modifications	Modifying a graph
Data selection updating	Changing the data
To add or delete columns	Adding or deleting columns
How to change color or patterns	Changing the color or patterns
Titles and legends can be included	Adding titles and legends

FIGURE 11-23 • Nonparallel and Parallel Headings
Headings that use the same sentence structure—parallel headings—are easier for users to follow.

the contents, they may be confused and unsure whether they are where they thought they were going.

Design Headings to Organize the Page

Headings do more than outline your document. They also help readers find specific parts quickly, and they show the relationship among the parts. To help readers, headings have to be easily distinguished from the text and each level of heading has to be easily distinguished from all the other levels. Figure 11-24 is a good example of a print document with four levels of headings. You can see how the writer uses boldface to distinguish all headings from the text and then uses type size, capitalization, and placement on the page to distinguish each level of heading from the other levels.

These seven suggestions will help you design useful headings:

- Limit the number of heading levels.
- Create a pattern for the headings and stick to it.
- Match size to importance.
- Put more space before a heading than after it.
- Keep each heading with the section it covers.
- Use headings frequently.
- Consider using numbers with your headings.

Limit the Number of Heading Levels Student papers and technical documents that are meant to be read on paper shouldn't need more than four levels of headings. If you have more than four levels, consider dividing the material into two chapters. Online documents shouldn't need more than two levels of headings because readers see much less at one time online than in a paper document.

Create a Pattern for the Headings and Stick to It Although your choices depend in part on the technology you are using, you almost certainly have several options for showing levels of headings.[13] Figure 11-24 demonstrates a variety of ways to show different levels of headings. You can combine these to create the pattern for your headings. For example, you can change size, placement, *and* capitalization to show the different levels of headings. Look again at Figure 11-24 to see how the writer has combined size and placement to create a pattern in which the level of each heading is obvious. To see how a writer can use a consistent pattern of headings in a complete report, look ahead to Figure 16-3.

Match Size to Importance Changing the type size is one way to indicate levels of headings. If you use different type sizes, make sure that you

Controlling Soil-Borne Pathogens in Tree Nurseries

Types of Soil-Borne Pathogen and Their Effects on Trees

Simply stated, the effects of soil-borne pathogens......................................

....

The soil-borne fungi

At one time, it was thought that the soil-borne fungi...................................

Basiodiomycetes. The Basiodiomycetes are a class of fungi whose species

....

Phycomycetes. The class Phycomycetes is a very diversified type of fungus. It is the ....

The plant parasitic nematodes

Nematodes are small, unsegmented...

....

Treatments and Controls for Soil-Borne Pathogens

....

....

....

FIGURE 11-24 • Four Levels of Headings in a Report

match the size to the level of importance. If the headings are different sizes, readers expect first-level headings to be larger than second-level headings, second-level headings to be larger than third-level headings, and so on, as shown in Figure 11-24. The lower-level headings can be the same size as the text, but no level of heading should be smaller than the text. That would violate readers' expectations. If you use different type sizes for different heading levels, don't make the differences too great.

Put More Space before a Heading than after It Headings announce the topic that is coming next in your document. Therefore, you want the heading to lead the reader's eye down the page or screen into the text that follows. One way to do that is to have more space, on the page or screen, before the heading than after it, as in Figures 11-4 and 11-9.

If you are going to use a rule with the heading, consider putting it *above* the heading rather than below it. A rule above the heading creates a "chunk" that includes both the heading and the text that it covers. A rule above the heading also draws the reader's eye down into the text that follows instead of up and away from that text.

Keep Each Heading with the Section It Covers Don't leave a heading at the bottom of a page when the text appears on the next page. Make sure you have at least two lines of the first paragraph on the page with the heading. In some cases, you may want each topic to be on a separate page so that the heading and all the text of a topic appear together. The letter in Figure 11-7 is done this way. The formal reports in Chapter 16 also illustrate effective ways of breaking pages. Most word processing programs have functions that help you keep headings from being stranded at the bottom of a page and that allow you to set up your document so that all headings of a certain level start on a new page.

Use Headings Frequently Frequent headings break up the monotony of text on the page or screen. They also help readers who are skimming to grasp the main points of the document quickly. Review Figure 11-7. In a report, you probably want a heading for every subsection, which might cover two or three paragraphs. In general, in print, you want to have clues to the text's arrangement on every page; online, you should have a heading on every screen or window. On a World Wide Web page, you want to keep each topic short and give each topic a heading.

Consider Using Numbers with Your Headings In many companies and agencies, the standard for organizing reports and manuals is to use a numbering system with headings. Figure 11-25 shows the three most commonly used systems:

- The traditional outline system
- The century-decade-unit system (often called the Navy system)
- The multiple-decimal system

The rationale for these systems is that you can refer to a section elsewhere in the report by the number of its heading. Numbering systems, however, have several disadvantages. In all of these systems, if you want to add or remove a section, you have to renumber at least part of the report. Unless your software does this for you automatically, renumbering is tedious and highly

Traditional outline system

TITLE
I.　FIRST-LEVEL HEADING
　　A.　Second-Level Heading
　　　　1.　Third-level heading
　　　　2.　Third-level heading
　　B.　Second-Level Heading
II.　FIRST-LEVEL HEADING
　　A.　Second-Level Heading
　　　　1.　Third-level heading
　　　　2.　Third-level heading
　　B.　Second-Level Heading

Century-decade-unit system

TITLE
100　FIRST-LEVEL HEADING
　　110　Second-Level Heading
　　　　111　Third-level heading
　　　　112　Third-level heading
　　120　Second-Level Heading
200　FIRST-LEVEL HEADING
　　210　Second-Level Heading
　　　　211　Third-level heading
　　　　212　Third-level heading
　　220　Second-Level Heading

Multiple-decimal system

TITLE
1　FIRST-LEVEL HEADING
　1.1　Second-Level Heading
　　　1.1.1　Third-level heading
　　　1.1.2　Third-level heading
　1.2　Second-Level Heading
2　FIRST-LEVEL HEADING
　2.1　Second-Level Heading
　　　2.1.1　Third-level heading
　　　2.1.2　Third-level heading

FIGURE 11-25 • Three Types of Numbering System

susceptible to error. Many readers have trouble following these numbering systems, especially if you need more than three levels. The multiple-decimal system is particularly difficult for most people to use. For example, by the time you get to a heading marked 1.1.1.1 (and some government reports go to a fifth level, 1.1.1.1.1), you may find it difficult to remember what the main division 1.0 actually was.

If you are not required to use a numbering system, we suggest that you not institute one. Better alternatives are available now. You can show the hierarchy of heading levels distinctly with changes in type size and placement instead of numbers, as you have seen in examples in this and other chapters of this book.

However, many government agencies and many companies, especially those that prepare documents for the government, require one of these numbering systems. Therefore, it pays to be familiar with them. If you use a numbering system with your headings, you must also use the numbers before the entries in your table of contents.

Use Page Numbers and Headers or Footers in Print Documents

In addition to clearly worded and visually accessible headings, you can use other devices to make your content and organization clear in printed documents. Two good ways are to number each page and to include running headers, as shown in each page of this book or footers, as described shortly.

Number the Pages You have been numbering the pages of essays, research papers, and book reports for years, but you may not have considered the importance of page numbering as a document design tool. Page numbers help readers keep track of where they are and provide easy reference points for talking about a printed document. Always number the pages of your drafts and final documents that people are going to read on paper.

Note that if the document is going to be used online, page numbers aren't usually helpful. In most online documents, readers can skip around in the document, jumping from one topic to another in any order. One place where page numbers are useful online, however, is in a set of visuals for an oral presentation. These may be created with software and projected directly from the computer or printed on transparencies and shown on an overhead projector (see Chapter 19, Oral Reports). To help your audience know where you and they are in the presentation, you may want to number your slides. You may want to let the audience know how many slides there are with a notation like this:

Slide 1 of 10

Short manuscripts and reports that have little prefatory material almost always use Arabic numerals (1, 2, 3), like the page numbers in this book. The commonly accepted convention is to center the page number below the text, near the bottom of the page, or to put it in the upper right-hand corner. Always leave at least one double space between the text and the page number. Put the page number in the same place on each page. Page numbers at the bottom of the page often have a hyphen on each side, like this:

```
-  17  -
```

As reports grow longer and more complicated, the page-numbering system also may need to be more complex. If you have a preface or other material that comes before the main part of the report, it is customary to use small Roman numerals (i, ii, iii) for that material and then to change to Arabic numerals for the body of the report. The opening pages of this book use Roman numerals, and the balance use Arabic numerals.

In a report, the introduction may be part of the prefatory material or the main body. The title page doesn't show the number but is counted as the first page. The page following the title page is number 2 or ii.

When numbering the pages, you have to know whether the document is going to be printed or photocopied on one side of the paper or two. If both sides of the paper will have printing on them, you may have to number some otherwise blank pages in word processing files. New chapters usually start on a right-hand page—that is, on the front side of a page that is photocopied on both sides. The right-hand page always has an odd number. If the last page of your first chapter is page 9, for example, and your document will be photocopied double-sided, you have to include an otherwise blank page 10 so that the first page of your second chapter will be a right-hand page (in this case, page 11) when the document is printed, copied, and bound.

The body of a report is usually paginated continuously, from page 1 to the last page. For the appendixes, you may continue the same series of numbers, or you may change to a letter-plus-number system. In that system, the pages in Appendix A are numbered A-1, A-2, and so on. The pages in Appendix B are numbered B-1, B-2, and so forth. If your report is part of a series, or if your company has a standard report format, you will need to make your page numbering match that of the series or standard.

Numbering appendixes with the letter-plus-number system has several advantages:

- It separates the appendixes from the body. Readers can tell how long the body of the report is and how long each appendix is.
- It clearly shows that a page is part of an appendix and which appendix it belongs to. It makes pages in the appendixes easier to locate.

- It allows the appendixes to be printed separately from the body of the report. Sometimes the appendixes are ready before the body of the report has been completed, and being able to print the appendixes first may save time and help you meet a deadline.
- It allows the pagination of either an appendix or the body to be changed without requiring changes in the other parts.

Include Headers or Footers In long paper documents, it helps readers if you give them information about the document at the top or bottom of the page. If the information is at the top of the page, it is a **header**. This book uses headers printed in $8^1/_2$-point type to help you find chapters quickly as you look through the pages. If the information is at the bottom of the page, it is a **footer**. The document in Figure 11-4 uses a footer.

A typical header for a report would show the author's name, the title of the report, and the date. It might look like this:

```
Jane Fernstein        Feasibility Study        June 2001
```

The page numbers would likely appear at the bottom of the page.

A typical header for a letter would show the name of the person receiving the letter, the page number, and the date. It might look like this:

```
Dr. Jieru Chen              -2-              June 16, 2001
```

Or

```
Dr. Jieru Chen
Page 2
June 16, 2001
```

Figure 11-7 uses this type of header.

The header does not appear on the title page of the report or on the first page of a letter. Most word processing programs allow you to set up your file so that the header starts on the second page.

Online documents should also have indicators that tell people both what document they are in and what part of the document they are looking at.

▶ APPRECIATING THE IMPORTANCE OF DOCUMENT DESIGN

Both in print and online, the way your document looks is critical. The layout of the page or screen makes a visual impression that affects readers. Readers will spend more time with pages and screens that are visually pleasing. Document design is more than just aesthetics, however. The choices you make about document design, including page or screen layout, typography for the different elements, and the wording as well as placement of headings, can all either help or hinder readers as they try to find what they need and to understand what they find. The chapters that follow help you develop good ideas for designing specific types of documents, both in print and online, and for incorporating more features, especially graphics, into your designs.

▶ PLANNING AND REVISION CHECKLISTS

You will find the Planning and Revision Checklists that follow Chapter 2, Composing, and Chapter 4, Writing for Your Readers, valuable in planning and revising any presentation of technical information. The following questions specifically apply to document design. They summarize the key points in this chapter and provide a checklist for planning and revising.

GENERAL QUESTIONS

Planning

- Have you considered how people will use your document?
- Have you checked on the software and hardware that you will use to prepare both drafts and final copy? (Do you know what options are available to you?)
- Have you found out whether you are expected to follow a standard format, and
- Have you thought about how you will make the arrangement obvious to your readers? (What will you do to make it easy for people to read selectively in your document?)

Revision

- Is your document clean, neat, and attractive?
- Is your text easy to read?
- Will your readers be able to find a particular section easily?
- If your document is supposed to conform to a standard, does it?

QUESTIONS ABOUT SETTING UP A USEFUL FORMAT

Planning

- Have you set the margins so that there is enough white space around the page, including space for binding, if necessary?
- Have you set the line length and line spacing for easy reading?

- Have you decided how you are going to show where a new paragraph begins?
- Have you decided whether to use a justified or ragged right margin?
- Have you planned which features to surround with extra white space, such as lists, tables, graphics, and examples?

Revision

- Have you left adequate margins? Have you left room for binding?
- Is the spacing between the lines and paragraphs consistent and appropriate?
- Can the reader tell easily where sections and paragraphs begin?
- Have you left the right margin ragged? If not, look over the paper to be sure that the justification has not made overly tight lines or left rivers of white space.
- Have you used the white space to help the reader find information?
- Have you put white space around examples, warnings, pictures, and other special elements?
- Have you used lists for steps in procedures, options, and conditions?

QUESTIONS ABOUT MAKING THE TEXT READABLE

Planning

- Have you selected a type size and typeface that will make the document easy to read?
- Have you planned for highlighting? Have you decided which elements need to be highlighted and what type of highlighting to use for each?
- Do you know whether you can use color? If you can, have you planned what color to use and where to use it in the document?

Revision

- Is the text type large enough to be read easily?
- Have you been consistent in using one typeface?
- Have you used uppercase and lowercase letters for the text and for most levels of headings?
- Have you used highlighting functionally? Is the highlighting consistent? Does the highlighting make important elements stand out?

QUESTIONS ABOUT MAKING INFORMATION EASY TO LOCATE

Planning

- Have you planned your headings? Have you decided how many levels of headings you will need? Have you decided on the format for each level of heading?
- Will the format make it easy for readers to tell the difference between headings and text? Will the format make it easy for readers to tell one level of heading from another?
- Have you decided where to put the page numbers and what format to use?
- Have you decided on headers or footers (information at the top or bottom of each page)?
- Have you found out whether you are expected to use a numbering system? If you are, have you found out what system to use and what parts of the document to include?

Revision

- Have you checked the headings? Are the headings informative? Unambiguous? Consistent? Parallel?
- Will readers get an overall picture of the document by reading the headings?
- Is the hierarchy of the headings obvious?
- Can readers tell at a glance what is heading and what is text?
- If readers want to find a particular section quickly, will the size and placement of the heading help them?
- Have you checked the page breaks to be sure that you do not have a heading by itself at the bottom of a page?
- Are the pages of a paper document numbered?
- Are there appropriate headers or footers?
- If you are using a numbering system, is it consistent and correct?

► EXERCISES

1. Figure 11-26 was sent to all employees of Mega University to inform them that a payroll change would be enacted. The memo instructs employees to complete the change form, which was attached, and return it.

   The problem? Few employees returned the completed change form by the deadline, and many were returned to the wrong office. Because of lack of compliance, the memo was reissued shortly before the deadline, with a phrase handwritten at the top: Please comply immediately.

FISCAL DEPARTMENT MEMORANDUM NO. 92-15

TO: Vice Presidents, Deans, Directors, and Department Heads

SUBJECT: Electronic Deposit of Paychecks

Senate Bill 3, as passed during the first called session of the 72nd Legislature, mandated that the state comptroller's office pay state employees through the Federal Reserve System's Automated Clearing House system for those state employees paid from funds on deposit in the State Treasury. The Mega-State University System has decided to extend this procedure to all employees, regardless of funding source.

An informational memorandum and enrollment forms are currently being distributed to all Mega University employees through the payroll clerks in their campus departments. Employees are being asked to return completed enrollment forms to the Budget and Payroll Services Office, Room 009, YMCA Building, by May 1, 2001. In order to demonstrate compliance with Senate Bill 3 for audit purposes, *all budgeted employees* (including graduate assistants) will be required to complete and return the enrollment forms whether they request participation in or seek exemption from the direct deposit program. Wage employees (including student workers) are also eligible and must complete an enrollment form if they choose to participate.

Direct deposit will begin for biweekly-paid employees on the June 15 pay date and for monthly paid employees on the July 1 pay date. Beginning with these dates, our previous practice of delivering checks to local financial institutions will be discontinued. Paychecks for employees who delay return of the enrollment form or request exemption from direct deposit will be given to their campus departments for distribution.

Provision of the direct deposit service should be beneficial to employees in the conduct of their financial affairs. Please encourage your employees to complete and return their enrollment forms by the May 1 deadline. If you have questions, please call Danny Smith or Ed Jones in the Budget and Payroll Services Office at 645-1711.

Jane Brunari,
Assistant Vice President & Controller

FIGURE 11-26 • Original Memo, Exercise 1

Phone lines were jammed with faculty trying to contact the office of the controller.

What happened? Employees saw the subject line, which did not clearly state what the memo was about (or its importance). Most employees were already having the university deposit their paychecks automatically, so these employees did not read the memo. They assumed that automatic deposit and electronic deposit were the same. Lack of effective document design buried the important information items—what to do, why, and where to return the form.

The result? A major directive from the vice president's office was ignored because faculty did not read it and were not encouraged to do so. More than 2,500 memos had to be distributed, and the electronic deposit of paychecks could not be initiated on time for all employees.

By employing document design principles discussed in this chapter, technical writing students were able to redesign the memo. Figures 11-27 and 11-28 represent two efforts by students like you. As you study them, you can see that each is effective but different. You can also see how the design principles can reshape a document to instantly reveal the importance of the message.

Which revision do you like best? Study the original and design your own revision.

2. Now you are ready to try your hand at a revision on your own. Assume that the memo in Figure 11-29 was sent to instructors at your school. The memo announces that they have been selected to administer the experimental teaching evaluation forms that the university wants to test. The main part of the memo, paragraph 2, provides instructions on how to administer the evaluations. The teachers who receive this memo are not expecting to receive it and are totally unfamiliar with the new teaching evaluation, a copy of which is attached to the memo.

   Redesign the memo to help teachers administer the evaluation correctly and let them know what they should do after they give the evaluation.

3. Revise the memorandum in Figure 11-30, which is to be sent to plant engineering managers, so that it clearly explains the company's policy for paying for continuing education courses.

4. Revise an earlier writing assignment, using the design guidelines you have learned in this chapter.

April 4, 2001

Fiscal Department Memorandum No. 92-15

To: Vice President, Deans, Directors, and Department Heads

From: Jane Brunari, Assistant Vice President & Controller

Subject: **Mandatory Enrollment Forms for All Budgeted**
               Employees Due May 1, 2001

<u>New Direct Deposit Enrollment Forms Required</u>

The payroll clerks in all departments are distributing new direct deposit enrollment forms to employees. **All university budgeted employees (including graduate assistants)** *must* complete an enrollment form for our new direct deposit system, even if they are currently having their checks direct deposited. Those who do not wish to have their checks direct deposited must also fill out the new forms. **Wage employees (including student workers)** must complete an enrollment form *only* if they wish to have their checks direct deposited. Employees must return the enrollment form to the **Budget and Payroll Services Office, Room 009, YMCA Building by May 1, 2001**. Those employees who fail to return the completed forms by the deadline will automatically have their paychecks sent to their departments for distribution.

<u>Description of New Direct Deposit System</u>

Although the university has direct deposited employee paychecks in the past, we are changing our system to comply with the mandates of Senate Bill 3. This new direct deposit system (the Federal Reserve System's Automated Clearing House system) extends direct deposit to all state employees paid with State Treasury funds.

<u>Transition from Old System to New Direct Deposit System</u>

We will begin direct deposit under this new system on the **June 5** pay date (for biweekly paid employees) and the **July 1** pay date (for monthly paid employees). To facilitate the change from the old system to the new one, please encourage employees to complete the new form, even if they are currently having their checks delivered to local financial institutions or do not wish to have their checks direct deposited.

With your cooperation, the transition to the new direct deposit system should be smooth and relatively painless. If you have any questions about this new system, please call Danny Smith or Ed Jones in the Budget and Payroll Services Office at **645-1711**. Thank you for helping us with this process.

FIGURE 11-27 • First Revision, Exercise 1

April 9, 2001

FISCAL DEPARTMENT MEMORANDUM NO. 92-15

TO: Vice Presidents, Deans, Directors, and Department Heads

FROM: Jane Brunari
             Assistant Vice President & Controller

SUBJECT: Payroll Deadline for All Employees: May 1, 2001

New Payroll Procedure

As of June 15, 2001, all paychecks will be distributed through the Federal Reserve System's Automated Clearing House. To facilitate our change to the new system, the Budget and Payroll Services Office must receive a completed enrollment form from every budgeted employee (including graduate assistants) by May 1.

What You and Your Employees Must Do

- Pick up forms and informational memos for the new program from payroll clerks in all campus departments.
- Return completed forms to the Budget and Payroll Services Office, YMCA Building Room 009, by May 1, 2001.

Employees who delay returning the form will not receive their paychecks on time, regardless of whether they choose to participate. These employees, along with those who request exemption from direct deposit, will receive their paychecks through their campus departments. Paychecks will no longer be delivered to local financial institutions.

Employees already being paid through electronic deposit must complete an enrollment form to be entered into the new system. Wage employees (including student workers) may participate in the program but are not required to do so.

If you have any questions, please call Ed Jones or Danny Smith in the Budget and Payroll Services Office at 645-1711.

FIGURE 11-28 • Second Revision, Exercise 1

DATE: November 12, 2001

FROM: Karen Jones
               Associate Director of Testing

TO: Faculty

As you know, the university has made every effort to see that teaching evaluations, which are given once a year, are as accurate a reflection as possible on the effectiveness of your teaching. We know that this goal is your desire. To help us better achieve this goal, we are launching a pilot program to test a new kind of evaluation. You were one of 50 faculty who agreed to test the new evaluation system. Because you are getting this memorandum, you are one of the faculty chosen for the trial evaluations. After you receive your scores, we will send you a response form to allow you to express your views on the evaluation. We will then set up an interview with you so that we can more fully discuss your views of the accuracy of the results and changes you think should be made.

When you receive the questionnaire, a copy of which is attached, we want you to do a number of things. Please announce that the questionnaire will be given and urge students to attend class that day. If some students are absent the day you give the questionnaire, give those students a questionnaire the next class period. For the trial questionnaire, it is imperative that every student in the trial sections complete a questionnaire. Have someone else administer the questionnaire—either a colleague or your department secretary. Be sure you are not present while the students are completing the questionnaire. Have the person who is monitoring the questionnaire collect all of them and place them back in the envelope. These should be sealed in front of the students. The person monitoring the questionnaire should return these to the testing office (104 Haggarty) immediately after the test. The tests should be left at the test desk, which is the first desk on the right after you enter the office. Give the test to the clerk in charge of the trial test evaluation. Her name is Micki Nance. She will be there from 8–11 and 1–4 every class day during the test week, which will be the first week in December (December 3–7). Sign the sheet to indicate that you have returned your trial test. You will receive your printout by the first week in February. When you receive your printout, it will include a date that tells you when we will want talk to you further. The response card, indicating your feelings about the accuracy of the trial evaluation, should be completed and returned immediately.

If you have any questions, please call Sammy Carson at ext. 9912.

FIGURE 11-29 • Original Memo, Exercise 2

TO:	Plant Engineering Managers	DATE:	September 3, 2001

FROM: John Bridgers
         District Superintendent

SUBJECT: Company Education Policy

Here is the company's policy on education, which many of you have asked about. Please keep it for your files for reference.

Policy 44.7. Advanced Education and Training. This policy applies to all employees except technicians and maintenance personnel. In order to encourage management personnel to achieve increasing professional competence in their disciplines and to enhance advancement potential, personnel who register for credit at the undergraduate or graduate level in accredited institutions will be reimbursed for tuition costs, registration fees, required textbooks, lab equipment, and other required materials upon completion of these courses. Certification that the specific course(s) will enhance the employee's professional growth must be provided by the employee's direct supervisor and countersigned by the supervisor's superior, unless the employee's supervisor holds the rank of vice president. Successful completion, defined as a grade of B or higher, must be attained in any course before the employee can apply for compensation. Costs of travel to the institution and costs of nonrequired materials such as paper, photocopies, and clerical help will not be reimbursed nor submitted to the company clerical workers. Submission to the Training Division of all receipts for all expenses, approval of the direct supervisor that the course fills the requirements of this policy, and documentation of successful completion are required before reimbursement will be permitted by the Training Division. Supervisors may allow release time for their employees to enroll in credit courses when work schedules permit. Release time is encouraged only when scheduled meetings of extremely important courses occur during regular working hours. If possible and necessary, personnel may be required to make up working time outside normal working hours. If the credit college course can be taken outside the individual's normal working hours, no release time will normally be allowed. To receive reimbursement, personnel should submit Training Division Form 6161 to the Training Division in accordance with the instructions on that form.

FIGURE 11-30 • Original Memo, Exercise 3

TO: SWMTR II Departmental Coordinators and Time Reporters

FROM: SWMTR System Administrator

SUBJECT: Deletion of Security Codes

This memorandum reminds time reporters to delete their security codes when they are no longer reporting payroll time data, informs new time reporters to establish unique security codes, and emphasizes the importance of using innovative passwords.

Security codes should be deleted when a time reporter leaves a group or is no longer responsible for inputting payroll. When new time reporters are assigned, they must obtain new security codes. The security codes of a prior time reporter should not be used by the new time reporter. These security code procedures are documented in the Time Reporter Training Manual, Section IV.

Security codes may be added or deleted by sending a completed SW4570 form (Security Code Request) to SWMTR Administrator at One Palm Center, 17-A-2, St. Louis, Missouri 63101. Payroll numbers that are to be added or deleted to a security code must also be included on the SW4570. Also submit an SW4570 if you are not receiving your verification reports. Include your current security code, check the "Add Payroll Number" Box, and list all payroll numbers for which you are responsible under "New Payroll Numbers."

The last five positions of the security code are referred to as the "password." In SWMTR Memorandum 860721, dated March 4, 1995, it was stated that passwords should be made up of completely random numbers. For security purposes, you should not use a sequence of consecutive digits or the same digit repeated five times. The inputters database shows that approximately 22% of the time reporters are using this type of password. Passwords should be made more discrete so that the number schemes are not easily broken.

Additional information or questions should be referred to your local SWMTR II departments coordinator of your local payroll office.

FIGURE 11-31 • Memo for Exercise 7

5. Find an online document or World Wide Web site from which you can print a few screens of information. Critique the organization and design of the information. What about it works well, based on the principles in this chapter? What about it does not work well?

6. Locate, to share with your class, a document that you have read that you found difficult to use because of poor document design. Revise the document according to the principles presented in this chapter. Make transparencies of both the original document and your revision. Be prepared to give a short oral analysis of both documents. Explain the problems with the original document and why you revised it in the way you chose.

7. The instructions memorandum shown in Figure 11-31 was written to explain how to delete security codes. Use principles of document design to make the memo easier to read and understand. This memo will be used as a reminder—to help employees remember how to handle deletion of security codes. It will be read carefully by those who do not know how to delete security codes.

It's only your third week on the job, but you decide that a better graphics accelerator on your office computer is critical. You have to write a memo to your boss to justify the request. You don't have much time to write this memo, and you know your boss won't have much time to read it. You could write several paragraphs comparing and contrasting your existing equipment with the graphics accelerator you'd like to have, but you decide it would be a lot easier on your boss if you display the specifications in a simple table. And to emphasize the substantial difference in image quality, you choose two pictorial illustrations that dramatically display the distorted images generated by your existing equipment versus the crisp images that the new graphics accelerator would give you. Side by side on the page, the two pictures build a persuasive case: you could never have said it better.

chapter 12

Using Illustrations

▶ Choosing Illustrations
 Consider Your Purpose
 Consider Your Audience
 Consider Your Audience Again
 Consider Your Purpose Again

▶ Creating Illustrations
 Designing Tables
 Designing Bar and Column Graphs
 Designing Circle Graphs
 Designing Line Graphs

▶ Designing Illustrations Ethically

In communicating technical information, you will often need to use illustrations either in addition to words or instead of words to convey your message. Learning how to create effective tables, graphs, diagrams, and drawings will give you additional tools for helping readers to understand your subject.

As in all technical communication, using illustrations has ethical implications. In every diagram and drawing, every table and graph, you have a moral responsibility to offer a clear and correct impression of your subject.

▶ CHOOSING ILLUSTRATIONS

How do you determine whether illustrations are really desirable? The answer is to consider your rhetorical situation, including both purpose and audience.

Consider Your Purpose

- What do you want to have happen as a result of the document?
- What do you want the reader to do or think after reading your document?
- How will illustrations help you to achieve your objective?

For example, Andrew Crowell, the owner of Crowell Heating & Cooling in Rising Star, New Mexico, is writing a recommendation report regarding the installation of new air conditioning equipment for a local business. He wants the potential client to approve this recommendation quickly, to clinch the sale. Andrew decides that illustrations will dramatize the benefits of the new equipment. He includes a photograph of the same equipment being installed, for a previous client, wanting both to help the prospective client to envision a similar installation and to reinforce Crowell's track record with such installations. And he includes a bar graph spotlighting the high cooling costs with the current system versus the lower costs projected for the new equipment. Andrew believes the two illustrations will focus attention on the persuasive evidence.

Erica Vasquez of Wild Computers has a different challenge. She is writing a set of instructions for customers on how to install additional memory chips in their computers. She wants such installations to proceed without incident, reinforcing the image of Wild Computers as easy to operate and easy to upgrade. She wants people to read the instructions and feel confident that they can perform the installations; she doesn't want users getting stuck in the middle of the procedure, feeling frustrated, and calling Wild for technical support. Erica believes that a flowchart, outlining the steps in the procedure, will give customers a comforting overview. She will also need to include lots of drawings to show users exactly how to open the case, insert the chips, and close the case.

Consider Your Audience

What are the expectations of your readers regarding illustrations? If they expect illustrations, you will need to deliver illustrations or risk disappointing and distracting your audience. If your audience doesn't expect illustrations, you will need to gauge carefully the likely positive or negative impact of including graphics. For example, readers of financial reports expect to see tables of sales figures, profits and losses, stockholders' equity, and long-term debt. If your financial report doesn't display this information in tables, your readers probably will be confused and irritated. On the other hand, World Wide Web users, expect to see illustrations (including animated illustrations). A site that is all paragraphs is considered primitive and uninviting. Readers of résumés, however, still expect words on a page and might interpret illustrations as a distraction to mask a weak set of credentials.

In addition to the expectations of your audience, consider their background, attitude, and environment.

- If your readers have little or no knowledge of your subject, illustrations may create a virtual experience by showing what the subject looks like, summarizing its specifications, highlighting its components, revealing its organization, or displaying its operation.
- If your readers have limited language abilities, illustrations may help them circumvent the difficulties of deciphering words on a page.
- If your readers aren't motivated to read your document, illustrations may encourage them to read by making your document look more inviting and accessible.
- If your audience has little time to read your document, illustrations may assist by capsulizing information in a quick snapshot of your subject.
- If your readers are in a distracting environment, illustrations may focus their attention with a display of information that is eye-catching and engaging.

For example, Andrew Crowell believes the prospective client will be nicely surprised by the two illustrations. In conversations regarding the new cooling equipment, Andrew has noticed that the client is often impatient with long explanations and likes to go straight to the point. Instead of offering a boring, all-prose recommendation report, therefore, Andrew integrates illustrations that focus on key issues and expedite the job of reading.

Similarly, Erica Vasquez knows that most of her readers have never before installed additional memory chips in their computers. She knows that to motivate users to read the instructions and perform this procedure, she must make the job look as easy as possible. And instead of using words and requiring readers to picture objects and actions for themselves, Erica includes a series of drawings that show customers what they need to do and what their computers should look like at every step along the way. For the minority of customers who are experienced in such installations, Erica believes a flow-chart outlining the steps will provide sufficient guidance. And for the inexperienced majority, the flowchart will make the whole procedure look coherent and systematic.

Once you decide to use illustrations, how do you decide which illustrations to use? Once more, you will have to consider your rhetorical situation, chiefly your audience and purpose.

Consider Your Audience Again

Is your audience familiar with this kind of illustration? Does your audience have the ability to interpret the illustration? If your audience is unfamiliar with circle graphs, for example, displaying the information in such a manner will be ineffective without considerable verbal explanation. And if considerable explanation of an illustration is necessary, you are probably using the wrong kind of illustration for your audience. If your audience is international, you must also be sensitive to cultural variations in the interpretation of illustrations. For example, the convention of using bubbles in drawings to depict what people are thinking (see Figure 12-1) will be readily understood in some cultures but can cause confusion in others. International variations in the design of objects such as trash containers, mailboxes, or electrical outlets also can lead to misunderstanding or misinterpretation of pictures displaying such objects. (see Figure 12-2).

Consider Your Purpose Again

- **If the purpose of your document is to summarize information, use a table.**
- **If you wish to exhibit or emphasize information, use a figure.**

Tables are rows and columns of numbers and words. Tables offer readers the details of a subject. If you want your readers to be able to remember or retrieve specific pieces of information, tables will serve your purpose.

For example, Tom Skiludi of National Oil & Gas, headquartered in Pittsburgh, is reporting to the northeast regional supervisor on the year's operations. He knows the supervisor will pass the figures on to the company's chief financial officer. Tom chooses a table as the efficient way to display the information (see Table Exhibit 12-1). Figures come in a wide variety and dramatize different kinds of information (see Table 12-1).

To emphasize or reinforce the meaning of data, start with a table and then use a figure to spotlight the implications of the data. For example, in reporting

FIGURE 12-1 • Depiction of Thinking
This drawing is from a research report prepared by the federal Department of Justice. Aimed at American audiences, the drawing communicates effectively by using a readily understood convention of bubbles to depict that the school administrator is considering different security techniques. For a person unfamiliar with the practice of using bubbles to imply thought, however, the drawing is almost impossible to decipher.
Source: National Institute of Justice. The Appropriate and Effective Use of Security Technologies in U.S. Schools: A Guide for Schools and Law Enforcement Agencies. NCJ178265. (Washington, DC: GPO, 1999), 2.

Table 1. National Oil & Gas, Northeast Region Operations		
	2001	**2000**
Gas throughput (billion cubic feet)		
Distribution	453.5	427.6
Transmission	659.7	640.2
Gas production (billion cubic feet)	224.5	263.8
Oil production (thousand barrels)	3458.8	3144.9

TABLE EXHIBIT 12-1 • Sample Table
This is a simple and clean table, offering specific numerical information. Notice that the words are left aligned while the numbers are right aligned. White space is used (instead of thin rules) to separate the rows and columns of information.

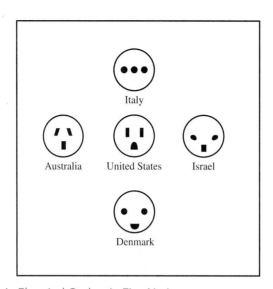

FIGURE 12-2 • Variations in Electrical Outlets in Five Nations
Electrical outlets differ from one nation to the next. With no universal standard for representing this common feature of schematic illustrations, you must adapt drawings and diagrams of electrical outlets according to the national origins of your audience.

▲ TABLE 12-1	The Purposes of Figures		
Illustration	**Image**	**Purpose**	**Example**
Line graph		To show the degree and direction of change relative to two variables	A city's growing population during a 40-year period
Bar graph		To compare and contrast two or more subjects at the same point in time	The populations of major cities according to the 2000 census
Column graph		To reveal change in a subject at regular intervals of time	The number of registered voters in your city during the last five elections
Circle graph		To display the number and relative size of the divisions of a subject	The distribution of majors at a university

(continued)

▲ TABLE 12-1	The Purposes of Figures (*continued*)		
Illustration	Image	Purpose	Example
Flowchart		To show the sequence of steps in a process or procedure	The process for installing a computer software application
Organizational chart		To map the various divisions and levels of responsibility within an organization	The hierarchy of military officers in the U.S. Air Force
Diagram		To identify the parts of a subject and their spatial relationship	The rooms of a building
Drawing	 ON/OFF	To exhibit selected features of an object or process	The on/off button on a machine
Photograph		To show what a subject looks like in realistic detail	A crime scene

on the year's operations, Tom considered several possible illustrations, including a line graph to dramatize the company's rising oil production and a pair of circle graphs to highlight the stability in the relative proportions of gas distribution and transmission. He decided, however, on a bar graph because it would readily focus attention on a potentially ominous piece of information: While gas transmission and distribution both increased in 2001, gas production decreased (see Figure 12-3).

Ordinarily, you will use a table to arrange your data for easier analysis and interpretation. Graphics programs will then allow you to select a dramatic way of displaying the data.

Often a variety of illustrations will serve your purpose. Consider, for example, the various tables and figures in the U.S. Environmental Protection

Agency's chemical accident investigation report of the Tosco Avon Refinery in Martinez, California. On page v of this 105-page report, the purpose and audience are identified:

> A key objective of the EPA chemical accident investigation program is to deter-
> mine and report to the public the facts, conditions, circumstances, and causes or
> likely causes of chemical accidents that result, or could have resulted, in a fatality,
> serious injury, substantial property damage, or serious off-site impacts, including a
> large scale evacuation of the general public. The ultimate goal of an accident in-
> vestigation is to determine the root causes in order to reduce the likelihood of re-
> currence, minimize the consequences associated with accidental releases, and to
> make chemical production, processing, handling, and storage safer.

The report describes the investigation of an accident in the refinery's hydrocracker (a device that splits the molecules of hydrocarbon oil at high temperature and pressure). A hydrocarbon and hydrogen release and a subsequent fire killed one operator and injured forty-six others. The cause was a rupture of one of the reactor effluent pipes due to excessively high temperature.

Among the illustrations in the report are maps of the refinery and the hydrocracker that show the site of the accident (see Figures 12-4 and 12-5). A

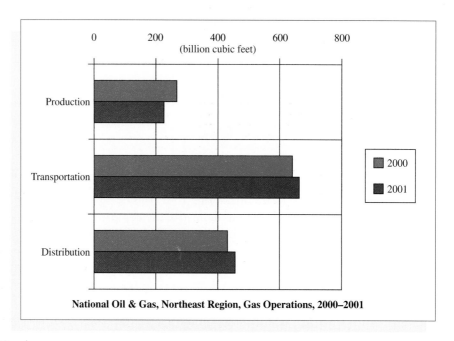

National Oil & Gas, Northeast Region, Gas Operations, 2000–2001

FIGURE 12-3 • Bar Graph
Notice that though the 2001 bars exceed the 2000 bars for both Transportation and Distribution, the reverse is the case for Production, which is located prominently at the top of the figure. In addition, the vertical grid lines make it easier to decipher the approximate numerical values depicted by each bar.

flowchart explains the hydrocracking process (see Figure 12-6). A table lists the operating parameters of the reactor (see Table Exhibit 12-2) and two line graphs reveal spiking temperatures in the reactor prior to the explosion (see Figure 12-7). A series of photographs shows the damage to the equipment from the explosion (see Figure 12-8). Three tables summarize the chronology of incidents leading to the tragic accident and the various errors committed by operators at the refinery (see Table Exhibits 12-3, 12-4, and 12-5). Without the illustrations, the EPA investigators could never have achieved their purpose or communicated effectively with their audience.

Notice, however, the absence of pictures of human beings. There are no drawings of people making mistakes in their operation of the hydrocracker unit (human error is relegated to a table) and no photographs of the people killed and injured in the accident. This omission diminishes the importance of the people at this facility, both as contributors to the accident and as its victims. The illustrations focus the viewer's attention on buildings and machines. The impression thus communicated is that the chief cause of the accident was technological—a mechanical failure—and the chief consequence was also technological—a bunch of ruptured pipes. The human dimension of the incident is literally invisible.

As the illustrations in this report demonstrate, you have a variety of ways to help your readers perceive your meaning. In choosing illustrations, always consider your purpose and your audience. Consider illustrations while you are planning your document, but continue to look for ways to visualize your message even as you are writing and revising.

Operating Parameter	Limit	Consequences of Deviation
Maximum reactor temperature	800°F	Possible temperature runaway. Possible vessel failure and fire due to temperature runaway.
Maximum temperature for reactor outlet	690°F	Possible downstream feed/effluent exchanger fire. Possible fire, explosion if ignition source present.
Maximum reactor bed average differential temperature	40°F	Possible temperature runaway. Possible vessel failure and fire due to temperature runaway.
Maximum reactor differential temperature	75°F	Possible temperature runaway. Possible vessel failure and fire due to temperature runaway.

TABLE EXHIBIT 12-2 • Critical Operating Limits
This is a simple table and poorly designed. Notice that the headings are displayed in the same plain type as the information in each cell of the table. The heavy lines separating the cells are unnecessary. Notice also that the temperatures are left-aligned instead of right-aligned, as numerical information typically is. Nevertheless, the table serves to organize the information so that it is easy to access and easy to understand.
Source: U.S. Environmental Protection Agency, Office of Solid Waste and Emergency Response. EPA Chemical Accident Investigation Report: Tosco Avon Refinery, Martinez, California. EPA 550-R-98-009. (Washington, DC: GPO, 1998), 19.

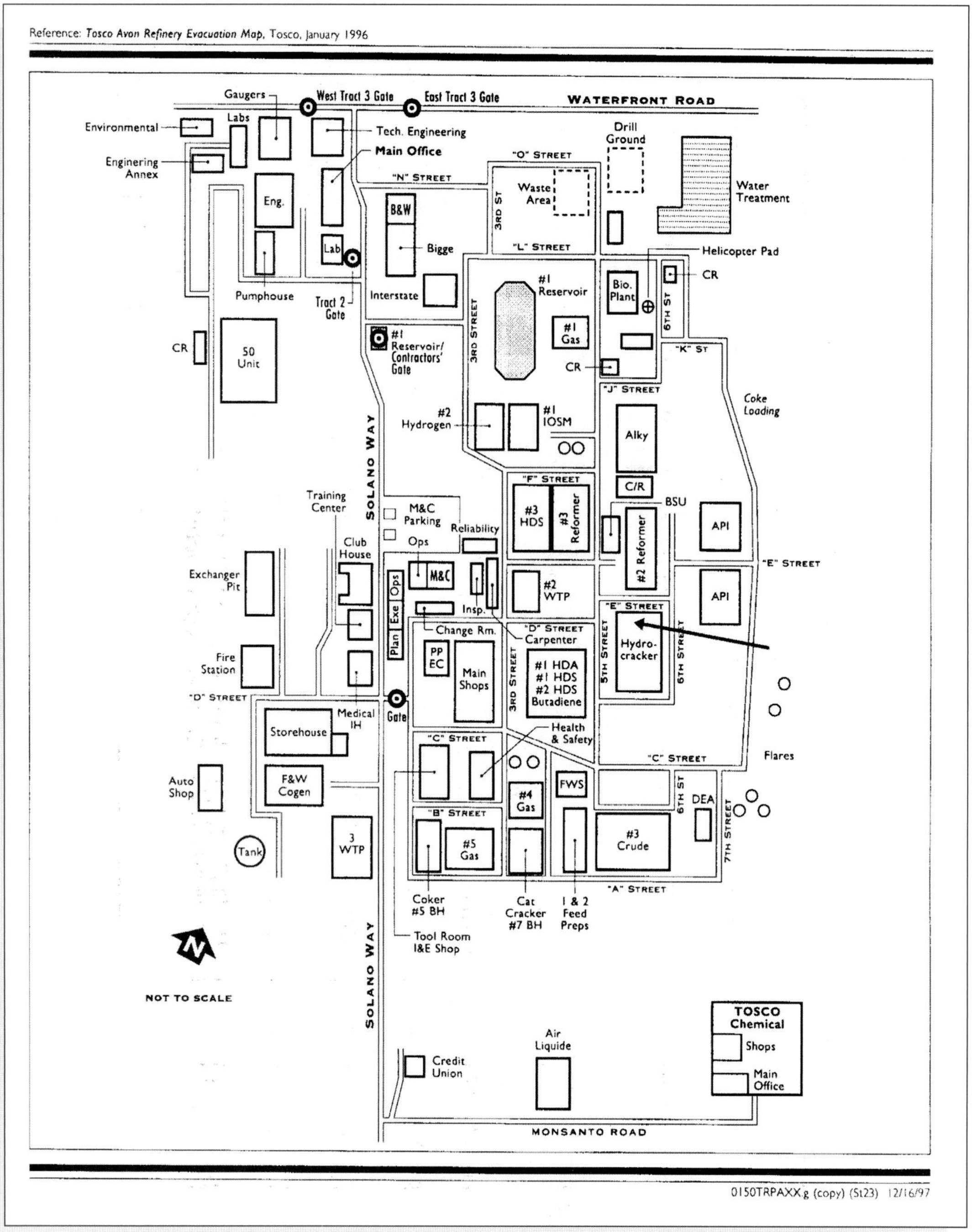

FIGURE 12-4 • Map of Refinery

In this map of the refinery facility, notice the clear labeling of each building. The labels occur inside the buildings whenever possible and are usually horizontal for easier reading. A directional arrow is given to indicate the geographical orientation of the map. A note below the arrow specifies that the map is a pictorial approximation of the relative positions of the buildings instead of a precise scale drawing.
Source: U.S. Environmental Protection Agency, Office of Solid Waste and Emergency Response. EPA Chemical Accident Investigation Report: Tosco Avon Refinery, Martinez, California. EPA 550-R-98-009. (Washington, DC: GPO, 1998), 4.

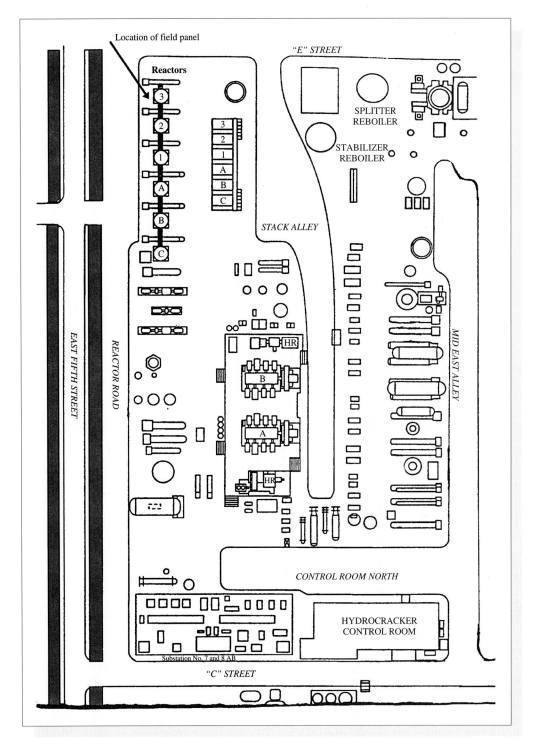

FIGURE 12-5 • Map of Hydrocracker Unit

In this map of the hydrocracker unit, only the objects necessary to understanding the accident have been identified. The unidentified graphic elements serve to clarify the relative positions of crucial objects. Notice that the labeling is almost always horizontal for easier reading.

Source: U.S. Environmental Protection Agency, Office of Solid Waste and Emergency Response. EPA Chemical Accident Investigation Report: Tosco Avon Refinery, Martinez, California. EPA 550-R-98-009. (Washington, DC: GPO, 1998), 12.

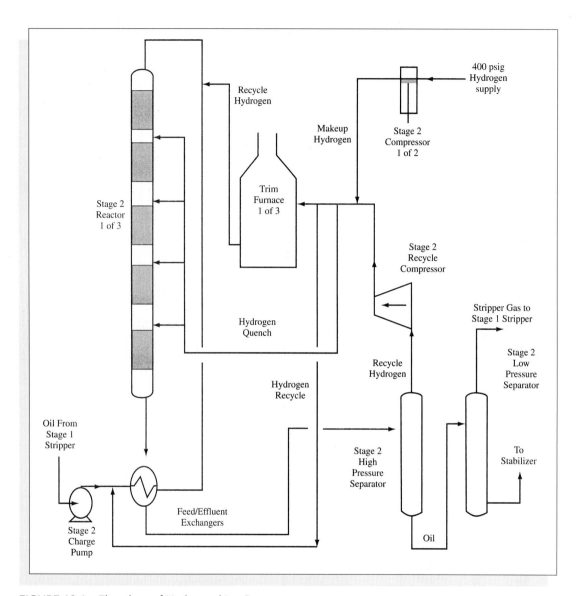

FIGURE 12-6 • Flowchart of Hydrocracking Process
This flowchart of the hydrocracking process, though it claims to be simplified, might be unclear to a nonspecialist audience because of its several crisscrossing lines and arrows. For example, it is difficult to decipher where the process starts and stops. This figure seems to be designed for readers with a specialized education or experience. Before including such a figure in your report, you would have be certain that your audience could interpret it.
Source: U.S. Environmental Protection Agency, Office of Solid Waste and Emergency Response. EPA Chemical Accident Investigation Report: Tosco Avon Refinery, Martinez, California. EPA 550-R-98-009. (Washington, DC: GPO, 1998), 7.

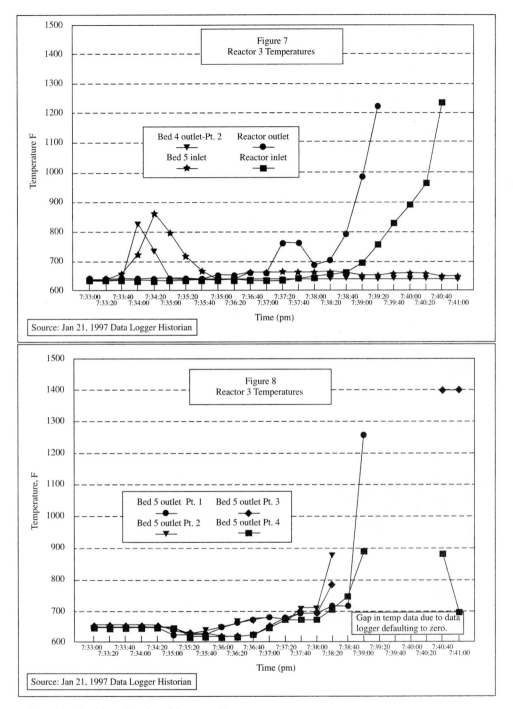

FIGURE 12-7 • Line Graphs of Reactor Temperatures

These two line graphs are a fairly dramatic display of the spiking temperatures in the reactor. The four data lines on each graph are quite crowded and the different shapes for each line are almost indistinguishable, but the basic message of both graphs is still clear: The operation was proceeding normally but abruptly changed at roughly 7:38:40.

Source: U.S. Environmental Protection Agency, Office of Solid Waste and Emergency Response. EPA Chemical Accident Investigation Report: Tosco Avon Refinery, Martinez, California. EPA 550-R-98-009. (Washington, DC: GPO, 1998), 20.

FIGURE 12-8 • Photographs of Damaged Equipment

This series of photographs reveals the exterior of the hydrocracker unit in full color, offering viewers a vivid and realistic depiction—a "you are there" experience that helps them to visualize exactly what happened. No drawings of the unit would have quite the dramatic impact that the photographs do. Notice the careful labeling of objects in each photograph that serves to direct and focus the viewer's attention.

Source: U.S. Environmental Protection Agency, Office of Solid Waste and Emergency Response. EPA Chemical Accident Investigation Report: Tosco Avon Refinery, Martinez, California. EPA 550-R-98-009. (Washington, DC: GPO, 1998), 24–26.

FIGURE 12-8 • *Continued*

FIGURE 12-8 • *Continued*

January 10 Day shift	Stage 1 and 2 were in operation. Temperature monitoring for Stage 2 was switched from data logger to new I/A computer system. (See Section 3.3.3.1 of this report for further discussion)
January 11	An internal leak was detected in a Stage 1 heat exchanger, the stripper feed preheater.
January 12-15	Stage 1 and 2 of the Hydrocracker were shutdown and internal heat exchanger leaks on Stage 1 were repaired. Various control valves were replaced on Stage 2.
January 16	Stage 1 was put into operation. Reactor A feed/effluent exchanger began to leak externally from a flange but then stopped leaking on its own.
January 17	Reactor A exchanger began to leak again. Leak was repaired by applying sealant to clamp on exchanger.
January 18	Feed was introduced to Stage 2.
January 19 Day shift	Stage 2 was operating. Compressor B relief valve was replaced.
10:20 pm	A temperature excursion occurred in Bed 4 of Reactor 1. Some temperatures exceeded 900°F. Operators did not depressure Stage 2 but controlled temperature by other means. Operators reported problems with I/A temperature monitoring system.
January 20 Day shift	The use of I/A system was discontinued and the data logger was put back into service.
Swing shift	Feed rate to Stage 1 was increased.

TABLE EXHIBIT 12-3 • Time Line of Key Events Preceding the Day of the Accident

This is a simple table that serves to summarize the sequence of events leading to the accident. Notice that the dates are displayed in bold, thus emphasizing the chronological organization of this information. The heavy lines separating the cells, especially the lines separating times within a single day, are an unnecessary distraction.

Source: U.S. Environmental Protection Agency, Office of Solid Waste and Emergency Response. EPA Chemical Accident Investigation Report: Tosco Avon Refinery, Martinez, California. EPA 550-R-98-009. (Washington, DC: GPO, 1998), 27.

January 21 4:50 am	Reactor A effluent/feed exchanger clamp began to leak again and the leak could not be controlled. Feed to Reactor A was diverted to Reactor B and C, causing reactor cooling and high nitrogen content in effluent.
8:10 am	Nitrogen content of Stage 1 effluent was 196 ppm, above the specification of 14 ppm.
10 am	Stage 2 catalyst beds were poisoned from high nitrogen levels in the feed and cracking was greatly reduced. Nitrogen content from Stage 1 was 352 ppm. Sealant was injected into clamp on Reactor A heat exchanger.
2 pm	Two extra operators were added on swing shift to help with Stage 1 problems. During swing shift, operators gradually increased temperatures in Stage 2 to drive nitrogen off the catalyst.
7:34 pm	A temperature excursion occurred in Reactor 3, Bed 4. Inlet temperature to Bed 5 increased rapidly as a result.
7:35 pm	The quench valve above Bed 5 opened wide. Data logger temperatures bounced from zero to normal or high and back. Makeup hydrogen to Stage 2 began to decrease. Bed 4 outlet temperature point decreased to 637°F.
7:36 pm	Bed 5 inlet temperature decreased to 633°F. Reactor 3 outlet temperature increased to 650°F. A No. 2 Operator went outside to check temperatures on the external panel sometime before 7:37 pm..
7:37 pm	Bed 5 outlet temperatures were increasing. Operator manually closed quench valve to Bed 5. Hydrogen makeup to Stage 2 dropped to zero.
7:38 pm	Quench valve to Bed 5 was reopened. Bed 5 outlet, reactor inlet and outlet temperatures continued to rise; some of these exceeded 1200°F.
7:39 pm	Operators heard a garbled radio message from No. 2 Operator. Two operators went outside to check on No. 2 Operator.
7:40 pm	Bed 5 temperatures and the reactor outlet temperature read off scale on strip charts and defaulted to zero on data logger. Operators requested assistance of instrument technician.
7:41 pm	One of the Bed 5 outlet points read 1398°F on the data logger. A section of the Reactor 3 effluent piping ruptured causing an explosion and large fire. The No. 2 Operator was killed.

TABLE EXHIBIT 12-4 • Time Line of Key Events the Day of the Accident
This is essentially a continuation of the preceding table, organizing the sequence of events on the day of the accident. The heavy lines separating the cells again are unnecessary.
Source: U.S. Environmental Protection Agency, Office of Solid Waste and Emergency Response. EPA Chemical Accident Investigation Report: Tosco Avon Refinery, Martinez, California. EPA 550-R-98-009. (Washington, DC: GPO, 1998), 28.

Personnel Errors	Control room operator errors
Design	Temperature and pressure indicating system, control room, field temperature panel, effluent piping system, reactor
Human Factors	Design of the control room information devices - charts, loggers
Management Policy and Implementation	Including services and management expectations
Maintenance	Maintenance plan and implementation
Readiness	Monitoring system ready to operate
Hazard Analysis Process	Evaluating the installation and design of the new temperature logging system
Procedures	Routine and emergency operating procedures appropriateness and completeness
Information System	Information available to the operators regarding process monitoring system
Supervision	Detecting and correcting hazards, enforcing safety and emergency practices.

TABLE EXHIBIT 12-5 • Human Errors Contributing to Accident
This is a simple table and poorly designed. Notice that the headings are displayed in the same plain type as the information in each cell of the table. The heavy lines separating the cells also are unnecessary. Nevertheless, the table does a good job of summarizing important information and making that summary readily accessible.
Source: U.S. Environmental Protection Agency, Office of Solid Waste and Emergency Response. EPA Chemical Accident Investigation Report: Tosco Avon Refinery, Martinez, California. EPA 550-R-98-009. (Washington, DC: GPO, 1998), 31.

▶ CREATING ILLUSTRATIONS

In deciding when and how to use illustrations, remember the following guidelines:

- **Simplify your illustrations.** Keep your illustrations as simple as possible so that your reader has no difficulty understanding your message. Avoid distracting your reader with unnecessary details or decorative flourishes.
- **Use computer applications critically.** Computer graphics software and clip art allow you to include in your document all manner of illustrations. To ensure the effectiveness of your tables and figures, however, you must impose your judgment on the choices available from the computer. Graphics software, for example, might create artistic but misleading graphs, and

clip art might exhibit a pictorial style that isn't quite serious enough or detailed enough to do justice to your subject. It is your job to choose illustrations that display your information clearly and correctly, in a format that can be quickly grasped.

- **Consider size and cost.** Calculate the impact of illustrations on the expected length of your document. Illustrations will often increase the size of a document and add to the cost of production and distribution.
- **Choose illustrations carefully.** Realize that you usually have a choice of illustrations. If a table or figure that you initially consider using does not convey your point quickly and clearly, look for other ways of displaying the information visually.
- **Title your illustrations.** Give each table and figure a title that clearly indicates the content of the display.
- **Number your illustrations.** If you use several illustrations in your report, number them. Number the tables and figures separately (e.g., Table 1, Table 2, Figure 1, Figure 2). Place the number and title above a table and below a figure.
- **Alert your readers.** Always alert your readers to illustrations by referring to them in the text. Every time you refer to the illustration, use the table or figure number.
- **Position your illustrations strategically.** Place each illustration as close to the passage it explains as possible. Announce the table or figure—what it is or shows—then insert the illustration, and add any verbal explanation your reader will need to fully understand the illustration. Don't lead readers through a complicated explanation and only afterward refer to the illustration. Send them to the illustration immediately; then they can shift back and forth between the explanation and the illustration as necessary.
- **Identify your sources.** If you borrow or adapt a table or figure from another source, identify that source below the illustration.

Designing Tables

- Every column in a table should have a heading that identifies the information below it. In a table of numbers, include the unit of measurement, such as "miles per hour." For large numbers, add a designation such as "in thousands" or "in millions" to the column heading (and delete the corresponding zeros from the numeric data). Headings should be brief. If headings need more explanation, include this information in a footnote below the table. Use lowercase letters, numbers, or symbols (e.g., ★ or +) to indicate footnoted material.
- If possible, box your table to separate it from surrounding paragraphs.
- Keep tables as simple as possible. Include only data relevant to your purpose.

• Consider omitting lines between rows and columns to avoid giving your table a crowded appearance. If possible, use white space to separate rows and columns.

Table Exhibits 12–6–12–8 show three ways of presenting tabular data. The first two examples contain serious design flaws.

Web Sites Collecting Personal Information,[1]
By Sample and Company Size

Sample	Total		Large		Medium		Small	
	Percent	Number	Percent	Number	Percent	Number	Percent	Number
Comprehensive (A)	92% (89.8%-94.1%)[2]	621/674	93% (86.8%-96.4%)	125/135	90% (85.7%-93.3%)	241/268	95% (91.7%-97.5%)	235/247
Health (B)	88% (80.9%-92.6%)	120/137	83% (68.6%-93.0%)	35/42	92% (80.0%-97.7%)	44/48	91% (78.3%-97.5%)	40/44
Retail (C)	87% (79.9%-91.7%)	123/142	90% (73.5%-97.9%)	27/30	85% (71.9%-93.1%)	44/52	88% (76.3%-94.9%)	50/57
Financial (D)	97% (92.0%-99.1%)	121/125	100% (92.7%-100%)	49/49	94% (84.1%-98.8%)	49/52	100% (85.2%-100%)	23/23
Most Popular (F)	97% (92.3%-99.4%)	108/111	—	—	—	—	—	—
Children (E) [3]	89% (83.6%-92.6%)	188/212	—	—	—	—	—	—

[1] "Personal Information" is defined to include any of the following: personal identifying information (*e.g.*, name, postal address, e-mail address, telephone number); demographic information (*e.g.*, age, gender, education level, income); and preference information (*e.g.*, hobbies, interests).

[2] Figures in parentheses represent the 95% binomial confidence interval for each calculated percentage.

[3] For the Children's Sample only, the data reflect personal information collected from children.

TABLE EXHIBIT 12-6 • Web Sites Collecting Personal Information by Sample and Company Size
This table summarizes information according to two categories. The table has a clear and concise label. Notice that the headings in the first column and the top row are displayed in bold to distinguish them from the information in the remaining cells of the table. Subheadings are displayed in a smaller size of type, and heavier lines separate the heading cells from the information cells. Numerical information, however, is centered in each cell instead of being aligned on the right. Statistical details are effectively displayed in a smaller size of type. If no information in a particular category is available, a dash is used to indicate the absence of information. Footnotes offer important explanations that clarify or qualify the information displayed.
Source: Federal Trade Commission. Privacy Online: A Report to Congress. (Washington, DC: GPO, 1998), D-3.

**Percent of Web Sites Collecting Various Types of Personal Information,[1] By Sample
(Expressed as Percent of Web Sites Collecting Any Personal Information)**

Sample	Name	E-mail Address	Postal Address	Telephone #	Fax #	Credit Card #	Social Security #	Age/Date of Birth	Gender	Education	Occupation	Income	Hobbies	Interests	Hardware/Software
Comprehensive (A)	68%	98%	58%	54%	26%	19%	3%	8%	5%	2%	6%	5%	0%	2%	4%
Health (B)	58%	100%	51%	47%	13%	8%	3%	12%	8%	2%	3%	0%	1%	3%	3%
Retail (C)	77%	100%	70%	67%	31%	31%	6%	7%	2%	4%	5%	3%	0%	5%	2%
Financial (D)	73%	93%	65%	59%	27%	7%	20%	17%	4%	6%	21%	20%	1%	1%	2%
Most Popular (F)	93%	97%	81%	61%	26%	44%	3%	36%	33%	11%	22%	11%	6%	18%	19%
Children (E)[2]	74%	96%	49%	24%	6%	0%	1%	46%	25%	7%	3%	3%	9%	18%	13%

[1] "Personal Information" is defined to include any of the following: personal identifying information (*e.g.*, name, postal address, e-mail address, telephone number); demographic information (*e.g.*, age, gender, education level, income); and preference information (*e.g.*, hobbies, interests).

[2] For the Children's Sample only, the data reflect personal information collected from children.

TABLE EXHIBIT 12-7 • Percent of Web Sites Collecting Various Types of Personal Information
This table is difficult to read. The title is long, complicated, and partially parenthetical. The headings in the top row are displayed vertically instead of horizontally. Numerical information is centered in each cell instead of aligned on the right. In addition, because every number in every cell is a percentage, the use of a percent sign in every cell of the table body is unnecessary, creating a cluttered, hard-to-read display.
Source: Federal Trade Commission. Privacy Online: A Report to Congress. (Washington, DC: GPO, 1992), D-5.

Designing Bar and Column Graphs

- Avoid putting excessive information on a bar or column graph and thereby complicating the reader's ability to decipher it. Consider using a separate graph to communicate each point.
- Be sure to label the *x*-axis and the *y*-axis—what each measures and the units in which each is calibrated. Readers can't understand your graph if they don't know what you are measuring or how it is measured.
- For bar graphs, start the *x*-axis at zero and equally space the intervals on the *x*-axis to avoid distorting the length of the bars. For column graphs, start

Of those Web Sites That Collect Personal Information,[1]
Percent with an Information Practice Disclosure,[2] by Sample and Company Size

Sample	Total		Large		Medium		Small	
	Percent	Number	Percent	Number	Percent	Number	Percent	Number
Comprehensive (A)	15% (12.4%-18.2%)[3]	94/621	29% (21.1%-37.6%)	36/125	14% (9.6%-18.7%)	33/241	11% (7.0%-15.3%)	25/235
Health (B)	16% (9.8%-23.6%)	19/120	20% (8.4%-36.9%)	7/35	18% (8.2%-32.7%)	8/44	10% (2.8%-23.7%)	4/40
Retail (C)	15% (8.9%-22.1%)	18/123	7% (0.9%-24.3%)	2/27	20% (9.8%-35.3%)	9/44	10% (3.3%-21.8%)	5/50
Financial (D)	17% (10.4%-24.4%)	20/121	27% (14.9%-41.1%)	13/49	10% (3.4%-22.2%)	5/49	9% (1.1%-28.0%)	2/23
Most Popular (F)	73% (63.8%-81.2%)	79/108	—	—	—	—	—	—
Children (E)[4]	(50.6%-65.1%)	109/188	—	—	—	—	—	—

[1] "Personal Information" is defined to include any of the following: personal identifying information (*e.g.*, name, postal address, e-mail address, telephone number); demographic information (*e.g.*, age, gender, education level, income); and preference information (*e.g.*, hobbies, interests).

[2] An "Information Practice Disclosure" can be either a **Privacy Policy Notice**, defined as a comprehensive description of a Web site's information practices that is located in one place on the site and may be reached by clicking on an icon or hyperlink, or an **Information Practice Statement**, defined as a discrete statement that describes a particular use or practice regarding consumers' personal information and/or choice offered to consumers about their personal information. In some cases, Web sites have both a Privacy Policy Notice and one or more Information Practice Statement(s).

[3] Figures in parentheses represent the 95% binomial confidence interval for each calculated percentage.

[4] For the Children's Sample only, the data reflect personal information collected from children.

TABLE EXHIBIT 12-8 • Of Those Web Sites That Collect Personal Information, Percent with an Information Practice Disclosure
This table is designed effectively with distinctive headings, though the numerical information is centered instead of right aligned. Making the table look difficult, however, are other design features: the long and complicated label and the excessive footnoting. The definition of "Information Practice Disclosure," in particular, might easily be shifted to accompanying paragraphs of text instead of displayed as a footnote to this table.
Source: Federal Trade Commission. Privacy Online: A Report to Congress. (Washington, DC: GPO, 1998), D-3.

the *y*-axis at zero and equally space the intervals on the *y*-axis to avoid distorting the height of the columns.

- Color can enhance the effect of a graph, but excessive color can reduce comprehension and distort information. Use the same color for all bars or columns that are representing the same items. Avoid using color as simple decoration.

- Make the graph accurate. Computer graphics allow a tremendous range of special effects. However, artistic graphs are not always either effective or accurate. Three-dimensional bars and columns are often deceptive because readers have difficulty visually comparing the relative lengths of the bars and heights of the columns. If you choose three-dimensional bar or column graphs, watch for distortion.

- Try to write captions or labels on or near the bars. Avoid legends (or keys) that slow reader comprehension. When bars are divided into too many divisions, which cannot be interpreted without consulting a legend, the result can be confusion rather than effective communication. However, placing labels on bars can be difficult if you use colored bars. Even black text will often be difficult to read on any colors but very light ones. For that reason, many graphics software programs offer you the use of legends. In short, legends are fine if you don't have too many segments or bars—more than four—and if the legend is close to the bars.

- For divided bar and column graphs with extensive divisions, use color or shading to distinguish divisions instead of crosshatching patterns. Crosshatching often creates distracting optical illusions.

- Avoid crowding the bars or columns within a graph. Such visual clutter makes a graph look difficult to interpret. Using three-dimensional bars or columns will also reduce the number that will fit in a given space. Effective and inviting graphs leave generous space between the bars or columns.

See Figures 12-9–12-13 for examples of column and bar graphs.

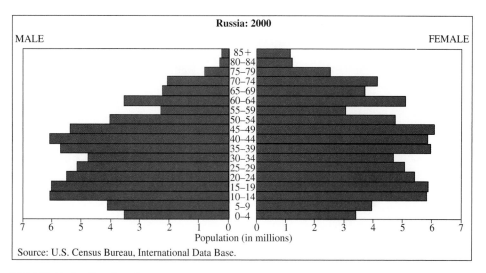

Source: U.S. Census Bureau, International Data Base.

FIGURE 12-9 • Bar Graph

This bar graph displays the population of Russian men and women of various ages in the year 2000, making it easy for viewers to compare and contrast among the different groups. It is readily apparent, for example, that men and women start off roughly equal in number and remain so until about age 40; at that point and continuing thereafter, the number of women exceeds the number of men. The simple design of the graph, including the use of the same color for every bar for both men and women, eliminates all potential distractions.

Source: U.S. Census Bureau, International Data Base. Population Pyramids for Russia. http://www.census.gov/cgi-bin/ipc/idbpyry.pl. April 15, 1999.

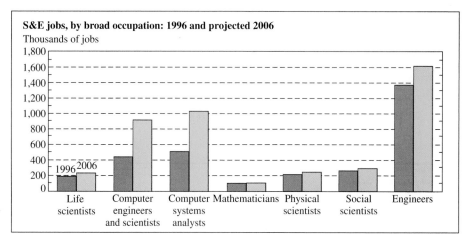

FIGURE 12-10 • Column Graph

This column graph would be better designed as a bar graph (i.e., with horizontal bars instead of vertical columns). The series of vertical columns aligned on the x-axis from left to right might be initially perceived as a chronological progression—the same subject displayed at consecutive points in time. In fact, the figure displays different subjects at the same points in time—1996 and 2006. Displaying the information as a bar graph would avoid any initial misunderstanding and speed the viewer's access to the information. Otherwise, the figure is quite effective in displaying the number of jobs for scientists and engineers. The two-dimensional columns keep the display simple, and the color-coding of the columns makes it easy to compare and contrast across the different occupations and time periods.

Source: National Science Board, *Science & Engineering Indicators—1998*. (Arlington, VA: National Science Foundation, 1998), 3-22.

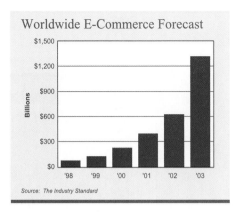

FIGURE 12-11 • Column Graph
This column graph is clean and concise. The blue columns are in clear contrast to the white background, and the horizontal gridlines aid the viewer's eye in determining the quantity depicted by each column. In the report from which this graphic comes, however, none of the 18 tables and figures are numbered, making it difficult to refer to specific illustrations without the nuisance of using their full title.
Source: U.S. Government Working Group on Electronic Commerce. Toward Digital eQuality. Second Annual Report. (Washington DC: GPO, 1999), iii.

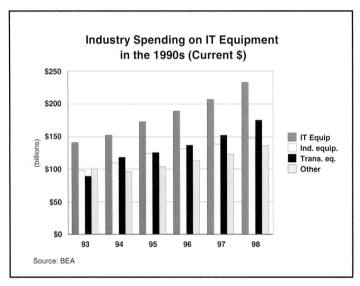

FIGURE 12-12 • Multiple-Column Graph
This is a multiple-column graph depicting the year-to-year changes in spending by industry on various kinds of equipment. The columns are displayed in two dimensions with visibly distinct shadings. The six groups of columns, however, are so close together that it is difficult to differentiate among the groups; because the same amount of space is used for the column width and the width of the space between columns, the spaces themselves look like additional columns. Inserting more space between the groups would make the graph easier to decipher. In addition, the purpose of this figure is to emphasize spending on information technology (IT) equipment, but it is the black columns of transportation equipment that receive visual emphasis and thus the viewer's initial attention. Using the black shading for the IT columns would better suit the purpose of the graph. The legend to the right could also be improved by consistent style: the word "equipment" is abbreviated differently three times and omitted for the last item.
Source: U.S. Department of Commerce, The Emerging Digital Economy II. (Washington, DC: GPO, 1999), 22.*Source*: U.S. Government Working Group on Electronic Commerce. Toward Digital eQuality. Second Annual Report. (Washington DC: GPO, 1999), iii.

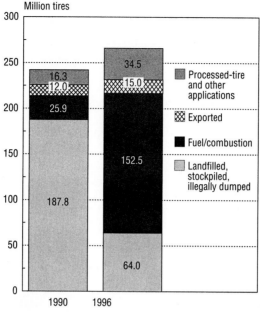

FIGURE 12-13 • Divided Column Graph

This divided column graph does a good job of emphasizing its key points but could be better designed nevertheless. It is readily apparent, for example, that the number of scrap tires going to landfills has decreased dramatically from 1990 to 1996, while the number being used for fuel has increased substantially and the number being processed has roughly doubled. The divisions that have seen the most obvious changes are also the divisions of highest contrast: The viewer notices them immediately. In addition, the numbers in each division give viewers access to specific information, essentially merging the details of a table with the emphasis of a figure. The cross-hatching for the exported spare tires division, however, makes it difficult to read the numbers and is inconsistent with the shading of the other divisions. A lighter shading or no shading would avoid this distraction. And instead of the legend, arrows pointing from the labels to the divisions in the 1996 column would be easier for viewers to interpret.

Source: U.S. Department of Transportation, Bureau of Transportation Statistics, Transportation Statistics, Annual Report 1998: Long Distance Travel and Freight. BTS98-S-01. (Washington, DC: GRO, 1998), 126.

Designing Circle Graphs

- Restrict the number of segments in a circle graph to seven or eight. There is simply a limit to the number of segments into which a circle can be divided before comprehension of the relative sizes is jeopardized. If necessary, combine several smaller segments and create a second circle graph to display the composition of that combined segment.

- Use shading or color to differentiate segments and make them easier for readers to see.

- Watch for possible distortion when you use three-dimensional circle graphs.

- Clearly label all segments. Whether they are placed inside or outside the circle, labels should be horizontal for easier reading.
- As you segment the graph, begin with the largest section in the upper right-hand quadrant. The remaining segments should be arranged clockwise, in descending order.

See Figures 12-14–12-16 for examples of circle graphs.

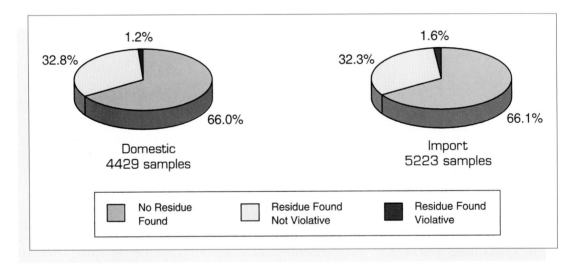

FIGURE 12-14 • Circle Graphs
These paired circle graphs compare and contrast the occurrence of pesticide residues on domestic and imported foods. Both graphs are designed with the largest segment starting in the upper right quadrant, followed systematically by the smaller and smallest segments. Together the two graphs emphasize that the difference in residues on domestic versus imported foods is insignificant: that is, the two circles look almost identical, and the numbers that identify the relative size of each segment reinforce that message. The graphs might be easier to read if the segments were fully labeled, but the legend is clear and concise. And while nothing is gained by making the graphs three-dimensional, nothing is distorted here either.
Source: U.S. Food and Drug Administration. Food and Drug Administration Pesticide Program: Residue Monitoring 1997. (Washington, DC: GPO, 1997), 15.

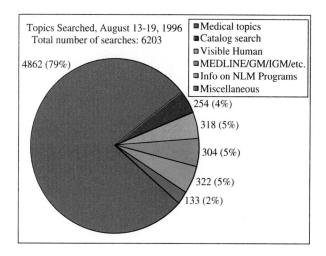

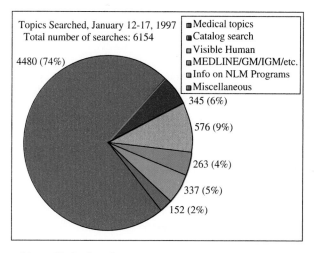

FIGURE 12-15 • Two or More Circle Graphs

These circle graphs compare and contrast the number of searches on a World Wide Web site before and after changes to the design of the site. The pair communicate the intended point effectively while violating conventions of the circle graph. If the largest segment started in the upper right quadrant as convention stipulates, the smaller segments would all be relegated to the upper left quadrant—a position of lesser emphasis. Proceeding from the largest segment to the smallest segment would also be ineffective. It is the identical positioning and sequencing of the segments that makes the differences between the two graphs more obvious: Viewers will readily notice that the yellow segment almost doubles in size. In the graphs, color is used effectively to differentiate the six segments. Nevertheless, the graphs would be easier to read if the segments were fully labeled: With six segments to identify, the legends are fairly complicated and require more time for reading and interpreting.

Source: Naomi, Miller, *Improving the NLM Home Page: From Logs to Links.* Poster presented at the annual meeting, of the Medical Library Association, May 26–27, 1997. U.S. National Library of Medicine. http://www.nlm.nih.gov/psd/web poster/web poster.html. February 11, 1999.

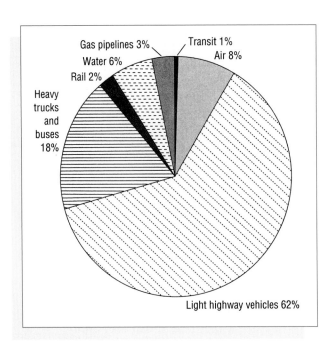

FIGURE 12-16 • A Distracting Circle Graph
While this circle graph is nicely labeled, the sections offer a distracting array of shadings and cross-hatchings, from diagonal dashes to horizontal lines to dots to two levels of gray. Inexplicably, black is used twice. Moreover, instead of starting with the largest segment in the upper right quadrant and progressing to the smallest segment, the graph displays a seemingly arbitrary order of segments and leaves it to the viewer to sort by size. Visually and logically, the graph is considerably more complicated than it needs to be.
Source: U.S. Department of Transportation, Bureau of Transportation Statistics. Transportation Statistics Annual Report 1998: Long Distance Travel and Freight. BTS98-S-01. (Washington, DC: GPO, 1998), 109.

Designing Line Graphs

- Label each axis clearly. Like bar and column graphs, line graphs must have clearly labeled scales to show the variables you are measuring. Ordinarily, the independent variable is placed on the horizontal *x*-axis, and the dependent variables are placed on the vertical *y*-axis and the diagonal *z*-axis (in a three-dimensional graph).

- Choose the scale of each axis to show the appropriate steepness of the slope of the line. Typically, the scales start at zero, with the intervals equally spaced on each axis.

- The major difficulty in designing line graphs lies in choosing the spacing for each axis so that the steepness (slope) of the line accurately measures the actual trend suggested by the data. Computer graphics will allow you to adjust the intervals on the *x*- and the *y*-axis, but your job is to decide whether the slope of the graph accurately depicts your data or gives a distorted impression.

- Avoid using more than three data lines on one graph unless they are spaced apart and do not overlap. Graphs with several intersecting data lines are usually difficult for readers to interpret.
- Keep the data lines on your graph distinctive by using different colors or styles for each line.
- If possible, label each data line. Avoid legends (or keys) that slow reader comprehension.

See Figures 12-17–12-20 for example of line graphs.

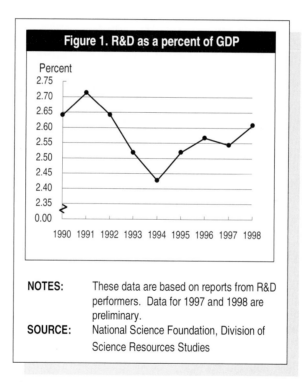

NOTES: These data are based on reports from R&D performers. Data for 1997 and 1998 are preliminary.

SOURCE: National Science Foundation, Division of Science Resources Studies

FIGURE 12-17 • Line Graph
This is a simple, clean line graph. Both scales are readily interpreted, and the single data line is plainly visible. Notice that the break in the y-axis (jumping from 0 to 2.35) is clearly identified with diagonal slashes.
Source: Steven Payson, R&D as a Percent of GDP Is Highest in Six Years. Data Brief. National Science Foundation, Division of Science Resource Studies. NSF 99-302. October 16, 1998, p. 1.

FIGURE 12-18 • A Bad Multiple Line Graph

This is a fairly confusing line graph. The excessively numerous data lines are inadequately differentiated by the black circles, diamonds, and triangles. The five lines also crisscross several times, creating a visual tangle that is difficult for viewers to decipher. Each data line is labeled, but three of the lines are assigned abbreviations (two of which are likely unfamiliar to viewers); because a definition key is necessary, quick understanding of the graph is once again hindered.
Source: U.S. Department of Transportation, Bureau of Transportation Statistics. Transportation Statistics Annual Report 1998: Long Distance Travel and Freight. BTS98-S-01. (Washington, DC: GPO, 1993), 113.

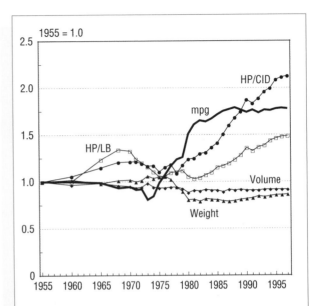

KEY: HP/CID = ratio of horsepower to engine size; mpg = miles per gallon; HP/LB = horsepower per pound.

SOURCE: U.S. Department of Transportation, National Highway Traffic Safety Administration, "Production Weighted Data from Manufacturer's Fuel Economy Reports," data tables, 1997.

FIGURE 12-19 • A Better Multiple Line Graph

In this line graph, the multiple data lines are readily distinguishable, simplifying visual interpretation of the figure. The data lines, however, are labeled with undefined abbreviations, yet again hindering quick understanding. Viewers of this line graph would have to search through the accompanying text for explanations of the abbreviations. If abbreviations in a graph cannot be avoided, a definition key is essential.
Source: U.S. Department of Transportation, Bureau of Transportation Statistics. Transportation Statistics Annual Report 1998: Long Distance Travel and Freight. BTS98-S-01. (Washington, DC, GPO, 1998), 118.

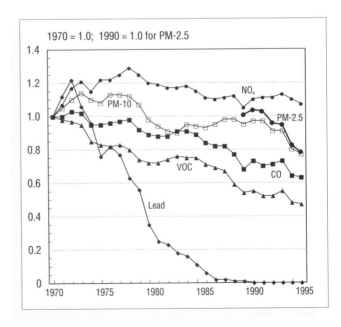

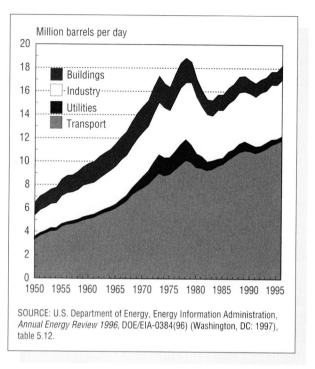

FIGURE 12-20 • Line Graph Variant
In this line graph, the multiple data lines never intersect, making it possible to color in the space between the data lines for additional emphasis. (Such a figure is often called a surface graph, but it is essentially a design variation of the line graph). A simple legend is used to identify the different subjects.
Source: U.S. Department of Transportation, Bureau of Transportation Statistics. Transportation Statistics Annual Report 1998: Long Distance Travel and Freight. BTS98-S-01. (Washington, DC: GPO, 1998), 110.

▶ DESIGNING ILLUSTRATIONS ETHICALLY

Displaying information ethically requires that you make careful choices about the design of your illustrations.

For example, the scale of the *x*- and *y*-axes on a line graph has a significant impact on the data display. In designing a graph, you ordinarily start the *x*- and *y*-axes at 0. Exceptions are possible if beginning at some other point ("suppressing the zero") will not distort information. If several line graphs are to be compared and contrasted, it would be unethical to suppress the zero on some of the graphs but not on others: readers might focus only on the data lines and overlook the difference in the starting points of the *x*- and *y*-axes (see Figures 12-21 to 12-25).

Pictographs (graphs using pictorial images) can be deceptive if the pictures are likely to distract the viewer or allow the graphic information to be misinterpreted (see Figures 12-26).

Using distorted graphs, however, isn't the only error that will result in the creation of unethical illustrations. It is unethical to create a drawing that makes a product look bigger or somehow better than it actually is. It is unethical to design a flowchart that disguises a procedure's complexity by making things look relatively simple. It is unethical to stage or doctor a photograph to create a positive or negative impression of your subject that isn't fully justified.

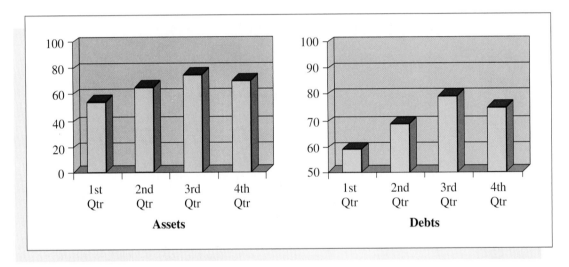

FIGURE 12-21 • Deceptive Paired Column Charts
Positioned side by side, the two graphs create a distorted impression. All the columns in the debts graph are smaller than the corresponding columns in the assets graph, giving the incorrect impression that throughout the year, debts were smaller than assets. The assets graph starts the y-axis at 0, but the debts graph suppresses the zero, and the percentages on the y-axis of the assets graph are given in increments of 20, whereas the debts graph uses increments of 10. Readers will be deceived unless they notice these differences in the two scales. The three-dimensional columns are distracting and hinder a clear comparison of the two graphs.

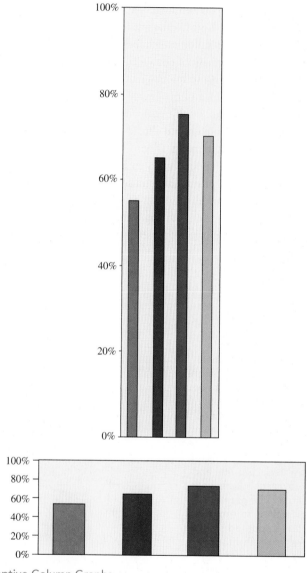

FIGURE 12-22 • Deceptive Column Graphs
It is also possible to distort graphic information by stretching one axis and shrinking the other, thereby making the differences among the data points either more or less apparent. Tall and narrow columns exaggerate differences in the data, while short and wide columns disguise such differences.

In addition, if you illustrate information regarding people, you must strive to be sensitive to their humanity. For example, to use a circle graph to depict the human beings killed in various kinds of automobile accidents genuinely diminishes the dignity of the victims, reducing real people to objects in a statistical display. To illustrate this information ethically, you might superimpose the circle graph on a photograph of a victim, thus offering a vivid reminder of the tragic impact on human beings of your subject. In certain cases, however, it is desirable to avoid illustrations altogether, conveying delicate information with words only. If you believe human life is unique or special, choose unique or special ways to illustrate it (see Figure 12-27).

The use of unethical illustrations damages your credibility and hinders your audience's understanding of your subject. (You may want to refer frequently to Chapter 6, Writing Ethically, to help you remain aware of issues that pertain to the ethical presentation of technical information.)

FIGURE 12-23 • Deceptive Line Graph

If readers look quickly at this graph of sales figures, they might come away with the impression that sales are rising. They might not notice that the time line on the x-axis is reversed; that is, instead of the earlier date on the left and the later date on the right as one would ordinarily expect, the horizontal scale starts with 2000 and proceeds backward in time to 1996. Sales, in fact, are falling. The extra-thick data line and the small labels on the x-axis contribute to the deception, as does the color. The green, in particular, would suggest money to American audiences. In addition, the graduated shading of the background (darker at the bottom and lighter at the top) lifts the reader's eye and reinforces the misperception of rising sales.

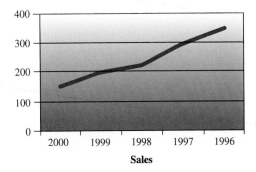

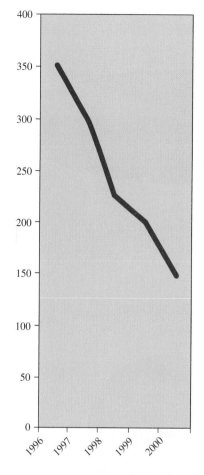

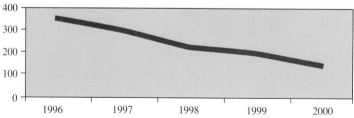

FIGURE 12-24 • More Deceptive Line Graphs
It is also possible to distort graphic information by stretching one axis and shrinking the other, thereby making the data line either more vertical (depicting a rapid and dramatic change) or more horizontal (depicting a slow and moderate change).

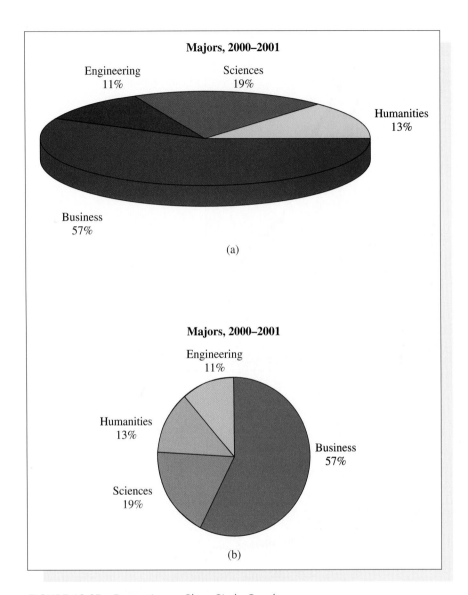

FIGURE 12-25 • Deceptive vs Clear Circle Graphs
The first circle graph (a) is quite deceptive: Even though the labeling of each section is correct, the visual impression is that the Humanities major is the smallest group instead of the second smallest group (i.e., Engineering is the smallest). The light coloring of the Humanities major section versus the dark coloring of the other sections distorts the relative size of the light section: the blue, brown and green sections essentially collapse so that the reader perceives a large dark section versus a small light section. Also disrupting the reader's understanding of the relative size of each section are the slight elevation of the circle graph and the three-dimensional perspective as well as the arbitrary ordering of the sections. The second circle graph (b), on the other hand, offers a clear and unambiguous display of information because of its two-dimensional view with a systematic ordering of the sections (largest to smallest) and a systematic coloring (from darkest to lightest).

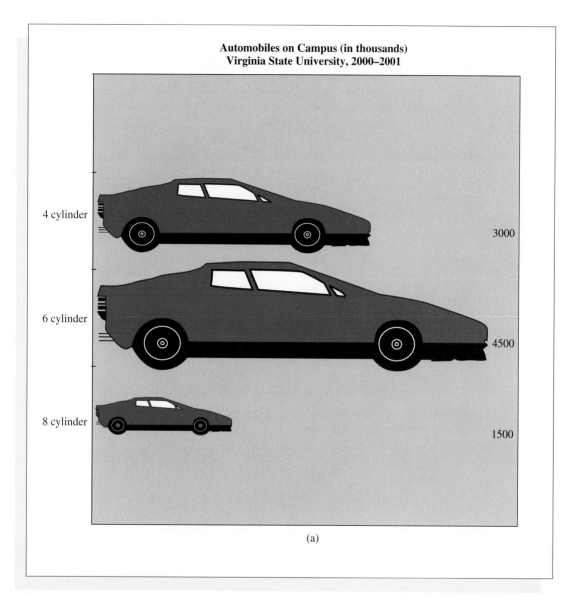

Automobiles on Campus (in thousands)
Virginia State University, 2000–2001

4 cylinder   3000

6 cylinder   4500

8 cylinder   1500

(a)

FIGURE 12-26 • Deceptive vs Clear Pictographs

The first pictograph (a) is potentially deceptive. Even though the numerical information is clearly specified in words, the visual impression is distorted. The picture for the 6-cylinder category is both three times wider and three times taller than the picture for the 8-cylinder category, making it nine times larger instead of only three times larger. Similarly, the picture for the 4-cylinder category is twice as wide and twice as tall as the picture for the 8-cylinder category, making it four times larger. The visual message, as a consequence, contradicts the verbal message. Since the visual message (bright red automobiles) is more conspicuous than the verbal message (in small, light type), the reader could easily misunderstand this illustration. To avoid such confusion, design the visual message to reinforce the verbal message by using one picture for a specific number (e.g., 1000) and duplicating that picture (or portions of it) to depict multiples of that number, as shown in the second example (b).

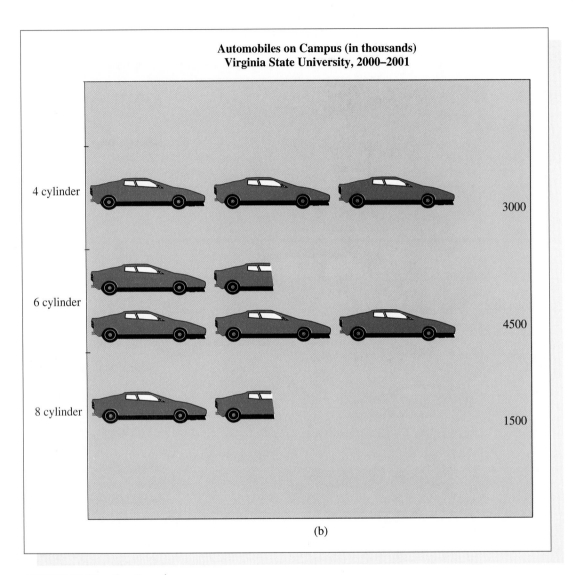

Automobiles on Campus (in thousands)
Virginia State University, 2000–2001

(b)

FIGURE 12-26 • *Continued*

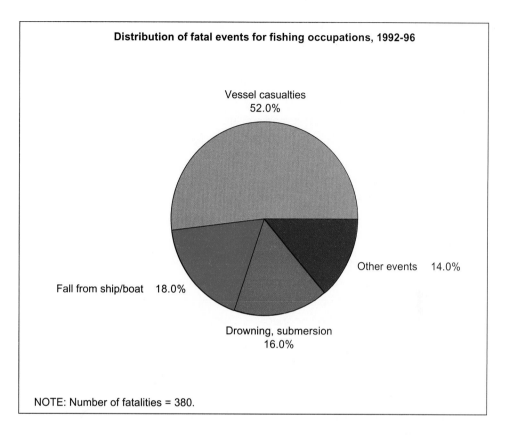

FIGURE 12-27 • Unethical Circle Graph
This is a circle graph of dubious ethics, cruelly depicting the loss of 380 human lives as you might the loss of 380 fish. While the text accompanying this graphic specifies such tragic accidents as "being pulled overboard by a hook caught in one's clothing" or "being caught in winches and other machinery," the visual display conveys none of this horror. The drownings, hypothermia, electrocutions, impalements, and eviscerations that plague the fishing industry—the genuine dangers to human beings engaged in this occupation—are nowhere illustrated. To depict this loss of human lives with a conventional circle graph (and to label it with the euphemism "fatal events") shows a considerable insensitivity to the victims and their survivors.
Source: Persons Overboard/Sunk Vessels: Fishing Jobs Continue to Take Deadly Toll, *Issues in Labor Statistics*, June 1998, p. 1.

▶ PLANNING AND REVISION CHECKLISTS

Planning Illustrations

- How important are illustrations to your presentation?
- How complex are your illustrations likely to be?
- How expert is your audience in reading illustrations?
- What kinds of illustrations is your audience familiar with?
- Are you working with any concepts that can be presented visually or in a combination of words and graphics?
- Do you have any definitions that should be presented visually in whole or in part?
- Do you have any processes or algorithms that could be depicted visually in a flowchart?
- Will you be presenting information on trends or relationships? Should some of this information be presented in tables and graphs?
- Do you have masses of statistics that could be summarized in tables?
- Do you need to depict objects? If so, what do you need to display about the objects? Do you need to focus attention on specific aspects of the objects? Do you require the realism of photographs?
- What are the design conventions of your illustrations?
- How much prose explanation of your illustrations are you likely to need?

Revising Illustrations

- Are your illustrations suited to your purpose and audience?
- Do your illustrations communicate information ethically?
- Are your illustrations effectively located and easy to find?
- Are your illustrations numbered and labeled?
- Do your verbal and visual elements complement each other?
- Are your illustrations genuinely informative instead of simply decorative?
- When necessary, have you helped your readers to interpret your illustrations with commentary or annotations?
- Will your readers easily understand the processes you have displayed visually?

- Have you included necessary units of measure in your tables and graphs?
- Are your tables simple, clear, and logical? Are the numbers in your tables aligned correctly (whole numbers on right-hand digits and fractional numbers on the decimal points)?
- Do your graphs need a grid for more accurate interpretation? Have you avoided the use of keys or at least kept them simple? Have you plotted your graphs according to the conventions: independent variable horizontally, dependent variable vertically? If you have used a suppressed zero, will it be obvious to your readers?
- Have you acknowledged the sources for borrowed or adapted tables and figures?

▶ EXERCISES

1. Analyze the effectiveness of Figures 12-28 (a) and (b). How would you revise the figures to clarify the visual display of information?

2. Analyze the ethics of Figure 12-29. How would you revise this display to minimize the possibility of deception?

3. Examine several technical publications (e.g., brochures, manuals, pamphlets) in your field of study. Choose examples of four effective or ineffective illustrations. Write a report for majors in your field that analyzes the effectiveness or ineffectiveness of each illustration. Develop conclusions and recommendations on the use of illustrations in your field. Be sure to integrate a copy of each illustration with your analysis of it.

4. Examine the various kinds of illustration used in several of the professional journals in your major field of study. Which types of illustration do you ordinarily find? Which types don't you find? Which occur most often? Which occur least often? Reproduce sample tables and figures to demonstrate the conventions for illustrations in your field. Give an oral presentation to your class in which you report your findings.

5. You are the director of marketing for Howell & Field, Inc., which raises turkeys in Texas, Oklahoma, Nebraska, and Kansas. You receive a call from Juanita Elizondo, Howell & Field's vice president of operations, who wants you to give an oral sales report to the company's board of directors. Your presentation should take approximately 10 minutes. Prepare several illustrations to explain Howell & Field's sales figures for 1996–2000.

Sales (Thousand of pounds)

	1996	1997	1998	1999	2000
Texas	90.4	98.6	99.8	104.6	97.6
Oklahoma	60.3	62.4	60.6	58.4	54.8
Nebraska	58.4	60.6	65.6	67.8	72.4
Kansas	40.8	48.5	52.5	56.3	58.9

6. After your sales presentation, Elizondo asks you to write a report for a group of prospective investors from Australia. She specifically wants you to make projections for 2001–2005 based on the 1996–2000 figures. Design the illustrations that you will include in your written report.

7. Aeschylus Corporation, which designs 3-D computer games, is looking for new employees, especially individuals able to conceive and design state-of-the-art computer software products. It has been a small private corporation for five years and hopes to achieve a major expansion. The president of Aeschylus, Robin Pierce, has asked your organization, Creative Consultants, to develop a brochure for prospective new employees, incorporating appropriate illustrations. You've interviewed Pierce and have gathered quite a bit of information on the company that you believe will be pertinent:

History	Founded in 1996, in Kansas City, Missouri, by Robin Pierce, B.S. in Computer Science, 1992, University of St. Louis; MBA, 1994, Missouri University
Sales	1996: $200,000; 1997: $750,000; 1998: $2 million; 1999: $7 million; 2000: $16 million

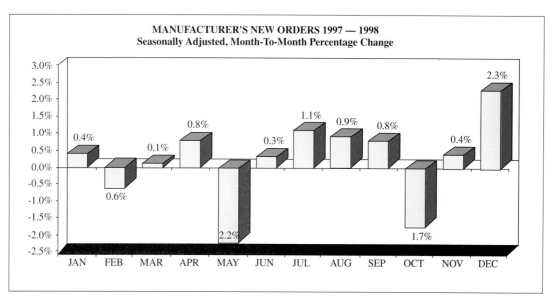

Source: U.S. Census Bureau, *Highlights from the Preliminary Report on Manufacturers' Shipments, Inventories, and Orders.*
http://www.census.gov/indicator/www/m3/index.htm, February 9, 1999.

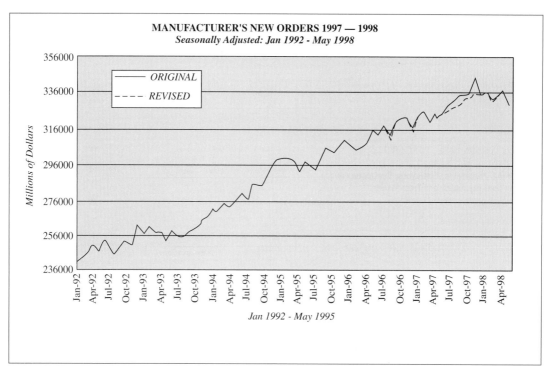

Source: U.S. Census Bureau, *Highlights from the Preliminary Report on Manufacturers' Shipments, Inventories, and Orders.*
http://www.census.gov/indicator/www/m3/bench/bch98no.gif, February 9, 1999.

FIGURE 12-28 • Graphs for Exercise 12-1

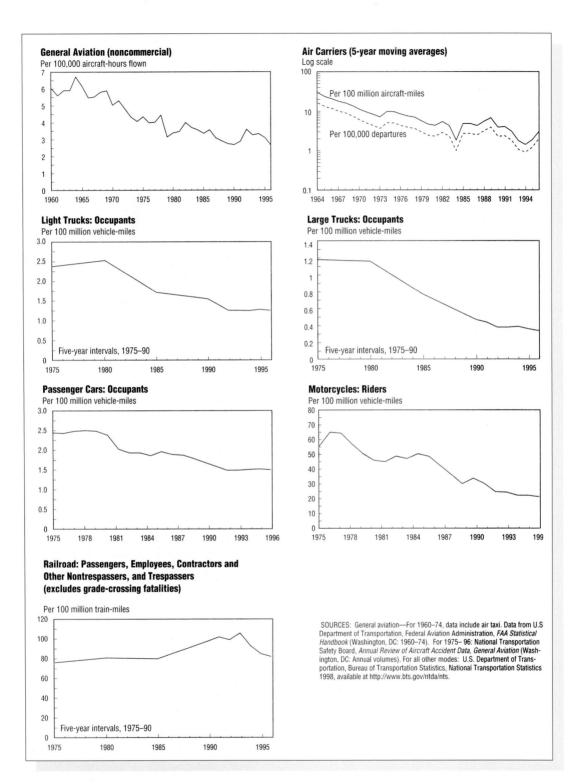

FIGURE 12-29 • Graphs for Exercise 12-2

Source: U.S. Department of Transportation, Bureau of Transportation Statistics. Transportation Statistics Annual Report 1998: Long Distance Travel and Freight. BTS98-S-01. (Washington, DC: 1998, GPO), 84.

Employees	with specialists in design (3), graphics and animation (4), programming (5), video and movie editing (3), production (2), quality assurance (1), documentation (1), sound (1), and music (1)
Products	6 current products, looking to diversify, especially in action–adventure, newest product: Street Maniac (driving game); biggest seller: Trojan War (fantasy role-playing)
Facilities	State-of-the-art computer equipment, serves both PC and Macintosh systems
Location	1224 Howard Avenue, Kansas City: new building, spacious offices
Salary and benefits	Competitive with industry; excellent medical coverage, 4 weeks vacation each year

Design a brochure for Aeschylus Corporation that incorporates as wide a variety of illustrations as possible.

8. In designing your brochure for Aeschylus Corporation, you are surprised by a moral dilemma. Robin Pierce is willing to hire people with disabilities and would like you to include that information in the brochure. At this time, Aeschylus has no permanently disabled employees. However, programmer Jacqueline Brown, who injured her back in a skiing accident, is temporarily restricted to a wheelchair. In a meeting with your design group, Pierce suggests including a photograph of all the Aeschylus employees (with Brown in the wheelchair) to show prospective employees that people with disabilities are welcome. You mention the idea to your staff photographer, Kishor Mitra, but he objects, claiming such a picture would be deceptive and thus unethical. As project leader, you have to determine which side should prevail and then write one of two memos: either to convince Pierce, your client, that such a photograph would be wrong, or to persuade Mitra, your employee, to set up the photograph.

Applications

PART III puts the skills and techniques you have learned in Parts I and II to work. It demonstrates job hunting strategies and covers the major report forms of technical communication, explaining how to organize and write them in both correspondence and report formats. Chapter 15 shows you how to propose work to be done and how to report progress in that work. Chapter 16 discusses how to analyze data and report your conclusions and recommendations in such formats as feasibility reports. Chapter 17 deals with how to turn your research into a report suitable for publication, and Chapter 18 describes how to plan, organize, and write a set of instructions. In Chapter 19, you learn how to plan and deliver an oral report. Chapter 19 also emphasizes the visual elements so important in technical reporting of any kind.

SCENARIO

You've just hung up after a telephone conversation with a client who called you to complain about a delayed shipment. You promised to investigate. And she promised to give you 48 hours.

The wise thing to do at this point is to create a written trail of your oral conversation. You write your client a brief e-mail message summarizing your understanding of the conversation and print out a copy for your file. You want a written record of your promise to the client and your client's promise to you. This written memo will confirm your expectations of each other. And if you or she has misunderstood the telephone conversation, your message will immediately identify that misunderstanding and create the opportunity to clarify it. For example, she might have said "within 48 hours," clearly expecting your call before that deadline, but if all you heard was "48 hours," you might have thought that you had 48 hours to investigate and could call in your report shortly thereafter. While a difference of only minutes might be involved, such a misunderstanding could jeopardize the business relations between your two organizations. A timely exchange of written messages could avoid later confusion and disappointment.

In this situation, you don't have a lot of time, so e-mail is the quick and inexpensive choice to communicate your message, but you could also write a letter and either fax it to your client or use overnight delivery service.

chapter 13

Correspondence

- ▶ Determining Your Purpose

- ▶ Analyzing the Audience

- ▶ Composing Letters, Memos, and E-Mail

- ▶ Finding the Appropriate Style
  Direct versus Indirect Style
  Conversational Style

- ▶ Special Considerations for E-Mail

- ▶ Special Considerations for International Correspondence

- ▶ Keeping Copies of Correspondence

On the job you will face a wide variety of situations that require you to write e-mail messages, letters, or memos. Oral communication—in person or by telephone—will dominate your day-to-day interactions, but much of your communication will also be written.

You will meet face-to-face to emphasize the importance or urgency of your message and to personalize the communication. A face-to-face conversation offers the greatest opportunity to establish a close human relationship: The parties see each other, offer greetings, and occupy the same space at the same time. A full exchange of verbal and visual information is possible, with ability to ask and answer questions.

You will telephone if a face-to-face conversation is impractical or if, having established a close human relationship, you nevertheless wish to emphasize the importance or urgency of your communication. Telephone conversations offer a limited opportunity to personalize the communication because only the voices of the individuals are available (unless the call allows video as well as audio transmission). You do, however, retain the ability to ask and answer questions. Again, neither caller receives a written copy of the information communicated.

You will write to create a record of decisions or promises. You will write to offer details that people might misinterpret or misunderstand if received orally. You will write because your audience expects certain information to be delivered in writing. And you will write whenever you would like to receive a written reply.

▶ DETERMINING YOUR PURPOSE

On the job you will compose correspondence for a variety of purposes, such as to report, inquire, or complain. In determining your purpose, ask yourself the following questions:

- What do I want to have happen as a result of my letter, memo, or e-mail?
- What do I want my reader to think or do after reading my message?
- Given the result that I want (and guided by ethical considerations), what must I do in my letter to achieve that result?

Table 13–1 displays several purposes of correspondence, the desired result, and common strategies used for achieving the desired result.

Consider, for example, the following situation. Maria Montez is a second-year engineering student at Florida Technological Institute. She is enrolled this semester in a technical writing course. A major project for the course is a presentation to the class on a critical issue in her major field of study. Maria is aware of the difficulties that engineers encounter because Americans continue to use the traditional "pounds and inches" system of weights and

▲ TABLE 13-1	Purpose of Correspondence	
Purpose	Desired Result	Common Strategies
Reporting	The reader takes the right action or makes the right decision.	• Use headings to identify the sections of your report. • State the subject and purpose of your message. • If your report or recommendation has been requested, identify the requesting individual and the circumstances leading to the request. • Summarize your report. Emphasize the key points important to the decision-making process as well as conclusions and recommendations. • Offer the details that support your conclusions and recommendations. Integrate illustrations as necessary. • Specify your conclusions and recommendations.
Inquiring (solicited)	You obtain the desired information, and your reader is willing to provide you additional information if you request it.	• Identify the advertisement or offer that solicited your inquiry. • Identify yourself and establish your need for the information. • Request the information. Specify the precise product or process in which you are interested. If appropriate, explain how the company might make a sale to you, thereby prompting a quick and complete reply to your inquiry.
Inquiring (unsolicited)	You obtain the desired information, and your reader is willing to provide you additional information if you request it.	• Identify yourself. • State clearly and specifically the information or materials that you want. • Establish your need for the requested information or materials. • Tell the recipient why you have chosen him or her as a source for this information or material. • Close courteously. Never write "thank you in advance," a phrase that presumes the reader will comply with your request.
Replying to inquiries	The reader receives all the information requested and doesn't have to write again to request more information.	• If possible, answer the questions in the order in which they appear in the inquiry. • Repeat enough of the original questions to remind the reader of the subject and identify which question you are answering. • Try to be as complete as possible, to assist your reader fully and to avoid the need for a second exchange of correspondence on the subject. • If appropriate, refer the reader to additional sources of information on the subject.
Complaining	The reader makes the adjustment that you desire.	• Be firm but polite. • Assume that the organization will try to correct the situation fairly. • Be specific about the problem and the inconvenience or injury you have suffered as a result. • Provide necessary documentation (e.g., dates, times places, names, product numbers). • Encourage the organization to make a fair adjustment. • If possible, suggest the adjustment you would like the organization to make.

(continued)

▲ TABLE 13-1	Purpose of Correspondence *(Continued)*	
Purpose	Desired Result	Common Strategies
Offering adjustments	The reader is satisfied with the adjustment you offer and maintains his or her relationship with your organization.	• Be friendly. • Focus on keeping the customer's goodwill. • Express regret about the problem and thank the customer for bringing it to your attention. • Explain the circumstances that caused the problem. • Describe specifically what the adjustment will be. • Resolve any special problems that may have accompanied the complaint. • Close politely.
Refusing adjustments	The reader accepts your refusal and maintains his or her relationship with your organization.	• Be friendly and polite. • Express regret about the problem and thank the customer for writing. • Explain the reason for the refusal in detail. Show the customer that you have given the complaint serious consideration. Prepare the reader for the negative decision. • State the refusal clearly but kindly. If possible, offer a partial or alternative adjustment. • Close the letter in a friendly way, leading the reader's attention away from the negative decision. Focus on the future instead of the past. Never apologize for the negative decision or solicit the reader's understanding of your reasons for reaching it.
Thanking	The reader feels appreciated for his or her efforts and is inclined to assist you again on a subsequent project.	• Be brief. • Be explicit in your expression of gratitude. • Identify specifically the reader's contribution. • Describe the positive impact of the the reader's efforts. • Close politely.

measures instead of adopting the metric system, which is the international standard. She believes the American rejection of the metric system arises from a failure to educate people effectively. Her research leads her to Professor Nicholas Hanson at the University of Cleveland, whose name is cited in the professional literature as a leading advocate of the metric system. He has also himself written a journal article on the economic benefits that would arise from implementation of a single international standard for weights and measures. But none of the articles available really address the question of how to teach Americans to understand the metric system.

Maria decides that she will write a letter to Professor Hanson to solicit his advice. She is a little pressed for time: It's February 1 and the presentation is scheduled for April 3. Professor Hanson's journal article gives his e-mail address at the University of Cleveland. But Maria decides a formal letter would be better, chiefly because she wants Professor Hanson to know that she has taken the time to compose her request and hasn't just hurried off a quick e-mail message to him. She's asking him to take the time to answer her questions and believes he will take her more seriously and give her more cooperation if he sees that she has invested some time of her own in this request.

Since Professor Hanson is a busy man, fully occupied with his teaching and research duties, Maria gets right to the point and immediately states her purpose for writing. She also decides to use short paragraphs to make the letter easy for the reader to skim through quickly. She proceeds to explain who she is. To give herself credibility, she specifically mentions that she has been reading journal articles on this subject. And she explains to Professor Hanson why she has chosen to contact him for information, slipping in a nice compliment while doing so. She then concisely asks her questions. Finally, she expresses her appreciation and, by including her e-mail address, tries to make it as easy as possible for Professor Hanson to reply. And Maria knows he is likely to reply a lot sooner by e-mail (see Figure 13-1).

Professor Hanson is impressed with Maria's letter. She seems like a serious student and he is pleased to offer his advice. He also appreciates being able to reply to Maria's letter by e-mail because it saves him time. And Maria will immediately receive the information she requested.

Because Maria is a student, Professor Hanson isn't sure how much she already knows about the metric system. He chooses to avoid technical language, but he includes a lot of examples, listing them to make them easier to read. Although he is pleased to answer Maria's letter, he doesn't want to be bothered by additional questions, especially if answers are readily available from other sources. He has a looming deadline on a research project and just doesn't have time to answer questions from students who aren't enrolled in his courses. He doesn't offer to provide additional information, therefore, referring Maria instead to a pertinent source (see Figure 13-2).

Maria is grateful for the information that Professor Hanson has provided. It gives her oral presentation a good sense of direction: she will compare the two methods of teaching the metric system and demonstrate the superiority of learning to think in metric weights and measures. She is also surprised that her earlier search on the World Wide Web using the keywords "metric system" didn't identify the U.S. Metric Association. She will visit its Web site to see if it has teaching materials available.

Maria composes a quick e-mail message to Professor Hanson. She wants him to know she appreciates his assistance so that he'll be willing to help again the next time a student writes to him with a question (see Figure 13-3).

▶ ANALYZING THE AUDIENCE

In composing correspondence, consider your readers: Who are they? What do they know already? What is their purpose in reading your letter or memo? How receptive will they be to your message?

Maria Montez
1225 55th Street
Gatesville, FL 32039
mmontez@fti.edu

Professor Nicholas Hanson
Department of Civil Engineering
University of Cleveland
Cleveland, OH 44125

Dear Professor Hanson:

I am writing to request information about effective ways to teach people the metric system of weights and measures.

I am a second-year student at Florida Technological Institute. For a course in technical writing that I am currently taking, I am giving a presentation on the proper way to educate Americans in the use of the metric system. The presentation is scheduled for April 3.

In the journals in which I have been researching the subject, you are frequently mentioned as a major authority in the field. Would you be kind enough to give me your opinion about how metrics should be taught?

The specific aspect of this question that concerns me is whether metric measurements should be taught in relation to present standard measurements, such as the foot and pound, or whether they should be taught independently of other measurements. I see both methods in use.

Any help you can give me will be greatly appreciated, and I will, of course, cite you in my presentation. For your convenience, I include my e-mail address: mmontez@fti.edu.

Sincerely yours,

Maria Montez

FIGURE 13-1 • Maria's Letter of Inquiry

Dear Ms. Montez:

The question of how to teach people about the metric system concerns a great many educators. I suppose it's inevitable that those familiar with the present system will be tempted to convert metric measurements to ones they already know. For example, people will say, "A kilogram, that's about two pounds."

In my opinion, however, such conversion is not the best way to teach metrics. Rather, people should be taught to think in terms of what the metric measurement really measures, to associate it with familiar things. Here are some examples:

* A paper clip is about a centimeter wide.

* A dollar bill weighs about a gram.

* A comfortable room is 20 degrees C.

* Water freezes at 0 degrees C.

* At a normal walking pace, we can go about 5 kilometers an hour.

These are the kinds of association we have made all our lives with the present system. We need to do the same for metric measurements. As in learning a foreign language, we really learn it only when we stop translating in our heads and begin to think in the new language.

I hope this answers your question. You can get valuable materials about metrics by writing to the U.S. Metric Association, 10245 Andasol Avenue, Northridge, CA 91325 (fax: 818-368-7443; http://lamar.colostate.edu//~hillger).

Sincerely,

Nicholas Hanson

FIGURE 13-2 • Professor Hanson's E-Mail Reply to Maria's Letter of Inquiry

Dear Professor Hanson:

Thank you for your quick reply to my questions. Your advice has been a great help as I prepare my oral presentation.

I also appreciate the reference to the U.S. Metric Association. I will check its Web site for more information.

Sincerely,

Maria Montez

FIGURE 13-3 • Maria's E-Mail Thank You

On the job, you will write to individuals and groups of people. And even if you are chiefly addressing a single reader, you may also be directing copies of your message to others. In such cases, you must think about the knowledge and experience of both your primary reader and your secondary readers. If, for example, those receiving copies are unfamiliar with the topic under discussion, you will have to provide background information.

In another common situation, you may be explaining a technical problem and its solution to a colleague with technical knowledge equal to yours.

If, however, you are sending a copy of your message to your boss, who lacks that technical expertise, you would be wise to start your discussion with a summary (see pages 618–622). Fill the boss in quickly on the key points and tell him or her the implications of your message.

In addition, consider your reader's purpose in reading your message. You have a purpose in writing your letter, memo, or e-mail message, but your reader has a purpose as well. For example, your reader may be reading to evaluate your recommendation and accept or reject it. Your purpose then must be to provide enough information to make that evaluation and decision possible. Or your purpose may be to explain why you missed a deadline. Your reader will be reading to determine whether your reasons are valid and acceptable. You will then need to provide enough information to justify your position.

You also need to determine your audience's attitude toward you, your subject, and your purpose. Do you have a good relationship with your audience? Do they ordinarily accept or reject your explanations and recommendations? Is your audience positively or negatively disposed to your subject and purpose? If you are registering a complaint about poor customer service, for example, you need to know how receptive your audience is to such complaints. If the audience is typically unsympathetic or doesn't know you or trust you, you will have to provide substantial evidence to build a persuasive case. A sympathetic audience who trusts your judgment will probably require less evidence of you.

Consider the following situation. Morad Atif, the manager of Building Services at Accell, Inc. would like to purchase new reversible power drills for a crew of twenty-five technicians. He has examined the options available and decided on a drill that he believes is suitable, but he still must receive approval from the company's financial officer, Tamika Williams. He has discussed the subject with Williams but a written request is still required. Williams likes to have good records.

Morad knows that buying the drills isn't as much the issue as the choice of drills. The previous manager was fired for accepting gifts from equipment suppliers. Morad is new on the job and he believes that suspicion still lingers: he'll have to prove that he is trustworthy and that his recommendations are credible.

Morad adopts a direct style, getting right to the point of the memo in the opening sentence. He knows that he has to come across as straightforward. He mentions the price and briefly justifies the new equipment. In the paragraphs that follow, he'll focus on the choice of drills, using a bulleted list to give the evidence visual emphasis. He'll also start the list with a reason that might be especially persuasive to the financial officer: cost. And he'll close the list with a reason that might also be pertinent: prevention of loss of equipment. He also decides to list the price information for the convenience of his reader, since Williams will later need to retrieve cost information from this memo for the company's financial records.

To prompt a quick decision, Morad closes the memo with a question and a tentative deadline (see Figure 13-4). Otherwise, he worries, his request might not be given priority.

▶ COMPOSING LETTERS, MEMOS, AND E-MAIL

How do you decide among letters, memos, and e-mail? Consider the following factors:

- **What is the usual practice of your organization?**

  For example, day-to-day business updates might be communicated by e-mail, but policy changes are distributed through memos, and the only letters are messages to and from the district supervisor. Ordinarily, you will adopt the usual practices of your organization.

- **What is the relative efficiency or practicality of each communication medium?**

  E-mail is rapidly replacing a substantial portion of traditional paper correspondence. The reasons for this change are e-mail's higher speed and lower cost.

ACCELL. Inc.
313 Slide Avenue, Portland, OR 97194-2113, USA, 1-800-555-6234
www.accell.com

DATE: September 5, 2001

TO: Tamika Williams, Financial Officer

FROM: Morad Atif, Manager of Building Services

SUBJECT: Request for Approval on Purchase of Power Drills

I am writing to request your approval of the purchase of 25 reversible power drills for my technicians. The total purchase price including tax is $810. The new drills will considerably speed the crew's ability to do its job while reducing fatigue and injury.

Company sales representatives recommended several models for the specific requirements of my technicians, and I examined the Towson 7190, Bedford 23088, Decker 404, Joppa 9420, and Stark 560.

I decided on the Towson drill for the following reasons:

- The Towson drill is the least expensive of the five considered.
- The variable speed trigger offers versatility.
- The double reduction gears guarantee additional torque for bigger and tougher jobs.
- The locking mechanism is recessed to avoid accidental lock-on, thus providing extra safety.
- The chuck key (used to change drill bits) comes on a plastic clip attached to the power cord, making it convenient to change drill bits and virtually eliminating the chance that a technician will lose this important item.

Here is the price information:
25 Towson 7190 drills @ $30/drill = $750
8% tax = $60
total = $810

To meet my assigned productivity objectives, I would like to make this purchase immediately. Would it be possible to receive your approval by Friday, September 7?

FIGURE 13-4 • Morad's Memo Requesting Approval

First, e-mail is quicker than conventional mail. E-mail allows you to send the message you type without the intermediate step of transferring it to paper. Your message goes from your computer to your reader's computer within minutes instead of a day or days. And you could receive the answer to your letter within the half-hour. Potentially, e-mail has the immediacy of oral conversation.

Second, e-mail is a less expensive medium for correspondence: it eliminates the costs of paper, print cartridges, envelopes, and postage as well as the costs associated with the distribution, filing, and storage of paper messages. E-mail messages are composed, distributed, received, filed, and stored electronically. For a typical organization, the savings are substantial: for example, the rising costs of paper and postage are minimized and fewer file folders and file cabinets are required for sorting and storing correspondence.

E-mail communication, however, has its risks. In the rapid exchange of ideas that e-mail encourages, you might fail to be as careful in choosing your words and phrases as you ordinarily would be. You might write something that isn't quite what you intended, leading to a message that is incorrect, ambiguous, or impolite. Such a message could damage your credibility and your relationship with your audience. E-mail might be as quick as oral conversation, but your readers can't hear your voice or see your face: they have only your written words with which to judge the accuracy, civility, and sincerity of your message.

In addition, because e-mail is a newer medium of communication, existing as bits instead of atoms, people often think of it as less important or official. Keep in mind, however, that e-mail is written communication: it has the potential permanence and legal significance of paper correspondence. E-mail requires thoughtful composing, editing, and proofreading.

Finally, though e-mail is *potentially* as quick as oral conversation, it isn't *necessarily* as quick. For example, the message you send today may not elicit a response today. It may be read tomorrow, next week, next month, or never. The absence of a guaranteed timely response to e-mail messages could leave you impatient or irate when some people are slower to reply.

Letters and memos address subjects of sufficient importance to justify the extra time, effort, and cost involved in preparing and transmitting a paper version of your message. That is, a letter or memo requires paper, ink, envelope, and your attention to the printing process. Once printed, the letter or memo must be delivered to its recipient. It passes through your organization's internal mail delivery system: it is picked up, sorted, and distributed—a labor-intensive process. If the recipient is outside your organization, postage will add again to the cost of your message. Or you could fax your letter or memo. This process isn't especially efficient, but it does enable you to send simple drawings and marked-up copies of paper documents.

Choose e-mail to exchange messages on day-to-day business and subjects of limited importance. Typical e-mail messages are brief, but you could attach a file to your e-mail message—like sending a cover letter with a report attached to it. Special software compresses the file and translates it to binary code for transmission. To reverse the process and access the file, your reader must have similar software.

- **What is your rhetorical situation?**

If your organization has no consistent practices regarding correspondence or if your communication situation is extraordinary, you will need to consider your audience, your subject, and your purpose in writing:

- **What is your purpose?** Are you writing to inquire, to complain, to thank? Is your message informative or persuasive? A letter or memo often seems more careful and deliberative, more official and authoritative, than e-mail, and thus usually more credible and persuasive.
- **Who is your audience?** Ordinarily, letters and e-mail go to people outside the company or organization, while memos and e-mail go to people within it. Within organizations, letters are usually restricted to special circumstances that require formal communication, such as a letter of resignation. In addition, the more important your audience is or the less familiar you are to your audience, the more likely it is you will choose the formality of a letter to communicate.

▶ FINDING THE APPROPRIATE STYLE

After analyzing your audience and considering your purpose, you have to decide on a suitable writing style.

Direct versus Indirect Style

In the United States, the preferred style of correspondence is direct communication: news, explanation, and closing. Americans consider this style candid and efficient: getting to the point immediately with the critical information, offering explanation or clarification, and ending politely. If the audience will be pleased with the news, the direct style is appropriate. Direct communication is also the right choice for situations of urgency, offering the earliest and easiest access to critical information.

In two rhetorical situations, however, the indirect style is usually the better choice: when you anticipate a negative reaction to your news and when you are writing to an international audience. If the news will disappoint or irritate your audience or if your message is of little or no urgency, the indirect style will cushion the negative impact of the news. And international audiences often prefer the indirect style, considering it more civilized and courteous. In the indirect style, you establish a human relationship with the audience before you discuss the news. Ordinarily, you start with a gracious opening, provide whatever background information or reasonable arguments are necessary to help the audience understand and accept the news, report the news itself, and offer a polite closing.

Consider the following situation. Nicholas Cooper is the president of Cooper & Cooper, a hog processing corporation. Laura Pauley the president of Red River Farming, a major hog supplier, has called to request that the contract price on hogs be raised. Because of increased labor costs, rising feed prices, and new environmental and agricultural regulations, Red River Farming is losing money on its hog operations at the existing price.

Nicholas explains that he would like to consider this request and fax a reply as soon as possible. While he is sympathetic to the plight of Red River Farming, Cooper & Cooper has also experienced a couple of rough years because the public consumption of hog products—bacon, ham, sausage—seems to be dropping. He'd like to be candid with Pauley, but he would also like to avoid antagonizing a major supplier. He tries a direct style (see Figure 13-5).

After reviewing the letter, Nicholas decides to try being indirect. He starts by thanking Pauley for her letter without mentioning its subject. He emphasizes the good relationship of the two companies and specifically compliments Red River Farming. It isn't until the second paragraph that he addresses Pauley's request, using sympathetic language such as "I understand." He offers the same justification for not raising the price that he used in the direct version, but here he takes two sentences, thus making his point more emphatic. In the third paragraph, he solicits Pauley's understanding of his position by using expressions such as "As you know" and "I'm sure you understand." In the fourth paragraph, he raises the subject of contract negotiations, as in the direct letter, but without the pessimistic warning that could leave Pauley dispirited. Nicholas decides to be positive: There's always a chance that things could change. He closes by once again emphasizing the relationship of the two companies. The message of this indirect letter is the same as in the direct version, but the refusal is implied instead of explicitly stated. That is, Nicholas hasn't exactly said "no" but he has offered all the reasons why he may have to (see Figure 13-6).

Keep in mind, however, that direct and indirect are opposite points on a continuum of correspondence, and the letters, memos and e-mail messages you write will usually be more or less direct, more or less indirect, according to the rhetorical situation. For example, your audience might be both American and international. Or your information might be of various levels of urgency, requiring both immediate decisions and a series of later actions from your audience. And your message may please some of your readers but disappoint

---

Cooper & Cooper

414 Williams Street, Lawrence KS 66045-1200

1-800-555-1919

www.cooper&cooper.com

Laura Pauley, President
Red River Farming
P.O. Box 299
Amarillo, TX 78404-0299

Dear Ms. Pauley:

I have received your letter requesting an immediate increase in the contract price that Cooper & Cooper pays for hogs from Red River Farming.

I regret that we will be unable to raise the contract price. According to our contract, which expires on December 31, 2001, you receive 25 cents per pound. This is the highest amount we pay to any of our other suppliers, and some receive less.

In general, the price of hogs and the demand for pork products has been declining instead of rising. To remain competitive in the market we have to buy our hogs at a cost that reflects market conditions.

We will begin negotiations later this year on a new contract. However, if hog prices remain as is or decrease further, a price increase in the new contract seems unlikely.

Sincerely,

Nicholas Cooper

Nicholas Cooper
President

FIGURE 13-5 • Nicholas's Letter Using a Direct Style

others. Your job as a writer will be to analyze carefully your entire rhetorical environment.

Conversational Style

In your correspondence, aim for a simple conversational style.

Everything we said about style in Chapter 5, Achieving a Readable Style, applies especially to letters, memos, and e-mail. Professionals on the job receive so much correspondence every week that they truly can't afford to be

---

Cooper & Cooper

414 Williams Street, Lawrence KS 66045-1200

1-800-555-1919

www.cooper&cooper.com

Laura Pauley, President
Red River Farming
P.O. Box 299
Amarillo, TX 78404-0299

Dear Ms. Pauley:

Thank you for your letter of August 10, 2001. We have long appreciated our association with your company. Your hog shipments have consistently been of high quality, reflecting the expertise and efficiency of your company's operations.

I understand that the current contract price we pay for your hogs no longer seems satisfactory to you. This price, however, is the same as the price we pay our other suppliers. In fact, in several cases, it is a higher price.

To continue buying hogs from your company, we must remain competitive in a difficult market. As you know, the demand for pork products has been declining instead of rising. I'm sure you understand our dilemma as we understand yours.

Our current contract expires at the end of this year. We will begin negotiations on a new contract in a few months. At that time we will know more accurately than we do now where hog prices are heading.

In the meantime, we hope that our long relationship will continue to the mutual profit of both our companies.

Sincerely,

Nicholas Cooper

Nicholas Cooper
President

FIGURE 13-6 • Nicholas's Letter Using an Indirect Style

paralyzed by messages that are difficult to read or difficult to understand. They don't have time. They need messages with short paragraphs, lists, simple sentence structure, and common words. Above all, avoid fancy language and the formality of the passive voice.

And avoid clichés. They'll make your letter seem formulaic, filled with canned expressions instead of specifically suited to your audience, subject, and purpose. And clichés will make you sound like a pompous official instead of a caring and articulate human being.

Instead of	Write
We beg to advise you that . . .	I'd like you to know that . . .
We are in receipt of your letter that . . .	I received your letter that . . .
It is requested that you send a copy of the specified document to our office.	Please send me a copy of your latest progress report.

In short, ask yourself whether you would or could say in conversation what you have written. If you know you never would say it, don't write it. Restate it in simpler language for a more readable style.

Finally, always focus on the human being reading your letter, memo, or e-mail. Develop a you-attitude, using the word "you" more often and "I" less often. Try to see things from the reader's point of view. Suppose, for example, you were writing a letter of job application to a prospective employer. You might write:

> I believe that my employment with XYZ Corporation will be a great learning experience for me and allow me to develop my skills as a mechanical engineer.

Here you are seeing the subject of employment from your point of view, emphasizing the benefits to you. Your reader, however, is more interested in learning how XYZ Corporation will profit by hiring you, how you will contribute to XYZ's objectives and operations. Adopting the you-attitude, you might write:

> My training as a mechanical engineer will support your mission at XYZ Corporation to design environmentally friendly automotive products. Specifically, my recent studies in high-temperature superconductivity will help you to develop state-of-the-art motors and generators.

Here, you are seeing the subject from XYZ's perspective, offering details that demonstrate your understanding of the organization.

Finally, keep your correspondence concise. Avoid overwhelming or intimidating readers with more information than they want or need. Remember that your readers don't get paid to read your letters, memos, and e-mail messages. Their job is to take actions and make decisions based on the information you have provided. The longer you keep your readers reading, the longer you keep them from making a decision or taking an action. The longer you keep your readers reading, the less productive they are. And the less productive your organization is.

While brevity in letters, memos, and e-mail is good, always avoid seeming brusque or impatient. Occasionally, a longer message gives a better impression, especially if your news is disappointing. In such situations, people appreciate your taking the extra time to explain in detail.

▶ SPECIAL CONSIDERATIONS FOR E-MAIL

Because e-mail has characteristics of both oral and written communication, of both informal and formal communication, writers adopt a variety of styles for their e-mail messages. While e-mail has the structure of a memo (with its designations of FROM, TO, and SUBJECT), it is usually written as a business or personal letter, with a salutation at the beginning of the message and the writer's "signature" at the end.

If your relationship with the reader is strictly professional, you might compose e-mail as though it were a business letter, starting with a greeting such as "Dear Dr. Smith:" or "Dr. Smith:" and closing with a "Sincerely," and your e-mail signature (i.e., name, title, and e-mail address). If your relationship is both professional and personal (e.g., if you've talked face to face or by telephone), you might adopt a friendlier greeting such as "Dear Bill," or "Bill," omit the "Sincerely," and close with your e-mail signature. Or if your message is strictly business, you might omit the salutation altogether and proceed directly to the news of your message.

Whichever opening or closing you choose, consider also the etiquette of your e-mail message.

- **Be polite.** Never compose and send e-mail when you're feeling irritated or discouraged; you might put on record something you'll later regret. Consider also your reader's feelings, and be sensitive to the power of the written word. Without the cushion of your smile or the delicacy of your voice, certain words may be perceived as insulting or offensive. To minimize misunderstandings, especially avoid satiric, ironic, or sarcastic comments. If you believe your words might be misinterpreted, you might incorporate emoticons to signal your attitude: for example, :-) for a smile, ;-) for a wink, or :-(for a frown. Keep in mind, however, that emoticons are often perceived as frivolous or trivial and would diminish the professional quality of an e-mail message intended for a supervisor or a high-level business contact.

- **Never write a message you wouldn't want others to see.** Any recipient can copy and distribute your message to others without your permission. Your message also may be monitored by your organization, which pays for your e-mail access, and hence, owns the messages handled by its Internet service provider. In addition, like the paper correspondence of your organization, your e-mail messages could be subject to subpoena and legal review.

- **Respect the privacy of e-mail messages.** Exercise discretion before copying and distributing an e-mail message without the sender's permission. The sender might have intended portions of his or her message for your eyes only.

- **Keep your messages brief.** Don't ask your reader to scroll through paragraphs of unnecessary information to locate the news of your message. If you are replying to a previous message, copy only the pertinent passages of the original message.

- **Answer your e-mail promptly, especially requests for information.** Your reader may be unable to take action or make a decision until he or she has received your reply.

- **Keep your paragraphs short.** Short paragraphs organize your message visually and simplify reading.

- **Edit and proofread carefully.** While typographical errors are characteristic of e-mail messages, numerous typos may diminish your credibility and distract from your message. Audience analysis is important here: Some readers will tolerate such errors, but others won't. If your relationship with your audience is strictly professional, apply strict standards to your grammar, spelling, and punctuation.

▶ SPECIAL CONSIDERATIONS FOR INTERNATIONAL CORRESPONDENCE

In Chapter 7, Writing for International Readers, we discuss the importance of understanding the culture of your readers. We advise you to adjust your communication style for the differences between American and other cultures:

- Use indirect style. Establish or reinforce your personal relationship with the reader before discussing your purpose for writing.

- Use a formal style.

- Avoid criticizing individuals or groups. Such criticism is often perceived as bringing disgrace both to the people criticized and to you for being rude enough to express criticism. Instead of identifying problems, focus on solutions. Emphasize easier, quicker, and cheaper ways of achieving superior results.

- Address business issues from a wider human, social, and organizational perspective.
- Avoid rushing people to make decisions. Allow time for group consensus to build.
- Keep your language common and simple. Your message may need to be translated for your intended readers, and unusual words or idiomatic expressions could prove difficult to interpret.

Consider the following situation. Theresa Ricco is a sales representative of Wild Computers. She is back in the office after a sales trip to the People's Republic of China, writing a letter to a potential client. Using direct style, she writes a letter that is clear and to the point. The language is simple and the paragraphs brief. It is a crisp and efficient piece of correspondence and typical of the letters she usually writes. While this letter might be ideal for American audiences, however, a Chinese audience might consider it discourteous—possibly thinking that Theresa didn't care enough to write a longer or personal letter (see Figure 13-7).

A careful analysis of the audience inspires Theresa to try a different kind of letter. Choosing the indirect style, Theresa starts the letter with good wishes, shows familiarity with Chinese culture, and offers personal information about herself, such as that she is married. In the second paragraph, she proceeds to thank and compliment the reader. In the third paragraph, she describes her company, reminding the reader of matters that she no doubt covered orally during their meeting—information that establishes her company's credibility (important to the Chinese). In the fourth paragraph, she finally arrives at the point of this letter, the offer of information about her company's products. Finally, she adopts the kind of formal closing that a Chinese writer might use.

This letter, while considerably longer, is more likely to be positively received. Like all effective correspondence, it is tailored to its audience (see Figure 13-8).

▶ KEEPING COPIES OF CORRESPONDENCE

Keep a file—paper or electronic—of every substantive letter, memo, and e-mail message that you write or receive. By controlling this correspondence, you have more control over the subjects discussed in that correspondence. And you will establish a reputation among your clients and colleagues for being organized, efficient, and indispensable.

For example, a dispute might arise on the job about details in a letter or memo or e-mail message written several weeks ago. If you have a copy of that correspondence, you are the person who can resolve that dispute. You

---

WILD COMPUTERS www.wildcomputers.com
100 Water Street, Seattle, Washington 98194, USA, 1-800-555-WILD

July 10, 2001

Mr. Gu Bao-hui
General Manager
Suzhou Winmedia Co., Ltd.
25 Qinghua Road
Suzhou 215008
P. R. CHINA

Dear Mr. Gu:

During my visit to your company, you expressed interest in our products and asked for additional information.

I am enclosing a brochure that lists our products and services. If you will let me know your exact requirements, I will be happy to provide you with more details.

I look forward to your reply.

Sincerely,

Theresa Ricco

Theresa Ricco
Sales Representative

Enclosure

FIGURE 13-7 • Theresa's Letter Using a Direct Style

don't have to trust your incomplete recollection of the message or rely on the incomplete recollection of others. You have the facts in a file at your fingertips.

By keeping copies of your correspondence, you will also protect yourself from being misrepresented, misquoted, or misinterpreted. If colleagues claim you never answered their request, you can present a copy of your response. If others forget what you wrote, you have copies to remind them. If clients claim you promised x and y, you have copies to prove you promised y and z. Controlling your on-the-job correspondence thus gives you more control of your working environment.

WILD COMPUTERS www.wildcomputers.com
100 Water Street, Seattle, Washington 98194, USA, 1-800-555-WILD

February 19, 2001

Mr. Gu Bao-hui
General Manager
Suzhou Winmedia Co., Ltd.
25 Qinghua Road
Suzhou 215008
P. R. CHINA

Dear Mr. Gu:

I hope that you and your family enjoyed the happiest of New Year celebrations. I arrived home from my trip to China just in time to welcome the Year of the Snake at a special dinner with my husband.

I wish to thank you for taking the time to meet with me during my visit to Suzhou. That meeting left me with a deep impression of your kindness and sincerity.

As I mentioned to you during my visit, my company is located in Seattle, a primary location for the computer industry in the United States. We have established a reputation for innovative products and friendly service to customers. We have been selling computer hardware for 15 years to 25 countries all over the world. We started selling computers to China in 1995.

I would like to know if you think Wild products could help your organization be more productive and profitable. I have enclosed a price list of our equipment. I would be pleased to provide more information.

I believe that our acquaintance could bring good fortune to us both.

Sincerely,

Theresa Ricco

Theresa Ricco
Sales Representative

FIGURE 13-8 • Theresa's Letter Using an Indirect Style

► PLANNING AND REVISION CHECKLISTS

You will find the planning and revision checklists that follow Chapter 2, Composing, and Chapter 4, Writing for Your Readers, valuable in planning and revising any presentation of technical information. See also Letter and Memorandum Format in Appendix B. The following questions specifically apply to correspondence. They summarize the key points in this chapter and provide a checklist for planning and revising.

Planning

- What is your subject and purpose?
- What do you want to have happen as a result of your correspondence? What will you do to achieve your objective?
- Who are your primary readers? Secondary readers? Do your primary and secondary readers have different needs? How will you satisfy all your readers?
- Why will your readers read your correspondence?
- What is the attitude of your readers toward you? Toward your subject? Toward your purpose?
- If you are addressing international readers, do you understand their cultural practices? What adjustments in your correspondence will their cultural practices require?
- Will you write a letter, memo, or e-mail message?
- Will you choose a direct or indirect style?

Revision

- Is your topic and purpose clearly identified?
- Have you satisfied your reader's purpose in reading?
- Have you adopted a style suitable to your reader's culture?
- Have you avoided jargon and clichés?
- Does your correspondence demonstrate a you-attitude?
- Is your message clear, concise, complete, and courteous?

► EXERCISES

1. Write an unsolicited inquiry to a company that manufactures a product you wish to know more about. Request sample materials or information. If the company has a home page on the World Wide Web, you probably can make your request by e-mail from the "Contact Us" link on the site. Otherwise, write a letter.

2. Identify a service or product that has recently caused you dissatisfaction. Find out the appropriate person or organization to address, and send your complaint to that person or organization—by letter or by e-mail.

3. Exchange the letter of complaint you wrote for Exercise 2 for a classmate's letter of complaint. Write two different answers to your classmate's letter. In one letter, offer the adjustment requested. In the other letter, refuse the adjustment requested.

4. Compose the memo called for in the following situation.

> Civil Engineering Associates of Purvis, Ohio, was established in 1990 by Robert B. Davidson and Walter F. Posey, both graduates of the University of Ohio. Business for the company was good, and CEA took on six additional partners between 1991 and 1999: Alvin T. Bennett, Wayne S. Cook, Frank G. Reynolds, John W. Castrop, George P. Ramirez, and Richard M. Burke— all graduates of the University of Ohio.
>
> For the last five years, the partners of CEA have met every Friday for a working lunch at Coasters, a local restaurant and bar that features attractive young waitresses wearing provocative swimsuits. The customers are almost exclusively men, and the interaction between customers and waitresses is often flirtatious.
>
> This year CEA hired Elizabeth P. Grider, a Texas State University graduate, as a new partner in the firm. She has attended two of the working lunches at Coasters and is uncomfortable in this environment. She does not feel, however, that she can just skip the events, which are the only regular occasions on which all the partners gather. Projects and work assignments are often discussed and decided at these Friday meetings. In addition, the lunches offer the opportunity for her, as the new kid on the block, to try to establish a comfortable working relationship with her partners. She realizes that "Friday at Coasters" is a long-standing tradition at the firm and she is reluctant to upset the status quo, but she wishes another venue, acceptable to everyone, could be found.
>
> As Elizabeth P. Grider, write a memo to the senior partner, Robert B. Davidson, explaining your problem and recommending one or more solutions. You would like to speak to Davidson directly, but you think that writing a memo allows you to organize your thoughts. And after the meeting, you could leave the memo with Davidson as a written record of your position.

5. Robert Braxton, 1296 Sycamore Avenue, Idaho Falls, ID 83401, is disappointed with the color laser printer he purchased from your company, INK.com, 4307 88th Street, St. Louis, MO 65407. He has written a letter to you to complain.

Braxton is a freelance technical editor. Earlier this year Braxton ordered one of your Horizon 9900 color laser printers. Braxton paid $5,870, including taxes, for the 9900, which is your top-of-the-line printer. He says he had no trouble setting it up and that initially it worked fine. But today, the printer jammed while printing flyers for Braxton's technical editing service. To clear the jam, he had to remove the print cartridge. In the process, the cartridge cracked and dumped ink all over the inside of the printer. And as he removed the jammed sheet of paper, two of the guide rollers loosened. Braxton has enclosed the mangled flyer and photographs of the damage. The photographs display the damage clearly but also show that he was using a refilled print cartridge instead of a new cartridge, as clearly specified on page 9 of the user's manual. In addition, the paper that jammed the printer was a heavy weight (60-lb) cotton bond paper instead of the light to medium weight (16-lb to 24-lb) paper recommended on page 33 of the user's manual.

Braxton has a $283 estimate for cleaning and repairs from his local computer store and wants you to agree to pay the bill. You are concerned about the situation because Braxton has recommended the Horizon 9900 to several of his business clients, who have written you asking for more information. The possible additional sales would be important to your new company. However, you know that Braxton should have read the user's manual more carefully and obviously bears much of the blame for the damage to his printer.

You decide to offer to send him a new print cartridge without charge, but no more. You will also instruct Braxton to refer to page 9 and 33 in the user's manual and you will emphasize as politely as possible that the instructions clearly specify using new print cartridges and 16-lb to 24-lb paper.

Write the letter to Braxton. Determine what additional actions are required to avoid similar complaints. Write the letters, memos, or e-mail messages necessary to direct such additional actions.

6. Compose the letter called for in the following situation.

You are a member of the permissions department at Educational Books, Inc., 25 Astoria Avenue, New York, NY 10027. One of your responsibilities is to be sure that books published by your company are not unfairly copied for classroom use. One of your company's textbook authors, Maria Lynn Davalos, is a visiting professor at Guixin University. According to Professor Davalos, one of the professors at Guixin University, a Chinese national, is copying several chapters of one of your company's textbooks for distribution to his students. The book, *Communicating in Technology and Business*, by Jane Fisher, is available for worldwide sale. Such extensive copying clearly violates international copyright law, as covered by the Berne Convention for the Protection of Literary and Artistic Works. However, you also have heard from several sources that instructors in China often ignore the law chiefly because textbooks are expensive for their relatively poor students.

You learn from your informant that the Chinese professor, Li Kua-fan, teaches English. He is a senior and respected member of the faculty. You wish to persuade the professor that requiring students to buy the book would be fairer to your company and the book's author and also in the best interest of his students. You will need to write a letter to the professor to accomplish that objective.

Before writing your letter, however, you will need to familiarize yourself with the Berne Convention so that in your letter you may refer to specific clauses. Also find out what you can about Chinese society and the Chinese school system today that might lead a respected professor to engage in the extensive copying of coryrighted material. What might be the arguments he would use to justify such copying? To be fully persuasive, you will need to anticipate and address such arguments.

SCENARIO

You and Ms. Cranshaw, your college career placement counselor, are discussing your upcoming job hunt. "I have one word for you," she says, "Internet. Get online and look at America's Job Bank." You take her advice, and at http://www.ajb.dni.us/ you find the Bank.

In a preliminary exploration, you find the link to the Career Resource Library. There you find links to career information, job search tips, job banks and city and state guides, and employers.

Following the employer link, you find the corporate profile for Data Instruments, a firm that interests you. You learn, among many other things, that it has 500 employees, sales last year of over $50 million, and a strong benefits package, including a 401K plan. The profile includes an e-mail address for a human resources executive named Bruce MacDonald.

You follow another link to a guide to posting your résumé online. There you find eleven fee-based databases and thirty-four free ones. Several seem to be a good fit for you.

Following a link to jobs in the computer industry, you find an embarrassment of riches, hundreds—even thousands—of jobs available in every state. You realize that America's Job Bank is going to be worth hours of your time in exploration. For a more condensed version of some of the same information, we recommend the chapter that follows.

chapter 14

The Strategies and Communications of the Job Hunt

- ▶ Preparation
  Self-Assessment
  Information Gathering
  Networking

- ▶ The Correspondence of the Job Hunt
  Letter of Application
  The Résumé
  Follow-Up Letters

- ▶ Interviewing
  The Interview
  Negotiation
  Before and After the Interview

As a college student or a recent college graduate, you can't, unfortunately, take for granted that you'll get a good job right out of college. In some cases, you may actually be competing with experienced workers for the job you want. To help you in this environment, we cover in this chapter the major steps of the job hunt: preparation, letters of application, résumés, and interviews.[1]

▶ PREPARATION

What you can take for granted is that job hunting is nearly a full-time occupation. If you are still in college, it has to be at least a part-time occupation. Most professional jobs require that you follow a regular schedule and work 40 to 50 hours a week. Job hunting also requires that you schedule your time around various activities and that you, if you are still in college, spend at least 15 to 20 hours a week in the hunt. Your first task is to prepare for the hunt. That involves self-assessment, gathering information about possible jobs, and networking.

Self-Assessment

The goal of self-assessment is twofold. First and most important, you want to avoid pounding a square peg (you) into a round hole (the wrong job). You want to determine what jobs among those that are available would suit you the best: What kind of work can you do well, and what kind of work pleases you? Second, in the job hunt, you'll be creating résumés, completing applications, and answering interview questions. Self-assessment will ensure that you list details that you will need about past work and educational experiences—such as dates, names, and job responsibilities.

In your self-assessment you should ask questions such as the following:

What are my strengths?
What are may weaknesses?
How well have I performed in past jobs?
Have I shown initiative?
Have I improved procedures?
Have I accepted responsibility?
Have I been promoted or been given a merit raise?
How can I present myself most attractively?
What skills do I possess that relate directly to what the employer seems to need?
How and where have I obtained those skills?

To go about your self-assessment in a serious and systematic way, use the questionnaire provided in Figure 14-1.

Work Experience (Use a sheet like this for each position you have held, including military service.)

Company: _____

Address: _____

Supervisor's Name and Title: _____

Dates of Employment: _____

Position(s)/Title(s)/Military Rank: _____

Duties and responsibilities: _____

_____

Accomplishments (including awards or commendations): _____

_____

Skills, Knowledge, and Abilities Used: _____

_____

Duties Liked and Disliked: _____

_____

Education and Training

School, College University	Dates of Enrollment	Degree or Major	Certificate	Date	GPA

Career Related Courses: _____

_____

Scholastic Honors, Awards, and Scholarships: _____

_____

College Extracurricular Activities: _____

_____

Other Training (include courses sponsored by the military, employers, or professional associations, etc.):

_____

Courses, Activities Liked and Disliked: _____

_____

Skills, Knowledge, and Abilities Learned: _____

_____

FIGURE 14-1 • Self-Assesment Questionnaire

Source: U.S. Department of Labor. *Job Search Guide: Strategies for Professionals* (Washington, DC: GPO, 1993).

Professional Licenses: _____
_____
_____

Personal Characteristics (e.g. organizational ability, study habits, social skills, like to work alone or on a team, like or dislike public speaking, detail work): _____
_____
_____

Personal Activities
Professional (association memberships, positions held, committees served on activities, honors, publications, patents, etc.): _____
_____
_____

Community (civic, cultural, religious, political organization memberships, offices or positions held, activities, etc.): _____
_____
_____

Other (hobbies, recreational activities, and other personal abilities and accomplishments): _____
_____
_____

Overall Assessment
Tale a look at all the work sheets you have completed: Work Experience, Education, and Personal Activities. Considering all you have done, list your strengths and positive attributes in each of the areas below.
Skills, Knowledge, and Abilities: _____
_____
_____

Accomplishments: _____
_____
_____

Personal Characteristics: _____
_____
_____

Activities Performed Well: _____
_____
_____

Activities Liked: _____
_____
_____

FIGURE 14-1 • (continued)

When you have completed your self-assessment, you will have a good record of past job and educational experiences. You should have a good idea of what skills you have and what it is you really like to do. If you are uncertain about how your skills and experience match to jobs available, three publications from the U.S., Department of Labor can help you make the match:

- *Guide for Occupational Exploration.* Lists over 12,000 occupations and guides you in relating your skills and likes to possible careers.
- *Occupational Outlook Handbook.* Describes the educational requirements, and salary ranges, duties, job prospects for most occupations.
- *Dictionary of Job Titles.* Describes in detail over 12,000 occupations.

College libraries and placement offices should have these books. In addition, the *Occupational Outlook Handbook* is available online at ⟨http://stats.bls.gov/ocohome.htm⟩.

What if, at the end of your self-assessment, you either can't decide what you want to do or, worse, decide that your college major is in a field that no longer interests you? In either case you might seek professional job counseling. Many college placement offices offer such help.

If you are reasonably sure of your career direction, your next step is to find where the jobs are that will lead in that direction.

Information Gathering

Two good ways exist to discover and gather information about companies and organizations that offer the jobs you are seeking. You can research on the Internet and in print publications. Both sources contain the information you need about where the jobs are, how to apply for them, roughly how much they pay, and how big a future such jobs have. However, undoubtedly, the quickest and most up-to-date source is the Internet.

Internet   The Internet is a rich source of information for the job hunter, so rich, in fact, that we can offer only a sampling of what is available.

- America's Job Bank ⟨www.ajb.dni.us⟩ offers information on every aspect of job hunting, either directly or through links to other sites. For example, it has links to a career resource library that offers information under four categories:

    Occupational: career information and exploring specific occupations.

    Job search aids: information on employers, application letters, résumés, and interviewing.

    Job and résumé banks: state and local resources and information on posting your résumé online

    Relocation information: city and state guides

On America's Job Bank, you can find state and employer profiles, salary information, and lists of the fastest growing occupations. In short, this is a site that will be an invaluable aid in your job hunt.

- *Career Magazine* ⟨www.careermag.com⟩ offers information about job fairs, job openings, and employers. The employer profiles are extensive. An excerpt from the entry on American Express states that

American Express is a great place to build an exciting future. With a growing, global customer base and more than $17 billion in revenues, we're focusing on expanding our premier brand presence through service innovation; diverse product offerings; and uncompromising commitment to satisfying our customers, shareholders, and employees. By steadily creating and seizing opportunities for international growth, we have become a respected provider of diversified business and financial services. As important, our initiatives as an employer have resulted in American Express being selected by *Fortune, Hispanic News, Working Woman,* and *LatinaStyle* as a great place to work. . . . American Express is comprised of nine business units, each focused on being a giant company in its market segment. With this much action, is it any wonder that ambitious innovators have plenty of opportunities for learning and career progression with American Express?

  The employer profiles offer lists of current job openings with links that tell you how to apply for them.

- *CareerWeb* ⟨www.cweb.com⟩ has a job-search listing and offers employer information; links that allow the posting of résumés are provided in both cases. The site offers articles on how to conduct a job search. The *Online Career Center* ⟨www.monster.com⟩ offers similar information and assistance.

- *Hot Jobs* ⟨www.hotjobs.com⟩ has employer information and job listings. It provides information on developing scannable electronic resumes and your own web site.

- The *Princeton Review* ⟨www.review.com⟩ offers good advice on interviewing, negotiating, and public speaking for both new college graduates and experienced professionals.

- U.S. Government Office of Personnel Management ⟨www.usajobs.opm.gov⟩ has information for those interested in a job with the federal government. You can find here a list of jobs at all levels for which the government is taking applications. For example, when this chapter was being written, this site listed 18 entry-level engineering jobs with the government and provided a link to apply for the jobs online.

- JobTrak ⟨www.jobtrak.com⟩ has over 800 colleges and universities that post their job listings on this site. If your school participates, you can post your résumé online and even sign up for interviews. JobTrak has an excellent career index that describes career employment outlooks and provides salary ranges. (It provides a salary calculator so you can compare the worth of a salary from one geographic region to another.) City information includes climate and demographic data. JobTrak offers good job-hunting tips, including instruction on designing scannable electronic résumés. Many companies post part-time jobs on this site, an advantage for students looking for work while still in school.

- JobFind ⟨www.jobfind.com/postresume.htm⟩ provides help in posting a résumé online.

Print Sources Following is a list of print sources of job information with brief descriptions of what you will find in them. Most of these sources are available in college libraries and placement offices.

- *National Business Telephone Directory* (Gale Research, Detroit, MI). An alphabetical listing of companies across the United States, with their addresses and phone numbers. It includes many smaller firms (20 employees minimum).
- *The Hidden Job Market: A Guide to America's 2000 Little-Known Fastest Growing High-Tech Companies* (Peterson's Guides, Princeton, NJ). Concentrates on high-tech companies with good growth potential.
- *Dun & Bradstreet Million Dollar Directory* (Parsippany, NJ). Provides information on 180,000 of the largest companies in the country. Gives the type of business, number of employees, and sales volume for each. It also lists the company's top executives. An abbreviated version of this publication also exists, which gives this information for the top 50,000 companies.
- *Standard & Poor's Register of Corporations, Directors and Executives* (New York, NY). Information similar to that in Dun & Bradstreet's directory. Also contains a listing of the parent companies of subsidiaries and the interlocking affiliations of directors.
- *The Career Guide—Dun's Employment Opportunities Directory* (Parsippany, NJ). Aimed specifically at the professional job seeker. Lists more than 5,000 major U.S. companies that plan to recruit in the coming year. Unlike the other directories from Standard & Poor and Dun & Bradstreet, this guide lists personnel directors and gives information about firms' career opportunities and benefits packages. Also gives a state-by-state list of headhunters and tips on interviewing and résumé writing.[2]

Another useful source, *Hoover's Handbook of American Business*, provides profiles of American Corporations. It is published by Hoover Business Press, Austin, TX.

In addition, numerous employment guides address themselves to specialized audiences. For examples Peterson's (Princeton, NJ) publishes *Peterson's Job Opportunities for Engineering and Science Majors* and *Peterson's Job Opportunities for Health and Science Majors*. Both books contain employer profiles, advice on researching job information, and advice on using the Internet for job searches.

To supplement these sources with the most recent information available, consult magazines and newspapers that regularly carry business news, such as *Forbes*, *Business Week*, and the *Wall Street Journal*. To see what has appeared recently in the business press about a company that interests you, consult the *Business Periodical Index*. For general coverage, see *The New York Times Index* and the *Reader's Guide to Periodical Literature*. Analyze the company to see what it is most proud of and to determine its goals. If you are interested in federal employment, seek out *Federal Career Opportunities*.

We cannot emphasize strongly enough the importance of these information-gathering activities. Many job seekers do not even know such rich information sources exist. Others who do know nevertheless neglect them. You now know what the sources are and where to find others. The rest is up to you.

Networking

Networking is a way of finding both job information and job opportunities. Networking starts with broadcasting the news that you are looking for a job. Whom do you tell? Start with family and friends, including grandparents, aunts, uncles, cousins, and in-laws. Expand to professors, clergy, and favorite high school teachers. Don't overlook family doctors, dentists, lawyers, bankers, barbers, and hairdressers. If there are professional associations that cover fields you are interested in, join them. For information about such organizations, see *Career Guide to Professional Organizations*. If there are local chapters of such organizations within a reasonable distance, attend their meetings.

Call on or phone local businesses or organizations, particularly those that have jobs you might be interested in, and ask for the names of people who have or manage jobs like the ones you want. Phone these people and ask if you can come by for a talk. Make it clear that you are not looking for a job interview but rather an informational interview, to seek advice about looking for work or how to prepare for a certain kind of job.

If you have a name you can use—for example, a relative or teacher—in making the initial contact, it will help. But don't let not having a name deter you. Try to make the contact anyway. You can expect a lot of people to put you off, but you will likely be pleasantly surprised at how many people will talk to you. People like to give advice in general, and in particular, they like to talk about their occupations. Furthermore, organizations are on the lookout for enterprising self-starters. In calling on the organization, you are showing yourself to be such a person.

In your contacts with local businesses and professional organizations, you are the interviewer. To help people remember you, have business cards made up that look like the one in Figure 14-2. If you have a profession, such as computer programmer, list it on the card beneath your name. To help your-

```
┌─────────────────────────────────────────────┐
│                                             │
│              ─────────────                   │
│                                             │
│               Jane E. Lucas                 │
│                                             │
│              (213) 596-4236                 │
│                                             │
│              jlucas@bga.com                 │
│                                             │
│              ─────────────                   │
│                                             │
└─────────────────────────────────────────────┘
```

FIGURE 14-2 • Business Card

self remember whom you have seen and what you have learned, keep good records as you proceed. Write down names (accurately spelled), addresses, and phone numbers. Record what seems to be important to these people about work in general and the specific work that interests you.

All this may strike you as an informal way of looking for work, and it is. But research shows that most people find work in precisely this way. This is true partly because many jobs are filled, not through a formal search, but through contacts of the kind we are telling you to develop. Also, two-thirds of all jobs are in companies with fewer than twenty-five employees.[3] Small companies often don't conduct formal searches such as sending recruiters to college campuses. You have to search them out, and networking is an effective way to do it.

More formally, you can network with organizations specifically set up to help people find work. Foremost among these, if you are a college student, is your college placement office. Many large firms regularly call on college placement offices when seeking new employees. Also, the placement office schedules campus interviews for graduating students, and many offices have job fairs once or twice a year. Job fairs, to which many companies send representatives, are good places to gather information and to network. In addition, the placement office maintains a library of books about how to seek employment and usually has a file of brochures and articles about companies and organizations that might interest you.

If you have already graduated from college, investigate whether your college alumni association offers help in seeking employment. Many do. Other formal possibilities are private employment agencies and public employment agencies.

Hunting a job is a hard job in itself. There is a great deal of help out there, but you can't be passive. You have to actively search out job information and opportunities. Another way to do that is with letters of application and résumés, which we take up next.

► THE CORRESPONDENCE OF THE JOB HUNT

In some cases, the first knowledge prospective employers will have of you is the letter of application and résumé that you send to them. A good letter of application, sometimes called a *cover letter*, and a well-done résumé will not guarantee that you get a job, but bad ones will probably guarantee that you do not. In this section we describe how to prepare the letter of application and both paper and electronic résumés. We also tell you about several follow-up letters you'll need to write during the job hunt.

Letter of Application

Plan the mechanics of your letter of application carefully. Buy the best quality white bond paper. This is no time to skimp. Prepare your letter on a word processor, of course, or have it done. Use a standard typeface. Do not use italics. Make sure your letter is mechanically perfect, free of grammatical errors. Be brief, but not telegraphic. Keep the letter to one page. Don't send a letter that has been duplicated in any way. Accompany each letter with a résumé. We discuss résumés later.

Pay attention to the style of the letter and the résumé that accompanies it. The tone you want in your letter is one of self-confidence. You must avoid both arrogance and humility. You must sound interested and somewhat eager, but not fawning. Don't give the impression that you *must* have the job, but, on the other hand, don't seem uncaring about getting it.

When describing your accomplishments in the letter and résumé, use action verbs. They help to give your writing brevity, specificity, and force. For example, don't just say that you worked as a sales clerk. Rather, tell how you maintained inventories, sold merchandise, prepared displays, implemented new procedures, and supervised and trained new clerks. Here's a sampling of such words:

administer	edit	oversee
analyze	evaluate	plan
conduct	exhibit	produce
create	expand	reduce costs
cut	improve	reorganize
design	manage	support
develop	operate	was promoted
direct	organize	write

You cannot avoid the use of *I* in a letter of application. But take the you-attitude as much as you can. Think about what you can do for the prospective employer. The letter of application is not the place to be worried about salary and pension plans. Above all, be mature and dignified. Forget about tricky and flashy approaches. Write a well-organized, informative letter that highlights those skills your analysis of the company shows it desires most. Here we will discuss the beginning, the body, and the ending of an application letter.

The Beginning Beginnings are tough. Do not begin aggressively or cutely. A beginning such as "WANTED: An alert, aggressive employer who will recognize an alert, aggressive young forester" will usually send your letter wastebasket-bound. If you can do so legitimately, a bit of name dropping is a good beginning. Use this beginning only if you have permission and if the name you drop will mean something to the prospective employer. If you qualify on both counts, begin with an opener such as this:

> Dear Ms. Marchand:
>
> Professor John J. Jones of State University's Food Science faculty has suggested that I apply for the post of food supervisor that you have open. In June I will receive my Bachelor of Science degree in Food Science from State University. Also, I have spent the last two summers working in food preparation for Memorial Hospital in Melbourne.

Remember that you are trying to arouse immediate interest about yourself in the potential employer. Another way to do this is to refer to something about the company that interests you. Doing so establishes that you have done your homework. Then try to show how some preparation on your part relates to this special interest. See Figure 14-3 for an example of such an opener.

Sometimes the best approach is a simple statement about the job you seek, accompanied by a description of something in your experience that fits you for the job, as in this example:

> Your opening for a food supervisor has come to my attention. In June of this year, I will graduate from State University with a Bachelor of Science degree in Food Science. I have spent the last two summers working in food preparation for Memorial Hospital in Melbourne. I believe that both my education and my work experience qualify me to be a food supervisor on your staff.

Be specific about the job you want. Quite often, if the job you want is not open, the employer may offer you an alternative one. But employers are not impressed with vague statements such as, "I'm willing and able to work at any job you may have open in research, production, or sales." As the vice president of one firm told us, "We have all the people we need who can do *anything*. We want people who can do *something*."

The Body In the body of your letter you highlight selected items from

635 Shuflin Road
Watertown, CA 90233
March 23, 2001

Mr. Morell R. Solem
Director of Research
Price Industries, Inc.
2163 Airport Drive
St. Louis, MO 63136

Dear. Mr. Solem:

Opener showing knowledge of company

Specific job mentioned

I read in the January issue of *Metal Age* that Dr. Charles E. Gore of your company is conducting extensive research into the application of X-ray diffraction to problems in physical metallurgy. I have conducted experiments at Watertown Polytechnic Institute in the same area under the guidance of Professor John J. O'Brien. I would like to become a research assistant with your firm and, if possible, to work for Dr. Gore.

Highlights of education

In June, I will graduate from WPI with a bachelor of science degree in Metallurgical Engineering. At present, I am in the upper 25 percent of my class. In addition to my work with Professor O'Brien, I have taken as many courses relating to metal inspection problems as I could.

Highlights of work experience

For the past two summers, I have worked for Watertown Concrete Test Services, where I have qualified as a laboratory technician for hardened concrete testing. I know how to find and apply the specifications of the American Society for Testing and Materials. This experience has taught me a good deal about modern inspection techniques. Because this practical experience supplements the theory learned at school, I believe I could fit into a research laboratory with a minimum of training.

Reference to résumé

You will find more detailed information about my education and work experience in the résumé enclosed with this letter. I can supply job descriptions concerning past employment and the report of my X-ray diffraction research.

Request for interview

In April, I will attend the annual meeting of the American Institute of Mining, Metallurgical, and Petroleum Engineers in Detroit. Would it be possible for me to talk with some member of Price Industries at that time?

Sincerely yours,

Jane E. Lucas

Jane E. Lucas

Enclosure

FIGURE 14-3 • Letter of Application

your education and experience that show your qualifications for the job you seek. Remember always that you're trying to show the employer how well you will fit into the job and the organization.

In selecting your items, it pays to know what things employers value the most. In evaluating recent college graduates, employers look closely at the major, academic performance, work experience, and extracurricular activities. They also consider recommendations, standardized test scores, and military experience, if any.

Try to include information from the areas that employers seem to value the most, but emphasize those areas in which you come off best. If your grades are good, mention them prominently. If you stand low in your class—in the lowest quarter, perhaps—maintain a discreet silence. Speak to the employer's interests, and at the same time highlight your own accomplishments. Show how it would be to the employer's advantage to hire you. The following paragraph, an excellent example of the you-attitude in action, does all these things:

> I understand that the research team of which I might be a part works as a single unit in the measurement and collection of data. Because of this, team members need a general knowledge and ability in fishery techniques as well as a specific job skill. Therefore, I would like to point out that last summer I worked for the Department of Natural Resources on a fish population study. On that job I gained electro-fishing and seining experience and also learned how to collect and identify aquatic invertebrates.

Be specific about your accomplishments. By being specific, you avoid the appearance of bragging. It is much better to say, "I was president of my senior class" than to say, "I am a natural leader."

One tip about job experience: The best experience relates to the job you seek, but mention any job experience, even if it does not relate to the job you seek. Employers feel a student who has worked is more apt to be mature than one who has not.

Don't forget hobbies that relate to the job. You're trying to establish that you are interested in, as well as qualified for, the job.

Don't mention salary unless you're answering an advertisement that specifically requests you to. Keep the you-attitude. Don't worry about pension plans, vacations, and coffee breaks at this stage of the game. Keep the prospective employer's interests in the foreground. Your self-interest is taken for granted.

If you're already working and not a student, you construct the body of your letter of application much as we've described. The significant difference is that you will emphasize work experience more than college experience. Do not complain about your present employer. Such complaints will lead the prospective employer to mistrust you.

In the last paragraph of the body, refer the employer to your enclosed résumé. Mention your willingness to supply additional information such as references, letters concerning your work, research reports, and college transcripts.

The Ending The goal of the letter of application is to get you an interview with the prospective employer. In your ending, you request this interview. Your request should be neither humble nor overaggressive. Simply indicate that you are available for an interview at the employer's convenience, and give any special instructions needed for reaching you. If the prospective employer is in a distant city, indicate (if you can) some convenient time and place where you might meet with a representative of the company, such as the convention of a professional society. If the employer is really interested, you may be invited to visit the company as its expense.

The Complete Letter Figure 14-3 shows a complete letter of application. Take a minute to reread it. The beginning of the letter shows that the writer has been interested enough in the company to investigate it. The desired job is specifically mentioned. The middle portion highlights the writer's course work and work experience that relate directly to the job she is seeking. The close makes an interview convenient for the employer to arrange.

A word processor is a great convenience when you're doing application letters. It allows you to store basic paragraphs of your letter that you can easily modify to meet the needs and interests of any organization you are writing to. Such modification for each organization is truly necessary. A personnel officer skims your letter and résumé in about thirty seconds. If you have not grabbed her or his interest in that time, you are probably finished with that organization.

The Résumé

A résumé provides your prospective employer with a convenient summary of your education and experience. As in the letter of application, good grammar, correct spelling, neatness, and brevity—ideally, only one page—are of major importance in your résumé. Although the traditional paper résumé is still commonplace, more and more organizations are using electronic media for screening their job candidates. Therefore, it's important to have versions of your resume available in the following formats:

- Traditional paper
- Scannable format
- E-mail format
- World Wide Web format

Because résumés of different kinds are similar in content and organization regardless of format, we discuss those aspects first.

Content and Organization The three most widely used résumés are chronological, functional, and targeted résumés. All have advantages and disadvantages.

Chronological Résumé The advantages of a chronological résumé (Figure 14-4) are that it's traditional and acceptable. If your education and experience show a steady progression toward the career you seek, the chronological résumé portrays that progression well. Its major disadvantage is that your special capabilities or accomplishments may sometimes get lost in the chronological detail. Also, if you have holes in your employment or educational history, they show up clearly.

Put your address at the top. Give your phone number, and don't forget the area code. If you have a fax number and an e-mail address, include them as well.

For most students, educational information should be placed before work experience. People with extensive work experience, however, may choose to put that first. List the colleges or universities you have attended in reverse chronological order—in other words, list the school you attended most recently first; the one before, second; and so on. Do not list your high school.

Give your major and date, or expected date, of graduation. Do not list courses, but list anything that is out of the ordinary, such as honors, special projects, and emphases in addition to the major. Extracurricular activities also go here.

As you did with your educational experience, put your work experience in reverse chronological order. To save space and to avoid the repetition of *I* throughout the résumé, use phrases rather than complete sentences. The style of the sample résumés makes this technique clear. As in the letter of application, emphasize the experiences that show you in the best light for the kinds of job you seek. Use nouns and active verbs in your descriptions. Do not neglect less important jobs of the sort you may have had in high school, but use even more of a summary approach for them. You would probably put college internships and work–study programs here, though you might choose to put them under education. If you have military experience, put it here. Give the highest rank you held, list service schools you attended, and describe your duties. Make a special effort to show how your military experience relates to the civilian work you seek.

You may wish to provide personal information. Personal information can be a subtle way to point out your desirable qualities. Recent travels indicate a broadening of knowledge and probably a willingness to travel. Hobbies listed may relate to the work sought. Participation in sports, drama, or community

RÉSUMÉ OF JANE E. LUCAS

635 Shuflin Road
Watertown, California 90233
(213) 596-4236
jlucas@bga.com

Education	
1999–2001	Watertown Polytechnic Institute
	Watertown, California

Fragmentary sentences used

Candidate for Bachelor of Science degree in Metallurgical Engineering in June 2001. In upper 25% of class with GPA of 3.2 on 4.0 scale. Have been yearbook photographer for two years. Member of Outing Club, elected president in senior year. Elected to Student Intermediary Board in senior year. Oversaw promoting and allocating funds for student activities. Wrote a report on peer advising that resulted in a change in college policy. Earned 75% of college expenses.

Highlights of education

Special activities

1997–1999 San Diego Community College
San Diego, California

Received associate of arts degree in general studies in June 1999. Made dean's list three of four semesters. Member of debate team. Participated in dramatics and intramural athletics.

Honors and activities

Business Experience
1999–2000 Watertown Concrete Test Services
Summers Watertown, California

Qualified as laboratory technician for hardened concrete testing under specification E329 of American Society for Testing and Materials (ASTM). Conducted following ASTM tests: Load Test in Core Samples (ASTM C39), Penetration Probe (ASTM C803-75T), and the Transverse Resonant Frequency Determination (ASTM C666-73). Implemented new reporting system for laboratory results.

Special work skills

1999–2001 Watertown Ice Skating Arena
Watertown, California

During academic year, work 15 hours a week as ice monitor. Supervise skating and administer first aid.

1995–1999 Summer and part-time jobs included newspaper carrier, supermarket stock clerk, and salesperson for large department store.

Summary of early employment

Personal Background Grew up in San Diego, California. Travels include Mexico and the eastern United States. Can converse in Spanish. Interests include reading, backpacking, photography, and sports (tennis, skiing, and running). Willing to relocate.

References Personal references available upon request.

February 2001

FIGURE 14-4 • Chronological Résumé

activities indicates a liking for working with people. Cultural activities indicate you are not a person of narrow interests.

If you indicate you are married, you might want to say that you are willing to relocate. Don't say anything about health unless you can describe it as excellent.

You have a choice with references. You can list several references with addresses and phone numbers or simply put in a line that says "References available upon request." Both methods have an advantage and a disadvantage. If you provide references, a potential employer can contact them immediately, but you use up precious space that might be better used for more information about yourself. Conversely, if you don't provide the reference information, you save the space but put an additional step between potential employers and information they may want. It's a judgment call, but, on balance, we favor saving space by omitting the reference information. Your first goal is to interest the potential employer in you. If that happens, then it will not be difficult to provide the reference information at a later time.

In any case, do have at least three references available. Choose from among your college teachers and past employers, people who know you well and are likely to say positive things about you. Get their permission, of course. Also, it's a smart idea to send them a copy of your résumé. If you can't call on them personally, send them a letter that requests permission to use them as a reference, reminds them of the association with you, and sets a time for their reply, like this:

Dear Ms. Pickford:

In June of this year, I'll graduate from Watertown Polytechnic Institute with a B.S. in metallurgical engineering. I'm getting ready to look for work. May I have permission to use you as a reference?

During the summers of 1999 and 2000, I worked as a laboratory technician in your testing lab at Watertown. They were good summers for me, and I qualified, with your help, to carry out several ASTM tests.

I want to start sending my résumé out to some companies by mid-March and would appreciate having your reply by that time. I enclose a copy of my résumé for you, so that you can see what I've been doing.

Thanks for all your help in the past.

Best regards,

At the bottom of the traditional paper resume, place a dateline—the month and year in which you completed the resume. Place the date in the heading of scannable and e-mail résumés.

Functional Résumé A main advantage of the functional résumé (Figure 14-5) is that it allows you to highlight the experiences that show you to your best advantage. Extracurricular experiences show up particularly well in a functional résumé. The major disadvantage of this format is the difficulty, for the first-time reader, of discerning a steady progression of work and education.

The address portion of the functional résumé is the same as that of the chronological. After the address, you may include a job objective line if you like. A job objective entry specifies the kind of work you want to do and sometimes the industry or service area in which you want to do it, like this:

```
Work in food service management.
```

or like this:

```
Work in food service management in a metropolitan hos-
pital.
```

Place the job objective entry immediately after the address and align it with the rest of the entries (as shown in Figure 14-6).

For education, simply give the school from which you received your degree, your major, and your date of graduation. The body of the résumé is essentially a classification. You sort your experiences—educational, business, extracurricular—into categories that reveal capabilities related to the jobs you seek. Remember that in addition to professional skills, employers want good communication skills and good interpersonal skills. Possible categories are *technical, professional, team building, communication, research, sales, production, administration,* and *consulting.* (See JobTrak.com for other categories.)

The best way to prepare a functional résumé is to brainstorm it. Begin by listing some categories that you think might display your experiences well. Brainstorm further by listing your experiences in those categories. When you have good listings, select the categories and experiences that show you in the best light. Remember, you don't have to display everything you've ever done, just those things that might strike a potential employer as valuable. Finish off the functional resume with a brief reverse chronological work history and a date line, as in the chronological résumé.

Targeted Résumé The main advantage of the targeted résumé (Figure 14-6) is also its main disadvantage: You zero in on one goal. If you can achieve that goal, fine—but the narrowness of the approach may block you out of other possibilities. The targeted résumé displays your capabilities and achievements well, but, like the functional résumé, it's a format that may not have complete acceptance among all employers.

The address and education portions of the targeted résumé are the same as those in the functional résumé. The whole point of a targeted résumé is that you are aiming at a specific job objective. Therefore, you express your job objective as precisely as you can.

RÉSUMÉ OF JANE E. LUCAS

635 Shuflin Road
Watertown, California 90233
(213) 596-4236
jlucas@bga.com

Education 2001	Candidate for degree in metallurgical engineering from Watertown Polytechnic Institute in June 2001.
Technical	• Qualified as laboratory technician for hardened concrete testing under specification E329 of American Society for Testing and Materials (ASTM). • Conducted following ASTM tests: Load Test in Core Samples (ASTM C39), Penetration Probe (ASTM C803-75T), and the Transverse Resonant Frequency Determination (ASTM C666-73). • Will graduate in upper 25 percent of class with a GPA of 3.2 on a 4.0 scale.
People	• Elected president of Outing Club. • Elected to Student Intermediary Board. • Oversaw promoting and allocating funds for student activities. • Participated in dramatics and intramural athletics.
Communication	• Wrote a report on peer advising that resulted in a change in institute policy. • Participated in intercollegiate debate. • Worked two years as yearbook photographer. • Completed courses in advanced speaking, small group discussion, and technical writing.
Work Experience **1999, 2000 Summers**	• Watertown Concrete Test Services, Watertown, California: laboratory technician.
1999–2001	• Watertown Ice Skating Arena, Watertown, California: ice monitor.
1995–1999	• Summer and part-time jobs included newspaper carrier, supermarket stock clerk, and salesperson for large department store. • Earned 75 percent of college expenses.
References	References available upon request.

February 2001

Margin notes:

Academic, work, and extracurricular activities categorized by capabilities

Summary of work experience in reverse chronological order

FIGURE 14-5 • Functional Résumé

RÉSUMÉ OF JANE E. LUCAS

635 Shuflin Road
Watertown, California 90233
(213) 596-4236
jlucas@bga.com

Job Objective	Research assistant in a testing or research laboratory.
Education	Candidate for degree in metallurgical engineering from Watertown Polytechnic Institute in June 2001.

Capabilities listed separately

Capabilities
- Find and apply specifications of the American Society for Testing and Materials (ASTM).
- Conduct X-ray diffraction tests.
- Work individually or as a team member in a laboratory setting.
- Take responsibility and think about a task in terms of objectives and time to complete.
- Report research results in both written and oral form.
- Communicate persuasively with nontechnical audiences.

Achievements that support capabilities listed

Achievements
- Will graduate in upper 25 percent of class with a GPA of 3.2 on a 4.0 scale.
- Earned 75 percent of college expenses.
- Qualified as laboratory technician for hardened concrete testing under specification E329 of ASTM.
- Conducted major ASTM tests and implemented new reporting system for laboratory results.
- Completed courses in advanced speaking, small group discussion, and technical writing.
- Wrote a report on peer advising that resulted in a change in institute policy.

Summary of work experience in reverse chronological order

Work experience

1999, 2000 Summers
- Watertown Concrete Test Services, Watertown, California: laboratory technician.

1999–2000
- Watertown Ice Skating Arena, Watertown, California: ice monitor.

1995–1999
- Summer and part-time jobs included newspaper carrier, supermarket stock clerk, and salesperson for large department store.

References   References available upon request.

February 2001

FIGURE 14-6 • Targeted Resume

Next you list your capabilities that match the job objective. Obviously, you have to understand the job you are seeking to make the proper match. Capabilities are things you could do if called upon to do so. To be credible, they must be supported by achievements or accomplishments, which are listed next in your résumé. You finish off the targeted résumé with a reverse chronological work history and a date line, as in the functional résumé.

As with the functional résumé, brainstorming is a good way to discover the material you need for your targeted résumé. Under the headings Capabilities and Achievements, make as many statements about yourself as you can. When you are finished, select those statements that best relate to the job you are seeking.

Paper Résumés As Figures 14-4, 14-5, and 14-6 illustrate, in a paper résumé, you use variations in type and spacing to emphasize and organize information. Make the résumé good-looking—leave generous margins and white space. Use distinctive headings and subheadings. The use of a two-column spread is common, as is the use of boldface in headings. You might use 12-point sans serif type for headings and 10-point serif type for the text. (See Chapter 11) Be careful, though, not to overdo the typographical variation, which can quickly change a sensible arrangement that showcases your information into a hodgepodge that overshadows the content. Use good paper in a standard color such as white or off-white. It's best if your letters and résumés are on matching paper.

To whom should you send letters and résumés? When answering an advertisement, you should follow whatever instructions are given there. When operating on your own, send the materials, if at all possible, to the person in the organization for whom you would be working—that is, the person who directly supervises the position. This person normally has the power to hire for the position. Your research into the company may turn up the name you need. If not, don't be afraid of calling the company switchboard and asking directly for a name and title. If need be, write to human resources directors. Whatever you do, write to *someone* by name. Don't send "To Whom It May Concern" letters on your job hunt. It's wasted effort.

Sometimes, of course, you may gain an interview without having sent a letter of application—for example, when recruiters come to your campus. Bring a résumé with you and give it to the interviewer at the start of the interview. He or she will appreciate this help tremendously. Furthermore, the résumé, by giving the interviewer a point of departure for questions, often helps to structure the interview to your best advantage.

Electronic Résumés Not surprisingly, with the increasing use of computers and the Internet in business, traditional paper formats frequently have to be modified to become electronically useful. We describe three such modifications: the scannable résumé, the e-mail résumé, and the World Wide Web résumé.

Scannable Résumé A scannable résumé is a paper résumé that has been modified so that it can be electronically scanned. Many organizations now scan the paper résumés they receive and enter the information into a special database for quick retrieval by keywords. (See Figure 14-7.) For example, if the company needs an environmental specialist, the hiring manager scours the database for words such as *environment* and *ecology*. Only job candidates with the keywords on their résumé will be considered. In a scannable résumé, therefore, you must make sure that the keywords of your occupation, often nouns, are present in abundance. You must get through the computer to be considered by a human reader.

For your résumé to be scannable, you must also modify its format. Ordinarily, a scanner reads résumés from left to right and often makes mistakes if it encounters such features as italics, underlining, changes of typeface, and small sizes of type. In designing your scannable résumé, therefore, adopt the following guidelines:

- Display all information in a single column.
- Align all information on the left margin.
- Use spaces instead of tabs to separate headings from text, or place headings on a separate line.
- Use a single typeface.
- Use all capital letters for your name and major headings.
- Use 12-point type.
- Do not use italics and underlining.
- Do not use rules and borders.
- Submit a clean and crisp laser-printed copy.
- Do not fold or staple the résumé.

E-Mail Résumé Often organizations bypass paper résumés entirely, preferring to solicit and receive candidate information electronically. Such organizations, for example, might announce their job openings on the World Wide Web and invite applications with a link to the e-mail address of the hiring manager.

Like the scannable résumé, the e-mail résumé is subject to keyword searches. Compose it accordingly, being sure to include the appropriate key words. (See Figure 14-8.)

In creating an e-mail résumé, do not use boldface, italics, variations in type size or typeface, and so forth. Essentially, creating an e-mail résumé is like typing with a typewriter, including the uniform spacing of letters. In

JANE E. LUCAS
635 Shuflin Road
Watertown, CA 90233
(213) 596-4236
jlucas@bga.com
February 2001

JOB OBJECTIVE
Research assistant in a testing or research laboratory

EDUCATION
Watertown Polytechnic Institute, Watertown, CA
B.S., metallurgical engineering, June 2001
GPA: 3.2 on 4.0 scale

TECHNICAL
Qualified as laboratory technician for hardened concrete testing under specification E329 of American Society for Testing and Materials (ASTM).
Conducted following ASTM tests: Load Test in Core Samples (ASTM C39), Penetration Probe (ASTM C803-75T), and the Transverse Resonant Frequency Determination (ASTM C666-73).

PEOPLE
Elected President of Outing Club.
Elected to Student Intermediary Board.
Oversaw promoting and allocating funds for student activities.
Participated in dramatics and intramural athletics.

COMMUNICATION
Wrote a report on peer advising that resulted in a change in Institute policy.
Participated in intercollegiate debate.
Worked two years as yearbook photographer.
Completed courses in advanced speaking, small group discussion, and technical writing.

WORK EXPERIENCE
Watertown Concrete Test Services, Watertown, CA; laboratory technician; summers, 1999, 2000
Watertown Ice Skating Arena, Watertown, CA; ice monitor; 1999–2001.
Summer and part-time jobs included newspaper carrier, supermarket clerk, and salesperson for large department store; 1995–1999.
Earned 75 percent of college expenses.

REFERENCES
References available upon request.

FIGURE 14-7 • Functional Résumé in Scannable Format

JANE E. LUCAS
635 Shuflin Road
Watertown, CA 90233
(213) 596-4236
jlucas@bga.com
February 2001

JOB OBJECTIVE
Research assistant in a testing or research laboratory

EDUCATION
Watertown Polytechnic Institute, Watertown, CA
B.S. metallurgical engineering, June 2001
GPA: 3.2 on 4.0 scale

CAPABILITIES
Find and apply specifications of the American
Society for Testing and Materials (ASTM).
Conduct X-ray diffraction tests.
Work individually or as a team member in a
laboratory setting.
Take responsibility and think about a task in
terms of objectives and time to complete.
Report research results in both written and
oral form.
Communicate persuasively with nontechnical
audiences.

ACHIEVEMENTS
Earned 75 percent of college expenses.
Qualified as laboratory technician for hardened
concrete testing under specification E329 of ASTM.
Conducted major ASTM tests and implemented
new reporting system for laboratory results.
Completed courses in advanced speaking, small
group discussion, and technical writing.
Wrote a report on peer advising that resulted
in a change in institute policy.

WORK EXPERIENCE
Watertown Concrete Test Services, Watertown, CA;
laboratory technician; summers, 1999, 2000
Watertown Ice Skating Arena, Watertown, CA; ice monitor;
1999–2001
Summer and part-time jobs included newspaper carrier,
supermarket clerk, and salesperson for large department
store; 1995–1999.

REFERENCES
References available upon request.

FIGURE 14-8 • Targeted Résumé in E-Mail Format

addition, the line length is restricted to sixty-five characters (including spaces), or approximately five inches. If you are creating your résumé with a word processing program, keep these restrictions in mind: Set the width of your page for 5 inches, and eliminate all special characters and formatting. Follow these guidelines:

- Display all information in a single column.
- Align all information on the left margin.
- Use spaces instead of tabs to separate headings from text or place headings on a separate line.
- Use all capital letters for your name and major headings.

World Wide Web Résumé Technologically sophisticated companies all over the world use the search engines of the World Wide Web to scour for résumés of promising job candidates. Creating a World Wide Web résumé, therefore, offers you a worldwide opportunity to locate a job. (See Figure 14-9.)

HotJobs.com offers help in developing a Web site. Also, see Developing a World Wide Web site in Appendix B.

Incorporate a variety of internal links so that visitors to your résumé site will interact with the pages. For example, the address of a former employer could be a link that opens a window to his or her e-mail address. The listing of your major and minor could link to a page that identifies pertinent courses. The mention of a special project could link to a detailed description of the online version of that project.

A WWW résumé has multimedia possibilities. In addition to the usual listing of information, you could add pertinent graphics, sound, and animation. Use audio to speak directly to prospective employers about your most important job skills.

Especially remember to register your site with all appropriate search engines—this is how prospective employers will locate you. Also, remember to fill your résumé with the keywords that prospective employers will use to conduct their search. Finally, be sure to include a link to your e-mail address. That is how interested employers will most likely contact you.

As discussed earlier, the WWW offers a rich variety of job-finding services. When you e-mail your résumé to such a service or submit specific biographical information electronically, it is then automatically compiled in a standardized resume format. The service then adds your résumé to its international database of available employees, thus making your résumé readily accessible through the Internet to prospective employers all over the world.

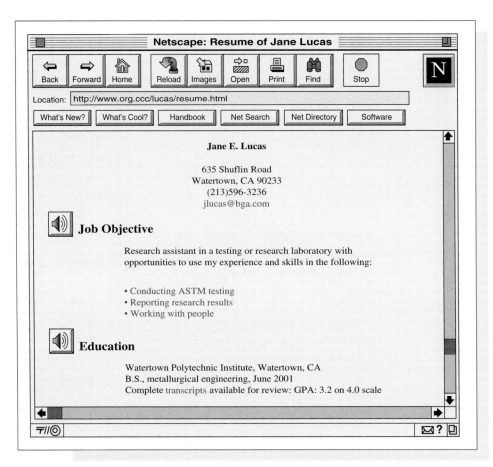

FIGURE 14-9 • World Wide Web Résumé
Links are indicated in color.

Follow-Up Letters

Write *follow-up letters* (1) if after two weeks you have had no answer to your letter of application; (2) after an interview; (3) if a company fails to offer you a job; and (4) to accept or refuse a job.

No Answer When a company has not answered your original letter of application, write again. Be gracious, not complaining—something like this:

Dear Mr. Souther:

On 12 April I applied for a position with your company. I have not heard from you, so perhaps my original letter and résumé have been misplaced. I enclose copies of them.

If you have already reached some decision concerning my application, I would appreciate your letting me know.

I look forward to hearing from you.

Sincerely yours,

After an Interview Within a day's time, follow up your interview with a letter. Such a letter draws favorable attention to yourself as someone who understands business courtesy and good communication practice. Express appreciation for the interview. Draw attention to any of your qualifications that seemed to be important to the interviewer. Express your willingness to live with any special conditions of employment, such as relocation. Make clear that you want the job and feel qualified to do it. If you include a specific question in your letter, it may hasten a reply. Your letter might look like this one:

Dear Ms. Marchand:

Thank you for speaking with me last Tuesday about the food supervisor position you have open.

Working in a hospital food service relates well to my experience and interests. The job you have available is one I am qualified to do. A feasibility study I am currently writing as a senior project deals with a food service's ability to provide more varied diets to people with restricted dietary requirements. May I send you a copy next week when it is completed?

I understand that the work you described would include alternating weekly night shifts with weekly day shifts. This requirement presents no difficulty for me.

Tuesdays and Thursdays are best for me for any future interviews you may wish, but I can arrange a time at your convenience.

Sincerely yours,

After Being Refused a Job When a company refuses you a job, good tactics dictate that you acknowledge the refusal. Express thanks for the time spent with you, and state your regret that no opening exists at the present time. If you like, express the hope of being considered in the future. You never know; it might happen.

Accepting or Refusing a Job Writing an acceptance letter presents few problems. Be brief. Thank the employer for the job offer, and accept the job.

Settle when you will report for work, and express pleasure at the prospect of working for the organization. A good letter of acceptance might read as follows:

Dear Mr. Solem:

Thank you for offering me a job as research assistant with your firm. I happily accept. I can easily be at work by 1 July as you have requested.

I look forward to working with Price Industries and particularly to the opportunity of doing research with Dr. Gore.

Sincerely yours,

Writing a letter of refusal can be difficult. Be as gracious as possible. Be brief but not so brief as to suggest rudeness or indifference. Make it clear that you appreciate the offer. If you can, give a reason for your refusal. The employer who has spent time and money in interviewing you and corresponding with you deserves these courtesies. And, of course, your own self-interest is involved. Some day you may wish to reapply to an organization that for the moment you must turn down. A good letter of refusal might look like this one:

Dear Ms. White:

I enjoyed my visit to the research department of your company. I would very much have liked to work with the people I met there. I thank you for offering me the opportunity to do so.

However, after much serious thought, I have decided that the research opportunities offered me in another job are closer to the interests I developed at the university. Therefore, I have accepted the other job and regret that I cannot accept yours.

I appreciate the courtesy and thoughtfulness that you and your associates have extended me.

Sincerely yours,

► INTERVIEWING

The immediate goal of all your preparation and letter and résumé writing is an interview with a potential employer. Interviews come about in various ways. If you network successfully, you will obtain interviews that allow you to ask questions of people already on the job. If you impress the person you are talking to, such information-seeking interviews may turn into interviews that assess your potential as an employee. Your letters and résumés may obtain interviews for you. Recruiters may come to your campus and schedule screening interviews with graduating students. As their name suggests, screening interviews are preliminary interviews from which the recruiters choose people to go further in the process.

Going further often means multiple interviews at the organization's headquarters. In one day, you might interview with a human resources staff person, the person who would be your boss if you were employed, and, perhaps, his or her boss. If you make it to the point of being offered a job, you will likely have an interview in which you negotiate the details of your job, salary, and benefits. All this can be quite stressful. The better prepared you are, the easier it will go. Screening and follow-up interviews follow a somewhat similar pattern. We discuss them first and then give you some advice about negotiation.

The Interview

If you have prepared properly, you should show up at the interview knowing a good deal about the organization. A comment by one interviewer emphasizes the importance of this:

> It's really impressive to a recruiter when a job candidate knows about the company. If you're a national recruiter, and you've been on the road for days and days, you have no idea how pleasant it is to have a student say, "I know your company is doing such and such, and has plants here and here, and I'd like to work on this particular project." Otherwise I have to go into my standard spiel, and God knows I've certainly heard myself give that often enough.[4]

You should have the following with you: your résumé, in both regular and scannable formats; a portfolio of your work, if appropriate; pen and notebook; a list of your references; and your card (see Figure 14-2).

For interviews, you should be well groomed and dressed conservatively. Arrive at the place of the interview early enough to be relaxed. Shake hands firmly but not aggressively, and make eye contact. Give the interviewer a copy of your résumé, and, when the interviewer sits down, sit down comfortably. Body language is important. Be neither rigid or slouching.

Most interviews follow a three-part pattern. To begin, the interviewer may generate small talk designed to set you at ease. Particularly at a screening interview, the interviewer may give some information about the company. This

- What can you tell me about yourself?
- What are your strengths and weaknesses?
- What do you want to be doing five years from now?
- Do you know much about us? Why do you want to work for us?
- We're interviewing ten people for this job. Why should you be the one we hire?
- What in your life are you most proud of?
- Here is a problem we had (interviewer describes problem). How would you have solved it?
- If you won $10 million in a lottery, how would you spend the rest of your life?
- Why do you want a career in your chosen field?
- Which school subjects interested you the most (least)? Why?

FIGURE 14-10 • Frequently Asked Interview Questions

is a good chance for you to ask some questions that demonstrate that you have done your homework about the company. But don't force your questions upon the interviewer.

Most of the middle portion of the interview will be taken up with questions aimed at assessing your skills and likes and how you might be of value to the organization. Well-done self-assessment obviously is a necessity in answering such questions. Figure 14-10 lists some of the commonly asked questions. If you prepare answers for them, you should be able to handle most of the questions you are likely to receive. Certainly, have well-thought-out answers to questions concerning both your short-range and long-range goals. In your answers, relate always to the organization. To the question, "What do you want to be doing five years from now?" the answer, "Running my own consulting firm," might bring the interview to an early close.

To the question, "What can you tell me about yourself?" the interviewer really doesn't expect an extended life history. This question provides you the opportunity to talk about your work and educational experiences and your skills. Try to relate your skills and experience to the needs of the organization. Don't overlook the people and communication skills essential to nearly every professional job. In your answer to this and other questions, be specific in your examples. If you say something like "I have good managerial skills," immediately back it up with an occasion or experience that supports your statement.

The question "Why to you want to work for us?" allows you to display what you have learned about the organization. In answering this question, you should again show that what you have to offer meshes with what the company needs.

The question about how you would spend your life if you won $10 million is an interesting one. "Lolling around the beach" is obviously the wrong answer, but "I'd continue to work for your corporation," might create a bad impression, as well. What the question is intended to get at are those worthwhile things in your life that you really enjoy doing. Building houses for Habitat for Humanity or setting up sports programs for inner-city youths might qualify as good answers. So might investing in the establishment of an e-commerce company.

In answering questions about your strengths and weaknesses, be honest, but don't betray weaknesses that could eliminate you from consideration. "I can't stand criticism," would likely finish you off. "Sometimes, I don't know when to quit when I'm trying to solve a problem," given as a weakness could be perceived as a strength.

In the last part of the interview you will likely be given a chance to ask some questions of your own. It's a good time to get more details about the job or jobs that may be open. Ask about the organization's goals. "What is the company most proud of?" is a good question. Don't ask these questions just to ask questions. The interview is a good time for you to find out if you really want to work for an organization. Not every organization is going to be a good fit for what you have to offer and what you want to do. Unless the interviewer has raised the question of salary and benefits, don't ask questions about these matters.

If you really want to go to work for the organization, make that clear before the interview ends. But don't allow your willingness to appear as desperation. At some point in the interview, be sure to get the interviewer's name (spelled correctly!), title, address, phone number, e-mail address, and fax number. You'll need them for later correspondence. When the interviewer thanks you for coming, thank him or her for seeing you and leave. Don't drag the interview out when it's clearly over. The *Princeton Review* ⟨www.review.com⟩ is an excellent source of information on how to conduct yourself during an interview and the negotiations that may follow the interview.

Negotiation

Interviewers seldom bring up salary and benefits until they either see you as a good prospect or are sure they want to hire you. If they offer you the job, the negotiation is sometimes done in a separate interview. For example, your future boss may offer you the job and then send you to negotiate with the human resources staff.

Sometimes, the negotiator may offer you a salary. At other times, you may be asked to name a salary. Now is the time to put to good use the information you gathered on the Internet sources for salary we cited on pages 360–361. You may also have received useful salary information through your networking activities.

Your research in these sources will give you not a specific salary but a salary range. If asked to name a salary, do not ask for the bottom of the range. Ask for as near the top as you reasonably can. The negotiator will respect you the more for your knowing what you are worth. However, balance the compensation package—vacations, pension plans, health care, educational opportunities, and so forth—against the salary. Some compensation packages are worth a good deal of money and may allow you to take a lower salary.

Also the location of the job plays a role. Monstermoving.com ⟨http://Monstermoving.com⟩ provides information and analysis that allows you to compare the worth of salaries by location. For example, a $45,000 salary in 1999 Savannah, Georgia, would provide the same lifestyle as a $50,000 salary in Minneapolis, Minnesota.

Before and After the Interview

If you have not participated in job interviews before, you should practice. Get together with several friends. Using the information that we have given you and that you have gathered for yourself, role play several interviews. As two of you play interviewer and interviewee, the others act as observers. They should look for strengths and weaknesses in your answers, diction, grammar, and body language. The members of the group need to appraise one another honestly. Practice until you feel comfortable with the process.

When an interview is over, write down your impressions as soon as you can. How did your clothes compare to the interviewer's? Were there unexpected questions? How good were your answers? What did you learn about the organization? What did you learn about a specific job or jobs? Did anything make you uncomfortable about the organization? Do you think you would fit in there? By the next day, get a thank-you note (letter, e-mail, or fax) off to the interviewer.

► PLANNING AND REVISION CHECKLISTS

You will find the planning and revision checklists that follow Chapter 2, Composing, and Chapter 4, Writing for Your Readers, valuable in planning and revising any presentation of technical information. The following questions specifically apply to the job hunt. They summarize the key points in this chapter and provide a checklist for planning and revising.

PREPARATION

Planning and Revision

- Have you completed the self-assessment questionnaire in Figure 14-1?
- Do you have a complete record of your past job and educational experiences?
- Do you know your strengths and weaknesses, your skills, and your qualifications for the jobs you seek? Do you have clear career objectives?
- Do you need professional career counseling?
- Have you researched the Internet and sources to find job information?
- Have you found organizations that fit your needs?
- Have you started your networking?
- Have you had business cards made up?
- Have you called on businesses and set up informational interviews?
- Have you joined a professional organization relevant to your career field?
- Have you located agencies and individuals who can help you in your job hunt?
- Have you kept good records of your networking?

THE CORRESPONDENCE OF THE JOB HUNT

Planning

- For your letter of application:

    Do you have the needed names and addresses?

    What position do you seek?

    How did you learn of this position?

    Why are you qualified for this position?

    What interests you about the company?

    What can you do for the organization that it needs?

Can you do anything to make an interview more convenient for the employer?

How can the employer reach you?

- For your résumé:

  Do you have all the necessary details of your past educational and work experiences (dates, job descriptions, schools, majors, degrees, extracurricular activities, etc.)?

  Which résumé format will suit your experience and capabilities best? Chronological? Functional? Targeted? Why?

  Do you need to prepare your résumé in electronic formats? What keywords will you use?

  In a functional résumé, which categories would best suit your experience and capabilities?

  Do you know enough about the job you are seeking to use a targeted résumé?

  Do you have permission to use the names of three people as references?

- What follow-up letters do you need? To follow up on no answer to your application? To follow up on an interview? To respond to a job refusal? To accept or refuse a job?

Revision

- Do your letter of application and résumé reflect adequate preparation and self-assessment?
- Are your letter of application and résumé completely free of grammatical and spelling errors? Are they well designed and good looking?
- For the letter of application:

  Have you the right tone—self-confidence without arrogance?

  Does your letter show how you could be valuable to the employer? Will it raise the employer's interest?

  Does your letter reflect interest in a specific job?

  Have you highlighted the courses and work experience that best suit you for the job you seek?

  Have you made it clear you are seeking an interview and made it convenient for the employer to arrange one?

- For the résumé:

  Have you chosen the résumé type that best suits your experiences and qualifications?

  Have you limited your résumé to one page?

Have you put your educational and work experience in reverse chronological order?

Have you given your information in phrases rather than complete sentences?

Have you used active verbs to describe your experience? Appropriate keywords?

Does the personal information presented enhance your job potential?

Do you have permission to use the names of those you list as references?

If you are using a functional résumé, do the categories reflect appropriately your capabilities and experience?

Has your targeted résumé zeroed in on an easily recognizable career objective?

Do the listed achievements support the capabilities listed?

- Have you followed up every interview with a letter? Are the follow-up letters you have written gracious in tone? Do the letters invite further communication in some way?
- Does your letter of acceptance of a job show an understanding of the necessary details, such as when you report to work?
- Does your letter of refusal thank the employer for time spent with you and make clear that you appreciate the offer?

THE INTERVIEW

Planning

- Have you found out as much about the organization as you can—its products, goals, locations, and so forth?
- Have you practiced interviewing using the questions in Figure 14-10?
- Have you the proper clothes for an interview?
- Do you have good questions to ask the interviewer?
- Do you know the salary range for the jobs you seek?

Revision

- How did your clothes compare to the interviewer's?
- Did you answer questions well? Which answers need improving?
- Did the interviewer ask any unexpected questions?
- How did the interviewer respond to your questions? Did he or she seem to think they were relevant?
- How well do you think you did? Why?
- Do you think your career goals and this organization are a good fit?

► EXERCISES

1. Work out a schedule for your job hunt. Allocate time and set dates for completing the following stages:

   - Self-assessment
   - Gathering job information
   - Networking
   - Preparing a letter of application
   - Preparing a résumé
   - Practicing the interview

2. Complete for yourself a summary of your self-assessment. Complete and turn in to your instructor a summary of your job information search, a networking plan, a sample letter of application and résumé, and a summary of the salary ranges for entry-level jobs in your field.

3. In groups of four, plan and carry out practice interviews. Everyone in the group should get the chance to play interviewer and interviewee once.

4. Write a letter to some organization in which you apply for full- or part-time work. Brainstorm and work out in rough form the three kinds of résumé: chronological, functional, and targeted. Choose the one that suits your purposes best, and work it into both regular paper and scannable form to accompany your letter. (It may well be that you are actually seeking work and can write your letter with a specific organization in mind.)

5. Prepare a fact sheet for yourself that contains the following information that will be useful to you in your job hunt:

   - Current and future job prospects in your field. What are the qualifications needed for the jobs available?
   - Salary ranges for jobs for which you are qualified.
   - Three places where you might post your résumé.
   - Five companies that hire people in your field, accompanied by brief profiles of two of the companies.
   - Useful information about a city that interests you as a place to live.
   - Information about the job-hunting assistance offered by a state in which you might wish to live.

- Jobs available in the federal government in your discipline.

Format your fact sheet in a way that makes it most useful to you. However, provide your instructor with a copy of it.

6. Using both this chapter and Chapter 7, Writing for International Readers, as your guides, prepare a letter of application to an employer in a country in either Latin America or Asia.

SCENARIO

Glenville, a community of 70,000 people, has just received a tract of undeveloped land, approximately 70 acres, and a small development grant from the estate of a prominent citizen. The city council believes that the site will make a beautiful park. The council discusses several possible ways of using the land to provide recreation facilities while still maintaining the natural beauty of the land.

The council decides to use a landscape design service. The problem they face is how to find and select the best company. The council decides to announce the project in the newspapers of Glenville and surrounding communities.

Helen Costillo notes: "Look, we don't know all that can be done with this land. We need input from several designers who can give us suggestions."

Paul Zetchen agrees but is concerned about the cost: "The estate has allotted about $40,000 toward development costs, but that won't begin to cover the work. We need to know how much development will cost."

Karen Schneider argues for credentials: "We want to know that the companies that we talk to are qualified—what other projects have they done like this? How much did those projects cost? How long did it take to do the job? Mason Valley had to fire one company that worked on their sports park because the company couldn't get the work done. Poor drainage was also a problem. What a mess!"

Laverne Roth then adds: "I don't want any trees removed that do not have to be removed. From my perspective, habitat preservation is critical. This land is too beautiful to be leveled by bulldozers!"

City Manager Catharine Cauthen then adds: "Let's mention these concerns in the notice we write for the newspapers. Let's also contact Felixville, which developed a new park when they began planning and find out who they talked to. We can then send letters to those companies.

"Let me draft a notice, then we can see if we need to include anything else. We want to target design firms that are environmentally conscious and experienced, as well as creative. What do we want firms to include in their proposals? We need to decide." The council members nod in agreement.

chapter 15

Proposals and Progress Reports

▶ The Relationship between Proposals and
Progress Reports

▶ Proposals
The Context of Proposal Development
Effective Argument in Proposal Development
Standard Sections of Proposals

▶ Progress Reports

▶ Physical Appearance of Proposals and Progress Reports

▶ Style and Tone of Proposals and Progress Reports

▶ Other Forms of Proposals and Progress Reports

Many times as an employee in an organization, you will generate a variety of documents relating to one particular problem or situation. You may send several e-mail memoranda to colleagues within the organization; you may write letters to individuals outside the organization concerning the problem or situation; you may write memo reports "To File" that document your activities on the problem or situation; you may also write a detailed formal report, such as a formal feasibility study (discussed in Chapter 16, Recommendation Reports) at the conclusion of your work on the situation. In short, you will write various documents to different audiences about one project, problem, or topic. Proposals and progress reports are two additional types of document that are often written in response to a project or problem.

▶ THE RELATIONSHIP BETWEEN PROPOSALS AND PROGRESS REPORTS

The proposal, as its name implies, describes work that is suggested, the reasons it should be done, and the methods proposed to accomplish the work. The progress report, as its name implies, describes and evaluates a project as work is being done. Thus, if an individual or an organization decides to begin a work or research project, particularly one that requires several months or even several years to complete, the individual or organization will usually need to *propose* the project and then *report the progress* on that project at intervals agreed upon when the proposal is accepted and the resulting agreement or contact is being negotiated. The topic of the progress report emanates from the project that is proposed; the content and organization of the progress report are often directed by the content and organization of the written proposal.

In other instances, employees may need to report progress on the full range of projects or problems on which they are working. In situations like these, the employee writes a progress report (or status report, as it may be called) to inform supervisors or other individuals about what has been accomplished in completing a job or solving a problem. By keeping these individuals up-to-date on work activities, the employee uses the status report to document what has been accomplished and by whom. The progress or status report thus becomes an official and even a legal record of work.

To help you understand how to design and write proposals and progress reports, we first discuss the development of proposals and use a student's research project proposal as an example. We then discuss progress reports in general. To illustrate the progress report, we discuss the student's progress report on her research project. Because progress—or status—reports are often written by employees to communicate and document their activities, we also present an example of a status report written by an employee who needs to update his supervisor on one of his assignments.

In the world of work, proposals are most often used by organizations to solicit work contracts. Thus, we show you a situation in which a communications firm writes a letter proposal to launch a writing workshop in a business organization. We also show you a progress report, written by one of the writing workshop instructors to his supervisor to evaluate the workshop and point out problem areas.

After you study this chapter, you should be able to develop the typical sections included in a proposal as well as in progress reports or status reports. As the examples in the chapter will show you, progress reports and proposals—in fact, any kind of document we discuss in this book—can be submitted in a memo or letter format, as discussed in Chapter 13 or as a longer, formal document, as discussed in Chapter 16. The length of each document as well as the audience and the context in which the document is generated and received will determine which format you use.

▶ PROPOSALS

All projects have to begin somewhere and with someone. In universities, in business, and in research organizations, the starting point is often a proposal. In simplest terms, a proposal is an offer to provide a service or a product to someone in exchange for money. Usually, when the organization—frequently a federal, state, or city government or a business enterprise—decides to have some sort of work done, it wants the best job for the best price. To announce its interest, the soliciting organization may advertise the work it wants done and invite interested individuals or organizations to contact the organization. In a university setting, the research and grants office may notify departments that money is available for research projects in a specific area. Faculty members are invited to submit project proposals that explain how much time they will need to complete the project; any financial resources required for equipment, salaries, and release time from regular teaching duties; and the goals and benefits of the research to the individual researcher and the university. Thus, the proposal process usually begins with an organization that is interested in having work or research done in response to a specific need or problem. The proposal is the written document that launches a proposed solution to this need or problem by individuals or groups qualified to deal with the matter.

When an organization disseminates a description of the work it wants done, this document is usually called a request for a proposal (RFP) or a statement of work (SOW). The soliciting organization may send selected companies an RFP that includes complete specifications of the work desired, or it may describe the needed work in general terms and invite interested firms to submit their qualifications. This type of request is usually called a request for qualifications (RFQ). The responding organization explains its past accomplishments, giving the names of companies for which it performed work, describing the work it did, and giving references who can substantiate the organization's claims. Based on the responses it receives, the soliciting organization will send full descriptions of the work to the groups it believes to be best qualified.

Alternatively, the soliciting organization may describe the kind of work it wants done and invite interested companies to describe briefly what they offer—their experience with similar projects, the qualifications of their personnel, their approach to the project, and the approximate cost. This kind of request is also called a request for qualification (RFQ). These are often published in newspapers. An example appears in Figure 15-1.

Firms that respond with a price that best approximates what the soliciting organization wants to pay will be sent a full description of the work needed and invited to submit full proposals.

To understand some of the many ways that proposals initiate projects, consider the following examples.

1. Professor X of the university's sociology department notes in the *Federal Register* that the U.S. Department of Health and Human Services (HHS) is soliciting studies of educational problems experienced by school-age children of single parents. Because Professor X has established a research record in this field and is looking for new projects, she decides to request a copy of the RFP. After studying it carefully, she decides to submit a proposal. In her proposal she describes her planned research and explains its benefits. She states her qualifications to conduct the research and details the costs of the project.

2. A county in Texas decides that it wants to repave a heavily used rural road and extend the paving another five miles beyond the existing pavement. The county public works office runs an advertisement in several county and state newspapers, briefly describing the work. Public works officials also send copies of the advertisement to road construction firms that have reputations for doing quality work at a fair price. The construction companies interested in submitting bids will notify the county officials and will be invited to attend a bidders' conference at which requirements of the job are discussed further. Public works officials may take potential contractors on a tour of the area. Those who decide to bid on the paving project will have four weeks to submit bids that meet the minimum specifications given in the published RFP and at the bidders' conference.

3. Alvin Cranston, a manager for a local telephone company, is charged with redesigning the operator service facilities for the company. Alvin

REQUEST FOR QUALIFICATIONS
For the construction of a
Clubhouse & Assorted Structures
for Universal City, Texas

The City of Universal City, Texas, through its agent, Granite Golf Management, Inc., seeks to identify interested and qualified companies to construct an 8,338-sf clubhouse with 5,834-sf underground cart storage, 5,000-sf maintenance building, and associated comfort stations and pump house/lift stations. Firms interested in being part of this process and having experience in construction of all the buildings herein described are invited to attend a prebid meeting March 3, 2001, 3:00 P.M. at Universal City, City Hall, 2150 Universal City Blvd, Universal City, TX 78148. Conference center and work plans may be picked up on February 26, 2001, between 9 A.M. and 12 P.M. and February 27, between 2 P.M. and 5 P.M. Limited special arrangements can be made by calling 210.659.6123.

If your firm is interested in being included in the bidding process and receiving more information for this project, please provide us with the following information:

1. Company name; if incorporated, give date and state of incorporation.
2. If your firm is not a corporation, specify type of entity.
3. If your firm is a partnership or individually owned, please give names of partners/owners and a résumé on each.
4. Number of years doing business under firms, current name, number of employees, and annual revenue. Any former name(s) under which firm has operated.
5. Jurisdictions and trade categories, registration numbers, and/or license numbers that indicate the categories in which your firm is legally qualified to do business, and the states of jurisdictions where those licenses or registrations allow you to do business.
6. Categories of work that your firm performs with its own labor.
7. Projects completed in the past five years where you provided similar services (scope of work). Enclose résumés for your key people to be utilized in planning or direct supervision of this project.
8. If you or any officer or member of your firm has failed to complete a project, or is involved in a litigation regarding a project, please give details.
9. Construction projects currently in process where you are providing similar services to those you wish to provide for this project, name of owner, percent complete and projected completion date.
10. Trade and bank references and name of surety bonding company, including agent's name and address.

Firms selected to be part of the bid process are required to provide financial statements prior to awarding contracts. Qualified firms interested in participating in the bid process may use AIA Form A305 for submission of qualifications which shall be submitted no later than the prebid meeting, March 2, 2001, to:

Granite Golf Management, Inc.
Jim Smith
9706 Gates Drive
Universal City, TX 78148
210.659.2267 phone
210.659.5546 fax

We expect construction to begin no later than September 1, 2001.

FIGURE 15-1 • Example Request for Qualifications in a Local Newspaper

knows that he will need to consider a number of issues (lighting, furniture, computers, as well as building layout), so he decides to publish a request for qualifications in telephone trade publications. He also asks the company's marketing department to help him locate a list of companies that specialize in ergonomic design. He writes each of the companies on the list and explains, in general terms, what his company wants to do and invites the design firms to submit their qualifications for performing such work.

4. Biotech Corporation is considering the development of a new organic dispersant for combating major oil spills in freshwater lakes. The company wants to know how much containers for transporting this new dispersant would cost, what kinds of containers are currently available to transport the dispersant by rail or air, and whether chemical transport container companies would be interested in providing the containers and shipping the dispersant to purchasers.

In short, each aspect of the solicitation process, the RFP, the RFQ, and the SOW, has an appropriate use, but one or more of them is necessary to initiate action on a project.

The Context of Proposal Development

Because proposals are time-consuming to write—most require substantial research and analysis on the part of the proposing organization—individuals and organizations wishing to respond to an RFP study it carefully. They do not want to submit a proposal that is unlikely to be accepted. Thus, the proposer—whether a university professor seeking research funds or a highway construction firm seeking to win a contract from a county to repave its rural roads—will approach the decision to prepare a proposal carefully.

The individual or the company must first decide whether to respond to the proposal. This decision is based on careful study of the RFP or RFQ with a number of questions in mind: Can we do the work requested? Can we show that we can do this work, based on what we have already done? Can we do it within the time limit given in the RFP? Businesses responding to RFPs are also interested in economic issues: How much will our proposed approach cost? How much money can we make? Who else will be submitting proposals? What price will they be quoting for the same work? Will we be competitive? What other projects are we currently involved in? Could problems arise that would make us unable to complete the job on time and at the price we quote? Do we have personnel qualified to work on this project?

Many business entities requesting proposals will hold a bidders' conference at which companies interested in submitting a proposal can ask questions about the project or seek clarification of the needs described in the RFP. Most RFPs require that proposals be submitted by a deadline and contain specific information. Proposals that do not contain the information requested may be omitted from consideration. Therefore, once an organization decides to submit a proposal, staff members carefully study the RFP and identify the information requirements. Each information requirement is given to an individual or a group who will be responsible for furnishing necessary material and data.

Some proposals, such as university research proposals, may be written by one person. In complex proposals, however, different sections may be written by individuals in different areas of the organization. An editor or proposal writer will then compile the final document. This writer/editor may be assisted by readers who help check the developing proposal to be sure that all requested information is included and that the information is correct. Once the proposal has been written and submitted, it becomes a legally binding document. The proposing company or individual is legally committed to do what is described in the proposal, at the cost stated and within the time limit stated. For that reason, the proposing organization carefully checks all information for accuracy. Figure 15-2 will help you visualize the proposal process.

When a large number of bidders submit proposals in response to an RFP, the soliciting organization may select several finalists and allow each finalist to give an oral version of the proposal. During this oral presentation, the soliciting group asks questions; representatives of the proposing groups have one more opportunity to argue for the value of what they are proposing, the merits of their organization, and the justification for the cost attached to the proposed work.

Effective Argument in Proposal Development

All writing is persuasive, in that it must convince the reader that the writer has credibility and that the writer's ideas have merit. However, the success of a proposal rests totally on the effectiveness of the argument—how convincingly the writer argues for a plan, an idea, a product, or a service to be rendered and how well the writer convinces the reader that the proposing organization is the best one to do the work or research needed. In planning the content of the proposal, the proposer must harmonize the soliciting company's needs with the proposer's capabilities. The writer must be acutely sensitive to what readers will be looking for but not propose action that is outside the capability of the proposing individual or organization. The proposing individual or organization has an ethical responsibility to explain accurately and specifically what work can be done and not done so that there is no possibility of deceiving readers by making promises that cannot be fulfilled.

The following questions are useful in analyzing the effectiveness of the argument, whether in a written or an oral proposal:

What does the soliciting organization really want?

What is the problem that needs to be solved?

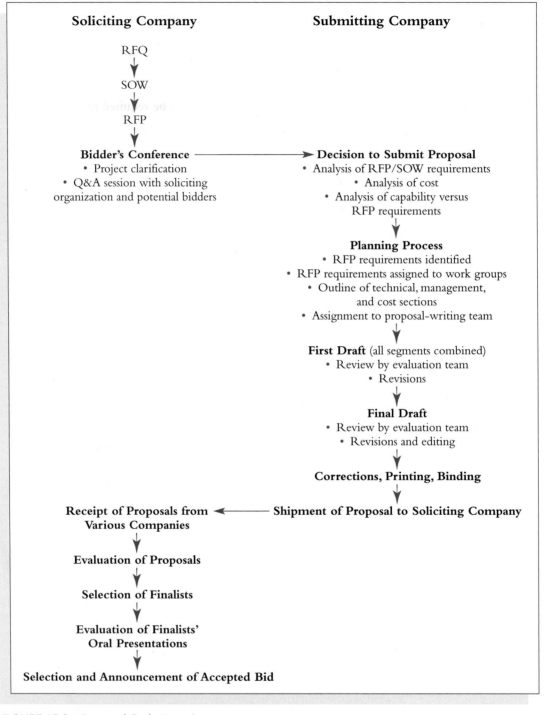

FIGURE 15-2 • Proposal Cycle in an Organization

What approaches to the solution will be viewed most favorably?

What approaches will be viewed unfavorably?

What objections will our plan elicit?

Can we accomplish the goals we propose?

To answer these questions, the proposer may be required to do research on the organization, its problems, its corporate culture and the perspective and attitudes stemming from its corporate culture, and its current financial status, goals, and problems. As each part of the proposal is developed, the writer should examine it from the intended reader's perspective.

What are the weakness of the plan, as we—the writers—perceive them?

How can we counter any weaknesses and reader's potential objections?

How can we make our plan appealing?

How can we show that we understand their needs?

How can we best present our capability to do this project?

What are our strengths?

From our own knowledge of our organization, what are our weaknesses— in personnel, in overall capability to complete this project as proposed?

Do we need to modify our proposed plan to avoid misleading readers about our ability to perform certain tasks on time, as proposed, and at cost?

Can we sell our idea without compromising the accuracy of what we can actually do?

As a proposal writer, you should consider each question and determine what evidence you will need to support the merits of your idea and the arguments needed to refute any objections. Every sentence in your proposal should argue for the merits of your plan and your or your organization's ability to complete it. Although the proposal is designed to be a sales document, you are still ethically obligated to present a plan that meets the soliciting organization's needs and requirements. In considering the ethical issues that confront proposal writers, you will want to review Chapter 6, Writing Ethically.

Standard Sections of Proposals

Proposals generally include three main divisions: a summary, a main body, and attachments. The main body focuses on the three main parts of the proposal: what the proposal's objectives are (technical proposal), how the objectives will be achieved (management proposal), and how much the project will cost (cost proposal). You may find it helpful to visualize the structure in this way:

Project summary
Project description (technical proposal)
    Introduction
    Rationale and significance
    Plan of the work
    Facilities and equipment
Personnel (management proposal)
Budget (cost proposal)
Appendixes

Major proposals are submitted in complete report format, which requires a letter of transmittal, a title page, a submission page (perhaps), a table of contents, and a summary. Shorter proposals may be written in a memo or letter format. Whatever the format, the main elements will be required, although how they appear will vary with each proposal. In most RFPs, the soliciting organization explains what should be included in the proposal (either specific information to be included or major elements), as shown in the RFP in Exercise 1 at the end of this chapter (Figure 15-9). Often, RFPs indicate the maximum number of pages allowed in a proposal. Writers are well advised to follow these instructions carefully to ensure that the proposal is not rejected during the initial screening process because it fails to follow preparation guidelines stipulated by the RFP.

Summary The summary is by far the most important section of the proposal. Many proposal consultants believe that a project will be accepted or rejected based solely on the effectiveness of the summary, which is your readers' first introduction to what you are proposing. The summary should concisely describe the project, particularly how your work meets the requirements of the soliciting organization, your plan for doing the work, and your or your company's main qualifications. The summary should be a concise version of the detailed plan, but it should be written to convince readers that you understand what the soliciting firm needs and wants, that what you are proposing can be done as you describe, and that your approach is solid because you have the required knowledge and expertise. After reading the summary, readers should want to read more of your proposal.

Project Description (Technical Proposal) The technical proposal describes what you or your company proposes to do. The description must be as specific as possible. The technical proposal has a number of elements, described below.

Introduction The proposal introduction should explain what you are proposing, why you are proposing this idea, and what you plan to accomplish.

The introduction contains the same elements as any introduction. In short proposals, the summary and introduction can be combined.

Rationale and Significance Much of your success in convincing readers that you should be granted a contract to do the work you propose rests on your success in convincing them that you understand the project. In the section on rationale and significance, you need to make it clear that you understand readers' needs—as stated in the summary or introduction—and that you have designed your goals by analyzing and defining their needs. Although you will clearly be selling your idea, you should recognize and answer any questions your readers may have as you argue the merits of your project. Convincing your readers that you fully understand what they are looking for is critical in establishing your credibility. In short,

- You may want to define the problem, to show that you understand it.
- You may want to explain the background of the problem, how it evolved, by providing a historical review of the problem.
- If you are proposing a research project, you may want to explain why your research needs to be done and what results can be expected from your research.
- You may want to describe your solution and the benefits of your proposed solution.

Of greatest importance, however, is the *feasibility* of the work you propose. Is your proposed work doable? Is it suitable, appropriate, economical, and practicable? Have you given your readers an accurate view of what you can and will do?

Plan of the Work The section on the work plan is also critical, particularly to expert readers who will attempt to determine whether you understand the breadth of the work you are proposing. In this section, you will describe how you will go about achieving the goals you have stated. You will specify what you will do in what order, explaining and perhaps justifying your approach as you believe necessary. A realistic approach is crucial in that a knowledgeable reader will sense immediately if your plan omits major steps. A flawed work plan can destroy your credibility as well as the merits of the goals or the solution you are proposing.

Scope The work plan section may need to describe the scope of the proposed work. What will you do and not do? What topics will your study or your work cover and not cover? What are the limits of what you are proposing? What topics will be outside the scope of your project? As the writer of the proposal, you have both an ethical and a legal obligation to make clear to your readers the limits of your responsibility.

Methods A work plan may also require a statement of the methods you will use. If you are going to do on-site research, how will you do this research? If you plan to collect data, how will you analyze it? How will you guarantee the validity of the analysis? If you are going to conduct surveys, how will you develop them? If you plan to do historical research or a literature review of a topic, how will you approach such a review to ensure that your findings are representative of what is currently known about a subject area? A precise, carefully detailed description of your work methods can add to your credibility as one who is competent to perform the proposed work.

Task Breakdown Almost all proposals require you to divide your work into specific tasks and to state the amount of time allotted to each task. This information may be given in a milestone chart, as illustrated in the third main section of the student research report shown shortly (Situation 1, Figure 15-3). The task breakdown indicates how much time you plan to devote to each task. A realistic time schedule also becomes an effective argument. It suggests to readers that you understand how much time your project will take and that you are not promising miracles just to win approval of your proposal or business plan.

   If a project must be completed by a deadline, the task breakdown and work schedule should indicate exactly how you plan to fit every job into the allotted time. However, do not make time commitments that will be impossible to meet. Readers who sense that your work plan is artificial will immediately question your credibility. Remember, too, that a proposal is a binding commitment. If you cannot do what you propose, what the soliciting organization requires within the required time, you can destroy your professional credibility and leave yourself open to litigation.

Problem Analysis Few projects can be completed without problems. If you have carefully analyzed the problem or work you intend to do, you should anticipate where difficulties could arise. Problems that may be encountered can often be discussed in the rationale section. However, if you discover major obstacles that you believe will occur during the course of the project, you may wish to isolate and discuss these in a separate section. Many organizations that request work or solicit research proposals are aware of problems that may arise. Reviewers in these organizations look carefully at the problem analysis section, wherever it occurs, to see whether the proposer has anticipated these problems and explained the course of action that will be followed in dealing with them. Anticipating and designing solutions to problems can further build your credibility with readers, who will not be impressed if you fail to diagnose points in your work plan that could be troublesome and even hinder your completion of the project as proposed.

Facilities The facilities section of the proposal is important if you need to convince the reader that your company has the equipment, plant, and physical capability to do the proposed work. Facilities descriptions are particularly crucial if hardware is to be built at a plant site owned by your organization. Even in study proposals, your readers may want to know what research resources you will use. Sometimes existing facilities are not adequate for a particular job and your company must purchase specific equipment. The facilities section enables you to explain this purchase and how it will be included in the cost proposal.

Researchers may need to travel to visit special libraries or research sites. The amount of money needed for this travel will be part of the cost proposal. Thus, the nature of any extra research support, its importance, and its cost to the project should be explained here.

Personnel (Management Proposal)

Any technical proposal or project is only as good as the management strategy that directs it. The management proposal should explain how you plan to manage the project: who will be in charge and what qualifications that person or team has for this kind of work. Management procedures should harmonize with the methods of pursuing the work described in the technical proposal.

Descriptions of your management philosophy and hierarchy should clearly reflect your company's management philosophy and culture. Readers should see the same kind of management applied to the proposed work as to the company and other projects it manages. Any testimony to or evidence of the effectiveness of the management approach will lend credibility to the technical proposal. Proposal reviewers must be convinced that you and your organization have a sound approach supported by good management of that approach.

In research proposals, the researcher who is soliciting funds will want to explain his or her expertise in the subject area proposed. This explanation may focus on educational background, previous projects successfully undertaken, published research on the topic, and general experience.

Cost (Cost Proposal)

The cost proposal is usually the final item in the body of the proposal, even though cost may ultimately be the most crucial factor in industrial proposals. Cost is usually given last and appears as a budget for the length of the proposal period. The technical and management sections of the proposal, with their descriptions of methods, tasks, facilities, required travel, and personnel, should help justify the cost. They should have already explained the rationale for items that will produce the greatest cost. However, any items not previously discussed in the technical and management sections—such as administrative expenses, additional insurance benefits costs, and unexpected legal costs—should be explained. An itemized budget is often submitted as a separate document. It includes items such as the proposing organization's liability for not meeting project deadlines, for cost overruns, and for unforeseen strikes and work stoppages. Many budget sections include standard statements such as descriptions of union contracts with labor costs, insurance benefits costs, nonstrike costs, and statements of existing corporate liability for other projects—any existing arrangements that affect the cost of the proposed contract. Clearly, the goal is to explain exactly how much the project will cost and how the cost is determined. How extensive the budget is depends on the magnitude of the project.

Conclusion The proposal includes a final section that repeats what the proposal offers the potential client or the soliciting agency, why you or your company should be selected to perform the work, and the benefits that the project, when completed, will yield for the client. The conclusion presents the final restatement of your central argument.

Appendixes As in any report, the appendix section includes materials to support information you give in the main body of the proposal—in the technical, management, or cost proposal. For example, the appendix might include résumés of principal investigators, managers, or researchers. These résumés should highlight their qualifications as they pertain to the specific project.

To help you understand proposals written by students, study the following situation and the corresponding student research proposal (Figure 15-3).

Situation 1 (Figure 15-3)

Anessa Jones is a senior agricultural engineering major. As part of her senior design project, Anessa has been asked by the Lombardy Irrigation Company to design a plan to restore the Lombardy Irrigation Ditch, which was dug in 1866, the year the company was founded. The ditch is no longer operational. Anessa presented the following proposal to the president of Lombardy, Harold R. Cole, to explain how she proposes to design a plan to restore the ditch for irrigation use. Anessa has to be finished with this project by the end of the fall semester. Thus, she describes her work plan, time line for completing the project by December 14, and project report schedule.

▶ PROGRESS REPORTS

When a soliciting organization requests a proposal, it often states that a specific number of progress reports will be required, particularly if the project covers a long time period. As their name suggests, progress reports, sometimes

```
┌─────────────────────────────────────────────────────────────────────────┐
```

**Proposal
for
Lombardy Irrigation Ditch Restoration Plan**

DATE SUBMITTED: October 1, 2001

Summary and Introduction

This project proposes to develop a restoration plan for the Lombardy Irrigation Company in Rio Frio, Texas. In 1866, the company was founded, and an irrigation ditch was dug adjacent to the Frio River in Real County, Texas, to divert water from the Frio River to water crops and livestock. The community of Rio Frio grew up around the ditch and relied on the water it provided for more than 100 years.

Water has since stopped running the entire length of the ditch because of faulty design, frequent flooding, and lack of maintenance. The Lombardy Irrigation Company wants a restoration plan that will include a ditch design, soil volume estimates for any excavation, cost estimates for construction, and vegetation control and ditch maintenance recommendations.

As an engineering consultant, I am qualified to perform the research, calculation, and design required by the client. The completion date for the research will be December 3, 2001.

Introduction

Background

Description of the Problem

The original ditch had a bottom width of 6 feet; a water depth of 5 feet; a top width of 7 feet; a slope of 4 1/6 feet per 1000 feet; and a flow rate of 109.62 cubic of feet per second (cfs). This configuration translates to a cross section with 10:1 side slopes, which is almost vertical. The design, combined with the location of the ditch about 50 feet from the river, contributed to ditch failure.

The company currently maintains water rights to divert 3,460 acre-feet of water per year from the Frio River and rights to use 1600 acre-feet of water per year for irrigation purposes. Over the years, land uses adjacent to the ditch have become less agricultural and more residential. Restoring the Lombardy Irrigation Ditch is necessary for historical value and for the water value, although few farms are left along the ditch that would use the water for irrigation. This situation make cost analysis of the project difficult, since most of the economic gain from the ditch would come from increased tourism of the area, higher property values along the ditch, and other factors that cannot be predicted with certain at this time.

A simple solution would be to redesign the canal and install an impermeable liner to prevent water loss and increase velocity. This solution is impractical because of economic considerations, land constraints, and the certain objections of adjacent landowners. Lombardy thus has the problem of finding the most economical way to restore the ditch to its original carrying capacity, taking into account socioeconomic factors and technical design factors.

Plan to Restore Lombardy Irrigation Ditch
October 1, 2001   1

```
└─────────────────────────────────────────────────────────────────────────┘
```

FIGURE 15-3 • Proposal

Project Goal

I propose to develop a restoration plan to bring the Lombardy Ditch Irrigation system in Rio Frio, Texas, back to its full carrying capacity. The plan will include a ditch design, soil volume estimates for any excavation, cost estimates for construction, and vegetation control and ditch maintenance recommendations.

Scope of the Proposed Work

The project will include an economic analysis of plan implementation; a ditch design including any excavation, side-slope stabilization, and line requirements; recommendations for vegetation control and ditch maintenance; and a suggested timeline for implementing the plan. The economic, social, and legal implications of ditch modification will be considered throughout all phases of the design and resulting recommendations.

Plan of the Proposed Work

The proposed plan has three specific phases, during which the following will be accomplished: a site inspection, a field survey, a literature review, a ditch design, and a final restoration plan. To conclude these tasks by the proposed December 14 date, I will work according to the following schedule:

Project Duration—Weeks: 10/8/01–12/14/01

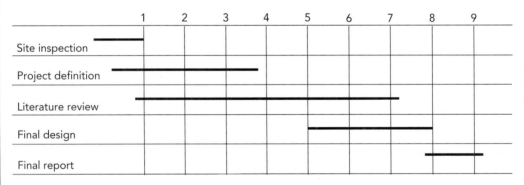

Site Inspection

Visiting the site will allow me to determine the cause of the problem and to help identify possible solutions. During a site inspection, I will collect soil and water samples, take photographs of unique elements in and around the ditch, and talk to community residents to learn about their concerns. Soils sample will identify soil characteristics in the area, including soil bulk density and permeability. A water sample will show turbidity of the water, or how much sediment the water is carrying that could be deposited in the ditch. A velocity meter will be used at the head gate of the ditch to estimate the flow rate from the river into the ditch. The flow rate will be used in the final ditch design.

Plan to Restore Lombardy Irrigation Ditch
October 1, 2001

2

FIGURE 15-3 • *(continued)*

Field Survey

The site inspection phase will include a survey of the ditch to determine the current slope and average cross section of the ditch. I will use this data to calculate soil excavation volumes and estimate construction costs. If the company decides to implement the plan, the construction contractor will use the survey to help with construction work.

Literature Review

A literature review will provide information about canal design, linear materials, soil survey information, historic Frio River flood dates, and other canal structures. This information will be critical to the final design and development of the recommendations for maintenance. A working bibliography of sources is included as Appendix A.

Ditch Design

The ditch design must address both land constraints and socioeconomic concerns of the area. The company owns the ditch and 10-foot easement on each side. The actual ditch cross section must fall within these boundaries because it is not feasible for the company to purchase more right-of-way from the adjacent landowners. Construction of the ditch is also an issue because there is not enough space to bring in heavy earthmoving equipment for ditch construction. The final design will include any excavation, side-slope stabilization, and linear requirements for the ditch.

Final Restoration Plan

The proposed final plan will include the ditch design, soil volume estimates for any excavation, cost estimates for construction, and vegetation control and ditch maintenance recommendations. I will provide an economic analysis of plan implementation, side-slope stabilization recommendations, and technical implications of plan implementation. A working outline for the final report is included as Appendix B.

Qualifications and Experience

I am completing the B.S. in agricultural engineering this fall. An integral part of my education has required me to develop expertise in design work, field surveying, and soil volume calculation. My résumé, included as Appendix C, describes my experience in these areas. During the three summers I worked as an engineering intern to the agricultural engineer group in Comal County, we diagnosed and developed designs for solving four large-scale irrigation problems in the county After graduating from Texas A&M, I will be employed by Hydro Collins Engineering Group in San Antonio, Texas, as a consulting engineer. Collins has hired me because of my background and interest in solving problems such as the one faced by Lombardy and my knowledge of irrigation and terrain problems in the Rio Frio area.

Plan to Restore Lombardy Irrigation Ditch
October 1, 2001

3

FIGURE 15-3 • (continued)

Budget

The budget for this project includes all expenses for completing the project by December 14.

Table 1: Estimated Budget for Proposed Restoration Plan

Item	Time	Cost
Travel, $0.45/mile	250 miles	$ 112.50
Surveying equipment rental, $65/day	3 days	195.00
Surveying, $20/hour	24 hours	480.00
Engineering services, $50/hour	80 hours	$4,000.00
Total		$4,787.50

Anticipated Problems

Completing the project on time and at cost could be hindered by weather. Usually, the county is relatively dry during the fall. However, additional days have been figured into the project schedule to allow for adverse weather than would delay surveying. Therefore, I see no problem in completing the project by December 14, as proposed.

Progress Reports

At our initial meeting, you requested that progress reports be submitted to you by e-mail every two weeks. Thus, assuming initiation of the project by October 15, I would send e-mail progress reports on the following dates:

November 9, 2001
December 3, 2001

Final Report will be submitted December 14, 2001, to your office.
Oral briefing. Date to be determined.

Conclusion

This project, as proposed, will furnish the design necessary to return the Lombardy Ditch to operative condition. Preliminary assessment of the problem and my initial research suggests that traditional methods can be used to redesign the ditch. With a minimum of expenditure for analysis and design, I can provide you a working plan for the ditch. All recommendations will focus on ensuring that reclamation is not only design-effective but also cost-effective.

Appendixes

Appendix A: Working Bibliography
Appendix B: Working Outline for Final Report
Appendix C: Résumé [Not included here.]

Plan to Restore Lombardy Irrigation Ditch
October 1, 2001

FIGURE 15-3 • (continued)

Appendix A

Working Bibliography

Aisenbrey, A. J., Jr., R. B. Hayes, H. J. Warren, D. L. Winsett, and R. B. Young. 1974 *Design of small canal structures*. Denver, CO: U.S. Department of the Interior, Bureau of Reclamation.

Certificate of Adjudication for Lombardy Irrigation Company. May 1984. No. 21-3158, Real and Uvalde Counties, Texas.

Deed of Trust of Lombardy Irrigation Company. March 1916. Real County, Texas.

Drainage and water table control. December 3–15, 1992. *Sixth International Drainage Symposium*, Nashville, TN: American Society of Agricultural Engineering.

Gunatillake, G. G. W. August 1987. Linings for irrigation canals. Student report. Department of Agricultural Engineering, Texas A&M University.

Haan C. T., B. J. Barfield, and J. C. Hayes. 1994 *Design hydrology and sedimentology for small catchments*. New York: Academic Press.

James, Larry G. 1988 *Principles of farm irrigation design*. Malabar, FL. Krieger.

Jones, C. W. August 1981. *Performance of granular soil covers on canals*. Denver, CO: U.S. Department of the Interior, Bureau of Reclamation.

Kraatz, D. B. 1977. *Irrigation canal lining*. Rome: Food and Agriculture Organization of the United Nations.

Morrison, W. R., E. W. Gray, Jr., D. B. Paul, and R. K. Frobel. September 1981. *Installation of flexible membrane lining on Mt. Elbert Forebay Reservoir*. Denver, CO: U.S. Department of the Interior, Bureau of Reclamation.

Sally, H. L. 1965. *Lining of earthen irrigation canals*. Los Angeles: Asia Publishing House.

Schwab, G. O. 1981. *Soil and water conservation engineering*. 3d ed. Baltimore: Durham-Hill.

Siddiqui, I. H. 1979. *Irrigation canals: planning, design, construction and maintenance*. Lahore, Pakistan: National Book Foundation.

Slagle, S. E. October 1992. Irrigation canal leakage in the Flathead Indian Reservation, northwestern Montana. U.S. Geological Survey, Water Resources Investigations Report No. 92-4066: Helena, MT: USGC.

Stevens, J. W., and D. D. Richmond. 1970 *Soil survey of Uvalde County, Texas*. Washington, DC: U.S. Department of Agriculture, Soil Conservation Service.

Plan to Restore Lombardy Irrigation Ditch
October 1, 2001

5

FIGURE 15-3 • (*continued*)

Appendix B

Proposed Report Outline

I. Executive Summary

II. Introduction
   A. Background
   B. Problem Definition
   C. Scope of Work

I. Literature Review
   A. Soil Information
   B. Channel Types
   C. Liner Types
   D. Channel Design

I. Design Alternatives

II. Final Ditch Design
   A. Slope and Cross Section
   B. Lined Areas
   C. Other Structures

I. Implementation Plan

II. Maintenance Plan

III. Vegetation Control Recommendations

IV. Technical Implications

V. Cost Analysis
   A. Tree Removal
   B. Construction
   C. Annual Maintenance

Plan to Restore Lombardy Irrigation Ditch
October 1, 2001

FIGURE 15-3 • *(continued)*

known as status reports, tell readers how work is progressing on a project. They are usually submitted at specific intervals that are agreed upon at the beginning of a project. Their immediate purpose is to inform the authorizing person of the activities completed on a project, but their long-range purpose should be to show the proposing organization's or the individual's competence in pursuing a task and completing it.

As we mention at the beginning of this chapter, as an employee you may write progress reports routinely to report the status of the range of projects you are working on. These progress reports explain what you have done so that others interested in the progress are kept informed. They also help you or your work group provide evidence of your activities. Whether a progress report is written to describe work on a particular project or to report general employee activity, it has three main purposes that provide *documentation* of work accomplished:

- To explain to the reader what has been accomplished and by whom, the status of the work performed, and problems that may have arisen that need attention.
- To explain to your client how time and money have been spent, what work remains to be done, and how any problems encountered are being handled.
- To enable the organization or individual doing the work to assess the work and plan future work.

Writers use several different strategies in designing progress reports. The report should begin with an introduction and a project description to familiarize the reader with the project. A summary of work completed follows. The middle section then explains what has been accomplished on specific tasks as well as what work remains, followed by a statement of work planned for the next progress report period. The final section assesses the work done thus far. Any problems that are encountered are also presented, along with methods of addressing those problems in the form of conclusions and recommendations. Cost can be dealt with in either the middle or the final section.

Structure by Work Performed The structure of a progress report might follow one of the two basic plans portrayed below. The middle section can be organized around work completed and work remaining, as shown in the left-hand column, or around tasks, as shown in the right-hand column. The beginning and the end have the same structure in both plans:

Beginning
- Introduction/project description
- Summary

Middle

• Work completed	or	• Task 1
Task 1		Work completed
Task 2, etc.		Work remaining
• Work remaining		• Task 2
Task 3		Work completed
Task 4		Work remaining
• Cost		• Cost

End

- Overall appraisal of progress to date
- Conclusion and recommendations

In this general plan, you emphasize what has been done and what remains to be done and supply enough introduction to be sure that the reader knows what project is being discussed.

Situation 1 Continued (Figure 15-4)

Anessa Jones's first e-mail progress report (Figure 15-4) shows how she used progress by main tasks to report the status of her restoration design for the Lombardy irrigation ditch. Her report follows the main elements of her work plan given in the proposal.

In her proposal that, Anessa has said she will send Harold Cole e-mail progress reports on two dates. Cole will want to know what Anessa has accomplished. These reports will be brief because each will cover 3–4 weeks of the project. Anessa will send e-mail copies of the reports to the faculty member in her department who is monitoring the project. The faculty director wants to know whether the work is on schedule to ensure that it is completed within one semester, the time allowed for the senior research project.

Beginning

Anessa begins the first report with a clearly worded subject line, followed by a brief introduction.

Because Lombardy is funding the project, Anessa explains how much she has spent on the project and notes that she is under budget on the cost of surveying equipment and engineering services.

Middle

In the Work Completed and Work Remaining sections, Anessa says that she has completed the site inspection, field survey, ditch design, and the literature review but has not begun to develop the restoration plan.

TO: hrc@pioneer.com

FROM: jones@aol.com

CC: d-canton@overland.com

RE: Progress Report #1-Lombardy Irrigation Ditch Restoration

This is the first of three e-mail progress reports on the status of my de-sign plan for restoring the Lombardy Irrigation Ditch.

COST TO DATE

Travel

Two trips to Frio County.	250 miles @ 0.45/mile	$225.00
Surveying Equipment	3 days	$95.00*
Engineering Services	50/hour × 20 hours	$1000.00***

*I was able to rent surveying equipment for $100 less than anticipated.

**I was able to complete the survey in 20 hours rather than 24 hours, as projected.

***I have currently used 25% of the required engineering services that I proposed.

WORK COMPLETED

Site Inspection and Field Survey

I have completed two site evaluations. During the second site evaluation, I completed a partial field survey of the ditch and actual water veloci-ty measurements through the headgate of the ditch. The survey data will be used to help calculate the amount of soil that will need to be removed when the new ditch is constructed and will tell us how much the soil removal will cost. The water velocity measurement will tell us if enough water is moving into the ditch from the river at the present time.

Ditch Design

I have also completed a new ditch design. The design is a trapezoidal chan-nel with a 5-foot bottom width, 13-foot top width, and a 5-foot depth of flow.

Literature Review

FIGURE 15-4 • E-Mail Progress Report

In addition to the sources listed in my proposal, I have continued to search for additional information. The sources used in my literature review are dated, as canal design is not new technology. I have been unable to find any cutting-edge information regarding the flow of water through a channel. In this project, I am applying standard technology to design a new ditch.

WORK REMAINING

Data Analysis

I have to analyze the data collected during the field surveys and generate a topographic map of the site. I am having a problem locating the software that I need to perform this task. I am working with a computer specialist in the Department of Agricultural Engineering to determine how to resolve this problem. An older type of software is available, which I can use if current software I need cannot be located easily.

Final Design for the Restoration

Work remaining includes contacting contractors to get cost estimates for the different types of work that will need to be done to restore the ditch. I will use this information to complete a cost analysis of restoring the ditch.

A major remaining task is recommending maintenance and vegetation control. I have contacted the Extension Service in Real County about this issue and will discuss this topic by phone next week.

An additional trip to the ditch will be needed, which will add another $112.50 to the initial projected cost. I had not anticipated that two trips, rather than one, would be needed.

ASSESSMENT OF PROGRESS TO DATE

The project should be completed on time and within the cost proposed. The unexpected travel cost will be offset by the savings in surveying equipment and time allocated to that activity. Because I have not encountered any problem that will delay or hinder completion, the project will be complete by December 14.

FIGURE 15-4 • (continued)

End

She provides an overall appraisal of her work and mentions the one problem she has experienced—the need to make an extra trip to Real County. While this trip has increased the proposed cost of travel, the overall cost remains as projected because costs of surveying equipment and engineering services are under budget.

As we note early in the chapter, employees often need to write progress reports to document their activities. These types of reports simply explain major accomplishments. Because business and technical organizations frequently stipulate a time frame for a project, status reports may emphasize completion dates as well as deadlines. Sometimes status reports indicate "action required" notices to keep the project on schedule. Figure 15-5, featured in situation 2, illustrates a status report written by an employee who is in charge of a project that must be completed according to a schedule.

Situation 2 (Figure 15-5)

Dean Smith, a training manager for a software development company, is responsible for developing training sessions for sales personnel. His main responsibilities are to provide all training to employees, to decide what training should be conducted, and then to develop the training courses. Dean routinely writes progress reports to the director of personnel, Sharon Sanchez, to keep her informed of his activities—training he thinks will need to be offered, training programs he is currently developing or planning to develop, and training programs he and other training staff are currently teaching or directing.

Response to Situation 2

Dean writes status reports to Sharon about once a month (or whenever he has something he wants her to know about). Because she is familiar with what Dean does, he does not need to include an elaborate introduction. He begins with a concise summary and then proceeds to describe pertinent activities. In this particular report, he is asking for increased funding for a training program. Thus he includes an action required statement in the heading.

For this routine progress report, Dean modifies the general plan as follows:

- **Beginning:** Introduction
      Purpose of the report—to report the status of a project
      Purpose of the work being performed
      Summary of current status
- **Middle:** Work completed on the project
      Task A
      Task B
      Task C
- **End:** Conclusion and perhaps recommendations

DATE: November 7, 2000

TO: Sharon Sanchez

FROM: Dean Smith

SUBJECT: TQI Workshop Plans for Spring 2001

            ACTION REQUIRED BY 12/8/00

Summary of Plans

Planning for our TQI workshops, scheduled for April and May, is nearly complete. Our TQI facilitators have produced detailed training schedules for technical service and customer relations. I have approved these, and materials are being ordered and prepared. A TQI program package, developed by HI-TOP Sales Materials, specifically for computer sales personnel, can be purchased for $3,600. The format would be an excellent follow-up for all employees. As you and I had already discussed, quality off-the-shelf TQI packages should be considered.

TQI Workshop Activities as of 11/17/00

TQI Preparations for Technical Service Personnel

Johnette Darden and her group have been preparing materials for the technical service employees. The workshop will help the staff to look at software purchases from the customer's perspective and to begin to look for ways of decreasing the time required to resolve customer complaints. The second part of the workshop will encourage TSP to examine faulty products and find ways of eliminating the problems by working with design. We will probably recommend a quality control unit be formed that uses people from both technical service and design.

TQI Preparations for Customer Relations

Responding to customer needs and filling orders rapidly will be the main focus of the TQI workshop for CR employees. Robert Newmann will be working with the group (1) to reassess what we are doing in our current customer relations efforts, and then (2) to improve and even eliminate processes that do not help us serve customers quicker and better.

FIGURE 15-5 • Routine Progress Report

Sharon Sanchez

Page 2

11/17/00

HI-TOP Sales Program Available for Purchase by 12/15

HI-TOP developed a superb TQI program for sales personnel about two years ago. The program was so effective that HI-TOP is now selling the program, which has received rave reviews from a half-dozen companies that sell hardware and software. I reviewed the program two days ago and think it would be an excellent follow-up for any TQI work we do. I would like to purchase the program and use it with both Technical Services and Customer Relations. We can continue to use the package with other TQI training.

An outline of the program is attached. As you can see, it addresses the major issues we believe our own TQI programs need to emphasize.

Please Note

HI-TOP will sell us the program package priced at $4,500 for $3,600 if we act before December 8. They are currently redesigning the program to include extensive teaching aids, which are nice but unnecessary for our purposes. The new package will be available 1/1 for $6,000. **The original package will not be available after 12/15.**

Please give me a call so that we can discuss.

FIGURE 15-5 • (*continued*)

For progress reports that cover more than one period, the basic design can be expanded as follows:

Beginning

- Introduction
- Project description
- Summary of work to date
- Summary of work in this period

Middle

- Work accomplished by tasks (this period)
- Work remaining on specific tasks
- Work planned for the next reporting period
- Work planned for periods thereafter
- Cost to date
- Cost in this period

End

- Overall appraisal of work to date
- Conclusions and recommendations concerning problems

Structure by Chronological Order If your project or research is broken into time periods, your progress report can be structured to emphasize the periods.

Beginning

- Introduction/project description
- Summary of work completed

Middle

- Work completed
  Period 1 (beginning and ending dates)
      Description
      Cost
      Period 2 (beginning and ending dates)
      Description
      Cost
- Work remaining
  Period 3 (or remaining periods)
      Description of work to be done
      Expected cost

End

- Evaluation of work in this period
- Conclusions and recommendations

Structure by Main Project Goals Many research projects are pursued by grouping specific tasks into major groups. Then, the writer describes progress according to work done in each major group and perhaps the amount of time spent on that group of tasks. Alternatively, a researcher may decide to present a project by research goals—what will be accomplished during the project. Thus, progress reports will explain activities performed to achieve those goals. In the middle of the plans below, the left-hand column is organized by work completed and remaining, and the right-hand column by goals.

Beginning

- Introduction/project description
- Summary of progress to date

Middle

• Work completed	or	• Goal 1
Goal 1		Work completed
Goal 2		Work remaining
Goal 3, etc.		Cost
• Work remaining		• Goal 2
Goal 1		Work completed
Goal 2		Work remaining
Goal 3, etc.		Cost
• Cost		

End

- Evaluation of work to date
- Conclusions and recommendations

Situation 3 (Figure 15-6)

Linbeth Consulting Company was founded to help U.S. businesses gain the knowledge and expertise necessary to do business abroad, either in specific countries or in specific market areas. When approached by companies interested in these company's services, Linbeth provides letter proposals explaining the services and how the client's specific situation might be approached. While working on a project, Linbeth consultants will frequently use an oral PowerPoint presentation to the client to explain the status on the research.

Doing Business in Mexico

A Status Report

Linbeth
Consulting, Inc.

March 15, 2001

Topics

▌ Project Description
▌ Summary of Progress to Date
▌ Work Remaining
▌ Analysis of NAFTA Economic Effects
▌ Problems Encountered
▌ Costs Incurred to Date

Project Description

▌ Describe the Mexican social, economic
and political structure
▌ Detail the regulatory climate in Mexico
▌ Highlight profit opportunities for Texas
businesses
▌ Clarify the implications of NAFTA on
U.S./Texas/Mexico business operations
▌ Clarify effects of culture on business

FIGURE 15-6 • Excerpt from a PowerPoint Progress Report

Summary of Progress

▮ Applicable demographics and statistics data are complete.

▮ Mexican regulations that affect business relationships have been compiled.

▮ Status of the Mexican economy through 1997 has been summarized.

▮ Status of the U.S. economy since passage of NAFTA has been summarized.

Work Remaining

▮ Analysis of assessments of NAFTA
  ▮ From Mexican perspective
  ▮ From Congressional reports
  ▮ From Department of commerce
  ▮ From border economic groups
  ▮ From Canada

Economic Profile of NAFTA

▮ Effects of NAFTA are not clear.

▮ Problem areas:
  ▮ Changes in environmental impact
  ▮ Changes in U.S. economy
  ▮ Real effects of NAFTA on the economy
  ▮ Results in specific product sectors

FIGURE 15-6 • (continued)

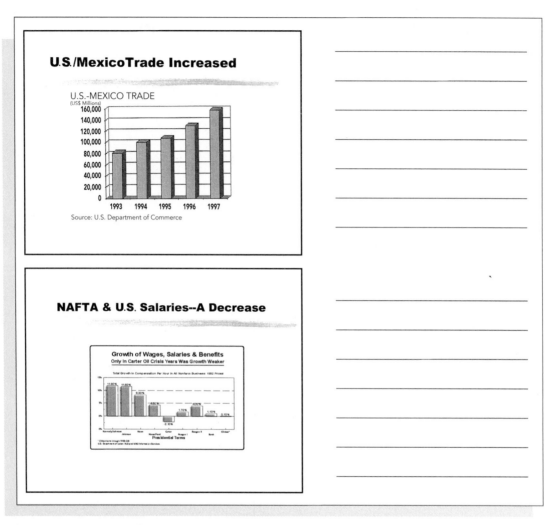

FIGURE 15-6 • (continued)

The segment of a PowerPoint progress report illustrated in Figure 15-6 was submitted to a company considering doing business in Mexico. We have included only eight slides from the presentation, but you can see how the narrative of the progress report surfaces in the presentation. Linbeth consultants provided copies of the presentation with space for notes. Copies would be available to other company employees. Note that the main segments of the progress report are clearly evident, even in this excerpt. In any kind of presentation software, such as PowerPoint, you can develop graphics and then paste them into the presentation, as exemplified in Figure 15-6.

▶ PHYSICAL APPEARANCE OF PROPOSALS AND PROGRESS REPORTS

The importance of the appearance of any proposal or progress report cannot be overestimated. A report that is neat and effectively formatted suggests the competence of the proposing organization or individual. Proposals and progress reports longer than letter or memorandum length should have a protective cover. The title page should be tasteful. The type or print should be of high quality. Colored paper and covers should convey a professional attitude. A professional appearance is the first argument for the merits of the proposal.

▶ STYLE AND TONE OF PROPOSALS AND PROGRESS REPORTS

The proposal and its related report documents are, in effect, sales documents, but writers have an ethical commitment to present information about a project in a clear and accurate manner. Proposals, once accepted, become legally binding documents. Because contracts are based on proposals, organizations must be prepared to stand behind their proposals. Thus, the style should be authoritative, vigorous, and positive, suggesting the competence of the proposer. Generalizations must be bolstered by detailed factual accomplishments. Problems should be discussed honestly, but positive solutions to problems should be stressed. Neither the proposal nor the progress report should resort to vague, obfuscatory language.

▶ OTHER FORMS OF PROPOSALS AND PROGRESS REPORTS

Proposals and progress reports can be prepared in a variety of formats: as memo reports, as formal reports, and as letters. Yet, no matter what the format, proposals and progress reports will incorporate the same elements described above and illustrated in the reports written by Anessa Jones the senior engineering student, and Dean Smith, the software development company training manager. To see how proposals and progress reports might appear in another format and another context, examine Situation 4, which describes an internal proposal and a letter progress report.

Situation 4 (Figures 15-7 and 15-8)

You are employed by Scruggs and Pate, a local accounting firm in Plano, Texas. S&P employs twenty accountants. Recently, the senior managing partner, Jared Hastings, tells you that the Chamber of Commerce, in cooperation with the American Accounting Association, has decided to launch a community education program to help people who own and or manage small businesses in Plano understand more about accounting. The two groups want to have a year of educational sessions, one each week for 40 weeks, which will be available to the public.

Jared Hastings tells you that he thinks that the presentations directed to local people provide a wonderful opportunity to educate the general public about accounting and to advertise Scruggs and Pate's expertise and its ability to make accounting concepts clear to potential clients.

Hastings asks the tax team to prepare a memo proposal. He will convey this document, attached to a letter, to Elizabeth Hartnett, project chair of the Chamber of Commerce, who is planning the workshops. Thus, the tax team has two audiences: Jared Hastings, their senior manager at Scruggs and Pate, and Elizabeth Hartnett.

Response to Situation 4

Proposal

This is a team proposal that clearly indicates that it is written to the two readers just described. The team explains (for Elizabeth Hartnett) why the topic is important (Project Description and Rationale) and (for Jared Hastings) how the firm will complete the project, which must be done during tax season. By presenting the milestone chart, they convey their planning and schedule. For Elizabeth Hartnett, the team describes the plan of the presentation, all proposed handouts, and the bibliography for those attending the presentation. See Figure 15-7 for the proposal to Jared Hastings. Note that this proposal gives only the work plan.

Status Report

Two weeks before the presentation, Jan Gharantz, writing for the tax group, sends Elizabeth Hartnet a letter progress report (Figure 15-8) to assure her that the project is developing as proposed and that the S&P tax team will be ready for the presentation April 29. She also states what equipment the team will bring and what equipment is to be available on site.

Scruggs & Pate

MEMORANDUM

TO: Mr. Jared Hastings   Date: March 11, 1999

FROM: Tax Group

SUBJECT: Proposal for Chamber of Commerce Community Education Program

Summary

In considering your request that we propose a segment for inclusion in the Chamber of Commerce education program, we have decided to prepare a presentation on the benefits small businesses receive through the Taxpayer Relief Act of 1997 (TRA). Because this act has been effective for only a short time, many entrepreneurs and small-business owners are not aware of certain provisions that can benefit them. An informative discussion of these provisions will enable small businesses to take full advantage of special deductions and use the tax law to work in their favor. For example, the Taxpayer Relief Act establishes special deductions that allow business owners to secure a greater return on their investment in the business. This provision encourages small businesses to take risks, invest, and grow.

By extensively researching this new law, we will expand our own expertise while providing information to prospective clients. Active involvement in the community will increase the name recognition of the firm and convey the fact that we care about our clients.

Project Description

Our presentation will provide the community information on important parts of the Taxpayer Relief Act of 1997. Our presentation will include four parts of the TRA that benefit small-business owners: home office deductions, health insurance deductions, educational assistance deductions, and the capital gain tax rate reduction.

The first segment will cover the expanded definition of the home office and explain how a business can benefit from the deduction. Next, we will discuss health insurance costs that self-employed individuals can deduct. The new deduction raises the percentage from 80% in 1996 to 100% in the near future. The third area is an educational assistance deduction. This part of the TRA allows an employer to deduct any undergraduate school fees and tuition for which the employer reimburses an employee. Finally, we will consider the decrease in capital gains tax. The new law cuts the top tax rate for individuals on long-term capital gains from 28% to 20%.

Rationale for Proposing This Topic

In today's competitive business market, small businesses must take advantage of every opportunity to grow, improve, and adjust. In the midst of preparing the organization and its people to perform to the best of their abilities, small business owners must focus their attention on improving prof-

---

2100 Brookhaven Parkway, Plano, Texas 75074

214 667-5400   **800 997-2376**   **FAX: 214 555-9734**

FIGURE 15-7 • Internal Proposal

itability, increasing employee training, maintaining competitive emplyee compensation, and keeping up with new technologies. However, it is essential for small-business owners and self-employed individuals both to understand how current tax laws will affect their goals and to develop means for achieving their goals.

The TRA of 1997 yields many benefits for small businesses to participate in restructuring, reorganizing, and offering employee education. It is difficult for a start-up firm to invest thousands of dollars into new equipment, educational assistance, and employee benefits because of cash-flow constraints, large liabilities, and competing interests However, when a company can save money on a particular type of investment, the money will be spent in that area. The new tax law allows for tax breaks when small businesses incur expenses for long-term investments and capital gains, educational assistance, expansion of a home office, and increased health insurance. Knowledge in these areas of the new law is vital for the growth of a company and will help facilitate the best possible decisions regarding investment opportunities.

Work Plan

Our presentation team will meet weekly on Fridays at 3:00 to review progress and integrate individual contributions. We plan to work strictly within this plan, as we will be working to through the heaviest part of tax season to prepare for this presentation.

Topic	Preparation Segments					
	3/9–15	3/16–22	3/23–4/1	4/2–12	4/13–19	4/20–29
Research	▬▬▬▬					
Combine research		▬▬▬▬				
Develop presentation			▬▬▬▬▬▬▬			
Develop visuals					▬▬▬	
Rehearsal						▬▬
Presentation date						▬

Resources

We plan to work with Tax and Accounting Ondisk and ABI/INFORM databases to broaden our knowledge of TRA 1997.

2100 Brookhaven Parkway, Plano, Texas 75074

214 667-5400　　　　　　　800 997-2376　　　　　　　FAX: 214 555-9734

FIGURE 15-7 • (continued)

Outline of the Presentation

The presentation, as we currently envision it, will have six parts:

Introduction and Overview   Jan Gharantz

Home Office Deduction   Brandi Schmidt
   Expanded definition
   Prior law/New law

Health Insurance Deduction   Christina Matthews
   Increased percentage now allowed
   Acceleration and future benefits

Educational Assistance   Christina Matthews
   Exclusion of reimbursement of undergraduate costs
   Employer deduction as a business expense

Capital Gains   Les Moletta
   Reduction of top tax rate
   Prior law/New law

Conclusion   Jan Gharantz

Recent Studies of TRA Applications

We plan to share with our audience numerous print articles and Web materials. These are resources that business owners with no tax experience may find helpful. We may include others if they become available and applicable to the needs of our audience:

Deloitte & Touche, LLP. 1997. "Capital Gains." http://www.Dtonline.com. 5 March 1998.

Ernst & Young, LLP. 1997. "Tax Alert." httpp://www.ey.com. 6 March 1998.

Farber, L. 1997. Answers to your tax questions. *Medical Economics*, January, 109.

Fried, C. 1998. Beat back fund taxes. *Money*, January, 88–93.

Gordanier, D. 1997. "Capital Gains Tax Law Changes." Testa, Hurwitz & Thibeault, LLP. http://www.tht.com. 9 March 1998.

Heim, J. 1993. Taxes and home office. *PC World*, December, 293–296.

Kerigan, K. 1997. President throws support behind tax deduction for home-based businesses. *The Business Journal*, July, 13–14.

Pryde, J. 1997. Business just got less taxing. *Nation's Business*, October, 25–27.

————, J. 1998. Improve tax break for small firms. *Nation's Business*. February, 25.

2100 Brookhaven Parkway, Plano, Texas 75074

214 667-5400   **800 997-2376**   **FAX: 214 555-9734**

FIGURE 15-7 • *(continued)*

Conclusion

The Taxpayer Relief Act of 1997 brings numerous benefits to small-business owners. Individuals who lack the time to research the new law will miss out on possible tax savings. We will focus on four specific sections of the law that are most beneficial to small business owners in our community. We believe that this topic meets the objectives established by the Chamber of Commerce: to broaden the business knowledge of new small-business owners in the community.

2100 Brookhaven Parkway, Plano, Texas 75074

214 667-5400   800 997-2376   FAX: 214 555-9734

FIGURE 15-7 • *(continued)*

Scruggs & Pate

April 11, 1999

Ms. Elizabeth Hartnett
Project Director
Plano Chamber of Commerce
P.O. Box 2156
Plano, TX 75074

Dear Ms. Hartnett:

The Tax Team of Scruggs & Pate is looking forward to our presentation on the Taxpayer Relief Act of 1997 and the new business orientation sponsored by the Plano Chamber of Commerce April 29. While we are slightly more than two weeks away from our presentation at the Convention Center, we are actually ahead in our preparation schedule that we provided in our work plan to Mr. Hastings on March 11.

Project Research

We have focused our research on business operations that are most affected by TRA. Your assistant, Jeanette South, has been most helpful in describing the types of new business that have opened in Plano in the past five years. This information has helped us select the examples we will use in explaining the benefits of TRA to small businesses. We will also identify the types of small business that will not benefit from TRA.

Presentation Development

We have prepared short informative handouts on the home office deduction, the health insurance deduction, educational assistance, and capital gains. Each handout contains a summary of provisions of TRA as it applies to those topics. We have also compiled a list of supplementary reading materials, most of which are available in the Plano Public Library. We will provide copies of several short research items that have been prepared by our research group.

Our PowerPoint presentation is designed to guide the audience through the handouts. We will have printed copies of our slides to enable listeners to take notes.

Rehearsal

We have rehearsed our presentation, and we are confident that we can cover the proposed topics in 45 minutes and provide the audience a 15-minute question period. We will be available throughout the morning session to talk with anyone about our presentation.

2100 Brookhaven Parkway, Plano, Texas 75074

214 667-5400   800 997-2376   FAX: 214 555-9734

FIGURE 15-8 • Letter Progress Report

April 11, 1999
Ms. Elizabeth Hartnett

Equipment Requirements

We will bring our own computer, projector, and 75 copies of all handouts. We will need a table for the equipment, a projection screen, and a microphone.

Arrival Time

We plan to arrive at the Convention Center by 8:00 the morning of April 29. Thus, we will be ready to begin our presentation promptly at 9:00. Attached to this letter are short résumés of the members of our tax team to help you during the introduction.

Conclusion

We thank you for the opportunity to be of service to new and prospective members of the Plano business community. The small-business enterprise is the heart of the Plano community, and we look forward to providing information to individuals interested in improving the tax situation for their business. We believe that individuals who wish to launch their own business will receive useful information from our presentation.

If you wish to contact us before April 29, you can call me at 666-2925, ext. 236.

Sincerely,

Jan Gharantz

Pc: Jared Hastings

2100 Brookhaven Parkway, Plano, Texas 75074

214 667-5400   800 997-2376   FAX: 214 555-9734

FIGURE 15-8 • (continued)

▶ PLANNING AND REVISION CHECKLISTS

You will find the Planning and Revision Checklists that follow Chapter 2, Composing, and Chapter 4, Writing for Your Readers, valuable in planning and revising any presentation of technical information. The following questions specifically apply to proposals and progress reports. They summarize the key points in this chapter and provide a checklist for planning and revising.

PROPOSALS

Planning

- Have you studied the RFP carefully?
- Have you made a list of all requirements given in the RFP?
- Who are your readers? Do they have technical competence in the field of the proposal? Is it a mixed audience, some technically educated, some not?
- What problem is the proposed work designed to remedy? What is the immediate background of the problem? Why does the problem need to be solved?
- What is your proposed solution to the problem? What benefits will come from the solution? Is the solution feasible (both practical and applicable)?
- How will you carry out the work proposed? Scope? Methods to be used? Task breakdown? Time and work schedule?
- Do you want to make statements concerning the likelihood of success or failure and the products of the project?
- What facilities and equipment will you need to carry out the project?
- Who will do the work? What are their qualifications for doing the work? Can you obtain references for past work accomplished?
- How much will the work cost? Consider such things as materials, labor, test equipment, travel, administrative expenses, and fees. Who will pay for what?
- Will you need to include an appendix? Consider including biographical sketches, descriptions of earlier projects, and employment practices.
- Will the proposal be better presented in a report format or in a letter or memo format?
- Do you have a student report to propose? Consider including the following in your proposal:

  Subject, purpose, and scope of report

  Task and time breakdown

Resources available

Your qualifications for doing the report

Revision

- Does your proposal have a good design and layout? Does its appearance suggest the high quality of the work you propose to do?
- Does the project summary succinctly state the objectives and plan of the proposed work? Does it show how the proposed work is relevant to the readers' interest?
- Does the introduction make the subject and the purpose of the work clear? Does it briefly point out the so-whats of the proposed work?
- Have you defined the problem thoroughly?
- Is your solution well described? Have you made its benefits and feasibility clear?
- Will your readers be able to follow your plan of work easily? Have you protected yourself by making clear what you will do and what you will not do? Have you been careful not to promise more results than you can deliver?
- Have you carefully considered all the facilities and equipment you will need?
- Have you presented the qualifications of project personnel in an attractive but honest way? Have you asked permission from everyone you plan to use as a reference?
- Is your budget realistic? Will it be easy for the readers to follow and understand?
- Do all the items in the appendix lend credibility to the proposal?
- Have you included a few sentences somewhere that urge the readers to accept the proposal?
- Have you satisfied the needs of your readers? Will they be able to comprehend your proposal? Do they have all the information they need to make a decision?

PROGRESS REPORTS

Planning

- Do you have a clear description of your project available, perhaps in your proposal?
- Do you have all the project tasks clearly defined? Do all the tasks run in sequence, or do some run concurrently? In general, are the tasks going well or badly?
- What items need to be highlighted in your summary and appraisal?
- Are there any problems to be discussed?
- Can you suggest solutions for the problems?

- Is your work ahead of schedule, right on schedule, or behind schedule?
- Are costs running as expected?
- Do you have some unexpected good news you can report?

Revision

- Does your report have an attractive appearance?
- Does the plan you have chosen show off your progress to its best advantage?
- Is your tone authoritative, with an accent on the positive?
- Have you supported your generalizations with facts?
- Does your approach seem fresh or tired?
- Do you have a good balance between work accomplished and work to be done?
- Can your summary and appraisal stand alone? Would they satisfy an executive reader?

► EXERCISES

1. Examine the RFP from the Department of Health and Human Services Figure 15-9 and answer these questions:

   - According to the RFP, what work does HHS want done or what product does it want? What problem does the RFP present to be solved?
   - Does the RFP specify a length for the proposal?
   - Does the RFP make clear the information the proposal must contain?
   - Does the RFP furnish an outline to follow? If so, what does the outline require?
   - Does the RFP require a specific format for the proposal? What is it?
   - Does the RFP make clear the criteria by which submitted proposals will be evaluated and who will do the evaluation?

2. Write an information report to your professor based on Figure 15-9, summarizing what content items the proposal should emphasize and what criteria will be used to evaluate the proposals.

3. You will probably be instructed to write a complete technical report as part of the requirements for your course in technical writing.

DEPARTMENT OF HEALTH AND HUMAN SERVICES

Centers for Disease Control and Prevention

[Announcement 99015]

Development and Support of Research Agenda Needs Related to Injury Prevention and Control; Notice of Availability of Funds

A. Purpose

The Centers for Disease Control and Prevention (CDC) announces the availability of fiscal year (FY) 1999 funds for a cooperative agreement with a multi-disciplined injury control research group to promote collaborative, educational, and scholarly activity in defining the research and training needs for injury control professionals and in developing the field of injury prevention and control.

This program addresses the "Healthy People 2000" priority areas of Unintentional Injury, Violent and Abusive Behavior, and Surveillance and Data Systems.

The purpose of this cooperative agreement is to assist an injury control research group in defining the training needs of the field of injury prevention and control, in synthesizing the expertise of the multiple disciplines of injury control, in disseminating injury research findings, and in serving as a resource for injury researchers and practitioners, all in the context of building and sustaining the field of injury prevention and control.

B. Eligible Applicants

Applications may be submitted by all public and private non-profit organizations and by governments and their agencies; that is, universities, colleges, research institutions, hospitals, and other public and private nonprofit organizations, State and local governments or their bonafide agents, including small, minority and/or women-owned businesses are eligible to apply.

Non-profit organizations must have their tax-exempt status as determined by the Internal Revenue Service (IRS) Code, Section 501(c). Tax-exempt status may be provided by either providing a copy of the current IRS Determination Letter or copy of the pages from the IRS most recent list of 501(c) tax-exempt organization. Proof of tax-exempt status must be provided with the application.

Note: Pub. L. 104-65 states that an organization described in section 501(c)(4) of the Internal Revenue Code of 1986 which engages in lobbying activities shall not be eligible to receive Federal funds constituting an award, grant (cooperative agreement), contract, loan, or any other form.

C. Availability of Funds

Approximately $50,000 is available in FY 1999 to fund one cooperative agreement. It is expected that the award will begin on or about August 1, 1999, and will be made for a 12-month budget period within a project period of up to five years. This funding estimate may vary and is subject to change.

Continuation awards within the project period will be made on the basis of satisfactory progress in meeting objectives and the availability of funds.

D. Program Requirements

In conducting activities to achieve the purpose of this program, the recipient will be responsible for the activities under 1. (Recipient Activities), and CDC will be responsible for the activities listed under 2. (CDC Activities).

1. Recipient Activities:

a. Promote collaborative, educational, and scholarly activity in defining the research and training needs of injury control professionals and in developing the field of injury prevention and control, both clinician and practitioner-oriented, through program development, teaching, and other activities drawing upon expertise from multiple disciplines, settings and perspectives.

b. Facilitate dissemination of the injury research findings of both the federally and non-federally funded community of injury control researchers to enable improvements in injury control policies and programs.

c. Provide a coordinated resource to other researchers and practitioners in accessing expertise in the development of program activities.

d. Sustain a focus on teaching the next generation of injury researchers and practitioners by participating in the development of improved educational opportunities in appropriate disciplines.

e. Promote rigorous evaluation of injury control initiatives through development and dissemination of improved methodologies for program implementation and evaluation.

f. Maintain active liaisons with other organizations, institutions, and agencies whose purposes and functions are similar in order to develop a more comprehensive presence in ongoing discussions defining injury-related issues.

2. CDC Activities:

a. Provide assistance in defining the research and training needs of injury control professionals in the developing field of injury prevention and control.

b. Provide assistance in the provision of a coordinated resource to other researchers, practitioners, and decision makers in accessing the expertise of the multiple disciplines of the field of injury prevention and control.

c. Provide continuing updates on scientific and operational developments related to injury prevention and control as part of a shared dissemination strategy.

E. Application Content

Applications for support of an injury prevention and control cooperative agreement should follow the PHS-398 (Rev. 5/95) application and Errata sheet, and should include the following information:

1. Face page
2. Description (abstract) and personnel
3. Table of contents
4. Detailed budget for the initial budget period: The budget should reflect the composite figures for the cooperative agreement as well as breakdown budgets for individual projects within the cooperative agreement.
5. Budget for the entire proposed project period including budgets pertaining to consortium/contractual arrangements.
6. Biographical sketches of key personnel, consultants, and collaborators.
7. Other support: This listing should include all other funds or resources pending or currently available. For each grant or contract, include source of funds, amount of funding (indicate whether pending or current), date of funding (initiation and termination), and relationship to the proposed program.
8. Resources and environment available to carry out described activities.
9. Operational plan including:

a. A detailed operational plan including value to field, and specific, measurable, and time-framed objectives consistent with the

---

FIGURE 15-9 • Request for Proposal

7894 **Federal Register** / Vol. 64, No. 31 / Wednesday, February 17, 1999 / Notices

proposed activities for each project within the proposed cooperative agreement.

b. A detailed evaluation plan that addresses outcome and cost-effectiveness evaluation as well as formative, efficacy, and process evaluation.

c. A description of the organization and its role in implementing and evaluating the proposed programs. The applicant should clearly specify how disciplines will be integrated to achieve the coordinating organization's objectives.

d. Charts showing the proposed organizational structure of the coordinating organization and its relationship to any broader institution of which it is a part, and, where applicable, to affiliate institutions or collaborating organizations. These charts should clearly detail the lines of authority as they relate to the coordinating organization, both structurally and operationally.

e. Documentation of the public health agencies and other public and private sector entities' involvement in the proposed program, including letters that detail commitments of support and a clear statement of the role, activities, and participating personnel of each agency or entity.

An applicant organization has the option of having specific salary and fringe benefit amounts for individuals omitted from the copies of the application which are made available to outside reviewing groups. To exercise this option: on the original and five copies of the application, the applicant must use asterisks to indicate those individuals for whom salaries and fringe benefits are not shown; the subtotals must still be shown. In addition, the applicant must submit an additional copy of page four of Form PHS-398, completed in full, with the asterisks replaced by the salaries and fringe benefits. This budget page will be reserved for internal staff use only.

Use the information in the Program Requirements, Other Requirements, Evaluation Criteria sections and the Errata Sheet (Addendum 3) to develop the application content. Your application will be evaluated on the criteria listed so it is important to follow them in laying out your program plan. Each application should be limited to 40 pages, excluding attachments.

F. Submission and Deadline

Submit the original and five copies of PHS 398 (OMB Number 0925-0001) and adhere to the instructions on the Errata Instruction Sheet for PHS 398). Forms are in the application kit.

On or before April 20, 1999, submit to: Sharron P. Orum, Grants Management Specialist, Grants Management Branch, Procurement and Grants Office Announcement #99015.

Centers for Disease Control and Prevention (CDC) 2920 Brandywine Road, M/S E-13 Atlanta, GA 30341-4146.

Applications shall be considered as meeting the deadline if they are received at the above address on or before the deadline date; or sent on or before the deadline date, and received in time for an objective review process. Applicants should request a legibly dated U.S. Postal Service postmark or obtain a legibly dated receipt from a commercial carrier or the U.S. Postal Service. Private metered postmarks shall not be acceptable as proof of timely mailing.

G. Evaluation Criteria

Each application will be evaluated individually against the following criteria by an independent review group appointed by CDC:

1. Background and Need (5 percent) The extent to which the applicant describes experience in related projects, and describes the context and needs related to the purpose of this program announcement.

2. Scope, Goals, and Objectives (15 percent) The extent to which the applicant provides relevant long-term goals and short-term objectives which are specific, measurable, time-phased, and achievable.

3. Operational Plan (40 percent) The extent to which the applicant provides an operational plan which addresses achievement of each of the objectives proposed. Does the applicant provide a description of each component or major activity, how it relates to objectives, and how it will be accomplished? Does the plan include a detailed time-line for completion of each component or major activity?

4. Administration and Management (20 percent) The extent to which the organizational structure is described and to which adequate management control systems are in place. Is proposed staffing adequate for completion of activities under this program announcement?

5. Evaluation Plan (20 percent) The extent to which the evaluation plan provides an adequate basis for monitoring and evaluating proposed activities.

6. Budget (not scored) The extent to which the budget is reasonable, clearly justified, and consistent with stated objectives and proposed activities.

H. Other Requirements

Technical Reporting Requirements Provide CDC with original plus two copies of:
1. progress report annually;
2. financial status report, no more than 90 days after the end of the budget period; and
3. final financial status report and performance report, no more than 90 days after the end of the project period.

Send all reports to: Sharron P. Orum Grants Management Specialist Grants Management Branch, Procurement and Grants Office Centers for Disease Control and Prevention (CDC) 2920 Brandywine Road, Mailstop E-13 Atlanta, Georgia 30341-4146.

The following additional requirements are applicable to this program. For a complete description of each see Addendum 1 in the application kit.

AR98-10—Smoke-Free Workplace Requirement

AR98-11—Healthy People 2000

AR98-12—Lobbying Restrictions

AR98-13—Prohibition on Use of CDC funds for Certain Gun Control Activities

AR98-15—Proof of Non-Profit Status

AR98-20—Conference Activities within Grants/Cooperative Agreements

I. Authority and Catalog of Federal Domestic Assistance Number

This program is authorized under Sections 301, 391, 392, 393, and 394 of the Public Health Service Act, [42 U.S.C. 241, 280b, 280b-1, 280b-1a, and 280b-2] as amended. Program regulations are set forth in 42 CFR Part 52. The catalog of Federal Domestic Assistance number is 93.136.

J. Where To Obtain Additional Information

Please refer to Program Announcement 99015 when you request information. To receive additional written information and to request an application kit, call 1-888-GRANTS4 (1-888-471-6874). You will be asked to leave your name and address and you will be instructed to identify the Announcement number of interest.

FIGURE 15-9 • (continued)

Forestry Research Associates
222 University Avenue
Madison, Wisconsin 53707
June 29, 2001
Mr. Lawrence Campbell, Director
Council for Peatlands Development
420 Duluth Street
Grand Forks, ND 58201
Dear Mr. Campbell:

Well, we have our Peatland Water-Table Depth Research Project under way. This is our first progress report. As you know, by ditching peatlands, foresters can control water-table depths for optimum growth of trees on those peatlands. Foresters, however, don't have good data on which water-table depths will encourage optimum tree growth. This study is an attempt to find out what those depths might be. We have to do several things to obtain the needed information. First, we have to measure tree growth on plots at varying distances from existing ditches on peatland. Then we have to establish what the average water-table depth is on the plots during the growing season of June, July, August, and September. To get meaningful growth and water-table depth figures, we have to gather these data for three growing seasons. Finally, we have to correlate average water-table depth with tree growth. Knowing that, foresters can recommend appropriate average water-table depths.

When the snow and ice went out in May, we were able to establish 14 tree plots on northern Minnesota peatlands. Each plot is one-fortieth of a hectare. The distances of the plots from a drainage ditch vary from 1 to 100 meters. The plots have mixed stands of black spruce and tamarack. During June, we measured height and diameter at breast height (DBH) of a random selection of trees on each plot. We marked the measured trees so that we can return to them for future measurements. We will measure them again in September of this year and in June and September of the next two years.

While we were measuring the trees, we began placing two wells on each plot. The wells consist of perforated plastic pipes driven eight feet into the mineral soil that underlies the plot. We should have all the wells in by the end of next week. We'll measure water-table depths once a month in July, August, and September. We will also measure water-table depths any time there is a rainfall of one inch or more on the plots.

We have our research well under way, and we're right on schedule. We have made all our initial tree measurements and will soon obtain our first water-table depth readings.

By the way, the entire test area seems to be composed of raw peat to a depth of about 20 cm with a layer of well-decomposed peat about a meter thick beneath that. However, to be sure there are no soil differences that would introduce an unaccounted-for variable into our calculations, we'll do a soil analysis on each of the 14 plots next summer. We will do this additional work at no extra cost to you. During the cold-weather months, between growing seasons, we'll prepare water-table profiles that will cover each plot for each month of measurement. At the completion of our measurements in the third year, we'll correlate these profiles with the growth measurements on the plots. This correlation should enable us to recommend a water-table depth for optimum growth of black spruce and tamarack. We have promised two progress reports per growing season and one each December. Therefore, we will submit our next report on September 28.

Sincerely,
Robert Weaver
Principal Investigator

FIGURE 15-10 • Progress Report

- Choose two or three topics you would consider to be suitable for a one-semester project.

- Write a feasibility report to your instructor examining each topic in terms of availability of information, suitability of the topic for the amount of time available during the semester, and the significance of each topic to your discipline or to your career goals. Decide which topic seems most feasible.

- Once your instructor has approved your choice of topic, write a proposal to your instructor, using memo format. In your proposal, include all elements commonly found in proposals.

- Write a progress report to describe the status of your semester report project. Design the progress report to reflect the tasks or project goals you used in developing your project proposal.

4. The progress report in Figure 15-10 is poorly organized and formatted. Reorganize it and rewrite it. Use a letter format, but furnish a subject line and the headings readers need to find their way through the report.

Oral Exercises

Before doing these exercises, see Chapter 19, Oral Reports.

5. Prepare an oral version of the proposal you wrote for Exercise 3, and plan on delivering it to your class. You will be allowed eight minutes maximum. Enhance your presentation with computer graphics or overhead transparencies to show anticipated costs, your project schedule, and any visuals that will help explain the significance of your project or the methods you propose to use.

6. Prepare an oral progress report to deliver to your class. You will be allowed five minutes maximum. Enhance your presentation with graphics to show work completed, work remaining, project costs to date, and status of your project.

SCENARIO

You are a captain and the base engineer at a large army post in Mississippi. It's an old base. Most of its housing, 2,000 units in all, dates back to the Korean War. The gas heating and electric air conditioning systems in the units are expensive to run and maintain. They frequently break down, and they heat and cool inefficiently. The heaters have recently caused several fires. You and the base commander have agreed that the equipment must be replaced. But with what?

You decide you need a feasibility study that will lead to a feasibility report to the base commander. As you study the problem, it's clear that the choice lies between updated (and more efficient versions) of the current equipment and geothermal heat pumps (GHPs).

The criteria for the choice begin to emerge: initial cost, maintenance cost, energy cost, efficiency, safety, and environmental impact. Luckily, you have a pilot program at Fort Polk in Louisiana to draw data from. Results there indicate that GHPs are better by every criterion. It becomes clear what your final recommendation will be. Now, you have to organize and write a report to support that recommendation.

For details on how to structure recommendation reports, read on in this chapter.

chapter 16

Recommendation Reports

▶ An Informal Report: The Church Repair Project
The Situation
Important Features of Report

▶ A Formal Report: The Oil Spill Problem
The Situation
Important Features of Report

▶ A Feasibility Report: Department Store Location
Logic of the Feasibility Study
Preparation of the Feasibility Report
The Situation
Important Features of Report

▶ A Final Word

Our purpose in this chapter is to give you a sense of the large class of reports known as recommendation reports. Recommendation reports present data, draw conclusions from the data, and make recommendations based on the data and the conclusions. If the person making the report has the authority to do so, the recommendations may be presented as decisions. The feasibility report, the last report presented in this chapter, has fairly standard features. However, many recommendation reports have no particular or prescribed format or organization beyond the need to do the following:

- Introduce the report.
- Present enough data in words and visuals to justify any conclusions drawn.
- Discuss and evaluate the data.
- Summarize the data.
- Draw conclusions from the data.
- Present recommendations based upon the data and the conclusions.

In presenting your report, choose a content, style, tone, and design suitable for your purpose and your audience. A careful reading of Parts I and II in this book will help you make the right choices. The methods of analysis presented in Chapter 10, Analyzing Information, are particularly useful for recommendation reports.

Your choice may be to present your report as a formal report, using all or some of the format features described in Report Format in Appendix B. Or you may choose a less formal method of presentation, such as a letter or memo (see Letter and Memorandum Format in Appendix B).

To help you with the choices you have to make, we present three sample reports in this chapter, each developed to meet a different situation. Studying these reports will show how the writers developed their reports to meet their situations. Applying what you learn will help you design and write your reports to meet your situations.

We show each report in an annotated figure. We describe the situation that generated the report and point out important features of the report.

► AN INFORMAL REPORT: THE CHURCH REPAIR PROJECT

Many reports are best designed and written as informal reports, usually presented as a letter or memo. Such was the case in our first example.

The Situation

Graham and Simpson is an architectural consulting firm that specializes in analyzing construction problems. The membership of a historic New England church has hired Graham and Simpson to determine why the chimneys of the church are leaking and to recommend solutions to the problem. Tim Fong, the managing engineer on the project, writes an internal report to Eben Graham, one of the principals of Graham and Simpson, who is dealing directly with the church repair committee (see Figure 16-1). Tim has two purposes in his report: (1) to report to Eben the progress his team has made, and (2) to alert Eben to the seriousness of the problems and let him know what his recommendations will be. With this information, Eben can deal with the church committee in an informed, responsible, and ethical way.

Important Features of Report

- For short internal documents, an informal memorandum design is often the best choice. The choice eliminates such things as title pages and tables of contents, needed for long reports but not usually needed for short reports. Information and analysis are presented quickly and with little formality.
- Both the subject line, functioning here like a report title, and the introduction make the subject and purpose immediately clear.
- The conclusions section both summarizes the damage and reaches conclusions concerning the damage. The summary and recommendations are presented up front in numbered lists. Executives like key information to appear early in reports and summaries, conclusions, and recommendations are certainly key information.
- The design of the "Field Observations" portion of the report allows the reader to easily find and easily read the information presented (see Chapter 11). Headings and subheadings guide the reader. Short paragraphs arranged in list fashion make the extent of the damage to the two chimneys immediately clear.
- Because the report is in part a progress report (see Chapter 15), in "General Observations of the Roof Structure" the writer describes future work. He concludes with sources for additional information in case the reader has questions.

▶ A FORMAL REPORT: THE OIL SPILL PROBLEM

Long complicated reports, particularly for an external audience, need a design that guides the reader to the information in the report. These more formal designs call for such features as title pages, letters of transmittal, and tables of content (see Chapter 11). Such is the case in the oil spill report. Although such design features create what is known as a formal report, their use is not really meant to increase formality. Rather, report writers use them to help readers find their way in a report.

Report purpose

Conclusions and recommendations up front

TO: Eben Graham   DATE: August 20, 2001

FROM: Tim Fong

SUBJECT: Status of Investigation of Masonry Deterioration and Leakage, The First Church, Nashua, NH

Jane Hazel, James Portales, and I have examined two of the chimneys of The First Church. The following points should aid you in preliminary conversations with First Church to inform them of the extent of damage. We will have a final letter report for the Church by 10/1/01 that will include repair estimates for all three chimneys and the roof.

Conclusions

The two chimneys we have examined are badly deteriorated and require extensive repairs to stop the leakage and to eliminate an increasing danger of falling debris.

(1) Leakage through faulty flashing can be stopped easily and effectively by repairing the flashings.

(2) Leakage through the stone masonry cannot be stopped effectively because the chimney masonry is badly deteriorated. The stones in the chimneys have shifted, thereby enlarging the stone joints and creating horizontal surfaces that catch water. Water entering the masonry can bypass the lead counterflashing internally and enter the building. Freeze–thaw action on the wet stone masonry has slowly pushed the stones apart. The stones in the chimneys are not mechanically tied together to prevent movement.

(3) Unless major repairs are made to the two chimneys and the bell tower, significant deterioration will occur in wood decking and masonry. The damage will cause dangerous conditions from falling debris. Eventually, the structural safety of the church will be threatened.

Recommendations

(1) We recommend removal of any chimney not needed. The work should include removal of the chimneys to below the roof level, repair of all deteriorated wood about the chimney, installation of a new roof deck, and installation of new roofing slate to match the existing roof.

FIGURE 16-1 • Church Repair Project

Eben Graham   -2-   August 20, 2001

(2) Any chimney scheduled to remain should be demolished and reconstructed with the exterior stones. Reconstruction should include new clay flue liners, steel reinforcing in the horizontal joints of the stone masonry, and new stainless steel or copper through-wall flashings. The roofing around the chimney should be repaired with new metal base flashing of the same metal used for the through-wall flashing.

(3) The wood components of the deck should be thoroughly examined and replaced or repaired, as required by the rotted conditions. Repairs should include exploratory operations into hidden conditions to ensure all deteriorated wood is repaired.

(4) Reconstruction of the interior finishes on the church should be delayed until all repair work is complete and tested.

Field Observations

We have examined both the interior and the exterior of both chimneys.

Support for
conclusions

Chimney No. 1

Chimney 1 has extensive problems with wood and masonry.

Interior Observations

* The chimney is constructed of brick below the roof deck.

* The underside of the roof deck and joists are water stained on four sides of the chimney. The heaviest staining occurs on the north side of the chimney, which is the low point of the surrounding roof.

* A gutter has been installed at the low side of the chimney to catch leakage water and direct it to trash barrels.

* The low header in the roof deck framing on the north side of the chimney opening is wet and extensively rotted, allowing easy insertion of a two-inch pocket knife. Large pieces of the rotted wood are easily removed by hand.

* The remaining structural components surrounding the chimney are sound, based on our visual examination from the attic space.

FIGURE 16-1 • (continued)

Eben Graham   -3-   August 20, 2001

Exterior Observations

* The chimney is capped with roofing cement and fabric membrane (see Photo 1).

* The mortar joints have been coated with a caulking material (see Photo 1 and Photo 2).

* A cricket made of copper sheet metal is located on the roof above the chimney (see Photo 3). There is one small crack in a soldered seam on the ridge of the cricket.

* After lifting the counterflashing on the cricket, we found a large hole in the membrane (see Photo 3). Water draining over the roof and onto the cricket enters through this hole into the building.

* Some of the granite blocks in the chimney have shifted, and the mortar joints are open slightly.

Chimney No. 2

Our examination shows that Chimney 2 is also in a highly deteriorated state.

Interior Observations

* The roof deck and structural components surrounding the chimney are stained from water leakage, but all components are sound, as far as we can tell without removing any decking.

Exterior Observations

* The chimney is capped with roofing cement and fabric membrane.

* The mortar joints have been coated with a caulking material.

* The flue lining is brick, which has deteriorated. The mortar joints of the lining are heavily eroded (see Photo 4).

* The granite blocks that form the exterior width of the chimney have shifted outward, leaving many of the horizontal and vertical stone joints open (see Photo 5).

Report & design separates the two chimneys

FIGURE 16-1 • (*continued*)

Eben Graham   -3-   August 20, 2001

* Some horizontal stone joints are completely open. We examined these joints at the corners of the chimney for the presence of metal ties between stones. We found no ties.

* We saw no defects in the metal flashings at the base of the chimney.

General Observations of the Roof Structure

Work remaining

We are currently examining the roof surfaces of The First Church to determine the presence of deterioration resulting from the leakage about the chimneys. We will send results of these findings to you by 9/25/01 along with photos that support our observations.

We still need to examine Chimney No. 3 carefully, but our visual observations suggest that the problems with No. 3 are similar to those of No. 1 and No. 2.

We plan to provide photos for Chimney No. 3 as well as sections of the roof, if visual inspection of the roofing near No. 3 suggests that water damage has occurred.

Please contact

Jane Hazel about interior observations (ext. 2165)
James Portales about exterior observations (ext. 2171).

I will be in Orono for the structural design conference until August 25.

FIGURE 16-1 • (continued)

The Situation

R. J. Meyers and Associates, Environmental Engineering and Consulting, has the task of determining whether oil spills at a British Petroleum facility can be controlled by containment booming. The Environmental Protection Agency (EPA) will not permit the use of chemical dispersants for controlling oil spills at this locality. Larry Payne, a consulting engineer with R. J. Meyers, has the task of investigating and solving the problem. The report in Figure 16-2 describes his investigation and details the recommendations he came to. Like many such reports, it has mixed elements. Although it is primarily a recommendation report, it is partly an instructional document (see Chapter 18) and partly a research report (see Chapter 17). To help his readers sort out and find the various elements of his report, Larry uses a formal report design.

Important Features of Report

- Larry writes the letter of transmittal in a somewhat informal style, indicating that he has a friendly relationship with the recipient, R. G. Rolan. If such a relationship did not exist, or if the letter were going to a culture that values formality, Larry would have to be more formal (see Chapter 7). As is common, the letter of transmittal briefly summarizes the report something that would be appreciated by a busy executive.

- The introduction serves several purposes. It makes subject and purpose clear. It indicates the plan of development of the report. Finally, it reassures the reader that the recommendations will meet all government regulations and reduce costs for British Petroleum (BP).

- The section of the report labeled "Summary: Oil Spill Response at BP's Marcus Hook Facility" is an excellent executive summary (see Report Format in Appendix B). It provides background information, explains the nature of the problem, gives the major implications (conclusions) of the data, and provides a summary of the recommendations. A busy executive would have every thing needed right here.

- Pages 3 through 9 provide instruction on boom containment and provide the theory that suggests that an angled boom deployment will be more effective than a straight-line deployment. The section is written on the assumption that readers of the report may not know how such booms work. If a reader wants the information it's in the report. For readers who don't want the information, the good design of the report with its headings and subheadings makes it easy to skip or skim over the technical parts. Chapter 18 and two sections in Chapter 9 (Mechanism Description and Process Description) are useful in learning how to write such instruction and description.

FIRST-LINE OIL SPILL RESPONSE RECOMMENDATIONS
FOR BRITISH PETROLEUM'S
MARCUS HOOK FACILITY

J. Larry Payne
R. J. Meyers and Associates
Environmental Engineering and Consulting

November 26, 2001

FIGURE 16-2 • The Oil Spill Problem

November 26, 2001

Letter of
transmittal

British Petroleum Oil Company Ltd.
520 Smith Street
Marcus Hook, PA 20190

Attention: R. G. Rolan
            Environmental Coordinator

Subject: First-Line Oil Spill Response Recommendations for
            British Petroleum's Marcus Hook Facility

Dear Bob:

Report purpose
and central
recommendation

Attached is our final report of first-line oil spill response recommendations for your personnel at the Marcus Hook facility. Our analysis indicates that containment booming can be effective if deployment techniques are adapted to swift water conditions.

Summary
arguments for the
recommendation

We have verified with Michael Flaherty of the EPA's Chemical Countermeasures Division that dispersant application within the Delaware River is not a viable response option. Therefore, containment booming as a response option is mandated by Annex X of the National Contingency Plan.

During our site assessment the first week of November, Clyde Strong and I worked with BP personnel to develop the angled method of boom deployment outlined in the report. We are confident that this strategy will work well for your personnel.

You will also note our recommendations to purchase an additional 3,500 feet of boom and 1 extra tow vessel. Since you have 1,500 feet of SLICKBAR boom, we've suggested that you stick with this brand. The SLICKBAR boom will cost less than half what a compactible boom will run and it will easily meet your needs based on our field trials. Another tow vessel similar to your MONARK will also be required.

Based on our analysis, BP's capital equipment investment will be less than your $200,000 ceiling (see the report for our estimates). The only other expenses you will need to consider are training costs to bring your

FIGURE 16-2 • (continued)

R. G. Rolan -2- November 26, 2001

personnel up to speed on the new deployment method. We'll be happy to discuss this with you in detail and submit a detailed proposal after the first of the year.

Finally, if you need information on equipment purchases give me a call. Should you decide to stay with SLICKBAR we'll need to get you in touch with John Sullivan and Russ Blair in Connecticut. If you want to consider a compactible boom, you'll need to contact Frank Meyer with Kepner Plastics in Torrance, California.

Thanks again for your hospitality and assistance in setting up the equipment trials. If you have any questions, please give us a call. If holidays intervene, call me at home (409) 779-8899.

Best regards,

J. Larry Payne

J. Larry Payne

JLP/mlp

enc:

Further information supporting the implementation of the solution

Note that the style of the transmittal letter is informal and personal. Sentences are concise and direct. The transmittal offers a brief summary of the report.

FIGURE 16-2 • *(continued)*

TABLE OF CONTENTS

INTRODUCTION
SUMMARY: OIL SPILL RESPONSE AT BP's MARCUS HOOK FACILITY

Background Information 1
Nature of the Problem 2
Major Implications 2
Summary of Recommendations 2

DETAILED DISCUSSION

Basic Boom Design 3
Modes of Boom Failure 5
Traditional Boom Deployment Methods 7
Adapting Containment Booms to Swift Current Applications 8

FINDINGS

Field Trial 10
Recommendations 11

FIGURE 16-2 • (*continued*)

INTRODUCTION

Report subject

Product volume and proximity to environmentally sensitive wetlands render BP's Marcus Hook facility susceptible to major oil spill difficulties. Viability of the only possible first-line response measure, containment booming, is severely compromised by swift currents in the Delaware River. This study provides the following:

Report purpose

1. A discussion of the background and nature of the problem.
2. An analysis of conventional booming methods and their limitations.
3. Recommended alterations in booming techniques to enhance BP's first spill response effectiveness.

Recommendations made by R. J. Meyers and Associates, Inc., comply with all pertinent local, state, and federal spill response regulations. Implementing these recommendations will significantly reduce BP's spill liability and cleanup costs.

SUMMARY: OIL SPILL RESPONSE AT BP's MARCUS HOOK FACILITY

Background information

The British Petroleum (BP) facility at Marcus Hook lies in one of the busiest product corridors in the United States. Maximum daily throughput capacity is 75,000 barrels of sweet crude oil. The average monthly processing rate exceeds 1 million barrels. Throughput volume alone signifies considerable potential for a major oil spill.

In addition, BP's facility sits in the midst of numerous environmentally sensitive areas that line the Delaware River. River currents running between 1.5 and 2.5 knots are capable of driving an uncontained oil spill into those wetlands, adversely affecting wildlife populations in Pennsylvania, New Jersey, and Delaware.

During the past decade BP has experienced three major spills at the Marcus Hook facility as well as a number of lesser incidents. Cleanup costs for these spills (excluding federal penalties, habitat restoration, and third-party damage claims) have ranged from an estimated low of $75 to an estimated high of $400 per barrel of oil spilled.

FIGURE 16-2 • (continued)

Nature of the Problem

The throughput volume, the environmentally sensitive location of the facility, and the swift river currents in the area require an immediate and effective first-line response strategy.

First-line spill response methods available to BP emergency crews are limited to containment booming operations. While large spills at sea can be dispersed with chemical agents or burned with incendiary devices, environmental factors and regulatory restrictions preclude these actions in the Marcus Hook area.

Major Implications

An evaluation of pertinent factors indicates that containment booming of an oil spill at BP's Marcus Hook facility constitutes the only first-line response action open to BP spill response personnel.

However, current speeds in the Delaware River (exceeding 1.5 knots) are not compatible with conventional containment booming strategies. Quite simply, traditional methods of containment booming fail catastrophically in such currents. If containment booming is to be effective, some means of adapting traditional methods to swift water situations must be devised.

Field studies conducted at the Marcus Hook facility in early November, 2001, demonstrated that conventional booming strategies could be modified to accommodate the local swift currents. Additional work in the area of angling boom directly into currents exceeding 0.75 knot is expected to further improve swift water containment capabilities.

Summary of Recommendations

Brief statement of recommendation discussed in detail on p. 11.

1. BP emergency response teams should receive prompt training in swift current boom deployment tactics.

2. 5,000 feet of round boom should be stockpiled at two locations for rapid deployment. (This requires purchasing 3,500 feet of boom at an estimated cost of $105,000)

3. 3.Two tow vessels should be equipped and available on a 24-hour basis for boom deployment. (This requires purchasing one vessel at an estimated cost of $56,500.)

4. Follow-up drills and hands-on training should be conducted regularly to improve BP's response capabilities.

-2-

FIGURE 16-2 • (continued)

DETAILED DISCUSSION

Basic Boom Design

Description of how boom containment works

Spill containment booms are designed to contain and control the movement of oil floating on the water's surface. Booms are not effective with emulsions, sinking products, or water-soluble materials. A flotation unit or freeboard corrals the floating slick on the surface while a flexible skirt or draft prevents oil from passing beneath the boom (see Figure 1).

Verbal discussion correlates with the visual aid.

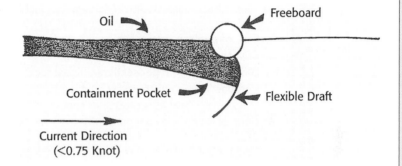

Figure 1. Cross-sectional view of round boom in low current.

Most containment booms rely upon round freeboard designs with flotation units ranging in diameter from 6 to 10 inches. Experience has shown that booms having round freeboards within this size range sufficiently limit splashover (oil sloshing over the top of the boom) in windy conditions. Field observations and informal boom tests conducted at the Environmental Protection Agency's Oil and Hazardous Material Simulated Environmental Test Tank (OHMSETT) in Leonardo, New Jersey, seem to support the contention that a round freeboard design helps limit splashover largely because of the reserve buoyancy inherent in the configuration.

FIGURE 16-2 • (*continued*)

Similar tests at OHMSETT indicate that boom drafts of between 12 and 16 inches in length work best to restrict carryunder (oil being entrained and carried beneath the boom by swift currents). Most boom drafts consist of flexible laminated plastic skirts that are attached to the freeboard. In low current situations (<0.75 knot) the skirt flexes with the current to form a cuplike containment pocket directly beneath the freeboard that aids containment and restricts carryunder (see Figure 1).

Many booms are manufactured from closed-cell plastic compounds that are resistant to hydrocarbons, industrial solvents, ultraviolet rays (sunlight), and salt water. In addition, booms should retain their flexibility during cold weather. Other major design considerations include:

1. Ease of deployment
2. Cost and availability
3. Length and weight per section or linear foot
4. Compactibility and storage requirements
5. Maintenance and repair requirements
6. General shape and configuration

Compactible or "compressible" booms are designed to fold up in an accordion fashion to facilitate storage. These types require little storage space compared to rigid booms and are characteristically easy to deploy. As the compressed sections are pulled into the water by a tow vessel, they expand and inflate themselves with ambient air. Compactible booms are becoming increasingly popular and demonstrate excellent wave conformity capabilities.

-4-

FIGURE 16-2 • (continued)

Modes of Boom Failure

Containment booms generally fail in one of two ways. In unprotected open water areas, oil may escape by splashing over the freeboard. Surface chop conditions usually result in minimal splashover. However, sustained winds in excess of 20 knots may result in catastrophic boom failure. Fortunately, BP's Marcus Hook facility is situated in a well-protected area with little threat of splashover.

However, booms are also subject to failure by carryunder. Carryunder, as noted earlier, is a failure mode whereby oil becomes entrained in swift water and is forcefully carried beneath the boom's draft later surfacing downstream (see Figure 2).

Visual aid is introduced, then discussed.

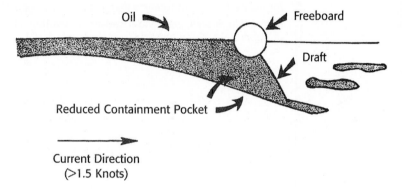

Figure 2.   Cross-sectional view of round boom failure in swift current.

While carryunder is simple and easy to understand in principle, the hydrodynamic factors involved are quite complex. As Figure 2 illustrates, swift water causes the boom's flexible draft to plane or roll with the current such that most of the containment pocket is lost. Consequently, some oil is pulled down the face of the boom directly into the swift current. As the oil

FIGURE 16-2 • (continued)

Methods of countering potential problems with boom containment

reaches the bottom of the boom's draft, water rushing past the skirt exerts a sort of venturi effect that actually pulls the oil beneath and past the boom.

A seemingly easy solution involves simply increasing the boom's draft length to compensate for the planing effect and help restore a larger containment pocket. Contrary to logic, extending the boom's draft has virtually no effect on the boom's ability to reduce carryunder in swift currents. OHMSETT tests show that increasing a boom's draft to even 36 inches does not appreciably limit carryunder. In fact, field trials in which the boom's draft was actually anchored to the streambed and held immobile against current flow reveal that carryunder persists in currents exceeding 1.5 knots. Various mathematical models have been proposed to account for this phenomenon. To date, no satisfactory model has been formulated. The fact remains that in currents comparable to those in the Marcus Hook area, carryunder causes conventional booming procedures to fail.

-6-

FIGURE 16-2 • (continued)

Traditional Boom Deployment Methods

Methods of implementing boom containment

As mentioned previously, containment booming is the only federally approved response tactic available for use by BP emergency response crews. Yet, past spills have demonstrated conclusively that conventional booms fail in swift currents. It appears that BP emergency teams are saddled with only one approved first line response tactic and that it is doomed to fail in the swift currents of the Delaware River.

Figure 3 is introduced.

Traditionally, spill containment booms are deployed in a straight line between two points as illustrated in Figure 3.

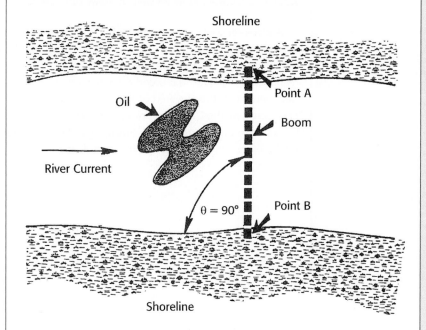

Figure 3.   Traditional straight–line boom deployment.

FIGURE 16-2 • (*continued*)

Figure 3 is discussed.

Note in Figure 3 that θ (the angle between the boom and the shoreline) is a 90° angle. The rationale underlying this straight-line deployment method is difficult to explain. It seems likely to have evolved as a result of untrained crews stringing the boom along the shortest distance between two points as a simple matter of convenience. Boom manufacturers, too, may have inadvertently contributed to this practice by demonstrating their products deployed in such a configuration. Finally, since some booms cost as much as $95 per linear foot, this straight-line deployment requires a minimal amount of boom to seal off a waterway.

Adapting Containment Booms to Swift Current Applications

A week-long site analysis of the Marcus Hook waterfront terminal was conducted by C. B. Strong and J. L. Payne November 2001. An evaluation of current speeds, available containment equipment, and traditional response techniques reinforced the notion that traditional boom deployment methods were not feasible. Recalling equipment tests conducted by the Canadian Environmental Protection Service (EPS) on the St. Lawrence River in 1980, Strong and Payne considered the boom to shoreline angle (u) to be the most easily manipulated deployment variable.

FIGURE 16-2 • (*continued*)

Logic suggested that by varying θ, the boom could be angled directly *into* the current to reduce the current load on the boom. A reduction in current loading along the face of the boom, it was thought, might also restrict carryunder. Strong and Payne also suggested that the boom—even if some carryunder occurred—would improve containment by deflecting oil out of the middle of the stream where currents tend to be greatest toward the calmer waters along the shoreline (see Figure 4).

Figure 4
visualizes written
recommendations.

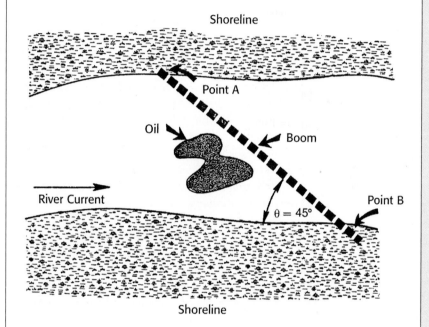

Figure 4.   Angled deployment deflection method.

The sharper angle θ is, with respect to the shoreline, the better the containment and deflection capabilities of the boom.

-9-

FIGURE 16-2 • *(continued)*

Research support-
ing the use of
boom containment

FINDINGS

Field Trials

Field trials conducted at Marcus Hook on November 5, 2001, showed that such an angled deployment strategy effectively contained a test slick of dyed rapeseed oil (a biodegradable product approved by the EPA for field tests) in a current estimated at 2.0 knots. The boom was deployed at an angle of roughly 40 degrees to the shoreline, compared with the traditional 90-degree angle.

Containment boom used during the trials was SLICKBAR MARK IV harbor boom. A total of 1,500 feet (three 500-foot sections joined with coupling plates) was towed into place by a 21-foot MONARK aluminum trihull workboat powered by twin 50-hp Johnson outboard motors. Both the boom and the workboat were part of BP's emergency response equipment available at Marcus Hook.

No difficulties were noted during the trials. The boom was easily towed into the 2.0-knot current by the workboat and performed well. Boom recovery operations were also routine.

While greater lengths of boom are required to implement this deployment strategy, there do not appear to be any major drawbacks. As noted, the trihull MONARK craft easily handled the boom in swift currents. However, attempting to deploy the boom from a single-engine shallow-draft boat is likely to create problems. Use of the facility's 17-foot Boston Whaler as a tracking or chase vessel revealed that this shallow-draft vessel was subject to problems caused by wind advection. Such a tendency to drift would probably combine with river currents in an additive fashion, making the boat unmanageable and dangerous to operate.

The SLICKBAR MARK IV round boom seemed well suited to the task. Towing characteristics were good, and the boom deflected the test slick well. There is some speculation that a compactible boom may reduce current drag and be a bit easier to tow. However, since the vessel had no trouble towing the facility's present boom, this advantage is slight.

Further trials need to be conducted to compare the performance of round booms with others in this deployment mode. It seems likely that round booms will perform better in swift currents than fence booms; however, this is mere speculation based on general characteristics of boom design.

-10-

FIGURE 16-2 • (continued)

Recommendations

Narrative statement of recommendations that are briefly listed on page 2

While BP's emergency response crews face a difficult situation in the event of an oil spill, the challenge can be dealt with effectively. Response teams must be trained promptly in the alternative method of swift water boom deployment outlined in this report. Traditional straight-line boom deployment techniques should be discontinued.

In addition, response crews must have access to appropriate containment equipment. At Marcus Hook, an additional 3,500 feet of SLICKBAR MARK IV should be purchased to complement the 1,500 feet already available at the facility. The boom (a total of 5,000 feet) should be stockpiled in two strategic locations (2,500 feet at each site) for rapid access and deployment. The estimated cost for the additional boom at $30 per foot is $105,000.

Although an argument can be made for replacing the SLICKBAR MARK IV boom with one of the increasingly popular compactible booms, such a move does not seem economically feasible. Replacing the SLICKBAR would require the purchase of 5,000 feet of boom. Costs for compactible boom range in excess of $60 per foot. Hence, minimum estimated costs for the boom would be $300,000. Since the SLICKBAR boom has already demonstrated its effectiveness in field trials, there seems to be little rationale for replacing it.

One additional tow vessel comparable to BP's 21-foot MONARK craft should be purchased and placed on standby to help deploy the boom. The estimated cost for a fully outfitted 21-foot MONARK vessel is $56,500. It is essential that two boats be available (one vessel for each 2,500-foot stockpile) to simultaneously deploy the boom. Again, the 21-foot MONARK has already demonstrated its suitability in field trials. The 17-foot Boston Whaler currently used as a backup by dockside personnel is not sufficient as a deployment vessel. This vessel's shallow draft and limited power are not suited to swift currents, and using it under such conditions would endanger the crew.

BP should provide adequate hands-on-training for all emergency response team members at the facility. Swift-water containment strategies should be emphasized, and the response personnel should become familiar with their equipment and its limitations. Cooperative training efforts with the Del-Bay Oil Spill Cooperative under the direction of Paul Eckert are recommended.

Once the necessary equipment has been purchased and response crews have received proper training and practice, BP's Marcus Hook group should be able to contend effectively with a major spill incident at the facility.

-11-

FIGURE 16-2 • (continued)

- Not content with providing only theory to validate the choice of angled boom containment, the author on page 10 reports field research conduced on the BP site that supports the theory.
- On page 11, the author provides a narrative statement of the recommendations that are listed on page 2. The narrative both states and supports the recommendations.

▶ A FEASIBILITY REPORT: DEPARTMENT STORE LOCATION

A feasibility report is a recommendation report that reports the results of a feasibility study. Feasibility is determined by the answers to questions concerning technological possibility, economic practicality, social desirability, environmental soundness, and so forth. The feasibility report presents, interprets, and summarizes the data relevant to feasibility. It presents the conclusions of the study and recommends actions to be taken.

Before discussing the preparation of a feasibility report, let's examine the feasibility study of which the report is the end product. Although exactly how you would conduct a feasibility study would depend upon your discipline and your level of expert knowledge, we can, in general terms, describe the conduct of a study for you.

Logic of the Feasibility Study

A feasibility study involves a choice among options. The options may involve doing something or not doing it. Or, given the decision that something should be done, the choice may lie among the options available to do it. At all levels of human activity, from the individual engrossed in personal and domestic problems to the highest level of policy making in government, we live in a society where such decision making goes on:

- Homeowners may discuss whether to replace the worn-out furnace with a new conventional furnace or to switch to a heat pump.
- A city council may debate whether to install a downtown heating plant and sell heat to local businesses.
- A company may study the feasibility of manufacturing a new product.
- A company may want to know whether land it owns near an interstate highway should be developed into a shopping mall, a business park, or some combination of both.
- The governments of the United States, Canada, and Mexico may study the feasibility of a $300 billion water system to bring water from Alaska and the Yukon to the rest of Canada and the United States and to Mexico.

At any level, a feasibility study involves steps like these:

- Setting the purpose and scope of the study
- Gathering and checking information
- Analyzing data
- Reaching conclusions
- Arriving at a decision or recommendation

Because formulating purpose and scope is so critical to the success of a feasibility study, we discuss them at some length here.

Purpose Before you do any research, define the precise purpose of all the work you will do. Usually, a single sentence is ideal for the purpose statement:

> The purpose of this investigation is to determine whether X Company of Old Town should establish a branch plant in New Town.

An announcement such as this may seem easy and self-evident, perhaps superfluous. But many investigators have floundered around and eventually bogged down simply because they did not clearly and consciously formulate the objective toward which they were striving.

Here are some additional examples of purpose statements:

- The purpose of this study is to determine the feasibility of using particle board to sheathe the interior of houseboats.
- The purpose of this investigation is to select the best methods for instructing elementary schoolchildren about the effects of toxic pollution on water quality.
- Our primary objective is to decide which of several microcomputers would be the best choice for the Department of Mechanical Engineering to purchase.

Scope Once the purpose of a feasibility study has been clearly and exactly decided, you must determine the methods of accomplishing your purpose. The methods chosen dictate the scope of the study, that is, the actions to be taken, the range of data to be gathered, the bounds to be set in studying the problem, and the criteria against which you will measure possible solutions. To illustrate, let us use our purpose statement example:

Purpose

- Should X Company of Old Town establish a branch plant in New Town?

Scope

- Does X Company now have, or can it develop, enough business in New Town to justify a branch there?

- Does New Town offer adequate physical facilities, utilities, and other services for plant operation there—office space, transportation, communications, and so forth?
- Can the required staff be obtained, whether by local hiring or moving personnel into the area, or both?
- Are local business practices and codes, tax structure, and so forth favorable for conducting business there?
- What effect, for better and worse, would opening a branch plant in New Town have upon overall company organization, operations, policy, and financial condition?

From such an initial statement of scope, the investigation can proceed, although the questions asked may be broadened and rephrased. As an investigator you should not remain blindly committed to your initial statement of scope but should reexamine it from time to time in the light of the information you gather. Look for holes, overlaps, superfluous items, and the like. Frequently, a person unacquainted with the study is in a far better position than you to spot shortcomings and illogicalities in the statement. Therefore, you should ask someone outside the study to review and react to the list of scope items you compile.

Preparation of the Feasibility Report

Your feasibility study will be complete when you have fulfilled your purpose and scope, that is, when you have gathered, checked, and analyzed your data, reached your conclusions, and arrived at your recommendation or decision. At that point you will need to plan your report.

Your feasibility report may include all or some of the following elements:

- Letter of transmittal or preface
- Title page
- Table of contents
- List of illustrations
- Glossary of terms
- Executive summary
- Introduction
- Discussion
- Summary
- Conclusions
- Recommendations

- Appendixes
- References

How many of these elements you include will depend upon audience factors and the length and complexity of the report. For example, a long report aimed at a narrow audience of several people should have a letter of transmittal. A long report for a more general audience would have a preface instead. A short feasibility report of only several pages may be cast as a memorandum or letter and essentially consist of only an executive summary, discussion, conclusions, and recommendations.

We discuss all the elements you may need for a feasibility report in Appendix B. As with all recommendation reports, the methods of analysis presented in Chapter 10, Analyzing Information, are particularly useful for feasibility reports.

A report based upon the feasibility of X Company establishing a branch plant in New Town could be based upon the criteria used in the investigation. The complete plan of the report, then might look like this:

Letter of Transmittal
Title Page
Table of Contents
Executive Summary: Should Company establish a branch plant in New Town, yes or no? Why?
Introduction
 Subject, purpose, and scope of study
 Reasons for conducting study
 Procedures used for conducting study
Analysis of Factors Determining the Establishment of a Branch
Plant in New Town
 Estimated profitability of new branch Facilities
  Existing office space
  Utilities
  Transportation
  Communication
  Land prices and availability
  Local construction prices
 Business climate
  Tax structure
  Building codes
  Business regulations
  Economic health

Personnel
  Local labor market
  Personnel available for transfer
Quality of life in New Town
  Schools
  Cost of living
Effect on X Company of establishing a branch plant
  Existing organization
  Existing operations
  Company policy
  Financial resources
Summary
Conclusions
Recommendations
References
Appendixes

Generally speaking, the readers of feasibility reports are not experts in the field of the study. The users of an environmental impact study—a type of feasibility report—may be citizens' groups and state legislators. In industry, the users of feasibility studies will be the executives responsible for making decisions. All these diverse audiences, are, in general, acting as executives, and reports for them should be written in a manner suitable for executives. Write in plain language, avoiding technical jargon when possible. Give necessary definitions and background information. Use suitable graphics. Emphasize consequences and function over methodology and theory. Interpret your data and state clearly the conclusions and recommendations that your best professional judgment leads you to.

For the most part, feasibility studies are conducted by experts in the field of the study or, in many cases, teams of experts from several fields. For example, environmental impact studies are specialized forms of feasibility study used in deciding whether some new project, perhaps a new highway, is environmentally sound. Such studies may bring together in a collaborative effort, civil engineers, wildlife biologists, soil scientists, archaeologists, and so forth.

However, students are capable of writing good feasibility reports. They can use real problems in their discipline that need solving, or they can role-play as problem solvers in an occupation they may some day have. The student Jennifer Youngren, whose report we show you now, chose to role-play an executive in a department store chain asked to choose the location for a new store.

The Situation

Kate Hanson, chief executive officer for Haley's Department Stores, must decide where to locate a new Haley's store in Cass, Ohio. The choice has been narrowed down to two empty store locations, one in a mall and one in the downtown area. She asks Jennifer Youngren, her chief financial officer, to investigate and make a recommendation. She asks Jennifer to pay particular attention to lease arrangements and the accessibility and nature of each location. The feasibility report in Figure 16-3 is the result of Jennifer's investigation. While the report is not particularly long, it is complex, and Jennifer chose to give it elements such as an executive summary and a table of contents to make the document more accessible to Kate.

Important Features of Report

- The title page carries all the information needed and is simple and uncluttered.
- The memo of transmittal submits the report, gives the occasion for it, and states its subject and purpose. Why, you may wonder, should Jennifer give Kate information she already knows. One reason is to remind a busy executive who has a great many things on her mind. Another is that the report goes on file as a part of the official record of the decision of where to locate the store. People who may examine the file in years to come will not be conversant with the details. Jennifer also forecasts her recommendation in the letter.
- The table of contents shows a simple two-level organization, as befits a fairly short report. Besides serving as a locating device, the table shows the logic and organization of the report.
- The executive summary summarizes the data and conclusions and announces Jennifer's recommendation to go with the downtown location.
- The introduction states the purpose, scope, and plan of development of the report.
- The discussion is organized to evaluate each location by the same criteria. A well-designed system of headings and subheadings makes the discussion easy to follow. The style used is plain, economical, and easy to read.
- The summary provides a table that is an excellent side-by-side factual comparison of the two sites. The conclusions, presented in narrative form, show that Jennifer has given both locations a fair appraisal. Because her choice of the downtown location involves some risk, she is careful to point out why she chose it. If Kate Hanson is like many executives, the introduction, summaries, conclusions, and recommendation of this report may be all she reads. If that is the case, she will have

Haley's Stores, Inc.
MEMORANDUM

Date: April 12, 2001

To: Kate Hanson
          Chief Executive Officer

From: Jennifer Youngren
          Chief Financial Officer   *J.Y.*

Submittal statement and occasion for report

I submit the following report, "Location Study for a new Haley's Department Store," in accordance with your request of March 5, 2001.

Purpose and scope of report

The report considers two locations for a new Haley's store in Cass, Ohio: (1) A regional mall four miles north of Cass on Interstate 71 and (2) downtown Cass. This study evaluated each location using the same criteria: nature of the location, accessibility of the location, neighboring establishments, terms of lease, and tax incentives.

Forecast of recommendation

Based upon the criteria, the report recommends the downtown location. I'll be happy to discuss the report and my recommendation at your convenience.

FIGURE 16-3 • Feasibility Study
Source: Reprinted by permission of Jennifer Youngren.

Location Study for a New Haley's Department Store

Prepared for

Kate Hanson
Chief Executive Officer
Haley's Stores, Inc.

By

Jennifer Youngren
Chief Financial Officer
Haley's Stores, Inc.
April 12, 2001

-1-

FIGURE 16-3 • (continued)

CONTENTS

Executive Summary iii

Introduction 1

Regional Shopping Mall Location 1
    Nature of the Location 1
    Accessibility of the Location 1
    Neighboring Establishments 2
    Terms of Lease 2
    Tax Incentives 3

Downtown Cass Location 3
    Nature of the Location 3
    Accessibility of the Location 3
    Neighboring Establishments 4
    Terms of Lease 4
    Tax Incentives 5

Summary and Conclusions 5

Recommendation 6

References 6

FIGURE 16-3 • (*continued*)

Executive Summary

Purpose and scope
of report

Haley's Stores, Inc., is considering two locations for its new store in Cass, Ohio: (1) a regional mall four miles north of Cass on Interstate 71 and (2) downtown Cass. This study evaluated each location using the same criteria: nature of the location, accessibility of the location, neighboring establishments, terms of lease, and tax incentives.

The mall location is attractive and bright, with neighboring stores to generate good customer traffic and with good parking. However, the lease would have an exclusivity clause that prohibits the sale of home furnishings by Haley's, amounting to an approximate loss of 20% of business.

Summary of data
and conclusions

Rent is cheaper in the downtown area, and there are tax incentives amounting to $1.2 million over six years. Parking problems, currently existing, will be largely solved by the time the new store could open.

The Cass City Council is embarking on an ambitious program designed to refurbish downtown, lower the crime rate, and increase travel in the city by both residents and day trippers.

Recommendation

Given downtown's lower expenses, the tax incentives, and the potential for a marked improvement in the environment, it seems to be the better location. I recommend it for our new store.

-3-

FIGURE 16-3 • (continued)

Purpose, scope, and plan of development of report

Introduction

This study evaluates two locations that Haley's Stores is considering for its new store in Cass, Ohio: (1) a regional mall four miles north of Cass on Interstate 71 and (2) downtown Cass. This study provides the following:

(1) An evaluation of each location using the following criteria: nature of the location, accessibility of the location, neighboring establishments, terms of lease, and tax incentives.

(2) Summary and conclusions.

(3) Recommendation.

Regional Mall Location

Discussion of data, using a simple but effective heading design

The mall being considered for a new Haley's Department Store is a regional mall located four miles north of Cass on Interstate 71. It was opened in 1995. It is anchored by Sears and JCPenny's.

Nature of the Location

The mall is a modern, well-designed, T-shaped, one-story building containing 98 establishments and 400,000 square feet. JCPenny's is at one end of the horizontal crossbar of the T and Sears is at the other end. The space we are studying is a vacant store, 60,000 square feet in area, located at the bottom of the T. It has been vacant for six months and requires no major repairs.

Accessibility of the Location

The accessibility of a mall is an important characteristic. The quality of access streets, the level of street congestion, and the presence of physical barriers all affect accessibility (Dunne, Lusch, & Gable, 1995, p. 213). The mall location has good accessibility. It is located directly off an exit of I-71. Other roads leading to the mall have been repaved recently and are in excellent condition. There are no natural barriers, such as rivers, barring access. The parking situation is also excellent. The mall has 10 parking spaces for every 1,000 feet of space, for a total of 4,000 spaces.

-4-

FIGURE 16-3 • (continued)

Neighboring Establishments

According to *Retail Marketing*, retailers benefit from store compatibility. A good neighbor is a store that is compatible with the retailer's line of trade. The theory of store compatibility says that when two similar businesses locate near each other, there will be an increase in sales greater than would be achieved if the two businesses were located away from each other (Lusch, Dunne, & Gebhardt, 1993, p. 394). Therefore, the location of JCPenny's and Sears in the mall should increase our traffic and increase sales. Numerous other high-quality single-line and specialty shops are also located in the corridor that leads to the empty store being considered. Eddie Bauer, Victoria's Secret, Banana Republic, and Radio Shack are all nearby. Also, a Chili's restaurant is located nearby at an exit that leads to a parking lot. In theory, traffic should be good. The extensive range of products offered by the large number of retailers in the mall creates heavy traffic in the corridors. This heavy traffic plus the neat, clean environment of the mall results in a low crime rate. Another advantage of good neighbors is that various merchants share common costs and cooperative planning (Boone & Kurtz, 1998, p. 507).

Terms of Lease

The length of a lease in the mall is for 10 years at a rental of $60,000 per month or 8% of gross sales, whichever is higher. However, mall leases have exclusivity clauses that in some instances prevent competition. Because JCPenny's has the exclusive right to be the only department store selling home furnishings in the mall, we would not be able to sell them. Home furnishings, on average, account for 20% of Haley sales, so this would be a serious matter for us. Also, our shopping hours would have to conform to the mall hours. In general, this would not be a problem for us.

Tax Incentives

No tax incentives exist for leasing space at the mall.

Downtown Cass Location

The second location considered is on the corner of 17th Street and Wabasha in downtown Cass.

FIGURE 16-3 • *(continued)*

Nature of the Location

The downtown site is a vacant building with 55,000 square feet of space. Sears was located in this building until it moved to the mall six months ago. The building and the buildings that surround it were mostly built from 1925 to 1940 and are beginning to show signs of aging. However, our construction consultant, Jim Meadors, says no serious structural problems exist and no major repairs are needed.

Accessibility of the Location

The current state of parking in the area is unsatisfactory. There are metered parking spaces on three sides of the building and a free parking lot behind it with 50 spaces. However, the Downtown Retail Council is using a government grant to build a parking ramp with 1,500 pay spaces that is scheduled for completion before we would occupy the building. Also, Cass subsidizes bus service that makes the downtown area inexpensively accessible from outlying areas.

Downtown streets have been recently repaved and are in good condition. Traffic is heavy from 8 to 9 o'clock in the morning, over the noon hour, and again from 5 to 6 o'clock in the evening. Because of congested traffic, deliveries to the store could sometimes be hindered.

Neighboring Establishments

A wide variety of small retailers surround the downtown site, such as optical shops, watch shops, antique stores, interior decorators, and shoe stores. The major neighbor is Lopez's, a moderately priced, local department store that should be quite compatible with us. Lopez's has many loyal customers because it has been in Cass since 1925 and provides civic leadership to the community. Surrounding buildings contain office space for small to moderate-sized businesses. Workers in these offices are a potential base of steady customers. Several attractive restaurants and coffee shops are nearby, which increases pedestrian traffic. Crime rates are higher downtown than they are at the mall.

The Cass City Council, working with the Downtown Retail Council, is embarking on an ambitious plan to make downtown more attractive. The city has hired additional police and is improving police training. Tax incen-

-6-

FIGURE 16-3 • (*continued*)

tives are being offered to building owners who improve their properties. As part of this program, several builders are remodeling old apartment houses into attractive condominiums, which should attract people to make downtown their home. A movie chain is converting an unused building into a multiplex theater. All these developments taken together should increase street pedestrian traffic in the evenings. This could be of significant benefit to us.

Terms of Lease

Lease terms require a 10 year commitment. The rent would be 6% of gross sales. There are no exclusivity clauses anywhere downtown, and we would be free to sell our full line of merchandise.

Tax Incentives

The City Council of Cass is anxious to have a department store once again in the empty building. To attract us, the council is offering tax incentives amounting to $1.2 million over six years.

Summary and Conclusions

The following table makes a point-by-point comparison of the two locations.

Table comparing factual data

Regional Mall	**Downtown**
60,000 square feet	55,000 square feet
Clean, modern environment	Aging environment
Easily accessible	Easily accessible
4,000 free parking spaces	1,500 pay parking spaces
High neighborhood compatibility	Good neighborhood compatibility
$60,000/month, or 8% of gross	6% of gross
No sale of home furnishings	No restrictions on sales
Low crime rate	High crime rate
No tax incentives	Tax incentives of $1.2 million

Conclusions

Comparing the two locations on the important points of space, environment, compatibility, parking, and crime rate indicates the mall to be a better choice. However, downtown has a clear edge in costs. The rent is cheaper, and the tax break is a powerful incentive. In addition, without being able to sell home furnishings, we lose approximately 20% of revenue at the mall.

FIGURE 16-3 • (*continued*)

Even with the higher costs, the mall seems the safer choice. The success of the downtown location depends to a marked degree on the success of the plans of the Cass City Council and the Downtown Retail Council. However, much of the plan is already in place. A parking ramp is nearly finished, nearby condominiums are under construction, and a multiplex theater is guaranteed. The situation at the mall is safe but static. The situation downtown is riskier but has far greater potential. A Haley's Department Store could become the centerpiece in a vibrant downtown community. Even though the move downtown entails risk, the lower rent, tax incentives, and the ability to sell home furnishings makes it a reasonable choice.

Recommendation

Haley's should locate its new store in downtown Cass.

Reference List

Boone, L. E., and Kurtz, D. L. (1998). *Contemporary marketing wired* (9th ed.). Orlando, FL: The Dryden Press.

Dunne, P., Lusch, R., & Gable, M. (1995). *Retailing* (2nd ed.). Cincinnati, OH: Southwestern College Publishing.

Lusch, R., Dunne, P., & Gebhardt, R. (1993). *Retail marketing* (2nd ed.). Cincinnati, OH: Southwestern College Publishing.

-8-

FIGURE 16-3 • (*continued*)

sufficient information to know how Jennifer has studied the problem and how she has arrived at her recommendation.

- The simply stated recommendation fulfills the purpose of Jennifer's report.

▶ A FINAL WORD

In this chapter we have shown you three recommendation reports, with special emphasis on the feasibility report. All three reports are excellent, and studying them is a good guide to planning, designing, and writing any kind of recommendation report. However, remember that these reports are simply examples that provide guidelines to creating your own recommendation reports. Any report you do should respond to your own purpose, content, and audience.

▶ PLANNING AND REVISION CHECKLISTS

You will find the planning and revision checklist inside the front cover valuable in planning and revising any presentation of technical information. The following questions specifically apply to recommendation reports. They summarize the key points in this chapter and provide a checklist for planning and revising.

Planning

- What is the purpose of your report? Have you stated it in one sentence?
- What is the scope of your report?
- Who is your reader? What is your reader's technical level?
- What will your readers do with the information?
- What information will you need to write the report?
- How long should the report be?
- What format should you use for the report?
- What report elements will you need?
- What elements do you need to include in your introduction?
- What arrangement will you use in presenting your report?
- What graphics will you need to present information or data?

Revision

- At a minimum, does your recommendation report do the following:
  Introduce the report?

Present enough data in words and visuals to justify any conclusions drawn?

Discuss and evaluate the data fairly?

Summarize the data?

Draw logical conclusions from the data?

Present recommendations based upon the data and the conclusions?

- Are your data accurate?
- Do your visuals immediately show what they are designed to show?
- Is your format suitable for your content, audience, and purpose?
- Have you properly documented all information sources?

▶ EXERCISES

1. Think of a piece of equipment your major department needs, such as a computer, camera, audio recorder, VCR, television, or test equipment. Explore the choices available for the particular piece of equipment needed. Write a report for the department head that evaluates the choices against appropriate criteria and that recommends which choice to buy. Submit your report as a memo (see Letter and Memorandum Format in Appendix B).

2. In groups of four or five, discuss some of the major problems students confront on campus. As a group, choose one of the problems as a project. Gather data that allow the group to define the problem accurately. Analyze the data and draw conclusions: Why does the problem exist? Based on the group's conclusions, develop possible solutions to the problem. After considering appropriate criteria—such as cost, personnel, and time—choose the most feasible solution to the problem.

   Write a report that presents the group's data, analysis, conclusions, and recommendations. Use a report format similar to that in Figure 16-3. Address the report to the dean of your college.

3. Imagine you are the army captain of our opening scenario who must write a feasibility report concerning geothermal heat pumps to the base commander. To gather information for your report visit http://www.eren.doe.gov/geothermal/ and check out the resources listed there. Use a report format similar to that in Figure 16-3. Submit your report to your instructor, who, for this exercise, will have the rank of brigadier general.

4. Seek out a subject for a feasibility study and report. In your local or campus newspaper identify any news items that call for feasibility studies. Is your community or school considering any actions that should be preceded by feasibility studies? Are there topics in your discipline that would lend themselves to feasibility studies?

- Using the material you have gathered, prepare a list like the one shown here, but substitute your own subject matter following the four colons:

  General field: Meteorology/physics

  Specific topic: Short-term weather forecasting

  Purpose: To determine the feasibility of devising and installing a lightning prediction system that will warn residents of a golf course community when lightning danger is imminent.

  Client: Regina Bereswill, General Manager of the community.

- Using the list you prepared, determine the scope of your treatment (see 465–466). Rough out the areas of information you will need and the sources and methods you will use to gather the information (see Chapter 8, Gathering, Evaluating, and Documenting Information).

- Submit to your teacher a proposal for a feasibility report based on the information you have developed above (see Chapter 15, Proposals and Progress Reports).

- Using the planning checklists inside the front cover and following this chapter, prepare an organizational plan for your report. Begin with an updated purpose, scope, and audience statement. Decide on an appropriate format for the report. Will it be a memorandum, letter, or a formal report? If a formal report, which format elements will you include? How many visuals, and what kinds, do you anticipate? Be prepared to justify your choices in a discussion with your teacher.

- Begin work on your report. Midway through the process, submit a progress report to your teacher (see Chapter 15, Proposals and Progress Reports).

- Write, revise, and edit the report you have planned and researched. Address it to the client, but submit it to your teacher.

5. Prepare an oral report for either Exercise 2 or 4. If Exercise 2, your fellow students are your audience. If Exercise 4, your proposed client is your audience. Your teacher will specify the time duration for your oral report (see Chapter 19, Oral Reports).

SCENARIO

With your major in food science, you were delighted to find work with Sheffield Farms, a medium-sized supermarket chain in the Middle West. Your first assignment was to a small group that studies consumer food preferences and habits. The group leader is Shirley Gomez. One of your tasks was to research the readability of the new food labels required by the Food and Drug Administration.

You had sought volunteers among people shopping in Sheffield Farm stores. You had provided them labels to read and then questioned them on their understanding of the information on the label. To a high degree they understood the information provided about fat, cholesterol, fiber, protein, and so forth. But as you were conducting your research, you wondered how many Sheffield Farms customers actually made decisions based on the labels.

You brought the idea up to Shirley. "Good thought," she said. "How would you go about it?"

"I can think of three ways," you said. "Observation for one. Simply watch to see how many people read a food label when they take food off a shelf. Another would be to ask people at checkout how often they read food labels. Third, we could take some common purchase like cereal out of customers' baskets, and without showing them the food label, try to find out how much of the information on the label they're actually aware of."

"Has anyone done this?" Shirley asked.

"My preliminary search in the journals and on the Web hasn't turned up anything like what I'm proposing," you said. "There has been a lot of focus group research about readability and decision making based on the labels, but I found nothing that checked their actual use by ordinary consumers. In any case, we haven't done anything like this with Sheffield customers. If we find that most our customers really don't use the labels, we might want to start an awareness program of some sort."

"Well, check the lit some more," Shirley said. "If you find the research you propose hasn't been done, you might have a journal article. In any case, the research report could be useful for us in-house," As an afterthought, she added, "Check your methodology with me before you begin, though. You can't be too intrusive, or you'll annoy our customers. Maybe you can offer people some small reward for answering your questions."

And so empirical research reports are born. Someone sees a need for the research and checks the literature carefully to see if it really needs to be done. If the need is perceived, the methodology for carrying out the research is planned and executed. When the results are in and analyzed, it's time to write the report, what this chapter is all about.

chapter 17

Empirical Research Reports

▶ Audience Adaptation

▶ Introduction and Literature Review
Statement of Objectives
Choice of Materials or Methodology
Rationale for Investigation
Verb Tense in Literature Reviews

▶ Materials and Methods
Design of the Investigation
Materials
Procedures
Methods for Observation, Analysis, and Interpretation
Voice in Materials and Methods Section

▶ Results

▶ Discussion

▶ A Final Word

How do spiders produce their silk? Why do some foods cook better in microwave ovens than others? Why do certain hunter-gatherer tribes in Africa exchange gifts? Does the neutrino (a subatomic particle) have mass?

To get answers to questions of this kind, you can do two things:

- You can find, through research in libraries and on the Internet, the answers that researchers have obtained.
- You can obtain firsthand answers for yourself, by the direct empirical methods of experimentation and observation.

An illustration may help to clarify our point. Suppose that we have a chunk of glass, crude and irregular, dumped out of the ladle and unmolded. We desire to find the impact strength of the chunk of glass. That is, how many pounds of force will be required to shatter it? We may approach our solution in two ways:

- We may read up on the chemical makeup of the chunk of glass. We may measure its geometric properties. We may pass white light through it to obtain a reading of its internal structure. By turning to suitable handbooks, we may then estimate the minimum impact force required to shatter the chunk.
- We can whack the chunk with a hammer, hitting harder and harder until it shatters. A pressure gauge or similar accessory will tell us how hard we had to hit to get the result we wanted. This is the pragmatic test, pure and simple.

The empirical research study places the emphasis on the second approach, but contains elements of the first approach. That is, before researchers embark on their observations or experiments, they wisely research the existing literature to see what is already known from past work in the area of the research.

The reports that result from such activities comprise four major sections that reflect how the research was carried out, what resulted, and an interpretation of the results:

- **Introduction and literature review**: research objectives and a review of past research in relevant areas
- **Materials and methods**: how the research was performed
- **Results**: the data revealed by the research
- **Discussion:** interpretation and evaluation of the results

When put into final form, the empirical research report may also contain the usual elements found in reports, such as tables of content, abstracts, and references. Where the research is reported—usually either in a journal article or a student thesis—will determine the exact format. Because we cover the additional parts in Appendix B, Formal Elements of Document Design, we deal here only with the sections just listed. Figure 17-1 shows a complete report. Skim through it before you continue on.

Status and Management of Pales Weevil in the Eastern United States

Scott M. Salom

Assistant professor, Virginia Polytechnic Institute and State University, Department of Entomology, Blacksburg, Virginia

The pales weevil—Hylobius pales (Herbst) is a subcortical feeding insect with a large geographic range and wide host-species range amongst conifers. It is a regeneration pest of forest and Christmas tree plantation, and nurseries, feeding on stems of seedlings and branch tips of saplings. It breeds in freshly killed stumps and slash. Across the geographic range of pales weevil, different conifer management objectives and constraints result in varying pest impacts and application of different pest management strategies. A questionnaire was sent to 32 states where pales weevil was believed to occur. Responses indicated that pales weevil is an important Christmas tree pest in the north central states, a pest of pine seedlings and Christmas trees in the northeastern states, and principally a pest of pine seedlings in the southern states. Pest management tactics used in the north central states focus on stump treatments (removal or application of insecticides). In the northeastern states, tactics include stump and seedling insecticide treatments and delayed planting of seedlings in recently harvested sites. In the South, the most popular tactic is to delay planting of seedlings. All these tactics are considered effective, yet they are also costly and those that include insecticides are not favored by land managers. Overall, there is a fair amount of dissatisfaction by foresters and landowners with currently available tactics. The need for development of more effective and less hazardous pest management tactics is discussed. Tree Planters' Notes 48(1/2): 4–11; 1997.

The pales weevil—*Hylobius pales* (Herbst) (Coleoptera: Curculionidae)—has long been considered a pest of seedlings and sapling stage coniferous trees in central and eastern North America (Carter 1916; Peirson 1921). A complete review of the systematics, distribution, biology, and recommended pest management practices for this insect has been presented by Lynch (1984).

Pales weevil is found throughout the eastern and central United States (figure 1), as well as southeastern Canada (Lynch 1984). In general, adult weevils are attracted by the resinous volatiles produced by dead and dying trees (Fox and Hill 1973; Hertel 1970; Peirson 1921; Thomas and Hertel 1969). They then feed and oviposit in the roots, dying stumps, or boles of fallen trees, where broods develop until the onset of winter (Anderson 1980; Doggett and others 1977). Subsequently, overwintering adults emerge the following spring, or brood adults emerge the following spring and summer, and feed on tender bark and cambial tissue of

Figure 1—*The states in which pales weevil is known to occur are shaded.*

seedling stems and roots, and sapling branch tips (figure 2).

Pales weevil has also been implicated as the principal vector of *Leptographium procerum* (Kendr.) to eastern white pine (*Pinus strobus* L.) and Scots pine (P. *sylvestris* L.) in Virginia (Lewis and Alexander 1986; Nevill and Alexander 1992a, b). Overlapping generations occur throughout the geographic range of pales weevil with the duration of the life cycle being about 1 year in southern Canada (Finnegan 1959) and northern United States (Peirson 1921) and less than 1 year in the southern

Figure 2—*Adult pales weevil feeding on bark tissue of twig (photograph courtesy of Stephen Cade).*

FIGURE 17-1 • Empirical Research Report
Source: Scott M. Solam, "Status and Management of Pales Weevil in the Eastern United States," *Tree Planters' Notes* 48 (1997): 4–10.

United States (Beal and McClintick 1943; Doggett and others 1977; Speers 1974).

The abundance of pales weevil is generally dependent on host availability. Because the weevils can feed on live tissue and breed in recently killed or dead material, they can be present in different conifer management settings. This may partially explain why pales weevil is capable of becoming a pest of nursery and plantation seedlings, and Christmas trees. Another reason for its success may be that pales weevil has been reported to feed on 11 coniferous genera including 29 tree species (Lynch 1984).

Currently, the following pest management tactics are available for reducing the impact of pales weevil:

1. Determining site hazard from host species composition and site preparation activities
2. Harvesting the site before mid-summer
3. Delaying the planting of new seedlings for 1 or 2 years after harvest
4. Treating seedlings with insecticide either before or after planting (Nord and others 1982)
5. Treating stumps with insecticides (Nielsen and Balderston 1975; Thomas 1971)
6. Removing stumps of recently harvested trees (Benjamin 1963)
7. Not harvesting the bottom whorl of branches, thus keeping stumps alive (Corneil and Wilson 1984a)

Following some preliminary inquiries, I found that the perceived impact of pales weevil on conifer seedlings and Christmas tree production varied from state to state, as did the application of pest management tactics (Salom 1992). Therefore, the objectives of this paper are to more completely characterize the following information throughout the geographic range of pales weevil:

▶ The impact of the pest on forest, nursery, and Christmas tree management
▶ The pest management tactics used to combat the problem
▶ The research needs as expressed by state forest health officers

State forest health officers were targeted because they keep abreast of forest pest activity and are often called upon to make recommendations or develop programs for residents of their state.

Methods

I developed a questionnaire to be completed by state forest entomologists or forest health officers for all states

in which pales weevil has been documented to occur (figure 1) (Lynch 1984). There were 9 questions in the questionnaire. The first 2 questions served to identify the respondent. A third question asked if pales weevil has ever been a pest of conifers in that state. If the answer was no, they were instructed not to answer any more questions. If the answer was yes, they completed the questionnaire. The remaining questions focused on situations in which pales weevil is a pest in their state. Respondents were then asked to rate the severity of pales weevil as a pest in their state. Severity classifications ranged from minor to serious relative to other pest problems within the state. The pest status of pales weevil was not based on economic data because such records are scarce. The respondents were then asked to list the host species most impacted from 1 (most impacted), 2 (second most impacted), and so on. The next question asked what management tactics are recommended. Again, respondents were asked to rank their recommendations with 1 (most frequent), 2 (second most frequent), and so on. Even though a tactic may be recommended, it may not be ideal. Therefore, the next question asked if state officials and users were satisfied with the currently used tactics. Lastly, respondents were asked to state their opinions on research needs for improving management of pales weevil.

The questionnaires were sent out to 1 state official in each of 32 states. In a few cases, more than 1 individual responded to the questionnaire, and the answers from within a state were then combined into a single response. Although some of the respondents may not have had intimate knowledge of pales weevil activity in their state, they were requested to obtain information from the person in the state best able to answer the questions or alternatively pass the questionnaire on to them. Because I considered it unlikely for each state to have more than a few individuals who could answer detailed questions about pales weevil, I focused on the most knowledgeable person in the state.

Results and Discussion

Responses were obtained from all 32 states. According to the respondents, pales weevil has never been a pest in Massachusetts and Connecticut. Therefore, the rest of the summary will not include information from these states. However, it should be noted that an important early paper on pales weevil by Peirson (1921) was based on studies carried out in Harvard Forest in Petersham, Massachusetts.

Pest status. Pales weevil was reported to cause serious damage to branches of Christmas trees in Wisconsin, Illinois, Pennsylvania, and New Jersey, and to a lesser extent in Indiana (figure 3a). Several of the

FIGURE 17-1 • (continued)

midwestern states and Maine reported moderate branch damage. Serious damage to Christmas trees seedlings was reported in Illinois, New York, New Jersey, and Maine (figure 3b). In addition, 11 other states rated this problem as moderate. Pales weevil was reported to be a serious seedling pest of forest plantations in almost all of the southern states plus Maryland (a border state) and New York (figure 3c). Although the southern states have long reported this problem, it was unexpected to have Maryland and New York included in this group. Pales weevil was generally reported as a minor pest in nurseries (figure 4), although New Jersey did report serious damage to branches of nursery trees (figure 4b).

The contrast in impacts between the southern and north central states is not unexpected. Although North Carolina and Virginia have become strong Christmas-tree-producing states, the main objective of foresters for growing conifers in the South is still pulpwood and sawtimber production. Even though several of the north central states are at the top of the Christmas tree production list (National Christmas Tree Association, unpublished report), the southern states surpass the northeastern and north central states combined in volume of conifer growing stock (2:1), volume of sawtimber (4:1), harvesting of growing stock (6:1), and harvesting of sawtimber (9:1) (Anonymous 1982).

Serious

Serious/moderate

Moderate

Moderate/minor

Minor

Not a pest

Figure 3—*Pest status of pales weevil in the eastern United States: for branches on Christmas trees (A), seedlings in Christmas tree plantations (B), and seedlings in forest plantations (C).*

FIGURE 17-1 • *(continued)*

A

B

Serious

Serious/moderate

Moderate

Moderate/minor

Minor

Not a pest

Figure 4—*Pest status of pales weevil in the eastern United States: for seedlings in nurseries (A) and branches on nursery trees (B).*

Host species. Among the surveyed states, the species of tree most frequently attacked by pales weevil is determined in part by both the geographic location and the relative importance and objectives of forest and Christmas tree managers. In the north central states of Indiana, Michigan, Minnesota, and Wisconsin, Scots pine is the most frequently attacked tree species, followed closely by eastern white and then red pine (*P. resinosa* Ait.) (table 1). Additional pine species were reported to be attacked in the northeastern states, yet both eastern white pine and Scots pines were the most highly ranked. In the South, loblolly pine (*P. taeda* L.) is reported to be the most attacked species. The second most attacked appears to be shortleaf pine (*P. echinata* Mill.). Despite being located north of Virginia, both Maryland and Delaware reported similar host species impacted as reported by most of the southern states. All species reported in this survey have been previously listed as susceptible hosts by Lynch (1984) and sources therein.

Pest management tactics. In the north central states, the treatments recommended most frequently for minimizing pales weevil damage are some form of stump treatments (table 2). Respondents were split between favoring insecticidal treatment of stumps or stump removal/slash management. Both approaches focus on reducing breeding material for pales weevil. The respondent from Wisconsin emphasized delayed planting over stump treatment, yet still ranked stump treatment with insecticides second.

Respondents in states that recommend stump removal and sanitation (table 2) are pleased with the results. In contrast, respondents in all states treating stumps with insecticides are interested in finding more "environmentally" friendly and less costly treatments. Although delaying planting 1 or 2 years is effective, it is unpopular with many growers. Even the respondent from Wisconsin, who ranked this tactic #1, is interested in finding an alternative approach.

In the northeastern states, recommendations varied (table 2). Respondents from New Jersey, Pennsylvania, Rhode Island, and West Virginia ranked insecticide treatment of stumps highest, whereas those from Maine, Maryland, and New York recommended delayed planting of seedlings the highest. Respondents from New Jersey and West Virginia gave a fairly high ranking (#2) to cutting stumps down to ground level and covering them with soil. Several of the respondents recommended treating seedlings with insecticides, yet only the Delaware respondent gave that tactic its highest rating (tied with stump removal and slash management).

Some of the respondents found treating stumps with insecticide acceptable, yet others would like an alternative to lindane, the most widely used insecticide for

FIGURE 17-1 • (continued)

Table 1— *Ranking of conifer species most affected by pales weevil (1 = most affected), as reported by surveyed states; all species are pines unless otherwise indicated*

State	Tree species ranking		
	1	2	3
Alabama	loblolly	longleaf	slash
Arkansas	loblolly	shortleaf	slash
Delaware	loblolly	Virginia	eastern white
Florida	slash	loblolly	
Georgia	loblolly	slash	shortleaf
Indiana	Scots	eastern white	red
Illinois	eastern white	Scots	Fraser fir
Kentucky	Scots	eastern white	loblolly
Louisiana	loblolly	shortleaf	slash
Maine	eastern white	balsam fir	
Maryland	loblolly		
Michigan	Scots	red & Jack	
Minnesota	Scots	red	
Mississippi	loblolly	shortleaf	longleaf
Missouri	Scots	eastern white	
New Hampshire	eastern white		
New Jersey	eastern white	Douglas-fir	spruce species
New York	red	Scots & eastern white	
North Carolina	loblolly	eastern white	longleaf
Ohio	eastern white	Scots	balsam fir
Oklahoma	loblolly	shortleaf	Virginia & Scots
Pennsylvania	eastern white	Scots	Douglas-fir
Rhode Island	eastern white	Scots	Fraser fir
South Carolina	loblolly	Virginia	eastern white
Tennessee	loblolly	eastern white	Virginia
Texas	loblolly	shortleaf	
Vermont	Scots	eastern white	
Virginia	loblolly	eastern white	Virginia
West Virginia	Scots	eastern white	
Wisconsin	Scots	red	eastern white

Table 2—*Pest management tactics recommended and used for managing pales weevil in the United States*

Region & state	Rank of control tactics*					
	A	B	C	D	E	F
North Central						
Illinois			1	2		
Indiana	2		1	3		
Michigan	3	2	1			
Minnesota				1		
Missouri				1		
Ohio			2	1		
Wisconsin	1		2			
Northeast						
Delaware		1.5		1.5		
Maine	1		2.5	2.5		
Maryland	1	2				
New Hampshire						1
New Jersey			1	3	2	
New York	1	2				
Pennsylvania			1			
Rhode Island		2	1			
Vermont			2	1		
West Virginia		3	1		2	
South						
Alabama	1					
Arkansas	1					
Florida	1	2				
Georgia	1	2				
Kentucky	1					
Louisiana	1					
Mississippi	1	2				
North Carolina	2	1				
Oklahoma	1					
South Carolina	1	2				
Tennessee	1	3	2			
Texas	2					1
Virginia	2	1	3			

1 = most commonly used or recommended tactic, 2 = next most common tactic, and 3 = least common tactic; No ranking indicates tactic not even considered.
* Treatment A = Delay planting 6 months to 2 years; treatment B = treat seedlings or trees with insecticides; treatment C = treat stumps with insecticides; treatment D = remove stumps, slash and /or sanitation; treatment E = cover stumps down to soil; treatment F = none.

stump spraying. Treatment of seedlings with insecticides is not a popular option with workers, as they would rather not work with hazardous materials. Covering stumps with soil is a satisfactory treatment for 2 states, New Jersey and West Virginia, but I am not aware of a published report recommending this treatment. Satisfaction with stump removal/sanitation was mixed. Some respondents stated that this tactic works, yet one respondent described sanitation as too time consuming.

In the South, all but 1 state respondent ranked delayed planting of seedlings as either the first or second most recommended treatment (table 2). This was followed by treating seedlings with insecticides. Stump treatments were rarely recommended, except in Virginia and Tennessee, which have significant Christmas tree industries. However, North Carolina and Georgia, both with strong Christmas tree industries, do not recommend stump treatments. In Texas, where pales weevil is

rarely a problem, the primary recommendation is to do nothing.

Delayed planting after harvesting was considered effective by all respondents in the South. However, some do not consider this approach economical, even though the delay is from 6 months to 1 year, rather than the 1 to 2 years needed in the northern states. Insecticide treatments of seedlings were also considered effective, yet satisfaction was also mixed for this tactic for the same reasons as stated above.

The differences in treatment recommendations between the southern and north central states may be largely a reflection of their different management objectives. With the emphasis in the north central states on Christmas tree production, intensive management of

FIGURE 17-1 • *(continued)*

plantations allows for stump treatments. Yearly harvesting and shearing practices associated with Christmas trees provide a consistent source of host volatiles and breeding material for the weevils. This makes delayed planting of seedlings less desirable and probably less effective. However in the South, where emphasis is on production of pulpwood and sawtimber, harvesting is generally intermittent on a temporal and spatial scale. Therefore, lack of continuously available breeding material makes delayed planting a more appealing and effective tactic.

Research needs. Respondents from the north central states indicated varied needs for research, including life history studies, better monitoring, biological control, and identification of pheromones. It is likely that recent research efforts and publications may not be reaching everyone equally. Much needed information on pales weevil life history (Hoffman and others 1997; Raffa and Hunt 1989; Rieske and Raffa 1990a;) and techniques for monitoring the pest (Raffa and Hunt 1988; Rieske and Raffa 1990b, 1991, 1993) is now available. Less effort has gone into the latter two areas.

Indiana reported a need to investigate the role of subcortical feeding insects in vectoring *Leptographium procerum* to trees that ultimately succumb to procerum root disease. Nevill and Alexander (1992a, b, c, d) studied this topic extensively. However, the actual timing of inoculation of the tree within the Christmas tree rotation has not been conclusively determined (Salom and Gray 1993) unpublished data). Respondents from the less impacted north central states did not feel any improvements were needed.

Respondents from the northeastern states focused on the need to develop either safer chemicals or non-chemical control tactics. One suggestion from the Maine respondent was to find a way to kill stumps. The respondent suggested that herbicide treatments might be less toxic and might solve the problem of available breeding material. Rennels and Fox (1969, 1970), however, reported little success in applying fuel oil, pentachlorophenol, or 2,4,5-T to stumps in an effort to inhibit pales weevil breeding.

In the South, the most pressing need is for the development of a method to predict weevil damage. Respondents from 6 of 12 southern states ranked this need the highest. This is not surprising. Nord and others (1982) stated that the biggest problem in managing for pales weevil is the inability to correlate number of weevils at a site with potential damage to seedlings. Sampling for field populations of pales weevil is based on three fundamental aspects of their biology:

▶ Adults are most active underground and are rarely active aboveground during sunny days (Corneil and Wilson 1984b)
▶ Adults are attracted to volatiles produced by dying conifers
▶ Populations are highly aggregated (Rieske and Raffa 1993)

Sampling for pales weevil is difficult and requires labor-intensive techniques, ranging from digging pits and filling them with insecticide-laced pine material (Doggett and others 1977) to using PVC drainpipe pitfall traps baited with ethanol and turpentine (Raffa and Hunt 1988). Studies have been conducted to predict weevil activity, mainly as damage to seedlings (Lawrence 1975) or pre-harvest Christmas trees (Rieske and Raffa 1993). Lawrence (1975) was unable to correlate weevil trap catches with weevil feeding on seedlings, but Rieske and Raffa (1993) did find a correlation between the number of females trapped and weevil activity in following years. However, it is unknown whether their data can be used as a reliable predictor of pales weevil activity. This may be partially due to the inherent problems associated with measuring damage to trees resulting from the complex of weevils present in the Wisconsin Christmas tree system. In Sweden, Nordlander (1987) had better success correlating trap catches of the closely related European pine weevil (*H. abietis* L.) to seedling damage.

Conclusions

There are several management options available for use against pales weevil. The differences in treatment recommendations for many of the states are partially a function of management objectives and constraints. It is apparent that recommended tactics can be effective, yet many landowners do not follow them, possibly a result of high cost or time allocation. The reasons why tactics were not often followed was not investigated in this survey.

An obvious weakness in the effective use of management tactics is an inability to correlate weevil density with damage. Such a tool would provide a relatively easy way to hazard-rate sites. Effective trapping techniques are critical for monitoring weevil densities. Such techniques became easier in the United States with the adoption of the PVC pitfall traps baited with ethanol and turpentine (Raffa and Hunt 1988). However, these traps are not effective in catching pales weevil in Virginia unless recently killed or cut host material is a component of the bouquet (Fettig 1996).

In this survey, insecticidal treatments were the least desirable, yet most often recommended tactic. The

FIGURE 17-1 • (*continued*)

development of less hazardous and equally effective compounds was seen as a priority by most respondents. In Virginia, a nursery application of permethrin to protect outplanted seedlings has been effective without some of the negative aspects associated with use of phosmet (preplanting) and chlorpyrifos (postplanting) insecticides (Tigner 1995). Active research efforts are being made into the possible treatment of seedling stems with non-toxic, biologically based anti-feedants (Salom and others 1994, 1996) or wax (Nordlander 1995). Although this research shows some promise, more work is needed.

Progress has been made over the years in minimizing the impact of pales weevil on conifer tree production in the eastern United States. Although many of the states reported that improved pest management tactics are needed for better acceptance by growers and land managers, most are satisfied with the level of control they are able to achieve with the tactics available. We all hope that continued research will lead to even better and less hazardous control tactics for pales weevil.

Address correspondence to: Dr. Scott Salom, Virginia Tech, Department of Entomology, Blacksburg, VA 24061; **e-mail**: salom@vt.edu

Acknowledgments

Adapted from a presentation made to Working Party 7.03.03 (Insects Affecting Reforestation) at the IUFRO 20th World Congress in Tampere, Finland, August 6–12, 1995. This paper would not have been possible without the help of the state forest entomologists and health specialists who responded to the questionnaire in a timely fashion. Tim Tigner was most helpful in reviewing earlier versions of the questionnaire and manuscript. I am also grateful to Jodi Gray, James Johnson, Frank Sapio, and Chris Fettig, who reviewed earlier versions of the manuscript.

Literature Cited

Anderson GW. 1980. Pine reproduction weevils (Coleoptera: Curculionidae) infesting Christmas trees plantations in southwest Virginia. Blacksburg, VA: Virginia Polytechnic Institute and State University. M.S. thesis. 65 p.

Anonymous. 1982. An analysis of the timber situation in the United States, 1952 2030. Rep. 23. Washington, DC: USDA Forest Service. 499 p.

Beal JA, McClintick KB. 1943. The pales weevil in southern pine. Journal of Economic Entomology 36: 792–794.

Benjamin DM. 1963. Control of weevils associated with replanted Scotch pine Christmas tree plantations following final harvest. Wisconsin Christmas Tree Producers Association New Bulletin 34: 1–2.

Carter EE. 1916. *Hylobius pales* as a factor in the reproduction of conifers in New England. Proceedings of the Society of American Foresters 11: 297–307.

Corneil JA, Wilson LF. 1984a. Live branches on pine stumps deter weevil breeding in Michigan (Coleoptera: Curculionidae). Great Lakes Entomologist 17: 229–231.

Corneil JA, Wilson LF. 1984b. Some light and temperature effects on the behavior of the adult pales weevil, *Hylobius pales* (Coleoptera: Curculionidae). Great Lakes Entomologist 17: 225–228.

Doggett CA, Grady CR, Green HJ, Kunselman MB, Layman H, Taylor S. 1977. Seedling debarking weevils in North Carolina. North Carolina Forest Service Forestry Note 31.

Fettig CJ. 1996. Development and evaluation of trapping studies for *Hylobius pales* (Herbst) and *Pissodes nemorensis* Germar (Coleoptera: Curculionidae) in Virginia Christmas tree plantations. Blacksburg: Virginia Polytechnic Institute and State University. M.S. Thesis. 82 p.

Finnegan RJ. 1959. The pales weevil, *Hylobius pales* (Hbst.), in southern Ontario. Canadian Entomologist 91: 664–670.

Fox RC, Hill TM. 1973. The relative attraction of burned and cutover pine areas to the pine seedling weevils *Hylobius pales* and *Pachylobius picivorus*. Annals of the Entomological Society of America 66: 52–54.

Hertel GD. 1970. Response of the pales weevil to loblolly pine seedlings and cut stems. Journal of Economic Entomology 63: 995–997.

Hoffman GD, Hunt DWA, Salom SM, Raffa KF. 1997. Reproductive readiness and niche differences affect responses of conifer root weevils (Coleoptera: Curculionidae) to simulated host odors. Environmental Entomology 26: 91–100.

Lawrence LK. 1975. Relationship between number of pales weevils trapped and subsequent seedling mortality. North Carolina Forest Service Forestry Note 23.

Lewis KA, Alexander SA. 1986. Insects associated with the transmission of *Verticicladiella procera*. Canadian Journal of Forest Research 16: 1330–1333.

Lynch AM. 1984. The pales weevil, *Hylobius pales* (Herbst): a synthesis of the literature. Journal of the Georgia Entomology Society 19: 1–34.

Nevill RJ, Alexander SA. 1992a. Distribution of *Hylobius pales* and *Pissodes nemorensis* (Coleoptera: Curculionidae) within Christmas tree plantations with procerum root disease. Environmental Entomology 21: 1077–1085.

Nevill RJ, Alexander SA. 1992b. Transmission of *Leptographium procerum* to eastern white pine by *Hylobius pales* and *Pissodes nemorensis* (Coleoptera: Curculionidae). Plant Disease 76: 307–310.

Nevill RJ, Alexander SA. 1992c. Pathogenicity of three fungal associates of *Hylobius pales* and *Pissodes nemorensis* (Coleoptera: Curculionidae) to eastern white pine. Canadian Journal of Forest Research 22: 1438–1440.

Nevill RJ, Alexander SA. 1992d. Root- and stem-colonizing insects recovered from eastern white pines with procerum rot disease. Canadian Journal of Forest Research 22: 1712–1716.

Nielsen DG, Balderston CP. 1975. Evaluation of insecticides for preventing reproduction of pales and northern pine weevils in pine stumps. Journal of Economic Entomology 68: 205–206.

Nord JC, Ghent JH, Thomas HA, Doggett CA. 1982. Control of pales and pitch-eating weevils in the South. For. Rep. SA-FR-21. Atlanta: USDA Forest Service.

Nordlander G. 1987. A method for trapping *Hylobius abietis* (L.) with a standardized bait and its potential for forecasting seedling damage. Scandinavian Journal of Forest Research 2: 199–213.

FIGURE 17-1 • *(continued)*

▶ AUDIENCE ADAPTATION

To illustrate the characteristics of empirical research reports, we draw upon Figure 17-1 and excerpts from several other research reports. We have been careful to select passages that you should be able to read regardless of your specialization. On several occasions, however, we do define terms that a non-specialist might not know. We place these definitions in brackets to distinguish them from the authors' work. Our need to define terms demonstrates a major point about audience adaptation in empirical research reports. Experts write these reports for their fellow experts, and thus they are free to use a professional vocabulary. When you write a research report, you may use the standard vocabulary and standard knowledge of your field and expect your audience to understand you. In fact, your audience would be annoyed if you took time to define familiar terms or explain well-understood concepts.

At times, however, even in reports written for your fellow experts, you may be moving to the fringe of what is standard knowledge. If you use a new term or a highly specialized one, you will have to define it, using the definition techniques we describe on pages 185–188. Nor is there any reason in writing for experts to set aside the concepts of good style discussed in Chapter 5, Achieving a Readable Style. A heavy, pretentious style, full of long convoluted sentences is a bad style, no matter the audience.

▶ INTRODUCTION AND LITERATURE REVIEW

When research reports are presented in journal articles, most often the introduction and literature review are integrated as they are in Figure 17-1. The major function of this integrated section is to describe the subject, scope, significance, and objectives of the research.

The literature review, as the name implies, reviews the scientific literature pertinent to the research being reported. In it the author defines the problem being investigated as a way of leading to a statement of objectives. The author may also use the literature review to explain a choice of materials or methodology, or show the rationale for the investigation.

Because space in journals is expensive, the integrated introduction and literature review is held to information absolutely necessary to the investigation. However, when a research report is presented as a student thesis rather than as an article, the literature review is often quite extensive and is given separately from the introduction. The purpose of such a detailed review is not only to introduce the research but to demonstrate the writers mastery of certain subject matter. In writing a thesis, always check with your adviser to determine the type of literature review required and the subject matter coverage desired.

Read now the introduction and literature review of the article in Figure 17-1.

As is typical of a scientific research article, this article is documented by parenthetical references (see Documentation in Appendix B). The authors use the literature cited to define the nature and scope of the problem. We know from the introduction that the researcher's objectives are to determine the impact of the pales weevil on forestry, nursery, and Christmas tree management, the management tactics used to combat the weevil, and the research needs of state forest health officers. We will expect before the article is finished to know how well those objectives were met.

Statement of Objectives

Objectives may be stated in various ways. Frequently, they are expressed as questions, as in this passage from a report on discourse communities:

1. What were the salient features of the discourse community under investigation that influenced or complemented writing activity?
2. What was the interrelationship of genres and the discourse community in which they were used?
3. What issues arose when writers had to learn new genres as they moved from academic contexts for writing to this professional context for writing?[1]

Sometimes, objectives are presented as a hypothesis, as in this study of the abilities of infants:

The general hypothesis of these studies were as follows:(a) Infants know that an object exists even when it is not visible or sounding, (b) they can learn and remember the outcomes of two auditory–visual events, and (c) they can subsequently engage in actions appropriate to the outcomes with no supporting perceptual signal.[2]

No matter how you present your objectives, be sure to present them with absolute clarity. No doubt should exist in the reader's mind concerning what you were up to in your research.

Choice of Materials or Methodology

Literature reviews are sometimes used to explain the choice of the materials used in the investigation, as in this passage:

Brentids [weevils] make good candidates for studies of sexual selection and individual variation because most species of the family exhibit pronounced sexual dimorphism [differences between the sexes in characteristics such as size and color] (Muizon, 1960; Haedo Rossi, 1961; Damoiseau, 1967, 1971). The males generally possess greater body length, a stouter rostrum [beak or snout], and more powerful mandibles [jaws], one of which may be grossly enlarged (Darwin, 1871). Within each sex there is impressive phenotypic variation in body size, especially in males, which fight one another with snout and mandible for access to females (Wallace, 1869; Meads, 1976). The most size-variable brentid may be *B. anchorago*: after examining a large series of this species, Sharp (1895) commented that "the variation in length is enormous, and perhaps not equaled in the case of any other species of Coleoptera, small males being only 10–11 mm long, while large examples of the same size attain 52 mm." Such variation in size is common within a single aggregation, and is important in male mating success, in female choice, and in patterns of mating in the aggregation as a whole.[3]

Similarly, the investigator could use the literature review to explain or justify a choice of methodology.

Rationale for the Investigation

Often the rationale for the investigation lies in past research. That is, past research may not have solved a problem adequately, or perhaps it was faulty in some way. There may be many reasons, and the investigator can use the literature review as a medium to express the reason or reasons for the research that he or she has conducted. The close of the introduction in Figure 17-1 presents such a rationale:

State forest health officers were targeted because they keep abreast of forest pest activity and are often called upon to make recommendations or develop programs for residents of their state.

Verb Tense in Literature Reviews

Choosing proper verb tense is frequently a problem in writing a literature review. It will help to keep these principles in mind. When referring to the actual work that researchers have already done, use the past tense. When referring to the knowledge their research produced, if the content is still considered to be true, use the present tense. Thus the literature review usually mixes together past and present tense as shown in this passage in which we have italicized the verb forms:

While significant improvements in ceramic technology *have been made* and *are currently being evaluated*, the issue of ceramic component reliability *has been raised* at this high temperature. An alternative to ceramic filter technology *is* sintered metal filter technology. Metal filter systems *offer* reduced potential for brittle failure. . . .[4]

▶ MATERIALS AND METHODS

The major criterion by which you can measure the success of a materials and methods (M & M) section is simply stated: An experienced researcher in the discipline should be able to use the information in this section to duplicate the research. For a second criterion, an experienced researcher should be able to use the information in this section to evaluate the research. If these criteria are not met, the M & M section fails.

M & M sections follow a fairly definite pattern incorporating some or all of the following parts:

- Design of the investigation
- Materials
- Procedures
- Methods for observation, analysis, and interpretation

The M & M section in Figure 17-1 consists of methods only. But every M & M section should contain all the information needed to meet the criteria of duplication and evaluation.

Design of the Investigation

When you have a complex design, give your readers an overview before you plunge them into the details. The overview need not, usually should not, be elaborate. Some turtle researchers gave it in one sentence and, indeed, included in the same sentence information about the materials used:

The effect of temperature on sex determination was studied in turtles of the subfamily Emydinae, genera *Graptemys* (map turtles), *Pseudemys* (sliders), and *Chrysemys* (painted turtles), from populations in the northern U.S. (Wisconsin) and southern U.S. (Alabama, Mississippi, and Tennessee).[5]

Materials

Materials can be human, animal, vegetable, or mineral. They are whatever you used by way of subjects, material, or equipment to do your research. In a report for the social sciences, instruments such as questionnaires would be described in this section. Remember that your descriptions of your materials have to be accurate enough to permit your readers to obtain or make similar materials. In the case of animals and plants, this usually means using the scientific as well as the common names. If you have a good deal of necessary information about your subjects or materials, use a table to display some of it. Equipment used throughout the experiment should be described, as in this passage:

> A bank of five parallel G.E. G8T5 germicidal lamps were used to generate ultraviolet light predominantly at 254 nm. The uncovered dishes to be irradiated were placed on a rotating platform 82 cm from the light source. A 10 cm diameter aperture midway between the light source and the rotating platform was used to collimate the incident light and to reduce shielding by the sides of the culture dishes.[6]

Procedures

In the procedures part, you describe for your readers step by step how you did your investigation. The description should be as complete as necessary, but remember that you are writing for an expert audience. When you are working with a procedure or equipment common in the discipline, you do not need to describe it in detail. However, if you anticipate that your readers might have some question about why you conducted some step as you did, take time to explain.

You can save a great many words by referring to procedures described elsewhere rather than repeating the information found in the original source as in this passage:

> The methods for digoxigenin labeling of RNA probes, tissue preparation, and in situ hybridization were as described by Bradley, et al. (1993).[7]

This is an excellent practice as long as you don't refer to sources inaccessible to your readers either by reason of geographic location or obscurity.

Methods for Observation, Analysis, and Interpretation

When such information is applicable, tell your readers how you observed your materials during the investigation and how you analyzed and interpreted your results. Because methods of observation, analysis, and interpretation are often quite standardized, this part can frequently be quite short.

Voice in Material and Methods Sections

In the passages we have quoted from M & M sections, the authors have used far more passive voice than active voice sentences. In most cases it is either obvious that the researchers performed the steps described, or it is unimportant who performed them. Under such circumstances, passive voice is as good a choice as active voice, perhaps even a better choice. But don't fear using active voice and first person when they seem appropriate to you. Most modern style books encourage such practices, and an occasional *I* or *we* reminds your readers that real people are at work. The author of the report in Figure 17-1 follows such advice and uses *I* freely.

Also, remember that passive voice used carelessly creates a great many dangling modifiers: "After drawing the blood, the calf was returned to the pen." Here the case of the blood-drawing calf can be cleared up with judicious use of active voice: "After drawing the blood, I returned the calf to the pen." (See pages 92–93, 198.)

▶ RESULTS

Because your results section answers the questions you have posed, it is the most important section of your report. Nonetheless, it is often the shortest section of an empirical report. It often takes a great deal of work to gain only a few bits of knowledge.

Begin your results section with an overview of what you have learned. The first sentence or two should be like the lead in a newspaper story, where the main points are quickly given, to be followed in later paragraphs by the details. Because the report in Figure 17-1 is organized into sections that reflect its multiple objectives, each section, rather that the whole begins with such an overview, with details presented in tables and graphs. If you make good use of tables and graphs, you do not need to restate such details. But you may want to refer to key data, both to emphasize their significance and to help your readers comprehend your tables and graphs.

▶ DISCUSSION

Many research reports combine the results and discussion sections as is done in Figure 17-1. Whether separate or combined, the discussion interprets and evaluates the results. It answers questions such as these:

• Was the hypothesis proved or disproved, or did the experimental results prove to be inconclusive?

- Are there any doubts about the results? Why? Was the methodology flawed? How could it be improved?
- How do the results compare with results from previous research? Are there areas of disagreement? Can disagreements be explained?
- What are the implications for future work?

Though the discussion section may cover a lot of ground, keep it tightly organized around the answers to the questions that need to be asked.

If major conclusions are not presented during the discussion or if there are certain conclusions the author wishes to emphasize, the report may contain a conclusions section, as is the case in Figure 17-1.

▶ A FINAL WORD

In this chapter we have given you general advice about reporting empirical research. If you are to become a professional in any field that requires such reporting, doing it well will be of vital importance to you. Therefore, we strongly urge you to examine representative journals and student theses in your discipline. Observe closely their format and style. Most journals have a section labeled something like "Information for Contributors." This section gives guidelines for manuscript preparation and style. Often it will refer you to the style manual, such as *The ACS Style Guide*, that governs the journal. Likely your library will have a copy of the manual you need. Read it carefully. It will supplement what you have learned here.

▶ PLANNING AND REVISION CHECKLISTS

You will find the planning and revision checklists that follow Chapter 2, Composing, and Chapter 4, Writing for Your Readers, valuable in planning and revising any presentation of technical information. The following questions specifically apply to empirical research reports. They summarize the key points in this chapter and provide a checklist for planning and revising.

Planning

- What is the subject of your research? The scope? The significance?
- What were your objectives? How can you best state your objectives? As hypotheses? As questions? As a statement of purpose?

- What do want to accomplish with your literature review? Definition of the research problem? Explanation of choice of materials and methods? Rationale for investigation?
- Is your report going to be a journal article or a thesis? If a thesis, have you consulted with your thesis adviser about it?
- Do you have the following well in mind for your materials and methods section?
  Design of the investigation?

  Materials?

  Procedures?

  Methods for observation and interpretation?
- Are all your results in? Can some of them be tabulated or displayed in charts or graphics?
- Which of these questions need to be answered in your discussion section?
  Do the results really answer the questions raised?

  Are there any doubts about the results? Why? Did you find at some point that the methodology was flawed? How could it be improved?

  Were the research objectives met?

  Was the hypothesis proved or disproved?

  How do the results compare with results from earlier research? Are there areas of disagreement? Can disagreements be explained?

  What are the implications for future work?

Revision

- Will your reader know the subject, scope, significance, and objectives of your investigation? Are your objectives stated absolutely clearly?
- Have you used past and present tenses appropriately in your literature review?
- Would an experienced researcher in your field be able to use your materials and methods section either to duplicate your investigation or to evaluate it?
- Have you used active voice and passive voice appropriately in your materials and methods section? If you have used passive voice, have you avoided dangling modifiers?
- Do the first few sentences of your results section present an overview of the results? Have you used tables and graphs when appropriate?
- Have you kept your discussion tightly organized around the questions that needed answering?

► EXERCISES

1. Empirical research is primarily concerned with fact-finding and interpretation. Do you see any similarity between empirical research and recommendation reports (Chapter 16)? In what major respects are they different?

2. Referring to Chapter 8, Gathering, Evaluating, and Documenting Information, determine how the methods used to gather information are affected by the nature and purpose of the investigation. How do the techniques discussed in Chapter 8 relate to empirical research?

3. Choose a research problem in your discipline, perhaps with the help of an instructor in that discipline. Research the literature in the problem until you can formulate an empirical study to deal with some aspect of the problem. Then write an introduction and literature review and a materials and methods section for the study. (What you will have when you finish is what a great many scientific and technical departments require as a proposal to conduct thesis research.) Submit your work to both your writing teacher and the teacher in the discipline.

4. Divide the class into groups by discipline and let each group choose a recorder to summarize its discussion. Each group is to choose an empirical research report published in a journal in its discipline. With the help of this chapter and the style manual that governs the journal, if one is available, the group then discusses the report's format, style, organization, and content. How closely does the report follow the principles of this chapter and the style manual? Does it differ in any significant ways?

   Following the group discussions, the summaries become the basis for a full class discussion.

5. Using an empirical research report from your field, do the following exercise.

   Imagine that you are at work on your first job after graduation. You have read an empirical research report that contains information that might be useful for the company for which you work. Report the research to decision-making executives in your company. Write the report in language they will understand. Executives will have little interest in methodology. Rather, they will want answers to questions such as these:

What was investigated? Why? What were the results? What were the conclusions of the researcher? What are the implications of the research for the company? What are your conclusions and recommendations as to possible actions the company might take to use the research?

Chapters 2, Composing, and 4, Writing for Your Readers, will be helpful for this exercise. Write your report as a memo (see Letter and Memorandum Format in Appendix B).

SCENARIO

You've been working for a new mail order house for four months. The pay isn't great, but the stock options are promising. As part of your executive training program, you've been assigned to working in the returns department. After a few weeks there, you notice something that both troubles and amazes you. About 10 percent of the items are returned without a copy of the invoice. Instead, they come accompanied by handwritten notes that are often illegible and missing key information like addresses, making adjustments difficult, if not impossible.

You read a copy of the instructions that go out with your merchandise. There it is in black and white, clear instructions about returning the invoice with the merchandise: "Complete the return section on the back of the invoice and return in the package with your merchandise."

You take the instructions down to the line where workers sort the returns. Showing them to the supervisor, you ask, "What's wrong with people? Why can't they do a simple thing like return an invoice?"

She smiles. "What's an invoice?" she asks.

"Well, it's an itemized bill that comes with the merchandise," you answer.

"Suppose you didn't know that. What would you return?" she says. "Remember Murphy's law: What can go wrong, will go wrong."

You take her advice to heart. Obviously Murphy's law is in operation here. Your job is to minimize the number of things that "can go wrong."

You think of a solution and get management to try it. You start by ordering invoices printed on blue paper. Then you simplify the instruction a bit: "Fill in the return section on the back of the blue slip that came with your order, and put it in the package with the items you are returning."

After two months of using the blue invoices, you find that only 2 percent of returns do not have an invoice with them—not perfect, but much better. You wonder what else can be done.

If you want more help in defeating Murphy's law while writing instructions, read on in this chapter.

chapter 18

Instructions

▶ Situational Analysis for Instructions
What Is the Purpose of My Instructions?
What Is My Reader's Point of View?
How and Where Will My Reader Use These Instructions?
What Content Does My Reader Really Need and Want?
How Should I Arrange My Content?

▶ Possible Components of Instructions
Introduction
Theory or Principles of Operation
List of Equipment and Materials Needed
Description of the Mechanism
Warnings
How-To Instructions
Tips and Troubleshooting Procedures
Glossary

▶ Accessible Format

▶ Reader Checks

Instructing others to follow some procedure is a common task on the job. Sometimes the instructions are given orally. When the procedure is done by many people or is done repeatedly, however, written instructions are a better choice. Instructions may be quite simple—as in Figure 18-1—or exceedingly complex—comprising a shelfful of manuals. They may be highly technical—dealing with operating machinery or programming computers, for example. Or they may be executive- or business-oriented—for example, explaining how to complete a form or how to route memorandums through a company. The task of writing instructions is not to be taken lightly. A Shakespearean scholar who had also served in the British Army wrote the following:

> The most effective elementary training [in writing] I ever received was not from masters at school but in composing daily orders and instructions as staff captain in charge of the administration of seventy-two miscellaneous military units. It is far easier to discuss Hamlet's complexes than to write orders which ensure that five working parties from five different units arrive at the right place at the right time equipped with the proper tools for the job. One soon learns that the most seemingly simple statement can bear two meanings and that when instructions are misunderstood the fault usually lies with the original order.[1]

To help you write instructions, we discuss the following in this chapter: situational analysis for instructions, the possible components of instructions, creating an accessible format, and checking with your readers.

DIRECTIONS
1. Clean toilet bowl thoroughly including under the rim.
2. To remove product, peel backing from blister package.
   Do not remove wrapping around product...it dissolves.
3. Remove toilet tank top. Flush toilet. Before tank refills, place product against rear right corner of tank under float. (See diagram.)
4. Initial blue color will appear after several flushes.
5. No removal necessary. Simply add a new 2000 FLUSHES ® Brand BLUE, when color is gone.

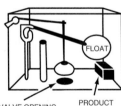

FIGURE 18-1 • Simple Instructions
Source: Reprinted with permission of Block Drug Company, Inc. © Block Drug Company, Inc., 1990.

▶ SITUATIONAL ANALYSIS FOR INSTRUCTIONS

In preparing to write instructions, follow the situational analysis we describe on pages 15–20 in Chapter 2, Composing. In addition, pay particular attention to the answers to these questions.[2]

What Is the Purpose of My Instructions?

Be quite specific about the purpose of your instructions. Keep your purpose in mind because it will guide you in choosing your content and in arranging and formatting that content. State your purpose in writing, like this:

> To instruct the plant managers, the corporate treasurer, and the plant accountant in the steps they need to follow to establish a petty cash fund.

What Is My Reader's Point of View?

Don't be satisfied with a general description of a reader as "the average consumer" or "a typical car owner." You'll achieve more accurate insights if you put yourself in the place of someone you know who fits that general description. For example, if I were my mother, what would be my point of view if I had to follow these instructions on how to complete this form? What questions and problems might I have? In what order might these questions and problems arise? Are there terms and concepts involved that I might not understand? What information do I really need? What information would be irrelevant? And so forth.

How and Where Will My Reader Use These Instructions?

Will your reader read your instructions carefully from beginning to end? Evidence indicates that he or she will not. Readers most often scan instructions and then begin reading carefully at those points where they need clarification. In other words, typically, they read them as a reference work rather than as an essay or a novel. Where will my reader use these instructions? In a comfortable, well-lighted workshop, well stocked with tools? In a cold, drafty, ill-lighted garage with only those tools hastily grabbed from the workshop? In the cockpit of a boat under emergency conditions, reading by a flashlight? Standing in line in a government office? The answers to such questions will help you organize and format your instructions.

What Content Does My Reader Really Need and Want?

Understanding your purpose and your reader's point of view is essential for answering this question. You can include many kinds of information in a set of instructions: theory, descriptions of mechanisms, troubleshooting advice, and so forth. We discuss such information shortly (see Possible Components of Instructions). You should include everything that is really relevant and nothing that is not relevant. If your reader is someone who has a need or a desire for theory, then furnish it. If theory is not needed or desired, furnishing it would be wasted effort for all concerned. Unneeded material is worse than irrelevant. It may obscure the relevant information so that the reader has difficulty finding it.

How Should I Arrange My Content?

Answers to all the previous questions aid you in arrangement decisions. If a good deal of theory is important and needed, your arrangement should probably include a separate section for it. If only brief explanations of theory are needed for the reader to understand a few steps in the instructions, place the explanations with the steps. For example, you might put the whys and wherefores of using a carpenter's level at that point in the instructions that describes how to use the level.

In order to arrange the actual instructions on how to perform a process, you must, of course, understand the process fully. If you can perform the process, taking notes as you go, do so. If that is not possible or convenient, at least analyze the process in your mind. Break it into its major steps and substeps. Be alert for potential trouble spots for your reader.

▶ POSSIBLE COMPONENTS OF INSTRUCTIONS

Sets of instructions may contain as many as eight components:

- Introduction
- Theory or Principles of Operation
- List of Equipment and Materials Needed
- Description of the Mechanism
- Warnings
- How-To Instructions
- Tips and Troubleshooting Procedures
- Glossary

We do not present this list as a rigid format. For example, you may find that you do not need a theory section, or you may include it as part of your introduction. You may want to vary the order of the sections. You may want to describe or list equipment as the reader needs it while performing the process rather than in a separate section. Often nothing more is needed than the how-to instructions. We describe the components of instructions primarily as a guide to your discovery of the material you will need.

Introduction

At a minimum, introductions to instructions state the purpose of the instructions and preview the contents. The following introduction from a student set of instructions does both, simply and efficiently:

> The purpose of these instructions is to provide a training manual as well as a field reference for installing the Hybrid Touch/Sound System for Paskett's visually impaired customers. These instructions cover preparing the customer's computer, installing the internal and external hardware, installing the software, testing, and cleaning up.[3]

Frequently, instructions may provide motivation for reading and following the instructions. They may also directly or indirectly indicate who the intended readers are. The following, from a publication concerning cholesterol, does all these things:

Intended audience

> High blood cholesterol is a serious problem. Along with high blood pressure and cigarette smoking, it is one of the three major modifiable risk factors for coronary heart disease. Approximately 25 percent of the adult population 20 years of age and older has "high" blood cholesterol levels—levels that are high enough to need intensive medical attention. More than half of all adult Americans have a blood cholesterol level that is higher than "desirable."

Motivation

Purpose of instructions

> Because high blood cholesterol is a risk to your health, you need to take steps to lower your blood cholesterol level. The best way to do this is to make sure you eat foods that are low in saturated fat and cholesterol. The purpose of this brochure is to help you learn how to choose these foods. The brochure will also introduce you to key concepts about blood cholesterol and its relationship to your diet. For example, it includes basic (but very important) information about saturated fat—the dietary component most responsible for raising blood cholesterol—and about dietary cholesterol—the cholesterol contained in food.

Preview of contents

> This brochure is divided in three parts. The first part of the brochure gives background information about high blood cholesterol and its relationship to heart disease. The second part introduces key points on diet changes and better food choices to lower blood cholesterol levels.
>
> Finally, in the third part more specific instructions are given for modifying eating patterns to lower your blood cholesterol, choosing low-saturated fat and low-cholesterol foods, and preparing low-fat dishes.

Reference to glossary

The "Glossary" provides easy definitions of new or unfamiliar terms. The appendices that follow the Glossary list the saturated fat and cholesterol content of a variety of foods.[4]

This introduction begins with motivation, stating that high blood cholesterol is a serious problem and providing support for that statement. The audience for the brochure, adult Americans, is indicated in an indirect manner. The purpose is clearly stated: "The purpose of this brochure is to help you learn how to choose these foods [that are low in saturated fat and dietary cholesterol]." Following the statements of motivation and purpose, the introduction previews what is to come in the rest of the brochure and refers to the glossary.

Introductions to instructions, then, are often not much different from the introductions we describe for you in Report Format in Appendix B. Short sets of instructions, however, may have very abbreviated introductions or, in some cases, no introduction at all. On the other hand, when introductions are longer than the one we have shown you, it's usually because the writers have chosen to include theory or principles of operation in the introduction. This is an accepted practice. We tell you how to give such information in the next section.

Theory or Principles of Operation

Many sets of instructions contain a section that deals with the theory or principles of operation that underlie the procedures explained. Sometimes historical background is also included. These sections may be called "Theory" or "Principles of Operation," or they may have substantive titles such as "Color Dos and Don'ts," "Purpose and Use of Conditioners," or "Basic Forage Blower Operation." Information about theory may be presented for several reasons. Some people have a natural curiosity about the principles behind a procedure. Others may need to know the purpose and use of the procedure. The good TV repair technician wants to know why turning the vertical control knob steadies the picture. Understanding the purposes behind simple adjustments enables the technician to investigate complex problems. What if nothing happens when the vertical control knob is turned? The technician with a theoretical background will know more readily where to look in the TV set to find a malfunction.

Theory sections do not need to be long or complicated. The following, from the student instructions on the Hybrid Touch/Sound System, explains the purpose of the system and outlines how it operates. It does a particularly good job in relating theory to the how-to instructions that will follow:

The Hybrid Touch/Sound System components and software convert a standard system to make that system available to visually impaired users while leaving the system available to sighted users. The system is comprised of separate touch systems and sound systems. Each can be installed without the other and still function. These instructions provide information for installing each system separately as well as together.

The Touch components and software allow a blind user to "see" the contents of the screen via Braille. This is accomplished by converting virtual visual output to a basic format, which is then transmitted to the Braille Board. The Sound components and software allocate the necessary storage space and memory to house and use the reading software. It also reconfigures the sound card to allow the user to give verbal commands to the computer. The software will control the system reconfigurations, and therefore the hardware components must be installed before the software.[5]

Sometimes a graphic can be used to cover theory, as in Figure 18-2.

Theory sections can be more complex as well. Figure 18-3 presents a portion of the theory section from the cholesterol brochure. It describes the relationship between cholesterol and atherosclerosis—that is, hardening of the arteries. Understanding the theory helps readers understand the guidelines for cholesterol levels set out in the rest of the section and motivates them to follow the guidelines. The entire section is written on a very personal level: What does this theory mean for the reader? Through the use of a simple for-

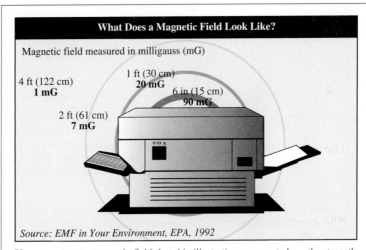

What Does a Magnetic Field Look Like?

Magnetic field measured in milligauss (mG)

4 ft (122 cm)
1 mG

1 ft (30 cm)
20 mG

6 in (15 cm)
90 mG

2 ft (61 cm)
7 mG

Source: EMF in Your Environment, EPA, 1992

You cannot see a magnetic field, but this illustration represents how the strength of the magnetic field—measured in milligauss—can diminish just 1 to 2 feet (30 to 61 centimeters) from the source. This magnetic field is a 60-Hz power-frequency field.

FIGURE 18-2 • Theory in a Graphic
Source: Department of Energy, *Emf in the Workplace* (Washington, DC: DOE, 1996), 7.

What You Need to Know About High Blood Cholesterol

Why Should You Know Your Blood Cholesterol Level?

There are important reasons for you to be concerned about your blood cholesterol level. Over time, cholesterol, fat, and other substances can build up in the walls of your arteries (a process called *atherosclerosis*) and can slow or block the flow of blood to your heart. Among many things, blood carries a constant supply of oxygen to the heart. Without oxygen, heart muscle weakens, resulting in chest pain, heart attacks, or even death. However, for many people there are no warning symptoms or signs until late in the disease process.

Heart disease is the leading cause of death in this country. Scientists have known for a long time that high blood cholesterol, high blood pressure, and smoking all increase the risk of heart disease.

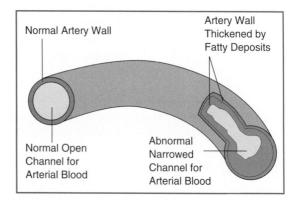

Normal Artery Wall

Artery Wall Thickened by Fatty Deposits

Normal Open Channel for Arterial Blood

Abnormal Narrowed Channel for Arterial Blood

Research now shows that the risk of developing atherosclerosis or coronary heart disease also increases as the blood cholesterol level increases. And it has now been proven that lowering high blood cholesterol, like controlling high blood pressure and avoiding smoking, will reduce this risk.

How High is Your Blood Cholesterol Level?

The medical community recently set guidelines for classifying blood cholesterol levels. They advise that a total cholesterol level less than 200 mg/dl is **"desirable"** for adults—above 200 mg/dl the risk of coronary heart disease steadily increases. The classifications of total blood cholesterol in the following chart are related to the risk of developing heart disease.

FIGURE 18-3 • Theory Section

Source: U.S. Department of Health and Human Services, *Eating to Lower Your Blood Cholesterol* (Washington, DC: GPO, 1989), 2–3.

Does Your Total Blood Cholesterol Level Increase Your Risk for Developing Coronary Heart Disease?

Desirable Blood Cholesterol	Borderline-High Blood Cholesterol	High Blood Cholesterol
Less than 200 mg/dl	200-239 moral	240 mg/dl and above

If your total cholesterol level is in the range of 200-239 mg/dl, you are classified as having **"borderline high"** blood cholesterol and are at increased risk for coronary heart disease compared to those with lower levels. However, if you have no other factors that increase your risk for coronary heart disease,* you should not need intensive medical attention. But you should make dietary changes to lower your level and thus reduce your risk of coronary heart disease.

On the other hand, if you have borderline-high blood cholesterol and have coronary heart disease or two other risk factors for coronary heart disease, you need special medical attention. In fact, you should be treated in the same way as people with **"high"** blood cholesterol— 240 mg/dl or greater—who could be at high risk for developing coronary heart disease and warrant more detailed evaluation and medical treatment.

Additional evaluation helps your physician determine more accurately your risk of coronary heart disease and make decisions about your treatment. Specifically, your doctor will probably want to measure your low density lipoprotein (LDL) cholesterol level—since LDL-cholesterol more accurately reflects your risk for coronary heart disease than a total cholesterol level alone. LDL-cholesterol levels of 130 mg/dl or greater increase your risk for developing coronary heart disease. After evaluating your LDL-cholesterol level and other risk factors for coronary heart disease, your physician will determine your treatment program.

Remember: *As your cholesterol level rises, your risk of developing coronary heart disease increases.*

*Risk factors for coronary heart disease include high blood pressure, cigarette smoking, family history of coronary heart disease before the age of 55, diabetes, vascular disease, obesity, and being male.

FIGURE 18-3 • *(continued)*

mat, graphics, questions, and plain language, the writers of the brochure make the theory quite accessible for the intended audience.

The theory section shown in Figure 18-3 uses some unfamiliar terms, such as *atherosclerosis*, which are defined in the glossary mentioned in the last paragraph of the introduction. However, the authors would have done their readers a kindness by mentioning the glossary again the first time it is needed and giving its page numbers. Remember to direct your readers. Locating a glossary for them is a good example of such direction.

As our excerpts illustrate, many diverse items of information can be placed in a theory or principles section. Remember, however, that the major purpose of the section is to emphasize the principles that underlie the actions later described in the how-to instructions. In this section, you're telling your readers *why*. Later, you'll tell them *how*. Theory is important, but don't get carried away with it. Experts in a process sometimes develop this section at too great a length, burying their readers under information the readers don't need and obscuring more important information that they do need. Make this section, if you include it at all, only as full and as complex as your analysis of purpose and readers demands.

List of Equipment and Materials Needed

In a list of equipment and materials, you tell your readers what they will need to accomplish the process. A simple example would be the list of cooking utensils and ingredients that precede a recipe. Sometimes if the audience is knowledgeable, the list of equipment is not used. Instead the instructions tell the readers what equipment they need as they need it: "Take a rubber mallet and tap the hubcap to be sure it's secure." However, skip the list of equipment only if you are sure the technicians for whom the instructions are intended are working in a well-equipped shop or routinely carry the necessary tools with them.

When a list is used, each item is mentioned by name, perhaps in tabular form. The list from our student instructions in Figure 18-4 uses side-by-side boxes of bulleted items to list the equipment and materials the technicians will need. Notice the caution about using demagnetized tools. Such cautions and warnings are common in instructions, and we say more about them later.

Sometimes, however, your audience analysis may indicate that more information then a simple list is needed. You may want, for instance, to define and describe the tools and equipment needed, as shown in Figure 18-5. If you think your readers are really unfamiliar with the tools or equipment being used, you may even give instruction in its use. If the equipment cannot be

---

EQUIPMENT AND MATERIALS

CAUTION: All tools must be demagnetized

• Phillips and Regular Screwdriver
• Component Pull (small and large)
• Grounding/Discharge Socket
• Jumper Tweezers
• Zip Plus Zip Drive, connection cable, and Zip Guest software
• Formatted, Blank Zip Disk (3 or more)

Hybrid System Components
- Braille Board (part BB1)
- Braille SCSI Board (part BB2)
- Visual Interpreter Video Card Attachment (part BB3)
- Audio Interpreter Audio Card Attachment (part BB4)
- Microphone/headset (part BB5)
- Software (CD and floppy included)

FIGURE 18-4 • Equipment and Materials List
Source: Dwayne Isbell, *Hybrid Touch/Sound System Installation.* Reprinted by permission of the author.

obtained easily, you'll do your readers a service by telling them where they can find the hard-to-get items. As always, your audience analysis determines the amount and kind of information presented.

Description of the Mechanism

Instructions devoted to the operation and maintenance of a specific mechanism usually include a section describing the mechanism. Similarly, if a mechanism is central in some process, it is frequently described. In such sections, follow the principles for technical description given on pages 192–194. Break the mechanism into its component parts, and describe how they function.

For example, springs can be developed as domestic water supplies through the use of a mechanism called a spring encasement. The following description, accompanied by the drawing in Figure 18-6, breaks a spring encasement into its component parts, describes the function of each part, suggests materials for the parts, and shows how the parts work together:

Spring encasements have six major components:

1. A system of perforated pipes to collect the water. Polyvinylchloride and cast-iron are common choices for all needed pipes.
2. A tank of reinforced concrete to store the collected water.
3. A heavy, cast-iron cover with lock to keep surface drainage and debris out of the storage tank.
4. A drain to clean out and empty the storage tank.

Basic Tools

You'll need a few basic tools for most home maintenance jobs, and some special tools for special jobs. Some are expensive, and are not needed very often. Is there a place where you can borrow or rent those?

Here are some basic tools and materials you may need for doing simple repairs on the outside of your house.

Nail Set

A *nail set* is a small metal device used to sink the heads of nails slightly below the surface you are driving them into (fig. 1).

Squares

The *framing square* is a handy measuring tool for lining up materials evenly and making square corners. It is usually metal (fig. 2).

The *try square* is smaller and is also used for lining up and squaring material. One side is made of wood and is not marked to measure with (fig. 3).

Miter Box

With a *miter box*, you can saw off a piece of board at an exact angle. It may be of wood, to use with a separate saw (fig. 4). Or it may be steel, with the saw set in the steel box (fig. 5).

Masonry Trowels and Jointer

The *trowel* is used to build or repair masonry walls, sidewalks, etc. It has a flat, thin, steel blade set into a handle. The "brick trowel" is the larger and is used for mixing, placing, and spreading mortar. The smaller "pointing trowel" is used to fill holes and repair mortar joints (fig. 6). This process is called "pointing."

The *jointer* is another masonry tool, used to finish joints after the wall is laid (fig. 7). Finish joints are made on the outside of a masonry wall to make it more waterproof and to improve appearance. The "V" and "concave" joints are the most weather tight. A different type of jointer is needed for each type of joint used.

FIGURE 18-5 • List of Tools
Source: U.S. Department of Agriculture, *Simple Home Repairs: Outside* (Washington, DC: GPO, 1986), 4.

5. A pipe to allow for overflow.

6. A connection to the distribution system.

When spring encasements are built on a slope, upslope from the collection system they should also have a surface-water diversion ditch and a cutoff wall of impermeable clay to control the water table around the tank.[6]

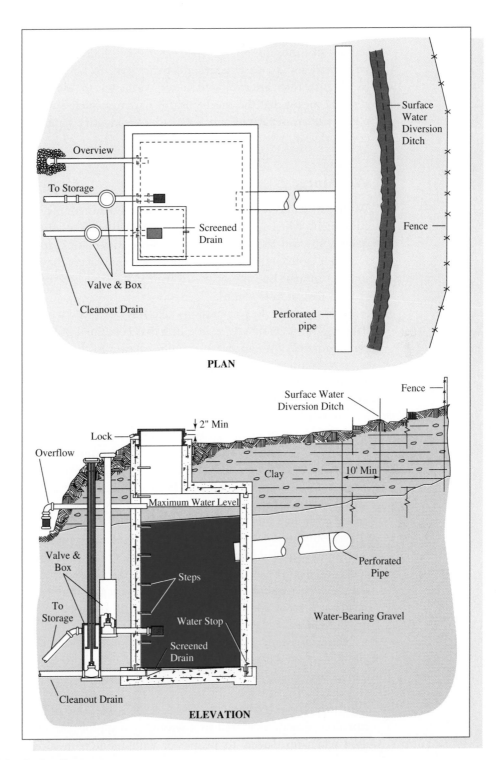

PLAN

ELEVATION

FIGURE 18-6 • Spring Encasement
Source: Environmental Protection Agency, *Manual of Individual and Non-Public Water Supply Systems* (Washington, DC: GPO, 1991), 70.

Mechanism descriptions are generally accompanied by numerous illustrations like those in Figures 18-6–18-8. Such illustrations show only necessary detail and, to be effective, normally have to be well annotated. Some, like Figure 18-8, are exploded views. We hasten to add that in this context *exploded* means that the mechanism is drawn in such a way that its component parts are separated and thus easier to identify. Figure 18-8 makes the concept clear.

Warnings

We live in an age of litigation. People who hurt themselves or damage their equipment when following instructions in the use of that equipment frequently sue for damages. If they can prove to a court's satisfaction that they were not sufficiently warned of the dangers involved, they will collect large sums of money. Because of this, warnings have become an increasingly important part of instructions.

How seriously do corporations take this need to warn people of possible dangers? We recently saw a shoe box that contained boating shoes. The box was decorated with an oceanographic chart. On the side of the box was a warning stating that, "this chart is not intended to be used as a navigational aid and is not reliable for that purpose.[7] Figure 18-9 shows that a device as simple to operate as an electric can opener comes with a set of warnings.

If they are extensive enough, the warnings may be put into a separate section, as they are in Figure 18-9. But often they are embedded in the how-to instructions. In either case, be sure they are prominently displayed in some manner that makes them obvious to the reader. You may surround them with boxes, print them in type different from and larger than the surrounding text, print them in a striking color, or mark them with a symbol of some sort. Frequently, you will use some combination of these devices.

Not only must you make the warnings stand out typographically, you must use language and, when appropriate, graphics that make the nature, severity, and consequences of the hazards involved absolutely clear. You must clearly state how to avoid the hazards. Any lack of clarity can result in a preventable accident, almost certainly followed by a costly lawsuit against your employer or your client.

No terminology is completely agreed upon for warnings. However, three levels of warning have been widely accepted, designated by the words *caution*, *warning*, and *danger*.[8]

Caution Use the word *caution* to alert the reader that not following the instructions exactly may lead to a wrong or inappropriate result. A caution is used when no danger to people or equipment is involved. Figure 18-10

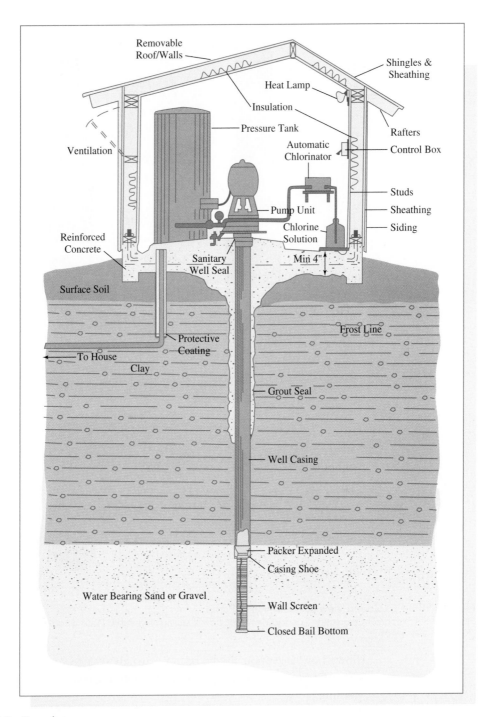

FIGURE 18-7 • Pumphouse
Source: U.S. Environmental Protection Agency, *Manual of Individual and Non-Public Water Supply Systems* (Washington, DC: GPO, 1991), 121.

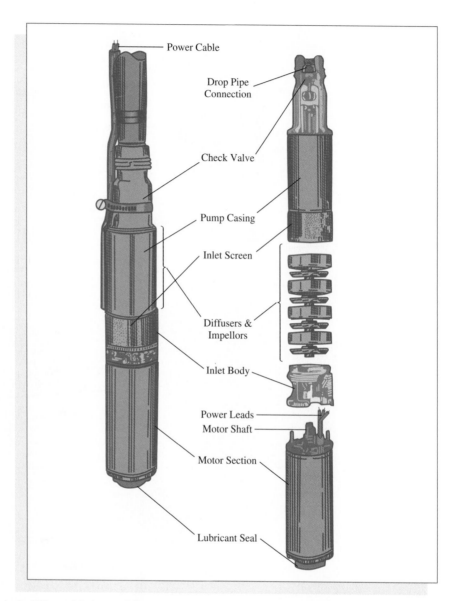

FIGURE 18-8 • Exploded View of Submersible Pump
Source: U.S. Environment Protection Agency, *Manual of Individual and Non-Public Water Supply Systems* (Washington, DC: GPO, 1991), 101.

shows how a caution might be used to advise a technician to follow the steps of a procedure in proper order. Sometimes, *note* is used for this level of warning.

Warning Use the word *warning* to alert the reader to faulty procedures that might cause minor-to-moderate personal injury or damage to equipment, as in the warning from a compact disc player manual shown in Figure 18-11.

IMPORTANT SAFEGUARDS

When using electrical appliances, basic safety precautions should always be followed, including the following:

1. Read all instructions.

2. To protect against risk of electrical shock, do not put power unit in water or other liquid.

3. Close supervision is necessary when any appliance is used by or near children.

4. Unplug from outlet when not in use, before putting on or taking off parts, and before cleaning.

5. Avoid contacting moving parts.

6. Do not operate any appliance with a damaged cord or plug or after the appliance malfunctions, or is dropped or damaged in any manner. Return appliance to the nearest authorized service facility for examination, repair or electrical or mechanical adjustment.

7. The use of attachments not recommended or sold by the appliance manufacturer may cause fire, electric shock or injury.

8. Do not use outdoors.

9. Do not let cord hang over edge of table or counter, or touch hot surfaces.

10. Do not open pressurized (aerosol-type) cans or cans of flammable liquids, such as lighter fluids.

SAVE THESE INSTRUCTIONS

FIGURE 18-9 • Warning Section
Source: Reprinted by permission of Underwriters Laboratories, Northbrook, IL.

The exclamation point inside the triangle in Figure 18-11 is a commonly accepted symbol, used to attract the reader's attention and to stress the importance of the message. You will see it used on all three levels of warnings.

Danger Use the word *danger* for the highest level of warning: a warning to prevent major personal injury or death. Obviously, you must make danger messages stand out typographically and write them with utter clarity. Figure 18-12 presents a good example.

Check Valve Test

- Place the mouthpiece shut-off valve in the Diving position.
- Place the mouthpiece in your mouth, squeeze the inhalation hose closed, and attempt to inhale through the mouthpiece. If it is possible to inhale with the inhalation hose closed off, the check valve is missing or defective.

CAUTION

If the mouthpiece shut-off valve is in the
Open position, the test will incorrectly
indicate a defective or missing check valve.

FIGURE 18-10 • A Caution Message

⚠ WARNING ⚠

- Do not use force to open or close the disc tray. Force may result in a damaged tray.
- Place nothing but a compact disc in the tray. Inserting objects other than discs in the tray may result in a damaged tray.

FIGURE 18-11 • A Warning Message

DANGER! RISK OF POSSIBLE ELECTRICAL SHOCK, INJURY, AND EVEN DEATH! USE PRECAUTION!

Follow all standard safety precautions when working with the components, computer, and electricity. Make sure that the computer is disconnected from the power supply and that the system has been discharged and grounded before touching or working. Note electrical hazards when you see this symbol.

FIGURE 18-12 • A Danger Message
Source: Dwayne Isbell, *Hybrid Touch/Sound System Installation*. Reprinted by permission of the author.

How-To Instructions

The actual instructions on how to carry out the procedure or operate the mechanism obviously lie at the heart of any set of instructions. The same general principles apply to all how-to instructions.

Style When writing how-to instructions, one of your major goals is to use a clear, understandable style. To write your instructions from the reader's point of view, use the active voice and imperative mood. The imperative mood is normal and acceptable in instructions. It's clear and precise and will not offend the reader. The instructions in Figure 18-13 illustrate the style.

By using the format shown in Figure 18-14, you can use the imperative mood even when several people with distinct tasks have to carry out the procedure. In the format shown, the headings in the left-hand column identify the responsible actor, allowing the imperative mood to be used in the right-hand column. It's an efficient system. (For more on the active voice and imperative mood, see pages 197–198.)

Most sets of how-to instructions use a list format. The list may use numbers, bullets or simply white space to keep the step distinct. Each step usually contains only one instruction and, at the most, two or three closely related instructions. Besides keeping each step distinct from other steps, listing has several other advantages as well.

- It makes it obvious how many steps there are.
- It makes it easy for readers to find their place on the page.
- It allows the reader to use the how-to instructions as a checklist.

EXTERNAL HARDWARE INSTALLATION

 DANGER! Risk of Possible Electrical Shock, Injury, or Even Death! Use precaution when connecting or disconnecting any device or hardware attached to the computer!

1. Disconnect grounding / discharge socket
2. Close chassis
3. If applicable, connect Braille Board to Braille SCSI port #1 (Note: ports are marked)
4. If applicable, connect microphone / headset to Braille SCSI port #2 (Note: ports are marked)
5. Reattach all hardware devices to parallel, SCSI, and serial ports where applicable
6. Connect computer to power source

FIGURE 18-13 • Imperative Mood Instructions
Source: Dwayne Isbell, *Hybrid Touch/Sound System Installation.* Reprinted by permission of the author.

DELUXE
CHECK PRINTERS, INC.

STANDARD OPERATING PROCEDURES

Procedure C-9
Establishing, Changing, or Eliminating the Petty Cash Fund
Accounts Payable and Purchasing Manual—C

SUMMARY: The petty cash fund is a fixed cash fund reserved for minor expenditures of $50 or less. This procedure explains how to establish change, or eliminate the petty cash fund.

NOTE: When a petty cash fund is established, the plant manager should assign responsibility to no more than two cash drawer custodians, with one individual having primary responsibility. The accounts payable clerk must not be a custodian of the petty cash fund.

See Procedure C-17 to disburse petty cash. See Procedure C-18 to replenish the petty cash fund. See Appendix f for petty cash fund controls.

RESPONSIBILITY	ACTION
Plant manager	1. Request authorization from corporate treasurer for one of the following: • establish petty cash fund • change amount of existing petty cash fund • eliminate existing petty cash fund
Corporate treasurer	2. Review request and approve or disapprove and notify plant accountant of decision.
Plant accountant	3. Notify plant manager of decision. 4. If establishing fund or increasing existing fund, have check prepared from Account 1030 (Regular Cash Account) for authorized amount payable to cash, debiting Account 1010 (Petty Cash Account) on check voucher. 4a. Place check in check cashing fund box and withdraw authorized amount of cash. 4b. Place cash in petty cash fund, and notify plant manager that petty cash fund is established or increased. —OTHERWISE— 5. If decreasing or eliminating existing fund, use Daily Report of Cash, form A-30-Q (Exhibit 24), to credit Account 1010.

Rewritten by: Kathy Huebsch

FIGURE 18-14 • Standard Operating Procedures
Source: Reprinted by permission of Deluxe Check Printers, Inc.

Use familiar, direct language, and avoid jargon. Tell your readers to *check* or *look over* equipment before or during use. Don't tell them to *conduct an investigation*. Tell your readers to *use* a wrench, not to *utilize* one. Fill your instructions with readily recognized verbs such as *adjust, attach, bend, cap, center, close, drain, install, lock, replace, spin, turn,* and *wrap*. For more on good style, see Chapter 5, Achieving a Readable Style.

If your how-to instructions call for calculations, include sample calculations to clarify them for the reader. As in this example:

> For a pesticide that is diluted with water, proportionally change the quantity of pesticide, the quantity of water, and the area, volume, or number of items treated. For example, one-half pound of pesticide in 1 gallon of water applied to 1,000 square feet is equivalent to 1 pound of pesticide in 2 gallons of water applied to 2,000 square feet.[9]

To further help readers with their calculations, the author provides the table reproduced in Figure 18-15.

Graphics Be generous with graphics. Word descriptions and graphics often complement each other. The words tell *what* action is to be done. The graphics show *where* it is to be done, and they often also show *how*. Our samples demonstrate well the relationship between words and graphics. Graphics are often annotated to allow for easy reference to them, as in Figure 18-16.

Pesticide Label Says Mix			Amount of Pesticide Per	
Amount Pesticide	**Per**		**1 qt. Water**	**1 pt. Water**
8 units	1 gal. water	EQUALS	2 units	1 unit
16 units	1 gal. water	EQUALS	4 units	2 units
32 units	1 gal. water	EQUALS	8 units	4 units
128 units	1 gal. water	EQUALS	32 units	16 units

Pesticide Label Says Apply			Amount of Pesticide Per		
Amount Pesticide	**Per**		**20,000 sq. ft.**	**10,000 sq. ft.**	**500 sq. ft.**
1 unit	1,000 sq. ft.	EQUALS	20 units	10 units	$1/_2$ unit
2 units	1,000 sq. ft.	EQUALS	40 units	20 units	1 unit
5 units	1,000 sq. ft.	EQUALS	100 units	50 units	$2^1/_2$ units
10 units	1,000 sq. ft.	EQUALS	200 units	100 units	5 units

FIGURE 18-15 • Table to Assist Calculations
Source: U.S. Environmental Protection Agency, *Citizen's Guide to Pesticides* (Washington, D.C.: GPO, 1991), 8.

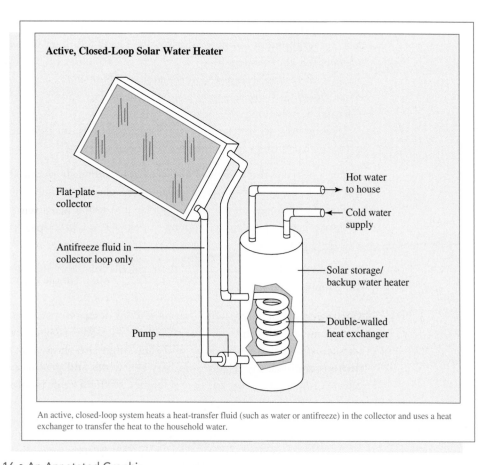

FIGURE 18-16 • An Annotated Graphic
Source: Department of Energy, *Solar Water Heating* (Washington, DC: DOE, 1996), 3.

Arrangement When writing performance instructions, arrange the process being described into as many major routines and subroutines as needed. For example, a set of instructions for the overhaul and repair of a piece of machinery might be broken down as follows:

• Disassembly of major components
• Disassembly of components
• Cleaning
• Inspection
• Lubrication
• Repair
• Reassembly of components

- Testing of components
- Reassembly of major components

Notice that the steps are in chronological order as are most how to instructions.

If steps are repeated, it's sometimes a legitimate practice to tell the reader to "repeat steps 2, 3, and 4." But whether you do so depends on your analysis of the reader's situation. Visualize your reader. Maybe he or she will be perched atop a shaky ladder, your instructions in one hand, a tool in the other. Under such circumstances, the reader will not want to be flipping pages around to find the instructions that need to be repeated. You will be wiser and kinder to print, once again, all the instructions of the sequence. But, if the reader will be working in a comfortable place with both feet on the ground, you will probably be safe enough saying, "Repeat steps . . . ."

Such reader and situation analysis can help you make many similar decisions. Suppose, for example, that your readers are not expert technicians, and the process you are describing calls for them to use simple test equipment. In such a situation, you should include the instructions for operating the test equipment as part of the routine you're describing. On the other hand, suppose your readers are experienced technicians following your instructions at a comfortable workbench, with a well-stocked library of manuals nearby. Then you can assume that they know how to operate any needed test equipment, or you can refer them to another manual that describes how to operate the test equipment.

For the most part, instructions have no conclusions. They simply end with the last instruction. On occasion, particularly when writing for a general audience, you might wish to close with a summary of the chief steps of the process or, perhaps, a graceful close (see page 632). However, such endings are not general practice.

Tips and Troubleshooting Procedures

Many sets of instructions contain sections that either give the reader helpful tips on how to do a better job or provide guidance when trouble occurs.

Tips You may present tips in a separate section, as illustrated in Figure 18-17. Or, just as likely, you may incorporate them into the how-to instructions, as in the following excerpt on setting flexible tile. In the excerpt, the last sentences in instructions 1, 2, 3, and 5 give the reader tips that should make the tasks go more easily:

1. Remove loose or damaged tile. A warm iron will help soften the adhesive.
2. Scrape off the old adhesive from the floor or wall. Also from the tile if you're to use it again.

| New Ways to Make Sauces and Soups | Sauces, including gravies and homemade pasta sauces, and many soups often can be prepared with much less fat. Before thickening a sauce or serving soup, let the stock or liquid cool-preferably in the refrigerator. The fat will rise to the top and it can easily be skimmed off. Treat canned broth-type soups the same way.

For sauces that call for sour cream, substitute plain low-fat yogurt. To prevent the yogurt from separating, mix 1 tablespoon of cornstarch with 1 tablespoon of yogurt and mix that into the rest of the yogurt. Stir over medium heat just until the yogurt thickens. Serve immediately. Also, whenever you make creamed soup or white sauces, use skim or 1% milk instead of 2% or whole milk. |

| New Ways to Use Old Recipes | There are dozens of cookbooks and recipe booklets that will help you with low-fat cooking. But there is no reason to stop using your own favorite cookbook. The following list summarizes many of the tips. Using them, you can change tried and true recipes to low-saturated fat, low-cholesterol recipes. In some cases, especially with baked products, the quality or texture may change. For example, using vegetable oil instead of shortening in cakes that require creaming will affect the result. Use margarine instead; oil is best used only in recipes calling for melted butter. Substituting yogurt for sour cream sometimes affects the taste of the product. Experiment! Find the recipes that work best with these substitutions. |

Instead of	Use
1 tablespoon butter	1 tablespoon margarine or 3/4 tablespoon oil
1 cup shortening	2/3 cup vegetable oil
1 whole egg	2 egg whites
1 cup sour cream	1 cup yogurt (plus 1 tablespoon cornstarch for some recipes)
1 cup whole milk	1 cup skim milk

Low-Fat Cooking Tips

Your kitchen is now stocked with great tasting, low-saturated fat, low-cholesterol foods. But you may still be faced with the temptation to fix your favorite higher fat meats, rich soups, and baked breads and cookies. The suggestions below will help you to reduce the amount of total and saturated fats in these foods.

New Ways to Prepare Meat, Poultry, Fish, and Shellfish

When you prepare meats, poultry, and fish, remove as much saturated fat as possible. Trim the visible fat from meat. Remove the skin and fat from the chicken, turkey, and other poultry. And, if you buy tuna or other fish that is packed in oil, rinse it in a strainer before making tuna salad or a casserole, or buy it packed in water.

Changes in your cooking style can also help you remove fat. Rather than frying meats, poultry, fish, and shellfish, try broiling, roasting, poaching, or baking. Broiling browns meats without adding fat. When you roast, place the meat on a rack so that the fat can drip away.

Finally, if you baste your roast use fat-free ingredients such as wine, tomato juice, or lemon juice instead of the fatty drippings. If you baste turkeys and chickens with fat, use vegetable oil or margarine instead of the traditional butter or lard. Self-basting turkeys can be high in saturated fat-read the label!

FIGURE 18-17 • Tips
Source: U.S. Department of Health and Human Services, *Eating to Lower Your Cholesterol* (Washington, DC: GPO, 1989), 23–24.

3. Fit tiles carefully. Some tile can be cut with a knife or shears, others with a saw. Tile is less apt to break if it's warm.
4. Spread adhesive on the floor or wall with a paint brush or putty knife.
5. Wait until adhesive begins to set before placing the tile. Press tile on firmly. A rolling pin works well.[10]

Troubleshooting Procedures You may incorporate troubleshooting procedures into your how-to instructions, as in this excerpt:

> Tighten screws in the hinges. If screws are not holding, replace them one at a time with a longer screw. Or insert a matchstick in the hole and put the old screw back.[11]

Perhaps more often, troubleshooting procedures will be in a section of their own, as in Figure 18-18, which illustrates a typical format, a three-

 DANGER! Risk of Possible Electrical Shock, Injury, or Even Death! Use precaution when removing and reinstalling any component as directed in Table 5. All danger warnings that are stated in this instruction set should be followed as you use the Troubleshooting Guide.

Problem	Probable Cause	Solution
Braille Board not showing any characters	• Braille Board not attached correctly • Software not installed correctly • Braille SCSI card not installed correctly • Braille Visual Hybrid Interpreter not installed correctly	• Check connections • Reinstall Braille Interpretation Software • Reinstall Braille SCSI and check jumpers • Reinstall Interpreter and check jumpers
Audio System not dictating and or not reading back	• Microphone/Speakers not attached Correctly • Software not installed correctly • Audio Interpreter not installed Correctly	• Check connections • Reinstall Audio I/O Control Language • Reinstall Audio Interpreter
Error message that says that the appropriate driver cannot be located	• Jumpers are set incorrectly	• Check all jumpers on all components to ensure that they are set correctly
None of the above solved the problem	• The system is too outdated to handle the Hybrid System components • Bad Hybrid component	• Upgrade the system to the minimum requirements • Order replacement component and reinstall replacement component

FIGURE 18-18 • Troubleshooting Chart
Source: Dwayne Isbell, *Hybrid Touch/Sound System Installation.* Reprinted by permission of the author.

column chart with headings such as "Problem," "Probable Cause," and "Solution." The solutions are given as instructions in the active voice, imperative mood.

Glossary

If your audience analysis tells you that your reader may not comprehend all the terminology you plan to use in your instructions, you'll need to provide definitions. If you need only a few definitions, you can define terms as you use them.

If you must provide many definitions, you'll probably want to provide a glossary as a separate section. See pages 185–188, where we discuss definitions, and page 188, where we discuss glossaries.

► ACCESSIBLE FORMAT

Your major goal in setting up your format in instructions should be to make the information accessible for your readers.

The theory section shown in Figure 18-3 demonstrates excellent accessibility. The type is large and readable, and the format is especially helpful for those readers who may scan the document. The headings standing apart to the left of the print allow the reader to scan quickly, looking for points of interest. Also, headings phrased as questions are more likely to arrest the attention of scanning readers and draw them into reading the text. Curiosity is put to work—they may want to know the answers to the questions.

In Figure 18-3, the graphic of the narrowed artery and the table showing cholesterol levels highlight the two key points in the section. The scanning reader who stops only long enough to absorb the information in the two graphics will at least learn the principal danger of high cholesterol and what a desirable cholesterol level is.

Look now at Figure 18-19, a government document intended to instruct readers in how to file a form to establish their relationship with "alien relatives" who may wish to immigrate to the United States. The document is an example of inaccessible format: Both the headings and the print are small. The page is cluttered and intimidating. The headings are not worded in a way that leads readers to the information they seek. Terms such as *Eligibility*, *Documents previously submitted*, and *Documents in general*, while meaningful to the person who wrote them, probably would not be helpful to the typical reader of these instructions. The format violates most of the principles discussed in Chapter 11, Document Design. Furthermore, the style of the instructions violates most of the principles discussed in Chapter 5, Achieving a Readable Style.

U.S. Department of Justice
Immigration and Naturalization Service

PETITION TO CLASSIFY STATUS OF ALIEN RELATIVE
FOR ISSUANCE OF IMMIGRANT VISA

READ INSTRUCTIONS CAREFULLY, FEE WILL NOT BE REFUNDED.

Not all of these instructions relate to the type of case which concerns you. Please read carefully those which do relate. Failure to follow instructions may require return of your petition and delay final action.

1. **Eligibility.** A petition may be filed by a citizen or a lawful permanent resident of the United States to classify the status of alien relatives as follows:

   a. *By citizen of the United States:* Except as noted in paragraph 2, a citizen of the United States may submit a petition on behalf of a spouse or sons and daughters (regardless of age or marital status). A United States citizen at least 21 years of age may submit a petition for a parent, brother, or sister. If the petition is for a son or daughter who is married or at least 21 years of age, or both, or for a brother or sister, do not submit petitions for the beneficiary's spouse or unmarried children under 21 years of age. If the petition is approved, the beneficiary's spouse and unmarried children under 21 years of age, if accompanying or following to join him/her, will automatically be eligible for the same preference status.

   b. *By a lawful permanent resident alien:* Except as noted in paragraph 2, an alien lawfully admitted to the United States for permanent residence may submit a petition on behalf of a spouse or an unmarried child regardless of age. However, if a lawful permanent resident alien is married to a citizen and wishes to petition for an unmarried child, such alien should consult the nearest office of the Immigration and Naturalization Service for advice as to whether it would be preferable, or *necessary*, for the United States citizen spouse to submit the petition instead. If the petition is for an unmarried son or daughter, do not submit petitions for the beneficiary's unmarried children under 21 years of age. If the petition is approved, the beneficiary's unmarried children under 21 years of age, if accompanying or following to join him/her, will automatically be eligible for the preference status.

2. **Petitions which cannot be approved.** Approval cannot be given to a petition on behalf of—

   a. A parent, brother, or sister, unless the petitioner is a United States citizen and at least 21 years of age.

   b. An adoptive parent, unless the relationship to the United States citizen petitioner exists by virtue of an adoption which took place while the child was under the age of 16, and the child has thereafter been in the legal custody of, and has resided with, the adopting parent or parents for at least 2 years. While the legal custody must be after the adoption, residence occurring prior to the adoption can satisfy the residence requirement.

   c. A stepparent, unless the marriage creating the status of stepparent occurred before the citizen stepchild reached the age of 18 years.

   d. An adopted child, unless the child was adopted while under the age of 16 and has thereafter been in the legal custody of, and has resided with, the adopting parent or parents for at lest 2 years. While the legal custody may be after the adoption, residence occurring prior to the adoption can satisfy the residence requirement.

   e. A stepchild, unless the child was under the age of 18 years at the time the marriage creating the status of stepchild occurred.

   f. A wife or husband by reason of any marriage ceremony where the contracting parties thereto were not physically present in the presence of each other, unless the marriage shall have been consummated.

   g. A grandparent, grandchild, nephew, niece, uncle, aunt, cousin, or in-law.

3. **Supporting documents.** The following documents must be submitted with the petition:

   a. *To prove United States citizenship of petitioner* (where petition is for relative of a citizen).

      (1) If you are a citizen by reason of birth in the United States, submit your birth certificate. If your birth certificate is unobtainable, see ``Secondary Evidence'' below for submission of document in place of birth certificate.

      (2) If you were born outside the United States and became a citizen through the naturalization or citizenship of a parent or husband, and have not been issued a certificate of citizenship in your own name, submit evidence of the citizenship and marriage of such parent or husband, as well as termination of any prior marriages. Also, if you claim citizenship through a parent, submit your birth certificate and a separate statement showing the date, port, and means of all your arrivals and departures into and out of the United States. (Do not make or submit a photostat of a certificate of citizenship.)

      (3) If your naturalization occurred within 90 days immediately preceding the filing of this petition, or if it occurred prior to September 27, 1906, the naturalization certificate must accompany the petition. Do not make or submit a photostat of such certificate.

   b. *To prove family relationship between petitioner and beneficiary.*

      (1) If petition is submitted on behalf of a wife or husband, it must be accompanied by a certificate of marriage to the beneficiary and proof of legal termination of all previous marriages of both wife and husband.

      (2) If a petition is submitted by a mother on behalf of a child (regardless of age), the birth certificate of the child, showing the name of the mother, must accompany the petition. If the petition is submitted by a father or stepparent on behalf of a child (regardless of age), certificate of marriage of the parents, proof of termination of their prior marriages, and birth certificate of the child, showing the names of the parents thereon, must accompany the petition.

      (3) If petition is submitted on behalf of a brother or sister, your own birth certificate and the birth certificate of the beneficiary, showing a common mother, must accompany the petition. If the petition is on behalf of a brother or sister having a common father and different mothers, marriage certificate of your parents, and proof of termination of their prior marriages must accompany the petition.

      (4) If petition is submitted on behalf of a mother, your own birth certificate, showing the name of your mother, must accompany the petition. If petition is submitted on behalf of a father or stepparent, your own birth certificate, showing the names of the parents thereon, and marriage certificate of your parents must accompany the petition, as well as proof of termination of prior marriages of your parents.

      (5) If either the petitioner or the beneficiary is a married woman, marriage certificate(s) must accompany the petition. However, when the relationship between the petitioner and beneficiary is that of a mother and child (regardless of age), the mother's marriage certificate need not be submitted if the mother's present married name appears on the birth certificate of the child.

      (6) If the petitioner and the beneficiary are related to each other by adoption, a certified copy of the adoption decree must accompany the petition.

FIGURE 18-19 • Government Instructions before Revision

c. *Secondary evidence.*

If it is not possible to obtain any one of the required documents or records shown above, the following may be submitted for consideration:

(1) Baptismal certificate.—A certificate under the seal of the church where the baptism occurred within two months after birth, showing date and place of the child's birth, date of baptism, and the names of the child's parents.

(2) School record.—A letter from the school authorities having jurisdiction over school attended (preferably the first school), showing the date of admission to the school, child's date of birth or age at that time, place of birth, and the names and places of birth of parents, if shown in the school records.

(3) Census Record.—State or federal census record showing the name(s) and places(s) of birth, and date(s) of birth or age(s) of the person(s) listed.

(4) Affidavits.—Written statements sworn to or affirmed by two persons who were living at the time, and who have personal knowledge, of the event you are trying to prove—for example, the date and place of birth, marriage, or death. The persons making the affidavits may be relatives and need not be citizens of the United States. Each affidavit should contain the following information regarding the person making the affidavit: his/her full name and address; date and place of birth; relationship to you, if any; full information concerning the event; and complete details concerning how he/she acquired knowledge of the event.

d. *Documents and secondary evidence unavailable.*

If you are unable to submit required evidence of birth, death, marriage, divorce or adoption because the event took place in a foreign country which does not record such events, and secondary evidence is unavailable, attach a statement to this effect, setting forth the date and place of each of your entries into the United States. Also attach any letters, photographs, remittances, or similar documents which tend to support the claimed relationship and three passport type photographs of yourself.

e. *Documents previously submitted.*

If your birth abroad, or the birth abroad of any person through whom citizenship is claimed by you, was registered with an American consul, submit with this petition any registration form that was issued. If any required documents were submitted to an attorney retained by the American consul in connection with such registration, or in connection with the issuance of a United States passport or in any other official matter, and you wish to use such documents in support of this petition instead of submitting duplicate copies, merely list such documents in an attachment to this petition and show the location of the consulate. If you wish to make similar use of required documents contained in any Immigration and Naturalization Service file, list them in an attachment to this petition and identify the file by name and number. Otherwise, the documents required in support of this petition must be submitted.

f. *Documents in general.*

All supporting documents must be submitted in the original. If you desire to have the original returned to you, and if copies are by law permitted to be made, you may submit photostatic or typewritten copies. Photostatic copies unaccompanied by the original may be accepted if the copy bears a certification by an immigration or consular officer that the copy was compared with the original and found to be identical. Any document in a foreign language must be accompanied by a translation in English. The translator must certify that he is competent to translate and that the translation is accurate. (Do not make a copy of a certificate of naturalization or citizenship.)

4. **Preparation of petition.** A separate petition for each beneficiary must be typewritten or printed legibly with pen and ink.

(If you need more space to answer fully any questions on this form, use a separate sheet(s), identify each answer with the number of the corresponding question, and date and sign each sheet.) Be sure this petition and attached Form 1-130A are legible.

5. **Submission of petition.** If you are residing in the United States, send the completed petition to the Office of the Immigrant and Naturalization Service having jurisdiction over your place of residence. If you are residing outside the United States consult the nearest American consulate as to the consular office or foreign officer of the Service designated to act on your petition. If you are a United States citizen petitioning for an immediate relative classification in behalf of your unmarried child, the petition must be submitted in sufficient time for action to be completed on the petition and for the child to obtain a visa and reach the United States before the date on which he/she will be 21 years of age.

6. **Approval of petition.** Upon approval of a petition filed by a United States citizen for his/her alien spouse, unmarried minor child, or parent, an immigrant visa may be issued to the alien without regard to the annual limitation on immigrant visa issuance. In the cases of all other aliens for whom immigrant visa petitions are approved, an immigrant visa number will be required. Availability of an immigrant visa number depends on the volume of demand by aliens in the same visa classification who have an earlier priority date on the visa waiting list.

7. **Fee.** A fee of thirty-five dollars ($35) must be paid for filing this petition. It cannot be refunded regardless of the action taken on the petition. DO NOT MAIL CASH. ALL FEES MUST BE SUBMITTED IN THE EXACT AMOUNT. Payment by check or money order must be drawn on a bank or other institution located in the United States and be payable in United States currency. If petitioner resides in Guam, check or money order must be payable to the ''Treasurer, Guam.'' If petitioner resides in the Virgin Islands, check or money order must be payable to he ''Commissioner of Finance of the Virgin Islands.'' All other petitioners must make the check or money order payable to the ''Immigration and Naturalization Service.'' When check is drawn on an account of a person other than the petitioner, the name of the petitioner must be entered on the face of the check. If petition is submitted from outside the United States, remittance may be made by bank international money order or foreign draft drawn on a financial institution in the United States and payable to the ''Immigration and Naturalization Service'' in United States currency. Personal checks are accepted subject to collectibility. An uncollectible check will render the petition and any document issued pursuant thereto invalid. A charge of $5.00 will be imposed if a check in payment of a fee is not honored by the bank on which it is drawn.

8. **Penalties.** Severe penalties are provided by law for knowingly and willfully falsifying or concealing a material fact or using any false document in the submission of this petition.

9. **Authority.** The authority for collecting the information required on this form is contained in 8 U.S.C. 1154(a). Submission of the information solicited is voluntary. The principal purpose for which the information is solicited is to determine the eligibility of the beneficiary for the benefits sought. The information solicited may also, as a matter of routine use, be disclosed to other federal, state, local, and foreign law enforcement and regulatory agencies, the Department of Defense including any component thereof (if either the beneficiary or petition has served, or is serving in the Armed Forces of the United States), the Department of State, Central Intelligence Agency, Interpol, and individuals and organizations, during the course of investigation to elicit further information required by this Service to carry out its functions. Failure to provide any or all of the solicited information may result in the denial of the petition.

FIGURE 18-19 • *(continued)*

Now look at Figure 18-20, which is the same document after it has been revised and given a new format to make it accessible. Certain things are immediately obvious. The print is bigger, and there is more white space. The headings are more meaningful and informative. They are phrased from the reader's point of view and are stated as questions that someone approaching this process might reasonably ask: "Who can file?" and "For whom can you file?" have replaced "Eligibility." Such new headings lead and inform readers rather than confusing them. The format and style of the instructions are now readable, showing a knowledge and application of the principles discussed in Chapters 5 and 11. The result is a readable document.

Finally, when a set of instructions runs more than several pages, you should furnish a table of contents (TOC) to help your readers find their way and to provide an overview of the instructions. The headings in the TOC should duplicate those in the instructions. (See pages 614–615.)

▶ READER CHECKS

When you're writing instructions, check frequently with the people who are going to use them. Bring them a sample of your theory section and discuss it with them. See if they understand it. Does it contain too much theory, or too little? Submit your how-to instructions to the acid test. Let members of the audience for whom the instructions are intended—but who are not familiar with the process—attempt to perform the process by following your instructions. Encourage them to tell you where your instructions are confusing. A procedure called protocol analysis can be a help at this point. In protocol analysis, you ask the person following your instructions to speak into a tape recorder, giving his or her observations about the instructions while attempting to follow them. Here is an excerpt from a set of such observations made by someone trying to use a computer manual and on-line help to aid him in a word processing exercise:

> Somehow I've got the caps locked in here. I can't get to the lower case. OK, I'm struggling with trying to come off those capitals. I'm not having any luck. So, what do I need to do? I could press help. See if that gets me anything. Using the keyboard. I'll try that. 2.0. I can't do that because it's in this mode. I'm getting upper case on the numbers, so I can't type in the help numbers. So I'll reset to get rid of that. Big problem. Try reset. Merging text, formatting, setting margins, fixing problems. I can't enter a section number because I can't get this thing off lock. Escape. Nothing helps. Well, I'm having trouble here.[12]

Such information pinpoints troublesome areas in instructions. If you were writing instructions that were to be used by many people, it would be a worthwhile investment of time and money to conduct a protocol analysis. In

U.S. Department of Justice
Immigration and Naturalization Service (INS)

Petition For Alien Relative

Instructions

Read the instructions carefully. If you do not follow the instructions, we may have to return your petition, which may delay final action.

1. Who can file?

A citizen or lawful permanent resident of the United States can file this form to establish the relationship of certain alien relatives who may wish to immigrate to the United States. You must file a separate form for each eligible relative.

2. For whom can you file?

A. If you are a citizen, you may file this form for:
1) your husband, wife, or unmarried child under 21 years old
2) your unmarried child over 21, or married child of any age
3) your brother or sister if you are least 21 years old
4) your parent if you are at least 21 years old

B. If you are a lawful permanent resident you may file this form for:
1) your husband or wife
2) your unmarried child

NOTE: If your relative qualifies under instruction A(2) or A(3) above, separate petitions are not required for his or her husband or wife or unmarried children under 21 years old. If your relative qualifies under instruction B(2) above, separate petitions are not required for his or her unmarried children under 21 years old. These persons will be able to apply for the same type of immigrant visa as your relative.

3. For whom can you *not* file?

You cannot file for people in these four categories.

A. An adoptive parent or adopted child, if the adoption took place after the child became 16 years old, or if the child has not been in the legal custody of the parent(s) for at least two years after the date of the adoption, or has not lived with the parent(s) for at least two years, either before or after the adoption.

B. A stepparent or stepchild, if the marriage that creating this relationship took place after the child became 18 years old.

C. A husband or wife, if you were not both physically present at the marriage ceremony, and the marriage was not consummated.

D. A grandparent, grandchild, nephew, niece, uncle, aunt, cousin, or in-law.

4. What documents do you need?

You must give INS certain documents with this form to show you are eligible to file. You must also give INS certain documents to prove the family relationship between you and your relative.

A. For each document needed, give INS the original and one copy. However, because it is against the law to copy a Certificate of Naturalization, a Certificate of Citizenship or an Alien Registration receipt Card (Form I-151 or I-551), give INS the original only. **Originals will be returned to you.**

B. If you do not wish to give INS the original document, you may give INS a copy. The copy must be certified by
1) an INS or U.S. consular officer, or
2) an attorney admitted to practice law in the United States, or
3) an INS accredited representative
(INS still may required originals)

C. Documents in a foreign language must be accompanied by a complete English translation. The translator must certify that the translation is accurate and that he or she is competent to translate.

5. What documents do you need to show you are a United States citizen?

A. If you were born in the United States, give INS your birth certificate.

B. If you were naturalized, give INS your original Certificate of Naturalization.

C. If you were born outside the United States, and you are a U.S. citizen through your parents, give INS
1) your original Certificate of Citizenship, or
2) your Form FS-240 (Report of Birth Abroad of a United States Citizen)

D. In place of any of the above, you may give INS your valid unexpired U.S. passport that was initially issued for at least 5 years

E. If you do not have any of the above and were born in the United States, see the instructions under 8, below. ``What if a document is not available?''

6. What documents do you need to show you are a permanent resident?

You must give INS your alien registration receipt card (Form I-151 or I-551). Do not give INS a photocopy of the card.

7. What documents do you need to prove family relationship?

You have to prove that there is a family relationship between your relative and yourself.

In any case where a marriage certificate is required, if either the husband or wife was married before you must give INS documents to show that all previous marriages were legally ended. In cases where the names shown on the supporting documents have changed, give INS legal documents to show how the name change occurred (for example, a marriage certificate, adoption decree, court order, etc.).

Find the paragraph in the following list that applies to the relative you are filing for.

If you are filing for your

A. **husband or wife,** give INS
1) your marriage certificate.
2) a color photo of you and one of your husband or wife, taken within 30 days of the date of this petition.

FIGURE 18-20 • Revised Government Instructions

These photos must have a white background. They must be glossy, un-retouched, and not mounted. The dimension of the facial image should be about 1 inch from chin to top of hair in ¾ frontal view, showing the right side of the face with the right ear visible. Using pencil or felt pen, lightly print name (and Alien Registration Number, if known) on the back of each photograph.

3) a completed and signed Form G-325A (Biographic Information) for you and one for your husband or wife. Except for name and signature, you do not have to repeat on the G-325A the information given on your I-130 petition.

B. **child** and you are the **mother,** give the child's birth certificate showing your name and the name of your child.

C. **child** and you are the **father or stepparent,** give the child's birth certificate showing both parents' names and your marriage certificate.

D. **brother or sister,** give your birth certificate and the birth certificate of your brother or sister showing both parents' names. If you do not have the same mother, you must also give the marriage certificates of your father to both mothers.

E. **mother,** give your birth certificate showing your name and the name of your mother.

F. **father,** give your birth certificate showing the names of both parents and your parents' marriage certificate.

G. **stepparent,** give your birth certificate showing the names of both natural parents and the marriage certificate of your parent to your stepparent.

H. **adoptive parent or adopted child,** give a certified copy of the adoption decree and a statement showing the dates and places you have lived together.

8. What if a document is not available?

If the documents needed above are not available, you can give INS the following instead. (INS may require a statement from the appropriate civil authority certifying that the needed document is not available.)

A. Church record: A certificate under the seal of the church where the baptism, dedication, or comparable rite occurred two months after birth, showing date and place of the child's birth, date of the religious ceremony, and the names of the child's parents.

B. School record: A letter from the school authorities of the school attended (preferably the first school), showing the date of admission to the school, child's date and place of birth, and the names and places of birth of parents, if shown in the school records.

C. Census record: State or federal census record showing the name, place of birth, and date of birth or the age of the person listed.

D. Affidavits: Written statements sworn to or affirmed by two persons who were living at the time and who have personal knowledge of the event you are trying to prove; for example, the date and place of birth, marriage, or death. The persons making the affidavits need not be citizens of the United States. Each affidavit should contain the following information regarding the person making the affidavit: his or her full name, address, date and place of birth; and his or her relationship to you, if any; full information concerning the event; and complete details concerning how the person acquired knowledge of the event.

9. How should you prepare this form?

A. Type or print legibly in ink.

B. If you need extra space to complete any item, attach a continuation sheet, indicate the item number, and date and sign each sheet.

C. Answer all questions fully and accurately. If any item does not apply, please write ``N/A.''

10. Where should you file this form?

A. If you live in the United States, send or take the form to the INS office that has jurisdiction over where you live.

B. If you live outside the United States, contact the nearest American Consulate to find out where to send or take the completed form.

11. What is the fee?

You must pay $35.00 to file this form. **The fee will not be refunded, whether the petition is approved or not.** DO NOT MAIL CASH. All checks or money orders, whether U.S. or foreign, must be payable in U.S. currency at a financial institution in the United States. When a check is drawn on the account of a person other than yourself, write your name on the face of the check. If the check is not honored, INS will charge you $5.00.

Pay by check of money order in the exact amount. Make the check or money order payable to ``Immigration and Naturalization Service.'' However,

A. if you live in Guam: Make the check or money order payable to ``Treasurer, Guam'', or

B. if you live in the U.S. Virgin islands: Make the check or money order payable to ``Commissioner of Finance of the Virgin Islands.''

12. When will a visa become available?

When a petition is approved for the husband, wife, parent, or unmarried minor child of a United States citizen, these relatives do not have to wait for a visa number, as they are not subject to the immigrant visa limit. However, for a child to qualify for this category, all processing must be completed and the child must enter the United States before his or her 21st birthday.

For all other alien relatives there are only a limited number of immigrant visas each year. The visas are given out in the order in which INS receives properly filed petitions. To be considered properly filed, a petition must be completed accurately and signed, the required documents must be attached, and the fee must be paid.

For a monthly update on dates for which immigrant visas are available, you may call (202) 632-2919.

13. What are the penalties for submitting false information?

Title 18, United States Code, Section 1001 states that whoever willfully and knowingly falsifies a material fact, makes a false statement, or makes use of a false document will be fined up to $10,000 or imprisoned up to five years or both.

14. What is our authority for collecting this information?

We request the information on this form to carry out the immigration laws contained in Title 8, United States Code, Section 1154(a). We need this information to determine whether a person is eligible for immigration benefits. The information you provide may also be disclosed to other federal, state, local, and foreign law enforcement and regulatory agencies during the course of the investigation required by this Service. You do not have to give this information. However, if you refuse to give some or all of it, your petition may be denied.

It is not possible to cover all the conditions for eligibility or to give instructions for every situation. If you have carefully read all the instructions and still have questions, please contact your nearest INS office.

FIGURE 18-20 • (continued)

any case, regardless of whether you use protocol analysis, if your readers can't follow your instructions, don't blame them. Rather, examine the instructions to see where you have failed. Often, you will find you have left out some vital link in the process or assumed knowledge on the part of your readers that they do not possess.

▶ PLANNING AND REVISION CHECKLISTS

You will find the planning and revision checklists that follow Chapter 2, Composing, and Chapter 4, Writing for Your Readers, valuable in planning and revising any presentation of technical information. The following questions specifically apply to instructions. They summarize the key points in this chapter and provide a checklist for planning and revising.

Planning

- What is the purpose of your instructions?
- What is your reader's point of view?
- How and where will your readers use these instructions?
- What content does your reader really need and want?
- How should you arrange your content? Which of the following components should you include as a separate section? Which should you omit or include within another component (for example, theory in the introduction)?

Introduction

Theory or principles of operation: How much theory do your readers really need or want?

List of equipment and materials needed: Are your readers familiar with all the needed equipment and material? Do they need additional information?

Description of the mechanism: Does some mechanism play a significant role in these instructions?

Warnings: Are there expected outcomes that will be affected by improper procedure? Are there places in the instructions where improper procedure will cause damage to equipment or injury or death to people?

How-to instructions: Can your instructions be divided into routines and subroutines? What is the proper sequence of events for your how-to instructions?

Tips and troubleshooting procedures: Are there helpful hints you can pass on to the reader? What troubles may come up? How can they be corrected?

Glossary: Do you have to define enough terms to justify a glossary?

- What graphics will help your instructions? Do you have them available, or can you produce them?

Revision

- Have you made the purpose of your instructions clear to your readers?
- Can your readers scan your instructions easily and find what they need?
- Do you have sufficient headings? Do your headings stand out? Are they meaningful to your readers? Would it help to cast some as questions?
- Is all terminology that may be unfamiliar to the reader defined somewhere?
- Is your print size large enough for your readers to read comfortably, given their likely location?
- Is all your content relevant? Do your readers need or want it? Have you made it easy for your readers to skim and to skip parts not relevant to them?
- Have you covered any needed theory adequately?
- Do your readers know what equipment and material they will need? Do they know how to use the equipment needed? If not, have you provided necessary explanations?
- Have you provided any necessary descriptions of mechanisms?
- Are your caution, warning, and danger messages easy to see and clear in their meaning? Are you sure you have alerted your readers to every situation in which they might injure themselves or damage their equipment?
- Have you broken your how-to instructions into as many routines and subroutines as necessary?
- Are your steps in chronological order, with no steps out of sequence?
- Are your how-to instructions written in the active voice, imperative mood?
- Have you used a list format, with short entries for each step of the instructions?
- Have you used simple, direct language and avoided jargon?
- If necessary, have you provided sample calculations?
- Have you used graphics whenever they would be helpful? Are they sufficiently annotated?
- Have you provided tips that may help your readers to do the task more efficiently?
- Have you anticipated trouble and provided troubleshooting procedures?
- If troubleshooting procedures appear in a separate section, is the section laid out in a way that clearly distinguishes problem, cause, and remedy?
- Do you have enough definitions to warrant a glossary?
- Are your instructions long enough to warrant a table of contents?

- Have you checked with your readers? Have you asked a typical reader to attempt to carry out the procedure using your instructions? Have you corrected any difficulties that such a check revealed?
- Have you checked thoroughly to eliminate any misspellings and mechanical errors?

▶ EXERCISES

1. Writing instructions offers a wide range of possible papers. Short papers might consist of nothing more than an introduction and a set of how-to instructions. Examples—good and bad—of such short instructions can be found in hobby kits and accompanying such things as toys, tents, and furniture that must be put together. Textbook laboratory procedures frequently exemplify short sets of instructions. Using the Planning and Revision Checklists for this chapter, write a short set of instructions. Here are some possible subjects:

   - Developing film
   - Drawing a blood sample
   - Applying fertilizer
   - Setting a bicycle gear
   - Completing a form
   - Accomplishing some do-it-yourself task around a house
   - Replacing a part in an automobile or some other mechanism
   - Cleaning a carpet
   - Balancing a checkbook
   - Writing or following a computer program

2. Using the Planning and Revision Checklists for this chapter, write a set of instructions that includes at least six of the eight possible components listed on page 506. The components do not have to be in separate sections, but they must be clearly recognizable for what they are. Here are some suggested topics:

   - Testing electronic equipment
   - Setting up an accounting procedure for a small business
   - Conducting an agronomy field test
   - Checking blood pressure
   - Painting an automobile
   - Setting up a Web site

3. The instructions for emergency disinfection in Figure 18-21 are usable in their current form, but they could be greatly improved. In a collaborative group, examine and discuss the instructions. Using the Revision Checklist for this chapter, decide on ways to improve them. At the end of the discussion, each member of the group should individually prepare a revision. Provide some typographical variation to make the instructions more accessible.

4. Divide the class into groups of five to seven. The instructor will supply each group with a toy building set, such as Lincoln Logs, Legos, Power Pack Motor Sets, Command-A-Bot, or Robot World. Using the set provided, each group will design and build a working mechanism and then write instructions for operating the device to perform some function. The instructions must include at least six of the eight components listed on page 506. The components do not have to be in separate sections, but they must be clearly recognizable for what they are.[13]

Emergency Disinfection

When ground water is not available and surface water must be used, avoid sources containing floating material or water with a dark color or an odor. The water tank from a surface source should be taken from a point upstream from any inhabited area and dipped, if possible, from below the surface.

When the home water supply system is interrupted by natural or other forms of disaster, limited amounts of water may be obtained by draining the hot water tank or melting ice cubes.

In case of a nuclear attack, surface water should not be used for domestic purposes unless it is first found to be free from excessive radioactive fallout. The usual emergency treatment procedures do not remove such substances. Competent radiological monitoring services as may be available in local areas should be relied upon for this information.

There are two general methods by which small quantities of water can be effectively disinfected. One method is by boiling. It is the most positive method by which water can be made bacterially safe to drink. Another method is chemical treatment. If applied with care, certain chemicals will make most waters free of harmful or pathogenic organisms.

When emergency disinfection is necessary, the physical condition of the water must be considered. The degree of disinfection will be reduced in water that is turbid. Turbid or colored water should be filtered through clean cloths or allowed to settle, and the clean water drawn off before disinfection. Water prepared for disinfection should be stored only in clean, tightly covered, noncorrodible containers.

METHODS OF EMERGENCY DISINFECTION

1. *Boiling.* Vigorous boiling for one minute will kill any disease-causing microorganisms present in water. The flat taste of boiled water can be improved by pouring it back and forth from one container into another, by allowing it to stand for a few hours, or by adding a small pinch of salt for each quart of water boiled.

2. *Chemical Treatment.* When boiling is not practical, chemical disinfection should be used. The two chemicals commonly used are chlorine and iodine.

   a. *Chlorine*

      (1) *Chlorine Bleach.* Common household bleach contains a chlorine compound that will disinfect water. The procedure to be followed is usually written on the label. When the necessary procedure is not given, one should find the percentage of available chlorine on the label and use the information in the following tabulation as a guide:

Available chlorine[1]	Drops per quart of clear water[2]
1%	10
4–6%	2
7–10%	1

[1]If strength is unknown, add 10 drops per quart of water.
[2]Double amount for turbid or colored water.

FIGURE 18-21 • Instructions for Emergency Procedures
Source: U.S. Environmental Protection Agency, *Manual of Individual and Non-Public Water Supply Systems* (Washington, DC: GPO, 1991), 173–74.

The treated water should be mixed thoroughly and allowed to stand for 30 minutes. The water should have a slight chlorine odor; if not, repeat the dosage and allow the water to stand for an additional 15 minutes. If the treated water has too strong a chlorine taste, it can be made more palatable by allowing the water to stand exposed to the air for a few hours or by pouring it from one clean container to another several times.

(2) *Granular Calcium Hypochlorite*. Add and dissolve one heaping teaspoon of high-test granular calcium hypochlorite (approximately 1/4 ounce) for each 2 gallons of water. This mixture will produce a stock chlorine solution of approximately 500 mg/L, since the calcium hypochlorite has an available chlorine equal to 70 percent of its weight. To disinfect water, add the chlorine solution in the ratio of one part of chlorine solution to each 100 parts of water to be treated. This is roughly equal to adding 1 pint (16 oz.) of stock chlorine solution to each 12.5 gallons of water to be disinfected. To remove any objectionable chlorine odor, aerate the water as described above.

(3) *Chlorine Tablets*. Chlorine tablets containing the necessary dosage for drinking water disinfection can be purchased in a commercially prepared form. These tablets are available from drug and sporting goods stores and should be used as stated in the instructions. When instructions are not available, use one tablet for each quart of water to be purified.

b. *Iodine*

(1) *Tincture of Iodine*. Common household iodine from the medicine chest or first aid package may be used to disinfect water. Add five drops of 2 percent United States Pharmacopeia (U.S.P.) tincture of iodine to each quart of clear water. For turbid water add ten drops and let the solution stand for at least 30 minutes.

(2) *Iodine Tablets*. Commercially prepared iodine tablets containing the necessary dosage for drinking water disinfection can be purchased at drug and sporting goods stores. They should be used as stated in the instructions. When instructions are not available, use one tablet for each quart of water to be purified.

Water to be used for drinking, cooking making any prepared drink, or brushing the teeth should be properly disinfected.

FIGURE 18-21 • *(continued)*

SCENARIO

You've been on the job for six months as a plant geneticist for a large seed company. As you're settling into work one morning, enjoying your second cup of coffee, and turning on your computer to run some figures on a seed corn project, your boss drops by your cubicle.

"Got an invitation here," your boss says. "The Rincon Kiwanis chapter wants a speaker, week from Thursday morning—twenty minutes and a question-and-answer period. Think you can handle it?"

"Ah, sure, yes, why not?" you manage.

"Good," says your boss. "I hear they're worried about genetically engineered plants, especially the ones with built-in insecticide capabilities. Work that in somehow." With that your boss drops off the invitation and saunters out.

"What have I got myself in for," you wonder. You think about some of the ways to plan a speech. Know your audience. Find out about the place where you'll be speaking. Plan your speech well, but deliver it extemporaneously. Visual aids? Maybe some of the slides you have from the corn project might work.

You remember reading that some people want insect-proof corn to be classified as an insecticide. Who are Kiwanians, anyway? Local business people, mainly? How do the Rincon Kiwanians feel about the genetic engineering of foods? Will they be hostile? You decide that a call to the president of the local chapter is in order. The telephone number is on the invitation. You reach for the phone.

For more about planning and delivering a speech, look into this chapter.

chapter 19

Oral Reports

► Preparation

► Delivery Techniques
The Extemporaneous Speech
The Manuscript Speech

► Arranging Content
Introduction
Body
Conclusion

► Presentation
Physical Aspects of Speaking
Audience Interaction

► Visual Aids
Purpose of Visual Aids
Criteria for Good Visual Aids
Visual Content
Visual Presentation Tools

Oral reports are a major application of reporting technical information. You will have to report committee work, laboratory experiments, and research projects. You will give reports at business or scholarly meetings. You will instruct, if not in a teacher-student relationship, perhaps in a supervisor-subordinate relationship. You may have to persuade a group that a new process your section has devised is better than the present process. You may have to brief your boss about what your department does, in order to justify its existence. In this chapter we discuss preparing and presenting your oral report and place heavy emphasis on the ways in which you can provide visual support.

▶ PREPARATION

In most ways, preparing an oral report is much like composing a written report. The situational analysis is virtually identical to the situational analysis described in Chapter 2, Composing. You have to consider your purpose and audience, discover your material, and arrange your material.

For an oral report, you may have to pay even more attention to questions about persona, audience attitude, and your relationship to the audience than you do for a written report (see pages 15–20). These questions are particularly crucial ones, as you need to know whether your audience will consider you trustworthy and credible. To be an effective speaker, you must establish an effective relationship between you and the audience. You must not only be sincere and knowledgeable about your subject but also conform to the audience's expectations about dress, demeanor, and choice of language.

If your audience is not North American, you must be aware of how they expect to be addressed (see Chapter 7, Writing for International Readers). Often, such awareness requires expert guidance. For example, certain hand gestures common in the United States may be considered obscene in other cultures. In some cultures, too casual dress for men would be insulting, and bare arms on a woman would be sacrilegious. Don't overlook the obvious: How well do your listeners understand English? Will an idiomatic expression such as "we're going to shoot the works on this project" leave them wondering what violence is intended? Chapter 7 lists some sources that will give you a start. Your library will provide further help, as will the World Wide Web.

Find out as much as you can about the conditions under which you'll speak. Inquire about the size of the room you will speak in, the time allotted for the speech, and the size of the audience. If you have to speak in a large area to a large group, will a public address system be available? Find out whether you will have a lectern for your notes. Check on the availability of any equipment you need, whether it be a computer program, such as Power-Point or Excel, or something as simple as an overhead projector to show transparencies. Plan to bring your own equipment if necessary.

Find out whether there will be someone to introduce you. If not, you may have to work your credentials as a speaker into your talk. Consider the time of day and day of the week. An audience listening to you at 3:30 on Friday afternoon will not be nearly as attentive as an audience earlier in the day or earlier in the week. Feel free to ask the sponsoring group any of these questions. The more you know beforehand, the better prepared and therefore the more comfortable you'll be.

▶ DELIVERY TECHNIQUES

There are four basic delivery techniques, but you really need to think about only two of them. The four are (1) impromptu, (2) speaking from memory, (3) extemporaneous, and (4) reading from a manuscript.

Impromptu speaking involves speaking "off the cuff." Such a method is too risky for a technical report, in which accuracy is so vital. In speaking from memory, you write out a speech, commit it to memory, and then deliver it. This gives you a carefully planned speech, but we cannot recommend it as a good technique. The drawbacks are (1) your plan becomes inflexible; (2) you may have a memory lapse in one place that will unsettle you for the whole speech; (3) you think of words rather than thoughts, which makes you more artificial and less vital; and (4) your voice and body actions become stylized and lack the vital spark of spontaneity. We consider the best delivery techniques to be extemporaneous speech and reading a speech from a manuscript, and we will discuss these in more detail.

The Extemporaneous Speech

Unlike the impromptu speech, with which it is sometimes confused, the extemporaneous speech is carefully planned and practiced. In preparing for an extemporaneous speech, you go through the planning and arranging steps described in Chapter 2, composing. But you stop when you complete the outline stage. You do not write out the speech. Therefore, you do not commit yourself to any definite phraseology. In your outline, however, include any vital facts and figures that you must present accurately. You want no lapses of memory to make your presentation of a technical report inaccurate.

Before you give the speech, practice it, working from your outline. Give it several times, preferably, before a live audience—perhaps a roommate or a friend. As you practice, fit words to your outlined thoughts. Make no attempt to memorize the words you choose at any practice session, but keep practicing until your delivery is smooth. When you can go through the speech without faltering, you are ready to present it. When you practice a speech, pay particular attention to timing. Depending on your style and the occasion, plan on a delivery rate of 120–180 words per minute. Nothing, *but nothing*, will annoy program planners or an audience more than to have a speaker scheduled for thirty minutes go for forty minutes or an hour. The long-winded speaker probably cheats some other speaker out of his or her allotted time. Speakers who go beyond their scheduled time can depend upon not being invited back.

We recommend that you type your outline. Use capitals, spacing, and underlining generously to break out the important divisions. Use boldface type if you use a word processor. But don't do the entire outline in capitals. That makes it hard to read. As a final refinement, place your outline in a looseleaf ring binder. By so doing you can be sure it will not become scattered or disorganized.

The extemporaneous speech has several real advantages over the speech read from manuscript. With the extemporaneous speech you will find it easier to maintain eye contact with your audience. You need only glance occasionally at your outline to keep yourself on course. For the rest of the time you can concentrate on looking at your audience.

You have greater flexibility with an extemporaneous speech. You are committed to blocks of thought but not words. If by looking at your audience you see that they have not understood some portion of your talk, you are free to rephrase the thought in a new way for better understanding. If you are really well prepared in your subject, you can bring in further examples to clarify your point. Also, if you see you are running overtime, you can condense a block by leaving out some of your less vital examples or facts.

Finally, because you are not committed to reciting specific words, you retain conversational spontaneity. You are not faltering or groping for words, but neither are you running by your audience like a well-oiled machine.

The Manuscript Speech

Most speech experts recommend the extemporaneous speech over reading from a manuscript. We agree in general. However, speaking in a technical situation often requires giving a manuscript speech. Papers delivered to scientific societies are frequently written and then read to the group. Often, the society will later publish your paper. Often, technical reports contain complex technical information or extensive statistical material. Such reports do not conform well to the extemporaneous speech form, and you should plan to read them from a manuscript.

Planning and writing a speech are little different from writing a paper. However, in writing your speech try to achieve a conversational tone. Certainly, in speaking you will want to use the first person and active voice. Remember that speaking is more personal than writing. Include phrases like "it seems to me," "I'm reminded of," and "just the other evening, I." Such phrases are common in conversation and give your talk extemporaneous overtones. Certainly, prefer short sentences to long ones.

Type the final draft of your speech. Just as you did in the outline for your extemporaneous speech, be generous with capitals, spacing, and underlining. Plan on about three typed pages per five minutes of speech. Put your pages in order, and place them in a looseleaf binder.

When you carry your written speech to the lectern with you, you are in no danger of forgetting anything. Nevertheless, you must practice it—again, preferably aloud to a live audience. As you practice, remember that because you are tied to the lectern, your movements are restricted. You will need to depend even more than usual on facial expression, gestures, and voice variation to maintain audience interest. Do not let yourself fall into a singsong monotone as you read the set phrases of your written speech.

Practice until you know your speech well enough to look up from the manuscript for long periods of good eye contact. Plan an occasional departure from your manuscript to speak extemporaneously. This will help you regain the direct contact with the audience that you so often lose while reading.

▶ ARRANGING CONTENT

For the most part, you will arrange your speech as you do your written work. However, the speech situation does call for some differences in arrangement and even content, and we concentrate on these differences. We discuss the arrangement in terms of introduction, body, and conclusion.

Introduction

A speech introduction should accomplish three tasks: (1) create a friendly atmosphere for you to speak in, (2) interest the audience in your subject, and (3) announce the subject, purpose, scope, and plan of development of your talk.

Be alert before you speak. If you can, mingle and talk with members of the group to whom you are going to speak. Listen politely to their conversation. You may pick up some tidbit that will help you get off to a favorable start. Look for bits of local color or another means to establish a common ground between you and the audience. When you begin to speak, mention some member of the audience or perhaps a previous speaker. If you can do it sincerely, compliment the audience. If you have been introduced, remember to acknowledge and thank the speaker. Unless it is a very formal occasion, begin rather informally. If there is a chairperson and a somewhat formal atmosphere, we recommend no heavier a beginning than "Mr. Chairman (or Madam Chairwoman), ladies and gentlemen."

Gain your audience's attention by mentioning some particularly interesting fact or bit of illustrative material. Anecdotes are good if they truly tie in with the subject. But take care with humor. Avoid jokes that really don't tie in with the subject or the occasion. Forget about risqué stories.

Be careful also about what you draw attention to. Do not draw attention to shortcomings in yourself, your speech, or the physical surroundings. Do not begin speeches with apologies.

Announce your subject, purpose, scope, and plan of development in a speech just as you do in writing. (See pages 622–628.) If anything, giving your plan of development is more important in a speech than in an essay. Listeners cannot go back in a speech to check on your arrangement the way that a reader of an essay can. So the more guideposts you give an audience, the better. No one has ever disputed this old truism: (1) Tell the audience what you are going to tell them. (2) Tell them. (3) Tell them what you just told them. In instructional situations, some speakers provide their audiences with a printed outline of their talk.

Body

When you arrange the body of a speech, you must remember one thing: A listener's attention span is very limited. Analyze honestly your own attention span—be aware of your own tendency to let your mind wander. You listen to the speaker for a moment, and then perhaps you think of lunch, of some problem, or an approaching appointment. Then you return your attention to the speaker. When you become a speaker, remember that people do not hang on your every word.

What can you do about the problem of the listener's limited attention span? In part, you solve it by your delivery techniques. (We discuss these in the next section of this chapter.) It also helps to plan your speech around intelligent and interesting repetition.

Begin by cutting the ground you intend to cover in your speech to the minimum. Build a five-minute speech around one point, a fifteen-minute speech around two. Even an hour-long talk probably should not cover more than three or four points.

Beginning speakers are always dubious about this advice. They think, "I've got to be up there for fifteen minutes. How can I keep talking if I have only two points to cover? I'll never make it." Because of this fear, they load their speeches with five or six major points. As a result, they lull their audience into a state of somnolence with a string of generalizations.

In speaking, even more than in writing, your main content should be masses of concrete information—examples, illustrations, little narratives, analogies, and so forth—supporting just a few generalizations. As you give your supporting information, repeat your generalization from time to time. Vary the way you state it, but cover the same ground. The listener who was out to lunch the first time you said it may hear it the second time or the third. You use much the same technique in writing, but you intensify it even more in speaking.

We have been using the same technique here in this chapter. We began this section on the speech body by warning you that a listener's attention span is short. We reminded you that *your* listening span is short—same topic but a new variation. We asked you what you can do about a listener's limited span—same topic with only a slight shift. In the next paragraph, we told you not to make more than two points in a fifteen-minute speech. We nailed this point down in the next paragraph by having a dubious speaker say, "I've got to be up there for fifteen minutes. How can I keep talking if I have only two points to cover?" In the paragraph just preceding this one we told you to re-peat intelligently so that "the listener who was out to lunch the first time you said it may hear it the second time or the third." Here we were slightly changing an earlier statement that "you listen to the speaker for a moment, and then perhaps you think of lunch. . . ." In other words, we are aware that attention sometimes wanders. When you're paying attention, we want to catch you. Try the same technique in speaking, because a listener's attention span is even more limited than a reader's.

Creating suspense as you talk is another way to generate interest in your audience. Try organizing a speech around the inductive method. That is, give your facts first and gradually build up to the generalization that they support. If you do this skillfully, using good material, your audience hangs on, won-dering what your point will be. If you do not do it skillfully or use dull ma-terial, your audience will tune you out and tune into their private worlds.

Another interest-getting technique is to relate the subject matter to some vital interest of the audience. If you are talking about water pollution, for ex-ample, remind the audience that the dirtier their rivers get, the more tax dol-lars it will eventually take to clean them up.

Visual aids often increase audience interest. Remember to keep your graphics big and simple. No one is going to see captions from more than three or four feet away. Stick to big pie and bar graphs. If you have tables, print them in letters from two to three inches high. If you are speaking to a large group, put your graphic materials on transparencies and project them onto a screen. Prepare your transparencies with care. Don't just photocopy typed or printed pages or graphics from books. No one behind the first row will see them. To be effective, letters and numbers on transparencies should be at least twice normal size. Word processing makes it easy to print graphics with large type. If you need an assistant to help you project visual aids, ask someone to help or bring someone with you.

Do not display a graphic until you want the audience to see it. While the graphic is being displayed, call your listeners' attention to everything you want them to see. Take it away as soon as you are through with it. If using a projector, turn it off whenever it is not in use. Be sure to key every graphic into your speaker's script. Otherwise, you may slide right by one.

Conclusion

In ending your speech, as in your written reports, you have your choice of several closes. You can close with a summary, a list of recommendations including a call for some sort of action, or what amounts to "Good-bye, it's been good talking to you." As in the introduction, you can use an anecdote in closing to reinforce a major point. In speaking, never suggest that you are drawing to a close unless you really mean it. When you suggest that you are closing, your listeners perk up and perhaps give a happy sigh. If you then proceed to drag on, they will hate you.

Remember that audience interest is usually highest at the beginning and close of a speech. Therefore, you will be wise to provide a summary of your key points at the end of any speech. Give your listeners something to carry home with them.

▶ PRESENTATION

After you have prepared your speech, you must present it. For many people, giving a speech is a pretty terrifying business. Before speaking they grow tense, have hot flashes and cold chills, and experience the familiar butterflies in the stomach. Some people tremble before and even during a speech. Try to remember that these are normal reactions, for both beginning and experienced speakers. Most people can overcome them, however, and it is even possible to turn this nervous energy to your advantage.

If your stage fright is extreme, or if you are the one person in a hundred who stutters, or if you have some other speech impediment, seek clinical help. The ability to communicate ideas through speech is one of humanity's greatest gifts. Do not let yourself be cheated. Some of the finest speakers we have ever had in class were stutterers who admitted their problem and worked at it with professional guidance. Remember, whether your problems are large or small, the audience is on your side. They want you to succeed.

Physical Aspects of Speaking

What are the physical characteristics of good speakers? They stand firmly but comfortably. They move and gesture naturally and emphatically but avoid fidgety, jerky movements and foot shuffling. They look directly into the eyes of people in the audience, not merely in their general direction. They project enthusiasm into their voices. They do not mumble or speak flatly. We will examine these characteristics in detail—first movement and then voice.

Movement A century ago, a speaker's movements were far more florid and exaggerated than they are today. Today we prefer a more natural mode of speaking, closer to conversation than oratory. To some extent, electronic devices such as amplifying systems, radio, and television have brought about this change. However, you do not want to appear like a stick of wood. Even when speaking to a small group or on television (or, oddly enough, on the radio), you will want to move and gesture. If you are speaking in a large auditorium, you will want to broaden your movements and gestures. From the back row of a 2,500-seat auditorium, you look about three inches tall.

Movement during a speech is important for several reasons. First, it puts that nervous energy we spoke of to work. The inhibited speaker stands rigid and trembles. The relaxed speaker takes that same energy and puts it into purposeful movement.

Second, movement attracts attention. It is a good idea to emphasize an idea with a pointing finger or a clenched fist; and a speaker who comes out from behind the lectern occasionally and walks across the stage or toward the audience awakens audience interest. The speaker who passively utters ideas deadens the audience.

Third, movement makes you feel more forceful and confident. It keeps you, as well as your audience, awake. This is why good speakers gesture just as emphatically while speaking on the radio as they would if the audience could see them.

What sorts of movements are appropriate? To begin with, movement should closely relate to your content. Jerky or shuffling motions that occur haphazardly distract an audience. But a pointing finger combined with an emphatic statement reinforces a point for an audience. A sideward step at a moment of transition draws attention to the shift in thought. Take a step backward and you indicate a conclusion. Step forward and you indicate the beginning of a new point. Use also the normal descriptive gestures that all of us use in conversation—gestures to indicate length, height, speed, roundness, and so forth.

For most people, gesturing is fairly natural. They make appropriate movements without too much thought. Some beginning speakers, however, are body-inhibited. If you are in this category, you may have to cultivate movement. In your practice sessions and in your classroom speeches, risk artificiality by making gestures that seem too broad to you. Oddly enough, often at the very point where your gestures seem artificial and forced to you, they will seem the most natural to your audience.

Allow natural gestures to replace nervous mannerisms. Some speakers develop startling mannerisms and remain completely oblivious of them until some brave but kind soul points them out. Some that we have observed include taking eyeglasses off and putting them back on; repeatedly knocking a heavy ring on the lectern; fiddling with a pen, pointer, chalk, necklace, microphone cord, ear, mustache, nose—you name it; shifting from foot to foot in time to some strange inner rhythm; and pointing with the elbows while the hands remain in the pants pockets. Mannerisms may also be vocal. Such things as little coughs or repeating comments such as "OK" or "You know" to indicate transitions can become mannerisms.

Listeners are distracted by such habits. Often they will concentrate on the mannerisms to the exclusion of everything else. They may know that a speaker put her eyeglasses on and off twenty-two times but not have the faintest notion of what she said. If someone points out such mannerisms in your speaking habits, don't feel hurt. Instead, work to remove the mannerisms.

Movement includes facial movement. Do not be a deadpan. Your basic expression should be a relaxed, friendly look. But don't hesitate to smile, laugh, frown, or scowl when such expressions are called for. A scowl at a moment in your speech when you are expressing disapproval makes the disapproval that much more emphatic. Whatever you do, do not freeze into one expression, whether it be the stern look of the man of iron or the vapid smile of a model in a television ad.

Voice Your voice should sound relaxed, free of tension and fear. In a man, people consider a deep voice to be a sign of strength and authority. Most people prefer a woman's voice to be low rather than shrill. If your voice does not have these attributes, you can develop them to some extent. A speech teacher can give you voice exercises. If, despite hard work, your voice remains unsatisfactory in comparison with the conventional stereotypes, do not despair. Many successful speakers have had somewhat unpleasant voices but through force of character or intellect they directed their audiences' attention to their ideas, not their voices.

Many beginning speakers speak too fast, probably because they are anxious to be done and sit down. A normal rate of speech falls between 120 and 180 words per minute. This is actually fairly slow. Generally, you will want a fairly slow delivery rate. When you are speaking slowly, your voice will be deeper and more impressive. Also, listeners have trouble following complex ideas delivered at breakneck speed. Slow down and give your audience time to absorb your ideas.

Of course, you should not speak at a constant rate, slow or fast. Vary your rate. If you normally speak somewhat rapidly, slowing down will emphasize ideas. If you are speaking slowly, suddenly speeding up will suggest excitement and enthusiasm. As you speak, change the volume and pitch of your voice. Any change in volume, whether from low to loud or the reverse, will draw your listeners' attention and thus emphasize a point. The same is true of a change in pitch: If your voice remains a flat monotone and your words come at a constant rate, you deprive yourself of a major tool of emphasis.

Many people worry about their accent. Normally, our advice is *don't worry*. If you speak the dialect of the educated people of the region where you were raised, you have little to worry about. Some New Englanders, for example, put *r*'s where they are not found in other regional dialects and omit them where they are commonly found. Part of America's richness lies in its diversity. In most countries accents vary from one region to another, but certainly not enough to hinder communication.

If, however, your accent is slovenly—"Ya wanna cuppa coffee?"—or uneducated, do something about it. Work with your teacher or seek other professional help. Listen to educated speakers and imitate them. Whatever your accent, there is no excuse for mispronouncing words. Before you speak, look up any words you know you must use and about whose pronunciation you are uncertain. Speakers on technical subjects have this problem perhaps more than other speakers. Many technical terms are jawbreakers. Find their correct pronunciations and practice them until you can say them easily.

Audience Interaction

One thing speakers must learn early in their careers is that they cannot count on the audience's hanging on every word. Some years ago an intelligent, educated audience was asked to record its introspections while listening to a speaker. The speaker was an excellent one. Despite his excellence and the high intelligence level of the audience, the introspections revealed that the audience was paying something less than full attention. Here are some of the recorded introspections:

> God, I'd hate to be speaking to this group. . . . I like Ben—he has the courage to pick up after the comments. . . . Did the experiment backfire a bit? Ben seems unsettled by the introspective report. . . . I see Ben as one of us because he is under the same judgment. . . . He folds his hands as if he was about to pray. . . . What's he got in his pocket he keeps wriggling around. . . . I get the feeling Ben is playing a role. . . . It is interesting to hear the words that are emphasized. . . . This is a hard spot for a speaker. He really must believe in this research. . . .
>
> Ben used the word "para-social." I don't know what that means. Maybe I should have copied the diagram on the board. . . . Do not get the points clearly

. . . cannot interrupt . . . feel mad. . . . More words. . . . I'm sick of pedagogical and sociological terms. . . . An umbrella dropped. . . . I hear a funny rumbling noise. . . . I wish I had a drink. . . . Wish I could quit yawning. . . . Don't know whether I can put up with these hard seats for another week and a half or not. . . . My head itches. . . . My feet are cold. I could put on my shoes, but they are so heavy. . . . My feet itch. . . . I have a piece of coconut in my teeth. . . . My eyes are tired. If I close them the speaker will think I'm asleep. . . .

Backside hurts. . . . I'm lost because I'm introspecting. . . . The conflict between introspection and listening is killing me. . . . If he really wants me to introspect, he must realize himself he is wasting his time lecturing. . . . This is better than the two hour wrestling match this afternoon. . . . This is the worst planned, worst directed, worst informed meeting I have ever attended. . . . I feel confirmation, so far, in my feelings that lectures are only 5% or less effective. . . . I hadn't thought much about coming to this meeting but now that I am here it is going to be O.K. . . . Don't know why I am here. . . . I wish I had gone to the circus. . . . Wish I could have this time for work I should be doing. . . . Why doesn't he shut up and let us react. . . . The end of the speech. Now he is making sense. . . . It's more than 30 seconds now. He should stop. Wish he'd stop. Way over time. Shut up. . . . He's over. What will happen now?. . .[1]

As some of the comments reveal, perhaps being asked to record vagrant thoughts as they appeared made some members of the audience less attentive than they normally would have been. But most of us know that we have very similar thoughts and lapses of attention while we attend classes and speeches.

The reasons for audience inattention are many. Some are under the speaker's control; some are not. The speaker cannot do much about such physical problems as hard seats, crowded conditions, a stuffy room, or physical inactivity. The speaker *can* do something about psychological problems such as the listeners' passivity and their sense of anonymity, their feeling of not participating in the speech.

Audience Analysis Even before they begin to speak, good speakers have taken audience problems into account. They have analyzed the audience's education and experience levels. They have planned to keep their points few and to repeat major points through carefully planned variations. They plan interesting examples. While speaking, they attempt to interest the audience through movement and by varying their speech rate, pitch, and volume.

But good speakers go beyond these steps and analyze their audience and its reactions as they go along. In an extemporaneous speech and even to some extent in a written speech, you can make adjustments based on this audience analysis.

To analyze your audience, you must have good eye contact. You must be looking at Ben, Bob, and Irma. You must not merely be looking in the general direction of the massed audience. Look for such things as smiles, scowls, fidgets, puzzled looks, bored expressions, interested expressions, sleepy eyes, heads nodded in agreement, heads nodded in sleep, heads shaken in disagreement. You will not be 100 percent correct in interpreting these signs. Many students have learned to smile and nod in all the proper places without ever hearing the instructor. But, generally, such physical actions are excellent clues as to how well you are getting through to your audience.

Reacting to the Audience

Reacting to the Audience If your audience seems happy and interested, you can proceed with your speech as prepared. If, however, you see signs of boredom, discontent, or a lack of understanding, you must make some adjustments. Exactly what you do depends to some extent on whether you are in a formal or informal speaking situation. We will look at the formal situation first.

In the *formal situation*, you are somewhat limited. If your audience seems bored, you can quickly change your manner of speaking. Any change will, at least momentarily, attract attention. You can move or gesture more. Having gained the audience's attention, you can supply some interesting anecdotes or other illustrative material to better support your abstractions and generalizations. If your audience seems puzzled, you know you must supply further definitions and explanations and probably more concrete examples. If your audience seems hostile, you must find some way to soften your argument while at the same time preserving its integrity. Perhaps you can find some mutual ground upon which you and the audience can agree and move on from there.

Obviously, such flexibility during a speech requires some experience. Also, it requires that the speaker have a full knowledge of the subject. If every bit of material the speaker knows about the subject is in the speech already, the speaker has little flexibility. But don't be afraid to adjust a speech in midstream. Even the inexperienced speaker can do it to some extent.

Many of the speaker's problems are caused by the fact that the speech situation is a one-way street. The listeners sit passively. Their normal desires to react, to talk back to the speaker, are frustrated. The problem suggests the solution, particularly when you are in a more informal speech situation, such as a classroom or a small meeting.

In the more *informal situation*, you can stop when a listener seems puzzled. Politely ask him how you have confused him and attempt to clarify the situation. If a listener seems uninterested, give her an opportunity to react. Perhaps you can treat her as a puzzled listener. Or, you can ask her what you can do to interest her more. Do not be unpleasant. Put the blame for the listeners' lack of interest on yourself, even if you feel it does not belong there. Sometimes you may be displeased or shocked at the immediate feedback you receive, but don't avoid it on these grounds. And do not react unpleasantly to it. You will move more slowly when you make speaking a two-way street, but the final result will probably be better. Immediate feedback reveals areas of misunderstanding—or even mistrust—of what is being said.

In large meetings where such informality is difficult, you can build in some audience reaction through the use of informal groups. Before you talk, divide your audience into small groups. Use seating proximity as the basis for your division if you have no better one. Explain that after your talk, the groups will have a period of time in which to discuss your speech. They will be expected to come up with questions or comments. People do not like to seem unprepared, even in informal groups. As a result, they will be more likely to pay attention to your speech in order to participate well in their groups.

Regardless of whether you use groups, often you will be expected to handle questions following a speech. If you have a chairperson, he or she will field the questions and repeat them, and then you will answer them. If you have no chairperson, you will perform this chore for yourself. Be sure everyone understands the question. Be sure *you* understand the question. If you do not, ask the questioner to repeat it and perhaps to rephrase it.

Keep your answers brief, but answer the questions fully and honestly. When you do not know the answer, say so. Do not be afraid of conflict with the audience. But keep it on an objective basis; talk about the conflict situation, not personalities. If someone reveals through his question that he is becoming personally hostile, handle him courteously. Answer his question as quickly and objectively as you can, and move on to another questioner. Sometimes the bulk of your audience will grow restless while a few questioners monopolize your time. If this occurs, release your audience and, if you have time, invite the questioners up to the platform to continue the discussion. Above all, during a question period, be courteous. Resist any temptation to have fun at a questioner's expense.

▶ VISUAL AIDS

Most technical talks require visual aids.

Purpose of Visual Aids

You will use a visual aid (1) *to support* and *expand* the content of your message and (2) *to focus the audience's attention* on a critical aspect of your presentation.[2]

Support The first purpose of any visual material is *to support your message*—to enlarge on the main ideas and give substance and credibility to what you are saying. Obviously, the material must be relevant to the idea being supported. Too often a speaker gives in to the urge to show a visually attractive or technically interesting piece of information that has little or no bearing on the subject.

Suppose, for the purposes of our analysis, that you were asked to meet with government representatives to present a case for your company's participation in a major federal contract. Your visual support would probably include information about the company's past performance with projects similar to the one being considered. You would show charts reflecting the ingenious methods used by the company's development people to keep costs down; performance statistics indicating your high-quality standards; and your best conception-to-production times, to show the audience how adept you are at meeting target dates.

In such a presentation, before an audience of tough-minded officials, you wouldn't want to spend your time showing them aerial views of the company's modern facilities or photographs of smiling employees, antiseptic production lines, and the company's expensive air fleet. Such material would hardly support and expand your arguments that the company is used to working and producing on a spartan budget.

Focus Your second reason for using visual aids is *to focus the audience's attention*. A good visual can arrest the wandering thoughts of your audience and bring their attention right down to a specific detail of the message. It forces their mental participation in the subject.

When you are dealing with very complex material, as you often will be, you can use a simple illustration to show your audience a single, critical concept within your subject.

Criteria for Good Visual Aids

What about the visual aids themselves? What makes one better than another for a specific kind of presentation? Before we consider individual visual aids, let's look at the qualities that make a visual aid effective for the technical speaker.

Visibility First, a visual aid must be *visible*. If that seems so obvious that it hardly need be mentioned at all, it may be because you haven't experienced the frustration of being shown something the speaker feels is important—and not being able to read it, or even make out detail. To be effective, your visual support material should be clearly visible from the most distant seat in the house. If you have any doubts, sit in that seat and look. Remember this when designing visual material: **Anything worth showing the audience is worth making large enough for the audience to see.**

Clarity The second criterion for a good visual is *clarity*. The audience decides this. If they're able to determine immediately what they are seeing, the visual is clear enough. Otherwise, it probably needs further simplification and condensation. The obvious mistake of showing a photograph that is out of focus or close-ups of a complex device that will confuse the audience is easy to understand. But what about the chart that shows a relationship between two factors on *x*- and *y*-axes when the axes are not clearly designated or when pertinent information is unclear or missing?

One way to achieve clarity is to choose fonts, type styles, and colors wisely (see Chapter 11, Document Design). The following are good ground rules:

- Use boldface type in a size that can be read easily.
- Limit yourself to two fonts per figure.
- Avoid all-cap styling except in single-line headings.
- Avoid visuals that use too many colors—more than four in any one visual is too many.

Visual material should be immediately clear to the audience, who should be able to understand it at a glance without specific help from the speaker.

Simplicity The third criterion for good visual support is *simplicity*. No matter how complex the subject, the visual itself should include no more information than absolutely necessary to support the speaker's message. If it's not carrying the burden of the message, it need not carry every detail. Limit yourself to *one* idea per visual—mixing ideas will totally confuse an audience, causing them to turn you off midsentence.

When using words and phrases on a visual, limit the material to key words that act as visual cues for you and the audience. If a visual communications expert giving a speech wished to present the criteria for a good visual, he might *think* something like this:

A good visual must be visible.
A good visual must be clear.
A good visual must be simple.
A good visual must be easy for the speaker to control.

What would he show the audience? If he knows his field as well as he should, he'll offer the visual shown in Figure 19-1.

The same information is there. The visual is being used appropriately to provide emphasis while the speaker supplies the ideas and the extra words. The very simplicity of the visual has impact and is likely to be remembered by the audience.

Controllability The fourth quality of a good visual aid is that the speaker can control it. As the speaker, you should be able to add information or delete

CRITERIA

Visibility

Clarity

Simplicity

Controllability

FIGURE 19-1 • A Simple Visual: Criteria for Visual Aids

it, to move forward or backward to review, and, finally, to *take the visual away* from the audience to bring their attention back to you.

Some very good visual aids can meet the other criteria and prove almost worthless to a speaker because they cannot be easily controlled. The speaker, who must maintain a flow of information and some kind of rapport with the audience, can't afford to let visual material interfere with this task. Remember, visual material is meant to *support* you as a speaker, not to replace you.

Visual Content

So far, we have discussed the purpose for using visual aids and criteria for good visual aids. The remaining two questions of concern to you are (1) What do I use? and (2) How do I use it? Let's consider them in that order. Visual content falls into seven categories:

- Graphs
- Tables
- Representational art, such as line drawings
- Photographs
- Words and phrases
- Cartoons
- Hardware

Graphs, tables, representational art, and photographs are discussed in detail in Chapter 12 Using Illustrations. You will want to apply the suggestions made there to the visuals you choose for oral reports. Apply also the visibility, clarity, simplicity, and control criteria. For example, the table in Figure 19-2 is too complicated for use as a visual aid for an oral report. The table in Figure 19-3 would work well. The graph in Figure 19-4 is too busy. Listeners would be spending their time trying to figure it out instead of attending to the speaker. The graph in Figure 19-5 would work well. The listener can

No. 31. Annual Inmigration, Outmigration, and Net Migration for Regions: 1960 to 1997

[In thousands. As of March. For persons 1 year old and over. Excludes members of the Armed Forces except those living off post or with their families on post. Based on Current Population Survey; see text. Section 1, and Appendix III. For composition of regions, see map, inside front cover. Minus sign (−) indicates net out-migration]

PERIOD	Northeast	Midwest	South	West	PERIOD	Northeast	Midwest	South	West
1980–81: Inmigrants ...	464	650	1,377	871	Net internal migration .	−328	−31	376	−17
Outmigrants	706	1,056	890	710	Movers from abroad....	267	132	451	396
Net internal migration	−242	−406	487	161	Net migration........	−81	101	827	379
Movers from abroad ...	207	180	412	514	**1985–86:** Immigrants....	441	842	1,284	792
Net migration	−35	−226	899	875	Outmigrants..........	675	775	1,134	775
1985–86: Inmigrants ...	602	1,011	1,365	810	Net internal migration .	−234	68	150	16
Outmigrants	752	996	1,320	710	Movers from abroad....	285	130	470	476
Net internal migration	−250	15	35	200	Net migration........	51	196	620	492
Movers from abroad ...	196	158	342	502	**1996–97:**				
Net migration	−32	173	377	702	Total immigrants.......	481	661	1,338	688
1990–91: Inmigrants ...	346	782	1,421	835	From Northeast	(X)	107	392	101
Outmigrants	932	797	987	888	From Midwest........	94	(X)	492	228
Net internal migration	−585	−15	433	167	From South..........	256	333	(X)	358
Movers from abroad ...	209	208	331	817	From West	131	221	454	(X)
Net migration	−376	193	784	784	Total outmigration	800	814	947	808
1992–93: Inmigrants ...	313	841	1,145	789	To Northeast.........	(X)	94	258	131
Outmigrants	647	608	1,044	770	To Midwest..........	107	(X)	333	221
Net internal migration	−834	233	101	–	To South	392	492	(X)	454
Movers from abroad ...	230	196	513	364	To West.............	101	228	358	(X)
Net migration	−104	431	614	363	Net internal migration ..	−119	−154	391	−118
1993–94: Inmigrants ...	348	706	1,336	746	Movers from abroad....	239	169	445	450
Outmigrants	676	737	960	763	Net migration........	120	15	836	332

X Not applicable.

Source: U.S. Bureau of the Census, *Current Population Reports*, P20–510, and earlier reports.

FIGURE 19-2 • A Complicated Table
Source: U.S. Department of Commerce, *Statistical Abstract of the United States*, 118th ed. (Washington, DC: GPO, 1998), 32.

grasp the main point of it immediately, with little help from the speaker. The hard fact is that many visuals taken from articles, books, or the Internet violate one or more of the criteria and are thus unsuitable for use in oral reports. You must either revise them or create your own visuals.

In the following sections, we discuss using words and phrases, cartoons, and hardware.

Words and Phrases There will always be circumstances in which you will want to emphasize key words or phrases visually, as in Figure 19-1. This type of visual can be effective in making the audience aware of major divisions or subdivisions of a topic, for instance.

In Brief

Ten most populous countries
in 1998:

	(million persons)
China	1,237
India	984
United States	270
Indonesia	213
Brazil	170
Russia	147
Pakistan	135
Bangladesh	128
Japan	126
Nigeria	111

FIGURE 19-3 • A Simple Table
Source: U.S. Department of Commerce, *Statistical Abstract of the United States*, 118th ed. (Washington, DC: GPO, 1998), 817.

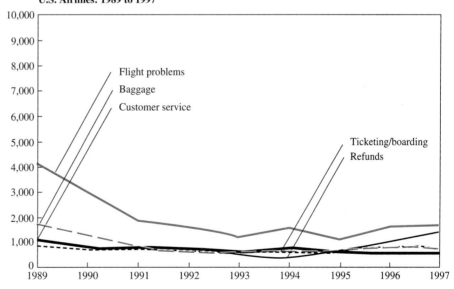

**Consumer Complaints Against
U.S. Airlines: 1989 to 1997**

Source: Chart prepared by U.S. Bureau of the Census. For data, see Table 1078.

FIGURE 19-4 • A Complicated Graph
Source: U.S. Department of Commerce, *Statistical Abstract of the United States*, 118th ed. (Washington, DC: GPO, 1998), 652.

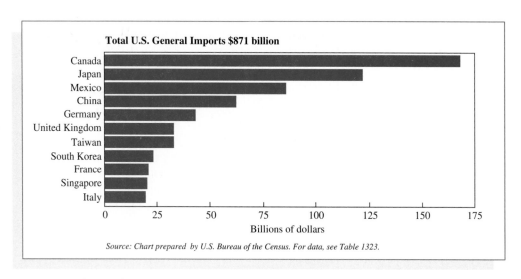

Total U.S. General Imports $871 billion

Source: Chart prepared by U.S. Bureau of the Census. For data, see Table 1323.

FIGURE 19-5 • A Simple Graph
Source: U.S. Department of Commerce, Statistical Abstract of the United States, 118th ed. (Washington, DC: GPO, 1998), 782.

There is danger, however, in the overuse of words—too many with too much detail. Some speakers tend to use visuals as a "shared" set of notes for their presentation, a self-limiting practice. Audiences who are involved in reading long, detailed piece of information won't recall what the speaker is saying

For technical presentations, there is still another problem with the use of words. Too often, because they may be parts of a specialized vocabulary, they do more to confuse the audience than to increase their understanding. Such terms should be reserved for audiences whose technical comprehension is equal to the task of translating them into meaningful thoughts.

Cartoons Cartooning is no more than illustrating people, processes, and concepts with exaggerated, imaginative figures—showing them in whatever roles are necessary to your purpose. (See Figure 19-6.) Not only does it heighten audience interest, but cartooning can be as specific as you want it to be in terms of action or position.

You might choose to use cartooned visual material in one of these situations:

• When dealing with a non expert audience
• When showing people-oriented action in a stationary medium (media other than motion pictures or video)

The resourceful speaker will use cartoons to help give additional meaning to other forms of visual support. For example, the use of cartoons as elements in a block diagram tends to increase viewer interest.

Trying To Look SUNsational?

Complexity Persists In Using Sunscreens

By Larry Thompson

You would think that all the questions about sunscreens have been answered by now. You slather it on before you go to the beach. It keeps you from being fried to a crisp. And, if you use enough, it helps prevent your skin from taking on that wrinkled, leathery look of photo-aged skin. Best of all, it protects you from the harmful ultraviolet rays that cause skin cancer.

ILLUSTRATIONS BY MICHAEL DAVID BROWN

FIGURE 19-6 • Cartooning
Source: FOA Consumer, July–August 2000, 15.

Like any other technique, cartooning can be inappropriate or overdone. For example, in a speech discussing a serious or grave situation, you will want to use only the most formal kinds of visual support material. On other occasions, cartooning may distract the audience or call too much attention to itself. Your purpose is not to entertain but to communicate.

Hardware After all this analysis of visual support material, you may wonder if it wouldn't be somewhat easier to show the real thing instead.

Certainly, there will be times when the best visual support you can have is the actual object you are discussing. Notably, the introduction of a new piece of equipment will be more effective if it is physically present to give the audience an idea of its size and bulk. If it is capable of some unique and important function, it should definitely be seen by the audience. (The greatest difficulty with the use of actual hardware is control. The device that is small enough for you to carry conveniently may be too small for the audience to see.)

Even when it's possible to present a piece of equipment physically, it's important to back it with supplementary visual materials. Chances are the audience will not be able to determine what is happening inside the machine, even if they understand explicitly the principle involved. With this in mind, you will want to add information, with appropriate diagrams, graphs, and scale drawings.

In this discussion of visual support, we've stressed the points of visibility, clarity, simplicity, and control over and over. The reason for this repetition is that these points are vital to the selection and use of visual support by the technical communicator. In the end, it is you who can best decide which visual support form your message and your audience require.

You are also faced with the choice of visual tools for presenting your visual material. The next section will deal with popular visual tools, their advantages, disadvantages, and adaptability to the materials we've already discussed.

Visual Presentation Tools

The major visual tools are these:

> Computer technology
> Overhead projection
> Slides
> Charts
> Movies and videos
> Chalkboards

We have listed these tools in descending order of importance. However, all of them are still in use and are valuable ways of presenting visual material to enhance an oral report.

Computer Technology Numerous computer graphics programs now make it possible to create a dazzling array of graphs, tables, and illustrations. You can create such visuals yourself with the help of the software, or, using a scanner or Internet downloads, you can import visuals from virtually any source into your programs. By using a printer, you can turn your visuals into transparencies for use in your presentations.

A program such as PowerPoint takes the process even further, allowing you to both create your visuals *and* present them. By using PowerPoint, for example, you could create a complete slide show and present it with a few keystrokes, eliminating altogether the need for making transparencies. With PowerPoint you can even create or import animated visuals and display them with an audio accompaniment.

With PowerPoint and computer graphics programs, you can also print out outlines and notes from your speech that you can hand out *after* you have finished for your audience to carry away as memory aids. *After* is a key word here. If you hand out such materials before your talk or during it, your audience will spend its time reading your outlines and notes instead of listening to you.

The good news is that such technology opens up possibilities for interesting and well-organized visual presentations unknown to speakers just a few years ago. The bad news is that the temptation to go too far with your visuals looms larger than ever before. It is so easy to type in or import text into graphics programs that speakers create wordy slides that engage the listener in reading rather than listening. Speakers create or import complicated graphs and tables that the listener has to study intently, thus losing the thread of the speaker's oral presentation. Remember the four criteria for the use of any visual:

Visibility
Clarity
Simplicity
Controllability

If your visual, no matter how beautiful, no matter how dramatic, does not meet all four criteria, don't use it.

Some of the presentation techniques in the sections that follow—particularly Overhead Projection and Movies and Videos—apply as well to computer presentations.

Overhead Projection Throughout this discussion of visual support, we've stressed the importance of maintaining a good speaker–audience relationship. It's an essential in the communication process. And it's fragile. Any time you turn your back to the audience, or darken the room, or halt the flow of ideas for whatever reason, this relationship is damaged.

The overhead projector effectively eliminates all of these rapport-dissolving problems. The image it projects is bright enough and clear enough to be used in a normally lighted room, without noticeable loss of visibility. And just as important from your point of view, it allows you to remain in the front of the room, *facing* your audience, throughout your presentation. The projector itself is a simple tool, and like all simple tools it may be used without calling attention to itself.

Visual material for an overhead projector is prepared on transparent sheets the size of typing paper. The methods for preparing these transparencies have become so simplified and inexpensive that the overhead has become a universally accepted visual tool in both the classroom and industry.

Perhaps the most important advantage of the overhead projector is the total speaker control it affords. With it, you may add information or delete it in a variety of ways or move forward or backward to review at will, and you can *turn it off* without altering the communicative situation in any way. By flipping a switch, you can literally remove the visual material from the audience's consideration, bringing their attention back to you and what you are saying. Because the projector is used in a lighted room, this on-and-off process seldom distracts the audience or has any effect on the speaker–audience relationship.

There are three ways to add information to a visual while the audience looks on—an important consideration when you want your listeners to receive information in an orderly fashion. In order of their discussion, they are (1) overlays, (2) revelation, and (3) writing on the visual itself.

The overlay technique (Figure 19-7a) combines the best features of preparing your visuals in advance and creating them at the moment they are needed.

It's the simple process of beginning with a single positive transparency and adding information by "overlaying" additional transparencies—that is, placing additional transparencies over the first so they are viewed by the audience as a single, composite illustration. Ordinarily, no more than two additional transparencies should be laid over the first, but it's possible to include as many as four or five. The technical person, who must usually present more complex concepts a step at a time to ensure communication, can immediately see the applications of such a technique.

The technique of revelation is simpler (see Figure 19-7b). It's the process of masking the parts of the visual you don't want the audience to see. A plain sheet of paper will work. By laying it over the information you want to conceal for the moment, you can block out selected pieces of the visual. Then, when you're ready to discuss this hidden information, you simply remove the paper. The advantage is clear enough. If you don't want the audience to read the bottom line on the page while you're discussing the top line, this is the way to control their attention.

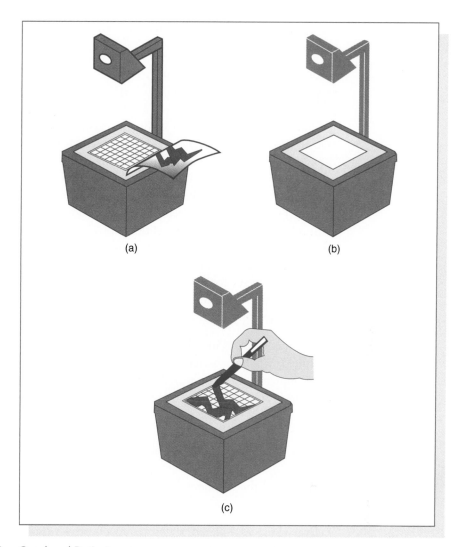

FIGURE 19-7 • Using Overhead Projectors
(a) Using overlays. (b) The technique for revelation. (c) Writing on transparencies.

Writing information on a transparency (Figure 19-7c) is nearly as easy as writing on a sheet of paper at your desk. You can use felt-tipped pens available for this purpose to create visual material in front of the audience. Often you can achieve your purpose by simply underlining or circling parts of your visual—a means of focusing audience attention on the important aspects of your message.

A final way of directing audience attention with overhead-projection transparencies is simply to use your pencil as a pointer. The profile shadow of the pencil will appear on the screen, directing the audience's attention to the proper place.

Slides The 35-mm slide, with its realistic color and photographic accuracy, has always been a popular visual tool for certain types of technical presentations.

Slide magazines allow you to organize your presentation and keep it intact. Remote controls allow you to operate the projector—even to reverse the order of your material—from the front of the room.

To use slide projectors effectively, however, you must turn off the lights in the room. Any time you keep your audience in the dark, you risk damaging the direct speaker–listener relationship on which communication hinges. In a sense, turning off the lights takes the control of the presentation out of your hands. Long sequences of slides tend to develop a will and a pace of their own. They tire an audience and invite mental absenteeism.

There are ways to handle the built-in problems of a slide presentation, simple techniques that can greatly increase audience attention and the effectiveness of your presentation.

- When using slides in a darkened room, light yourself. A disembodied voice in the dark is little better than a tape recorder; it destroys rapport and allows the audience to exit into their own thoughts. To minimize this effect, arrange your equipment so you may stay in the front of the room and use a lectern light or some other soft, nonglaring light to make yourself visible to the audience.
- Break the presentation into short segments of no more than five or six slides.
- Always tell the audience what they're going to see and what they should look for.

Everything considered, slides are an effective means of presenting visual material. But like any visual tool, they require control and preparation on your part. The important thing to remember is that they are there only to support your message—not to replace you.

Charts Charts take a couple of forms. The first is the individual hardboard chart, rigid enough to stand by itself and large enough to be seen by audience members, wherever they might be seated in the room. It is always prepared before the presentation, sometimes at considerable cost.

The second chart form is the flip chart, a giant-sized note pad that may be prepared before or during the presentation. When you have completed your discussion of one visual, you simply flip the sheet containing it over the top of the pad, as you would the pages of a tablet. The two types of charts have a common advantage. Unlike the chalkboard, they allow you to reshow a piece of information when necessary—an important aid to speaker control.

The following techniques will help you use charts more effectively during your presentation. They're really rules of usage, to be followed each time you choose this visual form for support.

- **Keep it simple**. Avoid complex, detailed illustrations on charts. A three-by-five-foot chart is seldom large enough for detailed visibility.
- **Ask for help**. Whenever possible, have an assistant on one side of your charts to remove each one in its turn. This avoids creating a break in your rapport with the audience while you wrestle with a large cardboard chart or a flimsy flip sheet.
- **Predraw your visuals with very light-colored crayon or chalk**. During the presentation, you can simply draw over the original lines in darker crayon or ink. This allows you to create an accurate illustration a step at a time for clarity.
- **Prime the audience**. Tell them what they are going to see and why before you show each visual.

Movies and Videos Whenever motion and sound are important to the presentation, movies and videos are the visual tools that can accomplish the effect. Like slides, they also provide an exactness of detail and color that can be critical to certain subjects. There is really no other way an engineer could illustrate the tremendous impact aircraft tires receive during landings, for instance. The audience will understand the subject only if they are able to view, through the eye of the camera, the distortion of the rubber when the plane touches down.

But movies and videos *are* the presentation. They cannot be considered visual support material in the sense of the term developed in this chapter. They simply replace the speaker as the source of information, at least for their duration. If they become the major part of the presentation, the speaker is reduced to an announcer with little more to do than introduce and summarize their content. This makes movies and videos the most difficult visual forms to control. Yet they can be controlled, and, if they are to perform the support functions we've outlined, they must be. Some effective techniques are given here.

- Prepare the audience by explaining the significance of what you're about to show them.
- Be sure that if a film or video is to be used, it makes up only a small part of the total presentation.

- Whenever possible, break the film or video into short three- or four-minute segments. Between segments you can reestablish rapport with the audience by summarizing what they have seen and refocusing attention on the important points in the next segment.

Chalkboards As a visual aid, the chalkboard leaves something to be desired. In the first place, preparing information on a chalkboard, especially technical information in which every sliding scrawl can have significance, takes time. And after the material is in place, it cannot be removed and replaced quickly. Second, the task of writing on a surface that faces the audience requires that you turn your back toward them while you write. And people don't respond well to backs. They want you to face them while you're talking to them. Add to these problems the difficulties of moving a heavy, semipermanent chalkboard around, and you begin to wonder why anyone bothers.

Low cost and simplicity are the reasons. The initial cost of a chalkboard is higher than you may think; but the cost of erasers and chalk is minimal. In spite of its drawbacks, a chalkboard is also easy to use. It may take time, but there's nothing very complicated about writing a piece of information on a chalkboard. This simplicity, of course, gives it a certain flexibility, making it essentially a spontaneous visual aid on which speakers can create their visual material as they go.

There are specific techniques for using a chalkboard that make it a more effective visual tool and help overcome its disadvantages. Let's consider them one at a time.

- **Plan ahead**. Unless there is a clear reason for creating the material as you go, prepare your visual material before the presentation. Then cover it. Later, you can expose the information for the audience at the appropriate point in your speech.
- **Be neat, and keep the information simple and to the point**. If your material is complex, find another way of presenting it.
- **Prime the audience**. Before showing your information, tell them what they're going to see and why they're going to see it.

This last point is especially important when you are creating your visual support as you go. Priming your listeners will allow you to maintain the flow of information and, at the same time, prepare them mentally to understand and accept your information.

▶ PLANNING AND REVISION CHECKLISTS

You will find the planning and revision checklists that follow Chapter 2, Composing, and Chapter 4, Writing for Your Readers, valuable in planning and revising any presentation of technical information. The following questions specifically apply to oral reports. They summarize the key points in this chapter and provide a checklist for planning and revising.

Planning

- What is the relationship between you and your audience?
- What is the attitude of your audience toward you and your presentation likely to be?
- Is your audience from a culture markedly different from yours? What adjustments to your persona and your presentation will any such difference require?
- What are the conditions under which you will speak?
- What equipment is available to you?
- Which delivery technique will be more appropriate? Extemporaneous? Manuscript?
- If you are speaking extemporaneously, have you prepared a speech outline to guide you?
- If you will be reading from a manuscript, have you introduced a conversational tone into your talk? Is your typed manuscript easy to read from?
- Do you have a good opening that will interest your audience and create a friendly atmosphere?
- Have you limited your major points to fit within your allotted time?
- Does your talk contain sufficient examples, analogies, narratives, and data to support your generalizations? Have you repeated key points?
- Can you relate your subject matter to some vital interest of your audience?
- Which visual aids do you plan to use?
  Graphs?
  Tables?
  Representational art?
  Photographs
  Words and phrases?
  Cartoons?
  Hardware?
- Which presentation tools will you use?
  Computer programs?
  Overhead projection?

Slides?

Charts?

Movies and videos?

Chalkboard?

- Have you prepared your graphics? Do they successfully focus the listeners' attention and augment and clarify your message? Do they meet the four criteria that govern good graphics?

Visibility

Clarity

Simplicity

Controllability

- Do you have a good ending ready, perhaps a summary of key points or an anecdote that supports your purpose?
- Have you rehearsed your talk several times?

Revision

Obviously, you can't revise a talk you have already given—unless, of course, you will have an opportunity to repeat it somewhere. But you *can* use revision techniques in your practice sessions. Most of the questions listed above under Planning lend themselves to use during revision. Also, you can critique your speeches, looking for ways to improve your delivery techniques in future speeches. The following questions are useful for critiquing a speech. You will find it helpful to ask someone in the audience to give you friendly but honest answers to all the questions listed in the Planning and Revision sections.

- Did your gestures support your speech? Did they seem normal and relaxed? Did you avoid nervous mannerisms?
- Was your speech rate appropriate? Did you vary rate, pitch, and volume occasionally? Could everyone hear you?
- Did you pronounce all your words correctly?
- Did you have good interaction with your audience? Were they attentive or fidgety?
- Did you talk fit comfortably into the time allotted for it?
- Did the questions that followed your talk indicate a good understanding of it? Did the questions indicate friendliness or hostility to your key points?
- Were you sufficiently informed to answer the questions raised?
- Were there any indications that members of your audience could not see or readily comprehend any of your visuals?

► EXERCISES

1. You are an instructor at your college. Prepare a short extemporaneous lecture on a technical subject from your field. The students in your audience are not in your field.

2. You are the head of a team that has developed a new product or process. Your job is to persuade a group of senior managers from your own firm to accept the process or product for company use. Assume these managers have a layperson's knowledge about your subject. Speak extemporaneously.

3. As a highly regarded expert on your subject, you have been invited to speak about it at the annual meeting of a well-known scientific association. You are expected to write out and read your speech. You are to inform your audience, which is made up of knowledgeable research scientists and professors from diverse disciplines, about your subject or to persuade them to accept a conclusion you have reached.

4. Imagine you work for a company that manufactures a product with which you quite familiar. You have been given the task of persuading the executives of a either a Latin American or an Asian corporation to purchase this product for their employees. Assume that the executives have a good working knowledge of English but are probably not conversant with American slang or idioms (see Chapter 7, Writing for International Readers).

5. Adapt for oral presentation a report you have already written. Speak extemporaneously.

Appendix A

Handbook

Any living language is a growing, flexible instrument with rules that are constantly changing by virtue of the way it is used by its live, independent speakers and writers. Only the rules of a dead language are unalterably fixed.

Nevertheless, at any point in a language's development, certain conventions of usage are in force. Certain constructions are considered to be errors that mark the person who uses them as uneducated. It is with these conventions and errors that this handbook primarily deals. We also include a section on sexist usage.

To make the handbook easy to use as a reference, we have arranged the topics covered in alphabetical order. Each convention and error dealt with has an abbreviated reference tag. The tags are reproduced on the back endpapers, along with some of the more important proofreading symbols. If you are in a college writing course, your instructor may use some combination of these tags and symbols to indicate revisions needed in your reports.

Abbreviations
Acronyms
Apostrophe
Brackets
Capitalization
Colon
Comma
Dangling Modifier
Dash
Diction
Ellipsis
Exclamation Point
Fragmentary Sentence

Hyphen
Italicization
Misplaced Modifier
Numbers
Parallelism
Parentheses
Period
Pronoun–Antecedent Agreement
Pronoun Form
Question Mark
Quotation Marks
Run-On Sentence
Semicolon
Sexist Usage
Spelling Error
Verb Form
Verb–Subject Agreement

_ab_

▶ **ABBREVIATIONS**

Every scientific and professional field generates hundreds of specialized terms, and many of these terms are abbreviated for the sake of conciseness and simplicity. A few principles for the use of abbreviations follow, the first probably being the most important:

- As a general principle, the style manuals that govern the various disciplines, discourage the indiscriminate use of abbreviations. The _Publication Manual of the American Psychological Society_ states this principle well:

  In general, use an abbreviation only (a) if it's conventional and if the reader is more familiar with the abbreviation than with the complete form or (b) if considerable space can be saved and cumbersome repetition avoided. In short, use only those abbreviations that will help you communicate with your readers. Remember, they have not had the same experience with your abbreviations as you have.[1]

- You must decide if your audience is familiar enough with the term to allow you to use it without definition. Second, you must decide if your audience is familiar enough with the abbreviation for you to use it without spelling it out. For example, here is how one writer introduces the term _electric and magnetic fields_ to a lay audience:

  Electric and magnetic fields (EMFs) are produced by power lines, electrical wiring, and electrical equipment. There are many other sources of EMFs. The focus of this booklet is on EMFs associated with the generation, transmission, and use of electric power. EMFs are invisible lines of force that surround any electrical device. Electric fields are produced by voltage and increase in strength as the voltage increases. The electric field strength is measured in units of volts per meter (V/m). Magnetic fields result from the flow of current through wires or electrical devices and increase in strength as the current increases. Magnetic fields are measured in units of gauss (G) or tesla (T). Most electrical equipment has to be turned on, that is, current must be flowing, for a magnetic field to be produced. Electric fields, on the other hand, are present even when the equipment is switched off, as long as it remains connected to the source of electric power.[2]

Placing the abbreviation *EMF* in parentheses following the first use of the term allows the use of the abbreviation throughout the rest of the article. Following the parentheses, the writer provides an extended definition. The amount of provided detail depends as always on purpose and audience. For a more expert audience it would probably be enough to put the abbreviation in parentheses without a definition.

- In some cases the abbreviation is so well known to a technical audience and the term itself is so cumbersome that the abbreviation without the term will suffice. For example, an article for a computer-knowledgeable audience would probably use *ACSII* without providing or defining the term, *American Standard Code for Information Exchange.* A term such as *DNA* is so well know, even if not thoroughly understood, that it can be used by itself, even in articles for lay people.
- Even when not used in the text, abbreviations are widely used to save space in tables and figures. When the abbreviations are standard abbreviations known to the audience, you don't need to spell them out or explain them. If they are not known, spell them out in the captions to the figure or table or in a note. If necessary, define them.
- Use Latin abbreviations like *cf.* (compare), *i.e.* (that is), and *e.g.* (for example) sparingly. In your text use them only in parenthetical explanations. Use them also in tables and figures where space constraints make their use practical and acceptable. Elsewhere, use the English equivalents.
- Do not begin a sentence with an abbreviation. If practical, spell the abbreviation out. If not, recast the sentence to move the abbreviation.

The formation of standard abbreviations follow a brief set of rules, illustrated by the following set of abbreviations and the rules that follow it.

absolute	abs
acre or acres	acre or acres
atomic weight	at. wt

barometer	bar.
Brinell hardness number	Bhn
British thermal units	Btu
meter	m
square meter	m^2
miwatt or miwatts	mW
miles per hour	mph
National Electric Code	NEC
per	per
revolutions per minute	rpm
rod	rod
ton	ton

1. Use the singular form of abbreviation for both singular and plural terms:

cu ft	either cubic foot or cubic feet
cm	either centimeter or centimeters

   But there are some common exceptions:

no.	number
nos.	numbers
p.	page
pp.	pages
ms.	manuscript
mss.	manuscripts

2. In abbreviating units measurement, use lowercase letters except for letters that stand for proper nouns or proper adjectives:

at. wt	*but*	Btu or B
mph	*but*	mW

3. For technical terms, use periods only after abbreviations that spell complete words. For example, *in* is a word that could be confused with the abbreviation for inches. Therefore, use a period:

ft	*but*	in.
abs	*but*	bar.
cu ft	*but*	at. wt

5. Spell out many short and common words:

acre	rod	per	ton

6. In compound abbreviations, use internal spacing only if the first word is represented by more than its first letter:

rpm	*but*	cu ft
mph	*but*	at. wt

7. With few exceptions, form the abbreviations of organization names without periods or spacing:

NEC   ASA

8. Abbreviate terms of measurement only if they are preceded by an arabic expression of exact quantity:

55 mph   *and*   20-lb anchor

but

We will need an engine of greater horsepower.

The principles and rules we have provided here will cover most general situations. But in preparing a manuscript for a specific discipline, be sure to consult the applicable style or publication manual.

acro

▶ ACRONYMS

Acronyms are formed in two ways. In one way, the initial letters of each word in some phrase are combined. An example would be WYSIWYG, an acronym for the computer phrase "What you see is what you get." In a second way, some combination of initial letters or several letters of the words in the phrase are combined. An example would be *radar* for *r*adio *d*etection *a*nd *r*anging.

Technical writing uses acronyms freely, as in this example from a description of a computer program that performs statistical analysis:

It has good procedural capabilities, including some time-series-related plots and ARIMA forecasting, but it doesn't have depth in any one area. Although it has commands to create EDA displays, these graphics are static and are printed with characters rather than with lines.[3]

Use acronyms without explanation only when you are absolutely sure your readers know them. If you have any doubts at all, at least provide the words from which the acronym stems. If you're unsure whether the words are enough, provide a definition of the complete phrase. In the case of the paragraph just quoted, the computer magazine in which it was printed provided a glossary giving both the complete phrases and definitions:

ARIMA (auto-regressive integrated moving-average): a model that characterizes changes in one variable over time. It is used in time-series analysis.

EDA (exploratory data analysis): The use of graphically based tools, particularly in initial states of data analysis, to inspect data properties and to discover relationships among variables.[4]

See also the Entry for Abbreviations. In general follow the same principles for using acronyms as for using abbreviations. Acronyms can be daunting to those unfamiliar with them. Even for an audience that knows their meaning, a too heavy use of acronyms can make your writing seem lumpish and uninviting.

apos

▶ APOSTROPHE

The apostrophe has three chief uses: (1) to form the possessive, (2) to stand for missing letters or numbers, and (3) to form the plural of certain expressions.

Possessives

Add an apostrophe and an *s* to form the possessive of most singular nouns, including proper nouns, even when they already end in an *s* or another sibilant such as *x:*

man's
spectator's
jazz's
Marx's
Charles's

Exceptions to this rule occur when adding an apostrophe plus an *s* would result in an *s* or *z* sound that is difficult to pronounce. In such cases, usually just the apostrophe is added:

Xerxes'
Moses'
conscience'
appearance'

To understand this exception, pronounce *Marx's* and then a word like *Moses's* or *conscience's.*

To form plurals into the possessive case, add an apostrophe plus *s* to words that do not end in an *s* or other sibilant and an apostrophe only to those that do:

men's
data's
spectators'
agents'
witnesses'

To show joint possession, add the apostrophe and *s* to the last member of a compound or group; to show separate possession, add an apostrophe and *s* to each member:

Gregg and Klymer's experiment astounded the class.
Gregg's and Klymer's experiments were very similar.

Of the several classes of pronouns, only the indefinite pronouns use an apostrophe to form the possessive.

Possessive of Indefinite Pronouns	*Possessive of Other Pronouns*
anyone's	my (mine)
everyone's	your (yours)
everybody's	his, her (hers), its
nobody's	our (ours)
no one's	their (theirs)
other's	whose
neither's	

Missing Letters or Numbers

Use an apostrophe to stand for the missing letters in contractions and to stand for the missing letter or number in any word or set of numbers from which a letter or number is omitted for one reason or another:

can't, don't, o'clock, it's (it is), and similar constructions
We were movin' downriver, listenin' to the birds singin'.
The class of '49 was Colgate's best class in years.

Plural Forms

An apostrophe is sometimes used to form the plural of letters and numbers, but this style is gradually dying, particularly with numbers.

6's and 7's (but more commonly, 6s and 7s)
a's and b's

brackets

▶ BRACKETS

Brackets are chiefly used when a clarifying word or comment is inserted into a quotation:

"The result of this [disregard by the propulsion engineer] has been the neglect of the theoretical and mathematical mastery of the engine inlet problem."

"An ideal outlet require [sic] a frictionless flow."
"Last year [2000] saw a partial solution to the problem."

Sic, by the way, is Latin for *thus*. Inserted in a quotation, it means that the mistake it follows is the original writer's, not yours. Use it with discretion.

cap

▶ CAPITALIZATION

The following are the more important rules of capitalization. For a complete rundown, see your college dictionary.

Proper Nouns

Capitalize all proper nouns and their derivatives:

Places
America   American   Americanize   Americanism

Days of the Week and Months
Monday   Tuesday   January   February

But not the seasons:
winter   spring   summer   fall

Organizations and Their Abbreviations
American Kennel Club (AKC)
United States Air Force (USAF)

Capitalize *geographic areas* when you refer to them as areas:
The Andersons toured the Southwest.

But do not capitalize words that merely indicate direction:
We flew west over the Pacific.

Capitalize the names of *studies* in a curriculum only if the names are already proper nouns or derivatives of proper nouns or if they are part of the official title of a department or course:

Department of Geology
English Literature 25
the study of literature
the study of English literature

Note: Many nouns (and their derivatives) that were originally proper have been so broadened in application and have become so familiar that they are no longer capitalized: *boycott, macadam, italicize, platonic, chinaware, quixotic.*

Literary Titles

Capitalize the first word, the last word, and every important word in literary titles:

But What's a Dictionary For
The Meaning of Ethics
How to Write and Be Read

Rank, Position, Family Relationships

Capitalize the titles of rank, position, and family relationship unless they are preceded by *my*, *his*, *their*, or similar possessive pronouns:

Professor J. E. Higgins
I visited Uncle Timothy.
I visited my uncle Timothy.
Dr. Milton Weller, Head, Department of Entomology

colon

▶ COLON

The colon is chiefly used to introduce quotations, lists, or supporting statements. It is also used between clauses when the second clause is an example or amplification of the first and in certain conventional ways with numbers, correspondence, and bibliographical entries.

Introduction

Place a colon before a quotation, a list, or supporting statements and examples that are formally introduced:

Mr. Smith says the following of wave generation:
> The wind waves that are generated in the ocean and which later become swells as they pass out of the generating area are products of storms. The low pressure regions that occur during the polar winters of the Arctic and Antarctic produce many of these wave-generating storms.

The various forms of engine that might be used would operate within the following ranges of Mach number:

M-0 to M-1.5	Turbojet with or without precooling
M-1.5 to M-7	Reheated turbojet, possibly with precooling
M-7 to M-10+	Ramjet with supersonic combustion

Engineers are developing three new engines: turbojet, reheated turbojets, and ramjets.

Do not place a colon between a verb and its objects or a linking verb and the predicate nouns.

Objects
The engineers designed turbojets, reheated turbojets, and ramjets.

Predicate Nouns
The three engines the engineers are developing are turbojets, reheated turbojets, and ramjets.

Do not place a colon between a preposition and its objects:
The plane landed at Detroit, Chicago, and Rochester.

Between Clauses

If the second of two clauses is an example or an amplification of the first clause, then the colon may replace the comma, semicolon, or period:

The docking phase involves the actual "soft" contact: the securing of lines, latches, and air locks.

Figure 2 illustrates the difference between these two guidance systems: The paths of the two vehicles are shown to the left and the motion of the ferry as viewed from the target station is shown to the right.

Generally, a complete sentence after a colon begins with a capital letter, whereas a simple list begins lowercase.

Styling Conventions

Place a colon after a formal salutation in a letter, between numerals representing hours and minutes, between a title and a subtitle, and between chapter and verse of the Bible:

Dear Ms. Jones:
at 7:15 P.M.
Working Women: A Chartbook
I Samuel 7:14–18

c

▶ COMMA

The most used—and misused—mark of punctuation is the comma. Writers use commas to separate words, phrases, and clauses. Generally, commas correspond to the pauses we use in our speech to separate ideas and to avoid ambiguity. You will use the comma often: About two out of every three marks of punctuation you use will be commas. Sometimes your use of the comma will be essential for clarity; at other times you will be honoring grammatical conventions. (See also the entry for Run-On Sentences.)

Main Clauses

Place a comma before a coordinating conjunction (*and, but, or, nor, for, yet*) that joins two main (independent) clauses:

> During the first few weeks we felt a great deal of confusion, but as time passed we gradually fell into a routine.

> We could not be sure that the plumbing would escape frost damage, nor were we at all confident that the house could withstand the winds of almost hurricane force.

If the clauses are short, have little or no internal punctuation, or are closely related in meaning, then you may omit the comma before the coordinating conjunction:

> The wave becomes steeper but it does not tumble yet.

In much published writing there is a growing tendency to place two very short and closely related independent clauses (called contact clauses) side by side with only a comma between:

> The wind starts to blow, the waves begin to develop.

Sentences consisting of *three* or more equal main clauses should be punctuated uniformly:

> We explained how urgent the problem was, we outlined preliminary plans, and we arranged a time for discussion.

In general, identical marks are used to separate equal main clauses. If the equal clauses are short and uncomplicated, commas usually suffice. If the equal clauses are long or internally punctuated, or if their separateness is to be emphasized, semicolons are preferable and sometimes essential.

Clarification

Place a comma after an introductory word, phrase, or clause that might be over-read or that abnormally delays the main clause:

> As soon as you have finished polishing, the car should be moved into the garage. (Comma to prevent over-reading)

Soon after, the winds began to moderate somewhat, and we were permitted to return to our rooms. (First comma to prevent over-reading)

If the polar ice caps should someday mount in thickness and weight to the point that their combined weight exceeded the equatorial bulge, the earth might suddenly flop ninety degrees. (Introductory clause abnormally long)

After a short introductory element (word, phrase, or clause) where there is no possibility for ambiguity, the use of the comma is optional. Generally, let the emphasis you desire guide you. A short introductory element set off by a comma will be more emphatic than one that is not.

Nonrestrictive Modifiers

Enclose or set off from the rest of the sentence every nonrestrictive modifier, whether a word, a phrase, or a clause. How can you tell a nonrestrictive modifier from a restrictive one? Look at these two examples:

Restrictive
A runway that is not oriented with the prevailing wind endangers the aircraft using it.

Nonrestrictive
The safety of any aircraft, whether heavy or light, is put in jeopardy when it is forced to take off or land in a crosswind.

The restrictive modifier is necessary to the meaning of the sentence. Not just any runway but "a runway that is not oriented with the prevailing wind" endangers aircraft. The writer has *restricted* the many kinds of runway he or she could talk about to one particular kind. In the nonrestrictive example, the modifier merely adds descriptive details. The writer doesn't restrict *aircraft* with the modifier but simply makes the meaning a little clearer.

Restrictive modifiers cannot be left out of the sentence if it is to have the meaning the writer intends; nonrestrictive modifiers can be left out.

Nonrestrictive Appositives

Set off or enclose every nonrestrictive appositive. As used here, the term *appositive* means any element (word, phrase, or clause) that parallels and repeats the thought of a preceding element. According to this view, a verb may be coupled appositively with another verb, an adjective with another adjective, and so on. An appositive is usually more specific or more vivid than the element for which it is an appositive; an appositive makes explicit and precise something that has not been clearly implied.

Some appositives are restrictive and, therefore, are not set off or enclosed.

Nonrestrictive

A crosswind, a wind perpendicular to the runway, causes the pilot to make potentially dangerous corrections just before landing.

Restrictive

In some ways, Mr. Bush the president has to behave differently from Mr. Bush the governor.

In the nonrestrictive example, the appositive merely adds a clarifying definition. The sentence makes sense without it. The appositives in the restrictive example are essential to the meaning. Without them we would have, "In some ways, Mr. Bush has to behave differently from Mr. Bush."

Series

Use commas to separate members of a coordinate series of words, phrases, or clauses if *all* the elements are not joined by coordinating conjunctions:

Instructions on the label state clearly how to prepare the surfaces, how to apply the contents, and how to clean and polish the mended article.

To mold these lead figures you will need a hot flame, a two-pound block of lead, the molds themselves, a file or a rasp, and an awl.

Under the microscope the sensitive, filigree-like mold appeared luminous and transparent and faintly green.

Other Conventional Uses

Date

On August 24, A.D. 79, Mount Vesuvius erupted, covering Pompeii with 50 feet of ash and pumice.

Note: When you write the month and the year without the day, it is common practice to omit the comma between them—as in June 1993.

Geographical Expression

During World War II, Middletown, Pennsylvania, was the site of a huge military airport and supply depot.

Title after Proper Name

A card in yesterday's mail informed us that Penny Hutchinson, M.D., would soon open an office in Hinsdale.

Noun of Direct Address

Lewis, do you suppose that we can find our way back to the cabin before nightfall?

Informal Salutation
Dear Jane,

dm

▶ DANGLING MODIFIER

Many curious sentences result from the failure to provide a modifier with something to modify:

Having finished the job, the tarpaulins were removed.

In this example it seems as though the tarpaulins have finished the job. As is so often the case, a passive voice construction has caused the problem (see pages 92–93, 198). If we recast the sentence in active voice, we remove the problem:

Having finished the job, the workers removed the tarpaulins.

dash

▶ DASH

In technical writing, you will use the dash almost exclusively to set off parenthetical statements. You may, of course, use commas or parentheses for the same function, but the dash is the most emphatic separator of the three. You may also use the dash to indicate a sharp transition.

The target must emit or reflect light the pilot can see—but how bright must this light be?

d

▶ DICTION

For good diction, choose words that are accurate, effective, and appropriate to the situation. Many different kinds of linguistic sins can cause faulty diction. Poor diction can involve a choice of words that are too heavy or pretentious: *utilize* for *use*, *finalize* for *finish*, *at this point in time* for *now*, and so forth. Tired old clichés are poor diction: *with respect to*, *with your permission*, *with reference to*, and many others. We talk about such language in Chapter 5, particularly in the section on pomposity (pages 96–98).

Sometimes the words chosen are simply too vague to be accurate: *inclement weather* for *rain*, *too hot* for *600°C*. See the section on specific words in Chapter 5 (pages 94–96) for more on this subject.

Poor diction can mean an overly casual use of language when some degree of formality is expected. One of the many synonyms for *intoxicated*, such as *bombed*, *stoned*, or *smashed*, might be appropriate in casual conversation but totally wrong in a police or laboratory report.

Poor diction can reflect a lack of sensitivity to language—to the way one group of words relates to another group. Someone who writes that "The airlines are beginning a crash program to solve their financial difficulties" is not paying attention to relationships. The person who writes that the "Steelworkers' Union representatives are getting down to brass tacks in the strike negotiations" has a tin ear, to say the least. Make your language work for you, and make it appropriate to the situation.

ell

▶ ELLIPSIS

Use three spaced periods to indicate words omitted within a quoted sentence; use four spaced periods if the omission occurs at the end of the sentence:

"As depth decreases, the circular orbits become elliptical and the orbital velocity . . . increases as the wave height increases."

"As the ground swells move across the ocean, they are subject to headwinds or crosswinds. . . ."

You need not show an ellipsis if the context of the quotation makes it clear that it is not complete:

Wright said the accident had to be considered a "freak of nature."

exc

▶ EXCLAMATION POINT

Place an exclamation point at the end of a startling or exclamatory sentence.

According to the Centers for Disease Control and Prevention, every cigarette smoked shortens the smoker's life by seven minutes!

With the emphasis in technical writing on objectivity, you will seldom use the exclamation point.

frag

▶ FRAGMENTARY SENTENCE

Most fragmentary sentences are either verbal phrases or subordinate clauses that the writer mistakes for a complete sentence.

A verbal phrase has a participle, a gerund, or an infinitive in the predicate position, none of which functions as a complete verb:

Norton, depicting the electromagnetic heart. (participle)
The timing of this announcement about Triptycene, (gerund)
Braun, in order to understand tumor cell growth. (infinitive)

When your fragment is a verbal phrase, either change the participle, gerund, or infinitive to a complete verb or repunctuate so that the phrase becomes part of a complete sentence.

Fragment
Norton, depicting the electromagnetic heart. She made a mockup of it.

Rewritten
Norton depicted the electromagnetic heart. She made a mockup of it.
Norton, depicting the electromagnetic heart, made a mockup of it.

Subordinate clauses are distinguishable from phrases in that they have complete subjects and complete verbs (rather than verbals) and are introduced by relative pronouns *(who, which, that)* or by subordinating conjunctions *(because, although, since, after, while).*

The presence of the relative pronoun or the subordinating conjunction is a signal that the clause is not independent but is part of a more complex sentence unit. Any independent clause can become a subordinate clause with the addition of a relative pronoun or subordinating conjunction.

Independent Clause
Women's unemployment rates were higher than men's.

Subordinate Clause
Although women's unemployment rates were higher than men's.

Repunctuate a subordinate clause so that it is joined to the complex sentence of which it is a part.

Fragment
Although women's unemployment rates were higher than men's. Now the rates are similar.

Rewritten
Although women's unemployment rates were higher than men's, now the rates are similar.

Various kinds of elliptical sentence without a subject or a verb do exist in English, for example, "No!" "Oh?" "Good shot." "Ouch!" "Well, now." These constructions may occasionally be used for stylistic reasons, particularly to represent conversation, but they are seldom needed in technical writing. If you do use such constructions, use them sparingly. Remember that major deviations from normal sentence patterns will probably jar your readers and break their concentration on your report, the last thing that any writer wants.

hyphen

▶ **HYPHEN**

Hyphens are used to form various compound words and in breaking up a word that must be carried over to the next line.

Compound Numbers

See Numbers.

Common Compound Words

Observe dictionary usage in using or omitting the hyphen in compound words.

governor-elect	court-martial
ex-treasurer	Croesus-like
Russo-Japanese	drill-like
pro-American	self-interest

But:

neophyte	sweet corn
newspaper	weather map
radioactive	radio beam
bloodless	blood pressure

Compound Words as Modifiers

Use the hyphen between words joined together to modify other words:

a half-empty fuel tank
an eight-cylinder engine
their too-little-and-too-late methods

Be particularly careful to hyphenate when omitting the hyphen may cause ambiguity:

two-hundred-gallon drums
two hundred-gallon drums
a pink-skinned hamster

Sometimes you have to carry a modifier over to a later word, creating what is called a *suspended hyphen:*

GM cars come with a choice of four-, six-, or eight-cylinder engines.

ital

▶ ITALICIZATION

Italic print is a distinctive typeface, like this sample: *Scientific American*. When you use a word processor, you can use an italic typeface or represent italics by underlining, like this:

Scientific American

Foreign Words

Italicize foreign words that have not yet become a part of the English language:

We suspected him always of holding some *arrière pensée*.
Karl's everlasting *Weltschmerz* makes him a depressing companion.

Also italicize Latin words for genus and species.

Cichorium endivia (endive)
Percopsis omiscomaycus (trout-perch)

But do not italicize Latin abbreviations or foreign words that have become a part of the English language:

etc.   bourgeois
vs.   status quo

A good collegiate dictionary should indicate which foreign words are still italicized and which are not.

Words, Letters, and Numbers Used as Such

The words *entrance* and *admission* are not perfectly interchangeable.
Don't forget the *k* in *picnicking*.
His *9s* and *7s* descended below the line of writing.

Titles

In general, italicize most titles, including the titles of books, plays, pamphlets, periodicals, movies, radio and television programs, operas, ballets, and record albums. Also italicize the names of works of art such as sculptures and paintings and the names of ships, airplanes, and spacecraft. Some examples follow:

The Chicago Manual of Style   *Sesame Street*
Othello   *Swan Lake*
Scientific American   *Mona Lisa*
Star Wars   *Sputnik II*

mm

▶ MISPLACED MODIFIER

As in the case of dangling modifiers, curious sentences result from a modifier's not being placed next to the element modified:

An engine may crack when cold water is poured in unless it is running.

Probably, with a little effort, no one will misread this example, but, undeniably, it says that the engine will crack unless the water is running. Move the modifier to make the sentence clear:

Unless it is running, an engine may crack when cold water is poured in.

It should be apparent from the preceding examples that a modifier can be in the wrong position to convey one meaning but in the perfect position to convey a different meaning. In the next example, the placement of *for three years* is either right or wrong. It is in the right position to modify *to work* but in the wrong position to modify *have been trying*.

I have been trying to place him under contract to work here for three years. (three-year contract)

As the examples suggest, correct placement of modifiers sometimes amounts to more than mere nicety of expression. It can mean the difference between stating falsehood and truth, between saying what you mean and saying something else.

num

▶ NUMBERS

There is a good deal of inconsistency in the rules for handling numbers. Often the question is whether you should write the number as a word or as a figure. We will give you the general rules. Your instructor or your organization may give you others. As in all matters of format, you must satisfy whomever you are working for at the moment. Do, however, be internally consistent within your reports. Do not handle numbers differently from page to page of a report.

Numbers as Words

Generally, in technical and scientific writing, you write out all numbers from zero to nine and rounded-off large numbers, as words:

six generators
about a million dollars

However, when you are writing a series of numbers, do not mix up figures and words. Let the larger numbers determine the form used:

five boys and six girls

But:

It took us 6 months and 25 days to complete the experiment.

Numbers as Sentence Openers

Do not begin a sentence with a figure. If you can, write the number as a word. If this would be cumbersome, recast the sentence to get the figure out of the beginning position:

Fifteen months ago, we saw the new wheat for the first time.
We found 350 deficient steering systems.

Compound Number Adjectives

When you write two numbers together in a compound number adjective, spell out the first one or the shorter one to avoid confusing the reader:

Twenty 10-inch trout
100 twelve-volt batteries

Hyphens

Two-word numbers are hyphenated on the rare occasions when they are written out:

Eighty-five boxes

or:

Eighty-five should be enough.

Numbers as Figures

The general rule for technical and scientific writing is to write all exact numbers over nine as figures. However, as we noted, rounded-off numbers are commonly written as words. The precise figure could give the reader an impression of exactness that might not be called for.
    Certain conventional uses call for figures at all times.

Dates, Exact Sums of Money, Time, Address
1 January or January 1, 2002
$3,422.67 but about three thousand dollars
1:57 P.M. but two o'clock
660 Fuller Road

Technical Units of Measurement
6 cu ft
4,000 rpm

Cross-References
See page 22.
Refer to Figure 2.

Fractions

When a fraction stands alone, write it as an unhyphenated compound:

two thirds
fifteen thousandths

When a fraction is used as an adjective, you may write it as a hyphenated compound. But if either the numerator or the denominator is hyphenated, do not hyphenate the compound. More commonly, fractions used as adjectives are written as figures.

two-thirds engine speed
twenty-five thousandths
3/4 rpm

paral

▶ PARALLELISM

When you link elements in a series, they must all be in the same grammatical form. Link an adjective with an adjective, a noun with a noun, a clause with a clause, and so forth. Look at the boldface portion of the sentence below:

A good test would **use small amounts of plant material, require little time, simple to run**, and **accurate**.

The series begins with the verbs *use* and *require* and then abruptly switches to the adjectives *simple* and *accurate*. All four elements must be based on the same part of speech. In this case, it's easy to change the last two elements:

A good test would use small amounts of plant material, require little time, **be simple to run**, and **be accurate**.

Always be careful when you are listing to keep all the elements of the list parallel. In the following example, the third item in the list is not parallel to the first two:

The process has three stages: (1) the specimen is dried, (2) all potential pollutants are removed, and (3) atomization.

The error is easily corrected:

The process has three stages: (1) the specimen is dried, (2) all potential pollutants are removed, and (3) the specimen is atomized.

When you start a series, keep track of what you are doing, and finish the series the same way you started it. Nonparallel sentences are at best awkward and off-key. At worst, they can lead to serious misunderstandings.

paren

▶ **PARENTHESES**

Parentheses are used to enclose supplementary details inserted into a sentence. Commas and dashes may also be used for this purpose, but with some restrictions. You may enclose a complete sentence or several complete sentences within parentheses. But such an extensive enclosure would confuse the reader if only commas or dashes were used to enclose it.

The violence of these storms can scarcely be exaggerated. (Typhoons and hurricanes generate winds over 75 miles an hour and waves 50 feet high.) The study . . . .

Lists

Parentheses are also used to enclose numbers or letters used in listing:

This general analysis consists of sections on (1) wave generation, (2) wave propagation, (3) wave action near a shoreline, and (4) wave energy.

Punctuation of Parentheses in Sentences

Within a sentence, place no mark of punctuation before the opening parenthesis. Place any marks needed in the sentence after the closing parenthesis:

A runway that is regularly exposed to crosswinds of over 10 knots (11.6 mph) is considered to be unsafe.

Do not use any punctuation around parentheses when they come between sentences. Give the statement *inside* the parentheses any punctuation it needs.

▶ PERIOD

Periods have several conventional uses.

End Stop

Place a period at the end of any sentence that is not a question or an exclamation:

Find maximum average daily temperature and maximum pressure altitude.

Abbreviations

Place a period after certain abbreviations:

M.D.   etc.
Ph.D.   Jr.

See also the entry for Abbreviations.

Decimal Point

Use the period with decimal fractions and as a decimal point between dollars and cents:

0.4 $5.60
0.05% $450.23

▶ PRONOUN–ANTECEDENT AGREEMENT

Pronoun–antecedent agreement is closely related to verb–subject agreement. For example, the problem area concerning the use of collective nouns explained under Verb–Subject Agreement is closely related to the proper use of pronouns. When a collective noun is considered singular, it takes a singular pronoun as well as a singular verb. Also, such antecedents as *each, everyone, either, neither, anybody, somebody, everybody*, and *no one* take singular pronouns as well as singular verbs:

Everyone had his assignment ready.

However, our sensitivity about using male pronouns exclusively when the reference may be to both men and women makes the choice of a suitable pronoun in this construction difficult. Many people object to the use of *his* as the pronoun in the preceding example. Do not choose to solve the problem by introducing a grammatical error, as in this example of incorrect usage:

Everyone had their assignment ready.

The use of male and female pronouns together is grammatically correct, if a bit awkward at times:

Everyone had his or her assignment ready.

Perhaps the best solution, one that is often applicable, is to use a plural antecedent that allows the use of a neutral plural pronoun, as in this example:

All the students had their assignments ready.

The same problem presents itself when we use such nouns as *student* or *human being* in their generic sense; that is, when we use them to stand for all students or all human beings. If used in the singular, such nouns must be followed by singular pronouns:

The student seeking a loan must have his or her application in by 3 September.

Again, the best solution is to use a plural antecedent:

Students seeking loans must have their applications in by 3 September.

See also the entry for Sexist Usage.

pron

▶ **PRONOUN FORM**

Almost every adult can remember being constantly corrected by parents and elementary school teachers in regard to pronoun form. The common sequence is for the child to say, "Me and Johnny are going swimming," and for the teacher or parent to say patiently, "No, dear, 'Johnny and I are going swimming.'" As a result of this conditioning, many adults automatically regard all objective forms with suspicion, and the most common pronoun error is for the speaker or writer to use a subjective case pronoun such as *I*, *he*, or *she* when an objective case pronoun such as *me*, *him*, or *her* is called for.

Whenever a pronoun is the object of a verb or the object of a preposition, it must be in the objective case:

It occurred to my colleagues and me to check the velocity data on the earthquake waves.

Just between you and me, the news shook Mary and him.

However, use a subjective case pronoun in the predicate nominative position. This rule slightly complicates the use of pronouns after the verb. Normally, the pronoun position after the verb is thought of as objective pronoun territory, but when the verb is a linking verb (chiefly the verb *to be*), the pronoun is called a *predicate noun* rather than an object and is in the subjective case.

> It is she.
> It was he who discovered the mutated fruit fly.

ques

▶ QUESTION MARK

Place a question mark at the end of every sentence that asks a direct question:

> What is the purpose of this report?

A request that you politely phrase as a question may be followed by either a period or a question mark:

> Will you be sure to return the experimental results as soon as possible.
> Will you be sure to return the experimental results as soon as possible?

When you have a question mark within quotation marks, you need no other mark of punctuation:

> "Where am I?" he asked.

quot

▶ QUOTATION MARKS

Use quotation marks to set off short quotations and certain titles.

Short Quotations

Use quotation marks to enclose quotations that are short enough to work into your own text (normally, fewer than three lines):

> According to Dr. Stockdale, "Ants, wonderful as they are, have many enemies."

Quotations longer than three lines should be set off by single spacing and indenting. See the entry for Colon for an example of this style. Do not use quotation marks when quotations are set off and indented.

Titles

Place quotation marks around titles of articles from journals and periodicals:

Nihei's article "The Color of the Future" appeared in *PC World*.

Single Quotes

When you must use quotation marks within other quotation marks, use single marks (the apostrophe on your keyboard):

"Do you have the same trouble with the distinction between 'venal' and 'venial' that I do?" asked the copy editor.

Punctuation Conventions

The following are the conventions in the United States for using punctuation with quotation marks:

Commas and Periods Always place commas and periods inside the quotation marks. There are no exceptions to this rule:

G. D. Brewer wrote "Manned Hypersonic Vehicles."

Semicolons and Colons Always place semicolons and colons outside the quotation marks. There are no exceptions to this rule:

As Dr. Damron points out, "New technology has made photographs easy to fake"; therefore, they are no longer reliable as courtroom evidence.

Question Marks, Exclamation Points, and Dashes Place question marks, exclamation points, and dashes inside the quotation marks when they apply *to the quote only or to the quote and the entire sentence at the same time*. Place them outside the quotation marks when they apply to the entire sentence only.

Inside
When are we going to find the answer to the question, "What causes clear air turbulence?"

Outside
Did you read Minna Levine's "Business Statistics"?

run-on

▶ RUN-ON SENTENCE

A run-on sentence is two independent clauses (that is, two complete sentences) put together with only a comma or no punctuation at all between them. Punctuate two independent clauses placed together with a period, a semicolon, or a comma and a coordinating conjunction (*and, but, for, nor,* or *yet*). Infrequently, the colon or dash is used also. (There are some exceptions to these rules. See the entry for Comma.) The following three examples are punctuated correctly, the first with a period, the second with a semicolon, the third with a comma and a coordinating conjunction:

Check the hydraulic pressure. If it reads below normal, do not turn on the aileron boost.

We will describe the new technology in greater detail; however, first we will say a few words about the principal devices found in electronic circuits.

Ground contact with wood is particularly likely to cause decay, but wood buried far below the ground line will not decay because of a lack of sufficient oxygen.

If the example sentences had only commas or no punctuation at all between the independent clauses, they would be run-on sentences.

Writers most frequently write run-on sentences when they mistake conjunctive adverbs for coordinating conjunctions. The most common conjunctive adverbs are *also, anyhow, besides, consequently, furthermore, hence, however, moreover, nevertheless, therefore,* and *too*.

When a conjunctive adverb is used to join two independent clauses, the mark of punctuation most often used is a semicolon (a period is used infrequently), as in this correctly punctuated sentence:

Ice fish are nearly invisible; however, they do have a few dark spots on their bodies.

Often the sentence will be more effective if it is rewritten completely, making one of the independent clauses a subordinate clause or a phrase.

Run-On Sentence
The students at the university are mostly young Californians, most of them are between the ages of 18 and 24.

Rewritten
The students at the university are mostly young Californians between the ages of 18 and 24.

semi

▶ SEMICOLON

The semicolon lies between the comma and the period in force. Its use is quite restricted. (See also the entry for Run-On Sentences.)

Independent Clauses

Place a semicolon between two closely connected independent clauses that are not joined by a coordinating conjunction (*and, but, or, nor, for,* or *yet*):

> The expanding gases formed during burning drive the turbine; the gases are then exhausted through the nozzle.

When independent clauses joined by a coordinating conjunction have internal punctuation, then the comma before the coordinating conjunction may be changed to a semicolon:

> The front lawn has been planted with a Chinese Beauty Tree, a Bechtel Flowering Crab, a Mountain Ash, and assorted small shrubbery, including barberry and cameo roses; but so far nothing has been done to the rear beyond clearing and rough grading.

Series

When a series contains commas as internal punctuation within the parts, use semicolons between the parts:

> Included in the experiment were Peter Moody, a freshman; Jesse Gatlin, a sophomore; Burrel Gambel, a junior; and Ralph Leone, a senior.

sexist

▶ SEXIST USAGE

Conventional usages often discriminate against both men and women, but particularly against women. For example, a problem often arises when someone is talking about some group in general but refers to members of the group in the singular, as in the following passage:

> The modern secretary has to be an expert with electronic equipment. She has to be able to use a computer and fix a fax machine. On the other hand, her boss still doodles letters on yellow pads. He has yet to come to grips with all the electronic gadgetry in today's office.

This paragraph makes two groundless assumptions: that all secretaries are female and all executives are male. Neither assumption, of course, is valid.

Similarly, in the past, letters began with "Dear Sir" or "Gentlemen." People who delivered mail were "mailmen" and those who protected our streets were "policemen." History books discussed "man's progress" and described how "man has conquered space."

Now we recognize the unfairness of such discriminatory usages. Most organizations make a real effort to avoid sexist usages in their documents. How can you avoid such usages once you understand the problem?

Titles of various kinds are fairly easy to deal with. *Mailmen* have become *mail carriers; policemen, police officers; chairmen, chairpersons* or simply *chairs;* and so forth. We no longer speak of "man's progress" but of "human progress."

The selection of pronouns when dealing with groups in general sometimes presents more of a problem. One way to deal with it is to move from the singular to the plural. You can speak of *secretaries/they* and *bosses/they,* avoiding the choice of either a male or a female pronoun.

You can also write around the problem. You can convert a sentence like the following one from a sexist to a nonsexist statement by replacing the *he* clause with a verbal phrase such as an infinitive or a participle:

The diver must close the mouthpiece shut-off valve before he runs the test.
The diver must close the mouthpiece shut-off valve before running the test.

If you write instructions in a combination of the second person (you) and the imperative mood, you avoid the problem altogether:

You must close the mouthpiece shut-off valve before you run the test.
Close the mouthpiece shut-off valve before running the test.

At times, using plural forms or second person or writing around the problem simply won't work. In an insurance contract, for example, you might have to refer to the policyholder. It would be unclear to use a plural form because that might indicate two policyholders when only one is intended. When such is the case, writers have little recourse except to use such phrases as *he or she* or *he/she*. Both are a bit awkward, but they have the advantage of being both precise and nonsexist.

You can use the search function in your word processing program to find sexist language in your own work. Search for male and female pronouns and *man* and *men*. When you find them, check to see if you have used them in a sexist or a nonsexist way. If you have used them in a sexist way, correct the problem, but be sure not to introduce inaccuracy or imprecision in doing so.

See also the entry for Pronoun–Antecedent Agreement.

sp

▶ SPELLING ERROR

The condition of English spelling is chaotic and likely to remain so. George Bernard Shaw once illustrated this chaos by spelling *fish* as *ghoti*—using the *gh* from *rough*, the *o* from *women*, and the *ti* from *condition*. If you have a spelling checker in your word processing program, it will help you avoid many spelling errors and typographical errors. Do remember, though, that a spelling checker will not catch the wrong word correctly spelled. That is, it won't warn you when you used *to* for *too*. You can obtain help from the spelling section in a collegiate dictionary, where the common rules of spelling are explained. You can also buy rather inexpensive books that explain the various spelling rules and provide exercises to fix the rules in your mind.

To assist you here, we provide a list of common words that sound alike, each used correctly in a sentence.

I **accept** your gift.
Everyone went **except** Jerry.

His attorney gave him good **advice**.
His attorney **advised** him well.

Her cold **affected** her voice.
The **effect** was rather froglike.

He was **already** home by 9 P.M.
When her bag was packed, she was **all ready** to go.

The senators stood **all together** on the issue.
Jim was **altogether** pleased with the result of the test.

He gave him **an** aardvark.
The aardvark **and** the anteater look somewhat alike.

The river **breached** the levee, letting the water through.
He loaded the cannon at the **breech**.

Springfield is the **capital** of Illinois.
Tourists were taking pictures of the **capitol** building.

Always **cite** your sources in a paper.
After the sun rose, we **sighted** the missing children.
She chose land near the river as the **site** for her house.

Burlap is a **coarse** cloth.
She was disappointed, of **course**.

His blue tie **complemented** his gray shirt.
I **complimented** him on his choice of ties.

Most cities have a governing body called a **council**.
The attorney's **counsel** was to remain quiet.

Being quiet, she said, was the **discreet** thing to do.
Each slice in a loaf of bread is **discrete** from the other slices.

"We must move **forward**," the president said.
Many books have **forewords**.

Am I speaking so that you can **hear** me?
He was **here** just a minute ago.

It's obvious why he was here.
The sousaphone and **its** sound are both big and round.

Lead (Pb) has a melting point of 327.5°C.
Joan of Arc **led** the French troops to victory.

Our **principal** goal is to cut the deficit.
Hold to high ethical **principles**.

A thing at rest is **stationary**.
Choose white paper for your **stationery**.

A **straight** line is the shortest distance between two points.
The **Strait** of Gibraltar separates Europe from Africa.

I wonder when **they're** coming.
Are they bringing **their** luggage with them?
Put your luggage **there**, in the corner.

He made a careful, **thorough** inspection.
He worked as **though** his life depended on it.
She **thought** until her head ached.

He **threw** the report on her desk.
His report cut **through** all the red tape.

Laurie moved **to** Trumansburg.
Gary moved to Trumansburg, **too**.
After one comes **two**.

We had two days of hot, sunny **weather**.
Whether he goes or not, I'm going.

Where **were** you on Monday?
The important thing is **we're** here today.
Where are you going tomorrow?

Whose house will you stay at?
Who's coming on the trip with us?

Is that **your** car you're driving?
You're right; it's my car.

vb

▶ VERB FORM

Improper verb form includes a wide variety of linguistic errors, ranging from such nonstandard usages as "He seen the show" for "He saw the show" to such esoteric errors as "He was hung by the neck until dead" for "He was hanged by the neck until dead." Normally, spending a few minutes with any collegiate dictionary will show you the correct verb form. College level dictionaries list the principal parts of the verb after the verb entry.

v/ag

▶ **VERB–SUBJECT AGREEMENT**

Most of the time, verb–subject agreement presents no difficulty to the writer. For example, to convey the thought "He speaks for us all," only a child or a foreigner learning English might say. "He speak for us all." However, various constructions exist in English that do present agreement problems, even for the adult, educated, native speaker of English. These troublesome constructions are examined in the following sections.

Words That Take Singular Verbs

The following words take singular verbs: *each, everyone, either, neither, anybody, somebody*. Writers rarely have trouble with a sentence such as "No one is going to the game." Problems arise when, as is often the case, a prepositional phrase with a plural object is interposed between the simple subject and the verb, as in this sentence: "Each *of these disposal systems* is a possible contaminant." In this sentence some writers are tempted to let the object of the preposition, *systems*, govern the verb and wrongly write, "Each of these disposal systems *are* a possible contaminant."

Compound Subject Joined by *Or* or *Nor*

When a compound subject is joined by *or* or *nor*, the verb agrees with the closer noun or pronoun:

> Either the designer or the builders are in error.
> Either the builders or the designer is in error.

In informal and general usage, one might commonly hear, or see, the second sentence as "Either the builders or the designer are in error." In writing you should hold to the more formal usage of the example.

Parenthetical Expressions

Parenthetical expressions introduced by such words as *accompanied by, with, together with*, and *as well as* do not govern the verb:

> Mr. Roberts, as well as his two assistants, is working on the experiment.

Two or More Subjects Joined by *And*

Two or more subjects joined by *and* take a plural verb. Inverted word order does not affect this rule:

Close to the academy are Cathedral Rock and the Rampart Range.

Collective Nouns

Collective nouns such as *team, group, class, committee*, and many others take either plural or singular verbs, depending on the meaning of the sentence. The writer must be sure that any subsequent pronouns agree with the subject and verb:

The team is going to receive its championship trophy tonight.
The team are going to receive their football letters tonight.

Note well: When the team was considered singular in the first example, the subsequent pronoun was *its*. In the second example the pronoun was *their*.

Formal Elements of Document Design

The formal elements of document design make technical documents, whether in print or on the Web, more accessible and readable for users. For example, a well-designed table of contents in a printed document allows readers to access and read the sections important to them. Similarly, a well-designed menu of links at the top and bottom of each Web page allows users to navigate the pages with a minimum of scrolling.

This appendix deals with five such formal elements:

- Report Format
- Letter and Memorandum Format (see page 637)
- Documentation (see page 649)
- Designing a World Wide Web Site (see page 675)
- Outlining (see page 681)

▶ REPORT FORMAT

Prefatory Elements
    Letter of Transmittal and Preface
    Cover
    Title Page
    Table of Contents
    List of Illustrations
    Glossary and List of Symbols
    Abstracts and Summaries

Main Elements
   Introduction

   Discussion

   Ending

Appendixes

Our approach to format is descriptive, not prescriptive; that is, we describe some of the more conventional practices used in technical reporting. We realize fully, and you should too, that many colleges, companies, and journals call for practices different from the ones we describe. Therefore, we do not recommend that you follow at all times the practices in this section. If you are a student, however, your instructor may, in the interest of class uniformity, insist that you follow this section fairly closely.

Chapter 11, Document Design, discusses strategies for achieving good design. In this section, we discuss the elements—the tools you can use to carry out those strategies. We divide the elements into three groups: prefatory elements, main elements, and appendixes. If you are writing a report that will require you to cite sources, see also the section on Documentation in this appendix.

▶ PREFATORY ELEMENTS

Prefatory elements help your readers to get into your report. The letter of transmittal or preface may be the readers' first introduction to the report. The table of contents reveals the structure of your report.

In the glossary, readers will find the definitions of terms that may be unfamiliar to them. All the prefatory elements discussed in this section contribute to the success of your report.

Letter of Transmittal and Preface

We have placed the letter of transmittal and preface together because they are often quite similar in content. They usually differ in format and intended audience only. You will use the letter of transmittal when the audience is a single person or a single group. Many of your reports in college will include a letter of transmittal to your professor, usually placed just before or after your title page. When on the job, you may handle the letter differently. Often, it is mailed before the report, as a notice that the report is coming, or it may be mailed at the same time as the report but under separate cover.

Typically, you use a preface for a more general audience when you do not know specifically who will be reading your report. The preface or letter of transmittal introduces the reader to the report. It should be fairly brief, but it should always include the following basic elements:

- Statement of transmittal or submittal (included in the letter of transmittal only)
- Statement of authorization or occasion for report
- Statement of subject and purpose

Additionally, you may include some of the following elements in a letter of transmittal or a preface:

- Acknowledgments
- Distribution list (list of those receiving the report—used in the letter of transmittal but not in the preface)
- Features of the report that may be of special interest or significance
- List of existing or future reports on the same subject
- Background material
- Summary of the report
- Special problems (including reasons for not meeting objectives)
- Financial implications
- Conclusions and recommendations

How many of the secondary elements you include depends on the structure of your report. If your report's introduction or discussion includes background information, there may be no point in including such material in the preface or letter of transmittal. See Figures B-1 and B-2 for a sample letter of transmittal and a sample preface.

If the report is to remain within an organization, the letter of transmittal will become a memorandum of transmittal. This changes nothing but the format. (See Letter and Memorandum Format in this appendix.)

Cover

A report's cover serves three purposes. The first two are functional and the third aesthetic and psychological.

First, covers protect pages during handling and storage. Pages ruck up, become soiled and damaged, and may eventually be lost if they are not protected by covers. Second, because they are what readers first see as they pick up a report, covers are the appropriate place to display identifying information such as the report title, the company or agency by or for which the report was prepared, and security notices if the report contains proprietary or classified information. Incidentally, students should not print this sort of information directly on the cover. Rather, they should put the information onto gummed labels,

Gatlin Hall
Weaver University
Briand, MA 02139
July 27, 2001

Dr. Ross Alm
Associate Professor of Geography
Department of Geography
Weaver University
Briand, MA 02139

Dear Dr. Alm:

Statement of transmittal

I submit the accompanying report entitled "Selected Characteristics of the People of the Commonwealth of Independent States" as the final project for Geography 334, the Commonwealth of Independent States.

Occasion for report

Statement of subject and purpose

This report explores the characteristics of the people of the European states of the CIS (Russia, Belarus, Ukraine, Moldova, Georgia, Armenia, and Azerbaijan) and the Central Asian states (Kazakhstan, Uzbekistan, Turkmenistan, Kyrgyzstan, and Tajikistan). The report considers population size, nationality, ethnic divisions, language, literacy rate, and labor force skills. I have attempted to provide a base for understanding how differences in these major characteristics will influence the relationships of these states within the Commonwealth.

I am indebted to Professor Janet Mattson who has allowed me to draw on her unpublished monograph on the Commonwealth.

Acknowledgment

Sincerely,

Anne K. Chimato

Anne K. Chimato
Geography 334

FIGURE B-1 • Letter of Transmittal

readily obtainable at the college bookstore, and then fasten the labels to the cover. A student label might look like the one in Figure B-3.

Finally, covers bestow dignity, authority, and attractiveness. They bind a bundle of manuscript pages into a finished work that looks and feels like a report and has some of the characteristics of a printed and bound book.

PREFACE

Occasion for report

Following the breakup of the USSR, the Commonwealth of Independent States (CIS) was formed from the former Soviet republics. These states have a need and a desire to coexist in harmony. How well they can do that will depend in some measure on how well these diverse states can work together without the power of a central government to hold them together. This report—part of the Central Intelligence Agency's public information program—lays a groundwork for understanding the difficulties involved by exploring the characteristics of the people of the European states of the CIS (Russia, Belarus, Ukraine, Moldova, Georgia, Armenia, and Azerbaijan) and the Central Asian states (Kazakhstan, Uzbekistan, Turkmenistan, Kyrgyzstan, and Tajikistan). The report considers population size, nationality, ethnic divisions, language, literacy rate, and labor force skills.

Statement of subject and purpose

Of particular interest is the wide distribution of different ethnic groups within these new states. Such ethnic divisions may cause future conflict as has been seen in Bosnia and Yugoslavia and in the dispute between Armenia and Azerbaijan over the ethnically Armenian enclave of Nagorno-Karabakh in Azerbaijan.

Feature of special interest

For detailed information on the geography, government, economy, and defense force of each of these states, see The World Factbook, published yearly by the Central Intelligence Agency and available through the U.S. Government Printing Office, Superintendent of Documents, Washington, DC 20402.

Another report on similar subject

FIGURE B-2 • Preface

**SELECTED CHARACTERISTICS OF THE PEOPLE OF
THE COMMONWEALTH OF INDEPENDENT STATES**

by

Anne K. Chimato

Geography 334   July 27, 2001

FIGURE B-3 • Student Label

Suitable covers need not be expensive and sometimes should not be. Students, particularly, should avoid being pretentious. All three purposes may be served by covers of plastic or light cardboard (perhaps 30- or 40-pound weight). You can buy such covers in a variety of sizes, colors, and finishes.

While you are formatting your report, remember that when you fasten it into its cover, about an inch of the left margin will be lost. If you want an inch of margin, you must leave two inches on your paper. Readers grow irritated when they must exert brute force to bend open the covers to see the full page of text.

Title Page

Like report covers, title pages perform several functions. They dignify the reports they preface, of course, but far more important, they provide identifying matter and help to orient the report users to their reading tasks.

To give dignity, a title page must be attractive and well designed. Symmetry, balance, and neatness are important. The most important items should be printed boldly; items of lesser importance should be subordinated. These objectives are sometimes at war with the objective of giving the report users all the data they may want to see at once. Here we have listed, in random order, the items that sometimes appear on title pages. A student paper, of course, would not require all or even most of these items. The first four items are usually sufficient for simple title pages.

- Name of the company (or student) preparing the report
- Name of the company (or instructor and course) for which the report was prepared
- Title and, sometimes, subtitle of the report
- Date of submission or publication of the report
- Code number of the report
- Contract numbers under which the work was done
- List of contributors to the report (minor authors)
- Name and signature of the authorizing officer
- Company or agency logo and other decorative matter
- Proprietary and security notices
- Abstract
- Library identification number
- Reproduction restrictions
- Distribution list (a list of those receiving the report). If the letter of transmittal does not contain this information, the title page should.

Of course, placing all of these items on an $8^1/_2$- by 11-inch page would guarantee a cluttered appearance. Include what you must, but no more.

Word processing programs allow report writers to use different type sizes and styles on a title page to indicate what is important and what is subordinate. Use this capability discreetly. Don't turn your title page (or any other part of your report) into a jumble of different typefaces. Generally, different type sizes and the use of boldface and plain style will suffice.

Figure B-4 illustrates a title page prepared with a word processor.

Selected Characteristics of the People of
The Commonwealth of Independent States

Prepared for

Dr. Ross Alm

Associate Professor of Geography

Geography 334

The Commonwealth of Independent States

by
Anne K. Chimato

Abstract

This report explores selected characteristics of the people of the European states of the CIS (Russia, Belarus, Ukraine, Moldova, Georgia, Armenia, and Azerbaijan) and the Central Asian states (Kazakhstan, Uzbekistan, Turkmenistan, Kyrgyzstan, and Tajikistan). The report considers population size, nationality, ethnic divisions, language, literacy rate, and labor force skills. It provides a base for understanding how differences in these major characteristics will influence the relationships of these states within the Commonwealth.

July 27, 2001

FIGURE B-4 • Title Page

Pay particular attention to the wording of your title. Titles should be brief but descriptive and specific. The reader should know from the title what the report is about. A title such as "Effects of Incubation Temperatures on Sexual Differentiation in Turtles: A Geographic Comparison" is illustrative. From it, you know specifically the research being reported. To see how effectively this title works, leave portions of it out, and see how quickly your understanding of what the article contains changes. For example, "Sexual Differentiation in Turtles" would suggest a much more comprehensive report than does the actual title. A title such as "Effects of Incubation Temperatures" could as well be about chickens as turtles. On the other hand, adding the words "An Investigation into" to the beginning of the title would add nothing useful. The test of whether a title is too long or too short isn't in the number of words it contains but what happens if words are deleted or added. Keep your titles as brief as possible, but make sure they do the job.

Table of Contents

A table of contents (TOC) performs at least three major functions. Its most obvious function is to indicate the page on which discussion of each major topic begins; that is, it serves the reader as a locating device. Less obviously, a TOC forecasts the extent and nature of the topical coverage and suggests the logic of the arrangement and the relationship of the parts. Still earlier, in the prewriting stage, provisional drafts of the TOC enable the author to "think on paper"; they act as outlines to guide the composition.

A system of numbers, letters, type styles, indentations, and other mechanical aids has to be selected so that the TOC will perform its intended functions. Figure B-5 shows a TOC suitable for student reports. We have annotated the figure to draw your attention to a few key points. However, the annotations are suggestions only. There are many acceptable variations in TOCs. For example, the leader dots in Figure B-5 carry the reader's eyes from the end of each title to the page number and tie the page together visually. However, use of leader dots is by no means universal. Some people feel the leader dots clutter the page and, therefore, don't use them. If you use a numbering system in your report (see pages 262–264), the TOC should reflect that system.

In Figure B-6, we reproduce a professionally created TOC that shows a good use of word processing capabilities. When you design your own TOC, avoid overcrowding. Seldom is there justification for going beyond three levels of headings; beyond three levels, users have almost as much trouble locating items in the TOC as they have in locating them by flipping through the report.

Be sure that page numbers in your TOC match the page numbers in your final draft. Remember that the wording of the TOC entries and the headings

Make all major headings distinctive. All capitals or boldface is a good choice.

Line up all numbers, arabic and roman, on right-hand digits.

Show hierarchy with indentation. If you have used a numbering system in the report, repeat it in the table of contents.

In subheadings, capitalize first and last words and all principal words. Do not capitalize an article, preposition, or coordinating conjunction unless it is a first or last word.

CONTENTS

	Page
LIST OF ILLUSTRATIONS	iii
INTRODUCTION	1
EUROPEAN STATES	2
Population Size	4
Nationality	6
Ethnic Divisions	7
Language	9
Literacy Rate	10
Labor Force Skills	11
CENTRAL ASIAN STATES	12
Population Size	14
Nationality	15
Ethnic Divisions	16
Language	18
Literacy Rate	19
Labor Force Skills	20
SUMMARY	21
NOTES	22

ii

FIGURE B-5 • Table of Contents

on the text pages must be exactly the same. Every entry in the TOC must also be in the report. However, every heading in the report need not be in the TOC. That is, if you have four levels of headings in your report, you might list only the top three levels in your TOC.

List of Illustrations

If a report contains more than a few illustrations, say more than three or four, it's customary to list the illustrations on a separate page or on the TOC page. Illustrations are of two major types: tables and figures. A table is any array of data, often numerical, arranged vertically in columns and horizontally in rows, together with the necessary headings and notes. Figures include photographs, maps, graphs, organization charts, and flow diagrams—literally any illustration that does not qualify as a table by the preceding definition. (For further details, see Chapter 12, Using Illustrations.)

If the report contains both tables and figures, it's customary to use the page heading "Illustrations" or "Exhibits" and to list all the figures first and then all the tables. If you have all of one kind of figure in your report, you can

FDA *Consumer*

The Magazine of the U.S. Food and Drug Administration

July–August 2000 • Vol. 34 No. 4

Saline Breast Implants Stay on Market as Experts Warn About Risks   9

Pharmacy Compounding: Customizing Prescription Drugs   11

Avoiding the Hazards of Medical Gases   13

Cover Story
Trying to Look SUNsational? Complexity Persists in Using Sunscreens   15

Bone Marrow Transplants Come of Age: New Hope for Deadly Diseases   22

Overcoming Juvenile Diabetes With a Little Planning and High-Tech Tools   28

Observations   2

Letters to the Editor   2

Updates   4

fda.gov   33

Summaries of Court Actions   34

Investigators' Reports   35

The Last Word   36

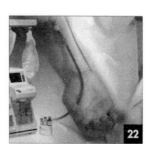

A diabetes patient uses a spring-loaded device to insert a tiny catheter into his abdomen, allowing precise doses of insulin to be delivered from a pump about the size of a pager. For the latest on juvenile diabetes, see page 28.

FIGURE B-6 • Professionally Produced Table of Contents
Source: FDA Consumer, July/August 2000, 1.

use the appropriate term as your heading; for example, "Maps" is used as a heading in Figure B-7. If you have various kinds of figures, use "Figures" as your heading.

Illustration titles should be as brief and yet as self-explanatory as possible. Avoid a cumbersome expression such as "A Figure Showing Characteristic Thunderstorm Recording." Say, simply, "Characteristic Thunderstorm Recording." On the other hand, do not be overly economical and write just "Characteristic" or "A Comparison." At best, such generic titles are only vaguely suggestive.

The simple list in Figure B-7 should satisfy most needs. Notice that arabic numerals are used for figures and roman numerals for tables. This practice is common but by no means standard. Make sure that your page numbers are correct and that the titles listed accurately repeat the titles in the report.

Glossary and List of Symbols

Reports dealing with technical and specialized subject matter often include abbreviations, acronyms, symbols, and terms not known to the nonspecialist. Thus, a communication problem arises. Technically trained persons have an

Line up all illustration and page numbers, arabic and roman, on the right-hand digit.

In titles, capitalize first and last words and all principal words. Do not capitalize an article, preposition, or coordinating conjunction unless it is a first or last word.

When titles run two or more lines, indent all lines after the first.

ILLUSTRATIONS

Maps   Page

1. European States of the CIS 2
2. Ethnic Divisions of the European States
      of the CIS 7
3. Central Asian States of the CIS 12
4. Ethnic Divisions of the Central Asian States
      of the CIS 16

Tables

I. Comparison of Selected Characteristics of the
      People of the European States of the CIS 3
II. Comparison of Selected Characteristics of the
      People of the Central Asian States of the CIS 13

iii

FIGURE B-7 • List of Illustrations

unfortunate habit of assuming that what is well known to them is well known to others. This assumption is seldom justified. Terms, symbols, and abbreviations change in meaning with time and context. In one context, ASA may stand for American Standards Association; in another context, for Army Security Agency. The letter K may stand for degrees Kelvin or for the element potassium. The meanings given to Greek letters may change from one report to the next, even though both were done by the same person.

Furthermore, writers seldom have complete control over who will read their reports. A report intended for an engineering audience may have to be read by managers, legal advisors, or sales representatives. It is wise to play it safe by including a list of symbols or a glossary or both. Readers who do not need these aids can easily ignore them; those who do need them will be immeasurably grateful.

The list of symbols is normally a prefatory element. A glossary may be a prefatory element or placed as an appendix at the end of the report. When you first use a symbol found in your list of symbols or a term found in the glossary, tell your reader where to find the list or the glossary. Figure B–8 illustrates a list of symbols. Figure B–9 illustrates a glossary.

Abstracts and Summaries

Abstracts and summaries are overviews of the facts, results, conclusions, and recommendations of a report. In many formats, such as empirical research reports and feasibility reports, abstracts or summaries will be placed near the front of the report. In that position, they both summarize the report and allow busy readers to decide whether they want to read further. Both executives and experts expect the abstract or summary to come early in the report.

In more discursive reports—such as magazine articles—summaries most often come at the end of the report, where they serve to draw things together for the reader. Many reports, particularly empirical research reports, have an abstract at the beginning and a summary at the end. These facts raise the question of when an overview is an abstract and when it is a summary. In general, these principles hold true:

- Abstracts are placed before technical reports, such as empirical research reports, meant for technical audiences.
- Summaries are placed before business and organizational reports such as proposals and feasibility reports. When the audience is primarily an executive audience, the summary will be known as an executive summary.
- An overview placed at the end of a report will probably be called a summary.

Because abstracts and executive summaries always appear as prefatory elements, we discuss them in this section. We discuss other types of summaries,

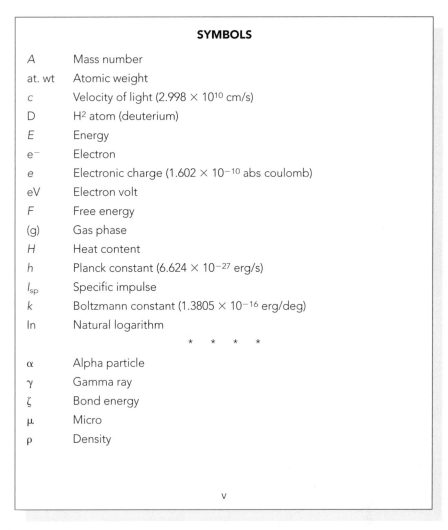

SYMBOLS

A	Mass number
at. wt	Atomic weight
c	Velocity of light (2.998×10^{10} cm/s)
D	H^2 atom (deuterium)
E	Energy
e^-	Electron
e	Electronic charge (1.602×10^{-10} abs coulomb)
eV	Electron volt
F	Free energy
(g)	Gas phase
H	Heat content
h	Planck constant (6.624×10^{-27} erg/s)
I_{sp}	Specific impulse
k	Boltzmann constant (1.3805×10^{-16} erg/deg)
ln	Natural logarithm

       ⋆   ⋆   ⋆   ⋆

α	Alpha particle
γ	Gamma ray
ζ	Bond energy
μ	Micro
ρ	Density

v

FIGURE B-8 • List of Symbols

conclusions, and recommendations on pages 629–630, where we discuss how to end a report.

Abstracts Discussed here are abstract style and two kinds of abstracts: informative and descriptive. Never use "I" statements in either kind of abstract. Report your information impersonally, as though it were written by someone else. The informative abstract in Figure B-10 illustrates the style. This is not an arbitrary principle. If you were to publish your report, your abstract would likely be reprinted in an abstracting journal, where the use of I would be inappropriate. Also, many companies, in the interest of good intracompany

Use parallel sentence fragments for glossary definitions (see Parallelism in Appendix A, Handbook).

Use complete sentences to add information to a definition.

GLOSSARY

Btu	the amount of heat required to raise the temperature of one pound of water one degree Fahrenheit.
degree day	a temperature standard around which temperature variations are measured.
design temperature	the maximum reasonable temperature expected during the heating or cooling season. Design calculations are based upon this number.
heat transmission coefficient	the quantity of heat in Btu transmitted per hour through one square foot of a building surface.
infiltration	the air leaking into a building from cracks around doors and windows.
sensible heat	heat that the human body can sense.
thermal conductivity	the quantity of heat in Btu transmitted by conduction per hour through one square foot of a homogeneous material for each degree Fahrenheit difference between the surfaces of the material.
thermal resistance	the reciprocal of thermal conductivity.

vii

FIGURE B-9 • Glossary

communication, publish the abstracts of all company research reports. The restriction on the use of I makes the use of passive voice common in abstracts. Because your full report contains complete documentation, you need not footnote or otherwise document the information in abstracts.

An informative abstract like that of Figure B-10 is most often intended for an expert audience; therefore, the author can use the technical language of the field freely. Write an informative abstract so that readers will understand

- The objectives of the research or the report
- The methodology used in the research
- The findings of the report, including the results and conclusions and, when appropriate, the recommendations

Most professional journals or societies publish stylebooks that include specifications for writing abstracts. Many journals, because of high publica-

<table>
<tr>
<td>Objective and
methodology</td>
<td>Although breast cancer can have a stressful impact on women of all ages, young women may be particularly vulnerable to the negative effects of the disease. Based on a developmental perspective, this article reviews studies on the emotional impact of breast cancer on young women, their spouses, children, and the marital relationship. Studies indicate that younger women experience more emotional distress than older women, although the inverse relationship between age and emotional distress is not consistent across all studies. Although age does not appear to have a direct relationship to husbands' adjustments, younger husbands reported more problems carrying out domestic roles and a greater number of life stresses than older husbands. Studies on the impact of breast cancer on children are limited in number and scope but indicate that the effects of breast cancer vary according to the developmental level of the child. Directions for further research on young women and their families are suggested.</td>
</tr>
<tr>
<td>Findings</td>
<td></td>
</tr>
</table>

FIGURE B-10 • Informative Abstract
Source: Laurel L. Northouse, "Breast Cancer in Younger Women: Effects on Interpersonal and Family Relations," *Monographs: Journal of the National Cancer Institute* 16 (1994): 183.

tion costs, set arbitrary limits of under two hundred words for abstracts. Because abstract writing uses many of the techniques used in summary writing, you might want to read what we say about that subject on pages 629–630.

The main purpose of the descriptive abstract is to help busy readers decide whether they need or want the information in the report enough to read it entirely. The descriptive abstract merely tells what the full report contains. Unlike the informative abstract, it cannot serve as a substitute for the report itself. Many reports contain descriptive abstracts, and many abstracting journals print them. The abstract included on the title page in Figure B-4 and the abstract in Figure B-11 are typical of the content and style of a descriptive

Abstract

This article argues that examining leaders and leadership techniques is a valid subject for technical and professional writing and communication classes. The article describes an assignment for studying leadership and provides related instructional materials.

FIGURE B-11 • Descriptive Abstract
Source: Mark Gellis, "Leadership, Teamwork, and the Professional Writing Class," *Journal of Technical Writing and Communication* 28 (1998): 251.

abstract. Whether a report is ten or a thousand pages long, a descriptive abstract can cover the material in less than ten lines. The descriptive abstract discusses the *report*, not the subject.

Executive Summary Placed at the front of a report, the executive summary ensures that the points of the report important to an executive audience are immediately accessible. To that end, it is written in a nontechnical language suited to an executive audience. Seldom more than one page long, double spaced, it emphasizes the material that executives need in their decision-making process. It need not summarize all the sections of the report. For example, writing for a combined audience of scientists and executives, a writer might include a theory section in a report. The executive summary might skip this section altogether or treat it very briefly.

In their decision making, executives weigh factors such as markets, risks, rewards, costs, and people. If your report recommends buying new equipment, they want to be assured that you have examined all reasonable alternatives and considered cost, productivity, efficiency, profits, and staffing. If you are reporting research, executives take your methodology for granted. They care very little for the physics, chemistry, or sociology behind a development. What they want to know are your results and the implications of those results for the organization.

Figure B-12 lists the questions that executives ask in different situations and that, therefore, an executive summary should answer. The annotated executive summary in Figure B-13 illustrates the style and the major parts of an executive summary.

Place an executive summary immediately before the introduction and label it Summary or Executive Summary. In short reports and memorandum reports, the executive summary often replaces the introduction and is followed immediately by the major discussion.

▶ MAIN ELEMENTS

The body of a report contains detailed information and interpretation. The body needs to be introduced and, normally, finished off with an ending of some sort that may include a summary, conclusions, recommendations, or simply a graceful exit from the report. We discuss all these elements in this section on main elements.

Introduction

A good introduction forecasts what is to follow in the rest of the report. It directs the reader's mind to the subject and purpose. It sets limits on the scope

Problems

What is it?

Why is solution undertaken?

Magnitude and importance?

What is being done? By whom?

Approaches used?

Are they thorough and complete?

Suggested solution? Best? Consider others?

What now?

Who does it?

Time factors?

New Projects and Products

Potential?

Risks?

Scope of application?

Commercial implications?

Competition?

Importance to company?

More work to be done? Any problems?

Required personnel, facilities, and equipment?

Relative importance to other projects or products?

Life of project or product line?

Effect on company's technical position?

Priorities required?

Proposed schedule?

Target date?

Tests and Experiments

What tested or investigated?

Why? How?

What did they show?

Better ways?

Conclusions? Recommendations?

Implications to company?

Materials and Processes

Properties characteristics, capabilities?

Limitations?

Use requirements and environment?

Areas and scope of application?

Cost factors?

Availability and sources?

What else can be used?

Problems in using?

Significance of application to company?

Field Troubles and Special Design Problems

Specific equipment involved?

What trouble developed? Any trouble history?

How much involved?

Responsibility? Others? Company?

What is needed?

Special requirements and environment?

Who does it? Time factors?

Most practical solution? Recommended action?

Suggested product design changes?

FIGURE B-12 • What Managers Want to Know

Source: James W. Souther, "What to Report," *IEEE Transactions on Professional Communication* PC-28 (1985): 6

of the subject matter and reveals the plan of development of the report. Early in your paper you also give any needed theoretical or historical background, and this is sometimes included as part of the introduction.

Subject Never begin an introduction with a superfluous statement. The writer who is doing a paper on read-only memory in computers and begins with the statement "The study of computers is a vital and interesting one"

SUMMARY

Problem definition

The university is steadily falling behind in the faculty and student use of computers. Our computer labs are filled with slow and obsolete computers that lack the memory and power to run programs currently being produced. We have faculty who are capable of designing computer programs for instructional use but who are reluctant to do so because their students do not have access to state-of-the-art computers. As a result, too many students are leaving the university as computer illiterates.

Information resources has considered three solutions to the problem:

Alternatives considered

1. Require all freshmen to buy a personal computer at an approximate cost of $1,000 each. At an interest rate of 8%, students could repay the university in 16 quarterly payments of $72.50 each.

2. Provide personal computers to those students and faculty who want them through the university bookstore at deep discounts. Purchasers would arrange any needed financing.

3. Upgrade the university computer labs by providing $1.5 million over the next fiscal year to provide personal computers, printers, software, and new furniture. Student lab fees of $25 per quarter will pay the cost of materials and employees to run the labs.

Recommendation

Effect of recommendation

We recommend solutions 2 and 3. We reject solution 1 on the grounds that we are a public institution and must not put educational costs out of the reach of our students. Solutions 2 and 3 would make enough computers available for the immediate future to encourage their use by both students and faculty.

FIGURE B-13 • Executive Summary

has wasted readers' time and probably annoyed them as well. Announce your specific subject loudly and clearly and as early as possible in the introduction, preferably in the very first sentence. The sentence "This paper will discuss several of the more significant applications of the exploding wire phenomenon to modern science" may not be very subtle, but it gets the job done. The reader knows what the subject is. Often, in conjunction with the statement of your subject, you will also need to define some important terms that may be unfamiliar to your readers. For example, the student who wrote the foregoing sentence followed it with these two:

> A study of the exploding wire phenomenon is a study of the body of knowledge and inquiry around the explosion of fine metal wires by a sudden and large pulse of current. The explosion is accompanied by physical manifestations in the form of a loud noise, shock waves, intense light for a short period, and high temperatures.

In three sentences the writer announces the subject and defines it. The paper is well under way.

Sometimes, particularly if you are writing for nonspecialists, you may introduce your subject with some interest-catching facts. The following example introduces an article on preventing childhood poisoning:

> Most people regard their home as a safe haven, a calming oasis in an often stormy world. But home can be a dangerous place when it comes to accidental poisoning, especially accidental poisoning of children. One tablet of some medicines can wreak havoc in or kill a child.
>
> Childhood poisonings caused by accidental overdoses of iron-containing supplements are the biggest concern of poison control experts, consumer protection groups, and health-care providers. Iron-containing supplements are the leading cause of pediatric poisoning deaths for children under 6 in the United States. According to the American Association of Poison Control Centers, from 1986 to 1994, 38 children between the ages of 9 months and 3 years died from accidentally swallowing iron-containing products. The number of pills consumed ranged from as few as 5 to as many as 98.[1]

Using a technique often seen in interest-catching introductions, the author of this example strengthens the reader's interest by immediately following her opening with a few eye-catching facts. Interesting-catching introductions are used in brochures, advertisements, and magazine and newspaper articles. You will rarely see an interest-catching introduction in business reports or professional journals. If you do, it will usually be a short one.

Purpose Your statement of purpose tells the reader *why* you are writing about the subject you have announced. By so doing, you also answer the reader's question "Should I read this paper or not?" For example, a Department of Labor report on job hunting includes this sentence: "Whether you are involuntarily unemployed, changing jobs, or looking for your first job, this Guide is designed to help you negotiate the many phases of the job search process."[2] Readers who have no reason to be interested in such a discussion will know there is no purpose in reading further.

Another way to understand the purpose statement is to realize that it often deals with the *significance* of the subject. Writers who had human–computer interaction as their subject announced their purpose this way:

> Why take yet another look at the way humans and computers interact? Because an important part of human–computer interaction is the way that people feel

about themselves and the computer's actions both during the interaction and after it is completed. These feelings affect their decision to buy or use a program, their attitude toward computing, and their effectiveness in future interactions. People may be happy and comfortable with the dialog, or they may not be. They may feel belittled and bewildered, or they may feel they are leading along a plodding machine that does not serve them well. Parallels can be drawn between human–computer dialogs and the dialogs that people have with each other.[3]

Scope   The statement of scope further qualifies the subject. It announces how broad the treatment of the subject will be. Often it indicates the level of competence expected in the reader for whom the paper is designed. For example, a student who wrote "In this report I explain the application of superconductivity in electric power systems in a manner suitable for college undergraduates" declared his scope as well as his purpose. He is limiting the scope to superconductivity in electric power systems and stating that his target audience is not composed of high school students or graduate physicists but of college undergraduates.

Plan of Development   In a plan of development, you forecast your report's organization and content. The principle of psychological reinforcement is at work here. If you tell your readers what you are going to cover, they will be more ready to comprehend as they read along. The following, taken from the introduction to a student's paper on enriching flour with iron, is a good example of a plan of development:

> This study presents a basic introduction to three major areas of concern about iron enrichment: (1) which form of iron is most suitable; (2) potential health risks from overdoses of iron, such as cardiovascular disease, hemochromatosis, and the masking of certain disorders; and (3) ignorance of the definitions, extent, and causes of iron deficiency.

You need not necessarily think of the announcement of subject, purpose, scope, and plan of development as four separate steps. Often, subject and purpose or scope and plan of development can be combined. In a short paper, perhaps two or three sentences might cover all four points, as in this example:

Subject

Purpose, scope, and plan of development

> Although breast cancer has a stressful impact on women of all ages, there is a growing concern that young women with breast cancer and their family members may be particularly vulnerable to the negative effects of the illness. However, little research has addressed the concerns or the impact of the illness on younger women's lives and the lives of their family members. Utilizing a developmental perspective, this article describes the emotional impact of breast cancer on young women, their spouses, children, and the marital relationship; it concludes with directions for future research.[4]

Also, introductions to specialized reports may have peculiarities of their own. These are discussed in Part III, Applications.

Theoretical or Historical Background

When theoretical or historical background is not too lengthy, you can incorporate it into your introduction. In the following excellent introduction, the writer begins with background, makes his subject and purpose clear, and closes with a paragraph that states his scope and plan of development:

> In recent years, two questions have received a good deal of attention in the field of business and technical writing, or professional communication, as I will call it. One question is old and one new, but both are closely related—at least to professional communication teachers and researchers who are trained in the profession of literary criticism. The first question is as old as technical and business writing courses, dating back to the 1910s: To what extent, if any, should business and technical writing courses serve the pragmatic needs of business and industry, and to what extent, if any, should those courses teach the concerns of literary studies? The second question is relatively new, but it has received a great deal of attention in recent years: What is the responsibility, if any, of the instructor of these courses to teach ethics? The two questions are related in complex ways because, for some teachers in the field of professional communication, putting business and technical writing courses at the service of business and industry is viewed as ethically suspect, and there have been a number of articles recently that argue or suggest that business and technical writing courses for students majoring in science, technology, and business should ask those students to critique the ethical basis of science, business, and industry from what is essentially the perspective of literary studies, as we shall see.
>
> Let me say from the outset that I believe that all teachers—and all professions and all institutions and indeed all human beings—have a responsibility to promote ethical behavior. So, too, every profession, institution, and human being ought to engage in critical reflection at times. The question is not whether teachers, courses, disciplines, professions, and institutions should promote ethical behavior but how, when, and for what purposes they should be promoted. These are far more complex questions, and they cannot be answered without instructors considering their methods, timing, and motives for raising ethical issues. In this article, I want to point out some potential difficulties—which are essentially ethical difficulties—in literature-trained faculty teaching ethics in professional communication courses, and I will warn against a too-hasty—uncritical, if you will—pursuit of certain kinds of critical reflection as a goal of these courses.
>
> First, I will examine the historical and an institutional context of my two central questions and look at two recent answers to them. Then I will turn to an obscure chapter in the history of business and technical communication—the teaching of "engineering publicity" at Massachusetts Institute of Technology (MIT) in

the early 1920s—to see the unusual answer of one institution to these questions at a crucial point in its history. Finally, I will suggest why I believe that answer is worth serious consideration by those of us involved in writing instruction and curricular planning for students who will enter business and professional communities, both outside and within academia (for we must remember that academics—even those in literary studies—are professionals as well).[5]

If the background material is extensive, however, it more properly becomes part of the body of your paper.

Discussion

The discussion will be the longest section of your report. Your purpose and your content will largely determine the form of this section. Therefore, we can prescribe no set form for it. In presenting and discussing your information, you will use one or more of the techniques described in Chapters 9 and 10 or the special techniques described in Part III, Applications. In addition to your text, you will probably also use headings (see pages 257–264) and visuals such as graphs, tables, and illustrations.

When thinking about your discussion, remember that almost every technical report answers a question or questions: What is the best method of desalination to create a water supply at an overseas military base? How are substances created in a cell's cytoplasm carried through a cell's membranes? What is the nature of life on the ocean floor? How does single parenthood affect the children in the family? Ask and answer the reporter's old standbys: Who? What? When? Where? Why? How? Use the always important "so-what?" to explore the implications of your information. However you approach your discussion, project yourself into the minds of your readers. What questions do they need answered to understand your discussion? What details do they need to follow your argument? You will find that you must walk a narrow line between too little detail and too much.

Too little detail is really not measured in bulk but in missing links in your chain of discussion. You must supply enough detail to lead the reader up to your level of competence. You are most likely to leave out crucial details on some basic point that, because of your familiarity with the subject, you assume to be common knowledge. If in doubt about the reader's competence at any point, take the time to define and explain.

Many reasons exist for too much detail, and almost all stem from writers' inability to edit their own work. When you realize that something is irrelevant to your discussion, discard it. It hurts, but the best writers will often throw away thousands of words, representing hours or even days of work.

You must always ask yourself questions like these: Does this information have significance, directly or indirectly, for the subject I am explaining or for the question I am answering? Does this information move the discussion forward? Does it enhance the credibility of the report? Does it support my conclusions? If you don't have a yes answer to one or more of these questions, the information has no place in the report, no matter how many hours of research it cost you.

Ending

Depending on what sort of paper you have written, your ending can be a summary, a set of conclusions, a set of recommendations, or a graceful exit from the paper. Frequently, you'll need some combination of these. We'll look at the four endings and at some of the possible combinations.

It's also possible in reports written with executives as the primary audience that the "ending" may actually be placed at the front of the report. Executives are more interested in summaries, conclusions, and recommendations than they are in the details of a report. Thus, many writers in business and government move these elements to the front of their reports. They may be presented in separate sections labeled Summary, Conclusions, and Recommendations or combined into an executive summary (see page 622). In either case, the body of the report may be labeled Discussion or even Annexes.

Summary Many technical papers are not argumentative. They simply present a body of information that the reader needs or will find interesting. Frequently, such papers end with summaries. In a summary, you condense for your readers what you have just told them in the discussion. Good summaries are difficult to write. At one extreme, they may fail to provide adequate information; at the other, they may be too detailed. You must pare the summary down to material essential to your purpose. This can be a slippery business.

Suppose your purpose is to explore the way the human digestive system absorbs iron from food. In your discussion you describe an experiment conducted with Venezuelan workers that followed isotopically labeled iron through their digestive systems. To enhance the credibility of the information presented, you include some details about the experiment. You report the conclusion that vegetarian diets decreased iron absorption.

How much of this should you put in your summary? Given your purpose, the location and methodology of the experiment would not be suitable material for the summary. You would simply report that in one experiment vegetarian diets were shown to decrease iron absorption.

In general, each major point of the discussion should be covered in the summary. Sometimes you may wish to number the points for clarity. The following, from a student's paper of about 2,500 words, is an excellent summary:

> The exploding wire is a simple-to-perform yet very complex scientific phenomenon. The course of any explosion depends not only on the material and shape of

the wire but also on the electrical parameters of the circuit. An explosion consists primarily of three phases:

1. The current builds up and the wire explodes.
2. Current flows during the dwell period.
3. "Post-dwell conduction" begins with the reignition caused by impact ionization.

These phases may be run together by varying the circuit parameters.

The exploding wire has found many uses: it is a tool in performing other research, a source of light and heat for practical scientific application, and a source of shock waves for industrial use.

Summaries should be concise, and they should introduce no material that has not been covered in the report. Read your discussion over, noting your main generalizations and your topic sentences. Blend these together into a paragraph or two. Sometimes you will represent a sentence from the discussion with a sentence in the summary. At other times you will shorten such sentences to phrases or clauses. The last sentence in the foregoing example represents a summary of four sentences from the writer's discussion. The four sentences themselves were the topic sentences from four separate paragraphs.

If you are using a word processor, you might do well to copy the material you are summarizing and then go through it, eliminating unwanted material to make your summary. Such a technique may be easier and more accurate than retyping the material.

Conclusions Some technical papers work toward a conclusion. They ask a question—such as "Are nuclear power plants safe?"—present a set of facts relevant to answering the question, and end by stating a conclusion—Yes, No, or, sometimes, Maybe. The entire paper aims squarely at the final conclusion. In such a paper, you argue inductively and deductively. You bring up opposing arguments and show their weak points. At the end of the paper, you must present your conclusions. Conclusions are the inferences drawn from the factual evidence of the report. They are the final link in your chain of reasoning. In simplest terms, the relationship of fact to conclusion goes something like this:

Facts	Conclusion
Car A averages 25 miles per gallon.	On the basis of miles per gallon,
Car B averages 40 miles per gallon.	Car B is preferable.

Because we presented a simple case, our conclusion was not difficult to arrive at. But even more complicated problems present the same relationship of fact to inference.

In working your way toward a major conclusion, you ordinarily have to work your way through a series of conclusions. In answering the question about nuclear power plant safety, you would have to answer many subquestions concerning such things as security of the radioactive materials used, adequate control of the nuclear reaction, and safe disposal of nuclear wastes. The answer to each subquestion is a conclusion. You may present these conclusions in the body of the report, but it's usually a good idea to also draw them all together at the end of the report to support the major conclusion.

Be sure that your conclusion or conclusions relate to the investigation or objectives proposed in the introduction. For example, the introduction to a tree planting experiment stated the following objective:

> This trial was established to determine whether a small volume of water applied after planting would have a beneficial impact on plant survival and growth.

The paper's conclusion spoke directly to the stated objective:

> Application of even a small amount of water to seedlings immediately after planting has a profound beneficial impact on both survival and early resumption of growth after planting. The marginal increase in cost of applying water to seedlings immediately after planting should be easily justified in terms of improved seedling establishment and subsequent growth.[6]

In longer papers, or when dealing with a controversial or complex subject, you would be wise to precede your conclusions with a summary of your facts. By doing so, you reinforce in your reader's mind the strength and organization of your argument. In any event, make sure your conclusions are based firmly upon evidence that has been presented in your report. Few readers of professional reports will take seriously conclusions based upon empty, airy arguments. Conclusions are frequently followed by recommendations.

Recommendations A conclusion is an inference. A recommendation is the statement that some action be taken or not taken. The recommendation is based on the conclusions and is the last step in the process. You conclude that Brand X bread is cheaper per pound than Brand Y and just as nutritious and tasty. Your final conclusion, therefore, is that Brand X is a better buy. Your recommendation is "Buy Brand X."

Many reports—such as feasibility reports, environmental impact statements, and research reports concerning the safety of certain foods or chemicals—are decision reports that end with a recommendation. For example, we are all familiar with the government recommendations that have removed certain artificial sweeteners from the market and that have placed warnings on cigarette packages. These recommendations were all originally stated at the end of reports looking into these matters.

Recommendations are simply stated. They follow the conclusions, often in a separate section, and look something like this:

Based upon the conclusions reached, we recommend that our company

- Not increase the present level of iron enrichment in our flour.
- Support research into methods of curtailing rancidity in flour containing wheat germ.

Frequently, you may offer a major recommendation followed by additional implementing recommendations, as in the following:

Major recommendation   We recommend that the Department of Transportation build a new bridge across the St. Croix River at a point approximately three miles north of the present bridge at Hastings.

Implementing recommendations
- The department's location engineers should begin an immediate investigation to decide the exact bridge location.
- Once the location is pinpointed, the department's right-of-way section should purchase the necessary land for the approaches to the bridge.

You need not support your recommendations when you state them. You should have already done that thoroughly in the report and in the conclusions leading up to the recommendations. It's likely, of course, that a full-scale report will contain a summary, conclusions, and recommendations.

Graceful Close A short, simple, nonargumentative paper often requires nothing more than a graceful exit. As you would not end a conversation by turning on your heel and stalking off without a "good-bye" or a "see you later" to cover your exit, you do not end a paper without some sort of close. In a short informational paper that has not reached a decision, the facts should be still clear in the readers' minds at the end, and they will not need a summary. One sentence, such as the following, which might end a short speculative paper on superconductivity, will probably suffice:

Because superconductivity seems to have numerous uses, it cannot fail to receive increasing scientific attention in the years ahead.

Sometimes, even a long, involved paper can profit from a graceful close. In the next example, the author of the introduction on pages 627–628 ends his scholarly paper with a reference to other work that supports his own:

Teachers of professional communication have a unique interdisciplinary perspective and thus a unique responsibility. They can—indeed they must—daily negotiate the distance between "the two cultures." C. P. Snow, who coined the phrase, was both a physicist and a man of letters, and it is salutary to recall that his famous essay (perhaps more often cited than read) is not an ethical indictment of the ethical position of scientific "culture," but just the opposite. Writing to his fellow literati, he says, "the greatest enrichment the scientific culture could give us is . . . a moral one." Snow praises scientific "culture" for its commitment to human improvement manifested in active involvement. Snow takes to task the other culture, the "mainly literary" one, for an ethical complacency "made up of defeat, self-indulgence, and moral vanity," a complacency to which "the scientific culture is almost totally immune." And he concludes, "It is that kind of moral health of the scientists which, in the last few years, the rest of us have needed most; and of which, because the two cultures scarcely touch, we have been most deprived" (414). Both cultures have changed much in the four decades since Snow published his essay, but perhaps each culture still has much to learn from the other, even about ethics.[7]

Combination Endings We have treated summaries, conclusions, and recommendations separately. Indeed, a full-scale report leading to a recommendation will often contain in sequence separate sections labeled Summary, Conclusions, and Recommendations. When such is the case, the summary will often be restricted to a condensation of the factual data offered in the body. The implications of the data will be presented in the conclusions, and the action to be taken in the recommendations.

However, in many reports, the major elements of factual summary, conclusions, and recommendations may be combined. A combination of summary, conclusions, and recommendations placed at the front of a report for a technical audience will probably be labeled an abstract. It will be, in fact, what we describe on pages 618–622: an informative abstract. The same combination located at the end of a report for any audience would probably be called a summary. A summary written specifically for an executive audience and located at the front of the report will be an executive summary (see Figure B-13).

It's unfortunate that there is a slight confusion of terms when these elements are used in different ways. Don't let the confusion in terminology confuse the essence of what is involved here. In all but the simplest reports, you must draw things together for your readers. You must condense and highlight your significant data and present any conclusions and recommendations you have. Notice how this summary of a scientific research report smoothly combines all these elements:

Summary

In many turtles the hatchling's sex is determined by the incubation temperature of the egg, warm temperatures causing femaleness and cool temperatures maleness. Consequently, the population sex ratio depends upon the interaction of (i) environmental temperature, (ii) maternal choice of nest site, and (iii) embryonic control of sex determination. If environmental temperature differs between

Summary

populations, then sex ratio selection is expected to adjust either maternal behavior or embryonic temperature-sensitivity to yield nearly the same sex ratio in the different populations.

  To test this hypothesis in part, we have compared sex determining temperatures among embryos of emydid turtles in the northern and southern U.S. We predicted that embryos of southern populations should develop as male at higher temperatures than those of northern populations. The data offer no support for this prediction among the many possible comparisons between northern and

Conclusion

Recommendation

southern species. The data actually refute the prediction in both of the North-South intraspecific comparisons. Further study is needed, in particular, of nest temperatures in the different populations.[8]

▶ APPENDIXES

Appendixes, as the name implies, are materials appended to a report. They may be materials important as background information or needed to lend the report credibility. They will not in most cases be necessary to meet the major purpose of the report or the major needs of the audience. For example, if you are describing research for an executive audience, they will likely be more interested in your results and conclusions than in your research methodology. If your audience consists totally of executives, you might include only a barebones discussion of your methodology in your report.

  But suppose you have a primary audience of executives and a secondary audience of experts. You could satisfy both audiences by placing a detailed discussion of your methodology in an appendix—out of the executives' way but readily accessible for the experts. Like most decisions in technical writing, what goes into the body of a report, what goes into an appendix, and what is eliminated altogether are determined by your audience and purpose.

  During the final stages of arranging your report, determine whether materials such as the following should be placed in appendixes:

- Case histories
- Supporting illustrations
- Detailed data
- Transcriptions of dialogue
- Intermediate steps in mathematical computation
- Copies of letters, announcements, and leaflets mentioned in the report
- Samples, exhibits, photographs, and supplementary tables and figures
- Extended analyses
- Lists of personnel
- Suggested collateral reading
- Anything else that is not essential to the sense of the main report

Before you place anything in an appendix, consider the effect on the report. Be certain that shifting an item to an appendix does not undermine your purpose or prevent the reader from understanding major points of the report.

▶ PLANNING AND REVISION CHECKLISTS

You will find the planning and revision checklists that follow Chapter 2, Composing, and Chapter 4, Writing for Your Readers, valuable in planning and revising any presentation of technical information. The following questions specifically apply to the elements of reports. They summarize the key points in this chapter and provide a checklist for planning and revising.

Planning

- Which does your situation call for, a letter of transmittal or a preface?
- Will you bind your report? If so, did you leave extra left-hand margin?
- Does your situation call for any information on your title page beyond the basic items: name of author, name of person or organization receiving the report, title of report, and date of submission?
- Have you used a system of headings that need to be repeated in your table of contents?
- Have you used a numbering system that needs to be repeated in your table of contents?
- Do you have enough illustrations to warrant a list of illustrations?
- Have you used symbols, abbreviations, acronyms, or terms that some of your readers will not know? Do you need a list of symbols or a glossary?
- Does your report require an abstract? If so, should it be informative or descriptive or both?
- Is your primary audience an executive one? Does the length of your report require an executive summary?
- What will be the major questions in the executives' minds as they read your report? Have you planned to answer these questions in the executive summary?
- Are your subject, purpose, scope, and plan of development clear enough that you can state them in your introduction?
- Do you need an interest-catching fact in your introduction?
- Do you need definitions or theoretical or historical background in your introduction?
- What information do your readers really need and want in your discussion? What questions will they have? What details do they want?
- What kind of ending do you need: summary, conclusion, recommendations, graceful exit, a combination of these?

- Do you have an executive audience? Should your "ending" come at the beginning of the report?
- Do you have material that would be better presented in an appendix rather than the discussion? Should you leave it out altogether?
- Do you have material you need to document—for example, direct quotes, research data and theories, illustrations—using either notes or author-date documentation? (See Documentation in this appendix.)
- Do you plan to publish your report? Does it contain material protected by copyright law? (See Copyright under Documentation in this appendix.) If so, begin seeking permission to use the material as early as possible.

Revision

- Does your letter of transmittal contain clear statements of transmittal, the occasion for the report, and subject and purpose of the report? Do you need any other elements, such as a distribution list?
- Does your preface contain clear statements of the occasion for the report and the subject and purpose of the report? Do you need any other elements, such as acknowledgments?
- Is your cover suitable for the occasion of the report? Is it labeled with all the elements necessary to your situation?
- Is your title page well designed? If you have used a word processor, have you kept your design simple? Does your title page contain all the elements required by your situation? Does your title describe your report adequately?
- Have you an effective design for your table of contents? Do the headings in your table of contents exactly match their counterparts in the report? Are the page numbers correct?
- Do you have a simple but clear numbering system for your illustrations? Do the titles in your list of illustrations exactly match the titles in the report? Are the page numbers correct?
- If needed, do you have a glossary and a list of symbols? Have you written your glossary definitions correctly?
- Are your abstracts written in the proper impersonal style? Does your informative abstract cover all the major points of your report? Have you avoided excessive detail? Does your abstract conform to the length requirements set for you?
- Does the executive summary answer the questions your executive audience will have? Have you included clear statements of your conclusions and recommendations? Have you held the length to one double-spaced page?

- Does the introduction clearly forecast your subject, purpose, scope, and plan of development? If they are needed, does the introduction contain definitions or theoretical or historical background?
- Does the discussion answer all the questions you set out to answer? Does it contain any material irrelevant to your subject and purpose?
- Does the ending draw things together for the readers? Does it condense and highlight your significant data? Does it present your conclusions and recommendations? Should the "ending" come at the front of the report?
- Does the appendix material belong in the appendix? If any material in an appendix is a key to a major point, move it to the discussion. If it seems irrelevant to the report, remove it altogether.
- Have you documented everything that needs to be documented in your report? Have you documented accurately? Do your notes or citations follow the format rules required in your situation? (See Documentation in this appendix.)
- If you plan to publish your report, do you have permission to use any copyrighted material it contains? (See Copyright Law under Documentation in this appendix.)

▶ LETTER AND MEMORANDUM FORMAT

Heading

Date Line

Inside Address

Attention Line

Reference Line

Subject Line

Salutation

Body

Complimentary Close

Signature Block

End Notations
  Identification
  Enclosure

Copy

Continuation Page

Almost any organization you join will have rules about its letter and memo formats. Either you will have a secretary to do your correspondence or you will have to learn the rules for yourself. In this section, we give you only enough rules and illustrations to allow you to turn out a good-looking, correct, and acceptable business letter or memo on your own. If for no other reason, you will find this a necessary skill when you go job hunting.

Figures B-14 and B-15 illustrate the block and semiblock styles on nonletterhead stationery. Figures B-16 and B-17 illustrate the block style and the simplified style on letterhead stationery.

The chief difference between memos and letters is format. Figure B-18 illustrates a typical memo format. Figure B-19 illustrates the heading used for the continuation pages of a letter or a memo. We have indicated in these samples the spacing, margins, and punctuation you should use. In the text that follows, we discuss briefly the different styles and then give you some of the basic rules you should know about the parts of a letter or memo. Before continuing with the text, look at Figures B-14–B-19. Particularly observe the spacing, placement, and punctuation of the various parts of letters and memos.

For most business letters you may have to write, any of the styles shown would be acceptable. For letters of inquiry or complaint, which typically do not address anyone specific in a company, we suggest the simplified style. For letters of application, we suggest the block or semiblock style without a subject line. Some people still find the simplified letter, without the conventional salutation and complimentary close, a bit too brusque. Unless you know for certain that the company you are applying to prefers the simplified form, do not take a chance with it.

If you are doing your own word processing, we suggest the block style as the best all-around style. It includes all the conventional parts of a letter, but everything is lined up along the left-hand margin. You do not have to bother with tab settings and other complications. Some people feel that a block letter looks a bit lopsided, but it's a common style that no one will object to. No matter which style you choose, leave generous margins, from an inch to two inches, all around, and balance the first page of the letter vertically on the page. Because letters look more inviting with lots of white space, you should seldom allow paragraphs to run more than seven or eight lines.

▶ HEADING

When you do not have letterhead stationery, you will have to furnish your heading. In the semiblock style, the heading is approximately flush right. In

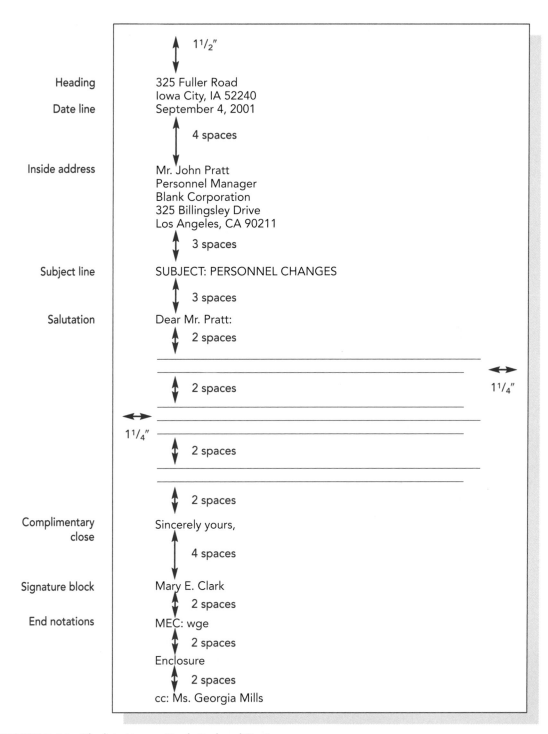

FIGURE B-14 • Block Letter on Nonletterhead Stationery

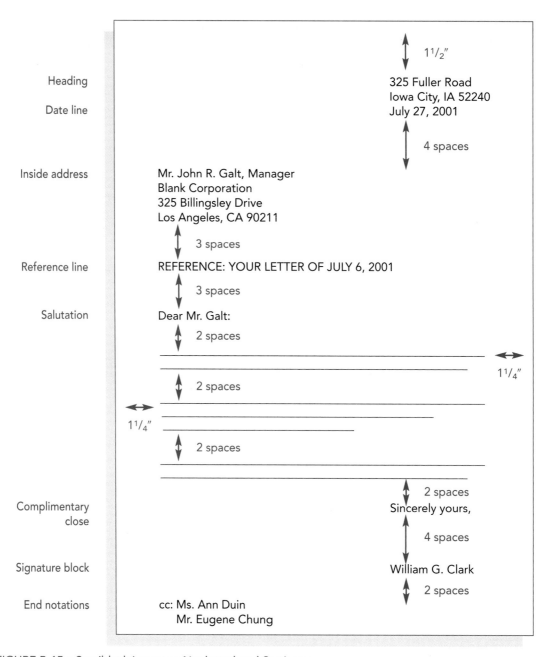

FIGURE B-15 • Semiblock Letter on Nonletterhead Stationery

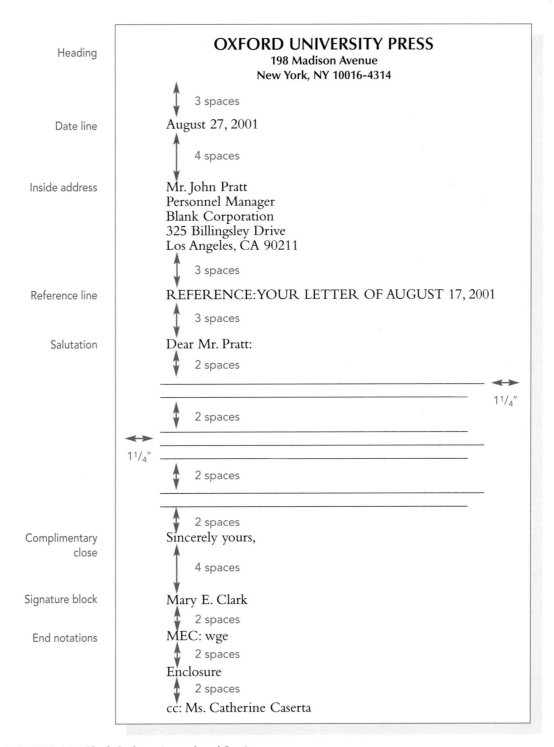

OXFORD UNIVERSITY PRESS
198 Madison Avenue
New York, NY 10016-4314

Heading

3 spaces

Date line — August 27, 2001

4 spaces

Inside address —
Mr. John Pratt
Personnel Manager
Blank Corporation
325 Billingsley Drive
Los Angeles, CA 90211

3 spaces

Reference line — REFERENCE: YOUR LETTER OF AUGUST 17, 2001

3 spaces

Salutation — Dear Mr. Pratt:

2 spaces

1¼″

2 spaces

1¼″

2 spaces

2 spaces

Complimentary
close — Sincerely yours,

4 spaces

Signature block — Mary E. Clark

2 spaces

End notations — MEC: wge

2 spaces

Enclosure

2 spaces

cc: Ms. Catherine Caserta

FIGURE B-16 • Block Style on Letterhead Stationery

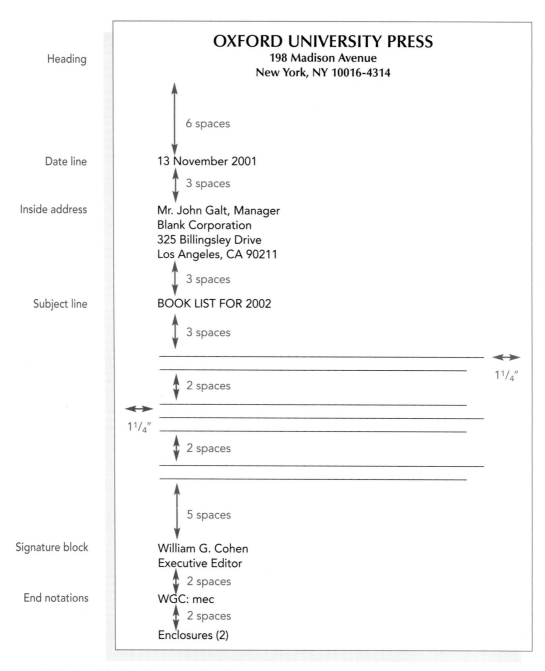

OXFORD UNIVERSITY PRESS
198 Madison Avenue
New York, NY 10016-4314

Heading

6 spaces

Date line   13 November 2001
3 spaces

Inside address   Mr. John Galt, Manager
Blank Corporation
325 Billingsley Drive
Los Angeles, CA 90211
3 spaces

Subject line   BOOK LIST FOR 2002

3 spaces

1¼"

2 spaces

1¼"

2 spaces

5 spaces

Signature block   William G. Cohen
Executive Editor
2 spaces

End notations   WGC: mec
2 spaces
Enclosures (2)

FIGURE B-17 • Simplified Style on Letterhead Stationery

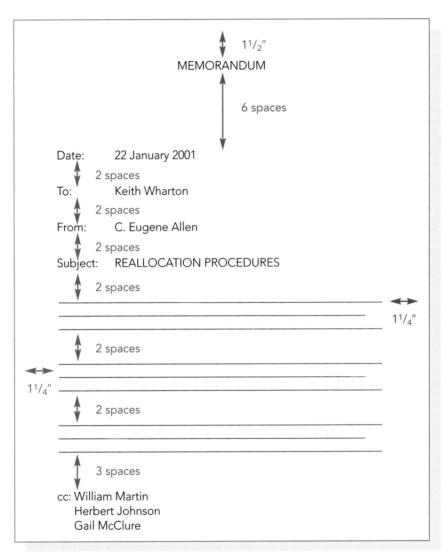

FIGURE B-18 • Memorandum Format

the other formats shown, the heading is flush left. Do not abbreviate words such as *street* or *road*. Write them out in full. You may abbreviate the names of states and provinces. Figure B-20 lists the two-letter abbreviations for states of the United States and provinces of Canada.

If you have business letterheads made up, have them printed on good quality white bond in a simple style. With word processing and a quality laser printer, it's possible to print your own letterheads. We have two cautions, however, if you choose to do so. First, keep in mind that only the most ex-

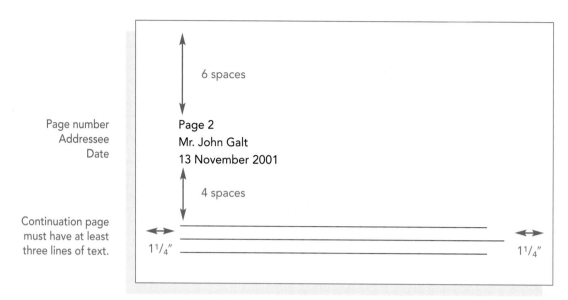

Page number
Addressee
Date

6 spaces

Page 2
Mr. John Galt
13 November 2001

4 spaces

Continuation page
must have at least
three lines of text.

1¼"

1¼"

FIGURE B-19 • Continuation Page

pensive printers will turn out printing as crisp and sharp as commercial printing will. Second, be careful not to design a too-elaborate letterhead. Keep it simple, in a standard design.

▶ DATE LINE

In a letter without a printed letterhead, the date line is part of your heading in the block, semiblock, and simplified styles. When you use printed letterhead, the date line is flush left in the block and simplified styles and approximately flush right in semiblock style. Place it three to six spaces below the printed letterhead, to help balance the letter vertically on the page. Write the date out fully, either as June 3, 20XX or 3 June 20XX. Do not abbreviate the month or use ordinal numbers or their abbreviations (e.g., 1st, 2nd) for the date.

▶ INSIDE ADDRESS

The inside address is placed flush left in all the formats shown. Make sure the inside address is complete. Follow exactly the form used by the person or company you are writing to. If your correspondent abbreviates *Company* as *Co.*, you should also. Use *S. Edward Smith* rather than *Samuel E. Smith* if that is the way Smith wants it. Do use courtesy titles such as *Mr.*, *Dr.*, and *Colonel* before the name. The usual abbreviations used are *Mr.*, *Ms.*, and *Dr.* Place

United States				Canada	
Alabama	AL	Missouri	MO	Alberta	AB
Alaska	AK	Montana	MT	British Columbia	BC
American Samoa	AS	Nebraska	NE	Labrador	LB
Arizona	AZ	Nevada	NV	Manitoba	MB
Arkansas	AR	New Hampshire	NH	New Brunswick	NB
California	CA	New Jersey	NJ	Newfoundland	NF
Colorado	CO	New Mexico	NM	Nova Scotia	NS
Connecticut	CT	New York	NY	Northwest Territories	NT
Delaware	DE	North Carolina	NC	Ontario	ON
District of	DC	North Dakota	ND	Prince Edward Island	PE
Columbia		Ohio	OH	Quebec (Province de Québec)	PQ
Florida	FL	Oklahoma	OK	Saskatchewan	SK
Georgia	GA	Oregon	OR	Yukon Territory	YT
Guam	GU	Pennsylvania	PA		
Hawaii	HI	Puerto Rico	PR		
Idaho	ID	Rhode Island	RI		
Illinois	IL	South Carolina	SC		
Indiana	IN	South Dakota	SD		
Iowa	IA	Tennessee	TN		
Kansas	KS	Texas	TX		
Kentucky	KY	Utah	UT		
Louisiana	LA	Vermont	VT		
Maine	ME	Virginia	VA		
Maryland	MD	Virgin Islands	VI		
Massachusetts	MA	Washington	WA		
Michigan	MI	West Virginia	WV		
Minnesota	MN	Wisconsin	WI		
Mississippi	MS	Wyoming	WY		

Notice that both letters of the abbreviation are capitalized and that no period is used.

FIGURE B-20 • Abbreviations for U.S. States and Canadian Provinces

one-word titles such as *Manager* or *Superintendent* immediately after the name. When a title is longer than one word, place it on the next line by itself. Do not put a title after the name that means the same thing as a courtesy title. For example, don't write *Dr. Marlene E. Smith, Ph.D.*

▶ ATTENTION LINE

On occasion you may wish to write to an organizational address but also draw your letter to the attention of some individual. It's a way of saying, in effect, "Anyone there can answer this letter, but if Mr. Smith is there he is the best person to handle the matter." When you use an attention line, type it flush left two spaces below the inside address. Capitalize only the *A*. You can use a colon or not between *Attention* and the name:

```
Attention Mr. Frank Rookard
```

or

```
Attention: Mr. Frank Rookard
```

▶ REFERENCE LINE

Use the reference line to refer to the letter or memo you are answering. For example,

```
REFERENCE: YOUR LETTER OF MAY 14, 2001
```

Place the reference line heading (sometimes abbreviated *RE.* or *REF.*) flush left in all styles. Type both the heading and the reference line itself in capital letters. Generally, you will follow the heading with a colon, although sometimes the colon is omitted. A letter may have both a reference line and a subject line, or the two may be combined, as in

```
REFERENCE: YOUR LETTER OF 12 JULY 2001
APPLICATION FOR A MORTGAGE AT 452 LITTLE COMFORT ROAD
```

▶ SUBJECT LINE

Place the subject line flush left in all styles. In the block and semiblock styles, it is usually preceded by the heading SUBJECT, though sometimes you will see a subject line with no heading. Generally, the heading is followed by a colon, but sometimes the colon will be omitted. Type both the heading and the subject line itself in capital letters. In the simplified style, omit the heading and type the subject line in all capital letters.

If you are answering a letter that has a subject line, repeat the subject line from the original letter. If you are making up your own subject line, be sure it's complete enough to be useful. If, for example, you're reporting progress on an architectural design for a building at 452 Little Comfort Road, don't write merely 452 LITTLE COMFORT ROAD. Rather, write PROGRESS REPORT ON THE ARCHITECTURAL DESIGN FOR THE BUILDING AT 452 LITTLE COMFORT ROAD.

Both subject lines and reference lines get your letters or memos off to good starts. They allow you to avoid cliché openers like "With regard to your letter of April 5, 2001.

▶ SALUTATION

Place the salutation flush left. Convention still calls for the use of *Dear*. Always use a name in the salutation when one is available to use. When you use a name, be sure it's in the inside address as well. Also, use the same courtesy title as in the inside address, such as *Dear Dr. Sibley* or *Dear Ms. McCarthy*. You may use a first-name salutation, *Dear Samantha*, when you are on friendly terms with the recipient. Follow the salutation with a colon.

What do you do when you are writing a company blindly and have no specific name to use? Some people use *Dear* followed by the name of the department being written to, such as *Dear Customer Relations Department*. Perhaps the best solution is to choose the simplified style, which uses no salutation.

In any case, do not begin letters with *Dear Person*, which is distasteful to many; *Dear Sir*, which is sexist; or *To Whom It May Concern*, which is old-fashioned.

▶ BODY

In word processing the body of an average-length letter or memo, use single spacing between the lines and double spacing between the paragraphs. In a particularly short letter, double-space throughout the body and use five-space indentations to mark the first lines of paragraphs. Avoid splitting words between lines. Never split a date or a person's name between two lines.

▶ COMPLIMENTARY CLOSE

In the block style, place the complimentary close flush left. In the semiblock style, align the close with the heading (or with the date line in a letterhead letter). Settle for a simple close, such as *Sincerely yours* or *Very truly yours*. Capitalize only the first letter of the close, and place a comma after the close.

▶ SIGNATURE BLOCK

Place your name four spaces below the complimentary close in the block and semiblock styles, five spaces below the last line of the body in the simplified style. Use your first name, middle initial, and last name or, if you prefer, your first initial and middle name, as in *M. Lillian Smith*. We don't recommend the use of initials only, as in *M. L. Smith*, because this form puts your correspondents at a disadvantage. People who don't know you will not know whether to address you as *Dear Mr.* or *Dear Ms.*

If you have a title, place it below your name. Sign your name immediately above your name. Your signature and your printed name should agree. In memos, it's customary to initial next to your printed name in the From line.

▶ END NOTATIONS

Various end notations may be placed at the bottom of a letter or memo, always flush left. The most common ones indicate identification, enclosure, and carbon copy.

Identification

The notation for identification is composed of the writer's initials in capital letters and the typist's initials in lowercase:

```
DHC: 1nh
```

Enclosure

The enclosure line indicates that additional material has been enclosed with the letter or memo. You may use several forms:

```
Enclosure

Enclosures (2)

Encl: Employment application blank
```

Copy

The copy line informs the recipient of a letter or memo that you have sent a copy of the letter to someone else. In form, the copy notation looks like this:

```
cc: Ms. Elaine Mills
```

See Figures B-14–B-18 for proper spacing and sequence of these three end notations.

Continuation Page

Use a continuation page or pages when you can't fit your letter or memo onto one page. Do not use letterhead stationery for a continuation page. Use plain bond of the same quality and color as the first page.

As shown in Figure B-19, the continuation page is headed by three items: page number, name of addressee, and date. When you have a continuation page, the last paragraph on the preceding page should contain at least two lines. The last continuation page must have at least three lines of text to accompany the complimentary close and the signature block.

► DOCUMENTATION

General Rules

Notes
  The Note System
  Model Notes

Author–Date Documentation: *The Chicago Manual of Style*
  Works Cited
  Parenthetical Citation
Author–Date Documentation: American Psychological
  Association
  Reference List
  Parenthetical Citation

Internet Documentation
  Model Notes and Citations
  Parenthetical Reference

Figures

Copyright Law

Different documentation systems are in use from college to college, journal to journal, company to company, discipline to discipline. Therefore, we cannot claim universal application for the instructions that follow. Use them barring conflicting instructions from your instructor, college, employer, or the stylebook of the journal or magazine in which you hope to publish.

Before we go into the mechanics of documentation, it might be wise to discuss why and when you need to document.

First of all, documenting fulfills your moral obligation to give credit where credit is due. It lets your readers know who was the originator of an idea or expression and where his or her work is found. Second, systematic documentation makes it easy for your readers to research your subject further.

When do you document? Established practice calls for you to give credit when you borrow the following:

• Direct quotes
• Research data and theories
• Illustrations, such as tables, graphs, and photographs.

You do not need to document general information or common knowledge. For example, even if you referred to a technical dictionary to find that creatinine's more formal name is methyglycocyamidine, you would not be obligated to show the source of this information. It is general information, readily found in many sources. If on the other hand you want to include in your paper an opinion that the cosmos is laced with strands of highly concentrated mass energy called *strings*, you would need to document the source of this opinion.

In general, give credit where credit is due, but do not clutter your pages with references to information readily found in many sources. If in doubt as to whether to document or not, play it safe and document.

To give you a wide familiarity with different documentation systems, we explain three major systems of documentation. The first uses notes—that is, footnotes or endnotes—and is based on the note system in *The Chicago Manual of Style*.[9] Notes are often used for documenting books and business reports. It is the system used throughout this book.

The second system uses author–date parenthetical citations keyed to a list of works cited and is based on the guidelines set out in *The Chicago Manual of Style*.[10] This system, or variations of it, is widely used in the physical and natural sciences.

The third system also uses parenthetical citations keyed to a list of works, but follows the system described in the *Publication Manual of the American Psychological Association*.[11] It is a system widely used in the social sciences.

As this book is being written, neither manual we have cited provides a way of documenting all the forms of information that can be taken from the Internet. No doubt they will in the future, but in the meantime writers are faced with the problem of how to document such sources. To help until the major systems catch up with these new demands, we provide a section on how to document Internet sources, based on systems offered on the Internet itself.[12] These systems are still works in progress and subject to further change.

Some general rules apply in the three major systems. We cover these rules first and then, in order, the note system, the author–date parenthetical systems, Internet documentation, and figure documentation.

▶ GENERAL RULES

The rules that follow apply whether you are using the note system or an author–date parenthetical system.

- You may use a short form of the publisher's name: for example, Wiley for John Wiley & Sons or GPO for the Government Printing Office. Be consistent throughout your notes or citations, however.
- When a city of publication is not well known, include an abbreviated form for the state, province, or country in your note or citation. For

states and provinces, use postal abbreviations: for example NY for New York and BC for British Columbia. (A list of state and province abbreviations is given in the the preceding section; see Figure B-20) For countries, use the abbreviations that can be found in most college dictionaries: for example, Arg. for Argentina.

- When information on pagination, publisher, or date is missing in your source, at the point where you would put that information, put: n. pag. for no pagination, n.p. for no place of publication or no publisher, and n.d. for no date.

▶ NOTES

Because of the ease of making notes with word processing, many organizations and companies use a note system. In this section we first explain the note system of documentation and then provide a series of model notes that you can use as guides in constructing your notes.

The Note System

Notes may be (1) displayed at the bottom of the page on which the documented material appears or (2) gathered together at the end of the report under the heading Notes. In the first method, the notes are called *footnotes* and in the second, *endnotes*. Footnotes are illustrated in Figure B-21, endnotes in Figure B-22. Endnotes are much more usual than footnotes in student and business reports and in journal articles. We use them in this book; see our Chapter Notes on pages 683–688.

Whether using footnotes or endnotes, number your notes in sequence through your paper. If your paper is divided into chapters, like this book, number your notes in sequence through each chapter. Except for spacing, the note form is the same for both footnotes and endnotes. In footnotes, single-space each note and double-space between notes. In endnotes, double-space the notes themselves and between notes. (If, however, you are preparing a manuscript for publication, double-space everything.)

In both footnotes and endnotes, the note number is indicated in the text by a superscript number, that is, a number placed above the line of type, as you can see in the many note numbers we give in this book and in Figure B-21. Place the number in the text where it is relevant and where it disrupts the text the least. Generally, you should place the note at the end of the grammatical unit—for example, sentence or clause—that contains the material you are documenting.

Notes, whether footnotes or endnotes, appear in the order that the superscript note numbers occur in the paper. For both footnotes and endnotes,

Current rhetorical theory indicates that this attempt, through analogy, to call on schemata for newspapers could affect readers' expectations about the writing in the newsletters, which in turn could influence the way these readers process the writing. Genre theory, for example, posits that generic patterns such as those in a newspaper, as part of our "cultural rationality,"[1] alert readers to ways of perceiving and interpreting documents.[2] In addition, theories of intertextuality, the concept that all texts contain explicit or implicit traces of other texts,[3] suggest that creating an analogy between newspapers and newsletters would affect readers' expectations, encouraging them to perceive and interpret material in a particular way.[4] We must ask, therefore, what readers' expectations about newspapers and hence, by analogy, about the newsletters, might be.

Place superscript note number after any punctuation at end of grammatical unit cited.

Use four spaces between text and notes.

Indent three spaces.

1. C. R. Miller, "Genre as Social Action," *Quarterly Journal of Speech* 70 (1984): 165.

Single-space each note; double-space between notes.

2. Miller, 159.

3. J. E. Porter, "Intertextuality and the Discourse Community," *Rhetoric Review* 5 (1986): 34.

Use a comma between name and page.

4. Porter, 38.

FIGURE B-21 • Footnotes on a Page
Source: Adapted with permission from Nancy Roundy Blyler, "Rhetorical Theory and Newsletter Writing," *Journal of Technical Writing and Communication* 20 (1990): 144.

indent three spaces from the left margin, place the number on line, and follow it with a period. Begin the body of the note one space to the right of the period. If the note is longer than one line, begin subsequent lines at the left margin. Figures B–21 and B–22 illustrate these details. Word processing can make placing and numbering footnotes and endnotes quite easy. Most pro-

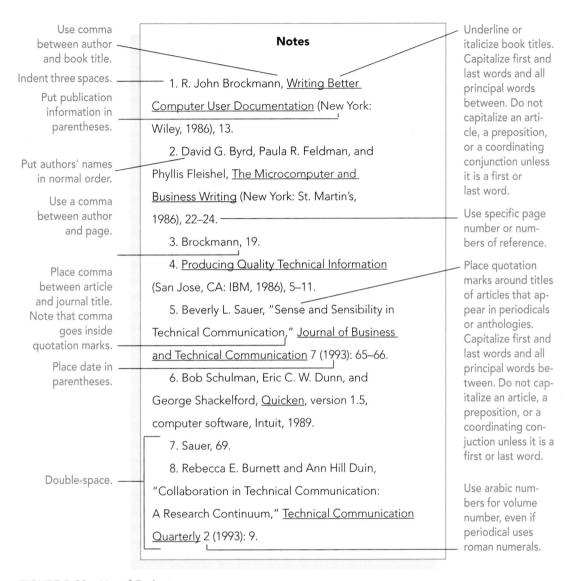

FIGURE B-22 • List of Endnotes

grams will number the notes automatically. Type the note at the place in the text where it is relevant. If you have specified endnotes, the program saves the note with the other endnotes and puts them all after the text. If you have specified footnotes, the program puts the note on the bottom of the page, adjusting the rest of the text for it. If you move the relevant text to another place later, the note moves with it. When you add or delete a note, the program renumbers all the other notes.

Model Notes

To construct your notes, consult the sample notes in Figures B-21 and B-22 and the examples that follow; we have annotated these figures to draw your attention to certain distinctive note features, such as italics, punctuation, and spacing. We categorize the model notes under the headings of **Books, Periodicals, Other**, and **Subsequent References**, and provide an example of most of the notes you are likely to need in school or business.

Books   The following examples illustrate various forms of book notes.

One author

1. Robert A. Day, *Scientific English: A Guide for Scientists and Other Professionals* (Phoenix, AZ: Oryx, 1992), 13–14.

Page numbers in notes are to the actual pages cited. When page numbers are two digits, use both digits in the second number, thus, 13–14. When page numbers are three digits or more, use only the last two digits in the second number, thus, 324–26, 1034–39.

Two or more authors

2. Edward von Koenigseck, James N. Irvin, and Sharon C. Irvin. *Technical Writing for Private Industry: The A-to-Z of O & M Manuals* (Malabar, FL: Krieger, 1991), 22–24.

An anthology

3. Linda P. Driskill, June Ferrill, and Marda Nicholson Steffey, eds., *Business and Managerial Communication: New Perspectives* (New York: Harcourt Brace Jovanovich, 1992), 112–15.

Use the abbreviation *ed.* for one editor, *eds.,* for two or more when, as in item 3, the book's editors are listed as authors. When the authors are contributors to an edited volume, as in item 4, use *ed.*, meaning "edited by," for one editor or more than one.

An essay in an anthology

4. Lee Odell, Dixie Goswami, Anne Herrington, and Doris Quick, "Studying Writing in Non-Academic Settings," in *New Essays in Technical and Scientific Communication: Research, Theory, Practice*, ed. Paul V. Anderson, R. John Brockmann, and Carolyn R. Miller (Farmingdale, NY: Baywood, 1983), 27–28.

Second or subsequent edition

5. Michael H. Markel, *Technical Writing: Situations and Strategies*, 3rd ed. (New York: St. Martin's, 1992), 17–18.

Article in reference book

6. "Petrochemical," *Columbia Encyclopedia*, 2001.

When a reference work is well known, you need cite only the name of the article, the name of the reference work, and the date of publication. If the work is arranged alphabetically, do not cite page numbers.

For less well-known reference works, give complete information. Cite the author of the article if known: otherwise, begin with the name of the article.

7. "Perpetual Calendar, 1775–2076," *The New York Public Library Desk Reference*, ed. Paul Fargis and Sheree Bykofsky (New York: Webster's New World, 1989), 9–13.

A pamphlet

8. *Cataract: Clouding the Lens of Sight* (San Francisco: American Academy of Ophthalmology, 1989), 1–2.

If the author of a pamphlet is known, give complete information in the usual manner.

Government or corporate publication

9. National Aeronautics and Space Administration, *Voyager at Neptune: 1989* (Washington, DC: GPO, 1989), 16.

Treat publications for which the "author" is a government agency or a division within a company much as you would any book, as shown in item 9. If you are sure your readers will understand that the government entity you cite is part of the federal government, you may omit the U.S. before its name, for example, Bureau of the Census.

Anonymous book

10. *Producing Quality Technical Information* (San Jose, CA: IBM, 1986), 5–11.

When no human, government, or corporate author is listed, begin with the title of the book.

Proceedings

11. Mary Fran Buehler, "Rules That Shape the Technical Message: Fidelity, Completeness, Preciseness," *Proceedings 31st International Technical*

Communication Conference (Washington, DC: Society for Technical Communication, 1984), WE-9.

Unpublished dissertation

12. Laura Gambel, "Trauma in Emergency Room Surgery," Ph.D. diss., University of Chicago, 1999, 16.

Periodicals   The following examples illustrate various forms of periodical notes.

Journal with continuous pagination

1. Thomas T. Barker, "Word Processors and Invention in Technical Writing," *The Technical Writing Teacher* 16 (1989): 127.

Journal that pages its issues separately

2. David P. Gardner, "The Future of University Industry Research," *Perspectives in Computing* 7.1 (1987): 5.

In this note, 7 is the volume number, 1 the issue number, and 5 the page number.

Commercial magazines and newspapers

A weekly or biweekly magazine:

3. Robert J. Samuelson, "The Health-Care Crisis Hits Home," *Newsweek*, 2 Aug. 1993, 38.

Monthly or bimonthly magazine:

4. Scott Beamer, "Why You Need a Charting Program," *MacUser*, June 1990, 126.

Newspaper

5. Louise Levathes, "A Geneticist Maps Ancient Migrations," *New York Times*, 27 July 1993, national ed., sec. C. p. 1.

Notice that when a date is not inside parentheses it is followed by a comma not a colon. When the masthead of the paper specifies the edition, put that information in your note. Newspaper content frequently changes from edition to edition on the same day.

Anonymous article

6. "Absolute," *New Yorker* 18 June 1990, 28.

When no author is given for an article, begin with the title of the article.

Other   In this section, we show you model notes for computer software, information services, letters, and interviews.

Computer software

1. Apple Telecom, 1996, Apple Computer, Inc., Cupertino, CA.

In citing computer programs, give as much information as you have available, including author's name, city of publication, publisher, version number, and so forth

Information service

2. R. Berdan and M. Garcia, *Discourse-Sensitive Measurement of Language Development in Bilingual Children* (Los Alamitos, CA: National Center for Bilingual Research, 1982), ERIC ED 234 636.

Letters

3. John S. Harris, letter to the author, 19 July 1999.

Interviews

4. Herman Estrin, personal interview, 16 Mar. 1998.

Subsequent References   After the first complete note on an item, subsequent references need only briefly identify the item. If a subsequent reference immediately follows the initial reference and the page number is the same, use Ibid. (a shortened form of the Latin word for "same"). If the page number is different use Ibid. with the new page number:

1. "Absolute," *New Yorker* 18 June 1990, 28.
2. Ibid.
3. Ibid., 32.

If one or more citations come between the initial reference and a subsequent one, identify the subsequent reference with the best information you have, be it the author's last name, a government agency, a shortened title, or whatever:

4. Day, 188.
5. *Cataract*, 9.

If you have two works by the same author, include a shortened version of the title to identify the correct work:

6. Conniff, "Eye on the Storm," 21.

▶ AUTHOR–DATE DOCUMENTATION: *THE CHICAGO MANUAL OF STYLE*

Author–date documentation combines parenthetical citations in the text with an alphabetized list of all the works cited. The system described in *The*

Chicago Manual of Style, sometimes with minor variations, is a common method of documentation in the physical and natural sciences. Shortly, we show you how to make parenthetical citations, but first we discuss how to construct the list of works cited.

Works Cited

In a section headed "Works Cited," you will list all the works that you cite in your paper. Figure B-23 illustrates how it is done. We have annotated Figure B-23 to draw your attention to certain distinctive citation features, such as

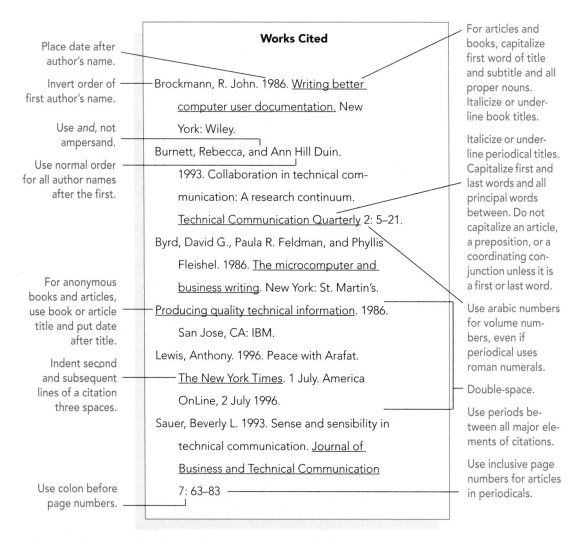

Works Cited

Place date after author's name.

Invert order of first author's name.

Brockmann, R. John. 1986. <u>Writing better</u> <u>computer user documentation.</u> New York: Wiley.

Use *and*, not ampersand.

Use normal order for all author names after the first.

Burnett, Rebecca, and Ann Hill Duin. 1993. Collaboration in technical com- munication: A research continuum. <u>Technical Communication Quarterly</u> 2: 5–21.

Byrd, David G., Paula R. Feldman, and Phyllis Fleishel. 1986. <u>The microcomputer and business writing</u>. New York: St. Martin's.

For anonymous books and articles, use book or article title and put date after title.

<u>Producing quality technical information</u>. 1986. San Jose, CA: IBM.

Lewis, Anthony. 1996. Peace with Arafat.

Indent second and subsequent lines of a citation three spaces.

<u>The New York Times</u>. 1 July. America OnLine, 2 July 1996.

Sauer, Beverly L. 1993. Sense and sensibility in technical communication. <u>Journal of Business and Technical Communication</u>

Use colon before page numbers.

7: 63–83

For articles and books, capitalize first word of title and subtitle and all proper nouns. Italicize or under- line book titles.

Italicize or under- line periodical titles. Capitalize first and last words and all principal words between. Do not capitalize an article, a preposition, or a coordinating con- junction unless it is a first or last word.

Use arabic numbers for volume num- bers, even if periodical uses roman numerals.

Double-space.

Use periods be- tween all major ele- ments of citations.

Use inclusive page numbers for articles in periodicals.

FIGURE B-23 • List of Works Cited: *The Chicago Manual of Style*

capitalization, italicization, and punctuation. For example, notice in Figure B–23 and the examples that follow that most titles use sentence capitalization: that is, they capitalize only the first word of a title and proper nouns. Notice also that the citation uses what is called "hanging indentation," that is, the second and subsequent lines of a citation are indented three to five spaces.

We have categorized the models that follow as **Books**, **Periodicals**, and **Other**.

Books   The following examples illustrate various forms of book citations.

One author
Day, Robert A. 1992. *Scientific English: A guide for scientists and other professionals*. Phoenix, AZ: Oryx.

Two or three authors
Von Koenigseck, Edward, James N. Irvin, and Sharon C. Irvin. 1991. *Technical writing for private industry: The a-to-z of o & m manuals*. Malabar, FL: Krieger.

Four or more authors
Rookard, Frank, Robert Matson, Gerald Fields, and Walter Mazura. 1995. *Communicating in business*. 4th ed. Savannah, GA: Osborn.

In the list of works cited, list all the authors of a work, no matter how many there are.

Anthology
Driskill, Linda P., June Ferrill, and Marda Nicholson Steffey, eds. 1992. *Business and managerial communication: New perspectives*. New York: Harcourt Brace Jovanovich.

Use the abbreviation *ed.* for one editor, *eds.* for two or more. Use *trans.* for one or more translators.

Essay in an anthology
Faigley, Lester. 1985. Nonacademic writing: The social perspective. In *Writing in nonacademic settings*, edited by Lee Odell & Dixie Goswami. New York: The Guilford Press.

Second or subsequent edition
Markel, Michael H. 1992. *Technical writing: Situations and strategies*. 3d. ed. New York: St. Martin's.

Article in a reference book
Petrochemical. 2001. *Columbia encyclopedia*.

When a reference work is well known, you need cite only the name of the article, the name of the reference work, the date of publication, and edition number (if it is not the first). If the work is arranged alphabetically, do not cite page numbers.

For less well-known reference works, give complete information. Cite the author of the article if you have that information; otherwise, begin with the name of the article.

> "Perpetual calendar, 1775–2076." 1989. *The New York Public Library desk reference*. Edited by Paul Fargis and Sheree Bykofsky. New York: Webster's New World. 9–13.

Pamphlet

Cataract: Clouding the lens of sight, 1989. San Francisco: American Academy of Ophthalmology.

If you know the author of a pamphlet, give complete information in the usual manner.

Government or corporate publication

National Aeronautics and Space Administration (NASA). 1989. *Voyager at Neptune: 1989*. Washington, DC: PO.

Treat publications for which the author is a government agency or a division within a company much as you would any book. When the corporate name is unwieldy, provide a shortened version in parentheses, which can then be used in the parenthetical citation.

Anonymous book

Producing quality technical information. 1986. San Jose, CA: IBM.

When no human, government, or corporate author is listed, begin with the title of the book.

Proceedings

Buehler, Mary Fran. 1984. Rules that shape the technical message: Fidelity, completeness, preciseness. *Proceedings of the 31st International Technical Communication Conference*. Washington, DC: Society for Technical Communication. WE 9.

Unpublished dissertation

Gambel, Laura. 1994. Trauma in emergency room surgery. Ph.D. diss. University of Chicago.

Periodicals   The following examples illustrate various forms of periodical citations.

Journal with continuous pagination

Barker, Thomas T. 1989. Word processors and invention in technical writing. *The Technical Writing Teacher* 16: 126–35.

Citations for periodicals list the inclusive pages of the article. When page numbers are two digits, use both digits in the second number: 13–14. When page numbers are three digits or more, use only the last two digits in the second number: 324–26, 1034–39.

Journal that pages its issues separately

Gardner, David P. 1987. The future of university/industry research. *Perspectives in Computing* 7(1): 4–10.

In this citation, 7 is the volume number, 1 is the issue number, and 4–10 are the inclusive pages of the article.

Weekly or biweekly magazine

Samuelson, Robert J. 1993. The health-care crisis hits home. *Newsweek*, 2 August, 38.

Monthly or bimonthly magazine

Beamer, Scott. 1990. Why you need a charting program. *MacUser*, June, 126–38.

Newspaper

Levathes, Louise. 1993. A geneticist maps ancient migrations. *New York Times*, 27 July, national edition.

When the masthead of the paper specifies the edition, put that information in your note. Newspaper content frequently changes from edition to edition on the same day.

Anonymous article

"Absolute." 1990. *New Yorker*, 18 June, 28–29.

When no author is given for an article, begin with the title of the article.

Other   In this section, we show you model citations for computer software, information services, letters, interviews, and two or more entries by the same author.

Computer software

Prometheus Version 1.06. (1993). MacKnowledge Communication Software.

In citing computer programs, give as much information as you have, including the author's name, the city of publication, the publisher, the version number, and so forth.

Information service

Berdan, R., and M. Garcia. 1982. *Discourse-sensitive measurement of language development in bilingual children*. Los Alamitos, CA: National Center for Bilingual Research. ERIC ED 234 636.

Letter

Harris, John S. 1995. Letter to the author. 19 July.

Interview

Estrin, Herman. 1994. Personal interview. 16 March.

Two or more works by the same author

Barker, Thomas. 1985. Video field trip: Bringing the real world into the technical writing classroom. *The Technical Writing Teacher* 11: 175–79.

————. 1989. Word processors and invention in technical writing. *The Technical Writing Teacher* 16: 126–35.

When you have two or more works by the same author or authors in your list of works cited, replace the author's name in the second citation with a 3-em dash (or three unspaced hyphens) and alphabetize by title.

Crowhurst, M. 1983a. *Persuasive writing at grades 5, 7, and 11: A cognitive-development perspective*. Paper presented at the annual meeting of the American Educational Research Association, Montreal, Canada.

————. 1983b. *Revision strategies of students at three grade levels*. Final report. Educational Research Institute of British Columbia. ERIC ED 238 009.

When your list of works cited includes two or more works written in the same year by the same author or authors, alphabetize by title, then mark each year with a lowercase letter, beginning with a.

Parenthetical Citation

When you have completed your list of works cited, refer your reader to it through parenthetical citations in your text. Figure B-24 shows a passage of text that includes parenthetical citations. We have annotated the figure to show you how the system works. Place the citation in the text where it is rel-

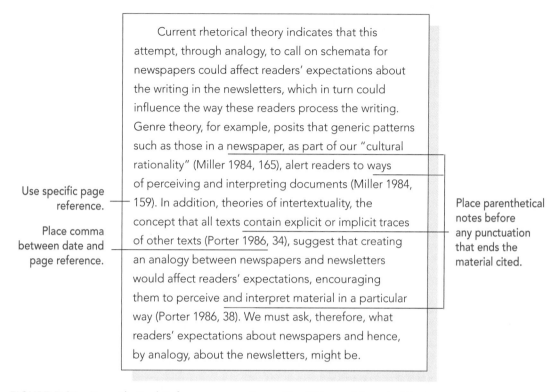

FIGURE B-24 • Parenthetical References on a Page: *The Chicago Manual of Style*
Source: Adapted with permission from Nancy Roundy Blyler, "Rhetorical Theory and Newsletter Writing," *Journal of Technical Writing and Communication* 20 (1990): 144.

evant and where it disrupts the text the least. Generally, you should place the citation at the end of the grammatical unit—the sentence or clause—that contains the material you are documenting.

The purpose of the parenthetical citation is to guide the reader to the corresponding entry in the list of works cited and, when appropriate, to cite the specific pages of the reference. Some model references follow.

Author and date
(Asher 1992)

This citation refers the reader to Asher's 1992 work in the list of works cited. Use this form when you are not citing a specific page.

Author, date, and page
(Asher 1992, 93)

This citation refers the reader to page 93 of Asher's 1992 work. Use this form when you're citing a specific page or pages.

Date and page
(1992, 97)

Use this form when you have already mentioned the author's name in the passage leading up to the parenthetical reference—for example, "As Asher's research shows. . . ."

Pages only
(324–27)

Use this form when you have mentioned both the author's name and the date in the passage leading up to the parenthetical reference—for example, "As Asher's research in 1992 shows. . . ."

Government or corporate author
(National Aeronautics and Space Administration 1994)

When you list a government agency or corporate division listed as the author in the works cited, you may use the name of the agency or division in your parenthetical citation. If the name is unwieldy, provide a shortened form in parentheses in the list of works cited and use that form in your references, like this:

(NASA 1994)

Title of work
(Producing quality technical information 1986, 14)

Use this form when you have no author's name and have listed the work by its title. As with the author–date reference, omit anything from the parenthetical citation that you have mentioned in the passage leading up to it.

Two or three authors
(Berdan and Garcia 1982)

Name all the authors of a work with two or three authors.

Four or more authors
(Odell et al. 1983, 28)

Use first author's name with *et al.* ("and others") to cite a work with four or more authors. However, list all the authors in the list of works cited.

Two or more works written by the same author in different years
(Jarrett 1992)
(Jarrett 1993)

When you have listed two or more works written by the same author but in different years, the dates will distinguish them.

Two or more works written by the same author in the same year
(Jarrett 1991a)
(Jarrett 1991b)

To distinguish two or more works written by the same author in the same year, mark the years with lowercase letters, in both the parenthetical citation and the list of works cited.

▶ AUTHOR–DATE DOCUMENTATION: AMERICAN PSYCHOLOGICAL ASSOCIATION

Another widely used author–date documentation system is provided by the American Psychological Association (APA). Like *The Chicago Manual of Style* system, the APA system combines parenthetical citations in the text with an alphabetized list of all the references cited. The APA system is a common method of documentation in the social sciences. First we discuss how to construct the reference list; then we show you how to make parenthetical citations.

Reference List

In a section headed "Reference List," you will list all the works that you cite in your paper. Figure B-25 illustrates how it is done. We have annotated Figure B-25 to draw your attention to certain distinctive features such as capitalization, transposition of names, punctuation, and spacing. For example, notice that in the APA system, in contrast to *The Chicago Manual of Style* system, not only the first author's name but also the names of subsequent authors are transposed.

We have categorized the models as **Books**, **Periodicals**, and **Other**.

Books The following examples illustrate various forms of book citations.

One author
Day, R. A. (1992). *Scientific English: A guide for scientists and other professionals*, Phoenix, AZ: Oryx.

Multiple authors
Von Koenigseck, E., Irvin, J. N., & Irvin, S. C. (1991). *Technical writing for private industry: The a-to-z of o & m manuals*. Malabar, FL: Krieger.

In the reference list, cite all authors, no matter how many.

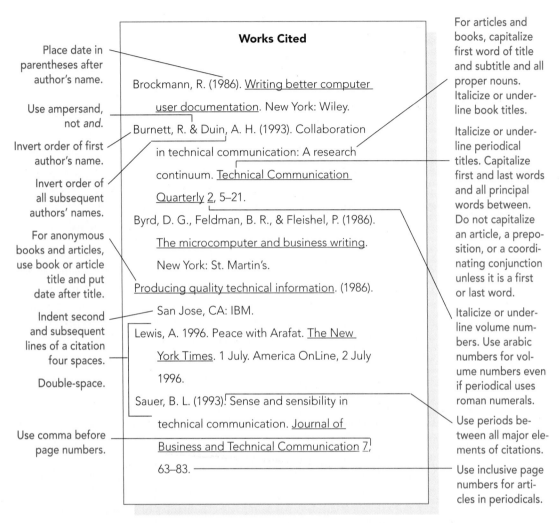

Works Cited

Place date in parentheses after author's name.

Use ampersand, not *and*.

Invert order of first author's name.

Invert order of all subsequent authors' names.

For anonymous books and articles, use book or article title and put date after title.

Indent second and subsequent lines of a citation four spaces.

Double-space.

Use comma before page numbers.

Brockmann, R. (1986). <u>Writing better computer user documentation</u>. New York: Wiley.

Burnett, R. & Duin, A. H. (1993). Collaboration in technical communication: A research continuum. <u>Technical Communication Quarterly</u> <u>2</u>, 5–21.

Byrd, D. G., Feldman, B. R., & Fleishel, P. (1986). <u>The microcomputer and business writing</u>. New York: St. Martin's.

<u>Producing quality technical information</u>. (1986). San Jose, CA: IBM.

Lewis, A. 1996. Peace with Arafat. <u>The New York Times</u>. 1 July. America OnLine, 2 July 1996.

Sauer, B. L. (1993). Sense and sensibility in technical communication. <u>Journal of Business and Technical Communication</u> <u>7</u>, 63–83.

For articles and books, capitalize first word of title and subtitle and all proper nouns. Italicize or underline book titles.

Italicize or underline periodical titles. Capitalize first and last words and all principal words between. Do not capitalize an article, a preposition, or a coordinating conjunction unless it is a first or last word.

Italicize or underline volume numbers. Use arabic numbers for volume numbers even if periodical uses roman numerals.

Use periods between all major elements of citations.

Use inclusive page numbers for articles in periodicals.

FIGURE B-25 • List of Works Cited: American Psychological Association
When using the APA style of documentation, check with your instructor to see if your paper will be considered a printed text, in which case use a hanging indent of five spaces. If your instructor expects your paper to be formatted as a manuscript, indent the first line of each entry five spaces like a paragraph. The examples in this figure are formatted as they would appear in a printed text.

Anthology

Driskill, L. P., Ferrill, J., & Steffey, M. N. (Eds.). (1992). *Business and managerial communication: New perspectives.* New York: Harcourt Brace Jovanovich.

Use the abbreviation *Ed.* for one editor, *Eds.* for two or more. Use *Trans.* for one or more translators.

Essay in an anthology

Faigley, L. (1985). Nonacademic writing: The social perspective. In L. Odell & D. Goswami (Eds.), *Writing in nonacademic settings* (pp. 231–246). New York: The Guilford Press.

Second or subsequent edition

Markel, M. H. (1992). *Technical writing: Situations and strategies* (3rd ed.). New York: St. Martin's.

Article in a reference book

Petrochemical. (2001). *Columbia encyclopedia*.

When a reference work is well known, you need cite only the name of the article, the name of the reference work, and the date of publication. If the work is arranged alphabetically, do not cite page numbers.

For less well-known reference works, give complete information. Cite the author of the article if you have that information; otherwise, begin with the name of the article.

Perpetual calendar, 1775–2076 (1989). In P. Fargis and S. Bykofsky (Eds.), *The New York Public Library desk reference* (pp. 9–13). New York: Webster's New World.

Pamphlet

Cataract: Clouding the lens of sight. (1989). San Francisco: American Academy of Ophthalmology.

If you know the author of a pamphlet, give complete information in the usual manner.

Government or corporate publication

National Aeronautics and Space Administration [NASA]. (1989). *Voyager at Neptune: 1989.* Washington, DC: GPO.

Treat publications much as would any for which the author is a government agency or division within a company book. When the agency or corporate name is unwieldy, provide a shortened version in brackets, which can then used in the parenthetical citation.

Anonymous book

Producing quality technical information. (1986). San Jose, CA: IBM.

When no human, government, or corporate author is listed, begin with the title of the book.

Proceedings

Buehler, M. F. (1984). Rules that shape the technical message: Fidelity, completeness, preciseness. *Proceedings of the 31st International Technical Communication Conference,* WE 9.

Unpublished dissertation

Gambel, L. (1994). *Trauma in emergency room surgery.* Unpublished doctoral dissertation. University of Chicago.

Periodicals   The following examples illustrate various forms of periodicals citations.

Journal with continuous pagination

Barker, T. T. (1989). Word processors and invention in technical writing. *The Technical Writing Teacher, 16,* 126–135.

For periodicals give the inclusive pages of the article. Use complete numbers for the second number, thus, 126–135, 1034–1045.

Journal that pages its issues separately

Gardner, D. P. (1987). The future of university/industry research. *Perspectives in Computing* 7(1), 4–10.

In this citation, 7 is the volume number, 1 is the issue number, and 4–10 are the inclusive pages of the article.

Weekly or biweekly magazine

Samuelson, R. J. (1993, August 2). The health-care crisis hits home. *Newsweek,* p. 38.

Monthly or bimonthly magazine

Beamer, S. (1990, June). Why you need a charting program. *MacUser,* pp. 126–138.

Newspaper

Levathes, L. 1993, July 27. A geneticist maps ancient migrations. *New York Times,* national ed., sec. C.

When the masthead of the paper specifies the edition, put that information in your note. Newspaper content frequently changes from edition to edition on the same day.

Anonymous article

Absolute. (1990, June 18). *New Yorker,* pp. 28–29.

When no author is given for an article, begin with the title of the article.

Other   In this section, we show you model citations for computer software, information services, letters, interviews, and two or more entries by the same author.

Computer software
Prometheus Version 1.06. (1993). MacKnowledge Communication Software.

In citing computer programs, give as much information as you have, including the author's name, the city of publication, the publisher, the version number, and so forth.

Information service
Berdan, R., & Garcia, M. (1982). *Discourse-sensitive measurement of language development in bilingual children.* Los Alamitos, CA: National Center for Bilingual Research. (ERIC ED 234 636).

Personal communication
Do not cite letters and personal interviews in reference list. Give a parenthetical text reference only, like this:

In the opinion of writer John S. Harris (letter to the author, July 19, 1994), publishing today is ...

Two or more works by the same author
Barker, T. (1985). Video field trip: Bringing the real world into the technical writing classroom. *The Technical Writing Teacher 11,* 175–179.

Barker, T. (1989). Word processors and invention in technical writing. *The Technical Writing Teacher 16,* 126–135.

When you have two or more works by the same author or authors in your list of references, list them in order by publication date, with the earliest work first and the most recent one last, and repeat the name or names.

Crowhurst, M. (1983a). *Persuasive writing at grades 5, 7, and 11: A cognitive-development perspective.* Paper presented at the annual meeting of the American Educational Research Association, Montreal, Canada.

Crowhurst, M. (1983b). *Revision strategies of students at three grade levels.* Final report. Educational Research Institute of British Columbia. (ERIC ED 238 009).

When your list of works cited contains two or more works published in the same year by the same author or authors, alphabetize by title, then mark each year with a lowercase letter, beginning with a.

Parenthetical Citation

When you have completed your list of references, refer your reader to it using parenthetical citations in your text. Place the citation in the text where it is relevant and where it disrupts the text the least. Generally, you should place the citation at the end of the grammatical unit—the sentence or clause—that contains the material you are documenting.

Figure B-26 shows a passage that contains parenthetical citations. We have annotated the figure to show you how the system works in the text. The purpose of the parenthetical citations is to guide the reader to the corresponding entry in the reference list and, when appropriate, to cite the specific pages of the reference. Some model references follow.

Author and date
(Asher, 1992)

When needed use specific page reference.

Place comma between name and date and between date and page reference.

Current rhetorical theory indicates that this attempt, through analogy, to call on schemata for newspapers could affect readers' expectations about the writing in the newsletters, which in turn could influence the way these readers process the writing. Genre theory, for example, posits that generic patterns such as those in a newspaper, as part of our "cultural rationality" (Miller, 1984, p. 165), alert readers to ways of perceiving and interpreting documents (Miller, 1984, p. 159). In addition, theories of intertextuality, the concept that all texts contain explicit or implicit traces of other texts (Porter, 1986, p. 34), suggest that creating an analogy between newspapers and newsletters would affect readers' expectations, encouraging them to perceive and interpret material in a particular way (Porter, 1986, p. 38). We must ask, therefore, what readers' expectations about newspapers and hence, by analogy, about the newsletters, might be.

Place parenthetical notes before any punctuation that ends the material cited.

Use p. for one page, pp. for two or more.

FIGURE B-26 • Parenthetical References on a Page: American Psychological Association
Source: Adapted with permission from Nancy Roundry Blyler, "Rhetorical Theory and Newsletter Writing," *Journal of Technical Writing and Communication* 20 (1990): 144.

This citation refers the reader to Asher's 1992 work in the list of works cited. Use this form when you are not citing a specific page.

Author, date, and page
(Asher, 1992, p. 93)

This citation refers the reader to page 93 of Asher's 1992 work. Use this form when you are citing a specific page or pages.

Date and page
(1992, p. 97)

Use this form when you have already mentioned the author's name in the passage leading up to the parenthetical citation, for example, "As Asher's research shows. . . ."

Pages only
(pp. 324–327)

Use this form when you have mentioned both the author's name and the date in the passage leading up to the parenthetical citation, for example, "As Asher's research in 1992 shows. . . ."

Government or corporate author
(National Aeronautics and Space Administration, 1994)

When you list a government agency or a corporate division as the author in the works cited, you may use the agency or corporate entity in your parenthetical citation. If the name is unwieldy, provide a shortened form in brackets in the list of works cited and use that form in your citations, like this:

(NASA, 1994)

Title of work
(Producing Quality Technical Information, 1986, p. 14.)

Use this form when you have no author's name and have listed the work by its title.

Multiple authors
(Berdan & Garcia, 1982)

Name all the authors of a work by two to five authors.

Six or more authors
(Odell et al., 1983, p. 28)

In a parenthetical citation for a book with six or more authors, use the first author's name with *et al.* ("and others"). However, in the list of references list all the authors.

Two or more works written by the same author in different years
(Jarrett, 1992)
(Jarrett, 1993)

When you have listed two or more works by the same author but written in different years, the dates will distinguish them.

Two or more works written by the same author in the same year
(Jarrett, 1991a)
(Jarrett, 1991b)

To distinguish two or more works written by the same author in the same year, mark the years with lowercase letters, in both the parenthetical citation and the list of references.

▶ INTERNET DOCUMENTATION

In this section, we discuss some of the special problems in documenting Internet material, provide model notes and citations, and provide guidance in forming parenthetical references.

For the following reasons, formats for print material documentation usually do not work well for documenting Internet material:

- Internet material seldom has page numbers.
- Publication dates are frequently not provided on the Internet. If they are, they are changeable. That is, many Web sites are works in progress, frequently revised and updated; moreover, revisions occur with little or no warning.
- The normal punctuation used in notes and citations may be mistakenly seen as part of an Internet address.
- Internet addresses must be stated exactly as given by the source; with every slash and period in exactly the right place and no extraneous spaces or punctuation. Improper spacing, wrong punctuation, or a misspelling in a standard citation may be embarrassing, but will probably not destroy the citation's usefulness. Similar errors in Internet citations will render them useless.
- Because the publication date is frequently missing for Internet citations, the date that the user accessed the material may be useful and should be included.

Model Notes and Citations

We provide six models that should cover most of your needs in documenting Internet material, no matter what system of documentation you are using. Whether you choose a note or an author–date style citation, punctuate the entry as shown in each model. However, if you are using notes, put the author's name in normal order and use the indentation style shown in Figure B-22. If your citation is in a *Chicago Manual* author–date reference list, transpose the first author's name and use the indentation style shown in Figure B-23. If the citation is in APA author–date style, transpose the name of all the authors and use the indentation style shown in Figure B-25.

File Transfer Protocol (FTP) Sites   FTP notes and citations contain the following information:

- Author or editor's name (if known), followed by a period
- Document title, within quotation marks, followed by a period
- Publication or revision date (if known), followed by a period
- FTP site address, in angle brackets
- Date of access, in parentheses, followed by a period

   1. Jeff Iverson. "Alabama." ⟨ftp://sumex-aim.stanford.edu:info-mac/education/alabama-hc.hqx⟩ (6 Sep. 1996).

World Wide Web (WWW) Site   WWW notes and citations contain the following information:

- Author or editor's name (if known), followed by a period
- Document title, within quotation marks, followed by a period
- Title of full work (if known), in italics, followed by a period
- Publication or revision date (if known), followed by a period
- WWW site address, angle brackets
- Date of access, parentheses, followed by a period

   Waggoner, Ben. "Introduction to the Viruses." *Life on Earth*. 1995. ⟨http://www.ucmp.berkeley.edu/alllife/virus.html⟩ (28 Oct. 1996).

Linkage   Because of the possibility for linking one document to another in Internet systems, showing that link is often the most convenient way to cite a document. The following note shows that the home page of the Department of Physics at Texas Tech, created by Alan Sill, can be found on the Nine Planets Home Page, maintained by the University of Arizona at the link named "Many Sites."

   2. Alan Sill. "Texas Tech Physics Department Home Page." Lkd. *The Nine Planets Home Page* at "Many Sites." ⟨http://seds.lpl.arizona.edu/nineplanets/nineplanets/nineplanets.html⟩ (27 July 1997).

Listserv Messages   Notes and citations for listserv messages contain the following information:

- Author's name (if known), followed by a period
- Author's e-mail address, angle brackets
- Subject line of message, in quotation marks, followed by a period
- Date of message, followed by a period
- Listserv address, in angle brackets
- Access date, in quotation marks, followed by a period

Selber, Stuart. ⟨selber@ttacsl.ttu.edu⟩ "Call for Articles on Managing International Technical and Scientific Communication." 29 Aug. 1996. ⟨CPTSC-L@CLVM.BITNET⟩ 30 Aug. 1996.

E-Mail Messages   Notes and citations for e-mail messages contain the following information:

- Author's name, followed by a period
- Author's e-mail address, in angle brackets
- Subject line from message, in quotation marks, followed by a period
- Date of message, followed by a period
- Kind of communication, for example, personal, business, professional, etc., followed by a period
- Date of access, in parentheses, followed by a period

3. Marlene Ellin. ⟨Mellinab@AOL. com⟩ "Reviews." 10 Sep. 1996. Business communication. (10 Sep. 1996).

Synchronous Communications   Notes and citations for synchronous communications (MOOs, MUDs, IRSs, chat rooms, and the like) contain the following information:

- Name of speaker (if known), followed by a period
- Type of communication (group discussion, interview, etc.), followed by a period
- Internet address in angle brackets
- Date in parentheses, followed by a period

Stephens, Harold. Group Discussion. ⟨http://204.31.29.22.8010⟩ (12 Jan. 1997).

Parenthetical Citation

When you are using an author–date system, make parenthetical references much as you do at any time. Use whatever information you have to work with. If you have an author or editor's name and a publication date, use both:

Chicago Manual style (Ellin 1996)
APA style (Ellin, 1996)

If you do not have a publication date, simply use the author or editor's name, thus:

(Sill)

If you do not have a name, use whatever comes first in the citation, for example, a title or a shortened title:

(International Professional Communication)

If you have two or more citations to the same person and no publication dates, use letters to distinguish them both in the list of references and in the parenthetical references (See page 671).

▶ FIGURES

Figures, such as tables and graphs, are documented separately from the text. As we explain in Chapter 12, Using Illustrations, sources are documented directly on the figure. In general, the form of figure citations follows that of a note in the note system or that of an entry in a list of works cited or list of references. Because figures have complete documentation internally, their citations do not appear with the other citations in a paper.

▶ COPYRIGHT LAW

Stringent copyright laws protect published work. When you are writing a student report that you do not intend to publish, you need not concern yourself with these laws. If you do intend to publish a report, however, you should become familiar with copyright law. You must get permission from the copyright holder to use illustrations and extended quotations. Look for information about the copyright holder on the title page of a publication. You can find a good explanation of copyright law in Chapter 4, Rights and Permissions, of *The Chicago Manual of Style*.

▶ DESIGNING A WORLD WIDE WEB SITE

Site Creation

Page Design

Site Maintenance

Sources
    Web Sites
    Books

To create a Web site, you will need access to a computer that has a direct Internet connection, the server software necessary to establish a World Wide Web service, and the space available for storage of World Wide Web pages. A variety of Internet service providers offer access to such World Wide Web servers.

You will also need authoring software. Many World Wide Web pages are written using HyperText Markup Language (HTML), a special coding that identifies the elements of each page, such as titles, headings, lists, and block quotations. You could do the HTML coding yourself or save time with free authoring software such as Microsoft FrontPage Express or Netscape Composer. Such programs apply HTML to your files by translating your designated formatting features to HTML tags. Even if you have authoring software, you probably should know the basics of HTML: This knowledge will help you to interpret the coding of pages you would like to imitate and will permit you to do a little quick editing of your pages whenever necessary (see Figure B-27).

▶ SITE CREATION

In creating your site, consider the following guidelines.

- Consider your purpose. A Web site that is trying to sell a product or service is different from one that is designed to entertain or to offer information. A newspaper or magazine site is different from a catalog site. Ask yourself two important questions: What do you hope to accomplish with your Web site? What do you want visitors to think or do at your Web site? Your answer to these two questions should guide the remainder of your design decisions.

- Consider your audience. A Web site aimed at children will ordinarily be quite different from one targeting adults. A Web site for engineers will typically differ from one for musicians. If your audience comprises a wide cross section of the general population, you will have to design for a variety of different education and income levels, different levels of motivation, and different kinds of hardware and software. If your audience is a fairly narrow group (e.g., the employees of a company), you will tailor your page to their specific desires and requirements.

- Explore and experiment. Navigate the World Wide Web for a while, locating pages you would like to imitate or designs you would like to

Before appropriate text

<li>   insert bullet

After appropriate text

<p>   insert paragraph break

               insert line break

Before and after appropriate text

<title>   indicates beginning of page title
</title>   indicates end of page title
<h2>   indicates beginning of heading level two
</h2>   indicates end of heading level two (the type size
                  of headings decreases from h1 to h4)
<b>   starts bold type
</b>   stops bold type
<blockquote>   starts indented block of text
</blockquote>   stops indented block of text
<center>   starts centered type
<a href=". . ."> indicates beginning of hypertext link
</a>   indicates end of hypertext link

Examples

Reference to a file on a different server:
<a href="http://www.tsu.edu/opt/jobs.html">Job Openings</a>

Reference to a file in a different folder on the same server:
<a href="opt/jobs.html">Job Openings</a>

Reference to a different file in the same folder:
<a href="jobs.html">Job Openings</a>

FIGURE B-27 • HTML Basics

adapt for your site. The almost unlimited variety of sites offers a good stimulus for your creativity. Look especially at sites whose audience and purpose are similar to your own.

- Strive for a consistent design for all the pages at your site. A consistent design will make your site more memorable and will help visitors to recognize when they have entered and when they have exited your site.

- Make your site inviting but simple. Don't litter your pages with meaningless graphics: Focus your reader's attention on your information instead of your decorations.

- Focus your efforts on the home page. The home page is where most visitors will enter your site. Make this page especially inviting and easy to navigate. If your home page is unattractive or confusing, visitors will exit your site without having browsed it.

- Be sensitive to the cultural differences of your international audience. Keep in mind that the World Wide Web is worldwide. Avoid idioms, slang, and biased language.

- Give your visitors opportunities to interact with your pages. Remember that a World Wide Web site is a dynamic medium, intrinsically different from the static paper page. Visitors don't simply want to read or view your World Wide Web pages: They want to interact with your material—to click on links and audio or video clips. They want to do things over the World Wide Web, such as order merchandise, download software, make reservations, or complete applications.

▶ PAGE DESIGN

In designing your pages, keep in mind the following common practices:

- Include a complete menu of links at the top and bottom of each page. Make it as easy as possible for visitors to navigate your pages with a minimum of scrolling.

- Avoid excessive links in the running text. Each link in the running text is a distraction from your message, requiring readers to make a choice—exit the page or continue reading. Give the complete menu of links at the top and bottom of the page and only crucial links in the running text.

- Include identifying information on each page. At the bottom of every page, place a copyright notice (e.g., © 2001 ABC Corporation), the date of the latest revision (e.g., *last revised February 1, 2001*), and your e-mail address. Visitors to your site will want to know who to credit as the source of the information, how up-to-date the information is, and who to contact with questions or comments.

- Choose a light, solid color for the background of your pages, such as light yellow, green, or blue. Text displayed on dark or patterned backgrounds can get visitors' attention but is also more difficult to read. Remember that the background is just that: background. If it's a distraction, it is ineffective and inefficient. Try to focus your reader's attention instead on the foreground—the text of your pages.
- Adjust the length of your pages to your information. Ordinarily, pages on the World Wide Web are relatively short: approximately one to three screens of information. If the material on a page is a long list, however, readers might prefer to scroll through the multiple screens of information and avoid the loading time that always accompanies a change of pages.
- Keep illustrations small. Large illustrations can be impressive but often take a long time to load. For indifferent visitors and people with older machines or slow Internet connections, that long load time can be annoying. Instead, include a thumbnail-sized illustration that interested visitors can view in detail by clicking it to load the larger version.
- Restrict animation to video or audio–video clips that the visitor specifically clicks on to view. Continuous motion (e.g., a blinking word) is a highly distracting element, reducing the reader's ability to pay attention to the other information on the page. The ability to animate your page doesn't mean that using animation is always a good idea.
- Use only two levels of heading. On a scrolling page, readers often have difficulty keeping track of the organization and hierarchy of information.
- Minimize your use of italics and script. These fonts are difficult to read on the screen.
- Use bold type selectively and consistently. Bold type is attention-getting and identifies information of special importance, but it loses its power of emphasis if you use it excessively or arbitrarily.
- Edit and proofread carefully. Errors in grammar and punctuation are distracting and jeopardize the credibility of your site.
- Use a variety of browsers, computers, and monitors to check the design of your site. A page that looks satisfactory with your browser on your monitor might be disappointing if viewed with a different browser on another monitor. Netscape Navigator and Internet Explorer, for example, don't always interpret HTML coding in identical ways. Macintosh monitors, also, operate at a higher brightness level than PC monitors, causing colors on a Macintosh to look lighter. And the higher the resolution of either monitor, the smaller that images display on the screen. If you are familiar with such variations, you will be able to adapt the design of your pages to the technology available to your audience.

- Use variations of typography to check the design of your pages. Each visitor to your site has partial control over how your pages will look on his or her screen. Specifically, visitors may decide for themselves on the following:

  Color of the links
  Underlining of the links
  Color of the type
  Size of the type
  Typeface

  Check the design of your pages by using variations of these five elements to see if your site still looks inviting and navigable.

▶ SITE MAINTENANCE

Once you have designed your site, you still have to maintain it. Remember the following guidelines.

- Register your site it with a variety of search engines. Doing so will make it easy for people to locate your site and see the information and services you have to offer.
- Keep updating your pages. Give visitors to your site a reason to return regularly. Offer new information and new opportunities to interact with your pages.
- Periodically check all your internal and external links to see that each is still active. (Internal links connect to other pages of your site; external links connect to pages at other sites.) Dead links annoy your visitors and jeopardize the efficiency and credibility of your site. Ordinarily, internal links break accidentally because of mistakes in the HTML coding that occur during updating or editing of your pages. External links break if a World Wide Web site closes or changes its address (usually because it changes its Internet access provider). A variety of programs are available to check links.
- If possible, avoid changing the address of your site. Changing your address will cause dead links at all the other sites with links to your pages. In addition, earlier visitors to your site who noted your location will be left with the wrong address. If you must change your address, notify visitors to your existing site of the coming change as soon as possible. Include on the existing site a link to your new site, and keep the existing site open for at least one month while you direct visitors to your new address. Use e-mail to advise appropriate discussion lists of your new address and register your new address with appropriate search engines.

▶ SOURCES

Consult the following for useful advice on designing a Web site.

Web Sites

Web Pages That Suck: www.webpagesthatsuck.com
WebMonkey: www.webmonkey.com
WebReference: www.webreference.com
WebReview: www.webreview.com
World Best Websites: www.worldbestwebsites.com
World Wide Web Consortium: www.w3.org

Books

Donnelly, Vanessa. *Designing Easy-to-Use Web Sites: A Hands-on Approach to Structuring Successful Websites*. New York: Addison-Wesley, 2000.

Lynch, Patrick J., and Sarah Horton. *Web Style Guide: Basic Design Principles for Creating Web Sites*. New Haven: Yale University Press, 1999.

Niederst, Jennifer. *Web Design in a Nutshell: A Desktop Quick Reference*. Sebastopol, CA: O'Reilly & Associates, 1998.

Nielsen, Jakob. *Designing Web Usability*. Indianapolis: New Riders, 2000.

Veen, Jeffrey. *The Art and Science of Web Design*. Indianapolis: New Riders, 2001.

▶ OUTLINING

As illustrated in the accompanying sample outline, an outline has a title, purpose statement, audience statement, and body. We have annotated the sample outline to point out major outlining conventions. Following the sample outline, we provide other major outlining principles.

Desalination Methods for Air Force Use

Purpose: To choose a desalination method for Air Force bases located near large bodies of salt water

Audience: Senior officers

First level, use capital roman numeral.

Second level, use capital letters.

Third level, use arabic numerals.

I. Statement of the problem
    A. Need for a choice
    B. Choices available
       1. Electrodialysis
       2. Reverse osmosis

III. Electrodialysis
    A. Theory of method
    B. Judgment of method
       1. Cost
       2. Purity

Capitalize only first
letter of entry and
proper nouns.

Fourth level, use
lowercase letters.

Use no punctuation
after entry.

C. Sources of data
   1. Air Force manuals
   2. Expert opinion
     a. Journals
     b. Interviews

II. Explanation of criteria
   A. Cost
   B. Purity
   C. Quantity

     3. Quantity
IV. Reverse osmosis
   A. Theory of method
   B. Judgment of method
     1. Cost
     2. Purity
     3. Quantity
V. Choice of method

- *Make all entries grammatically parallel.* (See the entry for Parallelism.) Do not mix noun phrases with verb phrases, and so forth. A formal outline with a hodgepodge of different grammatical forms will seem to lack—and, in fact, may lack—logic and consistency.

Incorrect

   I. The overall view
  II. To understand the terminal phase
 III. About the constant-bearing
      concept

Correct

   I. The overall view
  II. The terminal phase
 III. The constant-bearing
      concept

- *Never have a single division.* Things divide into two or more; so obviously, if you have only one division, you have done no dividing. If you have a I, you must have a II. If you have an A, you must have a B, and so forth.

Incorrect

   I. Visual capabilities
     A. Acquisition
  II. Interception and
      closure rate
 III. Braking

Correct

   I. Visual capabilities
     A. Acquisition
     B. Interception and
      closure rate
  II. Braking

- Do not have entries for your report's introduction or conclusion. Outline only the body of the report. Of course, the information in your purpose statement belongs in your introduction, and perhaps the information about audience belongs there as well.
- Use substantive statements in your outline entries. That is, use entries such as "Reverse osmosis" or "Judgment of method" that suggest the true substance of your information. Do not use cryptic expressions such as "Example 1" or "Minor premise."

Many word processing programs have an outlining feature that allows you to choose the outlining scheme you want—for example, I, A, B, 1, 2. The program automatically writes the appropriate numbers or letters for you and changes them when you change the outline.

Chapter Notes

Chapter 1: An Overview of Technical Writing

1. Paul V. Anderson, "What Survey Research Tells Us about Writing at Work," in *Writing in Nonacademic Settings*, ed. Lee Odell and Dixie Goswami (New York: Guilford, 1985), 30.
2. Anderson 40.
3. Anderson 54.
4. Philip W. Swain, "Giving Power to Words," *American Journal of Physics* 13 (1945): 320.

Chapter 2: Composing

1. Stephen S. Hall, "Aplysia and Hermissenda," *Science* 85, (May 1985) 33.
2. Lester Faigley and Thomas P. Miller, "What We Learn from Writing on the Job," *College English* 44 (1982): 562–63.
3. Lee Odell, Dixie Goswami, Anne Herrington, and Doris Quick, "Studying Writing in Non-Academic Settings," in *New Essays in Technical and Scientific Communication: Research, Theory, Practice*, ed. Paul V. Anderson, R. John Brockmann, and Carolyn R. Miller (Farmingdale, NY: Baywood, 1983), 27–28.
4. Lillian Bridwell and Ann Duin, "Looking In-Depth at Writers: Computers as Writing Medium and Research Tool," in *Writing On-Line: Using Computers in the Teaching of Writing*, ed. J. L. Collins and E. A. Sommers (Montclair, NJ: Boyton/Cook, 1985), 119.

Chapter 3: Writing Collaboratively

1. In this chapter we are indebted to the following: Rebecca E. Burnett, "Substantive Conflict in a Cooperative Context: A Way to Improve the Collaborative Planning of Workplace Documents," *Technical Communication* 38 (1991): 532–39. Mary Beth Debs, "Collaborative Writing in Industry," in *Technical Writing: Theory and Practice*, ed. Bertie E. Fearing and W. Keats Sparrow (New York: Modern Language Association, 1989), 33–42. *Collaborative Writing in Industry: Investigations in Theory and Practice*, ed. Mary M. Lay and William M. Karis (Amityville, NY: Baywood, 1991). In this anthology, we are particularly indebted to David K. Farkas, "Collaborative Writing, Software Development, and the Universe of Collaborative Activity," 13–30; James R. Weber, "The Construction of Multi-Authored Texts in One Laboratory Setting," 49–64; Barbara Couture and Jone Rymer, "Discourse Interaction between Writer and Supervisor: A Primary Collaboration in Workplace Writing," 87–108; Ann Hill Duin, Linda A. Jorn, and Mark S. DeBower, "Collaborative Writing: Courseware and Telecommunications," 146–169; and William Van Pelt and Alice Gillam, "Peer Collaboration and the Computer-Assisted Classroom: Bridging the Gap between Academia and the Workplace," 170–206. Evelyn Jaffe Schreiber, "Workplace Teams and Writing Groups: Team Management Theory and the Collaborative Writing Process," *Issues in Writing* 8 (fall/winter 1996): 54–75.

2. Schreiber, 59.

3. Ibid., 58.

4. For more on this, see Edgar R. Thompson, "Ensuring the Success of Peer Revision Groups," in *Focus on Collaborative Learning*, ed. Jeff Golub (Urbana, IL: NCTE, 1988), 109–116.

5. For this exercise we are indebted to Bridget M. Newall, "Evaluating, Web Sites, A Teaching Tip," ed. Gregory A. Wickliff, *Intercom*, June 1999, 34–35, 41.

Chapter 5: Achieving a Readable Style

1. John Henkel, "Drugs of the Deep," *FDA Consumer*, January–February 1998, 30.

2. Dixie Farley, "Bone Builders," *FDA Consumer*, September–October 1997, 27.

3. Steven R. Brantley, *Volcanoes of the United States* (Washington, DC: U.S. Geological Survey, 1994), 39.

4. U.S. Geological Survey, *Our Changing Continent* (Washington, DC: GPO, 1991), 3–4.

5. Janice C. Redish and Jack Selzer, "The Place of Readability Formulas in Technical Communication," *Technical Communication*, 4th quarter, 1985, 49.

6. Francis Christensen, "Notes Toward a New Rhetoric," *College English*, October 1963, 7–18.

7. Daniel B. Felker, Frances Pickering, Veda R. Charrow, V. Melissa Holland, and Janice C. Redish, *Guidelines for Document Designers* (Washington, DC: American Institutes for Research, 1981), 47–48.

8. Ibid., 64.

9. Ibid., 65.

10. Quoted in Janice C. Redish, *The Language of Bureaucracy* (Washington, DC: American Institutes for Research, 1981), 1.

11. CBE Style Manual Committee, *CBE Style Manual*, 5th ed. (Bethesda, MD: Council of Biology Editors, 1983), 38.

12. Ibid., 38.

13. For a perceptive essay on elegant variation, see H. W. Fowler, *A Dictionary of Modern English Usage* (New York: Oxford University Press, 1950), 130–33.

14. The excerpts from the St. Paul Fire and Marine Insurance Company's old and new personal liability catastrophe policy are reprinted with the permission of the St. Paul Companies, St. Paul, MN. 55102.

15. Kenneth W. Houp, Thomas E. Pearsall, Elizabeth Tebeaux, Susan Cody, and Ann Boyd, *Reporting Technical Information*, Canadian ed. (Scarborough, Ontario: Allyn & Bacon Canada, 1996).

16. *CBE Style Manual*, 36–37. Reproduced with permission from *CBE Style Manual*, 5th edition. Copyright 1983, CBE Style Manual Committee, Council of Biology Editors, Inc.

17. "Planners Outlaw Jargon," *Plain English*, April 1981, 1.

18. National Institutes of Health, *Inside the Cell* (Washington, DC: Department of Health and Human Services, 1990), 48.

Chapter 6: Writing Ethically

1. In writing this chapter, we have drawn upon the following books and articles: John Bryan, "Down the Slippery Slope: Ethics and the Technical Writer as Marketer," *Technical Communication Quarterly*, winter 1992, 73–88; Sam Dragga, "A Question of Ethics: Lessons from Technical Communicators on the Job," *Technical Communication Quarterly*, spring 1997, 161–178; William K. Franken, *Ethics* (Englewood Cliffs, NJ: Prentice-Hall, 1963); Dean G. Hall and Bonnie A. Nelson, "Integrating Professional Ethics into the Technical Writing Course," *Journal of Technical Writing and Communication* 17 (1987): 45–61; Mike Markel, "A Basic Unit on Ethics for Technical Communicators," *Journal of Technical Writing and Communication* 21 (1991): 327–50; H. Lee Shimberg, "Ethics and Rhetoric in Technical Writing," *Technical Communication*, 4th quarter 1978, 16–18; and Arthur E. Walzer, "The Ethics of False Implicature in Technical and Professional Writing," *Journal of Technical Writing and Communication* 19 (1989): 149–60.

2. George F. R. Ellis, quoted in W. Wayt Gibbs, "Profile: George F. R. Ellis: Thinking Globally, Acting Universally," *Scientific American*, October 1995, 55.

3. In writing this section on ethical graphics we have drawn on Edward R. Tufte, *The Visual Display of Quantitative Information* (Cheshire, CN: Graphics Press, 1983), 53–87.

4. Engineering Ethics Cases Section, *Online Ethics Center for Engineering and Science*. National Science Foundation. http://onlineethics.org/cases/engcases.html (1 February 1999).

5. Environmental Protection Agency, *Consumer's Guide to Radon Reduction* (Washington, DC: GPO, 1992).

6. The source for this exercise is Gray Matters Mini Cases, *Online Ethics Center for Engineering and Science*. National Science Foundation. http://onlineethics.org/text/corp/graymatters/case93.html (7 February 2000).

Chapter 7: Writing for International Readers

1. Geert H. Hofsted, *Culture's Consequences*, 2d ed. (Thousand Oaks, CA: Sage, 2000), *Cultures and Organizations: Software of the Mind*, London: McGraw-Hill, 1997.

2. Fong Trompenaars, *Riding the Waves of Culture*, 2d ed. (London: The Economist Books, 1993).

3. Edward T. Hall and Mildred Reed Hall, *Understanding Cultural Difference*. (Yarmouth, ME: Intercultural Press, 1990).

4. Lisa Hecklin, *Managing Cultural Differences: Strategies for Competitive Advantage*. (Reading, MA: Addison-Wesley, 1995).

5. Ibid., 35.

6. William Horton, "The Almost Universal Language: Graphics for International Documents," *Technical Communication*, 4th quarter, 1993, 682–693.

Chapter 9: Presenting Information

1. Steven R. Brantley, *Volcanoes of the United States* (Washington, DC: Department of the Interior, Geological Survey, 1995), 20–22.

2. Department of Commerce, *How We're Changing* (Washington, DC: Bureau of the Census, 1997), 1.

3. These quotations are from Geological Survey, *Safety and Survival in an Earthquake* (Washington, DC: GPO, 1991), 3–5.

4. William B. Gudykunst, *Bridging Differences: Effective Intergroup Communication* (Newbury Park, CA: Sage, 1991), 44.

5. Stephan Wilkinson, "Tiny Keys to Our Electronic Future," *Raytheon Magazine*, winter 1985, 4.

6. National Aeronautics and Space Administration, *Exploring the Universe with the Hubble Space Telescope* (Washington, DC: GPO, n.d.), 11.

7. "If All Our Reporters Were Laid End to End," *The Wall Street Journal*, 4 April 1983, 10.

8. Raymond H. Beal, Joe K. Mauldin, and Susan C. Jones, *Subterranean Termites: Their Prevention and Control* (Washington, DC: Department of Agriculture, 1989), 1.

9. Centers for Disease Control, *The Public Health Consequences of Disasters* (Washington, DC: Department of Health and Human Services, 1989), 33.

10. U.S. Congress, Office of Technology Assessment, *Biological Effects of Power Frequency Electric and Magnetic Fields* (Washington, DC: GPO, 1989), 19.

11. National Institutes of Health, *Inside the Cell* (Washington, DC: U.S. Department of Health and Human Services, 1990), 21.

12. Robert I. Tilling, Christina Heliker, and Thomas Wright, *Eruptions of Hawaiian Volcanoes: Past, Present, and Future* (Washington, DC: U.S. Geological Survey, 1987), 17.

13. National Aeronautics and Space Administration, *Planetary Exploration through Year 2000* (Washington, DC: GPO, 1988), 30–31.

14. David L. Wallace and John R. Hayes, "Redefining Revision for Freshmen," *Research in the Teaching of English* 25 (1991), 58–59.

Chapter 10: Analyzing Information

1. Department of the Interior, *Southeast Wetlands* (Washington, DC: GPO, 1994), 7.

2. Office of Technology Assessment, *Advanced Automotive Technology* (Washington, DC: GPO, 1995), 1–2

3. Department of Energy, *Earth-Sheltered Homes* (Washington, DC: GPO, 1997), 1–2, 8.

4. W. Jacquelyne Kious and Robert I. Tilling, *This Dynamic Earth* (Washington, DC: Department of the Interior, Geological Survey, n.d.), 1.

5. Department of State, Bureau of Oceans and International Environmental and Scientific Affairs, *Environmental Diplomacy* (Washington, DC: GPO, 1997), 14–15.

6. Lucy E. Edwards and John Pojeta, Jr., *Fossils, Rocks, and Time* (Washington, DC: Department of the Interior, Geological Survey, 1993), 11.

7. For a more detailed explanation of Toulmin logic, see Steven Toulmin, Richard Rieke, and Allan Janik, *An Introduction to Reasoning*, 2d ed. (New York: Macmillan, 1984) and Stephen Toulmin, *The Uses of Argument* (Cambridge: Cambridge University Press, 1958).

8. "Are We Seeing Global Warming," *Science*, 9 May 1997, 915.

9. Michael D. Lemmick, "Hot Air in Kyoto," *Time*, 8 Dec 1997, 79.

10. Gregg Easterbrook, "Hot Air Treaty," *U.S. News & World Report*, 22 Dec 1997, 46.

11. Quoted in Richard A. Kerr, "Greenhouse Forecasting Still Cloudy," *Science*, 16 May 1997, 1042.

12. Quoted in Kerr 1042.

13. Thomas R. Carl, Neville Nichols, and Jonathan Gregory, "The Coming Climate," *Scientific American*, May 1997, 83.

14. "Science and Solutions," *Global Climate Change*, 1997. fe.doe.gov/issues/globalclimate_intro.html (10 Jan 1999).

Chapter 11: Document Design

1. For a rationale for teaching design, see Stephen A. Bernhardt, "Seeing the Text," *College Composition and Communication* 37 (1986): 66–78. For a research-based summary of document design principles for paper documents, see Philippa J. Benson, "Writing Visually: Design Considerations in Technical Publications," *Technical Communication* 32, 4 (1985) 35–39.

2. Janice C. Redish, "Understanding Readers," in *Techniques for Technical Communicators*, ed. Carol Barnum and Saul Carliner (New York: Macmillan, 1993), 14–41.

3. William Horton lists many types of online documentation in his book, *Designing and Writing Online Documentation*, 2d ed. (New York: Wiley, 1994).

4. R. Kruk and P. Muter, "Reading of Continuous Text on Video Screens," *Human Factors* 26.3 (1984): 339–45; John Gould, "Why Is Reading Slower from CRT Screens Than from Paper?" *Proceedings of the Human Factors Society, 30th Annual Meeting* (Dayton, OH, Human Factors Society, 1986) 834–35.

5. Thomas N. Huckin, "A Cognitive Approach to Readability," in *New Essays in Technical and Scientific Communication: Research, Theory, and Practice*, ed. Paul V. Anderson, R. John Brockmann, and Carolyn R. Miller (Farmingdale, NY: Baywood, 1983) 90–101; Janice C. Redish, Robin M. Battison, and Edward S. Gold, "Making Information Accessible to Readers," in *Writing in Non-Academic Settings*, ed. Lee Odell and Dixie Goswami (New York: Guilford, 1985), 129–53.

6. These books will give you more information about designing effective paper documents: Jan V. White, *Graphic Design for the Electronic Age* (New York:

Watson-Guptill, 1988); and John Miles, *Design for Desktop Publishing* (San Francisco: Chronicle Books, 1987). These books will give you more information about designing effective online documents, help screens, and World Wide Web pages: Horton, *Online*; William K. Horton, Lee Taylor, Arthur Ignacio, and Nancy L. Hoft, *The World Wide Web Cookbook* (New York: Wiley, 1996). For information on the WWW about designing Web pages, check the links that are available through the home page of the Society for Technical Communication at http://stc.org.

7. White 20.

8. Rolf F. Rehe, *Typography: How to Make It Most Legible*, 3rd ed. (Carmel, IN: Design Research International, 1979), 34; Elizabeth Keyes, "Typography, Color, and Information Structure," *Technical Communication* 40.4 (1993); 638–54; and Elizabeth Keyes, David Sykes, and Elain Lewis, "Technology + Design + Research = Information Design," *Text, ConText, and HyperText*, ed. Edward Barrett (Cambridge, MA: MIT Press, 1988), 251–64.

9. M. Gregory and E. C. Poulton, "Even Versus Uneven Right Margins and the Rate of Comprehension in Reading," *Ergonomics* (1970): 427–34; Rehe 34.

10. M. A. Tinker, *Legibility of Print* (Ames, IA: Iowa State University Press, 1969); J. Foster and P. Coles, "An Experimental Study of Typographical Cueing in Printed Text," *Ergonomics* (1977): 57–66.

11. For more on using color effectively, see also Gerald M. Murch, "Using Color Effectively: Designing to Human Specifications," *Technical Communication* 32.4 (1985): 14–20; Horton, *Online*, 241–45; Horton et al., *Web Cookbook*, 242–43, 420–21.

12. Linda Flower, John R. Hayes, and Heidi Swarts, "in Revising Functional Documents: The Scenario Principle," *New Essays in Technical and Scientific Communication: Research, Theory, and Practice*, ed. Paul V. Anderson, R. John Brockmann, and Carolyn R. Miller (Farmingdale, NY: Baywood, 1983), 41–58.

13. White 95–106; Miles 42–46.

Chapter 14: The Strategies and Communications of the Job Hunt

1. In writing this chapter, we have drawn upon three publications from the U.S. Department of Labor: *Job Search Guide: Strategies for Professionals* (Washington, DC: GPO, 1993), *Tips for Finding the Right Job* (Wash-

ington, DC: GPO, 1992), and *Tomorrow's Jobs* (Washington, DC: GPO, 1998).

2. *Job Search Guide*, 24–25.

3. *Job Search Guide*, 22.

4. Avery Comarow, "Tracking the Elusive Job," *The Graduate* (Knoxville: Approach 13-30 Corporation, 1977), 42.

Chapter 17: Empirical Research Reports

1. Deborah Hicks, "Working through Discourse Genres in School," *Research in the Teaching of English* 31 (1997): 490.

2. Nathalie Goubert and Rachel K. Clifton, "Object and Event Representation in 6 1/2-Month-Old Infants," *Developmental Psychology* 34 (1998): 64–65.

3. Leslie K. Johnson, "Sexual Selection in a Brentid Weevil," *Evolution* 36 (1982): 251.

4. Rod Judkins, "Iron Aluminum Filters for Advanced PFBCs," ID 33106, Office of Fossil Energy, Department of Energy. http://www.fe.doe.gov/ (5 March 2000).

5. J. J. Bull, R. C. Vogt, and C. J. McCoy, "Sex Determining Temperatures in Turtles: A Geographic Comparison," *Evolution* 36 (1982): 326.

6. Gerald L. Chan and John B. Little, "Further Studies on the Survival of Non-Proliferating Diploid Fibroblasts Irradiated with Ultraviolet Light," *International Journal of Radiation Biology* 41 (1982): 360.

7. Sylvie Pouteau, Fiona Tooke, and Nicholas Battey, "Quantitative Control of Inflorescence Formation in *Impatiens balsamina*," *Plant Physiology* 118 (1998): 1192.

Chapter 18: Instructions

1. G. B. Harrison, *Profession of English* (New York: Harcourt, 1962), 149.

2. The questions posed here are based on questions presented by Janice C. Redish, Robbin M. Battison, and Edward S. Gold, "Making Information Accessible to Readers," *Writing in Nonacademic Settings*, ed. Lee Odell and Dixie Goswami (New York: Guilford, 1985), 139–43.

3. Dwayne Isbell, *Hybrid Touch/Sound System Installation*, 1. Student paper reprinted by permission.

4. Department of Health and Human Services, *Eating to Lower Your High Blood Cholesterol* (Washington, DC: GPO, 1989), 1.

5. Isbell, 1.

6. Adapted from Environmental Protection Agency, *Manual of Individual and Non-Public Water Supply Systems* (Washington, DC: GPO, 1991), 55–56.

7. Shoe box for Sebago Docksiders.

8. Charles H. Sides, *How to Write Papers and Reports About Computer Technology* (Philadelphia: ISI, 1984), 70.

9. Environmental Protection Agency, *Citizen's Guide to Pesticides* (Washington, DC: GPO, 1991), 8.

10. Department of Agriculture, *Simple Home Repairs: Inside* (Washington, DC: GPO, 1986), 7–8.

11. Ibid., 16.

12. Protocol analysis material furnished by Professor Victoria Mikelonis, U of Minnesota, St. Paul, MN.

13. For this exercise we are indebted to Stephanie Zerkel, "Technical Writing for Non-Traditional Students," A Teaching Tip, ed. Gregory A. Wickliff, *Intercom*, May 1998, 34–35.

Chapter 19: Oral Reports

1. These introspections were compiled at a session of the National Training Laboratory in Group Development in Bethel, Maine, which one of the authors attended.

2. The material on visual aids was adapted from material especially prepared for this chapter by Professor James Connolly of the University of Minnesota.

Appendix A: Handbook

1. *Publication Manual of the American Psychological Association*, 4th ed. (Washington, DC: APA, 1994), 83.

2. Department of Energy, *EMF in the Workplace* (Washington, DC: National Institute for Occupational Health and Safety, 1996), 5.

3. Minna Levine, "Business Statistics," *MacUser*, April 1990, 128.

4. Levine, 120.

Appendix B: Formal Elements of Document Design

1. Audrey T. Hingley, "Preventing Childhood Poisoning," *FDA Consumer*, March 1996, 7.

2. U.S. Department of Labor, *Job Search Guide: Strategies for Professionals* (Washington, DC: GPO, 1993), 2.

3. Lenore S. Ridgway, Roger A. Grice, and Emilie Gould, "I'm OK; You're Only a User: A Transactional Analysis of Computer–Human Dialogs," *Technical Communication* 39 (1992): 39.

4. Laurel L. Northouse, "Breast Cancer in Younger Women: Effects on Interpersonal and Family Relationships," *Monographs: Journal of the National Cancer Institute* 16 (1994): 183.

5. David R. Russell, "The Ethics of Teaching Ethics in Professional Communication: The Case of Engineering Publicity at MIT in the 1920s," *Journal of Business and Technical Communication* 7 (1993): 84–85. Reprinted by permission.

6. This excerpt and the one preceding it are from Warrick R. Nelson, "Trees Grow Better with Water," *Tree Planter's Notes*, 46 (1995): 46–47.

7. Russell, 107.

8. J. J. Bull, R. C. Vogt, and C. J. McCoy, "Sex Determining Temperatures in Turtles: A Geographic Comparison," *Evolution* 36 (1982): 331.

9. *The Chicago Manual of Style*, 14th ed. (Chicago: University of Chicago Press, 1993), 487–635.

10. Ibid, 637–699.

11. *Publication Manual of the American Psychological Association*, 4th ed. (Washington, DC: APA, 1994).

12. Janice R. Walker, *The Columbia Guide to Online Style*, 1996. Jwalker@chuma.cas.usf.edu (20 January 1999) and *ISO 690-2*, 1998. nlc-bnc.ca/iso/tc46sc9/standard/690-2ex.htm (22 January 1999).

Index

Abbreviations, 595, 638, 643, 644
 general rules, 574-577
 for U.S. and Canadian provinces, 645f
about.com, 169
Abstraction ladder, 94-96, 180-183
Abstracts, 618, 619-622
Acronyms, 577-578
Active space, 245
Active verbs, 91-92
Active voice, 30, 92-93, 197, 198, 497,
 521, 586
Adjectives, compound number, 592
Adverbial openers, 87-88
Alternatives, 222-223
Ambiguous and imprecise language, 112
American Psychological Association
 (APA) style, 650, 665-672
America's Job Bank, 359
Analogy, 179-180, 181f, 186, 190-192,
 205
Analysis, 210-229
 classical argument, 213-217
 comparision, 213, 222-223
 deduction, 213, 220-221
 induction, 213, 218-220
 pro and con argument, 213, 217-218
 Toulmin logic, 213, 223-226
And, subjects joined by, 605
Animation, 678-679
Apostrophe, 578-579
Appendixes, 188, 237, 265-266, 406, 634-
 635
Applied Science and Technology
 Abstracts, 166
Argument
 classical, 213-217
 pro and con, 213, 217-218
 in proposal development, 399-401

Aristotle, 14
Arrangement, 14, 31
 in chronological presentations, 178
 in collaboration, 38
 in discovery, 21
 elements of, 22-23
 of instructions, 506, 524-525
 of oral reports, 545-548
 in revision, 26-27
 Toulmin logic in, 226
ArticleFirst, 166
Articles, 168-169, 171
 askme.com, 169
Attention line, 645-646
Audience, 5-6, 16-20, *See also* Readers
 attitudes toward material, 18-19
 for chronological presentations, 178
 for correspondence, 333-337, 340
 for empirical research reports, 492
 for feasibility reports, 467
 illustrations for, 281-282
 international, *See* International read-
  ers/audience knowledge and experience of, 17
 for oral reports, 542, 551-554
 point of view, 17-18
 for World Wide Web site, 676

Backing, in Toulmin logic, 224, 226
Bar graphs, 285, 300-302, 303f
Blank space, 242-246, 261-262
Block style
 for letters, 638, 639f, 641f, 647
 for paragraphs, 247
Body
 of letters and memos, 647
 of oral report, 546-548
BOOKMARK function, 163

Books
 citing, 658-660, 666-667
 evaluating information from, 168, 171
 notes in, 653-655
Brackets, 579-580
Brainstorming, 20-21, 37-38
 britannica.com, 169
Buchwald, Art, 24-25
Business Dateline, 166
Business Periodical Index, 362

Call numbers, 164
Capitalization, 255, 580-581
Career Guide, The, 361
Career Guide to Professional Organizations,
 362
Career Magazine, 360
CareerWeb, 360
Carson, Rachel, 87
Cartoons, 560-562
Causality, 220
Caution message, 252, 516-518,
 520f
CBE Style Manual, 93, 94
Central statement of paragraph, 83
Century-decade-unit system (Navy
 system), 262, 263f
Chalkboards, 568
Chambers, 186
Charts, 566-567
Chicago Manual of Style, 39, 649-650, 657-
 664, 672, 675
China, 149
Christensen, Francis, 87, 88, 94
Chronological order
 presenting information in, 176-178,
  186, 194, 203-204, 216
 progress report structure by, 420-421

Circle graphs, 285, 305-306, 306f, 317f, 308f, 316f, 319f
Citation of sources, 111, 171-172, 295. *See also* Documentation
Claim, in Toulmin logic, 224, 226
Clarity, 6, 59, 556
Classical argument, 213-217
Classification, 180-184, 186, 205
Clauses, 582
  contact, 583
  independent, 583, 588, 600
  main, 583
  subordinate, 587, 588
Clichés, 344, 586
Collaboration, 34-53
  drafting in, 37f, 40
  editing in, 37f, 42-43
  group conferences in 47-50
  on the Internet, 44-47
  planning in, 37-39
  revision in, 37f, 41-42
  in the workplace, 43
Collective nouns, 605
Collectivism, 129-130, 141, 145
Colon, 581-582, 598
Color
  cultural associations with, 149t
  description of, 192
  in document design, 255-256
  in graphs, 301, 304, 305
  for World Wide Web sites, 678
Column graphs, 300-302, 303f, 304f, 305f, 312f, 313f
Comma, 582-586, 598
Communication goals, 56
Comparision, 213, 222-223
Complimentary close, 647
Composing, 12-33. *See also* Arrangement; Discovery; Drafting; Editing; Revision; Situational analysis
Compound number adjectives, 592
Compound words, 589
Compromisers, in groups, 50
Computer graphics, 285-287, 563
Computer screens, design of, 241-248
Conclusions, 212, 443, 469, 548, 630-631
Concrete language, 257
Conditional sentences, 89
Constant dollar, 114
Contact clauses, 583
Content
  planning, 73-75
  revision of, 26-27
Context, 75
Continuation page, 644f, 648
Contractions, 579
Conversational style, 342-345
Cooking, of data, 113
Coordinators, group, 39
Copyright law, 675

Correspondence, 328-353
  audience for, 333-337
  e-mail, 337-340, 345-346
  for international readers, 340-341, 346-347
  of the job hunt, 364-382
  keeping copies of, 347-348
  letters, 337-340
  memos, 337-340
  purpose of, 330-333, 340
  style for, 340-345, 346, 347
Cost proposals, 401, 405-406
Cover, report, 609-612
Criteria, 223
Criterion-based comments, 41
Criticism of work, 42
Culture. *See* International readers/audience

Danger message, 516, 519, 520f
Dangling modifier, 586
Dash, 586, 598
Data, manipulation of, 112-113
Date line, 644
Deadlines, 39, 40
Dead links, 680
Decimal point, 595
Deduction, 213, 220-221
Definitions, 185-188, 206
  extended, 186-187
  logical, 185-186
  placement of, 187-188
  proper use of, 5
  purpose of, 15-16
  sentence, 185-186
  for technical writers, 2
Department of Labor, U.S., 358-359
Description, 186, 188-203. *See also* Mechanism description; Process description
Descriptive abstracts, 619, 621-622
Dewey decimal system, 164, 165f
Diction, 586-587
Dictionary of Job Titles, 359
Direct style, 340-342, 347, 348f
Discovery, 14, 20-22, 31, 37-38
Discussion, 469, 484, 497-498, 628-629
Distribution lists, 59, 67-68
Division, 180-184, 186, 205
Documentation, 5, 39, 649-675
  author-date. *See* American Psychological Association style; *Chicago Manual of Style*
  checking, 28
  copyright law on, 675
  Internet, 672-674
  notes. *See* Notes
Document design, 27, 230-277, 607-682
  checking, 29
  consistency in, 239
  documentation, *See* Documentation

to facilitate information access, 256-266, 269
letter and memo format, 637-648
outlining, 681-682
for pages and screens, 241-248
planning, 237-238
possible decisions in, 232-236
report format. *See* Report format
revealing to readers, 239
situational factors in, 237
type in. *See* Type
on World Wide Web, 675-680
Drafting, 14-15, 31, 40-41
  in collaboration, 37f, 40
  dividing the work, 40
  elements of, 23-26
  by one person, 40-41
Dun & Bradstreet Million Dollar Directory, 361

Economic justification reports, 212
Editing, 14, 28-30, 32
  checking documentation, 28
  checking document design, 29
  checking graphics, 29
  checking mechanics, 28
  in collaboration, 37f, 42-43
Elegant variation, 97
Ellipsis, 587
Ellis, George F. R., 109
E-mail
  collaboration on, 44-45
  composing, 337-340
  documentation on, 674
  progress reports on, 415-416f
  résumés on, 376-379
  special considerations for, 345-346
Empirical research reports, 212, 482-501
  discussion, 484, 497-498
  introduction and literature review, 484, 492-495
  materials and methods, 484, 493-494, 495-497
  process description, 199-202
  results, 484, 497
  statement of objectives, 493
Empty words, 96-97
Encouragers, in groups, 50
Encyclopedia Americana Online, 164
Encyclopedia Britanica 164, 169
Encyclopedias, 163-164
Endings, 629-634
End notations, 648
Endnotes, 187, 188, 649, 651-653
Environmental impact statements, 212, 468
Ethics, 106-123
  behaving with, 116-118
  benefits of, 109-111

characteristics of acts lacking, 108-109
dealing with deviations from, 118-120
illustration design and, 308-320
recognizing deviations from, 111-116
Evaluation reports, 212
Evidence, 214-215
Exclamation point, 519, 587, 598
Executive reports, 199, 201f, 226
Executive summaries, 469, 618, 622, 624f
Exemplification, 178-179, 204, 212
Extemporaneous speeches, 543-544
Extended definitions, 186-187
External links, 680

Facts, 212
False implications, 112
Fatal Communication Error, 127
Faulkner, William, 87
Fault tree diagrams, 116-117
FAVORITES function, 163
Feasibility reports, 442, 464-479
example of, 470-478f
important features of, 469, 479
preparation of, 466-468
Feasibility studies, 464-466
Federal Career Opportunities, 362
Feeling expressers, in groups, 50
Femininity, of culture, 136, 147
Figures, 282, 286-287f, 675
First-person point of view, 93-94
FirstSearch, 166-167
Flaming, 161
Flip charts, 566-567
Flowcharts, 286, 291f, 309
Follow-up letters, 380-382
Fonts. *See* Typefaces
Footers, 264, 266
Footnotes, 187, 188, 296, 650-653, 673-674
Foreign words, italicizing, 590
Forging, of data, 113
Formal reports, 442, 443-464
example of, 449-463f
important features of, 448, 464
Formal situation, 553
Format, 42-43, 232-236, 267-268
example of poor, 235f
instruction, 528-531
letter and memos, 637-648
report. *See* Report format
Fractions, 593
Fragmentary sentences, 587-588
France, 149
FTP (file transfer protocol) sites, 44, 45, 673

Gatekeepers, in groups, 50
Generalizations, 178-179, 220
Germany, 149

Glossaries, 187-188, 237
example of, 189f
format for, 617-618, 620f
for instructions, 512, 528
GO menu items, 162-163
GPO Monthly Catalog, 166
Grammar checkers, 29-30
Graphics, 27, 246. *See also* Illustrations
analogy presentations and, 180, 181f
checking, 29
chronological presentations and, 177
computer, 288-292, 563
for instructions, 509, 523, 524f
for international readers/audience, 147-148
for oral reports, 547-548
Graphs, 5
bar, 285, 288f, 300-304
circle, 285, 305-306, 309f, 310-311f, 312f, 317f, 320f
column, 300-304, 305f, 306f, 307f, 308f, 314f, 315f
line, 285, 286, 293f, 306-307, 308-309, 313f, 314f, 316f
for oral reports, 557, 559f, 560f
picto, 113-116, 309, 318-319f
Grolier Multimedia Encyclopedia Online, 164
Grounds, in Toulmin logic, 224, 226
Group conferences, 47-50
Group maintenance roles, 50
Guide for Occupational Exploration, 359

Hall, Edward, 127
Hardboard charts, 566
Harmonizers, in groups, 50
Headers, 264, 266
Headings, 184, 239, 245
format for, 39
of letters and memos, 638-644
numbers with, 262-264
for page organization, 260-264
parallel, 259
for tables, 296
tips for writing descriptive, 257-260
on World Wide Web sites, 257, 262, 679
Hemingway, Ernest, 87
Hidden Job Market, The, 361
Highet, Gilbert, 87
Highlighting, 252-255
Hoecklin, Lisa, 127, 129
Hofstede, Geert, 127, 131-132
Honor in Science, 112
Hoover's Handbook of American Business, 361
Hot Jobs 360
HotJobs.com, 379
How-to instructions, 521-525
HTML (HyperText Markup Language), 676, 677f, 679, 680

Hyphen, 589, 592
Hypotheses, 218, 219, 493

Illustrations, 278-325. *See also* Figures; Graphics; Graphs; Photographs; Tables
audience for, 281-282
ethics in designing, 311-319
guidelines for creating, 297-311
list of, 615-617
purpose of, 280, 282-297
on World Wide Web sites, 678
Imperative mood, 197-198, 521
Impromptu speeches, 543
Indented style, 247
Independent clauses, 583, 588, 600
Indexes, 166-167
Index to Legal Periodocals & Books, 166
Indicative mood, 198
Indirect style, 340-342, 343f, 346, 347, 349f
Individualism, 128t, 129-130
Induction, 213, 218-220
Informal reports, 442-443, 444-447f
Informal situation, 553-554
Information, 156-173
analysis of. *See* Analysis
asking the right questions, 158
citation of sources, 171-172
evaluation of, 168-171
presentation of. *See* Presenting information
sources of, 158-167
Informative abstracts, 619, 620-621
Inside address, 644-645
Institute of Electrical and Electronics Engineers (IEEE) Code of Ethics, 109
Instructions, 194, 197, 245, 502-539
arrangement of, 506, 524-525
equipment and materials needed, 512-513, 514f
format for, 528-531
glossary, 512, 528
headings for, 258
how-to, 521-525
introduction, 507-508
mechanism description in, 513-516
purpose of, 505
readers of, 505-506, 531-534
theory or principles of operation, 508-512
tips and troubleshooting procedures, 525-528
warnings, 516-520
Internal links, 680
Internal proposals, 425, 426-429f
International readers/audience, 60, 124-153
correspondence for, 340-341, 346-347
examples of documents for, 139-143

International readers/audience *(continued)*
    graphics for, 147–148
    guide for written communication, 138–139t
    guides to doing business with, 149–151
    oral reports for, 542
    planning process and, 136–138
    situational analysis of, 19–20
    style for, 100–101, 340–341, 346, 347
    understanding, 127–136
    writing business communications to, 143–147
Internet
    collaboration on, 44–47
    documentation on, 672–674
    job hunt on, 359–361
Interviews, 159–160, 170
    job, 381, 382–386
Introductions
    of empirical research reports, 484, 492–495
    of feasibility reports, 469
    format for, 622–628
    of informal reports, 443
    of instructions, 507–508
    of oral reports, 545–546
Inverted constructions, 88
Italicization, 590

Japan, 145–147, 149
JobFind, 361
Job hunt, 354–391
    follow-up letters, 380–382
    information gathering, 359–363
    interviews, 381, 382–386
    letter of application, 364–368
    networking, 362–363
    résumé. *See* Résumés
    salary discussions, 386
    self-assessment, 356–359
JobTrak, 360–361, 372
Justification of type, 247–248

Kant, Immanuel, 108, 109
Keywords, 258–259

Labels, 609–610, 611f
Language
    ambiguous and imprecise, 112
    concrete, 257
    visual, 190–192
Letter progress reports, 425, 430–431f
Letters
    of application (cover letters), 364–368
    composing, 337–340
    difference between memos and, 638
    follow-up, 380–382
    format of, 637–648
    of transmittal, 608–609, 610f

Library, 163–167
Library catalog, electronic, 164–166
Library of Congress classification system, 164, 166f
Line graphs, 285, 286, 291f, 306–307, 308–309, 309f, 310f, 311f
Line length, 246–247
Links, 673, 678, 680
Lists, 245
    format for, 39
    in instructions, 521
    parentheses in, 594
    style of, 85–86
Listserv messages, 673
Literature review, 484, 492–495
Logic, 27
Logical definitions, 185–186
Logical fallacies, 221–222

Main clauses, 583
Major proposition, 213, 214, 215–216
Management proposals, 401, 405
Manuscript speeches, 544–545
Maps, 286, 289f, 290f
Margins, 242, 245, 247–248
Masculinity, of culture, 128t, 136, 147
Materials and methods (M&M), report section, 484, 493–494, 495–497
Mechanics, checking, 28
Mechanism description, 15, 187, 188–190, 192–194, 195f, 206–207, 513–516
Memoranda
    composing, 337–340
    difference between letters and, 638
    format of, 637–648
Metasearch engines, 162
Mexico, 131, 139, 141–143
Microjustifying of type, 247
Middle East, 149
Minor propositions, 213, 214–215
Misplaced modifier, 591
Mood, 194–198
MOOs (multiple user domain object-oriented), 45
Movies, 567–568
MUDs (multiple user dimension, dialogue, domain, or dungeon), 45
Multiple-decimal system, 262, 263f, 264
Multiple negatives, 91

National Business Telephone Directory, 361
Networking, 39, 362–363
Newsgroups, 160–161, 168, 170
Newspaper Abstracts, 166
New York Times Index, 166, 362
Nonrestrictive appositives, 584–585
Nonrestrictive modifiers, 584
Nor, compound subject joined by, 604
Notes, 111, 649, 650–657. *See also* Endnotes

Nouns
    collective, 605
    in headings, 257–258, 259
    predicate, 597
    proper, 580
Noun strings, 90–91
Numbers, 591–593
    as figures, 592–593
    with headings, 262–264
    for illustrations, 292
    page, 264–266
    as sentence openers, 592
    as words, 591–592

Occupational Outlook Handbook, 359
Office of Personnel Management, U.S., 360
O'Hara, John, 87
Online Career Center, 360
Online documents, 238, 249, 256, 257, 259–260, 266
Online Ethics Center for Engineering and Science, 118, 119–120
Openers
    adverbial, 87–88
    in front of the subject, 88–89
    numbers as, 592
Opinions, 212, 213, 220
Or, compound subject joined by, 604
Oral reports, 540–571
    arrangement of, 545–548
    delivery techniques, 543–545
    preparation for, 542–543
    presentation of, 548–554
    stage fright and, 548
    visual aids in, 547–548, 554–568
Organization
    in classical argument, 215–217
    headings in, 260–264
Outlining, 681–682
Overhead projection, 563–566

Page design, 241–248
    on World Wide Web, 678–679
Page numbers, 264–266
Pakistan, 139, 141
Paragraphs, 82–85, 246, 346
Parallelism, 259, 593–594
Parentheses, 594–595
Parenthetical expressions, 604
Parenthetical references, 662–665, 670–672, 674–675
Particularist cultures, 133–134
Passive of modesty, 94
Passive space, 245
Passive voice, 30, 92–93, 198, 497, 586, 620
Period, 576, 595, 598
Periodical Abstracts, 167
Periodicals, 656, 661, 668

Persona, 16-20
Peterson's Job Opportunities for Engineering and Science Majors, 361
Peterson's Job Opportunities for Health and Science Majors, 361
Photographs, 286, 292-294f, 309
Pictographs, 113-116, 309, 317-318f
Plagiarism, 111
Planning
  in collaboration, 37-39
  considering international differences in, 136-138
  for document design, 237-238
  for mechanism description, 193-194
  for process description, 202-203
  for reader communication, 56-75
Plan of development, 626-627
Plural forms, apostrophe for, 579
Pomposity, 96-98
Position, description of, 192
Possessives, apostrophe for, 578-579
Power distance, 128t, 131-133, 145
PowerPoint, 563
Predicate nouns, 597
Preface, 608-609, 611f
Presenting information, 174-209. *See also* Analogy; Chronological order; Classification; Definitions; Description; Division; Exemplification; Topical organization
Princeton Review, 385
Pro and con argument, 213, 217-218
Process description, 187, 188-190, 191f, 194-203, 207
Progress reports, 212, 392-395, 406-439
  defined, 394
  letter, 425, 430-431f
  physical appearance of, 425
  relationship between proposals and, 394-395
  structure by chronological order, 420-421
  structure by main project goals, 421-424
  structure by work performed, 413-420
  style and tone of, 425
Project description, 402-405
Pronouns, 595-597
Proper nouns, 580
Proposals, 212, 392-406, 425-439
  context of development, 398-399
  cost, 401, 405-406
  defined, 394
  effective argument in development, 399-401
  example of, 407-412f
  internal, 425, 426-429f
  management, 401, 405
  physical appearance of, 425

relationship between progress reports and, 394-395
  standard sections of, 401-406
  style and tone of, 425
  technical, 401, 402-405
Protocol analysis, 531, 534
Purpose, 5, 625-626
  chronological presentations and, 178
  of correspondence, 330-333, 340
  of feasibility studies, 465
  identifying, 15-16
  of illustrations, 280, 282-288
  of instructions, 505
  reader impact on, 57-58, 71-72, 78
  of visual aids, 554-555
  in World Wide Web site design, 676

Question mark, 597, 598
Questions, in headings, 257-258
Quotation marks, 597-598

Reader-based comments, 41
Readers, 54-79. *See also* Audience
  academic versus nonacademic, 57-59
  analyzing, 60-71
  determining, 57-60
  experts as, 60, 61, 64-65f, 70-71f
  indifferent, 58, 59, 78
  information overload, 58
  instructions for, 505-506, 531-534
  interest level of, 78
  knowledge and experience of, 77-78
  nonexperts as, 60, 62-63f, 67f, 68-70f, 76f
  primary, 59, 60, 68
  purpose influenced by, 57-58, 71-72, 78
  relationship to writer, 18, 78
  revealing document design to, 239
  secondary, 59
  unknown, 59-60
Reader's Guide to Periodical Literature, 362
Rebuttal, in Toulmin logic, 224-225, 226
Recommendation reports, 212, 440-481. *See also* Feasibility reports; Formal reports; Informal reports
Recommendations, 215, 443, 631-632
Reference line, 646
Reference lists, 665-669. *See also* Works Cited section
Report format, 607-637
  abstracts, 618, 619-622
  appendixes, 634-635
  cover, 609-612
  discussion, 628-629
  ending, 629-634
  glossary, 617-618, 620f
  introduction, 622-628
  letter of transmittal, 608-609, 610f
  list of illustrations, 615-617
  list of symbols, 617-618, 619f

preface, 608-609, 611f
  summary, 618-619, 629-630
  table of contents, 614-615, 616f
  title page, 612-614
Reports. *See* Analysis; Empirical research reports; Executive reports; Oral reports; Progress reports; Proposals; Recommendation reports
Request for a proposal (RFP), 395, 396, 398-399, 402
Request for qualifications (RFQ), 396, 397f, 398
Research. *See* Empirical research reports; Information
Restrictive appositives, 584-585
Restrictive modifiers, 584
Results, in reports, 484, 497
Résumés, 368-379
  chronological, 369-371
  electronic, 375-379
  e-mail, 376-379
  functional, 372, 373f, 377f
  paper, 375
  scannable, 376
  targeted, 372-375, 378f
  World Wide Web, 379, 380f
Revision, 14-15, 31-32
  in collaboration, 37f, 41-42
  criterion-based comments, 41
  elements of, 26-28
  reader-based comments, 41
Right margins, ragged, 247-248
Run-on sentences, 598-599

Salutation, 647
Sans serif type, 250-251
Scientific American, 83
Scientific method, 218
Scope, 403, 465-466, 626
Search engines, 162, 679
Semiblock letter style, 638, 640f, 647
Semicolon, 598, 599-600
Sentences, 5
  complexity and density of, 87, 88-91
  conditional, 89
  definitions for, 185-186
  fragmentary, 587-588
  in headings, 257-258
  length of, 86-87
  order of, 87-88
  run-on, 598-599
  structure of, 86-94
Separation of relationships, by culture, 130-131
Series, punctuation for, 585, 600
Serif type, 250-251
Sexist usage, 600-601
Shape, description of, 192
Sharing one's work, 28
Shaw, George Bernard, 601

Sigma Xi, 112
Signature block, 647
Simplified letter style, 638, 642f
Situational analysis, 30
  collaboration and, 37
  defined, 14
  for document design, 237
  elements of, 15-20
  for instructions, 505-506
Size, description of, 192
Slides, 566
Social Science Abstracts, 167
Society for Technical Communication
    (STC) Ethics Code, 109, 110f
Spacing, 246
Spelling checkers, 29, 601
Spelling errors, 601-603
Standard & Poor's Register of Corporations,
    Directors, and Executives, 361
Standard usage, 42-43
Statement of work (SOW), 395, 398
Steinbeck, John, 87
Style, 27
  choice of words, 94-96
  conversational, 342-345
  for correspondence, 340-345, 346, 347
  direct, 340-342, 347, 348f
  example of good, 98-100
  indirect, 340-342, 343f, 346, 347, 349f
  for instructions, 521-523
  for international readers/audience, 100-
    101, 340-341, 346, 347
  list, 85-86
  paragraph, 82-85
  for proposals and progress reports, 425
  sentence, 86-94
  table, 85-86
Style checkers, 29-30, 82
Style sheets, 38-39, 232
Subject, grammatical
  openers in front of, 88-89
  verb agreement with, 595, 604-605
  words between verb and, 89-90
Subject, of report, 623-625
Subject line, 646
Subject-verb-complement (SVC)
    structure, 86, 87, 88
Subject-verb-object (SVO) structure,
    86, 87, 88

Subordinate clauses, 587, 588
Summaries
  executive, 469, 618, 622, 624f
  of feasibility reports, 469
  format for, 618-619, 629-630
  of informal reports, 443
  of proposals, 402
Suspended hyphen, 589
Syllogisms, 220-221, 222
Symbols, list of, 617-618, 619f
Synchronous discussions, 44, 45-47, 674

Table of contents (TOC), 237, 238, 239
  of feasibility reports, 469
  format for, 614-615, 616f
  of instructions, 531
  matching headings to, 259-260
Tables, 5
  designing, 298-299
  exhibits, 283, 287, 295, 296, 297, 299,
    300, 301
  for instructions, 523
  for oral reports, 557, 558f, 559f
  purpose of, 282, 285, 286
  style of, 85-86
Technical proposals, 401, 402-405
Technical writers
  attributes of good, 6
  day in the life of, 7-10
  position in organization, 72-73, 78
Technical writing
  nature of, 4-6
  qualities of good, 7
  substance of, 2-4
Texture, description of, 192
Theoretical or historical background,
    627-628
Title page, 265, 469, 612-614
Titles, 292, 581, 590, 598
Tone, 73-75, 425
Topic, 15-16
Topical organization, 178, 186, 204
Toulmin logic, 213, 223-226
Traditional outline system, 262, 263f
Transitions, 84-85
Trimming, of data, 113
Trompenaars, Fons, 127, 133
Troubleshooting and tips, 525-528
Type, 248-256

highlighting with, 252-255
  in résumés, 375
  sans serif, 250-251
  serif, 250-251
  size, 249-250
Typefaces, 248, 250-251

Uncertainty avoiding, 128t, 141
Universalist cultures, 133-134
Utilitarians, 108

Verbal clauses, 88
Verbal phrases, 257-258, 587-588
Verbs, 86, 87, 88
  active, 91-92
  proper form, 603-604
  subject agreement with, 595, 604-605
  tenses of, 194-198, 494-495
  words between subject and, 89-90
Videos, 567-568
Visual aids, 547-548, 554-568
Visual language, 190-192
Visuals, misleading, 113-116
Vocabulary, 5, 97-98
Voice. See also Active voice; Passive voice
  in materials and methods sections,
    497
  in oral reports, 550-551
  in process description, 194-198

Warning message, 516, 518-519, 520f
Warnings, 252, 516-520
Warrant, in Toulmin logic, 224, 226
Wilson Business Abstracts, 167
Women, 136
Word processing programs
  document design with, 239, 242
  editing with, 29-30
  revision with, 41-42
Works Cited section, 658-662. See also
    Reference lists
World Wide Web sites, 168, 170-171,
    232
  designing, 675-681
  documentation on, 673
  evaluating information from, 169
  headings on, 257, 262, 679
  locating information on, 161-163
  résumés on, 379, 380f